SOCIAL WORK LAW IN SCOTLAND

14 Day Loan

AUSTRALIA
LBC Information Services–Sydney
CANADA and USA

Carswell–Toronto

NEW ZEALAND
Brooker's–Auckland

SINGAPORE and MALAYSIA
Sweet & Maxwell Asia
Singapore and Kuala Lumpur

SOCIAL WORK LAW IN SCOTLAND

Richard Mays
Senior Lecturer in Law, The Robert Gordon University,

Vikki L. Smith,
Committee Services Officer, Aberdeen City Council

&

Veronica M. Strachan,
Lecturer in Law, The Robert Gordon University

Published in 1999 by W. Green & Son Ltd
21 Alva Street
Edinburgh EH2 4PS

Typeset by York House Typographic Ltd
Printed and bound in Great Britain by
Redwood Books, Trowbridge, Wiltshire

No natural forests were destroyed to make this product;
only farmed timber was used and replanted

A CIP catalogue record for this book is available from the British Library

ISBN 0 414 01223 2

© W. Green & Son Ltd 1999

PREFACE

The writing of any book represents a considerable challenge. In many respects writing a book on social work law contains added problems. The parameters of social work law are ill-defined. As readers will appreciate it is an amalgamation of many discrete areas of law forged together in what we describe in chapter 1 as a "new emerging identity". It was the view of the writers and the publishers that there was a genuine need for a book which would provide readers with a "one stop" resource. Knowing what to include and what to omit ultimately proved difficult. In compiling what we hope will be an all embracing book, we have been guided by the syllabus for social work students compiled by the Central Council for Education and Training of Social Workers. Hopefully, we have managed to strike the correct balance of covering the subject in sufficient detail and retaining a manageable product. The law on the subject of course does not stand in isolation. Law is shaped by policy and indeed policy and practice are shaped by law. Although this is a law book and not a practice book, the reader will find areas where we have discussed the law in the context of practice to facilitate understanding and to provide context. While the book has been prepared with social work students and professionals in mind, we also anticipate that students of law and legal practitioners may find the book useful. There is increasing interaction between the two professions and it is our hope that this book will facilitate greater mutual understanding.

The commissioning of the book is perhaps indicative of the growing importance of social work. Not only is it being taught widely in universities and colleges throughout Scotland, not only does it employ large numbers of people, but it also impinges directly upon large sections of Scottish society. Once social work provision was viewed as applicable to an under privileged minority; today the practice of social work is widespread. Looking at the contents of this book it becomes apparent that everyone, if not directly affected by a core area of social work practice, has a family member, friend or neighbour who is affected. For this reason, and for our sense of care and compassion for fellow citizens, knowledge of social work law is of increasing importance.

Naturally, we have many people to thank. We are particularly appreciative of the assistance offered by several of our colleagues. Debbie Baillie read most of this manuscript and made many helpful suggestions for improvement. Colin Campbell offered useful comment on chapter 2. Iain Taylor commented on chapter 9. We were also ably assisted by our Research Assistants Lisa King and Euan Roberts and by our secretarial staff (Fiona Sturgeon, Audrey Howie and Eileen Ord). We also wish to thank others who read part of the manuscript and again who helped improve the end product – Professor Gill McIvor, Stirling University who read chapter 8, Delia Thornton, Hazelhead Academy, Aberdeen who read and commented upon chapter 5 and Patricia Saluja, Aberdeen who offered comment on chapter 9. We also wish to record our gratitude to our respective families and friends for their support without which compiling this book would have been a far more arduous task.

We would also like to place on record our thanks to the staff at W Green – Karen Taylor, Neil McKinlay, Russell Murphy and Heather Palomino for their forbearance and assistance. The book is altogether much better for their input.

We have attempted to state the law as at April 1, 1999. No significance should be read into the date.

Richard Mays
Vikki L. Smith
& Veronica M. Strachan

CONTENTS

Table of Cases

TABLE OF STATUTES

TABLE OF STATUTORY INSTRUMENTS

TABLE OF EUROPEAN LEGISLATION

Chapter 1

SOCIAL WORK LAW IN SCOTLAND

BACKGROUND

"Social work law" constitutes an amalgam of several disparate areas of law forged together **1.01** in a new and emerging identity. Not only has there been relatively recent recognition of this congregation of legal topics as a subject in its own right, but also much of the law itself is new. There are few other areas of law that can be viewed as more dynamic and the pace of this development shows no sign of abating. The emergence over the past 30 years of modern welfare services in large monolithic social work departments substantially explains why the collection of law is only now beginning to be considered a subject in its own right.

WHAT IS "SOCIAL WORK"?

There are varying definitions of the concept of "social work". All emphasise the personalised **1.02** nature of the concept and the idea of enablement rather than resolving problems for those in need of assistance. Bowers, for example, asserts that:

> "social casework is an art in which knowledge of the science of human relations and skills in relationships are used to mobilise capacities in the individual and resources in the community appropriate to better adjustment between the client and all or any part of his total environment."[1]

Similarly, the British Association of Social Workers describe the nature of the occupation of social work as extending:

> "its interest beyond the immediate issue to understanding the client's background, social situations, motivation, attitudes, values, personality and behaviour and attempts to encourage development and change by a wide variety of methods which amongst many others may well include the development of strong relationships with clients, insight giving techniques, behaviour modification and practical help."[2]

Often social work is best understood by reference to the client groups it seeks to serve. Problems relative to old age, handicap, mental illness, low income, family relationships and

[1]   Bowers (1949), p. 417, quoted in Younghusband, *Social Work in Britain 1950–1975: A Follow Up Study* (1978), at p. 26.
[2]   BASW (1975) quoted in Younghusband, *op. cit.*

children tend to be prominent in social work activities.[3] Cooper describes the subject by reference to the broad areas of involvement by defining social services as:

"the assortment of provisions common to modern industrialised societies and usually include up to six main services: education, employment and training, health, housing, income maintenance, and the sixth conglomerate of welfare provisions for those whose age, status or condition gives rise to the need for special social care and sometimes control."[4]

1.03   Social work services are both expansive and expanding.[5] The correlation between poverty and the provision of social services has been noted by many commentators. It has been said by one writer that "social work operates in conditions of material distress which often render its therapeutic orientations irrelevant."[6] However, while there is a strong connection, "social work is not only about the alleviation of poverty or struggles against inequality, but these issues remain fundamental to it."[7]

Parry *et al.* suggest that the tasks of social work can be categorised in four ways:

"(a) the provision of routine caring and supportive services of a non-expert kind, for example supportive visiting, a range of domicilary services, caring and supportive services for those in residential establishments;

(b) specialist skills, for example, different types of social work expertise (such as family counselling), occupational therapy, an expert service for the blind and deaf;

(c) the mobilisation of community activity, including participation in decision making, in the running of welfare services, and involvement in voluntary and paid capacities, in the provision of caring services;

(d) engaging in pressure for policy changes at local and national levels, backed by research, analysis and experiment undertaken by members of social services departments."[8]

Many of the social work texts refer to "personal social services" to describe social work provision. For example, Parker suggests that:

"the personal social services are usually considered to be those, lying outside the general fields of health and education, which are adjusted in some special way to the particular social needs of individuals, families or groups and which require personal contact between the provider and recipient. The skill involved in the provision of those services is often labelled 'social work'."[9]

"Personal" implies a service, tailored to individual or human needs as distinct from technical and environmental services, which tend to be more standardised.[10] It has been said that "personal social services directly affect only a minority of the population. It is a minority

3   Young, *Mastering Social Welfare* (2nd ed., 1989), at p. 177.
4   Cooper, *The Creation of the British Personal Social Services 1962–74* (1983), at p. 8.
5   See Bryne and Padfield, *Social Services Made Simple* (1990), at pp. 2–3.
6   Parry, Rusdtin, Satyamurti (Eds), *Social Work Welfare and the State* (1979), at p. 162.
7   *ibid.* at p. 166.
8   *ibid.* at p. 172.
9   Parker in Robson and Crick (Eds), *The Future of Social Services* (1970), at p. 105.
10   Cooper, *op. cit.*, at p. 8.

made up largely of people with the lowest incomes and the worst living conditions in our society."[11] Ironically, though demand does not diminish, like many public services there are periods of relative austerity which often lead to crisis for the recipients of those services.

A Historical Perspective

Welfare provision and care and concern for others in the community is not a modern phenomenon. There is a long history of voluntary provisions by private individuals, charitable organisations and religious orders.[12] The Trade Guilds and Friendly Societies (the forebears of modern trade unionism) were very active in providing for members and their families.[13] State mechanisms for such provision have an altogether shorter history. The public provision that originally existed was directed to poor law relief which carried considerable social stigma for the recipients. The transition has been a rapid one from "mere provision of material benefits by the state to a wide range of individually focused services which attempt to meet varied personal needs."[14] Whatever the case may be, there can be little doubt that social service provision has expanded beyond the very poor and now spans a much broader community.[15]

1.04

When reflecting on the historical development of social work law in Scotland undoubtedly two statutory developments will stand out. The Social Work (Scotland) Act 1968 represents essentially the founding statute of modern social work departments; it was instrumental in welding together disparate welfare agencies into modern unitary services. The second landmark statute is the Children (Scotland) Act 1995, which has substantially reformed the framework law relating to the care and protection of children and introduced other significant reforms. However, to focus exclusively on these two statutory enactments would be to neglect a large number of other statutory developments, principally since the Second World War, which have influenced and propelled the dramatic process of change, from relative disparity and obscurity, to cohesion and recognition.[16]

1.05

Historically, welfare provision throughout the United Kingdom was based on the Poor Law and its associated poorhouses. The Scottish Poor Law required recipients to be disabled as well as destitute.[17] Dickensian exposure of the hardship of children in poorhouses offered remarkable insight into the horrors of such institutions. The "old" Poor Law emphasised the need to undertake work in return for succour. Many localities established premises for such activities. Historical developments—population expansion, war, and the industrial revolution—combined to exacerbate poverty and escalate the problem of the poor to one of national importance. As a consequence, a Royal Commission on the Poor Laws was established in 1832. The Commission recommended *inter alia* the appointment of a central government board to administer the Poor Law and to oversee the work of parishes and their workhouses.

1.06

The revised system introduced by the Poor Law Amendment Act 1834—the "new" Poor Law—reflected many of the recommendations of the Commission. The general concept was that work was valuable and that all effort should be made to get the impoverished from Poor

---

[11] English (Ed.), *Social Services in Scotland* (1988), at p. 136.
[12] *Stair Memorial Encyclopaedia*, Vol. 22, *Social Work*, at p. 1.
[13] Ferguson, *Scottish Social Welfare, 1864–1914* (1958), at p. 4.
[14] *Stair Memorial Encyclopaedia*, Vol. 22, *Social Work*, at p. 1.
[15] *ibid.* at p. 2.
[16] Ferguson, *op. cit.*, at p. 10.
[17] *ibid.* at p. 2.

Law relief into work by providing disincentives to remain in receipt of Poor Law provision. The new Poor Law also sought to ensure that the sick and children should be housed separately from the able-bodied poor. Levitt explains that:

> "The Poor Law Amendment Act 1834 was important not only for what it did for people physically but also for what it did for them psychologically. The underlying message got across that poverty was a blameworthy condition to be in; that "lesser eligibility" was necessary to deter potential applicants; that poverty was to be relieved rather than prevented. The result was that large sections of the community regarded the Poor Law with fear and loathing."[18]

Whatever deficiencies there were in other fields of what is now known as social work law, there was a considerable amount of legislation designed to protect the interests of children in the 19th century. Naturally, it did not have the benevolence and scope of the legislation that was to follow. The 19th century developments in this field were prompted by the fact that "[t]he public conscience was ... more easily stirred on behalf of children than any other group."[19] Concern about children was considerable at the turn of the century and the advent of a new Liberal Government provided impetus for reform. The Children Act of 1908 provided that children being neglected could be removed to a place of safety. Various other prohibitions relating to children were introduced by the statute on such matters as smoking, consumption of alcohol, allowing children in brothels, or causing them to beg.

The philanthropy and paternalism that existed at the turn of the century focused primarily on children. The elderly and the chronically sick received limited attention. In 1909, the Report of the Royal Commission on the Poor Laws and the Relief of Distress[20] had noted that the vast majority of the elderly poor in institutions were in sub-standard large establishments, described by one commentator, as "human warehouses."[21] Under the Local Government Act 1929 administration of the Poor Law had transferred to county council, city, and large burgh councils. The service was re-styled as Public Assistance. The restructuring provided limited improvements to the way in which the elderly and chronically sick were treated in institutions. One description of such institutions said they were often:

> "grey stone buildings with narrow, often spiral, staircases as dark by day and poorly lit by a few weak electric light bulbs by night. There was no central heating and the few coal fires were rigidly forbidden between March and October. The dormitories were crowded and poorly furnished. The sitting rooms were largely bleak and barn-like. Washing and toilet arrangements are described as poor and difficult of access, some of it outside the main building."[22]

The alleviation of poverty of elderly people remained uninfluenced by the introduction of old age pensions in 1908. Moreover, their relative plight was seemingly overshadowed by other social problems of the day—unemployment, housing and childcare.

---

[18]   Levitt, *Poverty and Welfare in Scotland 1890–1948* (1990), at p. 9.
[19]   Watkin, *Documents on Health and Social Services 1834 to the Present Day* (1975), at p. 414.
[20]   Cmnd 4499.
[21]   Murphy, *British Social Services—The Scottish Dimension* (1992), at p. 35.
[22]   Description by Dr Nisbet in *The Care of the Elderly* (1952), paraphrased in Murphy, *op. cit.* at p. 39.

Post-war reform

In the historical analysis of social work provision, the catalytic events of the Second World **1.07**
War were of signal importance. The adversity of conflict had produced a collective consciousness of community and a desire for change. Importantly, "the state planning furnace, stoked
by experience ideals and new social values, stood fired and ready to forge new systems."[23]
The advent of a Labour Government committed to a programme of welfare reform ensured
that the immediate post-war period was one of considerable development and transition for
social services. The Poor Law was finally abolished in 1948 by the National Assistance Act
1948. The new approach to the provision of welfare represented a departure from past
practice.[24]

Under the newly created welfare state,

"a formula for basing social welfare on the promotion of individual need without recourse
to guilt or shame had been elaborated. The Government had struck a balance between
promoting the rights of individuals within a more advanced industrial society, guarantee-
ing working-class interests and ensuring the maintenance of order."[25]

In the immediate aftermath of the Second World War the social work profession could be
characterised by three constituent sources: the social workers in local authorities who dealt
with the welfare provision under the National Assistance Act 1948; the various groups of
specialist workers who owed their jobs to specialist legislation responding to an identified
need; and finally the semi-professional voluntary sector located ostensibly in charitable
organisations.[26]

The post-war welfare consciousness was also evident in a number of Commissions and **1.08**
committees set up to look at particular aspects of social need. In 1945 in England the Care of
Children Committee was set up under the chairmanship of Myra Curtis:

"[t]o enquire into existing methods of providing for children, who from loss of parents or
any cause whatever, are deprived from a normal home life with their own parents or
relatives; and to consider what further measures should be taken to ensure that these
children are brought up under conditions best calculated to compensate them for lack of
parental care."[27]

The Report was the first major inquiry into children deprived of a normal home life. It was
restricted to looking at children who were already in need of care by someone other than
their parents. Later the emphasis of legislation was to consider the plight of the child in the
context of the family and to seek to provide assistance before a need for care arose. Curtis
was of the view that the response to a child in need of care was a home or a good substitute
home. This home would be one where the child would receive affection and personal interest,
respect for his personality, a sense of belonging and security, stability, opportunity, and a
share in the common life of a small group of people in a homely environment.[28] The Curtis
Report was particularly favourable to the concept of adoption or alternatively fostering if it

23   Murphy, *British Social Services—The Scottish Dimension* (1992), at p. 17.
24   Levitt, *Poverty and Welfare in Scotland 1890–1948* (1990), at p. 199.
25   *ibid.* at p. 205.
26   English (Ed.), *Social Services in Scotland* (1988), at p. 106.
27   Cmnd 6922, HMSO (1946).
28   Watkin, *Documents on Health and Social Services, 1834 to the Present Day* (1975), at p. 421.

was sufficiently supervised. The Children Act 1948 which followed the Curtis Report set up an Advisory Council in Child Care in England and Wales and in Scotland. The Act (in language subsequently replicated in section 15 of the Social Work (Scotland) Act 1968) placed a duty on local authorities to receive a child into care where there was no parent or guardian, the child was abandoned or lost, or where the parent or guardian was temporarily or permanently by reason of incapacity unable to look after the child. The local authority could in certain circumstances assume all parental rights over the child. Unlike the later provisions in the Social Work (Scotland) Act 1968, local authorities were not given any powers to work with families to resolve difficulties and prevent the receipt into care of children. Their responsive approach was to rescue and place in a substitute home as Curtis had recommended.

1.09   In a spirit of equality, Scotland was granted its own Committee for Homeless Children under the chairmanship of Lord Clyde, though the Clyde Report was somewhat over-shadowed by the Curtis Report.[29] In Scotland at that time there were four main child care agencies: the Public Assistance Committees, the Education Committees, the Voluntary Homes and the Royal Society for the Prevention of Cruelty to Children. The Poor Law (Scotland) Act 1934 had conferred the obligation on local authorities to make arrangements for the lodging, boarding and maintenance otherwise than in a poorhouse, of children under 16 who were orphans, separated from their parents or had been deserted. It was estimated that this covered some 7000 children.[30] Throughout Scotland education authorities had duties under the Children and Young Persons (Scotland) Act 1937 which required them to bring children in need of care and protection before the juvenile court, and in addition to deal with children who were the subject of approved school orders. Childcare in this era either took place in voluntary sector children's homes or by boarding out. There were few public children's homes run by local authorities or foster homes. The Clyde Report was essentially supportive of rural boarding out (which had been a feature of wartime arrangements). The Report was critical of sending children to the poorhouse.

1.10   A further dimension of both Curtis and Clyde Reports was that they recommended the setting up of a unitary government department with the transference of existing responsibilities to it from separate government departments and a corresponding creation of single committees to exercise functions at local level. The response to the Clyde Report was to consolidate matters under the Home Department of the Scottish Office. Local authorities were required to set up Children's Committees and to appoint a children's officer who would supervise children separated from their parents.

1.11   The Second World War dramatically changed perceptions of the elderly. Titmuss notes that:

> "The problem of the aged and the chronic sick had been serious enough in peacetime; in war it threatened to be come unmanageable. Thousands who had formerly been nursed at home were clamouring for admission to hospitals, when families were split up, when houses were damaged or destroyed."[31]

1.12   The all round displacement and alienation occasioned by the war had dramatic effects on the plight of the elderly and provoked a considerable social problem. The demand for beds during wartime prompted the discharge of tens of thousands of patients into the community,

[29]   See Murphy, *British Social Services—The Scottish Dimension* (1992), at pp. 25–26.
[30]   See *ibid.* at p. 26.
[31]   Titmuss, *Problems of Social Policy*, HMSO 1950 at p. 559.

exacerbating an already growing problem.[32] The post-war response to this burgeoning problem was the Beveridge-inspired National Assistance Act 1948. The Act not only abolished the Poor Law, but enacted that there should be local government provision for the aged and the needy. The National Assistance Act 1948 was later to be accredited as a "launch pad for further legislative advance" in relation to the chronically sick and disabled.[33]

Mental health services

Prior to the war, the provision of mental health services was delivered via health departments **1.13** rather than local government. In 1948 new localised health authorities were set up. The law however continued to be of some antiquity. The principal statutes were the Lunacy Acts 1857–1913 and the Mental Deficiency (Scotland) Acts 1913 and 1940. The Mental Health (Scotland) Act 1960 heralded dramatic change. The emphasis no longer revolved round hospitalised treatment but rather sought to emphasis community treatment.

Criminal justice

Historical analysis also reveals that there has been social care provision for offenders in **1.14** Scotland for some considerable time. Probation was first established in Britain by the Probation of First Offenders Act 1887 and later extended in the Probation of Offenders Act 1907. Concern at the increased numbers of criminals prompted calls for reform, which arrived in the form of the Criminal Justice (Scotland) Act 1949. The 1949 Act required the constitution of ad hoc local authority committees. These committees included magistrates, Justices of the Peace, sheriffs and sheriff-substitutes. In addition, the probation officer's role was expanded to include assisting, advising, and befriending the probationer. Until 1949 the probation services that had existed were limited in scope and size; from 1950 and especially in the 1960s the service was to expand immeasurably.[34] Probation as a service came under further scrutiny under the Morrison Committee set up in 1959. This Committee was to conclude that probation had not developed as it should have because it was viewed as an inconsequential local authority function. The Committee formed the view that, in Scotland, probation should be provided by local committees with reduced local authority representation. In effect this meant only half the committee were to be local authority appointees. Sheriffs and sheriff-substitutes would remain; the remaining appointments would be nominees of the Secretary of State. A dissenting note was issued by a member of the Committee, Councillor John Mains, which was to prove both incisive and prophetic. His view was that social services had to be rooted in the community. Moreover, he was to attack the notion of specialism advocated by the Committee. He expressed the view that the trend was towards generic training of social workers. This view was later to be strongly endorsed by the Kilbrandon Report. The post-war developments in probation were such that one commentator asserted:

"probation moved from a poor basis, slowly at first, and then rapidly in comparison with other services to a position of a relatively well developed and staffed service in 1969 immediately prior to the reorganisation of social work."[35]

---

[32] Murphy, *British Social Services—The Scottish Dimension* (1992), at pp. 40–42.
[33] *ibid.* at p. 47.
[34] *ibid.* at p. 74.
[35] *ibid.* at p. 85.

Childcare

1.15   In the period immediately prior to the Kilbrandon Report, a further influential committee
reported: the McBoyle Committee[36]—a Committee of the Scottish Advisory Council on
Childcare—was requested by the Secretary of State to report on whether local authorities
should be given new powers and duties to forestall the suffering of children through neglect
in their own homes. The report drew much from the recommendations of the Ingelby
Committee in England and Wales which had a similar remit. Not surprisingly, the Committee
recommended that local authorities should indeed be given powers to provide a comprehensive service designed to prevent neglect. The recommendation included the giving of cash
or practical help in kind. The Committee identified the need to put greater emphasis on
services designed to provide assistance *in situ* of the family rather than bring children into
care. The McBoyle Committee did not however recommend amalgamation of existing
diversified services into one service, but did argue for greater co-operation and co-ordination
between the various social service providers. Important as the McBoyle Committee was, it
was somewhat overshadowed by the Kilbrandon Report.

The Move Towards Unification

In the years after the Second World War through to the passage of the Social Work
(Scotland) Act 1968, social work services were provided by four agencies: welfare, health,
probation and children's departments.[37] Welfare, health, and children's departments were all
local authority provided. Most Scottish local authorities established a welfare committee to
oversee the provision of welfare generally. The duty to provide welfare emanated from
sections 21 and 29 of Part III of the National Assistance Act 1948. These welfare provisions
offered scope for assistance to be given to the physically handicapped and, through innovative interpretation, problem families.[38]

Whilst there were reports on specific social care issues and areas of concern, there was until
the mid-1950s little or no emphasis on the role of the social worker and the organisation of
social work services. In 1955 the Younghusband Committee was established to consider the
issue of staffing in local authorities and health services, and in particular to consider if there
was a place for a general purpose social worker as a basic grade. The report in 1959 was to
conclude that there was such a need. In this context, the Younghusband Committee Report
constituted a significant development in the process of viewing social work as a coherent and
cohesive discipline and profession in its own right.

1.16   Relatively small as the profession was at that time, there was increased interest in the 1960s
amongst social workers in identifying the common elements of their profession and practice.[39] Indeed, it subsequently came to be recognised that one of the driving thrusts for
unification was the fact that social workers themselves began to see the importance of
recognising and dealing with the common elements behind the range of problems brought to
them by their clientele. The Working Party set up to examine the operation of the Social
Work (Scotland) Act 1968 subsequently noted that:

"[t]hose with experience in social work were not happy with the administrative structure
of the social services. In spite of the real achievements of co-ordinating committees, the

---

[36]   Cmnd 1966 (1963).
[37]   Murphy, *British Social Services—The Scottish Dimension* (1992), at p. 49.
[38]   *ibid.* at p. 53.
[39]   Ford in English (Ed.), *Social Services in Scotland* (1988), at p. 119.

administrative structure worked against attempts to give social help to individuals within the context of the family and community, and left gaps in provision that were not always recognised."[40]

By the mid-60s the process of unification in Scotland was well ahead of that in England. By now there appeared to be a better understanding of the nature of the problem of diversification and how it had come about. According to one commentator, **1.17**

"the defects in the prevailing organisation of local authority social work and welfare services were seen in the White Paper as arising from their piecemeal development in response to the identification at different times of certain groups of people who needed social help."[41]

Kilbrandon's proposals had included the unification of social work under education (Kilbrandon called these "social education departments"). Although the location of this unified service was not ultimately education, the notion of unification was, nonetheless, universally accepted. Until this point social workers had been variously employed as childcare officers, probation officers, welfare officers, mental health officers, psychiatric social workers and medical social workers.[42] Following Kilbrandon's Report, it became apparent that these and other services would need to be included in new "social work departments." To this end, a Joint Working Group was set up by the Government to consider the integration of social services into a coherent service. The Committee was charged with seeking the views of all the relevant professions on the proposal to amalgamate. In 1966 a White Paper entitled "Social Work and the Community"[43] expounded the Government's view of the desirability for a one-door approach to social work services. The nature of these new departments were described in the White Paper in the following terms:

"the existing powers of local authorities to provide advice and assistance, and to promote welfare, are set out mainly in the National Health Service (Scotland) Act 1947, the National Assistance Act 1948, the Children Act 1948, the Mental Health (Scotland) Act 1960, the Education (Scotland) Act 1962 and the Children and Young Persons Act 1963. These powers will be continued, with the adjustments necessary to fit the new organisation. They are already very wide, and only two substantial groups of people appear not to be fully covered. Services for old people under the National Assistance Act are limited to the provision of accommodation, meals and recreation. For adults who are not aged, handicapped, ill or parents of young children, there is at present no express power by which a local authority may at its own hand provide personal advice and guidance. It is proposed that the local authority should in the future have power to provide all citizens, of whatever age or circumstances, with advice and guidance in the solution of personal and social difficulties and problems."[44]

Finally, the Social Work (Scotland) Act 1968 brought together into a comprehensive service existing provision for children, offenders and people who were elderly, physically handicapped, and mentally handicapped.[45] The amalgamated function represented more **1.18**

---

[40] Mackenzie Report (also known as Rowntree Report): Report of a Working Party on the Social Work (Scotland) Act 1968, Dept of Social Study, Edinburgh University, 1969, at p. 8.
[41] English (Ed.), *Social Services in Scotland* (1988), at p. 120.
[42] See Murphy, *British Social Services—The Scottish Dimension* (1992), at p. 140.
[43] Cmnd 3065 (1966).
[44] Cmnd 3065 (1966), para 7.
[45] Murphy, *op. cit.* at p. 165.

than simply a combination of local authority services—several health authority functions were transferred as well. Most of the Act came into force in November 1969. Part III of the Act relating to children's hearings was delayed until April 15, 1971. The 1968 Act has significance attached to its title in respect that it is deemed to create professional recognition and to be "characterising the nature of the service to be provided to the community."[46] The new legal structure required local authorities (principally the county councils) to set up social work committees and to appoint Directors of Social Work. Reflecting on the 1968 Act, Murphy has said:

"in the first five years in the struggle for growth and survival, in many areas little more than a basic service was patchily provided. In others miracles were performed ... Viewed against the background of the Scottish scene of the time the production of the Act has the appearance of a miracle. The implementation of the Act, within the time and the resources available, if not a second miracle, was a triumph of hope over reality."

He went on to say:

"Local government re-organisation [in 1975] was the dawn of a new and richer era for social work. Since 1975, based on these foundations laboriously but successfully laid, and responding to a more favourable soil and climate, social work has established itself as a significant force in the land, and has made, by most comparisons, exceptional progress."[47]

Certainly the 1968 Act represented a break with the past rectifying poorly conceived welfare services as well as building a professional staffing structure.[48]

The underpinning philosophy of Kilbrandon's Report[49] is also largely credited as creating a distinctly Scottish pattern of social work services and approaches.[50] The particular proposals for children drew most acclaim. Cooper for example describes the Kilbrandon proposals as opening up a "fair, humane and holistic approach to children in need."[51] Though it is the childcare provisions which perhaps are most renowned, the developments of the 1960s were much wider in their significance. As one writer has explained, it is difficult to grasp the:

"sense of release and pioneering which the two reports, the White Paper and the Act generated in Scotland. For years the personal social services in Scotland had been static, sparse and old fashioned, but now they were given the potential to become among the most advanced in the world."[52]

Importantly, whilst the general pattern of development of social services has been similar throughout the United Kingdom as has the diagnosis of problems, the 1968 Act represented a divergence between Scotland and the rest of the United Kingdom. Viewing the newly created structures, one writer has argued that Scotland was the first country in the United Kingdom to develop a comprehensive system of personal social services.[53]

46   Cooper, *The Creation of the British Personal Social Services 1962–74* (1983), at p. 50.
47   *British Social Services—The Scottish Dimension* (1992) at p. 183.
48   Moore and Wood, *Social Work and the Criminal Law in Scotland* (2nd ed., 1992), at p. 287.
49   Cmnd 2306.
50   Moore and Wood, *op. cit.* at p. 1.
51   Cooper, *op. cit.* at p. 36.
52   Younghusband, *Social Work in Britain 1950–1975: A Follow Up Study* (1978), at p. 253.
53   Cooper, *op cit.* at p. 33.

In the period immediately following Kilbrandon there were several further drivers for change. Most importantly, there was a coincidence of "political and professional evangelism."[54] One illustration of the unity of purpose in practice was in the constitution of a Working Party on the Social Work (Scotland) Act 1968, set up in 1968 just before the Royal Assent was given to the 1968 Act. The Working Party sought to outline the tasks of the newly constituted social work departments and identified the need for policy statements.

The consensual nature of the developments throughout the 1960s undoubtedly helped to smooth the transition towards a unified coherent service. Moreover, that embryonic consensus can largely assume credit for cementing fairly solid foundations of the modern Scottish social work system.

Kilbrandon and the 1968 Act are not the final words in the development of either social work or social work law. Since Kilbrandon there has been considerable political change. First, there was, as noted above, local government reorganisation in 1975. In little over a five-year period from 1971 50 social work departments were reduced to 12 (albeit much larger departments). Then, in 1979, a Conservative Government was elected with a radically different agenda, one hostile to state provision and the allegedly suffocating and mollycoddling effect of state welfare provision. Throughout the 1980s and most of the 1990s the Conservative Government pursued a policy away from welfarism.[55]

SOCIAL WORK IN THE 1990S

Recently, there have been further changes which have substantially altered the shape of social work practice in Scotland. A second significant reorganisation of Scotland into unitary council authorities has again transformed the structural environment for the provision of social work services. Not surprisingly, this reform engendered some concern amongst social work professionals.[56] In 1997 "New Labour" was returned to central government power. Although there is little evidence of any immediate transformation, it seems inevitable that there will be subtle changes of policy and direction. However, it is not only political change that is transforming the landscape. Whilst the changed and changing political backdrop continues to alter the structural context in which social work services are offered, of equal significance are the clear perceptible shifts in philosophical approaches to the nature and provision of social work services in core areas of provision which have emerged throughout the last decade. Two particular areas stand out for special mention: the development of care in the community and the radical restructuring of childcare law in Scotland. The legislative enactments in both of these areas have substantially redefined the provision of certain key social work services.

1.19

Community care

In 1989 the Government published a White Paper entitled "Caring for People"[57] which established several principles on which community care would be based. These were:

1.20

    (a) promoting the development of domiciliary, day and respite services to enable people to live in their own homes wherever feasible and sensible;

---

54   Cooper, *The Creation of the British Personal Social Services 1962–74* (1983), at p. 42.
55   Moore and Whyte, *Social Work and the Criminal Law in Scotland* (3rd ed., 1998) at pp. 3–20.
56   See Davidson, Fairley and Stafford, *Local Government Restructuring and the Management of the Child Protection System* (1997).
57   Cmnd 849 (1989), p. 849.

(b) ensuring that service providers make practical support for carers a high priority;

(c) making proper assessment of need and good case management the cornerstone of high quality care, promoting the development of a flourishing independent sector along side good quality public services;

(d) clarifying responsibilities, so making it easier to hold authorities accountable for their performance; and

(e) securing better value for taxpayers' money by introducing a new funding structure for social care.[58]

The subsequent National Health Service and Community Care Act 1990 was introduced in three stages. The final stage, in 1993, signified the end of Department of Social Security funding of care for people entering private or voluntary residential nursing homes. Henceforth, local authorities were to assess needs, and purchase care for individuals. In the first year 85 per cent of their financial allocation was to purchase services in the independent sector.

The revolution in the provision of a considerable proportion of social work services has not been devoid of controversy. Resourcing has been at the root of most of the disharmony. Indicative of the nature of the concern occasioned by the transition towards expansion of care in the community provision, is the view that asserts that community involvement in caring is not the same as leaving families to cope the best they can but that this may be the reality of community care.[59] For all the transitional difficulties, the movement towards community care has engendered widespread support primarily on the basis that it promotes privacy, dignity and independence of living.[60]

Childcare

1.21 If the changes introduced by the 1990 Act were dramatic and far-reaching, the extensive changes to childcare law introduced by the Children (Scotland) Act 1995 have been no less so. The 1995 Act represents the culmination of considerable activity throughout the 1990s, all of which, in some way, influenced the ensuing legislation. The changes to childcare law must also be set in the context of the enhanced status of the child within Scottish society generally, and a political desire to reinvigorate the family as a social entity. In a White Paper in 1993 the Government had argued that,

> "The more traditional images of the family are being challenged by the very fact that many of our children now experience very diverse forms of family life as their parents cohabit, separate, marry, and remarry. Increasingly, children are being asked to adjust to living in a family with one parent absent, usually the father, or to living with a step parent, again usually a step father. Despite these changes families remain and will remain the foundation of care for children and the development of young people. In this changing world families will need support in ensuring a consistently high quality of care."[61]

The legal changes relative to children and childcare could have been said to have been fashioned in a cauldron of developments, reports and events over the preceding decade.

---

[58] See Wistow, Knapp, Hardy and Allen, *Social Care in the Mixed Economy, op. cit.*, para. 1.11; McKay and Patrick, *Care Maze* (1995), at p. 1.
[59] Parry, Rusdtin and Satyamurti (Eds.), *Social Work Welfare and the State* (1979), at p. 168.
[60] *A Framework for Mental Health services in Scotland: The Context* Consultation Draft, 1997.
[61] White Paper, *Scotland's Children—proposals for Child Care Policy and Law*, HMSO Cm. 2286, 1993.

First, there was a Review Group set up in 1988 to look at childcare law in Scotland which reported in October 1990. The United Nations Convention on the Rights of the Child was signed in April 1990 and ratified by the United Kingdom on December 16, 1991 subject to certain reservations and declarations.[62] In 1992 there was a report into the operation of children's hearings.[63] In between, the now infamous events in Orkney had resulted not only in considerable controversy, but had also given rise to a report by Lord Clyde.[64] Orkney was not the only place to face controversy; the Secretary of State had also asked Sheriff Kearney to inquire into the childcare policies of Fife Council. His report was published in 1992.[65] In February 1993 the Social Work Services Group (SWSG) published a consultation paper entitled "Emergency Protection of Children in Scotland."[66] Finally, the Government's own White Paper,—"Scotland's Children" argued,

> "the family is of fundamental importance to our society, and [the Government] are therefore committed to providing social welfare services designed to support and assist children within their families, so far as consistent with the children's welfare."[67]

Following the 1995 Act, all those associated with the care of children have had to re-examine their approach. The Act provides for a new child protection regime, seeks to combat child abuse, recasts the children's hearing system, and defines and delineates parental rights and responsibilities. In the process substantial parts of the Social Work (Scotland) Act 1968 are repealed. In short, the statute has radically overhauled much of the established social work law in the childcare field.

FUTURE DEVELOPMENTS

Any uncertainties as to the future should not blight the real progress made in a relatively short space of time. Writing in 1988, English noted that "in spite of substantial remaining gaps, enormous strides have been made during the two decades since the personal social services were reorganised with the creation of social work departments. The growth in numbers of staff have been accompanied by the provision in many areas of new and imaginative services. It remains to be seen in what ways the personal social services will evolve during the next two decades. Future developments will depend not only on the priorities of central and local government in distributing resources between alternative uses, but also the skill, and imagination exercised by social work departments and their staff in using the available resources to the best advantages of their clients."[68]

1.22

The past hundred years have been punctuated with several discernible trends and developments. First, there has been a shift from basic subsistence and piecemeal provision to the development of specialised services into areas hitherto untouched and the development of a comprehensive service. Secondly, there has been an obvious expansion of state provision at the expense of family, voluntary and employer provision. Thirdly, there has been greater emphasis put on the provision of personal services focusing on the individual rather than on the environmental and collective welfare. Fourthly, services are now universalistic in nature,

---

[62] See U.K.'s *First Report on UN Convention of the Right's of the Child* at p. 4.
[63] Finlayson, *Reporters to Children's Panels: Their Role Function and Accountability* (1992).
[64] *Report of the Inquiry into the Removal of Children from Orkney* (1992).
[65] *Report of the Inquiries into Child Care Policies in Fife* (1992–93, H.C. 191).
[66] *Consultation Paper and Proposals for Change* (Feb. 3, 1993).
[67] White Paper no. 61, para. 2.1.
[68] English (Ed.), *Social Services in Scotland* (1988), at p. 139.

engaging a far wider expanse of the population than hitherto. Fifthly, there has been a transition from the perception of social services as a gift towards viewing them as a right. Finally, there have been professional developments—greater training, expansion of knowledge, and greater development of sense of identity.[69] Given the short span of history of social work and social work law, only one confident prediction can be made—future development of the subject matter will ensue and:

> "whatever the future administrative structure of the personal social services, certain demographic, social and economic changes will lead to growth in the needs these services aim to meet. There is a basic fact of an increasing adverse balance of dependent to the independent in the population."[70]

1.23   The relationship between poverty and deprivation and social work has already been commented on. Poverty remains endemic in Scottish society. Parry *et al.* have commented that,

> "There is still widespread poverty, often related to particular stages in the life-cycle (old age, families with dependent children—especially one parent families, for example) but also arising from the way the income maintenance services are administered; there is still large-scale homelessness and overcrowding; there are still major shortcomings in the provision of health care. And social workers' clients tend to be drawn from sections of the population which are subject to these kinds of deprivation. These sections of the population tend also to be those who are affected by such factors as the decline of inner city areas, shortcomings in educational provision and communal facilities for children and young people, unemployment, especially for school leavers, and low paid oppressive types of work for those who are employed."[71]

In Scotland the statistical indicators represent alarming reading. Brown and Cook (1983) outlined representative indicators of poverty in the 1980s in Scotland. At that time they pointed to a picture of Scotland as one of the low pay economies of Britain,[72] extreme inequalities of wealth with 1 per cent of Scots owning 25 per cent of the wealth of the country, 500 individuals or companies owning half the land of Scotland, and the top 10 per cent of the nation owning 80 per cent of the wealth. Naturally the same writers offered reasons for this appalling state of affairs. Principally they pointed to changes in the extent and nature of work within the Scottish economy: the decline of heavy industries which had dominated the industrial landscape of Scotland, the growth in unemployment, the changing pattern of work, low pay and an inadequate "safety net" of the welfare state. Norris[73] had in an earlier treatment highlighted the obvious importance of work in the poverty equation. He explained that:

> "where the means of livelihood ... derive from participation in a free labour market, it is the processes and criteria which exclude people from full employment participation which are crucial in determining the characteristics of the poor. The poverty of the old, the sick and disabled and single-parent families is largely a reflection of their inability to enter the employment system."

---

[69]   See Bryne and Padfield, *Social Services Made Simple* (1990), at p. 4–5.
[70]   Parker in Robson and Crick (Eds.), *The Future of Social Services* (1970), at p. 106.
[71]   Parry, Rusdtin Satyamurti (Eds.), *Social Work Welfare and the State* (1979), at p. 162.
[72]   Brown and Cook (Eds.), *Scotland The Real Divide: Poverty and Deprivation in Scotland* (1983), at p. 13.
[73]   *Poverty: The Facts in Scotland* (1977), at p. 10.

Demographic changes were highlighted by Brown and Cook (1983) as large contributory **1.24** factors of poverty, particularly the growth in number of elderly "dependants" in the economy relative to those in work[74] and the changing nature of the family composition (they pointed to the decline of the nebulous concept of the nuclear family and the rise of single parenthood). They also pointed to the growing numbers of minority groupings (for example the disabled and the mentally handicapped) suffering deprivation and unmet need.

Currently, the numbers claiming benefit in Scotland stand at 135,300.[75] Homelessness based on the number of applicants (households) to housing authorities in Scotland stands at 41,094 (estimated at 75,000 people). Of that number, 16,500 are identified as in priority need, 14,400 are not in priority need and 4,800 have lost contact with the authorities.[76] According to SHELTER these figures remain high but slightly less than the peak reached in 1991/92. The number of people on council house waiting lists remains at a record high (194,579 households).[77] Rural homelessness remains acute particularly given the decline in the size of public authority stock.[78] At March 31, 1995 there were 88,112 dwellings in Scotland identified as below tolerable standard.[79] With these statistics and other social need indicators in mind, one can confidently predict continuing demand for social services well into the 21st century. The shape, form and financing of those services are less certain. What is predictable is that the provision of social work services will continue to reflect a "mixed economy" of public, private, voluntary and domestic provision.

THE PROVISION AND ORGANISATION OF SOCIAL WORK SERVICES

The role of local government

Provision of comprehensive social work services by local authorities has a relatively short **1.25** history. The Social Work (Scotland) Act 1968 imposes several key obligations on local authorities as to the assessment of need and the provision of social care services. Although each local authority is no longer required to establish a social work committee by law, in practice many will have such committees which will oversee the operation of the authority's social work department. The 1968 Act was, as has been noted, instrumental in bringing together a number of individualised social care services under unitary organisations. One of the consequences of having different functions under one structure has been the need for the social work committee to have a number of sub-committees dealing with particular functions. Following local government re-organisation it is still the case that most local authorities utilise sub-committees for particular functions.

Local authorities are required by law to appoint chief social work officers with prescribed qualifications.[80] That person may be designated as the Director of Social Work but that title is no longer mandatory. The chief social work officer has several key statutory functions

---

[74]   A point noted in an earlier study by Norris, *Poverty: The Facts in Scotland* (1977) at p. 2.
[75]   See news release, Feb. 17, 1999, The Scottish Office. The numbers claiming benefit is seen by the Government as an indicator of unemployment. The rate of unemployment is estimated at 5.5 per cent. The latest available estimates for the population of Scotland is 5, 136,600: General Registers Office, Scotland, June 1995.
[76]   Latest figures for 1996/97: Scottish Office, March 1998, *Operation of the Homeless Persons Legislation in Scotland*, 1986–87 to 1996–97, HSG/1998/1.
[77]   SHELTER Annual Survey, 1996.
[78]   *ibid.*
[79]   Scottish Office Statistics, Feb. 1997.
[80]   Social Work (Scotland) Act 1968 ("the 1968 Act"), s. 3 as amended by the Local Government etc. (Scotland) Act 1994, s. 45; see also Circular No. SWSG2/95 3737; Qualifications of Chief Social Work Officers (Scotland) Regulations 1996 (S.I. 1996 No. 515).

which involve overseeing the provision and purchase of social work services.[81] Prior to 1994 statute required the local authority to have adequate staff. This provision was considered unnecessarily prescriptive. Like many public services, in the taxing environment of social work, staff resources are often stretched to the limit.[82] In 1997 there were nearly 36,500 staff employed in social work departments in Scotland.[83] Roughly 17 per cent were involved with children, 41 per cent with the elderly, 9 per cent with adult offenders, 4 per cent with physically handicapped, 9 per cent with the mentally ill and handicapped with 26 per cent non-specific groups.[84] Overall it is estimated that there are 104,000 people employed in social work throughout Scotland.

Each local authority will organise its social work department in the fashion it pleases. There will doubtless be several senior officers below the rank of chief social work officer and some senior managers below them who supervise basic grade social workers and other professional and administrative staff who are part of the social work department. In recent times there has been a trend towards decentralised services. Such an approach is consonant with the philosophy of social work provision that there should be close community involvement between professional social workers and the client groups they serve. As well as community services, it is also incumbent on local authorities to provide social work services in hospitals and prisons.

The role of central government

1.26 The Social Work (Scotland) Act 1968 states that local authorities shall perform their functions under the Act under the general guidance of the Secretary of State.[85] The Secretary of State may make regulations governing the activities of the local authorities and the voluntary sector. In addition the Secretary of State may issue directions to local authorities, either individually or collectively, as to the manner in which they are to exercise any of their social work functions and the local authority must comply.[86] In addition to this the Secretary of State has powers of inspection.[87] This will be carried out on his behalf by the Social Work Services Inspectorate. The Secretary of State also has the power to "cause an inquiry to be held" into

(a) the functions of a local authority (under various social work enactments);

(b) the functions of an adoption society; and

(c) the functions of a voluntary organisation in so far as those functions relate to establishments.[88]

A further power of the Secretary of State relates to the furtherance of research into the functions of local government in relation to social welfare and voluntary organisations. A

[81] 1968 Act, s. 5(1B) as inserted by the Local Government etc. (Scotland) Act 1994, Sched. 13, para. 76(3).
[82] See *Walker v. Northumberland C.C.* (1995) 1 All E.R. 737 for a case where a social worker successfully sued his employer for mental injury occasioned by high work loads.
[83] Government Statistical Service, Scottish Abstract of Statistics No. 26, 1998–13, 494 were employed in central/strategic, fieldwork and special location staff, 10,866 in home care, 3,876 in day centre, 8,160 in residential establishments.
[84] *Guide to Scottish Local Government* (1995), p. 30.
[85] 1968 Act, s. 5(1) as amended by the Children (Scotland) Act 1995, s. 105(4) and Sched. 4, para. 15(4).
[86] 1968 Act, s. 5(1A) as inserted by the NHS and Community Care Act 1990, s. 51, as amended by the Local Government etc. (Scotland) Act 1994, s. 180(1) and Sched. 13, para. 76(3).
[87] 1968 Act, s. 6 as amended by the NHS and Community Care Act 1990, s. 53, and Sched. 9, para. 10(4).
[88] 1968 Act, s. 6A as inserted by the NHS and Community Care Act 1990, s. 54.

considerable amount of research is commissioned and funded each year. The Secretary of State is further empowered to make funding available for training.[89]

Prior to the implementation of the Social Work (Scotland) Act 1968, there was set up, **1.27** under the guise of central government, a central advisory service known as the Social Work Services Group (SWSG). The Group was formed to support the newly formed and localised social work departments who were thought to be in need of guidance. Several inspectorates for key social work services were brought together in the new body. Rather curiously, the new Group was attached to the Scottish Education Department where it has remained to this day. The SWSG provides social work departments with advice and guidance on professional, practical and policy issues. The principal objectives of the SWSG are:

(a) to develop community care for vulnerable people;

(b) to develop child care services;

(c) to maintain the children's hearing system;

(d) to develop social work services in the criminal justice system; and

(e) to promote the voluntary sector and volunteering.[90]

The relationship between local authorities and the SWSG is two-way: local authorities must provide SWSG with a considerable amount of statistical data which assists in long term planning. Moreover, local authorities will be questioned about service provision and generally the SWSG carries out a monitoring role on the part of the Secretary of State. In addition SWSG plays an integral part in the development and implementation of new legislation applicable to social work practice. As well as acting as advisers to local authorities, the Group also acts as an adviser to the Secretary of State. Moreover many of the functions attributed to the Secretary of State in the foregoing paragraph are carried out on his behalf by the SWSG, especially funding for training and research.[91]

The voluntary sector

The Social Work (Scotland) Act 1968 defines a "voluntary organisation" as a body the **1.28** activities of which are carried on otherwise than for profit, but does not include any public or local authority.[92] Many such organisations provide specialist services which supplement and often surpass services provided by the public sector. The 1968 Act envisages local authorities engaging the assistance of the voluntary sector in the provision of service.[93] Funding of such organisations is clearly a major concern. Without appropriate support many of the voluntary organisations would be unable to provide the valuable services they do. While many have privately raised funding or are perhaps able to secure funding from sources such as the lottery fund, most will depend on securing funding from either the local authority or central government. Both central and local government are empowered to make grants or loans to voluntary organisations. The Secretary of State may make provision for "expenses" of

---

[89] 1968 Act, s. 9 as amended by the Children (Scotland) Act 1995, s. 105(4), and Sched. 4, para. 15(8).
[90] Circular SWSG 10/95 5425, June 21, 1995.
[91] See Circular SWSG 7/98, May 1998.
[92] 1968 Act, s. 94.
[93] 1968 Act, s. 4.

voluntary organisations whose activity relates to his or the local authorities' functions.[94] On the other hand the local authority may "make contributions" by way of a grant or loan to voluntary organisations whose sole or primary purpose is social welfare.[95] In addition local authorities are empowered to make donations of equipment and premises as well as the services of local authority staff.[96] Assistance may come from departments of the local authority other than the social work departments and, in fact, assistance may come from health boards and other agencies not part of the local authority. It is often the case that funding from the Secretary of State is time-limited and the expectation is that the time will be utilised to develop alternative sources of funding. Local authorities may in addition to making grants or loans buy in supplementary provision, the latter being quite distinct from the former.

The charitable and voluntary sector has a long history of provision of social work services. It was that sector, often through the prompting of individuals dedicated to social reform, which many accredit with providing the first aspects of social care provision in Britain.[97] In the modern era they continue to fulfil an important dimension of social welfare services including a considerable number of residential facilities. With their strong commitment to the client group they serve, the expertise they have developed, and their community based support, voluntary organisations are often better placed to deliver many of the key social work services. Their strong relationship with local authorities ensures that they operate as an important adjunct to the mainstream provision of local authorities.[98]

The private sector

1.29 In the 1980s there was a discernible expansion of private sector provision of social care services.[99] Commentators have suggested that this expansion was not strategic but rather a response to the financial opportunity created by the mass expansion of social security provision.[1]

Modernising Social Work Services

The Government has recently published a consultation paper entitled *Modernising Social Work Services*, which among other things posts the idea of setting up a regulatory body to ensure high standards for social work services staff. The document argues that:

> "people using social work services have a right to expect high quality services delivered by a competent work force committed to continuous improvement ... The Government's prime concern in regulating staff in social work services is to ensure that people who use services are protected from bad practice, neglect, misconduct or worse."[2]

---

[94] 1968 Act, s. 10(1) as amended by the Children Act 1975, Sched. 3, para. 51(a), the Adoption (Scotland) Act 1978, Sched. 3, para. 11, the Local Government etc. (Scotland) Act 1994, s. 180(1) and Sched. 13, para. 76(7), and the Children (Scotland) Act 1995, s. 105(4) and Sched. 4, para. 15(9).

[95] 1968 Act, s. 10(3).

[96] 1968 Act, s. 10(4).

[97] *Stair Memorial Encyclopaedia*, Vol. 22, *Social Work*, at p. 1.

[98] *ibid.* at para. 10.

[99] Midwinter, *Local Government in Scotland: Reform of Decline?* (1995) at p. 69.

[1] Wistow, Knapp, Hardy and Allen, *Social Care in the Mixed Economy* (1994), at p. 28.

[2] "Modernising Social Work Services – A Consultation Paper on Workforce Regulation and Education" (1998) S.W.S.G., para. 1.5.

The proposed regulatory body will have responsibility for registration and discipline of social workers, the regulation of professional and vocational education and the publication of codes of practice.[3] Whilst the consultation is ongoing there must be some uncertainty as to the future for social work. What is clear is that there is pressure for enhancement of the professional status of the social worker and greater cohesion in the profession itself.

[3] "Modernising Social Work Services—A Consultation Paper on Workforce Regulation and Education" (1998) S.W.S.G, paras 11 and 12.

Chapter 2

THE SCOTTISH LEGAL FRAMEWORK

INTRODUCTION

Rudimentary knowledge of the legal context in which social work law operates is central to **2.01** any understanding of the subject. Knowledge of the sources of Scots law, the court system, the rules of evidence in those courts, and the personnel involved in the operation of the legal system is important for the social worker. At some point in their career, they will have some interaction with either the courts, the police, lawyers, or some other aspects of the legal system.

SOURCES OF SCOTS LAW

Legislation

A large volume of the law one now calls "social work law" is made up of legislation.[1] **2.02** Legislation comprises Acts of Parliament, Acts of the Scottish Parliament and subordinate, or delegated, legislation, as well as legislation of the European Communities.[2] Since the early 18th century, Great Britain has had a united Parliament. That Parliament and the legislation it has enacted is of considerable significance. Naturally, the inauguration of the new Scottish Parliament will have a significant impact on legislation, but at the time of writing all the statutes referred to in this book are enactments of the Westminster Parliament.

Acts of [the Westminster] Parliament are legislative enactments ordinarily passed by both **2.03** chambers of the House of Parliament (the House of Commons and the House of Lords) and given the Royal Assent on behalf of her Majesty the Queen. In certain circumstances it is possible to dispense with the approval of the House of Lords. The vast majority of legislative enactments which emanate from Parliament are government sponsored. In conformity with their election manifesto (and sometimes not) the government will present Bills to Parliament for approval. After various parliamentary stages including an intensive committee stage scrutiny of the detailed proposals the Bill passes from one chamber to the other. Finally on approval by both (or if appropriate the House of Commons alone) it is presented for the

---

[1] See Mays (ed.), *Scottish Social Work Legislation*.
[2] A discussion of European legislation is not included here. The reader is referred to specialist texts, *e.g.* Beaumont and Weatherill, *E.C. Law* (2nd ed. 1997), Chap. 5.

Westminster legislative process

Public Bill Orginating in the House of Commons

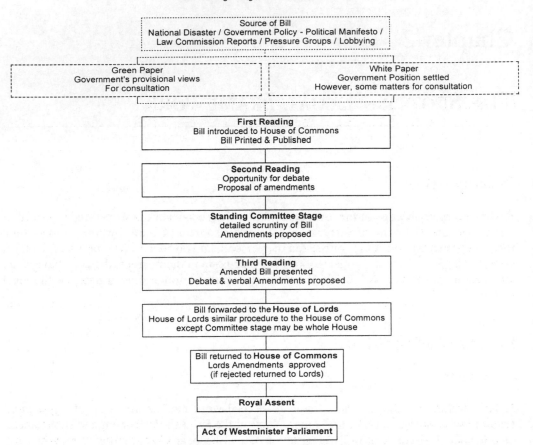

Royal Assent. This is done on behalf of the Queen by Royal Commissioners. The Act itself will state when the law is to come into force.

It is possible for an individual Member of Parliament to present a Bill for approval under the Private Member's Bill procedure, but the prospects of success are extremely restricted. Social reform can be a fertile area for private member activity but without cross party support, or Government support, it is almost impossible to see a proposal through to legislative enactment. Private Members' Bills can be introduced in a number of ways in the Commons. Members of Parliament may enter their names in a ballot, and normally three names are drawn. Those selected then have nine days in which to table the subject matter of their Bills which will then be debated on some six Fridays during the session. Members may also use the "10 minute rule" procedure by giving notice of a motion for leave to introduce a Bill. This procedure is available on Tuesdays and Wednesdays, and allows the member to speak for a brief period in support of his Bill, while an opponent may reply, and then the House will "divide" (vote) on the proposal. Peers in the House of Lords may also introduce Private Members' Bills. However, the real role of backbench Bills is often to attract, or maintain, publicity for a particular issue, or to put pressure on government to introduce a Bill of its own on the subject.

As a general position, it is the case that legislative provisions of the United Kingdom **2.04** Parliament will be given supremacy over any other domestic law. Only in situations where it conflicts with legislation of the European Union does that rule not hold good.[3]

Judges must interpret statutory provisions. In so doing, they hold considerable sway over how the law is understood and applied. There are certain approaches to interpreting statutes.[4] Some judges will apply words and phrases literally whilst others may adopt a more liberal approach.[5] To the student, or practitioner, the understanding of the language of a statutory provision may be difficult. One may need to resort to judicial pronouncements to gain further insight. Within the statute there will always be an interpretation section which will offer definitions of words and phrases used within that statute. The preamble to the statute may also offer guidance on the purpose and philosophy of the statute. It is also a feature of modern academic writing that law publishers are engaging academic writers to annotate provisions of legislation to offer guidance to those having to resort to legal materials. As useful as these are, it must be borne in mind that they are simply one person's view and advice.

The advent and impact of the Scottish Parliament

The Scottish Parliament has altered the way in which Scotland is governed and the making of **2.05** law relative to Scotland. Members of the Scottish Parliament have legislative capacity over a number of very important issues including social work and related domestic matters. The Scottish Parliament makes laws known as Acts of the Scottish Parliament.[6] The power of the Westminster Parliament to make laws pertaining to Scotland remains in force.[7]

When a legislative measure is introduced in the Scottish Parliament by the governing party, a member of the ruling Scottish Executive (the equivalent of the Cabinet) will make a statement that the Bill is within the legislative competence of the Parliament. The Presiding Officer of the Parliament has the power to rule that a Bill is outwith the legislative competence of the Parliament. There is also scope for Scottish Law Officers (the Lord Advocate, the Advocate General, or the Attorney-General) to refer the matter to the Judicial Committee of the Parliament for a ruling of whether a legislative provision is within the competence of the Scottish Parliament. In addition the Secretary of State has the power to intervene where he believes a Bill (a) is incompatible with international obligations, or interests in defence and security, or (b) modifies law relating to reserved matters. This intervention will be in the form of passing an order which prevents the legislative measure receiving the Royal Assent.[8]

In the normal course of events the legislative process will entail a general debate on the Bill with the opportunity to vote on general principles. Thereafter there will be an opportunity for MSPs to consider the details of the proposal followed by a final stage at which the Bill can be accepted or rejected. Bills may be reconsidered once they have been passed if the Judicial

---

[3] See Bradley and Ewing, *Constitutional and Administrative Law* (12th ed., 1997), at pp. 145–149; Case C −213/89 *R. v. Secretary of State for Transport, ex p. Factortame* [1990] 2 A.C. 85 (No. 2);[1991] 1 A.C. 603; Beaumont and Weatherill, *E.C. Law* (2nd ed., 1997), pp. 369–377.

[4] See Walker, *The Scottish Legal System*, (7th ed., 1997) pp. 391–410.

[5] See Walker, *op. cit.* pp. 395–413; White and Willock, *The Scottish Legal System* (1993), pp. 157–182; Walker, "Discovering the Intention of Parliament", 1993 S.L.T. (News) 121; Maher, "Statutory Interpretation: The Wilsonian Analysis" in MacQueen, *Scots Law into the 21st Century* (1996); Walker, "The Crumbling Pillars of Statutory Interpretation" in MacQueen, *supra*.

[6] Scotland Act 1998, s. 28(1).

[7] *ibid.*, s. 28(7).

[8] *ibid.*, ss. 31, 33 and 35.

Scottish legislative process

Provisional Outline of the Process

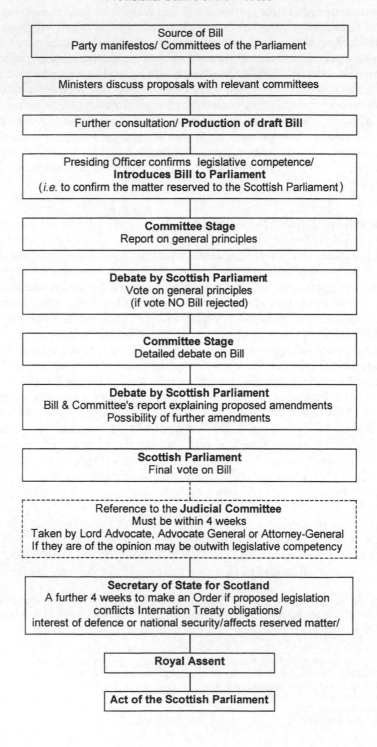

Source of Bill
Party manifestos/ Committees of the Parliament

Ministers discuss proposals with relevant committees

Further consultation/ **Production of draft Bill**

Presiding Officer confirms legislative competence/
Introduces Bill to Parliament
(*i.e.* to confirm the matter reserved to the Scottish Parliament)

Committee Stage
Report on general principles

Debate by Scottish Parliament
Vote on general principles
(if vote NO Bill rejected)

Committee Stage
Detailed debate on Bill

Debate by Scottish Parliament
Bill & Committee's report explaining proposed amendments
Possibility of further amendments

Scottish Parliament
Final vote on Bill

Reference to the **Judicial Committee**
Must be within 4 weeks
Taken by Lord Advocate, Advocate General or Attorney-General
If they are of the opinion may be outwith legislative competency

Secretary of State for Scotland
A further 4 weeks to make an Order if proposed legislation
conflicts Internation Treaty obligations/
interest of defence or national security/affects reserved matter/

Royal Assent

Act of the Scottish Parliament

Committee decide that the Bill is outwith the legislative competence of the Scottish Parliament, or the Secretary of State makes an order prohibiting the Royal Assent.[9]

Schedule 4 to the Scotland Act 1998 prohibits the Scottish Parliament from attempting to alter the Human Rights Act 1998, certain provisions of the European Communities Act 1972, and the Acts of Union 1706 and 1707. Nor can an Act of the Scottish Parliament modify, or confer power by subordinate legislation to modify, certain parts of the Scotland Act 1998 dealing with its constitution and legislative capacity. Furthermore, there are a number of matters reserved to the Westminster Parliament of the United Kingdom. Irrespective of these reservations, the Scottish Parliament will legislate for large areas of domestic law.

Delegated legislation

Delegated legislation is produced where Parliament delegates its law-making capacity to some other subordinate body or persons. Bodies or persons ordinarily entrusted with the framing of delegated legislation are government ministers, local authorities, courts and other public bodies. One finds a considerable amount of delegated legislation promulgated under the Children (Scotland) Act 1995 and other principal social work statutes. For example, detailed rules of procedure for the children's hearing system have been promulgated under delegated legislation.[10] Most delegated legislation comes into force once it is published, or shortly thereafter. **2.06**

If properly made in accordance with the procedure set down for it, delegated legislation becomes a powerful part of the general body of law called legislation. Because those persons to whom legislative capacity has been delegated have limited powers, individuals may challenge the validity of delegated legislation, either on the basis that the powers of the person or body have been exceeded (known as *ultra vires*), or that the correct procedure has not been followed. In contrast to the courts' approach to Acts of Parliament, there are numerous judicial decisions where the validity of delegated legislation has been challenged.[11]

Judicial precedent

All major legal systems operate a system of judicial precedent whereby cases that have been decided in the past guide decisions in cases before the courts today. Judicial precedents are prior decisions which contain important principles of law. On a practical level, previously decided case law represents an extremely important source of Scots law. Even where legislation exists (as it does in much of social work law) legal practitioners and social work practitioners will look to judicial precedent to offer guidance on principles of law, or illumination of statutory provisions. Although not always the case,[12] it is accepted in modern Scots law that in certain circumstances previous decisions are not only helpful, but may be binding on a court hearing a legal case. It is the principles of law and not the factual circumstances which are applied to the case in hand. Essential to the application of judicial precedent is an effective system of reporting of judicial principles and reasons. Scotland, like other countries, now has several journals and books reporting significant cases of legal **2.07**

---

9   Scotland Act 1998, ss. 35 and 36.
10 Act of Sederunt, Children's Hearings Rules 1996 (S.I. 1996 No. 3261).
11 See Bradley and Ewing, *Constitutional and Administrative Law* (12th ed., 1997), pp. 729–732; for a recent example see *Secretary of State for Defence v. Percy* [1999] 1 All E.R. 732.
12 See Walker, *The Scottish Legal System* (7th ed., 1997), at p. 414.

importance. In Scotland the main series of reports are the *Scots Law Times* (S.L.T.), *Session Cases* (S.C.) and *Justiciary Cases* (J.C.), the *Scottish Civil Law Reports* (S.C.L.R.) and the *Scottish Criminal Case Reports* (S.C.C.R.). Some of these law reports are now being presented on computer databases or in CD-ROM version.

The doctrine of *stare decisis* (standing by one's previous decisions) operates in such a way that where two golden rules are applicable to a case, this case must be followed by the court considering it. Those two rules are that: first the precedent is a decision of a court superior in the Scottish legal hierarchy to the court of the current case (see court hierarchies at pages 28 and 31), and secondly that the precedent had the same legal principle in dispute as the current case before the court. Where the court decides that the principle of law in dispute is the same, the precedent is said to be "in point". Essentially, this means that decisions of the House of Lords in Scottish cases are binding on all other courts in the Scottish civil court hierarchy where the principle of law is the same. The Inner House of the Court of Session binds the Outer House and the sheriff courts. Judicial precedents of the Outer House of the Court of Session are binding in the sheriff courts. Decisions of the sheriff principal only bind a sheriff in his own sheriffdom. Given that all sheriff courts are supposedly of equal standing, one sheriff court can never bind another. In criminal cases decisions of the Scottish Court of Criminal Appeal bind all other courts in the criminal hierarchy. Precedent plays a somewhat lesser role in the criminal courts. Much of their work revolves round an assessment of the facts in determining guilt. However, precedent is still important in many cases not only on points of law but also in determining sentences.

Where a precedent is "in point" and is from a higher court in the hierarchy, the judge must apply it—failure to do so will only result in an appeal and severe criticism of the judge. In many situations judges will attempt to evade application of a precedent by arguing that it is not in point and as such can be distinguished from the case in hand. Even where cases do not satisfy the two golden rules they may still have major significance. Precedents of courts of equal standing or from a senior court of another jurisdiction (*e.g.* England) may well be termed "persuasive" so that the judge may follow them if he wishes.

2.08   Not all cases that go to court are reported in the law reports. Indeed only a minority are. Those reports that do find their way into the law reports might only mention an aspect of a particular case which is considered important by those reporting it. In other instances a very fulsome report may be given of the judges' opinions. Usually when a case is reported the form it will take is that there will be an italicised section of catchwords of legal headings. There will then follow a brief summary of the facts and a statement of the point of law decided by the court. The statement of law will usually occur after the word "held". If one or more of the judges has not agreed with the majority opinion of the court there will almost certainly be an indication of this. This summary of the case is referred to as the "rubric". It is not technically part of the judgment but a useful summary of the case. Many students often get no further than reading the rubric of a case. In most law reports there will then follow a list of the sources of law to which the court was referred or did refer to determine the case. After these preliminaries one can expect the substantive body of the report which will detail the steps in the litigation, sometimes summarise arguments, perhaps extracts from earlier court hearings of the same case, and finally the text of the judges' opinions. Sometimes only one opinion will be delivered as the unanimous opinion of the court.

Other sources of Scots law

2.09   Such has been the development of Scots law over the past 300 years that it is rare when there is neither European law, legislation, or precedent which can be applied to the matter in hand.

Occasionally though that is the case, and one needs to go further back to find a source of law to provide guidance on a subject. One such repository of law is the institutional writings.[13] These are writings of historic scholars given an exalted status in Scots law[14] and are frequently referred to even in cases where there are other sources of law.

In addition, courts and legal practitioners will often refer to other legal textbooks not afforded the status of institutional writings but important nonetheless. Custom and equity may be other sources of law and is increasingly the laws of foreign jurisdictions are offering guidance on a number of legal issues.[15]

Codes, guidance and circulars

In addition to the formal sources of law outlined above, the professional social worker must have regard to a number of codes of practice, guidance notes and circulars. These may be issued by government, or other public bodies, such as the Equal Opportunities Commission or the Commission for Racial Equality.[16] In Scotland, guidance and circulars on aspects of social work practice are regularly issued by the Social Work Services Group.[16a] Whilst not given the same weight as law, codes and guidance are nevertheless extremely important as evidence of best practice and the expected standard. Some of the codes of practice may be in the form of National Standards (for example those in respect of dealing with criminal offenders).[17]

2.10

THE COURT SYSTEM

Civil law courts can be broadly viewed as existing for the resolution of disputes between two or more parties whether those parties be individuals, corporate entities, the State, or State bodies. In the social work context, it is more likely that disputes will arise between individuals, or between individuals and the State or voluntary organisations as providers of social work related services. The sort of civil law disputes that may affect the social work client are debt, housing matters, family law disputes such as contact or residence, or disputes involving childcare law, or indeed any disputes pertaining to most of the areas of law covered in this book.

2.11

Criminal law can be distinguished on the basis that it is a body of rules designed for the harmonious co-existence of society which the State on behalf of society enforces. Central to an understanding of the criminal law and the criminal prosecution system is the fact that transgression of the law is an offence against society as a whole and not principally the specific "victim" of the crime. The criminal law courts provide a mechanism for the State to prosecute those accused of crimes, and where a conviction ensues to impose appropriate punishment.[18] The distinction between criminal law and civil law gives rise to two separate court structures.

2.12

---

[13] Walker, *The Scottish Legal System* (7th ed.), p. 456–458.
[14] For a full list of the institutional writings see Walker, at *op. cit.*, at pp. 456–457.
[15] For a discussion of these sources see Walker, *op. cit.*, pp. 458–460.
[16] See paras 10.11 and 10.17 respectively.
[16a] See Chap. 1, para. 1.27.
[17] Discussed at para. 8.29.
[18] Further discussion of social workers and the criminal justice system is to be found in Chap. 8.

Criminal court structure

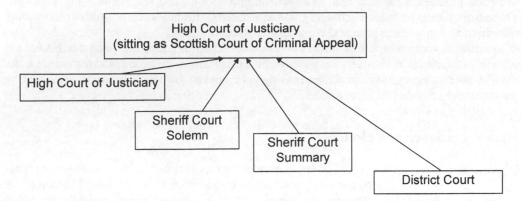

The criminal courts

The district court

2.13   The lowest court in the criminal court structure is the district court. There are 56 district courts located, in major towns and cities throughout Scotland. The courts are administered by the unitary local authorities.[19] As the lowest court in the country, not surprisingly, the court has jurisdiction over the most basic of offences. For example, such crimes as breach of the peace, minor assault, petty theft, and minor statutory offences will be tried in the district court. The geographic jurisdiction of the court only extends to the area of the district, and accordingly, only crimes committed within the district go before the court. Uniquely amongst the Scottish criminal courts, the district court is presided over by a person or persons not legally qualified. These lay persons are known as justices of the peace ("J.P."). In some district courts a J.P. will sit alone; in others there may be a panel of justices. The procedure in the district court is summary criminal procedure (see Chapter 8) and as such there is no jury present. The J.P.s determine the guilt of the accused and impose the sentence. In their role as judge, they are assisted in court by a legally qualified clerk who will be a full-time employee of the local authority. The clerk will offer legal advice and guidance where that is necessary. The longest prison sentence which can be imposed in the district court is 60 days, and the maximum fine up to level 4 on the standard scale, at present £2,500. Naturally, there are other punishments the court may impose (see Chapter 8). As one would expect, most punishments are at the lower end of the spectrum. Because of the volume of criminal court work, there is a special arrangement in Glasgow where a legally qualified stipendiary magistrate sits in the district court. The stipendiary magistrate has the same powers as a sheriff sitting in the summary criminal court (see below).

The sheriff court (summary)

2.14   Second lowest in the hierarchy of Scottish criminal courts is the sheriff court (summary). Scotland is divided into six sheriffdoms.[20] One will find sheriff courts located in the principal

---

[19]   The current structure of local government was established by the Local Government etc. (Scotland) Act 1994 and came into effect on April 7, 1995. The structure consists of 29 single tier councils, replacing the 53 district and 9 regional councils established in 1975.

[20]   Grampian, Highland and Islands; Tayside, Central and Fife; Lothian and Borders; Glasgow and Strathkelvin; North Strathclyde; South Strathclyde; Dumfries and Galloway.

towns and cities of each sheriffdom. A number of legally qualified judges known as sheriffs are appointed to each sheriffdom. As the name implies the court operates summary criminal procedure, and as such the sheriff acts as judge and jury in each case. In a similar fashion to the district court, the sheriff court has a geographic jurisdiction over summary crimes committed in its area. An accused can expect to be brought before the sheriff court for the area in which the offence took place. Offences tried in this court are still relatively minor but slightly more serious than those taken to the district court. Typically, cases such as assault, minor drugs offences, road traffic offences, and theft will be prosecuted before the sheriff court sitting as a summary court. The sheriff has the power to impose a sentence of up to six months' imprisonment, or a fine of £5,000, notwithstanding alternative forms of punishment.

The sheriff court (solemn)

From time to time, somewhat more serious offences will come before the sheriff court. These will be tried under solemn procedure, a feature of which is the involvement of a jury to determine guilt where guilt is denied. A sheriff will preside, sum up for the jury, and will pass sentence if there is a finding of "guilty". The sort of cases one can typically find being tried under solemn procedure include fraud, embezzlement, serious road traffic offences, serious health and safety offences, robbery, and aggravated assaults. Again the sheriff court has geographic jurisdiction over offences of this type in the locality of the area it covers. In keeping with the gravity of the crimes tried, the sentencing powers of the sheriff are somewhat more severe. In solemn procedure cases the sheriff can, amongst other things, impose a sentence of up to three years' imprisonment, or an unlimited fine. **2.15**

The High Court of Justiciary

The highest criminal trial court in Scotland is the High Court of Justiciary. The High Court of Justiciary is a "circuit court". Scotland is divided into four circuits—Home, North, West and South. Without a permanent home, the High Court of Justiciary sits at various times in different places throughout Scotland. The volume of business in places such as Glasgow and Edinburgh ensures that the Home and the West circuits are in almost permanent session. In keeping with its status as the highest criminal court in the land, it hears the most serious cases. Indeed certain cases are reserved to it. For example, murder, rape, treason, incest, and offences under the Official Secrets Act must be tried in the High Court of Justiciary. However, one can also expect to see other serious offences tried there. Armed robbery, culpable homicide, serious drugs offences, and sexual abuse cases are typical examples of the type of case regularly tried in Scotland's most senior trial court. The court operates solemn procedure[21] and as such a jury of 15 persons will determine the issue of guilt where that is in dispute. The judge, a Lord Commissioner of Justiciary will preside over the proceedings and impose sentence. The powers of sentence in this court are unlimited although where there is a mandatory penalty (such as life imprisonment for the crime of murder) the judge has no discretion. **2.16**

Criminal appeals and the Scottish Court of Criminal Appeal

All appeals from decisions of the Scottish criminal courts are heard in Edinburgh before the High Court of Justiciary sitting as the Scottish Court of Criminal Appeal. Three senior judges **2.17**

---

[21] See para. 8.12.

of the High Court of Justiciary will hear appeals against conviction on points of law and against sentence.

A miscarriage of justice in solemn cases may be based on (a) the existence and significance of evidence which was not heard at the original proceedings, and (b) the jury's having returned a verdict which no reasonable jury properly directed could have returned.[22] The fresh evidence need not come from a new witness.[23] However, the court must be convinced that there is a reasonable explanation as to why the evidence was not led at the original trial.[24] The appeal court will hear the explanation before it will hear the evidence. In summary cases the only basis for a miscarriage of justice is fresh evidence.[25] There has been criticism of the restrictive basis of establishing a miscarriage of justice.[26]

There are several ways an accused can subsequently challenge his conviction.[27] One which is complex and unlikely is a referral under the appeal court's *nobile officium*.[28] Another option is a Royal Pardon which has occurred only twice in recent Scottish legal history. However, from April 1999 cases may be referred to the Scottish Criminal Cases Review Commission which will have the power to investigate and refer the matter to the appeal court.

The civil courts

The sheriff court

2.18   The lowest court in the hierarchy of civil courts is the sheriff court. Its geographic jurisdiction is similar to that of the sheriff court in criminal matters. Disputes may result in legal action being initiated in this court. Common types of disputes include matrimonial disputes, disputes relating to children, debt, land and property disputes, personal injury cases, and contract disputes. Although there is no upper financial limit as to the value of any case taken in the sheriff court, the sheriff court's privative jurisdiction dictates that any disputes involving cash sums up to £1,500 must be initiated in the sheriff court.

Operating in the sheriff court there are three distinct forms of procedure—small claims, summary cause and ordinary procedure. The least formal and cheapest procedure is the small claim. It was destined to be litigant-friendly and accessible to persons without legal representation. The pecuniary limit of a small claim is currently £750. Claims with a financial value above £750 up to and including £1,500 ordinarily proceed by way of summary cause procedure.[29] It is also the case that actions for recovery of possession of heritable property by councils, housing associations, or private landlords ordinarily proceed by way of this procedure. Though more formal than small claims, it is still intended to be relatively speedy

---

[22]   Criminal Procedure (Scotland) Act 1995, s. 106(3), as amended by the Crime and Punishment (Scotland) Act 1997.

[23]   See Ferguson, "Fresh Evidence Appeals" (1995) 40 J.L.S.S. 264; Ferguson, "Miscarriages of Justices and the Criminal Appeal Court", (1998) 43 J.L.S.S. p. 100; Scott, "New Criminal Appeal Provisions—Back to the Future", 1997 S.L.T. (News) 249.

[24]   Criminal Procedure (Scotland) Act 1995, s. 106(3C), as amended by the Crime and Punishment (Scotland) Act 1997, s. 17.

[25]   Criminal Procedure (Scotland) Act 1995, s. 175, as amended by the Crime and Punishment (Scotland) Act 1997, s. 17(2).

[26]   See Ferguson, "Miscarriages of Justice and the Criminal Appeal Court" *op. cit.*, at p. 101.

[27]   See Poole, "Remedies in Miscarriages of Justice Cases", 1998 S.L.T. (News) 65.

[28]   See Poole, *op. cit.*; Ferguson, "The Scope of the Nobile Officium to Review Appeal Court Decisions", (1993) 38 J.L.S.S. 439.

[29]   Scottish Courts Administration are currently consulting on the pecuniary limits of these procedures and it seems likely that sometime in 2000 there will be an increase in the current limits.

Civil court structure

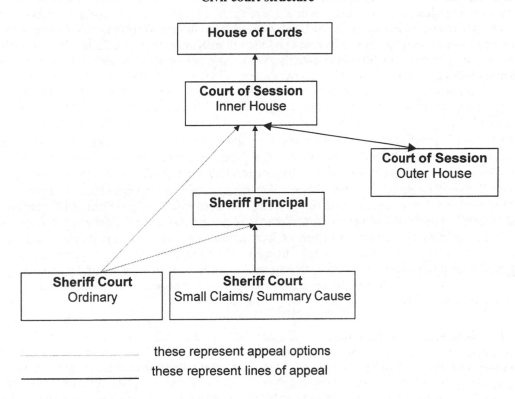

_____ these represent appeal options

_____ these represent lines of appeal

and inexpensive. Finally, ordinary procedure applies to all claims with a value over £1,500 and applies to the vast bulk of the case load before the sheriff court.[30]

The sheriff principal

Each sheriffdom has a sheriff principal who acts as a senior judge in each sheriffdom. His role is largely one of hearing appeals from decisions of the sheriffs in his own sheriffdom. Appeals may be taken from a final judgment of the sheriff principal to the Inner House of the Court of Session on any point of law.   **2.19**

Outer House of the Court of Session

The highest court of "first instance" (where a case may start) in Scotland is the Outer House of the Court of Session. The Court of Session is located in Edinburgh and is divided into an Outer House and an Inner House. The Outer House is presided over by a Lord Ordinary, a judge appointed by the Crown. Judges at this level, as Senators of the College of Justice, are the most senior judicial appointments in Scotland. There is seniority within the College of Justice and it will be the case that more lowly Lords Ordinary will preside in the Outer House of the Court of Session whilst the more senior judges will decide upon appeals in the Inner House. The Outer House of the Court of Session has national jurisdiction and accordingly   **2.20**

[30]   For a brief discussion of the various procedures see paras 9.70–9.78.

will hear cases of some complexity or importance from all over Scotland or cases having a national significance. Some actions must start there, for instance actions for declarator of marriage, and actions of judicial review.[31] By and large though there is no difference in the types of cases heard in the sheriff court and the Outer House and indeed often there is little difference in value. One would ordinarily expect very large value actions to be taken in the Outer House.

Inner House of the Court of Session

2.21   The Inner House of the Court of Session is almost exclusively an appeal court. For the purposes of convenience and workload, the court is divided into two courts—the First Division and the Second Division. Both courts have equal standing. The First Division is presided over by Scotland's most senior judge, the Lord President, whilst the second court is presided over by the second most senior judge, the Lord Justice-Clerk. Ordinarily, they will sit with two other fairly senior Lords Ordinary to determine an appeal. Each court comprises four judges in all but usually only three sit. One cannot elect which division to take one's case to, nor is there any appeal from one division to the other. From time to time, the First Division and the Second Division are conjoined in a court of five or seven judges where the court considers the matter to be important enough to warrant such a step. All appeals in the Inner House will be on a point or points of law only.

The House of Lords

2.22   In civil law matters, unlike criminal law, there is the possibility of an appeal being taken to the House of Lords located in London. Appeals are heard by legally qualified members of the House of Lords who are appointed to the Judicial Committee of the House of Lords to fulfil a judicial function. The most senior judge in the House of Lords is the Lord Chancellor. The other judges are known as the Lords of Appeal in Ordinary. Although the quorum is three, cases are usually heard by five judges. It is also usually the case that at least two of the judges operating in the House of Lords are of Scottish jurisdiction origin. However, there is no rule that in cases originating from Scotland a Scottish judge must be part of the court. In the normal course of things, a case will be heard by five judges, a majority of whom will be English. The scope for Anglicisation of Scots law is obvious, and has been severely criticised by several Scottish commentators.[32] Decisions of the court are by a majority. It is not uncommon for cases of social importance to have been decided on three to two verdicts. Very few cases proceed on appeal from Scotland to the House of Lords.

The European Court of Justice

2.23   Although not part of our domestic court structure, the European Court of Justice is of crucial importance. It operates to deliberate upon matters of European law brought to it under the Treaties applicable to the Community. A case brought before it may be an action against a Member State, or may be a referral by a court of a Member State for a preliminary ruling on a matter of European law. The Court comprises judges nominated by the Governments of the Member States. The president of the Court is appointed by the judges themselves from among them. The judges of the court are assisted by six advocates general who are appointed

---

[31]   Discussed below at para. 2.45 *et seq.*
[32]   See Walker, *The Scottish Legal System* (7th ed., 1997), p. 280.

for a six-year renewable term. The role of advocate general is of considerable importance. He considers the case and reaches his own personal conclusion as to what the law is, and how the case should be resolved. The advocate general neither represents the institutions of the community, the Member States, or the public. He will propose to the court a solution to any case brought before the court, relate the proposed solution to existing case law, and in some circumstances outline the probable development of case law on this issue. Once the court has heard the views of the advocate general, they will retire to deliberate upon their verdict. In most cases, the court will follow the views of the advocate general. Very few, if any, cases of relevance in the social work context are likely to be decided by this court. Social work tends to be a matter of domestic law and rarely raises issues of European significance, although it is possible. Decisions of the court are binding and must be applied by domestic courts.[33]

The European Court of Human Rights

Quite distinct and unconnected to the European Communities and its Institutions is the European Court of Human Rights, set up under the auspices of the Council of Europe. The significance of the European Court of Human Rights is likely to be enhanced with the recent enactment of the Human Rights Act 1998. The recognition of the European Convention on Human Rights did not confer rights on ordinary citizens enforceable in their own national courts. Currently, referrals are made to the Commission on Human Rights which may in turn refer a matter to the European Court of Human Rights. Referrals can only be made to the Commission once domestic remedies have been exhausted. Participating states may also refer matters to the court.

2.24

The Human Rights Act 1998

The preamble to the Human Rights Act 1998 said that it was intended to give further effect to rights and freedoms guaranteed under the European Convention of Human Rights. In this respect, it does not go nearly far enough for many of those who had sought the full enactment of a Bill of Rights into United Kingdom law. The 1998 Act did not enact the entire European Convention on Human Rights directly into United Kingdom law. Instead it sought to enact certain core values into legal interpretation. In section 2 (1) a duty is placed upon courts and tribunals to take account of (a) any judgment, decision, declaration, or advice of the European Court of Human Rights; (b) any opinion of the Commission given in a report adopted under Article 31 of the Convention; (c) decisions of the Commission; and (d) decisions of the Committee of Ministers. It is further enacted under section 3 (1) that "So far as it is possible to do so, primary legislation and subordinate legislation must be read and given effect in a way which is compatible with the Convention rights". However, in assessing compatibility no power is given in the legislation to alter the validity, or continuing operational enforcement of incompatible legislation.[34] All that a British court can do is to issue a declaration that legislation in the United Kingdom is incompatible with the core values adopted.[35] Only the highest courts, namely the House of Lords and the Scottish Court of Criminal Appeal may make declarations of incompatibility.[36] A further dimension to the

2.25

---

[33] For a full discussion on the workings of the European Court of Justice see Beaumont and Weatherill, *E.C. Law* (2nd ed., 1997), pp. 132–164; Lasok and Bridge, *Law and Institutions of the European Communities* (5th ed. 1991), Chap. 9.

[34] See Human Rights Act 1998, s. 3(1)(b) and (c).

[35] *ibid.*, s. 4(2).

[36] *ibid.*, s. 4(5).

legislation is that it is enacted that public authorities must act in a way which is compatible with Convention rights and in the Act.[37] Individuals will have the right to bring proceedings against public authorities where they believe that the public authority has acted in a way not compatible with an enacted Convention right.[38] Courts will have the power to grant relief, or remedy, or to make any order within its power to address any unlawful act by a public authority. Specifically, the civil court has the power to award damages or compensation. In awarding damages, the court will need to take account of any other relief or remedy granted, and be satisfied that the award is necessary to afford just satisfaction to the person to whom it is made.[39]

There are provisions in the statute under section 10 whereby a statute or other legislation which has been declared incompatible may be amended by Order of the Minister of the Crown as he considers necessary to remove the incompatibility.[40] This represents a remarkable innovation in United Kingdom law and clearly impacts upon the concept of parliamentary supremacy.

There can be no doubt that the Human Rights Act 1998 is likely to have considerable impact on the law of Scotland in the way in which legal practitioners and other professionals consider the law.[41] Moreover, there can be no doubt that it will impact considerably upon social work law and practice as an area of law dominated by the issue of rights, particularly, but not exclusively, in areas involving children, mental health, and criminal justice.

TRIBUNALS

2.26 It is a feature of the modern legal system that the operation and influence of tribunals is on the increase. There are tribunals for employment disputes, social security, disability, child support, and medical matters, as well as a range of other matters. Indeed it is believed that there are around 2,000 different tribunals operating in the United Kingdom.[42]

Tribunals exist to relieve the pressure on courts to resolve disputes, to provide a relatively informal arena for the resolution of some disputes, to allow the involvement of experts in settling particular disputes, to provide a relatively cheap mechanism for resolution of disputes, to infuse the system of adjudication with social policy considerations, and to deal with matters too trifling for the courts.[43] The extent to which any of these points is true is arguable. Certainly, tribunals are popular with government and the public. They play an increasingly pervasive part of modern life and social work professionals, or at least members of their client group, can expect to encounter some of these tribunals at some point in their career.

EVIDENCE IN COURT PROCEEDINGS

2.27 The basic rule is that all material facts which are in dispute in a court case must be established by evidence. Evidence is the information which tends to prove or disprove any fact. Evidence may come in several forms—the oral or written testimony of a witness, documentary

---

[37] *ibid.*, s. 6(1).

[38] Human Rights Act 1998, s. 7.

[39] See *ibid.*, s. 8.

[40] *ibid.*, s. 10(2) and (3).

[41] See Gane, "Human Rights Bill—Impact on the Law of Scotland" (1998) 43 J.L.S.S. 16–19; Miller, "Planning for Human Rights" (1997) 42 J.L.S.S. 282–283.

[42] See Ashton and Finch, *Administrative Law in Scotland* (1997), p. 185.

[43] *ibid.*

evidence, and other productions such as physical evidence (*e.g.* stolen goods, drugs, or a weapon).

In civil cases the person or body bringing the case to court is responsible for proving the facts upon which their case relies, and is known as the "pursuer". If he does not prove those facts, his case will fail. The task of the opposing party is simpler. To defend the case, he need only attack the evidence of the pursuer so that it fails to satisfy the court. He may of course lead his own evidence. In civil cases, a material fact, and the case as a whole, may be established on the balance of probabilities. As a consequence of provisions in the Civil Evidence (Scotland) Act 1988 the rules of evidence in civil cases are also less strict.

In the criminal court, a person is presumed innocent until proven guilty. The court must be convinced by evidence led by the prosecution beyond a reasonable doubt that the accused is guilty. There are strict rules of evidence, and corroboration (proof of material facts from more than one source) is required. Questions of fact in criminal cases are to be determined by the jury (or by the judge if there is no jury), while questions of law are to be determined by the judge. A question of fact concerns the truth or otherwise of something that can be appreciated by one of the five senses; sight, sound, smell, taste, touch, *i.e.* what someone said or did, where and when. Evidence will be heard to decide questions of fact. A question of law concerns the rule of law, for instance what interpretation should be given to a particular Act of Parliament or what weight or interpretation is to be given to a judicial precedent.

Rules of evidence

Evidence in any proceedings must be relevant, admissible and credible. Relevancy and admissibility are matters for the judge. To be relevant, evidence must bear upon the issues of the case. Not all relevant evidence is admissible. There are a number of exclusionary rules which render relevant evidence inadmissible.   **2.28**

Under the "best evidence" rule, a party should present the best available evidence to the court. Although in civil proceedings copy documents can now be produced and are treated as if they were the document itself.[44] Although one does not present hearsay evidence if one can present the evidence of an actual observer.[45]   **2.29**

The "rule against hearsay" is a controversial feature of the law[46] which provides that a fact may not be established by calling A, who did not see an event or hear a statement, to tell the court that he heard B who did. For example, if a child tells a social worker that he has been sexually abused by his father, the rule prevents the social worker giving evidence of what the child said to prove that the abuse took place. The social worker's evidence is hearsay; the child must tell the court himself. As a basic premise hearsay is excluded in criminal proceedings because it is unreliable.[47] The rule against hearsay in civil proceedings was abolished by section 2 of the Civil Evidence (Scotland) Act 1988 and it is allowed. However, even in many criminal cases hearsay statements are admissible. There are so many exceptions to the hearsay rule that it has been claimed that the rule has been "comprehensively circumscribed by the courts and statutory intervention".[48] Hearsay evidence which forms   **2.30**

---

[44]   Civil Evidence (Scotland) Act 1988, s. 6.
[45]   See generally Sheldon, *Evidence Cases and Materials* (1996), Chap. 6; Nicol, "Best Evidence in Criminal Cases", 1990 S.L.T. (News) 149; although note that the best evidence rule can be overcome with the admission of hearsay in civil cases: see *F v. Kennedy*, 1993 S.L.T. 1284.
[46]   See Sheldon, *Evidence Cases and Materials*, p. 197; Wilkinson, "The Hearsay Rule in Scotland", 1982 J.R. 213; *Report on Hearsay Evidence in Criminal Proceedings* (Scot. Law Com. No. 149, 1995).
[47]   See rationale for hearsay rule in Field and Raitt, *Evidence* (1996), pp. 171–173.
[48]   Sheldon, *Evidence Cases and Materials*, p. 197; see also Sheldon, "The Hearsay Rule Devoured", 1995 J.R. 504.

part of the whole circumstances immediately connected with the occurrence which is part of the facts at issue may be admissible.[49] The utterances are spontaneously related to the event and as such are an indication of what happened.[50] It follows that there must be proximity in time to the event and the hearsay.[51]

Section 259 of the Criminal Procedure (Scotland) Act 1995 also provides further statutory exceptions to the hearsay rule in criminal cases. It provides that evidence other than oral testimony may be admitted where:

(i) the witness is now deceased or by reason of bodily or mental condition unfit or unable to give evidence in any competent manner;[52]

(ii) the witness is outwith the United Kingdom and it is not reasonably practicable to obtain evidence by alternative means or secure his attendance;

(iii) the witness has been sufficiently identified but cannot be found and all reasonable steps have been taken to trace him;

(iv) the witness refuses to give evidence having been advised that it might be incriminating to him; and

(v) the witness refuses to give evidence or to take the oath.

Ordinarily, where a witness gives oral evidence, any prior statement will be inadmissible unless that witness has been advised at the time of making the statement that it will be admissible. However, prior statements of witnesses may be admissible where the statement is contained in a document, where the witness in the course of giving evidence indicates that the prior statement was made by him and he adopts it as evidence, and also at the time of making the statement the witness was a competent witness in the proceedings.[53] Although these rules do not apply to an accused in his own trial, the prior statements of that accused may be admissible at the instance of a co-accused.[54]

2.31 **Corroboration** is another rule of admissibility and is required in criminal proceedings. Corroboration requires that an item of evidence from an independent source supports another item of evidence.[55] Therefore in criminal cases the testimony of one witness alone cannot prove a fact.[56] Corroboration may be in the form of another witness testimony, documentary or other evidence. Although section 1 of the Civil Evidence (Scotland) Act 1988 abolished the requirement for corroboration in civil proceedings, corroborated evidence will always carry more weight.[57] The rules of corroboration and hearsay are not strictly applied in children's hearings.

In criminal cases a series of similar alleged acts may corroborate each other. The leading

---

49   Wilkinson, *Scottish Law of Evidence*, p. 22.

50   Field and Raitt, *Evidence* (1996), p. 173.

51   *Tepper v. R.* [1952] A.C. 480; *cf. H.M. Advocate v. Murray* (1866) 5 Irv. 232.

52   This provision was recently used in an unusual way for the first time in Aberdeen High Court where the main witness for the Crown was so profoundly deaf that he was unable to be examined or cross-examined. His evidence following agreement of the prosecution and the defence was taken from a statement from a policeman's notebook which he had signed. However, see *MacDonald v. H.M. Advocate*, 1999 S.C.C.R. 146, where a child became distressed in the witness box and refused to answer any more questions about abuse. It was suggested that s. 259 is directed more at the issue of refusal rather than difficulty or inability to give evidence.

53   See Criminal Procedure (Scotland) Act 1995, s. 260.

54   *ibid.*, s. 261.

55   Field and Raitt, *op. cit.* p. 142.

56   See *Morton v. H.M. Advocate*, 1938 J.C. 50, *per* Lord Justice—Clerk Aitchison at p. 55; Renton and Brown, *Criminal Procedure According to the Law of Scotland* (3rd ed., 1983), para. 18–52.

57   *L v. L*, 1996 S.L.T. 767.

Scottish case, *Moorov v. H.M.Advocate*,[58] concerned a number of charges of indecent assault of different women. The only direct evidence in each charge was the testimony of the woman assaulted. It was held that there was sufficient interrelation in time, place, and circumstances, between the assaults to amount to corroboration.[59] It is also the case that in respect of particular sexual offences, evidence of the victim's distress may corroborate her statement that she did not consent to the actions of the accused. It will not corroborate evidence of exactly what the accused did.[60]

The final rule for admissibility is **privilege**. This exonerates witnesses from answering **2.32** particular questions.[61] For example, communications between a husband and wife are privileged,[62] as are most communications between a solicitor and his client.[63] However, the same is not true of doctors, or social workers.[64] Privilege does not extend to a child when that child is asked to give evidence for or against a parent or relative. Courts will allow witnesses to refuse to answer questions, where it is deemed that the greater public good requires it (public interest immunity).[65] For example, in the case of *D v. NSPCC*,[66] the NSPCC could refuse to disclose the name of the person who had told them of their suspicions that a child was being abused because he was a police informer. Where there is no privilege, refusal to answer a question is punished as a criminal offence of contempt of court.

Important distinctions have to be drawn between fact and opinion, and evidence and **2.33** argument. Witnesses as to fact tell the court what they have perceived with their senses, but only an expert witness may express an opinion in court. It is for the judge to decide if he thinks the witness has sufficient knowledge to give expert evidence. He need not have formal qualifications. Expertise may be based on experience. Social workers may be in a good position to give expert evidence by reason of their qualifications and experience. The function of the expert is not to present ready made conclusions, but to provide the court with evidence on which it can reach its own conclusions.

Credibility is a matter for the jury or the judge where there is no jury. It is their task to decide whether to believe the witnesses. The court will take into account any motive the witness may have for putting matters into a particular light. In cases of assaults and sexual offences, evidence of a victim's statement is admissible to support his credibility, where the statement was made shortly after the event and no later than the first opportunity which the victim had to make a disclosure to a natural confidant.[67]

Child witnesses

The general principle is that all who are capable of giving intelligible evidence are competent **2.34** as witnesses, and that all who are competent are compellable. Children, no less than adults,

---

58 1930 J.C. 68.
59 See Field and Raitt, *Evidence* (1996), pp. 158–161.
60 "Distress as an Element of Corroboration" (1997) 42 J.L.S.S. 176–178; *Smith v. Lees*, 1997 S.C.C.R. 139; Davidson, "Corroboration in Distress", 1997 S.L.P.Q. 30; Shiels, "Distress as Corroboration" (1994) 39 J.L.S.S. 293; Field and Raitt, *op. cit.*, p. 162; *Moore v. H.M.Advocate* 1991 S.L.T. 278; *Meek v. H.M. Advocate*, 1983 S.L.T. 280; *Gracey v. H.M. Advocate*, 1987 S.L.T. 749; *McLellan v. H.M. Advocate* 1992 S.L.T. 991; *Cannon v. H.M. Advocate*, 1992 S.L.T. 709; *Stobo v. H.M. Advocate*, 1994 S.L.T. 28.
61 See Field and Raitt, *op. cit.*, Chap. 12.
62 Evidence (Scotland) Act 1853. s. 3 (in civil cases); 1995 Act, s. 264(2)(b), (in criminal cases).
63 Field and Raitt, *op. cit.*, pp. 262–265.
64 *ibid.*, p. 269.
65 *ibid.*, pp. 271–274.
66 [1978] A.C. 171.
67 *Morton v. H.M. Advocate*, 1938 J.C. 50; *Andersons v. McFarlane* (1899) 1 F. (J.) 36; *Begg v. Tudhope*, 1983 S.C.C.R. 32.

are often bystander witnesses to crimes. The increasing number of child abuse cases going to court in the late 1970s and early '80s focused public attention on the unsatisfactory way in which the legal system then treated the evidence of children.[68] A number of important changes were made through the Law Reform (Miscellaneous Provisions) (Scotland) Act 1990, Prisoners and Criminal Proceedings (Scotland) Act 1993, and ultimately by the reworking of these provisions in the Crime and Punishment (Scotland) Act 1997. Children as young as three have been called as witnesses. When giving evidence, children over the age of 14 are sworn in. Children under 12 give evidence unsworn, but are warned to tell the truth. Children between 12 and 14 give sworn or unsworn evidence, depending on their level of understanding.[69] Whether a child gives evidence on oath, or not, is at the judge's discretion.[70] Where a child gives evidence on oath without the judge ascertaining his age or whether he understands the nature of the oath, the evidence will nevertheless be admissible if no objection is taken.[71]

Children must undergo a competency examination before being allowed to give evidence. The judge must decide whether the child knows the difference between truth and lies by asking the child questions. There is no set form of questions; it is left to each judge to decide how he will approach the question. In *Rees v. Lowe*[72] the accused was charged with indecency towards a young girl. Before the girl gave evidence, the sheriff merely told her to answer questions as best she could. The accused was convicted but he appealed on the ground that the child's evidence was incompetent. The Scottish Court of Criminal Appeal quashed the conviction on the basis that it was the sheriff's duty to carry out a preliminary examination to see whether she knew the difference between what is true and what is false, and to admonish her to tell the truth. In proceedings which relate to conduct contrary to decency or morality, the court may direct that the public is excluded from court while the child's evidence is heard.[73]

2.35   The Lord Justice-General's Memorandum (of guidance) in 1990, on use of discretionary measures in criminal cases where children are witnesses, made the following recommendations: removal of gowns and wigs by judges, counsel and solicitors; seating the child at a table in the well of the court, along with judge and lawyers, rather than in the witness box; allowing a relative or other supportive adult to sit beside the child while he or she gives evidence; and clearing the courtroom of all people who are not involved in the proceedings.[74]

Unlike criminal cases, there is no guidance on evidence in civil proceedings. There is no reason, however, why the facilities available in criminal cases cannot be used at the judge's discretion. The rules of the court require a child to be served with the papers relating to the case in which he or she is the subject unless the court dispenses with service on the child. The court may appoint a curator *ad litem* to represent the child's interests.[75] In family actions where the interests of the child are involved, there has been since 1996 a system of child

---

[68]   *Evidence of Children and Potentially Vulnerable Witnesses* (1990), S.L.C No. 125.
[69]   Field and Raitt, *Evidence* (1996), p. 234.
[70]   *cf.* English decision of *R. v. Smith* [1994] Crim. L.R. 458; also *R. v. Norbury* (1992) 95 Cr. App. R. 256.
[71]   *Jardine v. Howdle*, 1998 S.L.T. 142.
[72]   1990 S.L.T. 507; see also *Kelly v. Docherty*, 1991 S.L.T. 419.
[73]   Children and Young Persons (Scotland) Act 1937, s. 45.
[74]   See Dent and Flinn (eds), *Children as Witnesses* (1992) Appendix, pp. 148–150.
[75]   A curator *ad litem* is appointed when the parents or guardians are for some valid reason unable to act on the child's behalf, for instance if the parents are dead and no guardian has been appointed, if the child is subject to a ground of referral as a result of an alleged abuse or neglect by the parent, or if the child and parent are involved in an action against one another. (see Wilkinson and Norrie, *Parent and Child*, p. 404). The curator *ad litem* is responsible for managing the affairs of the child and safeguarding his interests in all legal matters.

welfare hearings to address issues relating to the child which are held before the first major procedural hearing of the main family action.[76] The child may attend such hearings.

In other civil proceedings, a child cannot insist on giving evidence and can only give evidence if called to do so by one of the parties to the action. If a child wants to enter legal proceedings as a party, a solicitor must lodge a minute to this effect. It is then up to the judge to decide whether it is allowed. If a child wants to make sure his views are heard in court, he needs to instruct a solicitor who will act on his instructions. A child has the legal capacity to instruct a solicitor regarding any civil matter, where the child has a general understanding of what it means to do so (a person of 12 years or more is presumed to have such understanding).[77] The child can also apply for legal aid.[78]

The evidence of vulnerable persons in criminal cases

Measures in section 271 of the Criminal Procedure (Scotland) Act 1995[79] make provision for the giving of evidence by vulnerable persons. A vulnerable person includes children and someone over 16 suffering from significant impairment of intelligence and social functioning, or someone who has been found to be mentally disordered under mental health legislation. Evidence may be taken from a vulnerable person by a commissioner appointed by the court. The person appointed to take the evidence on commission must be an advocate, or solicitor, of five years' standing. The evidence before the commissioner is video-recorded. The accused will not be present in the room throughout the taking of evidence, but will be given the opportunity by suitable means to watch and hear the proceedings. As an alternative, a court may on application authorise the giving of evidence by a vulnerable person by live television link. If the application is granted, the vulnerable person gives evidence from a room adjacent to the court room, sitting beside a supportive adult in front of a unit which enables two-way transmission of picture and sound. The vulnerable person sees only the person in the court who is asking the questions. All those in the court room see the vulnerable person on similar screens, and the judge and the clerk of the court have additional screens which give an overview of the whole room in which the vulnerable person is sitting. As a further alternative, the court may on application authorise the use of a screen to conceal the accused but the accused must be given the opportunity to watch and hear the evidence being given. **2.36**

The court may only allow one of the foregoing alternatives on cause shown having regard to the possible effect on the vulnerable person, whether the vulnerable person would be better able to give evidence, and the views of the vulnerable person. The court will also have to take account of the offence in question, the nature of the evidence of the vulnerable person, any relationship between the accused and the vulnerable person, and where the person is a child, their age and maturity.

Witnesses in criminal cases

A party may examine or cross-examine any witness.[80] Whilst a spouse is always a competent witness for or against their spouse, he or she is never compellable.[81] It is not possible to object **2.37**

---

[76]   See Clelland, "The New Ordinary Cause Rules for Family Actions", 1997 SCOLAG 100.
[77]   Age of Legal Capacity (Scotland) Act 1991, s. 2(4A).
[78]   See *Journal of the Law Society of Scotland*, Feb. 1996, pp. 83–85.
[79]   As amended by the Crime and Punishment (Scotland) Act 1997, s. 29.
[80]   1995, Act, s. 263(1).
[81]   1995 Act, s. 264. The refusal to give evidence by a spouse cannot be commented upon by the prosecution: see subs. (3).

to any witness on the grounds of (a) conviction of or punishment for an offence, (b) interest, (c) agency or partial counsel, (d) the absence of due citation to attend the court, and (e) that the witness has been precognosed subsequent to the citation to attend.[82] An accused is always a competent witness for the defence at any stage of the case.[83] Only the defence can call the accused as a witness.[84] Whilst an accused can be asked questions which might incriminate him of the charges before the court,[85] he cannot be asked questions designed to show that he has been convicted of, or charged with, a prior offence unless:

(a) the proof that he has committed or been convicted of a prior offence is admissible evidence to show that he is guilty of the offence with which he is currently charged;

(b) the accused or his counsel or solicitor has asked questions of the witnesses for the prosecution with a view to establishing the accused's good character or impugning the character of the complainer, or the accused has given evidence of his own good character, or the nature of conduct of the defence is such as to involve imputations on the character of the complainer or of the witnesses for the prosecution or complainer; or

(c) the accused has given evidence against any other person charged in the same proceedings.[86]

A court shall not admit questioning or evidence which shows a complainer in sexual offences is not of good character in relation to sexual matters, or that she is a prostitute or an associate of prostitutes or has engaged in sexual behaviour which is not the subject-matter of the charge.[87]

Witnesses are not usually permitted to sit in the court prior to the giving of their evidence though an application for permission to do so may be made to the court. Even where the witness has been present in court without the permission of the court and the consent of the parties, he may still give evidence provided the court is satisfied that it was not the result of criminal negligence or criminal intent, and that the witness has not been unduly instructed or influenced by what took place during his presence, or that injustice will not be done by his giving evidence.[88] Certified transcripts of police interviews with the accused may be received into evidence. Transcripts must be served on the accused who has the right to challenge the transcript or its accuracy.[89]

THE PERSONNEL OF SCOTS LAW

Solicitors and Advocates

2.38 Lawyers in Scotland are grouped into two distinct branches of the legal profession. The largest grouping are solicitors. The other much smaller grouping are court specialists called "advocates". Solicitors are regulated by the Law Society of Scotland, whilst the governing body for advocates is the Faculty of Advocates.

---

[82] 1995 Act, s. 265(1).
[83] *ibid.*, s. 266(1).
[84] *ibid.*, s. 266(2).
[85] *ibid.*, s. 266(3).
[86] *ibid.*, s. 266(4).
[87] 1995 Act, s. 274; although note there are some exceptions to this rule in s. 275.
[88] 1995 Act, s. 267(1)–(2).
[89] 1995 Act, s. 277(1)–(2).

Some solicitors who specialise in court matters train to become what is known as solicitor-advocates. These solicitors have what is known as extended rights of audience in the supreme courts of Scotland. Hitherto only advocates had the right to speak in the Court of Session, the House of Lords, and the Scottish Court of Criminal Appeal. Solicitors who have not less than five years' continuous experience of court work may apply to practice in the superior civil or criminal courts or both. They must undergo an induction course, observe cases in appropriate court(s), attend (subject to certain exemptions) a training course in the work of the courts, and pass examinations on subjects related to practice in the superior courts.[90]

Generally speaking, advocates (sometimes known as counsel) are specialist court practitioners. It is often the case that advocates specialise in particular areas of law. Their mode of instruction is through the solicitor. It is the solicitor who will have considerable contact with the client, and where an advocate is instructed he will guide the written and oral pleadings. Advocates have access to the superior courts of Scotland, most importantly the Court of Session, High Court of Justiciary, the House of Lords and Judicial Committee of the Privy Council in London, and, in Luxembourg, to the Court of Justice of the European Communities. After about 10 to 15 years of successful practice they may apply through the Lord President to be appointed by the Queen to the Roll of the Queen's Counsel in Scotland. As a Q.C. or senior counsel, the advocate is entitled to require that he be accompanied by a junior to assist him in the conduct of a case, but he may choose not to be. Advocates may not be sued for professional negligence when in court, although it is likely that they may be in respect of negligent advice.[91] And most remarkably the advocate's "legal right is to conduct the cause without any regard to the wishes of his client and what he does bona fide according to his own judgment will bind his client".[92] **2.39**

Professor Walker has described the difference between solicitors and advocates in the following terms:

"The solicitor is to a large extent the general legal practitioner, the primary adviser, the negotiator and the man of business, whereas the advocate is called in cases of difficulty, for advice on tricky or important business, and in all cases where there is litigation of any consequence in prospect or in train ... The advocate has to be the legal expert, the quick thinker, the fluent and persuasive debater, usually involved in matters of controversy, whereas the solicitor has much more routine work to do and spends much time in consulting clients, negotiating and carrying through business, frequently non-contentious and attending to everyday affairs."[93]

Whilst much of what Professor Walker says is true, as an exact differential it gives a rather misleading perception of a legal elite which whilst possibly relevant some time ago bears little relation to modern reality. Solicitors, or more properly solicitors' practices, do often provide a more generalist and complete service than the sole practitioner advocate. Moreover, they do attend to negotiations and business matters and tender advice. However, to contend that the advocate is always more expert than the solicitor is misleading. It is not uncommon to see a solicitor and an advocate on opposing sides in the lower courts and for the solicitor to appear more "expert" than the advocate. Counsel is often instructed for reasons other than

90 See Admission as a Solicitor with Extended Rights (Scotland) Rules 1992.
91 See White and Willock, *The Scottish Legal System*, (1993) pp. 233–235.
92 *Batchelor v. Pattison & Mackersey* (1876) 3 R. 914, *per* Lord President Inglis at p. 918.
93 Walker, *The Scottish Legal System* (7th ed., 1997) at p. 350–351.

expertise. The virtual monopoly they have over practice in the senior courts ensures that certainly in respect of those courts they are undoubtedly more expert. It is possible to engage counsel where their expertise is beyond reproach and where they truly can be thought of as part of the legal elite. Perhaps less controversially one can say that both solicitors and advocates are often experts in their fields, that generally both fulfil a slightly different role towards the client and that sometimes the functions they perform overlap with each other.

Judges

2.40 In the foregoing discussion on the Scottish court system several different judges were identified as acting in those courts. The Justice of the Peace sitting in the District Court, the sheriff sitting in civil and criminal matters, the Senators of the College of Justice sitting in the superior Scottish courts and the Lords of Appeal in Ordinary sitting in the House of Lords in civil matters.

As indicated previously, the Justice of the Peace is not a legal practitioner but a lay person drawn from the community in which he serves. They are appointed by the Secretary of State for Scotland on the recommendation of local justices committees. These committees are charged with securing the services of suitable persons representative of the local community. Local authorities also have the right to nominate several of their members to serve as Justices of the Peace. Only a minority of all the Justices of the Peace in Scotland serve in the capacity as a judge in the district court.

Solicitors or advocates of at least 10 years' standing are eligible to be appointed as sheriffs. As well as the numerous full-time appointments, there are a considerable number of temporary appointments to help ensure the operation of the many sheriff court activities. Sheriffs may hold office until they are 72 years of age.

Senior judicial appointments in Scotland are made by the Queen on the recommendation of the Government (usually after consultation with the Lord Advocate and the Secretary of State for Scotland). There are currently 27 Senators of the College of Justice. Those eligible for appointment are sheriffs, sheriffs principal who have held office for five years, and advocates and solicitor-advocates who have had extended rights of audience in the superior courts of Scotland for a period of five years. In reality all appointments to senior judicial office have been lawyers who have practised as advocates at a very senior level. It is often the case that judges have previously been Dean, or vice-Dean, of the Faculty of Advocates, Lord Advocate or a senior Advocate Depute. Judges at this level are granted the honorary title of "Lord" although they have no entitlement to sit in the House of Lords. All judges have the same rank; promotion to the Inner House is by way of selection from amongst the body of judges. The two most senior judicial appointments may be appointed direct to their office. Indeed the last two serving Lords President were directly appointed to their posts over the other judges. Judges must retire at 75. However, there is no formal mechanism for appointing them, no scrutiny of appointments, and only very limited training. By 1993, eight non-retired temporary judges had been appointed, including two QCs and six sheriffs. Sheriff Aronson, appointed in 1992, was the first woman to sit having assumed the title of Lady Cosgrove.

Lords of Appeal in Ordinary sitting in the House of Lords are appointed by the Queen on the advice of the Prime Minister (in practice after consultation with the Lord Advocate and the Secretary of State for Scotland). Invariably Scottish appointees are judges promoted from the Court of Session.

Ombudsmen

Parliamentary Ombudsman

The first Ombudsman in the United Kingdom was the Parliamentary Commissioner for **2.41** Administration (PCA) set up in 1967. Arguably, the system has been successful to the extent that a number of other ombudsmen have sprung up in various avenues of public and private service.[94] The PCA deals with allegations of maladministration on the part of the Government in exercise of its functions. The PCA is appointed by the Queen[95] and is answerable to Parliament. The work of the PCA is scrutinised by Parliament's Select Committee on Public Administration to whom he submits his reports. Maladministration includes bias, neglect, inattention, delay, incompetence, ineptitude, perversity, turpitude and arbitrariness.[96] The definition is intended to be wide. It does not allow challenge to a decision which the complainant believes to be wrong on its merits, but rather is more concerned in how that decision was reached and the procedural methodology.

The PCA receives about 1300 complaints a year.[97] More than half are rejected as being outwith the Ombudsman's jurisdiction. Individual complaints of maladministration are passed to the Parliamentary Ombudsman through individual M.P.s. This need not be the person's own M.P. though it is likely that an M.P. receiving a request for referral from a person outside his constituency will notify the appropriate M.P., or indeed refer the person to that M.P. There has been much criticism of this filter mechanism over the years.[98] Complaints can be made either by the aggrieved party or, if deceased, their legal representative. The person will have to be resident in the United Kingdom at the time of making the complaint, or when the maladministration complained of took place.[99]

To assist the Parliamentary Ombudsman there is a Director of Screening who receives the complaints, seeks further information from M.P.s, and generally acts as a hub before the PCA formally investigates. It may become apparent at the screening stage that it is not appropriate for the Ombudsman to deal with the referral, and as a consequence informal advice may be given to pursue the matter through a different channel. The target screening period is three weeks.[1]

The Parliamentary Ombudsman has a discretion whether to pursue a complaint or not.[2] He cannot be compelled to investigate when he declines to do so.[3] The PCA cannot act on their own initiative, but must respond to a complaint by a member of the public routed through an M.P. Complaints may only be made within 12 months of the matter coming to the attention of the person making the complaint.[4] Usually, the PCA will not investigate a matter which has not exhausted legal remedies.[5] He may not investigate matters involving foreign affairs, national security, the commencement or conduct of court proceedings, the exercise of the Royal Prerogative of Mercy, commercial and contractual transactions entered into by

[94]   There are ombudsmen in respect of the European Parliament, local government, the health service, the legal profession, building societies, banking, travel agencies and insurance: see Ashton and Finch, *Administrative Law in Scotland* (1997), p. 166.
[95]   Parliamentary Commissioner for Administration Act 1967, s. 1(1) and (2).
[96]   See Ashton and Finch, *op. cit.*, pp. 173–175.
[97]   *ibid.*, p. 175.
[98]   *ibid.*, pp. 167–168.
[99]   Parliamentary Commissioner for Administration Act 1967 ("1967 Act"), s. 6(2) and (4).
[1]   Annual Report of the PCA, 1994 H.C. 307, App. B.
[2]   1967 Act, s. 5(3); *R. v. PCA, ex p. Dyer* [1994] 1 W.L.R. 621.
[3]   1967 Act, s. 5(5).
[4]   *ibid.*, s. 6(3).
[5]   1967 Act, s. 5(2) (a) and (b); where it is not reasonable for the complainant to pursue a legal remedy he may investigate; see also *Congreve v. Home Office* [1976] 1 All E.R. 697.

Government, and personnel matters of the civil service or armed forces or the grant of honours.

If he decides to investigate, the Parliamentary Ombudsman informs the relevant government department. He has the power to compel written or oral evidence from departmental officials. The government minister cannot impede the investigation. Wilful obstruction of the Ombudsman's investigation is an offence.[6] The average time for an investigation is around 70 weeks.[7] On completion of the investigation the Parliamentary Commissioner sends a copy of his report to the government department complained of and to the M.P. who first brought the case to him. The department is given an opportunity to comment on his findings. There is no such reciprocal right of the complainant to see the draft report.[8]

One of the perceived problems of the PCA is that his decisions are not legally enforceable. He may nevertheless recommend the payment of compensation on an *ex gratia* basis. Significantly, he has the power to lay a special report on the matter before Parliament and the Select Committee. In turn, the committee may require officials from the offending department to attend to explain themselves. In essence the system works entirely on the basis of public shaming and the expectation that the government will respond on a voluntary basis to the promptings and exhortations of the Ombudsman.

Local Government Ombudsman

2.42   Modelled on the Parliamentary Commissioner and introduced by the Local Government (Scotland) Act 1975, the Commissioner for Local Administration in Scotland seeks to fulfil a similar role in respect of local government as that undertaken by the Parliamentary Ombudsman. As well as considering complaints against local government, the Local Government Ombudsman (LGO) also deals with complaints against Scottish Homes. The largest proportion of cases which the LGO deals with are housing-related. Complaints no longer require to be fed through a councillor but can be sent direct to the LGO. This stands in contrast to the Parliamentary Ombudsman. Councils will usually have forms for complaint displayed prominently in their offices. Complaints must be raised within 12 months of the matter coming to the attention of the complainant. The LGO has the power to compel the local authority, or other body, to hand over information. The LGO cannot investigate where there exists a legal remedy. Nor can he investigate certain matters such as personnel matters, or matters pertaining to civil or criminal courts. If the LGO decides that the complaint is within his jurisdiction, he will refer a copy of the complaint to the local authority or other body in question and ask them to respond. On receipt of a complaint, many authorities will suspend any further action on the complainant's case pending the outcome of the complainant's referral. In that sense sometimes the complainant is better seeking redress through an alternative, less formal avenue. On receipt of the local authority's response, the LGO may decide to launch a formal investigation. Very few cases result in formal investigation.[9] Where an investigation does ensue, it usually lasts less than six months.

The powers of the LGO are limited in that all he can do is issue a report asking the local authority to adopt his recommendations. If they fail to do so he may issue another report expressing his displeasure. In the event that the local authority refuses to comply, he has the power to compel them to place an advert in a local newspaper detailing the complaint and the LGO's decision. The system works on the basis of application of public and peer pressure to

6   1967 Act, s. 9(1).
7   Annual Report of PCA, 1994 H.C. 307, App. B.
8   See *R. v. PCA, ex p. Dyer* [1994] 1 W.L.R. 621.
9   In 1994/5 there were 13 formal investigations in respect of 1,002 complaints.

conform. There have been notable examples where local authorities have not been deterred by such pressure.

The Scottish Legal Services Ombudsman

There is also a Scottish Legal Services Ombudsman (SLSO) set up in 1990. This purpose is to **2.43** investigate complaints of mishandling by the Law Society of Scotland of complaints against solicitors by members of the public. The remit has now expanded to encompass the Faculty of Advocates and the Conveyancing and Licensed Executry Services Board.[10] Ashton and Finch say of the SLSO that

> "He does not act as an appeal from the findings of a professional body and he does not act as a conciliator between the complainant and the member of the professional body. He reviews the actions of the professional body and reports whether they acted properly in handling the complaint."[11]

Following investigation the SLSO reports to the complainant and the professional body. He has no powers of enforcement, although he may take a case direct to the Scottish Solicitors Discipline Tribunal. Following the legislative amendment in 1997, the SLSO also has the power to recommend that the professional body pay compensation of up to £1,000 for any loss, inconvenience, or distress.[12]

The complainant writes direct to the SLSO. There must have been a prior complaint to the professional body about one of its members. The referral to the SLSO relates to how the professional body dealt with that complaint. The SLSO must first decide if the matter is within his competence and jurisdiction. Roughly a third of all cases are rejected at a preliminary stage for these reasons. The SLSO may refuse to investigate or discontinue an investigation.[13] The professional body is under a legal duty to consider the recommendations of the SLSO and inform him of their considerations and actions.[14] The SLSO may also report any matter to the Secretary of State.

The National Health Service Ombudsman

The National Health Service (Scotland) Act 1972 introduced the post of Health Service **2.44** Commissioner for Scotland.[15] The post has since its inception been concurrently held by the PCA. The Health Service Commissioner may investigate (a) an alleged failure in service by a health service body, (b) an alleged failure of a health service body to provide a service it was its function to provide, or (c) maladministration connected with any action taken by the health service body. There is no power to investigate where there is in existence an alternative judicial remedy. In 1996, jurisdiction was expanded to include complaints against

---

[10]   Law Reform (Misc. Prov.) (Scotland) Act 1990, s. 34(1), as amended by the Scottish Legal Services Ombudsman and Commissioner for Local Administration in Scotland Act 1997.
[11]   Ashton and Finch, *Administrative Law in Scotland* (1997), p. 181.
[12]   Law Reform (Misc. Prov.) (Scotland) Act 1990, s. 34A, as inserted by the Scottish Legal Services Ombudsman and Commissioner for Local Administration in Scotland Act 1997.
[13]   Law Reform (Misc. Prov.) (Scotland) Act 1990, s. 34(1C) and (1D), as inserted by the Scottish Legal Services Ombudsman and Commissioner for Local Administration in Scotland Act 1997.
[14]   Law Reform (Misc. Prov.) (Scotland) Act 1990, s. 34A, as inserted by the Scottish Legal Services Ombudsman and Commissioner for Local Administration in Scotland Act 1997.
[15]   The law is now consolidated in the Health Service Commissioners Act 1993.

those providing primary health care services, and to investigate cases involving clinical judgment.[16]

Not surprisingly given the concurrent role, reports of the Health Service Commissioner follow a similar pattern to that of the PCA.[17] Around half of all complaints are rejected as falling outside the HSC's jurisdiction. Reports are sent to the Secretary of State for Scotland, or to the regional or area health authority. Annual reports are made to the Secretary of State who lays them before Parliament. Complaints are not filtered through M.P.s; complainants have direct access. Complaints must ordinarily be made within 12 months of the matter complained of arising. A health service body may make a referral to the HSC for independent enquiry into a matter.[18] It is not appropriate to refer general matters, such as staffing levels—many referrals of this, and a similar type, are not investigated.

JUDICIAL REVIEW

2.45   The growth in the power and influence of government in the everyday lives of citizens has given rise to broadening concern. The court procedure by which citizens can legally challenge decisions of government or other public bodies is known as judicial review. Judicial review in Scotland is only possible in the Court of Session. Judicial review exists not to challenge the merits of government decisions, but rather to ensure that they are made fairly, in conformity with the law, and within the powers of the authority making them.

Decisions of public authorities can be challenged on the basis that the authority has exceeded the power granted to it. This is known as acting *ultra vires* (outwith its powers). There are of course many instances where a public authority is entrusted with a duty. Many of the social work statutes confer such duties. The failure to fulfil a duty may result in a legal challenge to the authority, and it is possible that a court order compelling compliance with that duty may be sought. Under the Court of Session Act 1988, the Court of Session may order the specific performance of a statutory duty on such conditions and penalties as seem fit where the duty is not complied with.[19] The duty must be specific and unequivocal.[20] It is a remedy of last resort after other avenues have been exhausted.[21] Moreover, the exercise of powers and duties often requires the exercise of discretion. Judicial review can be used to legally challenge the exercise of discretion on the basis that it has exceeded the legal power of the person or body exercising that legal discretion. In addition there will often be challenges on the basis of procedural impropriety.

Under the common law, there is a right to seek judicial review of a decision of a public authority. This right exists whether a statute confers a right of appeal or not. Judicial review may be used to review the decisions of public authorities, voluntary organisations, and some private bodies.[22] All decisions, acts and omissions of public authorities are potentially reviewable.[23]

[16]   See Bradley and Ewing, *Constitutional and Administrative Law* (12th ed., 1997), pp. 764–765; Health Service Commissioners (Amendment) Act 1996.
[17]   See Wade and Forsyth, *Administrative Law* (7th ed., 1994) at p. 103.
[18]   See Foulkes, *Administrative Law* (8th ed., 1995), p. 546.
[19]   The Court of Session Act 1988, s. 45(b).
[20]   Ashton and Finch, *Administrative Law in Scotland* (1997), pp. 220–221.
[21]   *ibid.*, p. 224; *O'Neil v. SJNC for Teaching Staff*, 1987 S.L.T. 648; *Strathclyde Buses v. SRC* 1994 S.L.T. 724.
[22]   See Clyde, "The Nature of the Supervisory Jurisdiction and the Public/Private Distinction in Scots Administrative Law" in Finnie, Himsworth and Walker (eds), *Essays in Scots Law* (1991).
[23]   Smith, "The Scope of Judicial Review Determined", 1997 J.R. 122; Smith, "Contract or Tripartite Arrangement—Rooney v. Chief Constable of Strathclyde Police", 1998 J.R. 193; Ashton and Finch, *op. cit.*, p. 243.

Social work and housing services are likely subjects of judicial review cases where the member of the public is generally dissatisfied with his treatment at the hands of the public authority. The importance of judicial review in this regard cannot be over-stated. The difficulty of accessing delictual remedies for a breach of statutory duty by a local authority (discussed in Chapter 10) make judicial review often the major avenue of judicial redress for those dissatisfied with the way in which the local authority has carried out its functions.

The remedies available to a person or body seeking judicial review are relatively limited.[24]   **2.46**
One can obtain a declarator[25] setting out one's rights or the duties of the authority; an order of reduction[26] cancelling the authority's decision; an interdict[27]; an order of specific performance[28]; damages[29]; and any other specific statutory remedy. Often the main remedy of reduction simply puts the person seeking judicial review back in the position he was in before the authority made the decision. So, for example, someone successfully winning a case against the allocation decision of a housing authority may not be allocated a house, but simply have the council's original decision not to allocate reduced. The local authority may subsequently reconsider the applicant's case, follow a correct procedure, and still not allocate. Furthermore, the court has a discretion as to whether to grant a reduction. Therefore, even if the applicant proves the case against the authority, the court may refuse to grant a remedy if they are of the opinion that it would not lead to a change in the decision.[30]

NON-LEGAL AND NON-FORMAL REMEDIES/ADVICE

As an adviser, advocate, or facilitator for the social work client, the social work professional   **2.47**
will often need to enlist the advice and assistance of others for the benefit of their client. It is a fact that first resort to legal remedies may be neither appropriate or particularly helpful. This is not to minimise the importance of the law, or the mechanisms that exist for enforcing legal rights. These can be powerful in the correct situation, and indeed may be the only resort in many cases. There exist, however, many agencies and avenues of advice and support which stop some way short of lawyers and the courts. In many instances these agencies can be more expert, more helpful and less expensive than enlisting the services of a lawyer and pursuing litigation. For example, there are a number of voluntary organisations that exist in a range of social work fields which provide valuable services and which can be the source of helpful advice and information. Consumer organisations such as Citizen's Advice Bureaux, Welfare Rights Organisations, and other groups for particular specialist client groups such as SHELTER, MENCAP, and ENABLE, may be the source of much help to the client and the professional alike. There are likewise a number of organisations which seek to assist the resolving of disputes by "alternative" means other than through the courts.[31]

---

[24]   See Ashton and Finch, *Administrative Law in Scotland* (1997), Chap. 14.
[25]   *e.g. Rossi v. Edinburgh Mags* (1904) 7 F. (H.L.) 85; *Stirling C.C. v. Falkirk Mags. 1911 S.C. 1282; Ayr Mags. v. Lord Advocate*, 1950, S.C. 102.
[26]   *e.g. Smith v. H.M. Advocate*, 1994 S.L.T. 1161 (partial reduction).
[27]   *e.g. Deane v. Lothian R.C.*, 1986 S.L.T. 22; *McColl v. Strathclyde RC*, 1983 S.L.T. 616.
[28]   *Docherty v. Monifieth Town Council*, 1970 S.C. 200.
[29]   Only available in limited situation: see *Kelly v. Monklands D.C.*, 1986 S.L.T. 169; *Ministry of Housing v. Sharp* [1970] 2 Q.B. 223.
[30]   *King v. East Ayrshire Council*, 1998 S.C. 182.
[31]   See Mays and Clark, *Alternative Dispute Resolution in Scotland*, (Scottish Office, 1996), Chap. 2; Clark and Mays, "Its Good to Talk—Community Mediation in Scotland", 1998 *The Police Journal*, pp. 4–14.

As many of the social and welfare services are provided by local and central government, the assistance of a councillor, or M.P., may be of great importance. The elected representative holds considerable influence with officialdom and in any situation involving an exercise of discretion it is he more than any other person or agency who may have the capacity to influence matters to the benefit of the individual. Informal routes in general often yield better results than formal ones. The involvement of lawyers and ombudsmen can often instil rigidity in the exercise of discretion and in that way work against the interests of the client. It is difficult in a book of this nature to offer anything other than general advice. It will be a question of being aware of all the relevant avenues and making a value judgment as to the best course of action in the given circumstances but, as a basic premise, formality of complaint and formality of process does not necessarily secure the most expeditious and beneficial resolution to the problem at hand.

Chapter 3

PARENTS, CHILDREN, FAMILY RELATIONSHIPS AND THE LAW

As an integral feature of social work, practitioners must deal with people from a variety of **3.01** backgrounds. Family history and family setting are often important issues in meeting a client's social work needs. Inevitably, a sound knowledge of the law relating to family life becomes a necessary supplement to the core knowledge of social work practice. Amongst the principal issues which are addressed in this chapter are those which are deemed central to the functions of social workers on a daily basis—the formation of family relationships and the legal significance of those relationships, the key relationship of parent and child, and the obligations which arise from it.

Society has undergone major transformation in the past few years. Divorce is commonplace, single parentage has increased, cohabitation is widespread, and there is remarriage and reconstitution of family in ever increasing numbers. The law has also undergone substantial transformation to respond in part to the changing social circumstances. More than ever, the law is important to families and as a consequence the law that regulates, fashions and underpins family relationships is important to those who work with families in a social work capacity.

MARRIAGE

The formation of the relationship of marriage in Scotland is primarily regulated by the **3.02** Marriage (Scotland) Act 1977. In addition to marriage by "regular" means by way of civil or religious ceremony, Scots law recognises one form of "irregular" marriage—marriage by cohabitation with habit and repute.[1] There are various restrictions on marriage. First, no one under 16 years of age may get married in Scotland.[2] Parental consent to marry is not necessary for young persons between 16 and 18.[3] Where either, or both, the parties to a marriage is under 16 the marriage is automatically void.[4] Certain parties stand in forbidden degrees of relationship to one another with the effect that any marriage between these

---

[1] For a discussion of marriage by cohabitation with habit and repute see Clive, *The Law of Husband and Wife in Scotland* (4th ed., 1998) pp. 48–65; Ashton-Cross, "Cohabitation with Habit and Repute", 1961 J.R. 21; Sellar, "Marriage by Cohabitation with Habit and Repute: Review and Requiem?" in Carey Miller and Meyes (eds), *Comparative and Historical Essays in Scots Law* (1992), pp. 117–136.

[2] Marriage (Scotland) Act 1977 ("1977 Act"), s. 1.

[3] See also Clive, "Parental Consent to Marry", 1968 S.L.T. (News) 129–132 for pre-1977 position.

[4] 1977 Act, s. 1(2).

parties is also void.[5] These relationships are all based upon consanguinity (blood relationship), affinity (through marriage), or adoption. Certain relaxations were introduced by the Marriage (Prohibited Degrees of Relationship) Act 1986 so that certain parties who were once related by affinity can now marry provided they have:

(a) both attained the age of 21 at the time of the marriage; and

(b) the younger party has not at any time before attaining the age of 18 lived in the same house as the other party and has not been treated by the other party as a child of the family.[6]

Thus, for example, this relaxation might allow a woman to marry the former husband of her mother provided they satisfy the conditions laid down in the statute.

Other persons who are related within the degrees of affinity[7] may marry provided both parties have attained the age of 21 and the marriage is solemnised (a) in the case of a man marrying his mother-in-law or daughter-in-law, after the deaths of his former wife and her father or the deaths of his son and his son's mother, and (b) in the case of a woman marrying her father-in-law or her son-in-law, after the deaths of her former husband and his mother or the deaths of her daughter and her daughter's father.

There is no congruity between the relationships of incest, for which there is criminal liability, and the forbidden degrees of marriage.[8] In some situations it is lawful to have sexual intercourse with a person who nevertheless one is forbidden to marry. Moreover, as forbidden relationships of affinity arise through marriage, no restrictions apply to partners of former cohabitees. It is not altogether certain why particular relations are prohibited from marrying each other. Principally, theories centre around two themes—genetic issues and social and policy considerations. The latter view must now be considered the predominant theory. The social disruption which would ensue from allowing persons of whatever relationship to marry is fairly obvious and indeed the relaxation of the forbidden degrees by affinity introduced in 1986 also suggest that social disruption lies at the root of prohibition.

3.03   Scots law does not recognise same sex marriage.[9] Various attempts have been made recently to challenge United Kingdom law on the basis that the prohibition is an infringement of Articles 8 and 12 of the European Convention on Human Rights. All such attempts have been unsuccessful.[10] The law is also such that transsexuals are not allowed to marry persons of their own sex.[11]

3.04   Another major impediment to marriage is that persons who are already married may not enter into marriage until that prior subsisting marriage is dissolved.[12] Further, as marriage is a consensual agreement, it is the case that a number of matters which may indicate that consent was not truly given may impact on the validity of the marriage. These grounds can be

---

[5]   1977 Act, s. 2(1); see Sched. 1 for a full list of the prohibited relationships; Ross, "Forbidden Degrees of Matrimony" (1987) 32 J.L.S.S. 20–22.

[6]   1977 Act, s. 2(1A) as inserted by the Marriage (Prohibited Degrees of Relationship) Act 1986, para. 2(b) of Sched. 2.

[7]   1977 Act, s. 2 (1B) as inserted by the Marriage (Prohibited Degrees of Relationship) Act 1986, para. 2(b) of Sched. 2: mother of former wife; father of former husband; former wife of son; former husband of daughter.

[8]   See Norrie, "Incest And Forbidden Degrees Of Marriage In Scots Law" (1992) 37 J.L.S.S. 216.

[9]   1977 Act, s. 5(4); *Corbett v. Corbett* [1971] P. 83.

[10]   *Rees v. U.K.* [1986] 9 E.H.R.R. 56; *Cossey v. U.K.* [1991] 13 E.H.R.R. 622; "Transsexuals, The Right To Marry And Voidable Marriages In Scots Law", 1990 S.L.T. (News) 353; *Report on Family Law*, Scot. Law Com. No. 135 (1992), p. 68; Lind, "Time for Lesbian and Gay Marriages" (1995) 145 N.L.J. 1553–4. Art. 12 of Sched. 1 to the Human Rights Act 1998 states, "Men and women of marriageable age have the right to marry and to found a family, according to the national laws governing the exercise of this right."

[11]   See *Report on Family Law*, Scot. Law Com. No. 135 (1992) at p. 68.

[12]   *Burke v. Burke*, 1983 S.L.T. 331.

variously stated as mental incapacity, intoxication, error or fraud, force and fear, or that the marriage is a sham. Mentally incapacitated people can marry but it is essential that they are capable of understanding the relationship of marriage and are capable of freely giving their consent.[13] Attempts to have marriage dissolved on the basis that one or other of the parties was intoxicated so as to affect their consent must have a highly improbable prospect of success in the modern era.[14] The formal preliminaries to marriage will point towards an intention to be married, and with it there will be implicit consent notwithstanding the intoxication of one or both of the parties at the time of the ceremony. Similarly, error will only succeed as a basis of dissolution in the most unlikely of circumstances either in respect of the identity of the party to be married, or the nature of the ceremony. One cannot seek to annul a marriage on the basis of error as to quality of the spouse.[15] Moreover, fraud is not thought to be a ground of nullity in Scots law.[16]

Altogether a more fertile ground of nullity is where the marriage is entered into under **3.05** force and fear or where the marriage is a sham marriage. In respect of force and fear it must be shown that the consent of the party was genuinely overcome by the application of pressure inducing fear in that person.[17] In recent years in Scotland, there has been legal controversy over arranged marriages common in certain ethnic groups. It had been thought that simple parental pressure and disapproval might not be sufficient force and fear to invalidate the marriage. However, it now seems clear following the cases of *Mahmood*[18] and *Mahmud*[19] that the courts are prepared to consider whether the consent of the party was genuinely overcome by the force and fear induced by parental pressure and opprobrium. Arranged marriages *per se* are not invalid—they will only be so when the court considers that parental pressure has been forceful enough to overcome the party's true consent to be married.

In "sham marriages" the supposition is that both parties do not truly consent to be married and that they are simply entering into a marriage of convenience for some ulterior purpose, often, but not exclusively, connected with immigration. Although the Scottish Law Commission has recommended that regular marriage should not be reducible on the basis that one or both parties had the belief that, despite the ceremony, no legal marriage would result from it,[20] Scots law continues to accept that sham marriages may be set aside on the basis that the parties did not consent.[21]

Where a marriage is declared void the law presupposes that it was void from the beginning **3.06** and treats it as though it did not take place at all. The normal route for a party wishing to annul their marriage would be to raise an action for declarator of nullity in the Court of Session.[22] Any party with an interest in having the marriage declared void may bring proceedings at any time.[23] Where a marriage is declared null and void, the courts have the power to order financial settlement using a process similar to that which applies in divorce

13   *Long v. Long*, 1950 S.L.T. (Notes) 32.
14   Contrast this with the dated case of *Johnston v. Browne* (1823) 2 S. 495.
15   *Lang v. Lang*, 1921 S.C. 44.
16   See Clive, *Husband and Wife* (3rd ed., 1992) at p. 88; *cf.* England, s. 12(e) and (f), Matrimonial Causes Act 1973.
17   See *Buckland v. Buckland* [1968] P. 296; *Mahmood v. Mahmood*, 1993 S.L.T. 589; *Mahmud v. Mahmud* 1994 S.L.T. 599.
18   1993 S.L.T. 589.
19   1994 S.L.T. 599.
20   *Report on Family Law*, Scot. Law Com. No. 135 (1992), para. 8.20.
21   *Orlandi v. Castelli*, 1961 S.C. 113; *Mahmud v. Mahmud*, 1977 S.L.T. (Notes) 17; *Akram v. Akram*, 1979 S.L.T. (Notes) 87; *Ebrahem v. Ebrahem*, 1989 S.L.T. 808.
22   Sheriff Courts (Scotland) Act 1907, s. 5(1) precludes these actions in the sheriff court; *cf.* Scot. Law Com. *Report on Family Law* (1992), para. 9.1.
23   Edwards and Griffiths, *Family Law* (1997), p. 265.

proceedings.[24] Fathers retain parental rights and responsibilities in respect of children born into the dissolved marriage (mothers automatically have them).[25] Where one of the parents believed the marriage to be valid (known as putative marriage) children are deemed to be legitimate children of the two parties. The importance and legal impact of legitimacy is of course much reduced in modern Scots family law.[26]

3.07   There is one ground upon which a marriage is voidable as opposed to void, in other words legally valid until such times as it is challenged and subsequently declared void. This takes effect from the start of the marriage notwithstanding any delay in seeking a challenge. Where one of the parties is incurably impotent a declarator can be sought to dissolve the marriage. Incurable impotency exists where one party is unable to have full and complete sexual intercourse with the other party and that incapacity is incurable.[27] The incurable impotency must have existed at the commencement of the marriage. A refusal to engage in sexual relations or the absence of procreative capacity will not be enough to make a marriage voidable, just as supervening impotency does not constitute a ground of nullity. A person may be personally barred from seeking a reduction in the marriage if he or she knew of their condition before the marriage and accepted it,[28] or where his or her actions were such that it would be inequitable to allow them to seek nullity. In situations where the party has acquiesced in artificial insemination of his wife, or adopted a child, there will be no prospect of the court granting a declarator of nullity.[29] It is possible for a party to found on their own incurable impotency.[30]

3.08   As indicated it is possible in Scots law to have a common law marriage by cohabitation with habit and repute formally and legally recognised. However, various prerequisites apply. First, the parties must be cohabiting as husband and wife. Simply engaging in sexual relations is not enough. Someone of Scottish domicile who seeks to have a declarator of marriage on the basis of cohabitation with habit and repute can only rely upon cohabitation after the parties reach the age of 16.[31] The cohabitation must take place in Scotland.[32] Moreover, the cohabitation must be for a sufficiently long period to establish habit.[33] The parties must have the repute of being husband and wife. Repute need not be universal but must be substantially unvarying and consistent and not divided.[34] Even although the parties have discussed going through a regular marriage ceremony this will not operate to bar any claim that they view themselves as husband and wife.[35] Before marriage by cohabitation with habit and repute can take place there must be no lawful impediment to the marriage. In situations where the parties have cohabited together for a long period of time, but throughout most of that time there has been an impediment, for instance a prior subsisting marriage, they can nevertheless expect a reasonably sympathetic view being taken by the courts of the short duration of the

---

[24]   Family Law (Scotland) Act 1985 ("1985 Act"), s. 17(1).
[25]   Children (Scotland) Act 1995, s. 3(2).
[26]   Edwards and Griffiths, *Family Law* (1997), para. 5.26 at p. 138.
[27]   *J v. J*, 1978 S.L.T. 128; *M v. M*, 1966 S.L.T. 152.
[28]   *L v. L*, 1931 S.C. 477.
[29]   *AB v. CB*, 1961 S.C. 347.
[30]   *F v. F*, 1945 S.C. 202.
[31]   See Thomson, *Family Law In Scotland* (3rd ed., 1996), p. 23; *AB v. CD*, 1957 S.C. 415.
[32]   *Dysart Peerage Case* (1881) L.R. 6 App. Cas. 489, *per* Lord Watson at pp. 537–538; *Walker v. Roberts*, 1998 S.L.T. 1133.
[33]   *Campbell v. Campbell* (1866) 4 M. 867; *Wallace v. Fife Coal Co.*, 1909 S.C. 682; *Kamperman v. McIver*, 1994 S.L.T. 763; *cf. Shaw v. Henderson*, 1982 S.L.T. 211; *Mullen v. Mullen*, 1991 S.L.T. 205.
[34]   *Low v. Gorman*, 1970 S.L.T. 356; see *Petrie v. Petrie*, 1911 S.C. 360; *Gow v. Lord Advocate*, 1993 S.L.T. 275; *Mackenzie v. Scott*, 1980 S.L.T. (Notes) 9; *Shaw v. Henderson*, 1982 S.L.T. 211.
[35]   *Dewar v. Dewar*, 1995 S.L.T. 467; see also *Walker v. Roberts*, 1998 S.L.T. 1133 where evidence of hostility to getting married did act as a bar.

impediment-free cohabitation.[36] Where a party wishes to have a marriage by cohabitation with habit and repute formally recognised they must raise an action of declarator of marriage in the Court of Session. Where the action is successful the court will set a date on which the marriage took place and thereafter the marriage will be registered similar to a regular marriage.[37]

The legal consequences of marriage

Whilst the social and legal significance of marriage is arguably diminishing there are nevertheless a number of important legal consequences which ensue from the relationship. Some consequences simply arise from cohabitation[38] but there are several consequences which are directly related to marriage. There is no longer a direct duty for a wife to reside with her husband where he chooses.[39] The obligation to stay impliedly arises from the law of divorce where irretrievable breakdown of marriage may be established by desertion or two years' non-cohabitation with consent of both parties, or five years' non-cohabitation. There is also an implicit duty to be faithful to your spouse.[40] **3.09**

An important legal consequence of marriage is a spouse's obligation to aliment the other during the subsistence of the marriage. Both husbands and wives owe the obligation of aliment to each other, *i.e.* to provide such support as is reasonable in the circumstances having regard to (a) the needs and resources of the parties; (b) the earning capacity of the parties; and (c) generally to all the circumstances of the case.[41] No account should be taken of the conduct of the parties unless it is manifestly inequitable to leave it out.[42] Although unusual, it is possible for one spouse to raise an action for aliment against the other whilst living in the same house.[43] It will be a defence to a claim for aliment to prove that the obligation is already being fulfilled while the spouse is in the house and that this will continue in the future.[44] Indeed as a general defence, it might be proved that the defender has offered to maintain the claiming spouse in the defender's home in circumstances which it is reasonable to expect the spouse seeking aliment to accept.[45] It is possible to have awards of interim aliment and for variations of interim aliment where there is a material change in circumstances.[46] Parties may also by agreement reach a voluntary arrangement on the level of aliment.[47] **3.10**

Another of the major legal consequences of marriage relates to rights in succession following the death of a spouse. Spouses have prior rights and legal rights. Under the Succession (Scotland) Act 1964 a spouse has "legal rights" over his or her spouse's estate irrespective of whether that spouse leaves a will. If there are children of the deceased a spouse is entitled to a third share of the moveable estate (basically everything which is not heritage). If there are no children then the surviving spouse is entitled to legal rights **3.11**

---

[36] See Edwards and Griffiths, *Family Law* (1997), p. 274.
[37] 1977 Act, s. 21.
[38] See para. 3.28.
[39] Law Reform (Husband and Wife) (Scotland) Act 1984, ss 2 and 4; *cf. Stewart v. Stewart*, 1959 S.L.T. (Notes) 70.
[40] See para. 3.15; *Donnelly v. Donnelly*, 1959 S.C. 97.
[41] 1985 Act, s. 4(1).
[42] *ibid.*, s. 4(3)(6).
[43] *ibid.*, s. 2(b).
[44] *ibid.*, s. 2(7).
[45] *ibid.*, s. 2(9); *Pryde v. Pryde*, 1991 S.L.T. (Sh. Ct.) 26.
[46] See *Ritchie v. Ritchie*, 1987 S.L.T. (Sh. Ct.) 7; *Neill v. Neill*, 1987 (Sh. Ct.) 143; *Harper v. Harper*, 1990 G.W.D. 40–2322; *Stenhouse v. Stenhouse*, 1990 G.W.D. 28–1609; *Bisset v. Bisset*, 1993 S.C.L.R. 284.
[47] 1985 Act, s. 7.

amounting to half of the moveable estate. In testate succession cases the provisions of the will are implemented in so far as they can be after the payment of legal rights to the spouse. Legal rights may be discharged by acceptance of the will's provisions or by agreeing to waive them during the lifetime of the deceased. Obviously, legal rights can be defeated by ensuring that one's estate comprises heritage alone or at leasts principally heritage.[48]

Where the deceased spouse leaves no will the surviving spouse may first claim prior rights.[49] This entitles the spouse to claim the dwellinghouse in which they were ordinarily resident prior to death up to a value of £110,000. Where the spouse leaves more than one house the surviving spouse may elect which home they will receive. Where the value of the deceased's share of the dwelling is more than £110,000 the spouse may elect to receive an equivalent cash sum. In addition to the dwellinghouse the surviving spouse may claim furnishings and plenishings up to a value of £20,000 and money up to the value of £30,000 if the deceased has children, or £50,000 if there are no children.[50] Following the claiming of prior rights, the surviving spouse may then claim legal rights as discussed above. The remainder of the estate will then be distributed in line with the normal rules of succession.

3.12   There are specific legal provisions surrounding the ownership of property which pertains to married persons. Generally speaking property, other than matrimonial property, owned by a married person is separately owned.[51] Accordingly, property acquired before marriage or in some instances during it will belong to a particular spouse. Savings from housekeeping are shared equally between spouses, as is anything purchased from those savings.[52]

3.13   There are special rules on competence and compellability of witnesses where one spouse is a witness against the other in criminal proceedings.[53] Husbands and wives are always competent but never compellable. One spouse may sue the other in a civil action.[54] Other than matrimonial proceedings, there are a number of possible matters where a dispute might ensue. A delictual claim is most likely. A spouse also has the right to sue a third party in circumstances where the injury or death of their spouse is caused by that person or persons.[55] The spouse may sue where appropriate for loss of society, loss of support, funeral expenses, and medical expenses. As spouse may also sue for recovery in respect of loss of services.[56] Cohabitees, in contrast, only have the right to seek loss of support, funeral expenses, and personal services.[57]

Separation and Divorce

3.14   It is an accepted fact that some relationships may come to an end. Where once it was viewed as a relationship for life, it has come to pass that frequently marriage like other relationships terminates. The modern era is one characterised by high divorce rates.[58] In consequence the law has had to respond not only to regulate the termination of the relationship of marriage

---

[48]   The Scottish Law Commission has called for legal rights to apply to heritable property as well as moveable. See *Report on Succession*, Scot. Law Com. No. 124 (1990).

[49]   Succession (Scotland) Act 1964, s. 8.

[50]   For current levels of prior rights see Prior Rights of Surviving Spouse (Scotland) Order 1993 (S.I. 1993 No. 2690).

[51]   1985 Act, s. 24; *Maclure v. Maclure*, 1911 S.C. 200; *Millar v. Millar*, 1940 S.C. 56; see also 1985 Act, s. 25.

[52]   1985 Act, s. 26; *Pyatt v. Pyatt*, 1966 S.L.T. (Notes) 73.

[53]   Criminal Procedure (Scotland) Act 1995, s. 264.

[54]   Law Reform (Husband and Wife) Act 1962, s. 2.

[55]   Damages (Scotland) Act, 1976 s. 1.

[56]   Administration of Justice Act 1982, ss. 7–9.

[57]   *ibid.*, s. 14.

[58]   See *Untying the Knot—Characteristics of Divorce in Scotland*, Scottish Office Report (1993).

but also to regulate the various affairs of the separating spouses. As a prelude to divorce, it is common for separating spouses to regulate their various affairs by way of a separation agreement. It will often be the case that in reaching agreement the spouses ensure a relatively straightforward passage when they come to seek divorce. Others will wish to press for divorce almost immediately the relationship has failed.

Divorce

The only ground on which divorce can be granted in Scotland is that the marriage has **3.15** irretrievably broken down.[59] Whether or not the marriage has broken down irretrievably will be determined by reference to five grounds[60]—adultery, behaviour, desertion, two years' non-cohabitation with both parties consenting to the divorce, or five years' non-cohabitation. The courts do not insist on attempts to conciliate to prove that the marriage has irretrievably broken down and there is no obligation on the parties to attempt to salvage the marriage. All they must do is establish one of the "fault grounds" to ascertain that the marriage has irretrievably broken down.

Adultery is voluntary sexual intercourse by a married person with a person of the opposite sex where that person is not their spouse. A single act of sexual intercourse is sufficient to constitute adultery. Pre-marital sexual relations cannot constitute adultery, nor can involuntary sexual relations amount to adultery.[61] For adultery to take place there must be penetration of the female sexual organ by the male sexual organ. Accordingly, other forms of sexual relations—oral sex or anal sex for example—do not amount to adultery. Artificial insemination is likewise not adultery.[62]

A party may invoke three defences to an action of adultery. Condonation is applied where the spouse argues that the other forgave the adultery and resumed marital relations in the full knowledge of that indiscretion.[63] Equally, it will be a defence to show that the spouse seeking a divorce on the grounds of adultery actually encouraged or induced the defender to commit adultery.[64] This is known as *lenocinium*.[65] Finally, where the parties collude to deceive the court, decree of divorce will be refused.[66]

A person may obtain a divorce on the basis that their spouse's behaviour since the marriage has been so bad that they cannot reasonably be expected to remain with them. Nearly a quarter of all divorce actions proceed on this basis.[67] The behaviour may be active or passive and may or may not be a result of mental abnormality.[68] Only behaviour since the date of marriage is relevant. One solitary instance of behaviour may be sufficient depending on the nature of what it is.[69] Behaviour is very widely construed and embraces a whole range of scenarios.[70] Each case will turn on its respective merits. Obviously violence, abuse or

---

[59]   Divorce (Scotland) 1976, s. 1(1).
[60]   Divorce (Scotland) Act 1976, s. 1(2); *Findlay v. Findlay*, 1991 S.L.T. 457 at p. 458.
[61]   *Stewart v. Stewart*, 1914 2 S.L.T. 310 (rape); see also *Hunter v. Hunter*, (1900) 2 F. 771.
[62]   *MacLennan v. MacLennan*, 1958 S.C. 105.
[63]   Divorce (Scotland) Act 1976, s. 1(3).
[64]   *Gallacher v. Gallacher*, 1928 S.C. 586; *cf. Thomson v. Thomson*, 1908 S.C. 179.
[65]   See Thomson, *Family Law in Scotland*, (3rd ed., 1996) pp. 102–103.
[66]   *Walker v. Walker*, 1911 S.C. 163; *Fairgrieve v. Chalmers*, 1912 S.C. 745; *McKenzie v. McKenzie*, 1935 S.L.T. 198.
[67]   See *Untying the Knot*, n. 58, *supra*.
[68]   Divorce (Scotland) Act 1976, s. 1(2)(b).
[69]   See *Gray v. Gray*, 1991 G.W.D. 8–477.
[70]   See *Knox v. Knox*, 1993 S.C.L.R. 381; *Findlay v. Findlay*, 1991 S.L.T. 457; *White v. White*, 1966 S.L.T. 288; *Stewart v. Stewart*, 1987 S.L.T. (Sh. Ct.) 48.

cruelty are examples of unreasonable behaviour, as are certain sexual improprieties stopping short of adultery.

Desertion as a ground of divorce is not commonplace. It occurs where a spouse "wilfully and without reasonable cause" deserts the spouse seeking the divorce and for two years after the desertion there has been no cohabitation between the parties,[71] and there has been a genuine and reasonable offer to adhere by the party seeking the divorce.[72] There must have been an intention to desert. Separation against one's will, for example imprisonment, cannot amount to desertion. Following the initial desertion the parties must not live together as man and wife. In this context engaging in sexual relations is not sufficient in itself to constitute living together; there must be cohabitation.[73]

The fourth basis of establishing irretrievable breakdown of marriage is that the parties have not cohabited for two years and both consent to the divorce. It is not important why the parties are not living together.[74] It is possible that parties may co-exist in close proximity (even in the same house) and not be cohabiting as man and wife.[75] However, the mere absence of sexual relations does not amount to non-cohabitation. The non-cohabitation must be for a continuous period of two years. In recognition of the fact that parties may attempt to reconcile, the law determines that resumption of cohabitation for periods not exceeding six months do not break the continuity of the two-year period but also do not count as part of it.[76] The spouse being divorced must consent to the granting of decree. They may withhold their consent for any reason or no reason.[77] Indeed consent to divorce may be withdrawn at any time.

The final avenue for a party seeking to establish irretrievable breakdown is that the parties have not cohabited for a continuous period of five years after the date of the marriage and immediately prior to bringing the action of divorce. The consent of the spouse being divorced is not required. Despite one assuming that a period of five years apart might convince anyone that the marriage is over, there is scope within the Divorce (Scotland) Act 1976 for the court to refuse to grant divorce. If it is thought that there will be grave financial hardship arising from the divorce then the court may refuse decree.[78] Only in the most unusual of circumstances can it be imagined that divorce will not ensue.[79]

Judicial separation

3.16   As an alternative to divorce, judicial separation remains an option for parties whose marriage is at an end. The grounds for obtaining a judicial separation are exactly the same as those for obtaining a divorce.[80] A party may obtain a judicial separation order and thereafter proceed to obtain a divorce. Parties judicially separating still have an obligation to aliment each other and cannot remarry. There remains the obligation of fidelity and behaviour.[81] A further consequence is that a husband loses any rights in succession to his wife's property

---

71   *Lennie v. Lennie*, 1950 S.C. (H.L.) 1.
72   Divorce (Scotland) Act 1976, s. 1(2)(c).
73   *Edmond v. Edmond*, 1971 S.L.T. (Notes) 8; see the Divorce (Scotland) Act 1976, s. 13(2).
74   There is a suggestion in England that the parties must have the intention to be apart. See *Santos v. Santos* [1972] 2 All E.R. 246.
75   Divorce (Scotland) Act 1976, s. 13(2).
76   *ibid.*, s. 2(4).
77   *Boyle v. Boyle*, 1977 S.L.T. (Notes) 69; *Donnelly v. Donnelly*, 1991 S.L.T. (Sh. Ct.) 9.
78   For a discussion on this see Thomson, *Family Law In Scotland*, (3rd ed., 1996), pp. 114–116.
79   *Nolan v. Nolan*, 1979 S.L.T. 293; *Norris v. Norris*, 1992 S.L.T. (Sh. Ct.) 51.
80   Divorce (Scotland) Act 1976, s. 4.
81   See Clive, *Husband and Wife* (3rd ed., 1992) at p. 363.

acquired after the parties separated if she dies leaving no will.[82] There have been calls for judicial separation to be abolished on the basis that it is no longer necessary.[83]

Financial provision on divorce

Scots law contains some far-reaching provisions designed to regulate the redistribution of financial assets following divorce. The philosophy inherent in these provisions is that so far as possible when the parties divorce there should be a "clean break" settlement of the financial matters. Section 8(2) of the Family Law (Scotland) Act 1985 provides that the court shall make an order justified by the principles set out in section 9 of the Act and one which is "reasonable" having regard to the resources of the parties.[84] **3.17**

Orders under the Family Law (Scotland) Act 1985

Section 8(1) of the 1985 Act permits a court to make various orders in respect of financial provision on divorce. Given the clean break philosophy of the legislation, the most common orders are for payment of a capital sum or for the transfer of property. Notwithstanding this, the court can order that a capital sum be paid in instalments. Moreover a capital transfer may be appropriate in addition, and not just as an alternative, to a property transfer order. Either order may be made at the date of divorce or at some other time specified by the court. It may also come into effect at a specified future date.[85] **3.18**

In the event that the court is satisfied that it is not possible to cater for financial provision by way of a capital transfer order and/or a property transfer order, it may order the payment of periodical allowance.[86] As the name implies this is a regular payment. It may be for a definite period, an indefinite period or until a specified event.[87] Periodical allowance ends with the death of the person to whom it is being paid but not necessarily upon the death of the payer.[88]

In addition to these main orders there are a number of incidental orders at the disposal of the court.[89] These incidental orders operate in conjunction with an order for financial provision.[90] They may order the sale of the property, the valuation of property or a declarator of ownership of any property.[91] A court may also grant an order which regulates occupancy of the matrimonial home and the usage of furniture and plenishings within it.[92] Besides these powers there are a number of others specific to certain situations including an order that security be given for any financial provision.[93] It is fair to claim that the courts have a broad array of powers which ensure ultimate flexibility in dealing with the issue of financial provision on divorce.

---

[82] Conjugal Rights (Scotland) Amendment Act 1861, s. 6.
[83] *Report on Family Law*, S.L.C. (1992), para. 12–19; Edwards and Griffiths, *Family Law* (1997), at p. 386; Clive, *Husband and Wife* (3rd ed., 1992), p. 361.
[84] *Crockett v. Crockett*, 1992 S.C.L.R. 591; *Wallis v. Wallis*, 1993 S.L.T. 1348 (HL).
[85] See generally 1985 Act, s. 12; *Little v. Little*, 1990 S.L.T. 785.
[86] 1985 Act, s. 13(2); *Mackin v. Mackin*, 1991 S.L.T. (Sh. Ct.) 22 at p. 24, *per* Sh.Pr. Ireland.
[87] 1985 Act, s. 13(3); *Mitchell v. Mitchell*, 1993 S.L.T. 426.
[88] 1985 Act, s. 13(7)(b), but it may be recalled by the payer's executor under s. 13 and (7)(a) (4).
[89] 1985 Act, s. 14.
[90] *MacClue v. MacClue*, 1994 S.C.L.R. 933.
[91] 1985 Act, s. 14(2).
[92] 1985 Act, s. 14(2)(d); *Little v. Little*, 1990 S.L.T. 785.
[93] 1985 Act, s. 14(2)(d); *Murley v. Murley*, 1995 S.C.L.R. 1138.

Principles of financial provision on divorce

3.19   The key to determining financial provision on divorce lies in the section 9 principles. The first of those states that the net value of the matrimonial property should be shared fairly among the parties to the marriage. Fair sharing is to be viewed as equal sharing unless special circumstances justify another approach.[94] Matrimonial property is defined as

> "all the property belonging to the parties or either of them at the relevant date which was acquired by them or him (otherwise than by gift or succession from a third party)—
>
> (a) before the marriage for use by them as a family home or as furniture or plenishings for such a home; or
>
> (b) during the marriage but before the relevant date".

The relevant date is the earlier of either the date the parties ceased to cohabit, or the date when a summons for divorce is served.[95] Some financial property acquired after the relevant date may nevertheless form part of the matrimonial property, for example, damages received after the relevant date but relating to an accident before that date.[96] Pensions and life policies are considered matrimonial property.[97] Similarly, a tax rebate received after the relevant date but relating to the period the parties were together may also be matrimonial property.[98] Redundancy payments may in some circumstances also be considered matrimonial property.[99]

Many things are excluded from the calculation of matrimonial property. Property acquired before marriage and not intended for use as matrimonial property is not included. Something bought prior to the marriage but which subsequently becomes shared in the marriage may still be considered matrimonial property.[1] The real test appears to be whether the property has been bought for family use.[2] Some problems arise in respect of homes purchased prior to marriage where the parties reside in that home during their marriage. If it can be shown that the original intention was not for use as a family home or indeed as that marriage's family home then the property will not be considered matrimonial property.[3] Section (9)(1)(a) specifically excludes property acquired during the marriage which has been inherited by or donated to one of the spouses. Gifts between spouses are not excluded. Where a gift prior to marriage is utilised to purchase a house which the parties reside in then it may be that the house will not be matrimonial property.[4] Where a gift or inheritance is sold and the proceeds used to purchase an asset then that asset can become matrimonial property.[5]

It is the net value of matrimonial property which must be divided fairly. Accordingly, any mortgage over heritable property must be deducted from the value. Outstanding debts as at

---

[94]   1985 Act, s. 10(1).
[95]   *ibid.*, s. 10(3) and (4).
[96]   *Skarpaas v. Skarpaas*, 1991 S.L.T. (Sh. Ct.) 15; *cf. Petrie v. Petrie*, 1988 S.C.L.R. 390.
[97]   1985 Act, s. 10(5); Bisset-Jones, "Recent Changes In Valuation And Division Of Pensions On Divorce", 1996 S.L.T. (News) 295; see Edwards and Griffiths, *Family Law* (1997), pp. 351–353 for advice on how pensions are calculated; *Brooks v. Brooks*, 1993 S.L.T. 184; *Crosbie v. Crosbie*, 1996 S.L.T. (Sh. Ct.) 86; *Gribb v. Gribb*, 1996 S.L.T. 719.
[98]   *MacRitchie v. MacRitchie*, 1994 S.L.T. (Sh. Ct.) 72.
[99]   *Tyrrell v. Tyrrell*, 1990 S.C.L.R. 244; *Smith v. Smith*, 1989 S.L.T. 668.
[1]   See *Mitchell v. Mitchell*, 1995 S.L.T. 426 at p. 426; *Buczynska v. Buczynski*, 1989 S.L.T. 558.
[2]   *Maclellan v. Maclellan*, 1988 S.C.L.R. 399; *cf. Jacques v. Jacques*, 1997 S.L.T. 459.
[3]   See Edwards and Griffiths, *op. cit.*, pp. 345–347; Meston "Matrimonial Property and the Family Home", 1993 S.L.T. (News) 62; Kinloch, "Wife's Claims where Home not Matrimonial Property", 1996 Fam.L.B. 20–4.
[4]   *Latter v. Latter*, 1990 S.L.T. 805.
[5]   *Jacques v. Jacques*, 1995 S.L.T. 963.

the relevant date must be deducted.[6] Where at the date of divorce the property has increased in value in the period since the relevant date, the increase in value will not be matrimonial property.[7]

Deviation from the basic rule that there should be fair sharing is permitted under section 10(1) which provides that "special circumstances" may allow such deviation. Section 10(6) goes on to suggest several circumstances where deviation might be appropriate:

(1) the source of the funds or assets used to acquire any of the matrimonial property were not derived from the income or efforts of the parties during the marriage

(2) where it seems appropriate, having regard to the nature of the matrimonial property, the use made of it (including use for business purposes or as a matrimonial home) and the extent to which it is reasonable to expect it to be realised or divided or used as security[8];

(3) where there has been any destruction, dissipation or alienation of property by either party[9];

(4) where there is any agreement between the parties on the ownership or division of the matrimonial property[10]; and

(5) where there is actual or prospective liability for any expenses of valuation or transfer of property in connection with the divorce.[11]

The matters specifically mentioned in section 10(6) are not designed to be exclusive. Other reasons can be entertained for a deviation from the fair sharing principle. However, one factor that may not be taken into account is the conduct of the parties unless it has had an impact on the financial assets.[12]

The second of the section 9 principles states that   **3.20**

"fair account should be taken of any economic advantage derived by either party from contributions of the other, and of any economic disadvantage suffered by either party in the interests of the other party or of the family."[13]

This provision is intended to ensure that where one spouse has stayed at home perhaps to look after children, they are not financially disadvantaged in the long term. In applying section 9(1)(b) the courts must take account of circumstances where:

"(a) the economic advantages or disadvantages sustained by either party have been balanced by the economic advantages or disadvantages sustained by the other party; and

---

6   *Jesner v. Jesner*, 1992 S.L.T. 999; *Mackin v. Mackin*, 1991 S.L.T. (Sh. Ct.) 22; *cf. McCormick v. McCormick*, 1994 G.W.D. 35–2078.
7   *Wallis v. Wallis*, 1993 S.L.T. 1348; see also Clive, "Financial Provision on Divorce – a Question of Technique", 1992 S.L.T. (News) 241; Thomson, "Financial Provision on Divorce – Not Technique but Statutory Interpretation", 1992 S.L.T. (News) 245; *Lewis v. Lewis*, 1993 S.C.L.R. 32: for a discussion on how to avert the unfairness of this see Edwards and Griffiths, *Family Law* (1997), pp. 348–350.
8   *Skarpaas v. Skarpaas*, 1993 S.L.T. 343; *Peacock v. Peacock*, 1994 S.L.T. 40; *Geddes v. Geddes*, 1993 S.L.T. 494; *Stephen v. Stephen*, 1995 S.C.L.R. 175; *Bannon v. Bannon*, 1993 S.L.T. 999.
9   *Short v. Short*, 1994 G.W.D. 21–1300; *Goldie v. Goldie*, 1992 G.W.D. 21–1225; *Fraser v. Fraser*, 1994 Fam.L.B. 10–3.
10   See Edwards and Griffiths, *op. cit.*, paras. 15.06 *et seq.*
11   See *e.g. Farrell v. Farrell*, 1990 S.C.L.R. 717; *cf. Adams v. Adams (No. 1)*, 1997 S.L.T. 144.
12   1985 Act, s. 11(7)(a).
13   1985 Act, s. 9(1)(b).

(b) any resulting imbalance has been or will be corrected by a sharing of the matrimonial property or otherwise."

In other words if it can be shown that the fair sharing of the matrimonial assets will correct the imbalance no award will be made under this section.[14]

3.21   Section 9(1)(c) states that "any economic burden of caring, after divorce, for a child of the marriage under the age of 16 should be shared fairly between the parties". The court must consider the age and health of the child, the educational, financial and other circumstances of the child and the needs and resources of the parties.[15] In addition to this, account may be taken of any support provided by the defendant spouse to dependants.[16] Awards may be in the form of periodical payments and/or a lump sum or property transfer orders.[17] Awards under this section are somewhat less important following the advent of the Child Support Act 1991. That Act and the Agency it created, the Child Support Agency (CSA), are central to the award of financial support for children.[18] Their involvement in a case may operate to bar a financial award under section 9(1)(c).

3.22   Under section 9(1)(d) a spouse who is financially dependant on the other spouse to a substantial degree may be awarded such financial provision as is reasonable to allow him or her to adjust over a period not exceeding three years from the date of divorce. Under section 11(4) the court in considering an award must take into account the duration and extent of the dependency. It has been suggested that where a spouse is able to survive without support in the period from separation to divorce, this may prejudice an award under 9(1)(d) on the basis that the spouse has shown themselves to be not substantially dependent on the other.[19] Payment under this heading is usually by way of periodical allowance although capital sum or property transfer are also competent.[20] The three-year period is designed to allow time for the dependant spouse to adjust perhaps by retraining. It is often the case that payments are for a much shorter duration than three years.[21]

3.23   Finally, section 9(1)(e) provides that a party who, at the time of divorce, seems likely to suffer serious financial hardship as a result of the divorce, should be awarded such financial support as is reasonable to relieve his or her hardship over a reasonable period. This principle is likely to become effective only when the others are inappropriate. It is likely to be applicable where at the time of divorce the spouse is old or so ill that he or she is unable to work.[22] Payment can be made by way of periodical allowance if the court considers that a capital sum or property transfer order is inappropriate or insufficient. In making an order under this section again the courts must have regard to the age, health and earning capacity of the applicant, the duration of the marriage, the standard of living of the parties during the marriage, and the needs and resources of the parties, as well as all other circumstances of the case.[23] Account may be taken of any support a spouse is giving to another person. Conduct will only be taken into account where it affects the financial resources of the parties or when it is manifestly inequitable to leave it out. As Professor Thomson notes, resort to section

---

[14]   See *Welsh v. Welsh*, 1994 S.L.T. 828; *Petrie v. Petrie*, 1988 S.C.L.R. 390; *De Winton v. De Winton*, 1996 Fam.L.B. 23–6; *cf. Clokie v. Clokie*, 1994 G.W.D. 3–149; *McCormick v. McCormick*, 1994 G.W.D. 35–2078.

[15]   1985 Act, s. 11(3).

[16]   *ibid.*, s. 11(6).

[17]   *ibid.*, s. 13(2); *Morrison v. Morrison*, 1989 S.C.L.R. 574; *Macdonald v. Macdonald*, 1994 G.W.D. 7–404.

[18]   See para. 3.42 below.

[19]   See Edwards and Griffiths, *Family Law* (1997), p. 366; *Dever v. Dever*, 1988 S.C.L.R. 352; *Millar v. Millar*, 1990 S.C.L.R. 666.

[20]   1985 Act, s. 13(2)(a).

[21]   *Muir v. Muir*, 1989 S.L.T. (Sh. Ct.) 20; *Sheret v. Sheret*, 1990 S.C.L.R. 799.

[22]   *Johnstone v. Johnstone*, 1990 S.C.L.R. 358.

[23]   See generally 1985 Act, s. 11.

9(1)(e) should be very rare. It is likely that in a marriage of considerable duration the parties will have accumulated sufficient assets to enable an award under one or other of the other principles.[24] In some circumstances the conferment of an award under section 9(1)(e) may result in the diminution of benefits from other sources, for instance those received from the state, and as such there could not be said to be hardship from the divorce.[25]

THE MATRIMONIAL HOME AND DOMESTIC VIOLENCE

The significance of the "matrimonial" home cannot be overstated in family law matters. Not only is it likely to be the principal matrimonial asset, it is also the seat of most domestic matters. Nowhere is the importance of the home more vividly illustrated than in situations where the relationship is dysfunctional, and a feature or cause of that dysfunctionalism is violence by one spouse towards the other. The spouse who is the victim of such behaviour often has two stark choices—to leave and find alternative accommodation, or to have the violent spouse leave.[26] To leave may appear to be the simpler solution, but if there are children and no alternative accommodation, matters become extremely difficult. Moreover, its seems somewhat unjust for the violent spouse to remain in the family home while the victim is compelled to leave. It is with these thoughts in mind that, in the 1980s, the Matrimonial Homes (Family Protection) (Scotland) Act 1981 was introduced which had as its principal object the desire to regulate occupancy of the matrimonial home and to offer additional protection to those victims of domestic violence. It is a law which conflicts at several points with the ordinary law of property.

3.24

Matrimonial homes are either rented or owned. The modern trend is away from rental to ownership.[27] Although the incidence is decreasing, it is not uncommon to find that title to the matrimonial home, or the tenancy agreement, is in the sole name of one spouse (usually the man). It is a basic tenet of property law that those with title have all the possessory rights of such property. Left unchallenged as a basic premise, it would mean that a spouse without title either in the title deeds or in the tenancy agreement would face severe hardship were a relationship to break up or become dysfunctional. He or she could simply be asked to leave the home. Alternatively, if they have nowhere to go, they may be compelled to remain in a violent environment. The Matrimonial Homes (Family Protection) (Scotland) Act 1981 ("the 1981 Act") among other things seeks to address these types of problems and dilemmas.

Under section 1(1) of the 1981 Act, where there is an entitled spouse, namely one who is the owner or tenant of the matrimonial home, and a non-entitled spouse (someone whose name is not on the title or tenancy agreement), the non-entitled spouse has the statutory right

(a) if in occupation, to continue to occupy the matrimonial home;

(b) if not in occupation, to enter into and occupy the matrimonial home.[28]

---

[24] Thomson, *Family Law in Scotland* (3rd ed., 1996), p. 144; *cf. Bell v. Bell*, 1988 S.C.L.R. 457.

[25] See *Barclay v. Barclay*, 1991 S.C.L.R. 205.

[26] Arguably there is a third way of mediation but this is fraught with problems: see Raitt, "Ethics of Mediation in Abusive Relationships" 1997 J.R. 76.

[27] Scottish Law Commission, *Report on Matrimonial Property* (Scot. Law Com. No. 86); see also Manners and Rauta, *Family Property in Scotland* (1981).

[28] Matrimonial Homes (Family Protection) (Scotland) Act 1981 ("1981" Act), s. 1(1) as amended by (the Law Reform (Miscellaneous Provisions) (Scotland) Act 1985, s. 13(2) ("1985 Act").

These rights are exercisable with any child of the family.[29] It would clearly be nonsensical to have the right to occupy if it could in practice be defeated by denying any child the right to occupy with you.

"Matrimonial Home" includes any house, caravan, houseboat or other structure which has been provided as or has become a family residence.[30] It is enough that it is intended to be used as a family home.[31] The rights of a non-entitled spouse commence as soon as the parties are married and a matrimonial home is acquired. Again, to facilitate the proper exercise of these statutory rights, a non-entitled spouse is authorised without needing the permission of the entitled spouse to pay any rent or mortgage, to carry out essential repairs and non-essential repairs approved by the court, or any other necessary step with a view to reasonable enjoyment of occupancy of the matrimonial home.[32]

Exclusion orders

3.25   An order may be sought under section 3 of the 1981 Act regulating the occupancy rights. However, of altogether more significance is the ability to have a spouse excluded from the matrimonial home under section 4 of the 1981 Act. An exclusion order can be sought by an entitled spouse[33] or a non-entitled spouse. Section 4(2) of the Act provides that the court,

"shall make an exclusion order if it appears to the court that the making of an order is necessary for the protection of the applicant or any child of the family from any conduct or threatened or reasonably apprehended conduct of the non-applicant spouse which is or would be injurious to the physical or mental health of the applicant or child."

Section 4(3) goes on to state that notwithstanding the provisions of section 4(2), the court shall not make an order if it would be "unjustified or unreasonable" to do so having regard to all the circumstances of the case including the conduct of the spouses in relation to each other, the respective needs and financial resources of the spouses, the needs of any child of the family and the extent to which the matrimonial home is used in connection with a trade, business or profession, and whether the non-applicant spouse has made any suitable alternative offer of accommodation.[34] Exclusion, as one will have noted from the terminology of the statute, may be ordered even in circumstances where there is no physical violence, although in practice it will be easier to satisfy sheriffs of the necessity of the order where physical violence is evident.[35]

Although many exclusion order cases turn upon the concept of "necessity", it is clear that such a test does not require the spouse to be in the matrimonial home at the time of seeking an order.[36] It is also equally apparent that the test of "necessity" can be satisfied without first resorting to other remedies such as matrimonial interdicts to see if they work.[37] Nevertheless, a judge in determining a case must decide if a lesser remedy would be sufficient to protect the applicant or the children, and if it would not, the judge must establish his reasons why it

---

[29]   1981 Act, s. 1(1A), added by Law Reform (Miscellaneous Provisions) (Scotland) Act 1985, s. 13(3).
[30]   1981 Act, s. 22.
[31]   *O'Neill v. O'Neill*, 1987 S.L.T. (Sh. Ct.) 26.
[32]   1981 Act, s. 2(1).
[33]   See, *e.g. Brown v. Brown*, 1985 S.L.T. 376; *Millar v. Millar*, 1991 S.C.L.R. 649.
[34]   1981 Act, s. 3(3) for details of the factors to be considered.
[35]   *Anderson v. Anderson*, 1993 Fam.L.B. 6–4.
[36]   See *Colagiacomo v. Colagiacomo*, 1983 S.L.T. 559; *Armour v. Anderson*, 1994 S.L.T. (Sh. Ct.) 14; *cf. Bell v. Bell*, 1983 S.L.T. 224; *Smith v. Smith*, 1983 S.L.T. 275; *Ward v. Ward*, 1983 S.L.T. 472.
[37]   *Roberton v. Roberton*, 1999 S.L.T. 38; *Brown v. Brown*, 1985 S.L.T. 376.

would not.[38] The necessity test is a difficult one to satisfy. It is not simply a balance of convenience test in the same way that interdicts are.[39] It is possible to obtain an exclusion order on the basis that the non-applicant's conduct is injurious to the mental health of the applicant or child, but not simply that the applicant is distressed about the breakdown of the marriage.[40] In *Roberton v. Roberton*[41] it was held that the sheriff was entitled to take a particular view of the applicant's mental health and to reject that it related solely to the breakdown of the marriage. Although the two-fold test is slightly confused, it is hard to imagine there will be many situations where the exclusion is thought necessary for the protection of the spouse or child, and it is then refused on the ground that it is unreasonable or unjustified.[42]

Rather helpfully, Lord Dunpark offered a four question test in the case of *McCafferty v. McCafferty*, which he said should be applied in all exclusion order applications.[43] He claimed one should ask the following questions:

(1) What is the nature and the quality of the alleged conduct ?

(2) Is the court satisfied that the conduct is likely to be repeated if cohabitation continues ?

(3) Has the conduct been or, if repeated, would it be injurious to the physical or mental health of the applicant or to any child of the family ?

(4) If so, is the order sought necessary for the future protection of the physical or mental health of the applicant or spouse ?

Matrimonial interdicts

A further avenue of protection for the victim of domestic violence is the matrimonial interdict. Such interdicts are available even where the spouses are living together. A matrimonial interdict including an interim interdict

3.26

(a) restrains or prohibits any conduct of one spouse towards the other spouse or a child of the family; or

(b) prohibits a spouse from entering or remaining in a matrimonial home or in a specified vicinity of the matrimonial home.[44]

It is important in framing interdict writs that the conduct to be restrained is not too widely defined.[45] It is not possible for a non-entitled spouse to seek to use a matrimonial interdict to exclude the entitled spouse from the matrimonial home.[46] It is however possible for an entitled spouse to use it as a remedy against a non-entitled spouse, but this may be countered with an application to have occupancy rights declared and enforced.

---

[38] *McCafferty v. McCafferty*, 1986 S.L.T. 650.
[39] *Smith v. Smith*, 1983 S.L.T. 275; *Hampsey v. Hampsey*, 1988 G.W.D. 24–1035; *Millar v. Millar*, 1991 S.C.L.R. 649.
[40] *Matheson v. Matheson*, 1986 S.L.T. (Sh. Ct.) 2.
[41] 1999 S.L.T. 38.
[42] *Brown v. Brown* 1985 S.L.T. 376, *per* Lord Dunpark at p. 378; *Millar v. Millar*, 1991 S.C.L.R. 649 at p. 651.
[43] 1986 S.L.T. 650.
[44] 1981 Act, s. 14.
[45] *Murdoch v. Murdoch*, 1973 S.L.T. (Notes) 13.
[46] *Tattersall v. Tattersall*, 1983 S.L.T. 506; the proper route is to seek occupancy rights and an exclusion order.

Matrimonial interdicts seek to regulate the conduct of one spouse towards the other. It is also common for a matrimonial interdict with a power of arrest to be ancillary to an exclusion order. The court must attach a power of arrest in a matrimonial interdict if it is requested by the applicant although it may refuse to attach a power of arrest to a non-molestation matrimonial interdict.[47] The effect of the power of arrest is that it permits a police officer to arrest the non-applicant spouse without warrant if he has reasonable cause for believing that the person is in breach of the interdict.

Where a power of arrest is attached to a matrimonial interdict the solicitor acting for the applicant will send a copy of the interdict and the attached power of arrest to the relevant chief constable and in this way notice of the court order is brought to the attention of the police. If called to an incident they are usually armed with the salient knowledge of the interdict to make an arrest. The non-applicant spouse suspected to be in a breach of interdict will be arrested and taken to the local police station. He may be liberated if the police are satisfied that there is no likelihood of violence to the other spouse, or child of the family. Alternatively, the police may refuse to release him.[48] If the non-applicant spouse is released, the matter is reported to the local procurator fiscal who may decide to bring proceedings. If the fiscal decides not to bring proceedings they must take all reasonable steps to inform the threatened spouse or his or her solicitor.[49] Where the spouse is not liberated following arrest but the fiscal has decided not to bring proceedings, the arrested person will be brought before a sheriff the day after arrest. The fiscal will inform the court of the facts disclosing a breach of interdict and request that he be detained for a further two days. Where the sheriff is satisfied that there has been a prima facie breach of interdict, that breach of interdict proceedings will take place, and that there is a substantial risk of violence by the arrested spouse towards the other spouse or child of the family, he may order that the person be detained for a further two days (Saturdays and Sundays are not computed as part of the two days).[50] The procedures for breach of interdict are, as is apparent, cumbersome and have been criticised by several writers.[51]

Other protection

3.27 The other protections contained in the 1981 Act concern provisions designed to ensure that the intention of the Act is not defeated by the non-applicant spouse "dealing" in the property. The occupancy rights of a non-entitled spouse are not defeated by the entitled spouse dealing in the matrimonial property.[52] Dealings include the sale or lease of the property, or the grant of a security over it. This is not to say that an entitled spouse cannot deal in the property; only that if they do, the non-entitled spouse still has occupancy rights. A purchaser is not entitled to occupy the property while the spouse is in the matrimonial home with occupancy rights over it, or part of it. A non-entitled spouse may renounce their occupancy rights in writing as long as the renunciation is before a notary public and is done freely without any coercion whatsoever.[53] As an alternative, the non-entitled spouse may consent to the dealing and this will have the effect of ending occupancy rights.[54] Where the

---

[47] 1981 Act, s. 15(1)(a) and (b).
[48] *ibid.*, s. 16(1).
[49] *ibid.*, s. 16(2).
[50] For this procedure see generally 1981 Act, s. 17.
[51] See for instance Clive, *Husband and Wife* (3rd ed. 1992), at p. 295; *Report on Family Law*, S.L.C. (1992), para. 11.45.
[52] 1981 Act, s. 6(1).
[53] *ibid.*, s. 1(5) and (6).
[54] *ibid.*, s. 6(3)(a)(i).

court believes that the non-entitled spouse is refusing unreasonably to consent they may dispense with that consent.[55] The 1981 Act recognises two situations where consent is unreasonably being withheld. First, the entitled spouse has been led to believe that the consent would be forthcoming and there has been no change of circumstances which would prejudice the non-entitled spouse. Secondly, the entitled spouse has taken all reasonable steps to obtain the consent but has been unable to obtain an answer to request for consent.

The occupancy rights of a non-entitled spouse cease if he or she has failed to occupy the matrimonial home for a continuous period of five years.[56] In practice though, the most common exemptions are to be found in section 6(3)(e) which states that occupancy rights are not enforceable against a third party where

"the dealing comprises a sale to a third party who has acted in good faith, if there is produced to the third party by the seller

(i) an affidavit sworn or affirmed by the seller declaring that the subjects of sale are not or were not at the time of the dealing a matrimonial home in relation to which a spouse of the seller has or had occupancy rights; or

(ii) a renunciation of occupancy rights or consent to the dealing which bears to have been properly made or given by the non-entitled spouse."[57]

If the affidavit turns out to be false the non-entitled spouse's remedy is against the entitled spouse.[58]

Where the spouses occupy their matrimonial home by virtue of a tenancy agreement it is possible for a non-entitled spouse, or an entitled spouse holding the tenancy in common with the other spouse, to seek a court order transferring the tenancy to their sole name paying just and reasonable compensation.[59] The landlord must be notified and may be conjoined in the legal proceedings. Even in situations where an entitled spouse ceases to occupy a tenanted property, the non-entitled spouse who remains in the home still enjoys the protection of the Rent (Scotland) Act 1984 (which amongst other things prevents harassment by a landlord and permits eviction only if authorised by a court order).[60]

COHABITATION

Rather unfortunately, Scots law does not accord a great deal of legal status to relationships of cohabitation.[61] Only in situations where a party can convince the court that there is marriage by cohabitation with habit and repute can they access the full rights accorded to married persons. The major legal consequences attendant in marriage such as inheritance,[62] financial provision following the termination of the relationship, aliment and rights in respect

3.28

---

55   1981 Act, s. 7.
56   1981 Act, s. 6(3)(f), added by Law Reform (Miscellaneous Provisions) (Scotland) Act 1985, s. 13(6)(c).
57   As amended by Law Reform (Miscellaneous Provisions) (Scotland) Act 1985, s. 13(6)(b) and Law Reform (Miscellaneous Provisions) (Scotland) Act 1990, Sched. 8, Para. 31(1) and Sched. 9.
58   1981 Act, s. 3(7).
59   1981 Act, s. 13(1) and (9).
60   1981 Act, s. 2(4).
61   For a summary of the differences between marriage and cohabitation see Nichols, *Living Together—A guide to the law of Marriage and Cohabitation in Scotland*, published by the CAB (1984); Love and Smith "The Cohabitants Fate", 1984 M.L.R. 341; Parry, *The Law Relating to Cohabitation* (3rd ed., 1993).
62   Edwards and Griffiths, *Family Law* (1997), p. 298.

of the family home, do not exist where the parties merely cohabit. It does not matter the extent, or even the quality, of cohabitation. A person living with another for a long period and perhaps having children with that person will be in little better position than a person who has been in a much more casual cohabiting relationship.

In some situations cohabiting couples are treated in the same way as married couples.[63] While Scots private law does not accord any specific rights to cohabitees it may be that general principles of Scots law will provide the cohabitee with a remedy.[64] For example, where one cohabitee has enriched himself at the expense of the other the doctrine of unjustified enrichment may be applicable. As things stand property acquired even for communal use in a family home will not necessarily be common property but will depend on who bought it, whether the purchaser was acting as an agent of the other person, and whether a presumption of ownership can be overcome.[65] Where both parties own a house jointly an action of division and sale will be competent which will allow the house to be sold and the respective parties realise their share.[66] Whilst there is a strong case for reform to iron out inequities between married spouses and cohabiting couples, there is no sign that changes are imminent.[67]

One area where there is some recognition of the rights of cohabitees is in the protections afforded to victims of domestic violence under the Matrimonial Homes (Family Protection) (Scotland) Act 1981 (discussed above). Nevertheless, the rights of cohabitees in this regard are somewhat less than those conferred on the married person. In respect of the 1981 Act a cohabiting couple are "a man and a woman who are living with each other as if they were man and wife".[68] Same sex partnerships are accordingly excluded. A cohabiting person bringing proceedings under the 1981 Act must prove that the parties are a cohabiting couple, though the parties need not be cohabiting at the time of bringing the action.[69] The cohabitee in contrast to the married spouse cannot gain interim occupancy rights.[70] This inevitably presents problems for cohabitants, particularly those with children who may have to wait several weeks to obtain an exclusion order.

Where the cohabitee is a victim of domestic violence they may resort to the matrimonial interdicts with power of arrest. If they wish to have their partner excluded they must first seek occupancy rights and then an exclusion order.[71] In the first instance they can only obtain up to six months' occupancy rights though this may be extended.[72] The exclusion order subsists during the occupancy rights. In all the circumstances the law clearly intends to give less rights to cohabitees than married couples. Moreover, the cohabitee is not protected from dealings in the property. The entitled cohabitee, where there is one, can sell the house to a third party who may in turn evict the cohabitee remaining in the house.[73] Where the cohabitee owns the home or is the tenant and faces violence from the non-entitled cohabitee, there is a common

---

[63]   Social security, certain matters of taxation, and delictual matters are some examples.
[64]   See Scottish Law Commission, *The Effects of Cohabitation in Private Law*, (1990), No. 86 p. 6.
[65]   *ibid.*, at p. 13.
[66]   See *Gray v. Kerner*, 1996 S.C.L.R. 331; "Remedies for Cohabitants when their Relationship breaks down", 1996 Fam.L.B. 22; see also McCulloch, "How Do You Get Them Out—Enforcing Decrees of Division and Sale", 1993 Fam.L.B. 6–2.
[67]   See generally Scot. Law Com. Report No. 86 (1990).
[68]   1981 Act, s. 18(1).
[69]   *Armour v. Anderson*, 1994 S.L.T. (Sh. Ct.) 14; *cf. Crossley v. Galletta*, 1993 S.C.L.R. 780; *Verity v. Fenner*, 1993 S.C.L.R. 223.
[70]   *Smith-Milne v. Gammack*, 1995 S.C.L.R. 1058 where the court expedited matters.
[71]   1981 Act, s. 18(4)(a); see "Occupancy Rights for Cohabiting Partners", 1995 Fam.L.B. 16–5.
[72]   1981 Act, s. 18(4).
[73]   *ibid.*, s. 18(5).

law right to evict that person. However, the cohabitee owner cannot seek an exclusion order under the 1981 Act.[74]

THE RELATIONSHIP OF PARENT AND CHILD

Parental rights and responsibilities

The Children (Scotland) Act 1995 ("the 1995 Act") attempts to make the first compre- **3.29** hensive statutory statement of parental rights and responsibilities in respect of their children. A parent has responsibility:

(a) to safeguard and promote the child's health, development and welfare;

(b) to provide direction and guidance to the child in a manner appropriate to the stage of the child's development;

(c) if the child is not living with the parent, to maintain personal relations and direct contact with the child on a regular basis; and

(d) to act as the child's legal representative.[75]

In fulfilling those responsibilities the Act also confers the following rights upon parents:

(a) to have the child living with the parent or otherwise to regulate the child's residence;

(b) to control, direct, or guide the child's upbringing in a manner appropriate to the child's stage of development;

(c) if the child does not live with the parent, to maintain personal relations and direct contact with the child on a regular basis;

(d) to act as the child's legal representative.[76]

Other Acts contain specific parental rights and these are not affected by the provisions of the 1995 Act.[77] Parental rights are only exercisable in the interests of the child.[78] The responsibility to provide guidance endures until the child is 18, but in all other respects parental responsibilities end when the child is 16.[79] The parent must so far as is reasonably practicable have regard to the views of the child in reaching any decision affecting that child if the child wishes to express any view.[80] The 1995 Act provides that a child of 12 years of age and over will be of sufficient age and maturity to express a view although younger children may be consulted if they are deemed to be of sufficient age and maturity.

A mother automatically has parental rights and responsibilities in respect of her child. The **3.30** child's natural father also automatically has rights and responsibilities if he is or was married to the child's mother at the date of the child's conception, or at any time thereafter.[81] This

---

[74] This is seen as a major flaw in the law: see Edwards and Griffiths, *Family Law* (1997), pp. 321–322.
[75] Children (Scotland) Act 1995 ("1995 Act"), s. 1(1).
[76] *ibid.*, s. 2(1).
[77] *ibid.*, s. 2(5): Note, however, the 1995 Act does supercede many common law rights.
[78] 1995 Act, s. 1(1) and 2(7).
[79] *ibid.*, s. 1(2)(a).
[80] *ibid.*, s. 6(1).
[81] See 1995 Act, s. 3(1).

includes any voidable marriage, or any marriage which was void but both parties believed to be valid.[82] In circumstances where the father is not, or has not, married to the mother he may acquire parental rights and responsibilities in two alternative ways. If the mother retains parental rights and responsibilities, she may enter into a voluntary agreement which confers parental rights and responsibilities on the child's father.[83] Such an agreement may be entered into even where the parents are under the age of 16. This type of agreement (known as a section 4 agreement) to be effective must be registered in the Books of Council and Session.[84] A registered agreement is irrevocable except by court order.[85]

Alternatively, a father may make an application to the court under section 11 of the 1995 Act for an order conferring parental rights and responsibilities. In determining any application, the welfare of the child is the paramount test for the court.[86] The father will only acquire parental rights and responsibilities if it is thought to be in the interests of the child.[87] It is possible for others who have an interest (genetic or otherwise) to seek a parental rights and responsibilities order under section 11(3)(a)(i). Where two or more persons have parental rights they may exercise them independently of the other.[88]

The law also recognises that a person over 16 may have responsibility for the care of a child under 16 without having parental rights and responsibilities. Section 5 of the 1995 Act imposes a duty on such persons to do all that is reasonable in the circumstances to safeguard the child's health, development and welfare. Specifically, they may give consent to any surgical, medical, or dental treatment or procedure where the child is unable to give their own consent, and it is not in the carer's knowledge that the parent would refuse to consent. In exercising this power, the carer must consult the child. Nothing in section 5 confers a right on anyone who has care and control of a child at school.

A parent may appoint a person to be their child's guardian in the event of the parent's death.[89] Appointments must be in writing and signed by the parent. For the appointment to be effective the parent must have been entitled to act as the child's legal representative. Any parental rights and responsibilities which a surviving spouse has continue to co-exist with those of the appointed guardian.

3.31   Undoubtedly, the principal responsibilities and rights of a parent are to have residence or contact with their child. The 1995 Act makes specific statutory provision for this. It is the right of a parent to have their child live with them or to regulate where they do live.[90] This right, like all rights, must be exercised in the child's interests. There are clear instances where it is not in the child's interest to be resident with their parent and as such the parental right of residence is one that can be lost.[91] Integral to the right of residence is the parent's right to determine residence of a temporary nature and accordingly the parent can control the child's temporary absence from home perhaps to stay with friends or other relatives. Where a non-custodial parent wishes a court order for their child to reside with him, or her, for particular

---

82   *ibid.*, s. 3(2)(a).
83   1995 Act, s. 4(1).
84   *ibid.*, s. 4(2).
85   *ibid.*, ss 4(4) and 11(11).
86   *ibid.*, s. 11(7)(a).
87   *Porchetta v. Porchetta*, 1986 S.L.T. 105; *Russell v. Russell*, 1991 S.C.L.R. 429, *per* Sheriff Gordon at p. 430; *Sanderson v. McManus*, 1996 S.L.T. 750.
88   1995 Act, s. 2(3), although a child cannot be removed from the U.K. without the consent of anyone who has parental rights relating to the child's residence or contact.
89   1995 Act, s. 7(1).
90   1995 Act, s. 2(1)(a); Professor Thomson suggests that this is integral to the promotion of the child's development: see *Family law in Scotland* (3rd ed., 1996), p. 200–201.
91   See *J v. C* [1970] A.C. 668 (HL); *Cheetham v. Glasgow Corporation*, 1972 S.L.T. (Notes) 50; *M v. Dumfries and Galloway R.C.*, 1991 S.C.L.R. 481.

periods such as holidays or weekends, the appropriate order is a contact order not a residence order.[92]

One of the innovations of the 1995 Act is the requirement that a non-resident parent maintain direct contact and personal relations with the child on a regular basis.[93] It is both a "right" and a "requirement". In so far as it is a right, it must be exercised in accordance with the welfare principle. Prior to the 1995 Act, it was very much the case that an absent father or mother would need to convince the court it was positively in the child's interest to have contact.[94] The inference of the Act is that there is a presumption that maintenance of contact is in the interests of the child. Naturally, given the statutory requirements of taking the child's own views into account, the child may well have a substantial say in whether a parent is denied contact with his child.

An area of considerable controversy in the 1990s has been a parent's right to discipline their child. The 1995 Act confers on the parent the right to control their child in accordance with the welfare principle. Ironically, that right includes the right to physically chastise the child. Many will consider being physically punished as inconsistent with the welfare principle and not in the child's interests. Notwithstanding this, the law permits the use of reasonable physical chastisement.[95] Where the parent uses excessive force they may face a common law charge of assault or criminal neglect.[96] The parent's motivation in chastisement is largely irrelevant; the real test relates to the severity of the force used.[97] Where there is excessive force used, there is likely to be a referral to a children's hearing of the child in question.[98] The right to physically chastise a child ends when the child reaches 16 years of age.[99]

3.32

One of the other areas where parents have corresponding rights and responsibilities is in the field of education. These rights and responsibilities are more fully discussed in Chapter 5. Suffice to say a parent has the obligation to ensure that their child is educated under education legislation[1] and also as part of their duty under section 2 of the 1995 Act to promote the development of their child.

An area of potential conflict given its dynamic in the Scottish nation is that of religion. Acting in accordance with the welfare principle, parents have a right to choose their child's religion from the outset. Although the Scottish courts have shown a preference for having some religion in a child's life, they have not shown any bias towards one particular religion or another.[2] Parental choice of religion should not conflict with the interests of the child. In circumstances where adherence to a particular religious persuasion is damaging to the child's health, it is likely that the courts will override the parents' wishes.[3] As a child matures, he may

---

[92] *McBain v. McIntyre*, 1997 S.C.L.R. 181.
[93] 1995 Act, s. 1(1)(c).
[94] *Porchetta v. Porchetta*, 1986 S.L.T. 105; *O v. O*, 1995 S.L.T. 238; *Crowley v. Armstrong*, 1990 S.C.L.R. 361.
[95] Children and Young Persons (Scotland) Act 1937, s. 12(7), which provides a specific defence to child assault.
[96] Children and Young Persons (Scotland) Act 1937, s. 12(1); *G v. Templeton*, 1998 S.C.L.R. 180; *A v. U.K.*, 1998 E.C.H.R. 23, Sept. 1998; see also on neglect Mays, "Home Alone Left Alone—Criminal Neglect Of Children" (1996) 64 S.L.G. 94.
[97] *B v. Harris*, 1990 S.L.T. 208.
[98] On the issue of reasonable chastisement see *B v. Harris*, 1990 S.L.T. 208; *Kennedy v. A*, 1993 S.L.T. 1134; *Cowie v. Tudhope*, 1987 G.W.D. 12–395; *Peebles v. MacPhail*, 1990 S.L.T. 245; Scot. Law Com. *Report on Family Law, supra Kennedy v. A*, 1993 S.L.T. 1134; see also Ross, "Reasonable Parenting—Borders of Acceptability", 1994 Fam.L.B. 7; and for the international human rights dimension see Smith, "To Smack or Not to Smack—A review of *A v. United Kingdom* in an international and European Context", 1999 *Web Journal of CLI* 1.
[99] See *Stewart v. Thain*, 1981 S.L.T. (Notes) 2.
[1] See generally Education (Scotland) Act 1980, discussed in Chapter 6.
[2] *McNaught v. McNaught*, 1955 S.L.T. (Sh. Ct.) 9; *McClements v. McClements*, 1958 S.C. 286; *MacKay v. MacKay*, 1957 S.L.T. (Notes) 17.
[3] Professor Thomson advises that it is likely that a child protection order will be sought with a direction that medical treatment be obtained under s. 58(5).

wish to choose his own religion. Previously academic commentators have argued that parental rights diminish in this context as the child gets older.[4] The current position is that a child on attaining the age of 16 has the right to choose their own religion. Below that age there is a suggestion that it is a parent's responsibility to consult the child on such issues.[5] It is likely that parents may agree with the child's wishes. Where the child's choice is likely to be against the welfare of the child it is thought that parental responsibility under the 1995 Act would demand that the parents object.

3.33   The statutory statement of parental responsibilities specifically states the requirement to promote the child's health and in that context, as a basic premise, parents have a right to consent to medical treatment or procedures as the child's legal representative.[6] The past two decades have seen much academic and judicial comment on this topic.[7] Like all decisions in respect of the child it is one governed by the welfare principle.[8] There will be circumstances where the refusal to consent will be overridden by the courts as not in the interests of the child's welfare.[9] Similarly, there will be situations where the parent's desire for a medical procedure or operation, for instance the sterilisation of a handicapped child, may not be in the child's interest.[10] In the normal course of events parents will give consent where the medical treatment is likely to benefit the child and that will be viewed as a proper exercise of parental rights and responsibilities. It is also the case that parents can consent to medical procedures and treatment in respect of their child even where that treatment or procedure is not positively in the interests of the child (for example, blood tests for paternity purposes).[11]

A person over 16 has the right to consent to medical treatment or procedures of his own accord.[12] In certain circumstances a child under 16 may also receive medical treatment or undergo a medical procedure in the absence of parental consent.[13] Indeed the child's desire to undergo medical treatment or procedure may overrule the parent's objection.[14] Professor Thomson canvasses a dilemma which the law has so far not resolved. Is a parent able to overrule a child where that child is competent but refuses medical treatment, and the parent considers the refusal of medical treatment not to be in their interest or to be against the welfare of the child?[15] One view is that the empowerment of the child excludes the parent's rights and responsibilities. Another is that the parent retains the right to direct the child presupposing that he knows about the proposed medical procedure.[16] It seems likely that the courts' own view of what is in the interests of the child will be the determinant of such controversial cases.[17]

In line with the duty to promote the health, development, and welfare of the child it is incumbent on parents to attend to the safety of their child and to ensure that adequate care arrangements are made for the child in the parents' absence. In circumstances where the

---

[4]   See Thomson, *Family Law in Scotland* (2nd ed., 1991) p. 204.
[5]   1995 Act, s. 1.
[6]   See Mason and McCall-Smith, *Law and Medical Ethics* (5th ed., 1999), pp. 248 *et seq.*
[7]   See Norrie and Wilkinson, *Parent and Child* (1993), pp. 182–189.
[8]   Edwards and Griffiths, *Family Law* (1997), at pp. 125–128.
[9]   *Re B (A Minor)* [1981] 1 W.L.R. 1421 (CA); *cf. Re C (A Minor)* [1990] Fam. 26; *Finlayson (Applicant)*, 1989 S.C.L.R. 601.
[10]   *Re B (A Minor)* [1976] 1 All E.R. 326; *cf. Re B (A Minor)* [1988] A.C. 199.
[11]   See Thomson, *Family Law in Scotland* (3rd ed. 1996), p. 207; *Docherty v. McGlynn*, 1983 S.L.T. 645.
[12]   See para. 3.36 below.
[13]   See Age of Legal Capacity (Scotland) Act 1991, s. 2(4).
[14]   see para. 3.36 below.
[15]   Thomson, *Family Law in Scotland*, p. 207.
[16]   See Professor Thomson's interesting discussion, *ibid.*, pp. 207–210; see also Norrie, "Medical Treatment: Overriding the Wishes of Children and Young Persons in Scotland", 1992 Fam.L.B. 1–3.
[17]   See discussion in Edwards and Griffiths, *op. cit.*, pp. 125–128.

child is abandoned, neglected or simply left alone parents may face criminal prosecution.[18] Interestingly, merely leaving a child alone unattended is not criminal neglect. Neglect is determined by looking at all the circumstances of the case—the age of the child, the arrangements for care, reasons for leaving the child alone and the duration for which the child is left with inadequate care as well as the surrounding dangers.[19]

It is customary in Scotland for children of married couples to take the name of the father. **3.34** It is not a legal requirement. Certainly parents have the right to name their child both in respect of the Christian name and the surname. Children born out of marriage may take either the father's or the mother's surname. Problems arise in practice in situations where the natural parents divorce and in particular if a custodial mother decides to remarry. It is not uncommon for such parents to seek to change the child's name to that of the step-parent. Here again the right of the parent is governed by the welfare principle.[20] An assessment of two competing claims must be taken—is it in the child's interest to have the same surname as the new family name or to retain the important link with the natural birth name? It will always be a matter of assessment on all the circumstances as to what is in the child's best interests. Courts have jurisdiction in such matters under section 11(1) as it is clearly a matter relating to the exercise of parental rights and responsibilities.

Children's rights

One of the emerging issues of the late twentieth century is the increasing recognition of the **3.35** important status of children in society. It is a fact that their rights have been expanded at a time when the rights of parents have arguably been diminished. This realignment in the parent-child relationship is hardly surprising given that children's rights and parental rights are essentially two sides of the same coin. The debate on this highly important area of law has been fuelled in part by the UN Convention on the Rights of the Child and a series of Law Commission and Scottish Office White Papers on the subject of *Scotland's Children*.[21] In addition there have been two major Acts of Parliament with important statutory provisions—the Age of Legal Capacity (Scotland) Act 1991 ("the 1991 Act") and the Children (Scotland) Act 1995.

Contract

The 1991 Act realigned and rationalised the age at which children attain full contractual **3.36** capacity. As a basic premise a person has full contractual capacity when they attain 16 years of age.[22] Equally, as a basic principle children under 16 years of age have no contractual capacity. However, the simplicity of these statutory provisions is dislodged somewhat by a range of caveats to these general rules. Those under 16 require their legal representative (usually their parent) to act in their stead. Where a child under 16 purports to enter into a contract by themselves then the contract is null and void. Where a parent enters into a contract on behalf of a child the contract will be valid even if not in the interests of the child;

---

[18]   Children and Young Persons (Scotland) Act 1937, s. 12; Mays, "Home Alone Left Alone—Criminal Neglect Of Children", *supra*.
[19]   See *M v. Orr*, 1995 S.L.T. 26; *H v. Lees*, 1994 S.L.T. 908, *D v. Orr*, 1994 S.L.T. 908.
[20]   See *Cosh v. Cosh*, 1979 S.L.T. (Notes) 72; *Flett v. Flett*, 1995 S.C.L.R. 189; *cf. Dawson v. Wearmouth* [1998] 1 All E.R. 271.
[21]   Cmnd 2286 (1993); Tisdall, *The Children (Scotland) Act 1995: Developing Policy and Law For Scotland's Children* (1998).
[22]   Age of Legal Capacity (Scotland) Act 1991, s. 1(1).

the child though will have a right of action against the errant parent for failing to fulfil their parental responsibilities properly.[23]

A child under the age of 16 may enter into a contract of a kind commonly entered into by a child of that child's age and circumstances on terms not unreasonable to the child.[24] There is some dubiety as to the meaning of "commonly"—does it mean "frequently" or "not unusually"?[25] One anticipates that this section permits children to enter into basic contracts such as suitable purchases at a local shop or school tuckshop. It is also the case that the 1991 Act does not affect the ability of a child aged 12 and over to make a will.[26] Moreover, a child over 12 has the right to consent or otherwise to the making of an adoption order or a freeing for adoption order.[27] Where a medical or dental practitioner is of the view that the child is of sufficient age and maturity to understand the nature and possible consequences of medical procedure or treatment the child may enter into a transaction for such medical procedure without parental consent.[28] Although this is viewed as a right of the child it is nevertheless one where a medical practitioner acts as gatekeeper. It appears from the statutory provisions (although they are not explicit on this question) that a child may refuse medical treatment.[29] It appears also to be the case that a child may consent to medical procedures ostensibly not in their own interest, for instance the donation of an organ tissue or blood to another.[30]

Children under 16 have the right to instruct a solicitor in any civil matter. Indeed the thrust of the 1995 Act is to engage children in family actions and it seems a prerequisite that legal advice is available to the child. A child aged 12 or above is presumed to have sufficient age, maturity and understanding to justify the engagement of a solicitor. There is nothing to stop a child under 12 engaging a solicitor where he too has such understanding of the enterprise in which he is engaged.[31] It is also possible for a child to obtain legal aid for the advice and instruction of a solicitor.[32]

Although the basic rule is that children who attain the age of 16 have full contractual capacity, the 1991 Act makes provisions for children aged 16–18 to challenge certain contracts entered into by them if they are unfairly prejudicial to them. The court has the power to set aside contracts deemed unfairly prejudicial until the person attains the age of 21.[33] There are exemptions and ways round any attack on a transaction with a child but discussion is outwith the scope of this book.

Delict

3.37 Where a child under 16 is injured by the actions of another they may have a remedy in delict. Ordinarily, if the person is under 16 this will be pursued on their behalf by their legal representative (probably their parent). A child may sue his parent for any wrongful action which results in damage to him or her.[34] Actions of this type are commonplace in respect of road traffic accidents where the child sustains damage as a result of a parent's negligence.

---

[23]   1995 Act, s. 10(1).
[24]   Age of Legal Capacity (Scotland) Act 1991, s. 2(1) (a) and (b).
[25]   See Norrie, "The Age of Legal Capacity (Scotland) Act 1991" (1991) 36 J.L.S.S. 434.
[26]   Age of Legal Capacity (Scotland) Act 1991, s. 2(2).
[27]   Age of Legal Capacity (Scotland) Act 1991 s. 2(3) and Adoption (Scotland) Act 1978, ss. 12(8) and 18(8).
[28]   Age of Legal Capacity (Scotland) Act 1991 s. 2(4).
[29]   See Thomson, *Family Law in Scotland* (3rd ed., 1996) pp. 167–168; 1995 Act, s. 90, 1991 Act, s. 2(4).
[30]   See though Norrie, "Medical Treatment: Overriding the Wishes of Children and Young Persons in Scotland", *supra*.
[31]   Age of Legal Capacity (Scotland) Act 1991, s. 2(4A), inserted by the 1995 Act, Sched. 4, para. 53(3).
[32]   See para. 2.35 above.
[33]   Age of Legal Capacity (Scotland) Act 1991 s. 3(1); see generally, Thomson, *op. cit.*, pp. 169–170.
[34]   *Young v. Rankin*, 1934 S.C. 499; *Wood v. Wood*, 1935 S.L.T. 431 (where the mother sued her son).

They are also thought to be possibilities where the child is damaged as a result of the parent's negligent or deliberate infliction of harm while the child is *in utero* (in the womb). Drinking, smoking, and drug addiction might provide interesting possibilities for such an action.

Children can be liable for their own delicts. In most circumstances they will have very few assets and as such will be considered "men of straw" and unable to meet any award of damages or legal expenses. Given that a court decree can subsist for a considerable time an action against a child may be more productive where the child is nearing working age and court-awarded damages can be derived from their future earnings. Only in circumstances where the parent has instructed or authorised the child to perpetrate the delictual wrong can a parent be vicariously liable for the delict of their child. Actions which hope to access the parent's wealth for the wrongs of their child are largely ineffectual. So, for example, where a youth deliberately assaults another there will be no right of action against the parent unless the child was acting as an agent of the parent. It is possible that a parent may be personally liable where they have inadequately supervised a child who perpetrates a civil wrong.[35]

The third facet of a child's rights in delict is that a child has title to sue a third party where that third party wrongfully, or negligently, injures or kills their parent or parents.[36] A child can sue a third party for damage or injury to his or her father even where the father is not married to his mother. The child can seek loss of support and "non-patrimonial" benefits.[37]

Miscellaneous statutory rights, responsibilities and protections

Many of a child's rights are enforceable against their parents but there are a number of rights, responsibilities and protections pertaining to the child which are conferred or imposed by society as a whole. For example, a child has the right to marry at the age of 16 without requiring parental consent.[38] In addition there are statutory rights to make a will, consent to or refuse adoption[39] and also a right to seek a child maintenance assessment order.[40] Likewise, there are a number of statutory age limits which restrict the rights of young persons that are not affected by the operation of the Age of Legal Capacity (Scotland) Act 1991. Some restrictions are well known, such as only being able to hold a driving licence at the age of 17,[41] while to buy or attempt to buy alcohol one must be 18 or over,[42] to place a bet in a betting office one must be 18,[43] and to have a tattoo inscribed on one's body a person must be 21. A child has criminal responsibility in Scots law at the age of eight.[44]

3.38

Sexual offences

The law also intervenes to proscribe certain sexual activities. There is a defence to the common law offence of sodomy or shameless indecency where homosexual partners are over 18 and the consensual sexual act takes place in a private place.[45] Where a woman has sex with

3.39

[35] See *Hastie v. Magistrates of Edinburgh*, 1907 S.C. 1102; *Hardie v. Sneddon*, 1917 S.C. 1.
[36] Damages (Scotland) Act 1976; it is possible for a child born after the parent has died to sue: see *Cohen v. Shaw*, 1992 S.L.T. 1022.
[37] See Thomson, *Family Law in Scotland*, (3rd ed., 1996) p. 171.
[38] Marriage (Scotland) Act 1977, s. 1.
[39] Age of Legal Capacity (Scotland) Act 1991, s. 2.
[40] Child Support Act 1991, s. 7.
[41] Road Traffic Act 1988, s. 101.
[42] Licensing (Scotland) Act 1976, s. 68(2).
[43] Betting, Gaming and Lotteries Act 1963, s. 222.
[44] Criminal Procedure (Scotland) Act 1995, s. 41; see para. 4.41.
[45] Criminal Law (Consolidation) Act 1995, s. 13(5); see McCall-Smith and Sheldon, *Scots Criminal Law*, (2nd ed., 1997) p. 205; Gane, *Sexual Offences*, (1992), at p. 76.

a boy under the age of 14 the common law offences of lewd and libidinous practices or shameless indecency may be relevant.[46] It is unlikely that heterosexual sexual acts by a women with a male over the age of 14 will be prosecuted though a charge of shameless indecency is thought competent.[47] It is an offence for a man to have sex with a girl under the age of 16. If the girl is below the age of 12 it is an offence of rape to have sexual intercourse with her even in circumstances where she consents.[48] Where the girl is aged between 12 and 13 the man will be charged with an offence under section 5 (1) of the Criminal Law (Consolidation) (Scotland) Act 1995, which carries a penalty of life imprisonment. Consent will not constitute an adequate defence. Where the girl is aged between 13 and 16 it is still a statutory offence but the law does countenance a defence whereby a man under the age of 24 who has not previously been charged with a like offence can satisfy the court that he had reasonable cause for believing that the girl was 16 or over.[49] Where the girl is under 16 years of age and the boy is over 16 years of age and there is close proximity in the ages of both, a prosecution is unlikely. In addition a girl below the age of 16 who consents to sexual intercourse with a man commits no offence but may nevertheless be referred to the children's hearing.

There are also statutory offences which prohibit sexual intercourse with a child in breach of trust,[50] procuring a girl for unlawful sexual intercourse,[51] intercourse with a stepchild,[52] incest,[53] indecent behaviour towards a girl aged between 12 and 16,[54] detention of a girl with the intention of having unlawful intercourse,[55] as well as a range of prostitution offences designed to prevent the involvement of children.[56]

Criminal neglect

3.40 In addition to the number of offences which restrict sexual abuse of children there is an offence in section 12 of the Children and Young Persons (Scotland) Act 1937. Anyone aged 16 or over, having custody, charge or care of a child or young person under 16 years of age, who wilfully assaults, ill-treats, neglects, abandons or exposes the child in a manner likely to cause unnecessary suffering or injury to health, including loss of sight, hearing, limb, organ or body, or any mental derangement, commits an offence. What amounts to neglect is open to some question. Certainly the wilful failure to provide food, clothing, medical aid or accommodation will be viewed as neglect.[57]

Aliment

3.41 Arguably, the principal right a child has against his or her parents is the right to financial support. Prior to 1991, the main financial assistance took the form of aliment. However, after 1991 the main form of financial assistance is child support (discussed below). Court actions

---

[46]   McCall-Smith and Sheldon, *Scots Criminal Law* (2nd ed., 1997), p. 205.
[47]   It is believed that there is a case currently with the Crown Office where consideration is being given to prosecuting a school teacher who allegedly had sexual relations with a male pupil who was over the age of 14.
[48]   Criminal Law (Consolidation) (Scotland) Act 1995, s. 5.
[49]   *ibid.*, s. 5(5)(b).
[50]   *ibid.*, s. 3(1).
[51]   *ibid.*, s. 7(1).
[52]   *ibid.*, s. 2.
[53]   *ibid.*, s. 1.
[54]   *ibid.*, s. 6.
[55]   *ibid.*, s. 8(1).
[56]   *ibid.*, ss. 9–12.
[57]   See *Stair Memorial Encyclopaedia*, Vol. 3, pp. 604–605, para. 1246.

for aliment remain for particular categories of young persons.[58] Aliment is the right to support from the parent and is governed by the Family Law (Scotland) Act 1985. The obligation to aliment falls upon both a father and a mother. There is no need for the parents to have been married for the obligation to financially support the child.[59] The obligation also extends to persons who have accepted the child as part of their household.[60] The obligation to aliment extends ordinarily to age 18 (even in respect of mentally handicapped children)[61] but may be applicable to children aged 18–25 who are reasonably and appropriately undergoing instruction at an educational establishment or training for employment, or for a trade, vocation or profession.[62]

Parents must provide such support as is reasonable in the circumstances having regard to the needs and resources of the parties, their earning capacities and all other circumstances.[63] It is possible to obtain an interim award of aliment. The child himself may bring the action against the parent or other person for aliment.[64] Where the child is under 16 the action may be brought by the child's parent, guardian or legal representative, or anyone seeking a residence order in respect of the child.[65] An action may be brought even where the child is still living with a person who has an obligation to aliment.[66] Obviously in those circumstances, it is possible for that person to defend an action by proving to the court that they are alimenting the child and will continue to do so.[67] An absent father cannot defend an action brought against him on the basis that he is willing to aliment the child if that child resides with him.[68]

Aliment will be paid in the form of periodical payments, usually weekly or monthly. An order may subsist for a definite period, indefinitely or until the occurrence of a specified event.[69] It is possible to have an award of aliment backdated.[70] It also possible to have an award varied or recalled where there is a material change of circumstances.[71] A variation may similarly be backdated and repayment ordered.[72]

Child support

Increasingly, resort is made to the provisions of the Child Support Act 1991 to obtain **3.42** financial provision for the support of children under 16 years of age. The system of aliment which operated alone prior to the child support provisions was criticised on the basis that awards were difficult to predict and inconsistent and on the ground that often aliment was

---

[58] See Edwards, "Aliment Actions in the Courts After April 1993", 1993 Fam.L.B. 2–6.
[59] Law Reform (Parent and Child) (Scotland) Act 1986, Sched. 1, para. 21.
[60] 1985 Act, s. 1(1)(d); note this does not apply to foster parents boarded out by a local authority or voluntary organisations: *Watson v. Watson*, 1994 Fam.L.B. 13–7.
[61] *McBride v. McBride*, 1995 S.C.L.R. 1021.
[62] 1985 Act, s. 1(5) (a) and (b); *Jowett v. Jowett*, 1990 S.C.L.R. 348.
[63] 1985 Act, s. 1(2) and 4(1); *Winter v. Thornton*, 1993 S.C.L.R. 389; *Walker v. Walker*, 1991 S.L.T. 649; *Bell v. McCurdie*, 1981 S.C. 64.
[64] 1985 Act, s. 2(4)(a).
[65] 1985 Act, s. 2(4)(c)(i) and (iii), as amended by Age of Legal Capacity (Scotland) Act 1991, Sched. 1, para. 40 and Children (Scotland) Act 1995, Sched. 4, para. 36(b).
[66] 1985 Act, s. 2(6).
[67] 1985 Act, s. 2(7).
[68] 1985 Act, s. 2(8); unless of course the child is over 16, in which case it may be a defences: s. 2(9); see also *McKay v. McKay*, 1980 S.L.T. (Sh. Ct.) 111.
[69] 1985 Act, s. 3(2); it is also possible for one-off special payments to be made for specific occurrences, *e.g.* hospital bills or school fees; in respect of the latter see *Macdonald v. Macdonald*, 1995 S.L.T. 72.
[70] 1985 Act, s. 3(1)(c).
[71] *ibid.*, s. 5(1).
[72] *ibid.*, s. 5(4); a variation of interim aliment cannot be backdated: *McColl v. McColl*, 1993 S.L.T. 617.

simply not paid.[73] Promoted as a measure to ensure that absent fathers started to pay for their children rather than the state through the benefit system, child support has engendered a fair measure of controversy. On the one hand it has been criticised as a cynical measure to reduce public expenditure on state benefits[74] and on the other it has been seen as an attack on second families.

Under the new statutory arrangements most cases of child maintenance are now assessed by the Child Support Agency ("CSA") rather than the courts and in addition the assessment is carried out by way of a formula. The initial criticisms which both the CSA and the law attracted resulted in modifications to the law in 1995.[75]

A person who has care of a child or who is the absent parent of a qualifying child may apply for a child maintenance assessment.[76] A qualifying child 12 years old or over may apply for an assessment in their own right as long as the parent with care or the absent parent has applied for an assessment, or the Secretary of State has been authorised to take action.[77] A person seeking an assessment authorises the collection and enforcement of the maintenance by the CSA. Where the parent who has residence of the child is in receipt of income support, family credit or disability working allowance that parent must authorise a compulsory assessment.[78] The parent will not need to give authorisation for an assessment where there are reasonable grounds for believing that there would be a risk to the parent of suffering undue harm or distress as a result of having to give the authorisation. In most circumstances the parent must provide information to trace the absent parent, to allow the assessment to be made. At inception this proved controversial; many single parents who had their children residing with them simply did not wish to have the absent parent in their lives in any shape or form. They had perhaps dissociated themselves from violent partners, or indeed the child had been the product of a casual relationship and they had no wish to resume contact with the natural father. Those on state benefits faced a 20 per cent reduction in their benefit if they refused to co-operate with the authorities.

Once the CSA has made an assessment, maintenance becomes a legal obligation. Where the assessment has been at the instance of the Secretary of State or where the person seeking the assessment has so authorised, collection and enforcement can be arranged by the Secretary of State. The major power open to the Secretary of State is an earnings order[79] which is an instruction to an employer to deduct the sums due from earnings and remit them to the Secretary of State. This order may be used to collect arrears and/or current maintenance due. A liability order[80] allows the recovery of arrears, and when this is made an earnings order would be inappropriate or ineffective. The liability order can be enforced by means of diligence such as poindings, warrant sales and inhibitions, but not an earnings assessment.

---

[73]   See White Paper, *Children Come First* (1990) Cm. 1264.
[74]   Graham and Knights, *Putting The Treasury First: The Truth About Child Support* (1994).
[75]   *Improving Child Support*, (1995) Cmnd 2745; Abbot, "The price of private parental responsibility", 1994 N.L.J. 681–682; Jones, "Child's Pay Not Child's Play", 1993 Law Gazette, S.L.G. 90/23, p. 28; McLean, "The Making of the Child Support Act of 1991: Policy Making at the Intersection of Law and Social Policy" (1994) 21 J. Law and Soc. 505–519; Diduck, "The Unmodified Family: The Child Support Act and the Construction of Legal Subjects" (1995) 22 J. Law and Soc., pp. 527–48; Ross and McKenzie, "*Financial Support For the Child in Disputed Parentage Cases*", 1995 J.R. 166–177 see continuing criticism of legislative amendments in Cavanagh, "*An Unworkable Act*" 1996 SCOLAG pp. 10–11; Mears, "Paper over the Cracks", 1995 Law Gazette 92/06 p. 16.
[76]   Child Support Act 1991 ("1991 Act"), s. 4.
[77]   *ibid.*, s. 7.
[78]   *ibid.*, s. 6.
[79]   *ibid.*, ss. 31–32.
[80]   *ibid.*, s. 33.

In assessing the child maintenance the CSA utilise a formula which has four elements—the maintenance requirement, assessable income, the rate of deduction and the protected level of income. The maintenance requirement is the basic amount required to meet the needs of the child but not necessarily the amount payable which will reflect other factors. Assessable income is the element of the absent parent or carer's income which is available for child maintenance. Some of the absent parent or carer's income will be exempt and deducted. An absent parent will ordinarily pay half of his assessable income until the maintenance requirement is met. This is the basic element of the amount payable. Once the maintenance requirement is met the absent parent's rate of deduction reduces to 15–25 per cent of their assessable income. This is called the additional element. There is an upper limit to the amount an absent parent must pay. The protected income level is the level below which the absent parent or his second family's income must not fall. The absent parent need not pay any more than 30 per cent of any net income in child maintenance. Nor will the absent parent or his second family have to pay maintenance which would leave them on a level of income which is not better than income support levels.

Assessments can be reviewed or appealed. Review is undertaken by child support officers. A maintenance assessment may be varied or recalled and cases are automatically reviewed every two years.[81] Alternatively, a review may be instigated at the instance of the absent parent, the carer parent, or the child.[82] It is also possible that reviews may occur at the instance of the child support officer where they decide that the original assessment was defective because it was made in ignorance of a material fact, based on a mistake or legally erroneous.[83] Review may also be made of the child support officer's decision.[84] In practice this latter type of review is commonplace. Further review of an assessment may be taken to Child Support Appeals Tribunals and child support commissioners.[85] On points of law there is further appeal to the Inner House of the Court of Session and on to the House of Lords.

ADOPTION

Adoption is the legal process whereby the legal relationship between a child and his natural **3.43** parents is severed and a new legal relationship between the child and his adoptive parents is created.[86] An adoption order can only be made in respect of a child who is under 18 years of age.[87] A child who is married or has been married cannot be adopted.[88] However, it is possible for a child to be re-adopted.[89] Although a process which severs and recreates a family relationship, it is one heavily overseen and regulated by the state, both with the involvement of the court and also the local authority.

All local authorities are required to provide an adoption service for their area.[90] Integral to the process of adoption is the an adoption agency. The law recognises two types of adoption agency—the local authority and other approved adoption societies.[91] Adoption societies,

---

[81] 1991 Act, s. 16.
[82] *ibid.*, s. 17.
[83] 1991 Act, s. 19, as substituted by Child Support Act 1995, s. 15.
[84] 1991 Act, s. 18.
[85] 1991 Act, ss. 21 and 22, and Scheds 3 and 4.
[86] For a brief discussion of the changing nature of adoption see Edwards and Griffiths, *Family Law* (1997), pp. 166–168; for more detail, see McNeil, *Adoption of Children in Scotland* (3rd ed., 1998).
[87] Adoption (Scotland) Act 1978, s. 12(1), as amended by Children (Scotland) 1995 Act, Sched. 2 para. 7.
[88] Adoption (Scotland) Act 1978 ("1978 Act"), s. 12(5).
[89] *ibid.*, s. 12(7).
[90] *ibid.*, s. 1.
[91] 1978 Act, s. 3, as amended by the Children (Scotland) Act 1995, Sched. 2, para. 3.

which require to be approved by the Secretary of State for Scotland, may provide the full range of adoption services or only some of those services. The local authority will have a full range of services including post-placement support for anyone with problems about adoption.[92] The work of adoption agencies has undergone a subtle transformation in modern times. Where once they acted as a service to place healthy babies, they now face the considerable problem of placing many highly disadvantaged children. Such children may have a long association with the social work department of the local authority. For example, the children may already be in care under other provisions (discussed in Chapter 4). The adoption agency, once it has decided that adoption is the best course of action for the child, must decide the best route to that objective whether it be placing the child for adoption or obtaining a freeing order for adoption which prepares the child for prospective adoption. Only local authorities can seek a freeing order.[93] The purposes of freeing is to sever the connection with the birth parents and remove the complication, at an early stage, of obtaining their consent to adoption. It is necessary before a freeing order will be granted to satisfy the court that a child has been placed for adoption or is likely to be placed.[94]

Adoption or Freeing Application

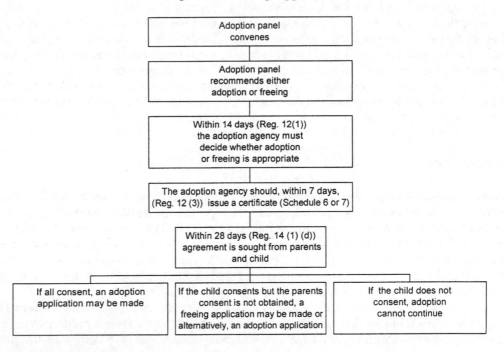

3.44   Obviously before proceeding to placing or any other adoption process, the local authority requires to carefully assess the child's needs, taking advice where appropriate from current carers and other professionals acquainted with the child. In preparing for placement a considerable amount of work will require to be undergone with the child. There will also require to be a great deal of work to link the child and the prospective adopters.[95] This

92   See *Scotland's Children*, Vol. 3, "Adoption and PROs", para. 4.
93   1978 Act, s. 18(1), as amended by the Children (Scotland) Act 1995.
94   1978 Act, s. 18 (3).
95   See *Scotland's Children*, Vol. 3, "Adoption and PROs", paras 17–19.

matching process is extremely delicate and sensitive and can often result in failure. Once a link is established attempts will be made to introduce the child to the prospective adopters. Again this is a delicate process which calls for a great deal of professional skill.[96]

Once the child is placed the adoption agency must visit the prospective adopters within one week of the placement.[97] A written report will be made of the visit. Initially at least, the child will have his own separate social worker who will maintain contact on a regular basis. If the placement is not working a decision to withdraw the child may be made but only after careful consideration. Where the placement is successful a decision is likely to be made for the prospective adopters to lodge an adoption petition in court.

Birth parents will also need support throughout the process. They will be offered counselling and advice both prior to the making of the decision to consent to the adoption of their child and also afterwards.[98]

In placing children, and particularly disadvantaged children, the adoption agency faces a considerable task. To facilitate that task they are permitted to organise regular publicity campaigns. They will also prepare information for prospective adopters including a written statement of the criteria which are applied to those wishing to be assessed as prospective adopters.[99] Applicants will complete a questionnaire which will be a prelude to assessment as prospective adopters.[1] The assessment will include medical and police checks.[2]

Adoption agencies are required to have adoption panels whose functions include considering: whether it is in the best interests of a particular child to be adopted; alternatives to adoption; the suitability of prospective adopters, and whether prospective adopters would be suitable adoptive parents for a particular child.[3]

Roughly half of all adoptions are step-parent adoptions where one of the birth parents has **3.45** entered a new relationship and both that person and their new partner wish to formalise the relationship between the child and the step-parent. It is also the case that other family members may wish to adopt a child. Naturally, these children are not placed by the adoption agency but are already *in situ* with the prospective adopters. Nevertheless there is a key role for the adoption agency and they must be notified of the intention to lodge an adoption petition in court.[4]

Irrespective of the mode of adoption there are general rules as to who can adopt. In adoptions where the child is placed with an adoption agency or the adoption is by a step-parent, parent or relatives, the child must be at least 19 weeks old by the time the order is made and must have lived with the prospective adopter for the preceding 13 weeks.[5] Single persons or married couples can adopt. Adopters must have been domiciled or habitually resident in the United Kingdom for one year prior to the application for adoption. Where the application is from a married couple they must be at least 21 years of age unless one of them is the natural parent of the child in which case that person need only be 18.[6] Where the applicant is single the court require to be satisfied that his or her spouse cannot be found, or that he or she is not married, or that the party's spouse is incapable of making an application

[96]   *Scotland's Children*, Vol. 3, "Adoption and PROs", paras 20–24.
[97]   Adoption Agencies (Scotland) Regulations 1996, reg. 19 (2).
[98]   Adoption Agencies (Scotland) Regulations 1996, reg. 1; see also *Scotland's Children*, Vol. 3, "Adoption and PROs", paras 30–58.
[99]   Adoption Agencies (Scotland) Regulations 1996, reg. 10(1).
[1]   *ibid.*, reg. 10(3).
[2]   See *Scotland's Children, op. cit.*, paras 76–88.
[3]   Adoption Agencies (Scotland) Regulations 1996, reg. 11; on the composition and role of the adoption panel see *Scotland's Children op. cit.* para. 93–137.
[4]   1978 Act, s. 22.
[5]   *ibid.*, s. 13.
[6]   1978 Act, s. 14(1A), substituted by Children Act 1989, Sched. 10, para. 33.

through mental or physical ill-health, or that the parties are separated and living apart and that separation is likely to be permanent.[7] Cohabitees cannot make a joint application to adopt. A single gay person in a stable relationship can adopt.[8] As noted earlier adoption agencies operate criteria for prospective adopters which are made available to those seeking to adopt.[9] The panel of men and women receive information about the child to be adopted and the prospective adopters as well as a case history and a home study report prepared by a social worker on the prospective adopters.

3.46   Following the amendments to the law introduced by the Children (Scotland) 1995 Act it is now possible for a step-parent alone to make an application for adoption. There is no longer any need for them to be conjoined in the application by the natural birth parent with whom thcy are now in a relationship.[10] Commentators have regularly lamented the fact that when a step-parent adoption takes place it often severs the legal ties with a natural birth parent, usually the natural father. The child and the birth parent inevitably lose rights *vis à vis* each other. Under the minimalist intervention strategy of the 1995 Act the court are implored only to make an order where they consider it better for the child's welfare to do so than not to do so.[11] The duty on the court is to take a decision on the basis that the welfare of the child throughout his life is paramount.[12] Despite the prompting of the law it is a fact that most step-parent adoptions are not contested and simply proceed without event. Whether matters will change under the new provisions remains to be seen. Birth parents have the right to withhold consent to an adoption order. One exception to this is that natural fathers who have never been married to the mother do not have such rights. Even in situations where the birth parent is withholding consent it is possible for the court to dispense with it on the basis that it is being withheld unreasonably.[13]

In all adoptions not involving an adoption agency (step-parent or other relative) at least three months' notice must be given to the local authority of the proposed adoption to allow suitable investigations to take place.[14] The local authority must be given access to the child in the home environment even where the child is living with parents, step-parents or relatives.[15]

Private arrangement of adoption other than in conformity with section 11(1) of the Adoption (Scotland) Act 1978 is a criminal offence.[16] The payment of money to procure an adoption or consent to adoption is also an offence,[17] although it may not bar the eventual adoption.[18] It is nevertheless possible for foster parents who adopt "hard to place" children in certain circumstances to continue to receive payments following adoption.[19]

As indicated earlier, in adoptions where the adoption agency has placed the child it is a requirement of law that the child must have been so placed for 13 weeks prior to the court granting the order. The agency must have sufficient time to observe the child in the home environment. During the placement, if informal consent has been given by the natural

---

[7]   1978 Act, s. 15.
[8]   *T, Petr*, 1997 S.L.T. 724.
[9]   Adoption Agencies (Scotland) Regulations (S.I. 1996 No. 3266), reg. 17 A.
[10]   See Margaret Ross, "Adoption and the Children (Scotland) Act 1995" (1995) J.L.S.S. 395.
[11]   1978 Act, s. 24(3), as amended by the 1995 Act, Sched. 2, para. 16; Ross, "Adoption and the Children (Scotland) Act 1995", *supra*.
[12]   1978 Act, s. 6A, as inserted by 1995 Act, s. 96.
[13]   1978 Act, s. 16(2); see also *A v. B*, 1987 S.L.T. (Sh. Ct.) 121.
[14]   1978 Act, s. 22.
[15]   *ibid.*, s. 13.
[16]   *ibid.*, s. 11(3).
[17]   *ibid.*, s. 51.
[18]   1978 Act, s. 24, as amended by the 1995 Act, Sched. 2, para. 16.
[19]   1978 Act, s. 51A, as inserted by the 1995 Act, Sched. 2, para. 25.

parents to the placement of the child with prospective adopters, the child cannot be removed by the parents without the consent of the adoption agency or the courts.[20] In all other respects, natural parents retain rights and responsibilities over their child until the adoption order is made unless the child is the subject of a supervision order or a parental rights and responsibilities order or freeing for adoption order.

The key test for adoption orders

Section 6(1) of the Adoption (Scotland) Act 1978 states that: **3.47**

"in reaching any decision relating to the adoption of a child, a court or adoption agency shall have regard to all the circumstances but

(a) shall regard the need to safeguard and promote the welfare of the child concerned throughout his life as the paramount consideration; and

(b) shall have regard so far as practicable—

(i)   to his views (if he wishes to express them) taking account of his age and maturity; and

(ii) to his religious persuasion, racial origin, and cultural and linguistic background."

A child aged 12 or more is to be presumed to be of sufficient age and maturity to form and express a view.[21] In all adoption applications where the child is 12 years of age or over an order cannot be made without the child's consent.[22] Even if the child is under 12 years of age his view should be given due consideration. In placing a child for adoption the adoption agency must have regard so far as is practicable to the religious views of the parents or guardians of the child as to the religious upbringing of the child. The child's religious persuasion is to be considered as a part of the welfare principle. Regardless of all this it is not a fast rule that children cannot be adopted by persons of a religious persuasion different from that of the parents, guardians or the child.

Application can be made to the Court of Session but it is more usual for the application to be made to the sheriff court for an adoption order. All hearings on adoption will take place in private.[23] The court must appoint a curator *ad litem* to safeguard the interests of the child. The curator will also provide the court with a report on the child's interests.[24] In addition to this a court reporter is required to witness the necessary consents to the adoption. It will often be the case that the reporter will also be the curator *ad litem*. The adoption agency or the local authority is required to submit a report on the suitability of the prospective adopters and the welfare of the child. These reports are of vital importance in assisting the court in its determination.[25]

Where the court has reservations about making an adoption order though does not wish to simply refuse it, it may postpone a decision for up to two years with or without a parental rights and responsibilities order being made instead of the adoption order.[26] It is also possible for a referral to the children's hearing system if the court considers that a ground of referral

[20]   1978 Act, s. 27.
[21]   1978 Act, s. 6(2); see *H v. M*, 1995 S.C.L.R. 401, where child of 6 was held to be too young to form a view.
[22]   1978 Act, s. 12(8).
[23]   *ibid.*, s. 57.
[24]   *ibid.*, s. 58.
[25]   See, *e.g. Central R.C. v. M*, 1991 S.C.L.R. 300.
[26]   1978 Act, s. 25, as amended by 1995 Act, Sched. 2, para. 17.

is established.[27] Where a child is already the subject of a supervision requirement and it is proposed that they be adopted, the hearing must be asked to review the case and provide advice to the court on the adoption application.[28] In making the adoption order the court may discharge the supervision requirement if it sees fit to do so.[29] It is also the case that the courts can, in granting an adoption order, make an order for contact with the birth parents but this is exercised rarely.[30]

Parental consent

3.48   It is essential that a parent or guardian of the child must freely and with full understanding of what is involved, agree unconditionally to the making of an adoption order.[31] A "parent" means the mother or father of the child where they both or either have parental rights and responsibilities.[32] A father who has never been married to the mother will not automatically have parental rights and responsibilities. He may acquire parental rights and responsibilities under section 4 (agreement with the mother) or under section 11 (court order) of the Children (Scotland) Act 1995. A guardian in the context of adoption is someone appointed by deed or court order.[33] A mother cannot give agreement until six weeks after the birth of the child.[34] Unless they are guardians, grandparents have limited scope for involvement in adoption proceedings.[35]

3.49   If a child has been freed for adoption there will be no need for a parent or guardian to consent. In the event that consent is required and is refused it is possible that the court may dispense with it. The grounds for dispensation are as follows:

(1) the parent or guardian is not known, cannot be found or is incapable of giving agreement;

(2) the parent or guardian is withholding agreement unreasonably;

(3) the parent or guardian has persistently failed, without reasonable cause, to fulfil one or other of his or her parental responsibilities in relation to the child;

(4) the parent or guardian has seriously ill-treated the child, whose re-integration into the same household as the parent or guardian is, because of the serious ill-treatment, or for other reasons, unlikely.[36]

Where the assertion is that the parent or guardian cannot be found or is not known the court will require to be satisfied by the report of the curator *ad litem* and any other available information of the steps taken to establish who the parents are or their whereabouts. If the basis of the dispensation of the agreement is that the parent is incapable of giving consent then medical evidence in the form of a medical report to that effect will be necessary. Establishment of the situation does not necessarily mean that agreement will be dispensed

27   Children (Scotland) Act 1995, s. 54.
28   1978 Act, ss. 73 and 22A, as inserted by the 1995 Act, Sched. 2, para. 15.
29   1978 Act, s. 12(9) and 18(9), inserted by 1995 Act, Sched. 2, paras 7(d) and 11(d).
30   *FB and AB, Petrs*, 1998 Fam.L.B. 35–6, *B v. C*, 1996 S.L.T. 1370; see Sutherland, "*D v. Grampian Regional Council: Parental Rights and Adoption*", 1996 S.L.P.Q. 159–165.
31   1978 Act, s. 16(1)(b).
32   1978 Act, s. 65(1), as amended by 1995 Act, Sched. 2.
33   1978 Act, s. 65(1), as amended by 1995 Act, Sched. 2, para. 9.
34   1978 Act, s. 16(4).
35   See Sutherland, "Grandparents and the Law", 1994 Fam.L.B. 7–3.
36   1978 Act, s. 16(2) as amended by 1995 Act, Sched. 2, para. 10.

with. In situations where the incapability is likely to be temporary the court will be reluctant to do so.

The persistent failure "without reasonable cause" to safeguard and promote the child's welfare will be exhibited by a pattern of conduct. The failure to pay aliment is likely to be viewed as an example of such conduct. Conversely, simply being absent from the house when one's marriage is disintegrating will not.[37] In *Angus Council Petitioners*[38] it was held that a mother's personality disorder did not constitute "reasonable cause" for her failure to safeguard and promote her child's welfare. Failure to pay aliment because of unemployment can amount to reasonable cause.[39] Again even if neglect is established the court must proceed to assess whether agreement should be dispensed with. There may be situations in which the prognosis of the parent's behaviour is favourable which leads the court to determine, in giving paramount consideration to the welfare of the child, that agreement should not be dispensed with.

In conformity with one of the themes of the 1995 Act of maintaining family contact, persistent failure of contact with a child without reasonable cause may result in parental agreement to adoption being dispensed with. Imprisonment and voluntarily not contacting the child over a period of time are examples likely to meet the objective assessment of without "reasonable cause".

In contrast, serious ill-treatment can be established by a solitary instance of sufficient gravity if it is the case that the child cannot be re-integrated back into the family home. Where re-integration is possible parental agreement will not be dispensed with. The operation of the twofold test is such that where the ground is established the welfare principle will operate in such a way that the court will invariably dispense with parental agreement.

Somewhat more controversial are the cases where the court has to decide that the parent is withholding their agreement unreasonably. It is not the case that, simply because the adoption order (having regard to the paramount interest of the child's welfare) would be better than no order, any refusal of the parent(s) will be rendered unreasonable.[40] The test is "would a reasonable parent have withheld consent?"[41] There need be no culpability on the part of the parent or guardian.[42] Where a child has been with the prospective adopters for a considerable period of time it is likely that a reasonable parent would see the likely disruption in removal and agree to the adoption.[43]

Once the order is made it is registered in the Adopted Children Register. When the **3.50** adopted person reaches the age of 16, he is entitled to obtain information in respect of his birth. The adopted person may be allowed access to court processes relating to the adoption[44] and also to see his original birth certificate.[45] In addition the adopted person may seek information from the adoption agency. Adopted persons seeking such information often do

---

[37] *Re D (Minors)* [1973] 3 All E.R. 1001; *cf. H and H, Petrs,* 1976 S.L.T. 80; see also *A and B v. C,* 1977 S.L.T. (Sh. Ct.) 55. See also Thomson, *Family Law in Scotland* (3rd ed., 1996), p. 248.

[38] Reported in 1998 Fam.L.B. 35–5.

[39] *A v. B,* 1987 S.L.T. (Sh. Ct.) 121.

[40] See Thomson, *Family Law in Scotland* (3rd ed., 1999), p. 250; *Re W (an infant)* [1971] A.C. 682 (HL), *per* Lord Hodson at p. 718.

[41] *P v. Lothian R.C.,* 1989 S.L.T. 739, *per* Lord Justice-Clerk Ross at p. 741; see also *Lothian R.C. v. A,* 1992 S.L.T. 858.

[42] See *Re D (infant)* [1977] A.C. 602 (HL).

[43] *O v. Central R.C.,* 1987 G.W.D. 22–813; *Lothian R.C. v. R,* 1988 G.W.D. 28–1172. Ross, "Adoption and the Children (Scotland) Act 1995", *supra.*

[44] Act of Sederunt (Child Care and Maintenance Rules) 1997, Sheriff Court r. 2.33(2)(a) and Court of Session r. 67.32(2)(a). These papers will have been transferred to the Scottish Record Office in Edinburgh.

[45] 1978 Act, s. 45(5), as amended by the Children Act 1989 and the Children (Scotland) Act 1995.

so as a prelude to searching for their birth parents. At the time of receiving the information they will also be entitled to receive counselling services to help them cope emotionally with their situation. Such counselling is not obligatory nor is it a prelude to the release of information. The adoption agency is restricted in its role in assisting a search for the birth parent. The desire to locate must come from the adopted person. However, it is suggested that initial contact with a located birth parent be made by a social worker.[46] Adopted persons under 16 years of age have no right of access to information but guidance suggests that it is important to explore the reasons why the young person has approached the adoption agency for information and with the adopted child's consent it is thought appropriate to inform the adoptive parents.[47]

Inter-country adoption

3.51 Inter-country adoption has gained some prominence in the 1990s. Whether it is because of the dearth of young healthy babies here in Scotland or concern for the plight of children in overseas nations wrought by deprivation, natural disaster, famine or armed conflict, it is a fact that more and more children are being brought to Scotland for adoption.[48] The process of inter-country adoption begins with an application for entry clearance to bring a child into the United Kingdom obtained from the Home Office.[49] The Home Office will consult with the Social Work Services Group which will require to be satisfied:

- that the adoption is likely to be in the interests of the child;
- what the reasons for the proposed adoption are, evidence of the child's identity and, with as much information about his circumstances, history and background as can be discovered, including a report on the British Association of Adoption and Fostering inter-country medical form;
- that there is evidence that the child is legally available for adoption and that the appropriate authorities support the adoption plans and have authorised the child's departure from the country of adoption for the purposes of adoption;
- that there is either a valid parental agreement, in a form acceptable to a United Kingdom court and given freely and with full understanding of the effects of a United Kingdom adoption order, or official certification that the child has been genuinely abandoned and the parents cannot be found; and
- that the prospective adopters are suitable adopters for a child from a particular country or countries.[50]

The assessment process will be carried out in this country, utilising the range of services available including local authority social workers. The linking process will be ongoing in the child's country of origin. The system provides for liaison between the two countries and for mechanisms which can ensure prior assessment of prospective adopters before the linking process begins. Obviously, the United Kingdom authorities have no control over the linking

---

[46] See *Scotland's Children*, Vol. 3, "Adoption and PROs," para. 234.
[47] *ibid.*, para. 236.
[48] *ibid.*, para. 238.
[49] Specific guidance was given for the adoption of Romanian children by the Immigration and Nationality Department in March 1991 issued by SWSG, ref 9/91.
[50] See *Scotland's Children*, Vol. 3, "Adoption and PROs," para. 244.

process. To ensure some congruity any assessment of prospective adopters in this country should make clear the age range of children and particular characteristics of the children which the prospective adopters are thought suitable for.[51] Once the Home Office has issued an entry clearance, the prospective adopters are free to bring the child back to Scotland.

---

[51]   *Scotland's Children*, Vol. 3, "Adoption and PROs", para. 260.

Chapter 4

CARE AND PROTECTION OF CHILDREN

INTRODUCTION

Law and policy formulation relative to the care and protection of children operates on **4.01** several key principles, namely that:

1. each child has a right to be treated as an individual;

2. each child who can form a view on matters affecting him or her has the right to express those views if he or she so wishes;

3. parents should normally be responsible for the upbringing of their children and should share that responsibility;

4. each child has the right to protection from all forms of abuse, neglect or exploitation;

5. so far as is consistent with safeguarding and promoting the child's welfare, the public authority should promote the upbringing of children by their families; and

6. any intervention by a public authority in the life of a child must be properly justified and should be supported by services from all relevant agencies working in collaboration.[1]

Although the law is becoming more prescriptive in the parent and child relationship (see Chapter 2), for the most part family autonomy is respected and in recent times there has been a political rhetoric of support for the family in what for many is its central function, to provide a stable, loving, and ultimately caring environment for the nurturing of children to adulthood and self-sufficiency. Inevitability, there arise occasions where nurturing within the child's own family is either impossible, impracticable, or ultimately detrimental to that child's health, welfare, or development. Where such situations arise, there is clearly a need for intervention whether in the form of assistance, or some other more direct action. In a civilised society, one should expect no less. The proper consideration given to children in our society ensures that a large segment of the collective services we call social work are dedicated to the care and protection of children.

---

[1] *Scotland's Children, Regulation and Guidance*, Vol. 1, "Support and Protection for Children and their Families", p. vii.

LOCAL AUTHORITY POWERS AND DUTIES

4.02 Local authorities have a number of legal responsibilities and powers in relation to childcare provision. Those responsibilities and powers emanate from several important statutory duties. Understanding these duties provides a useful starting point in the understanding of the broader body of law relating to the care and protection of children.

Children looked after by the local authority

4.03 In seeking to alter the tone of childcare legislation, children previously said to be in local authority care are now referred to as children "looked after" by the local authority.[2] Children are looked after by local authorities when they are provided with accommodation under section 25 of the Children (Scotland) Act 1995, or are the subject of a supervision requirement of a children's hearing, or are subject to any order, authorisation or warrant under which the local authority has responsibilities in respect of the child, or the child is living in Scotland but in respect of whom local authorities have responsibilities under the Children (Reciprocal Enforcement of Prescribed Orders etc.) England and Wales and Northern Ireland) (Scotland) Regulations 1996.

Local authorities have certain duties towards children looked after by them. They are:

(a) to safeguard and promote the child's welfare, taking the child's welfare as the paramount consideration;

(b) to make use of services that would be available for children were they cared for by their parents;

(c) to take steps to promote regular and direct contact between the child and any person with parental responsibilities, so far as is practicable, appropriate and consistent with the duty to safeguard the child's welfare;

(d) to provide advice and assistance with a view to the time when the child is no longer looked after by them;

(e) to find out and have regard to the views of the child, his parents and any other relevant person, so far as is practicable when making decisions about the child; and

(f) to take account as far as is practicable of the child's religious persuasion, racial origin, and cultural and linguistic background.[3]

The local authority may deviate from these obligations where necessary to protect members of the public from serious harm.

Devising a care plan

4.04 In practice the local authority is expected to develop a care plan for any child looked after by them. The care plan will be based on gathered information which will allow the short and long term assessment of the child's needs.[4] The arrangements put in place for the child should

---

[2] Children (Scotland) Act 1995 ("1995 Act"), s. 17(6).

[3] See 1995 Act, s. 17.

[4] See reg. 3(2)(a) of Arrangements to Look After Children (Scotland) Regulations 1996 ("1996 Regs"): the information required to be obtained is detailed in Sched. 1.

be committed to writing, and where possible agreed with the child's parents, or a person having parental responsibility for him/her. Discussion is encouraged even in circumstances where the child must be looked after by the local authority, such as with a supervision requirement by a children's hearing. The care plan is designed to ensure that those involved know their obligations under it.

Local authorities are expected to act as "good parents" to children looked after by them.[5] Care plans should reflect healthcare needs, health promotion, general assessment, surveillance and assessment of developmental progress, as well as treatment of illness and accidents, in order to promote the physical, social, and emotional health and development of the child.[6] The local authority is also expected to encourage and facilitate the child's educational development.[7] Where the child is placed with foster carers and the parent's have signed a consent form, those carers may authorise consent for medical, surgical and dental treatment where the child is not of sufficient age and maturity to give his or her own consent.

Reviewing the care plan

Local authorities must review the cases of all children looked after by them. Regulations set out how those reviews should be carried out.[8] The objectives of care review will be: **4.05**

(a) to provide an opportunity to take stock of the child's needs and circumstances at regular prescribed time intervals;

(b) to consult formally with parents and children;

(c) to assess the effectiveness of current care plans as a means of securing the best interests of the child;

(d) to provide an opportunity to oversee and make accountable the work of professional staff involved; and

(e) to formulate future care plans.[9]

Where the child is looked after by the local authority and placed away from his or her own home, the first review must take place within six weeks. A subsequent review will take place within three months of the first review, and thereafter at intervals of six months. Where the child is being looked after as a result of a children's hearing, a review meeting should take place prior to any further consideration by the children's hearing under section 73(4) and (5) where the local authority believe the supervision requirement should be ended or varied or is considering an application for a parental responsibilities order, a freeing for adoption order, or a placing for adoption.[10] The outcome of the review meeting will be communicated to the hearing.

There is a legal requirement on authorities to insist that any persons with whom the child is placed must notify them forthwith of any accident, injury or illness, disability, unauthorised absence, or the death of the child.[11] In respect of the death of the child, the local authority is

---

5   1996 Regs, reg. 13.
6   *Scotland's Children*, Vol. 2, "Children Looked After by Local Authorities", p. 12.
7   1996 Regs, reg. 5(2)(c).
8   *Scotland's Children*, Vol. 2, *op. cit.*, pp. 18–24; see also Annex 2, p. 35, for suggested format of reviews and issues to be discussed.
9   *ibid.*, p. 18.
10 1996 Regs, reg. 9.
11 *ibid.*, reg. 14.

required to notify the Secretary of State and as far as practicable the child's parents and other persons who have parental responsibilities for the child.[12] The Secretary of State will be notified via the Social Work Services Group who must be notified within one day of the death of the child.[13]

Home supervision

4.06 One of the means by which a child will be looked after by a local authority is under a supervision requirement of a children's hearing. Home supervision has the followings objectives:

(a) to provide effective measures for the care, protection, support, guidance, treatment or control of children living at home with their families;

(b) to enable children and their families to recognise and tackle successfully the difficulties and problems which led to the child being referred to a children's hearing;

(c) to reduce offending behaviour;

(d) to provide protective measures for a child from others or from himself or herself, where this is an issue;

(e) to ensure school attendance where this is an issue;

(f) to provide programmes of supervision which will maintain the confidence of panel members and the public in the effectiveness of home supervision as a decision of the hearing; and

(g) to provide programmes of supervision which aim to integrate the child in the community and maintain the confidence of the community.[14]

In ensuring any of these objectives, the social worker has a key role in maintaining contact as agreed in the care plan and in working directly with the child and his family.[15]

Residential supervision

4.07 In some cases children will be looked after by the local authority in residential care establishments. In this regard, there are key provisions in the Residential Establishments—Childcare (Scotland) Regulations 1996. The Regulations lay down rules for the operation of such establishments. Before a child is placed in a residential establishment the person in charge should be provided with a report on the child.[16] The managers of residential care establishments in conjunction with the person in charge are required to prepare a statement of functions and objectives of the establishment.[17] In addition the Regulations attempt to address the issue of staff, the number of children to be accommodated, and the quality of care. Within a residential care establishment there may be secure accommodation for those

---

[12] 1996 Regs, reg. 15; see *Scotland's Children*, Vol. 2 "Children Looked After by Local Authorities", Annex 4, p. 38

[13] *Scotland's Children*, Vol. 2, *op. cit*, p. 29.

[14] *ibid.*, p. 40.

[15] *ibid.*, pp. 43–45.

[16] Residential Establishments—Child Care (Scotland) Regulations 1996, reg. 17.

[17] *ibid.*, reg. 5; see also *Another Kind of Home* (HMSO, 1992).

children who require it and from which the child cannot leave. These units are regularly inspected by the Social Work Services Inspectorate and are governed by the Secure Accommodation (Scotland) Regulations 1996.[18]

Foster care

One of the most common ways in which a child is looked after by a local authority is by foster care. Fostering is principally governed by the Fostering of Children (Scotland) Regulations 1996, but also by the Arrangement to Look After Children (Scotland) Regulations 1996. The concept of fostering is that the child is looked after for a limited period of time before being returned to their own family. On a practical basis, foster care forms part of the local authorities' children's services plans. Those plans will identify particular need for fostering, and it is anticipated that the local authority will supplement volunteers with recruited foster parents.[19]

4.08

Each local authority, is required to form a fostering panel.[20] The fostering panel considers all those wishing to become foster parents and makes recommendations as to their suitability for a particular child, any child or certain categories of child.[21] A child may be fostered by a man and a woman living and acting jointly together, or a man or a woman living and acting alone.[22] Where the household contains other persons, a person can still be approved provided those persons are relatives of the prospective foster carers. If a foster carer dies, or leaves the household, it may not be necessary for the child to be removed if the local authority are satisfied that another member of the household can act as a foster parent.[23]

Those applying to become foster parents will require to be assessed by the local authority. They will be interviewed by or on behalf of the local authority and a report will be passed to the fostering panel.[24] The interviewing process may take place over a series of visits, and will involve the inspection of documents such as birth and marriage certificates. It may also entail what might be perceived as intrusive questioning as to the nature and extent of relationships within the household, lifestyle and standard of living, religion, views on discipline, and other analogous matters.[25] An assessment should take place as to amenities and schools available in the locality of the prospective foster parents. On receipt of a report by the fostering panel, if the local authority considers that a prospective foster carer is a suitable person with whom to place a child, they will approve that person as a foster carer.[26] Prospective foster carers may be invited to meet with the foster panel. Once approved, a written agreement is entered into between the foster carer and the local authority.[27] There are allowances payable to foster parents.[28] The local authority is charged with keeping under review foster carers and at intervals of not more than one year they must decide whether the foster carer continues to be a suitable person with whom to place children. Following review, the local authority may revise the terms of the agreement or revoke it in entirety. A foster carer may intimate that

---

18   See generally *Scotland's Children*, Vol. 2, "Children Looked After by Local Authorities", Chap. 6 for a summary and guidance of the key regulations.
19   *Scotland's Children*, Vol. 2, *op. cit.*, pp. 46–48.
20   Fostering of Children (Scotland) Regulations 1996, reg. 4(1).
21   *ibid.*, reg. 6(1).
22   *ibid.*, reg. 12(4).
23   *ibid.*, reg. 12(5).
24   The particulars to be considered are listed in Sched. 1 to the Fostering of Children (Scotland) Regulations 1996.
25   See *Scotland's Children*, Vol. 2, *op. cit.*, pp. 48–51.
26   See generally Fostering of Children (Scotland) Regulations 1996, reg. 7.
27   *ibid.*, reg. 8 and Sched. 2 for the matters to be covered in Foster Carer Agreements.
28   *ibid.*, reg. 9; see also for a full discussion on this issue *Scotland's Children*, Vol. 2, *op. cit.*, pp. 59–61.

they no longer wish to be considered as a foster parent and the local authority will simply terminate the agreement.[29]

4.09   Where a local authority is looking after a child under section 17 (6) (a) (b) and (d) of the Children (Scotland) Act 1995 (essentially those provided with accommodation), they must not place a child with foster parents unless those foster carers have been approved as foster carers in advance and they have satisfied themselves that placement with that particular foster carer is in the child's best interests. Special agreements require to be entered into by the local authority and the foster carers.[30]

In emergency situations the local authority may place a child for up to 72 hours with any approved foster carer. Before doing this, the local authority are required to satisfy themselves that foster placement is the most suitable way of meeting the child's needs.[31] Where a local authority are satisfied that the immediate placement of a child is necessary they may for a period not exceeding six weeks place the child with a person who is not an approved foster carer provided, after interviewing the person, inspecting the accommodation, and obtaining information about the person and others living in the household, that:

(a) the person is a relative or friend of the child;

(b) the person has entered into a written agreement to carry out specified duties in respect of the child; and

(c) they are satisfied that a foster placement is the most suitable way of meeting the child's needs.[32]

A local authority may enter into arrangements with voluntary organisations to discharge duties relative to foster care on their behalf.[33] Case records will be compiled and maintained for each foster carer and also each person who is not an approved foster carer with whom the local authority places a child, as well as a file for each prospective foster carer.[34] These records are to be maintained for at least 10 years, and the local authority is charged with their safekeeping and to ensure that the information which it contains is kept confidential.[35]

Under the Social Work (Representations Procedure) (Scotland) Directions 1996, foster carers have the right to make representations including complaints concerning the authority's discharge of, or failure to discharge, any of their legal functions in relation to a child, although prospective foster carers may not make representations about the failure to approve them as foster carers, nor can foster carers complain about termination of approval.[36]

The costs of care

4.10   Local authorities are entitled to recover financial contributions towards the costs of looking after children. If the child is under 16, recovery will be from anyone who has parental responsibilities over the child. Where the young person is over 16 and in paid employment, he or she will have liability. In most authorities, there will be a sliding scale of charges based

[29]   Fostering of Children (Scotland) Regulations 1996, reg. 10.
[30]   *ibid.*, reg. 12.
[31]   *ibid.*, reg. 13.
[32]   *ibid.*, reg. 14(1).
[33]   *ibid.*, reg. 16.
[34]   *ibid.*, reg. 18.
[35]   *ibid.*, reg. 19.
[36]   *Scotland's Children*, Vol. 2, "Children Looked After by Local Authorities", p. 59.

on the means of the person liable. Parents who are on state benefits will not normally be expected to make a contribution.[37] It is possible to enforce payment of a contribution by means of a contribution order obtained from the court.[38] Natural fathers who do not have parental rights may nevertheless be liable for a contribution to the costs of care of the child.

Duties of local authorities in respect of Children

It is the duty of a local authority to make available general advice, guidance and assistance to "persons in need" living in the area covered by the jurisdiction of the local authority.[39] This is written into the Social Work (Scotland) Act 1968 at Section 12. However, children are no longer included within these general welfare provisions and are now covered by the more specific terms of the Children (Scotland) Act 1995.[40] The 1995 Act introduced a broad duty to provide services to "children in need" and a number of additional duties complement this key obligation. Of course, children who have been receiving services under the 1995 legislation may become "persons in need" once they reach the age of 18.

4.11

Most fundamentally perhaps, a local authority is under a duty to (a) safeguard and promote the welfare of children in its area who are in need; and (b) so far as is consistent with that duty, promote the upbringing of such children by their families. There is an implicit presumption that the maintenance of children at home is to be preferred. However, the local authority's duty to safeguard and promote the welfare of the child must be given greater weight. In fulfilling its obligations, it will be incumbent on the local authority to have regard, so far as is reasonably practicable, to each child's religious persuasion, racial origin, and cultural and linguistic background.[41]

Information needs

Each local authority must prepare and publish a plan for the provision of relevant services for and in respect of children in their area. It must keep that plan under review and modify it where appropriate. In preparing the plan, each local authority must consult every Health Board and NHS Trust, such voluntary organisations as appear to the authority to represent the interests of persons who use, or are likely to use, the services in that area or who provide such services, the chairman of the children's panel for the area, and the housing associations and voluntary housing associations in the area.[42] Guidance indicates that plans should have five strategic aims:

4.12

    (a) to ensure the welfare of children;

    (b) to clarify strategic objectives in relation to services;

    (c) to promote integrated provision of services and effective use of available resources;

    (d) to ensure a consistent approach to planning by local authorities; and

---

[37] Social Work (Scotland) Act 1968, s. 78A inserted by Health and Social Services and Social Security Adjudicators Act 1983, s. 19(3).

[38] *ibid.*, ss. 80–83.

[39] *ibid.*, s. 12, as amended by 1995 Act, Sched. 4, para. 15(11).

[40] 1995 Act, s. 105(4) and Sched. 4, para. 15(11).

[41] *ibid.*, s. 22(2); see *Valuing Diversity*, The Scottish Office (1998).

[42] 1995 Act, s. 19.

(e) to establish a high standard of co-ordination, co-operation and collaboration between service departments within local authorities and with other agencies and organisations which have a contribution to make to effective local services.[43]

Many local authorities now publish the standards of service that the public can expect to receive. Information should be made available in doctors' surgeries, children's hearing centres, hospital outpatient departments, clinics, schools, libraries, community centres, nurseries, CABs, law centres, benefit agencies and churches.[44]

As well as drawing up a plan the local authority has a duty to prepare and publish information:

(a) about relevant services which are provided by them for and in respect of children (including services for and in respect of disabled children or children otherwise affected by disability) in their area or by any other local authority for those children; and

(b) where they consider it appropriate, about services which are provided by voluntary organisations and by other persons for those children, being services which the authority have power to provide, and which, were they to do so, they would provide as relevant services.[45]

Assessment and service provision

4.13   The assessment of a child's needs is crucial in identifying need and providing service. A child is in need of care and attention if he satisfies one of the following conditions:

(a) he is unlikely to achieve or maintain, or to have an opportunity of achieving or maintaining, a reasonable standard of health or development unless the local authority provides services for him;

(b) his health or development is likely significantly to be impaired unless such services are provided;

(c) he is disabled; or

(d) he is affected adversely by the disability of any other person in his family.[46]

Local authorities are required to screen referrals and in appropriate instances provide advice and assistance, refer to another agency, undertake an assessment, make enquiries under local child protection procedures, or undertake joint investigation into the child's welfare or safety.[47]

Services may be provided for a particular child, or for his family, or any other member of the child's family, if provided with a view to safeguarding or promoting the child's welfare. Its seems probable that assistance other than to children will be to the child's parent or guardian to enable them to care for the child. As with the general social work duty under section 12 of

---

[43]   *Scotland's Children*, *Regulation and Guidance*, Vol. 1, "Support and Protection for Children and their Families," p. 9. See generally Chap. 2 of Vol. 1.

[44]   *ibid.*, p. 22.

[45]   1995 Act, s. 20(1).

[46]   *ibid.*, s. 93(4).

[47]   *Scotland's Children*, Vol. 1, *op. cit.*, para. 14, p. 3; Fuller and Brown, *Joint Police and Social Work Investigations in Child Protection* (1991) SWRC, Stirling.

the 1968 Act,[48] assistance may be given in kind or in exceptional circumstances in cash.[49] Examples of goods in kind include household furniture or cooking equipment. Any cash may be given unconditionally, or may be subject to full or part repayment. The local authority must have regard to the child's and his or her parent's means before imposing such a condition, and in any event no repayment condition can be imposed on persons on income support or family credit or jobseekers allowance. There is clearly a considerable discretion given to the local authority as to whether it gives a cash payment or not and the terms it gives such payments on. One must however be cautious: the law does not delineate the resources available to the local authority for the many services it provides, and financial pressures may have a direct bearing on a local authority's attitude to cash assistance.

The services provided by the local authority in respect of any disabled child within its area shall be designed to minimise the effect of his disability, and also to minimise the effect on any child within their area who is adversely affected by the disability of any other person in his family. The services should be designed to give children the opportunity to lead lives which are as normal as possible. A person is to be treated as disabled if he is chronically sick or disabled or suffers from mental disorder. Where requested to do so the local authority must carry out an assessment of a child, or any member of his family, to determine the needs of the child in so far as they are attributable to his disability or to that of the other person.[50] A child may be entitled to more than one assessment depending on his particular needs, though the guidance suggests a streamlined, aggregate approach whereby one comprehensive assessment takes account of both special educational needs in terms of the Education (Scotland) Act 1980, and disability needs under the Chronically Sick and Disabled Persons Act 1970 and the Disabled Persons (Services, Consultation and Representation) Act 1986.

4.14

Where a child is found to be adversely affected by the disability of an adult family member, the local authority may be alerted for the first time to the need for community care services and will at that stage undertake an assessment of the adult in question if it has not done so already. This will inevitably have long term benefits for children who are caring for members of their famliy without an adequate support network.[51]

Providing accommodation

A local authority may provide accommodation for any child in its area if it considers that to do so would safeguard or promote his welfare. In certain circumstances the provision of accommodation becomes a duty. Section 25 (1) of the Children (Scotland) Act 1995 states:

4.15

"A local authority shall provide accommodation for any child who, residing or having been found in their area, appears to them to require such provision because—

(a) no-one has parental responsibility for him;

(b) he is lost or abandoned; or

(c) the person who has been caring for him is prevented, whether or not permanently and for whatever reason, from providing him with suitable accommodation or care."

---

[48] See para. 7.25.
[49] 1995 Act, s. 22.
[50] See generally, 1995 Act, s. 23.
[51] Legal provisions relative to children and adults who are chronically sick and disabled are given fuller treatment elsewhere in this book: see Chap. 7.

In the context of section 25, the accommodation provided is for a continuous period of 24 hours including, by implication, a place to sleep. A child is someone under the age of 18 although it is open to a local authority to provide accommodation for any person within the area who is at least 18 but not yet 21, if it considers that to do so would safeguard or promote welfare. Local authorities do not have a mandatory legal obligation to accommodate persons aged over 18 years in the same way that they must do if the child is under 18 and appears to require such assistance. Given the wording of the section, if a child has no local connection with the area but simply arrives in a locality the authority will nevertheless have a duty towards that person certainly in the first instance. They may look to the local authority applicable to the child's normal place of residence or origin to assume the duty to provide accommodation. Where the accommodation is being provided under the mandatory duty and the child happens to be ordinarily resident in another local authority area, it is incumbent on the local authority to contact the other authority in writing to advise that such provision is being made. The notified authority may subsequently take over the provision of accommodation for the child.

4.16 Before providing a child with accommodation under section 25, the local authority must have regard to his or her views (if he or she wishes to express them). A child 12 years of age or over will generally be considered to be of sufficient age and maturity to form a view. Notwithstanding this, children under 12 where they are of sufficient age and maturity should also have their views taken into account. The local authority cannot provide accommodation for a child where there is someone who has parental rights and responsibilities for him or her and that person is willing and able either to provide, or to arrange to have provided, accommodation for him or her and they object to the local authority providing accommodation. Moreover, a parent with subsisting responsibilities and rights has the right to remove their child from accommodation provided by the local authority. Parental rights and responsibilities will not be affected by the mere placing of a child in accommodation.

The power to object to the provision of accommodation does not apply to children aged over 16 who agree to be provided with accommodation, or when a person who has a residence order in their favour agrees that the child should be provided with accommodation. The power to remove a child from accommodation provided by the local authority is qualified with a condition that where the child has been in the said accommodation for a continuous period of six months or more, the person removing the child must give the local authority 14 days' written notice of their intention to remove the child.[52] This effectively offers the local authority a window of time in which to decide if it should seek an order which would thwart the parent's desire to remove the child or put in place some protective order.

In satisfying its obligations under the statute, the local authority may place a child with one of his relatives, with a foster family, or with any other suitable person "on such terms as to payment, by the authority or otherwise, as the authority may determine". Alternatively, it may place him in a residential establishment or make such other arrangements as appear appropriate which may include placing the child with a person or local authority accommodation elsewhere in the United Kingdom.[53]

Whilst providing accommodation for the child, and in making any decisions with respect to that child, the local authority must fulfil its statutory obligations under section 17 of the 1995 Act, set out at the beginning of the Chapter. It is open to the local authority to depart from

---

[52] For an illustration of parental attempt at recovery under the Social Work (Scotland) Act 1968, s. 15, see *M v. Dumfries and Galloway R. C.*, 1991 S.C.L.R. 481.

[53] 1995 Act, s. 26.

the obligations on the basis that it is necessary to do so to protect the public from serious harm whether or not that is physical harm. Under section 31(1) of the 1995 Act, there is a duty placed upon the local authority which is looking after a child to review the child's case at regular intervals.[54]

Young persons[55]

There is a further duty on the local authority, unless it is satisfied that a child's welfare does **4.17** not require it, to advise, guide, and assist any person in the area who is over school age but not yet 19 years old and who has previously been looked after by the local authority. This is qualified to the extent that children who ceased to be looked after before they ceased to be of school age need not be given help by the local authority. These important statutory innovations are designed to help young persons make the transition from local authority care into the wider community. An attempt to compensate for the absence of parental guidance at this formative stage of their lives is made by placing certain duties and powers on the local authority in whose care they have previously been. A young person who has been looked after by the local authority until he or she ceased to be of school age may, if over 19 but under 21, apply to the local authority to request advice, guidance, and assistance. Although not compelled to do so, the local authority may grant such an application. The assistance to young persons in both situations may be in cash or in kind. It is also open to the local authority to make grants to any person in its area who ceased to be looked after by the local authority at the time he or she ceased to be of school age or subsequently, to enable him or her to meet expenses in connection with education or training, or to make contributions to accommodation and maintenance costs to enable him or her to be near a place of employment or education and training. This support can go on beyond the young person attaining the age of 21 until he completes the education or training. Although a broad enabling power, there must be some doubt as to its practicable application.

Short term refuges for children at risk of harm[56]

Where it appears to a local authority that a child may be at risk of harm, it may at a child's **4.18** request provide the child with refuge in a residential establishment controlled, managed and designated by them. Alternatively, it may arrange for refuge with a person whose house has been approved and designated by them. Short term refuge ordinarily lasts for seven days but may in exceptional circumstances be for 14 days. Similar powers are given to those who provide residential establishments which are approved by the local authority. The limitation of this section is that it is only applicable to children old enough to request refuge themselves.[57] Obviously, the short duration of the refuge is ameliorated by the local authority's duty to safeguard and promote the welfare of the child and it may take further steps under the extensive powers of the 1995 Act. A child who is in refuge is not "looked after" and may not, based on their location in a residential establishment, enforce the numerous obligations of the local authority to provide children and their families with support.

In related provisions, the 1995 Act states that where a child is in residential accommodation in hospitals or nursing homes, and it appears that there has been no parental contact for

---

54   See also Arrangements to Look After Children (Scotland) Regulations 1996 (S.I. 1996 No. 3262).
55   See 1995 Act, ss. 29 and 30.
56   1995 Act, s. 38.
57   See Norrie, Annotations in Mays (ed.), *Scottish Social Work Legislation*, C191.2.

a continuous period of three months, or it is likely that the child will have no parental contact for a period of three months, the hospital or home must notify the local authority. The local authority must on notification take steps to safeguard and promote the child's welfare and consider whether to exercise its statutory powers.[58]

CARE AND PROTECTION COURT ORDERS

4.19   The Children (Scotland) Act 1995 empowers local authorities to intervene to provide care and protection where it is necessary to do so. The Act provides for several court orders which the local authority can seek in furtherance of their statutory obligations. These orders are relatively novel and in many respects practical experience of them is limited.

Child assessment orders

4.20   One of the interesting new orders introduced by the 1995 Act is the child assessment order (CAO). It is intended to allow local authorities, and local authorities alone, to undertake preliminary investigation and assessment where they have suspicions of neglect or abuse. It is not intended for cases where the child is thought to be at immediate risk.[59] The information provided by the assessment may allow the activation of other local authority measures under the Act for which direct evidence is necessary, or it may simply reassure the local authority that its initial fears are unfounded. Clearly an important new power, the Act and the guidance issued to accompany it, attempt to address some of the sensitivities of an order which has civil liberty implications. It is intended that there should be the minimum possible disruption to the child and the family's routine.

A sheriff, on application by the local authority, may grant a CAO for an assessment of the state of the child's health or development.[60] He may only do so if he is satisfied that:

(a)   the local authority have reasonable cause to suspect that the child in respect of whom the order is sought is being so treated (or neglected) that he is suffering or is likely to suffer significant harm;

(b)   such an assessment is required in order to establish whether or not there is reasonable cause to believe that the child is so treated (or neglected); and

(c)   such assessment is unlikely to be carried out, or carried out satisfactorily, unless the order is granted.

Significant harm in this context is harm that is serious and not of a minor or transient nature. It may be physical or emotional.[61] It is believed that the level of "reasonable cause" may be low given that the order is an investigatory order. A simple allegation of abuse may be sufficient to allow the authority to assert "reasonable cause". It is likely that a sheriff will allow an authority some latitude and as long as they have some basis for seeking the order there should be no impediment to it being obtained. The sheriff is not compelled to grant the order if the grounds exist: he still has discretion to refuse but this will be highly unlikely. He will focus on his obligation under section 16 of the 1995 Act to make the child's welfare

---

[58]   1995 Act, s. 36.
[59]   *Scotland's Children*, Vol. 1, "Support and Protection for Children and their Families", p. 54.
[60]   1995 Act, s. 55.
[61]   Norrie, Annotations in Mays (ed.), *Scottish Social Work Legislation*, C208.3.

throughout the child's life his paramount consideration. In any situation where abuse is alleged, it will be hard to dislodge a presumption that the child's welfare is better served by investigation and detection.

Before applying for a CAO the local authority should discuss its statutory duty to "cause inquiries to be made"[62] and offer the parents an opportunity to comment. The purpose of the initial discussions is to allow the parents an opportunity to give access to the child so that an assessment can be carried out voluntarily. It will also help establish , if such be the case that the parents "unreasonably" refused access. The local authority must serve notice and a copy of the application for a CAO on the persons named in the order. The child must also receive a copy unless the sheriff dispenses with service on the child as inappropriate. At least 48 hours' notice must be given. Those served with the application and notice have the right to appear or be represented at the child assessment hearing.   **4.21**

Where the sheriff considers that the conditions for the making of another of the new statutory orders, for instance a child protection order (CPO), are satisfied he must proceed to make such an order rather than simply a CAO.[63] It may well prove to be the case in Scotland that local authorities will be inclined to seek CPOs rather than CAOs primarily because if there are reasonable grounds for suspicion that the child is at risk it is better to move to protect the child than carry out further investigation.[64]

Child assessment orders[65] must specify both the date on which the assessment is to begin and the dates for commencement and duration of the assessment, which must be not more than seven days. They must also require any person to produce the child to an authorised person and to permit that person or another authorised person to carry out the assessment in accordance with the order. The CAO will be carried out by an authorised person in accordance with the order. It is the local authority which authorises any person to carry out the assessment. It is expected that the order should not normally entail the physical separation of the child from his family. However, where it is necessary, the CAO may permit the taking of the child to a place of safety for the purposes of the assessment and authorise the detention of the child for such period as may be specified in the order. Where the sheriff does authorise removal to, or detention in, a place of safety or other place, he may in granting the CAO make such directions as he considers appropriate as to the contact which the child will be allowed to have with any other person whilst there.

The appeal procedure against a sheriff's decision to grant a CAO is thought to be through the normal appeal process of decisions of a sheriff, that is, to the sheriff principal. However, constraints of time dictate that this is an unlikely occurrence unless the assessment is not to commence for some weeks and that fact itself would appear to be unlikely given the grounds for obtaining a CAO.   **4.22**

A child who has capacity under the Age of Legal Capacity (Scotland) Act 1991, s. 2 (4), may refuse to consent to any assessment which involves medical treatment or examination and thus defeat the object of the order.[66]

The local authority is expected to discuss with the family how the assessment is to be carried out. Professionals familiar with the family should be consulted on the best way to carry it out.[67] Once the assessment has been carried out the local authority will be in a position to determine what further action, if any, it should now take. This may involve

---

[62]   1995 Act, s. 53.
[63]   *ibid.*, s. 55(2). See p. 107–121 below.
[64]   Norrie, Annotations in Mays (ed.), *Scottish Social Work Legislation*, C208.2.
[65]   See generally 1995 Act, s. 55.
[66]   1995 Act, s. 90.
[67]   *Scotland's Children*, Vol. 1, "Support and Protection for Children and their Families", p. 57.

referral to the children's hearing or recourse to further orders available under the 1995 Act.

Exclusion orders

4.23   Another major innovation of the 1995 Act is the exclusion order which bears striking similarity to exclusion orders in domestic violence situations.[68] These orders, which represent a major aspect of the Government's anti-child abuse strategy, were originally mooted by Lord Clyde in his Report of the Inquiry into the Removal of Children from Orkney in 1992.[69] They operate in a simple way to exclude an alleged abuser from the home rather than have the child displaced. As Professor Thomson argues, they are "consonant with the aim of the 1995 Act that, so far as is consistent with the local authorities' duty to safeguard and promote the child's welfare, a child should be brought up by his or her own family".[70] Nevertheless they are a short term protective mechanism designed to offer respite and protection and the opportunity to search for a longer term solution. An order is thought to be appropriate where there is an acknowledgement from the alleged abuser that abuse has occurred, and there is no apparent reduction in risk to the child or other children; where the child has made a clear disclosure implicating the alleged abuser and the child's account is believed by the non-abusing parent, but denied or minimised by the alleged abuser; where the child or non-abusing parent is afraid to remain in the household with the alleged abuser; or where fear, distress or a conflict of loyalties caused by the alleged abuser's presence in the household prevent the non-abusing parent from meeting the child's needs and protecting the child from further harm.[71] There may be an absence of, or in any event limited, corroboration of the alleged abuse but nevertheless an exclusion order may be appropriate. There must be evidence of abuse and of continuing risk before an exclusion order can be granted. Before applying for an exclusion order it is thought that the local authority will consider other alternatives. It may be that exclusion can be obtained on a voluntary basis but such voluntary arrangements will have no force of law and may easily be reneged upon. Other options open to the local authority include applying for a CPO, or assisting the child and the non-abusing parent to leave the house. There will undoubtedly be circumstances where the child is better protected by removal. Whilst the exclusion order adds to the "weaponry" of the local authority in its efforts to protect the child, the fact that the whereabouts of the child and other members of the family are known may make the very people which the authority seeks to protect a sitting target.

A local authority may apply to the sheriff seeking an exclusion order with the effect that a named person is excluded from the child's family home.[72] A named person need not be the child's parent or someone who is living with the child. The sheriff must be satisfied that the following conditions pertain:

(a)   that the child has suffered, is suffering, or is likely to suffer, significant harm, as a result of any conduct, or any threatened or reasonably apprehended conduct, of the named person;

---

[68]   1998 Act, s. 76 and para. 3.25 above.
[69]   Sutherland, "Clyde and Beyond", 1993 J.R. 178 (Case and Comment).
[70]   Thomson, *Family Law in Scotland* (3rd ed., 1996) at p. 263.
[71]   *Scotland's Children*, Vol. 1, "Support and Protection for Children and their Families", p. 66.
[72]   See generally 1995 Act, s. 76.

(b) that the making of an exclusion order against a named person—

    (i) is necessary for the protection of the child, irrespective of whether the child is for the time being residing in the family home[73], and

    (ii) would be better to safeguard the child's welfare than the removal of the child from the family home; and

(c) that, if an order is made, there will be a person specified in the application who is capable of taking responsibility for the provision of appropriate care for the child and any other member of the family who requires such care and who is or will be residing in the family home.

It is interesting to note that the remedy is not available to the non-abusing parent directly; he must involve and enlist the assistance of the local authority who have sole right to bring exclusion order proceedings. In contrast, exclusion orders under the Matrimonial Homes (Family Protection) (Scotland) Act 1981 may be sought directly by either party to a marriage or cohabitation and may have the effect of protecting a child at risk of abuse. Furthermore, it follows from paragraph (c) above that exclusion orders will not be appropriate where the alleged abuse is by a lone parent who is the sole carer of the child or where both carers are thought to be abusing the child.

Making the order

In an application for an exclusion order under the 1995 Act, the welfare of the child is the paramount consideration.[74] This must be seen to qualify what would ordinarily be a considerable hurdle, that the exclusion order be "necessary". Where the order is thought to be in the paramount interests of the child it is going to take an unconscionable impediment for the sheriff to then decide that it is not "necessary". More than this though, the sheriff has a duty to consult the child before making an order. The sheriff must be satisfied that making an order is better then not making one at all. "Necessary" is not to be interpreted in such a way that an exclusion order is always refused where another order is available, such as a CPO.[75]

    4.24

Like other exclusion orders, no order seeking to exclude an alleged abuser can be granted on the basis of *ex parte* statements—the person to be excluded must be given the opportunity of being heard or represented before the sheriff.[76] Exclusion orders are only applicable in situations where the child is under 16 years of age, or under 18 where the child is already the subject of a supervision requirement of the children's hearing system.[77] Where the sheriff is satisfied that the conditions exist for the grant of an exclusion order but has not heard the named person or any other person who has been served notice of the proceedings, he may nevertheless grant an interim exclusion order.[78] Interim orders can usually be obtained

---

[73] A family home is defined as "any house, caravan, houseboat or other structure which is used as a family residence and in which the child ordinarily resides with a person who has parental responsibilities in relation to him or who ordinarily has charge of or control over him. It includes any garden or other ground and any building attached to or usually occupied with the house, caravan, houseboat or other structure": 1995 Act, s. 76(12), (13) and (14).

[74] See generally 1995 Act, s. 16.

[75] Norrie, Annotations in Mays (ed.), *Scottish Social Work Legislation*, C229.4. Professor Norrie goes on to suggest that an order will be necessary when it is the most appropriate of the available means of protecting the child from significant harm.

[76] 1995 Act, s. 76(3).

[77] *ibid.*, s. 93(2)(b).

[78] *ibid.*, s. 76.

within 48 hours of the initial application. An interim order has the same effect as a full order but will require the sheriff to hold a further hearing to afford the opportunity to those parties who are entitled to be heard but have not been. At that further hearing, the sheriff may confirm or vary the interim order until final determination of the proceedings. In any event, the sheriff may pronounce an interim order if he is satisfied that the grounds exist until such times as a final determination of the case takes place. Where the sheriff is satisfied that the conditions for making a child protection order under section 57 of the 1995 Act exist, he may make such an order.

The sheriff shall not make an exclusion order if it appears to him that to do so would be unjustifiable or unreasonable having regard to all the circumstances of the case.[79] In assessing those circumstances he may take into account (a) the conduct of the members of the child's family (whether in relation to each other or otherwise), (b) the respective needs and financial resources of the members of that family, and (c) the extent (if any) to which the family home and any relevant item in that home is used in connection with a trade, business or profession by any member of that family. In seeking to balance these considerations with the welfare of the child the court may face a difficult task. The legislation does not seek to address this anomaly. The sheriff must also have regard to the fact that the named person may be required to reside in the family home because it is a tenancy under the Agricultural Holdings (Scotland) Act 1991, or is let to the person by his employer as incidental to his employment.

The effect of an exclusion order[80]

4.25   An exclusion has the effect of suspending the named person's occupancy rights in the home of the child. It prevents the named person from entering the home without the express permission of the local authority who sought the order. Incidental to the exclusion order, the sheriff may grant ancillary orders which grant (a) a warrant for the summary ejection of the named person from the home, (b) an interdict prohibiting the named person from entering the home without the express permission of the local authority, (c) an interdict prohibiting the removal by the named person of any relevant item specified in the interdict except with the written consent of the local authority or of an appropriate person or by order of the sheriff, (d) an interdict prohibiting the named person from entering or remaining in a specified area in the vicinity of the home, (e) an interdict preventing the named person from taking any step in relation to the child, and (f) an order regulating the contact between the child and the named person.[81] In fact, the 1995 Act grants the power to the sheriff to make any order incidental to the exclusion order which he considers necessary. The named person may defend these ancillary orders on the basis that they are unnecessary. Where the sheriff grants warrant for summary ejection, he may make an order for preservation of the named person's goods and effects which remain in the family home.

Power of arrest[82]

4.26   Like the interdicts in the Matrimonial Homes (Family Protection) (Scotland) Act 1981, there is scope for attachment of the power of arrest both to the final order or any interim order. The sheriff may attach a power of arrest to any interdict granted under section 77 of the 1995 Act

---

[79]   1995 Act, s. 76.
[80]   See 1995 Act, s. 77.
[81]   The sheriff can make an order regulating contact whether applied for or not: see s. 77(6).
[82]   See 1995 Act, s. 78.

whether or not an application is made. A local authority may, at any time while an exclusion order has effect, apply for the attachment of a power of arrest. Only once the named person has been served with the interdict with the attached power of arrest will it become effective. When a power of arrest is attached to any interdict granted under section 77, it is incumbent on the local authority "as soon as possible" after the interdict with the power of arrest has been served on the named person to ensure that it, and the court order granting it, are delivered to the chief constable of the police area in which the family home is situated. Where the power of arrest relates to the taking of any step in respect of the child, the documents must be passed to the chief constable in the area where the step or conduct was prevented. Variations or recall of the interdict with the attached power of arrest must also be advised to the chief constable.

The power of arrest allows a constable to arrest without warrant the named person if he has reasonable cause for suspecting the person to be in breach of the interdict. Where a named person has been arrested, the officer in charge of the police station may liberate him if satisfied that that there is no likelihood of that person further breaching the interdict to which the power of arrest has been attached. Alternatively he may refuse to liberate him. Even where the police officer releases the named person he must notify the procurator fiscal forthwith of the facts and circumstances which led to the arrest. A person arrested and not released must be brought before a sheriff sitting as a court of summary jurisdiction in the area in which he was arrested on the first working day after the arrest. The procurator fiscal will present a petition containing a statement of the particulars of the person, the facts and circumstances which gave rise to the arrest, and a request that the person be detained for a period not exceeding two days. If it appears to the sheriff that the procurator fiscal's statement discloses a prima facie case of breach of interdict, that breach of interdict proceedings will be taken, and that there is a substantial risk of violence by the arrested person against any member of the family, or an appropriate person, resident in the family home, he may order that the named person be detained for a period not exceeding two working days.

Where a person is liberated by the police or is brought before a sheriff, it is the duty of the procurator fiscal at the earliest opportunity (and in respect of the latter situation before the person is brought before the sheriff) to intimate to the local authority which brought the application for an exclusion order or an appropriate person who will reside, or who remains in residence, in the family home (or the solicitor who acted for them or who acts for them now), that he has decided that no criminal proceedings should be taken in respect of the arrest of the named person.

4.27 Exclusion orders if granted exist for up to a maximum of six months after being made.[83] They may cease to have effect on that appointed date or cease earlier where (a) the order contains a direction by the sheriff that it shall, (b) the sheriff recalls the exclusion order, or (c) permission given by a third party to the spouse or partner of the named person, or to an appropriate person, to occupy the home to which the order relates is withdrawn. On application by the local authority, the named person or the spouse or heterosexual partner of the named person (if that person is not also excluded and is not also an appropriate person) may recall or vary the exclusion order as well as any ancillary or incidental order such as interdicts, warrants or directions. An exclusion order cannot be renewed. However, the safety net it hopefully provides allows the local authority to intervene with other measures if it considers it appropriate, and allows the family the opportunity to consider how best to secure the welfare of the child.

---

[83] 1995 Act, s. 79.

In response to the exclusion, local authorities are expected to discuss with the excluded person where they should go and the impact of the order on him. The excluded person is likely to be viewed as intentionally homeless and as such will be refused housing by the local authority under the homeless persons legislation. Nor is it likely that an excluded person will be in priority need.[84] The local authority may nevertheless provide other assistance to the excluded person. The local authority should discuss with both parents arrangements for contact between the excluded person and the child and any siblings. It is expected that the local authority will regularly review the need for an exclusion order to continue. The excluded person should nevertheless be enabled to fulfil parental responsibilities in respect of the child where that is practicable and in the interests of the child.[85]

Parental responsibility orders[85a]

4.28   There will be many situations where the local authority's duty to reinvigorate and reinforce the family unit under section 22 of the 1995 Act is simply not appropriate. In fact, there will be situations where re-establishing the child in his own family is wholly detrimental to that child's interests. Referral to a children's hearing might be one solution to the child's need for compulsory measures of supervision. However, there is another alternative and that is for the local authority to seek a parental responsibility order (PRO) which has the effect of vesting parental rights and responsibilities in relation to the child in the local authority and removing the same from the child's parents. An application for a PRO can be made whether or not a child is looked after by the local authority although the former situation is likely to be the norm. Where a child is being looked after by a local authority and a childcare review indicates that the child is in need of long term care away from his or her family, having sought the views of the child, the authority should consider whether a PRO might be appropriate to promote his long term welfare. In all situations where the local authority acts under a PRO, it is charged with the duties under section 17 relative to all children "looked after" by the local authority, including the duty to safeguard and promote his welfare.[86]

Rather controversially parental rights, prior to the Children (Scotland) Act 1995, could be assumed by simple resolution of the local authority without resort to any judicial process.[87] Under the old regime the child had to be in the "care" of the local authority.[88] While there was scope to legally challenge the assumption of the parental rights, the mechanism operated further to the event.[89] For many, it was incongruous that the local authority could take such an important step on its own initiative. The modified arrangements now contained in the 1995 Act ensure that the taking of parental rights from parents is overseen by a sheriff from the outset.

4.29   The local authority may apply to the sheriff for an order transferring (but only during the subsistence of the order) the appropriate parental rights and responsibilities.[90] In PRO proceedings a curator *ad litem* to the child may be appointed as well as a person known as a

---

84   See para. 9.22–9.24.
85   *Scotland's Children, Regulations and Guidance*, Vol. 1, "Support and Protection for Children and their Families", pp. 70–71.
85a   See generally 1995 Act, s. 86.
86   Discussed above at para. 4.03.
87   See Thomson, *Family Law in Scotland* (2nd ed., 1991) pp. 232–240.
88   See *Lewisham LBC v. Lewisham Juvenile Court Justices* [1979] 2 All E.R. 297; *Central R. C. v. B*, 1985 S.L.T. 413.
89   See *e.g. Lothian R. C. v. S*, 1986 S.L.T. (Sh. Ct.) 37.
90   1995 Act, s. 86(1).

reporting officer. Both roles may be fulfilled by the same person.[91] A PRO cannot be granted by the sheriff unless he is satisfied that each relevant person either:

(a) freely and with full understanding of what is involved agrees unconditionally that the order be made;

(b) is withholding such agreement unreasonably;

(c) has persistently failed, without reasonable cause, to fulfil one or other of the following parental responsibilities in relation to the child: the responsibility to safeguard and promote the child's health, development and welfare or, if the child is not living with him, the responsibility of maintaining personal relations and direct contact with the child on a regular basis; or

(d) has seriously ill-treated the child, whose reintegration into the same household as that person is, because of the serious ill-treatment or for other reasons, unlikely.[92]

In a decision under the previous legislation, it was argued that "persistent failure" had the connotation of consistent or repeated behaviour which need not necessarily be wilful.[93] Moreover, the issue of "reasonable cause" was to be construed as applying an objective standard of a reasonable parent.[94]

Those with parental rights and responsibilities before the making of the order retain the right to consent or object to the freeing for adoption of the child or the actual adoption of the child.[95] However, in satisfying the conditions for a PRO it appears likely that such consent or refusal might easily be dispensed with on similar grounds under the tests for adoption, which contain similar terminology.[96] In granting a PRO the sheriff may impose such conditions as he considers appropriate. He may discharge or vary a PRO on application by the local authority, the child or any parent of the child or a person who for the time being has parental rights and responsibilities in relation to the child.[97] PROs automatically terminate when the child attains 18 years of age, is adopted, or becomes subject to a freeing for adoption order.[98]

Effect of a parental responsibilities order[99]

Once the local authority has been granted a PRO, it must undertake full parental responsibilities in respect of the child. Notwithstanding that a PRO has been made, the local authority may allow, either for a fixed period or until the authority otherwise determine, that child to reside with a parent, guardian, relative or friend of his if it appears to the local authority that to do so would be for the benefit of the child. Where the local authority has allowed the child to remain with a parent, relative or friend, it may at any time call for the return of the child by giving notice in writing to that person.

4.30

Where a PRO is made or is in force, a child shall be allowed reasonable contact by the local authority with each person who had parental rights and responsibilities prior to the making

---

[91] 1995 Act, s. 87(4).
[92] *ibid.*, s. 86(2).
[93] See *Central R.C. v. B, supra, per* Lord Brand at p. 421.
[94] *Central R.C. v. B, supra, per* Lord Robertson at p. 418 and Lord Stewart at p. 422.
[95] 1995 Act, s. 86(3); see paras 3.48 *et seq.*
[96] See para. 3.49.
[97] 1995 Act, s. 86(5).
[98] *ibid.*, s. 86(6).
[99] *ibid.*, ss. 87–89.

of the order or who had a residence or contact order or analogous order prior to the PRO. The sheriff may make an order regulating contact on application by the local authority with the child, any relevant person in respect of the child, and any person not referred to in the previous sentence. Indeed the sheriff may make an order regulating contact in the course of granting a PRO irrespective of whether an application is made or not. He may on application by the child, the local authority, or any person with an interest, vary or discharge an order as to contact. Orders as to contact automatically cease on cessation of the PRO.

There are statutory criminal offences to cater for situations where persons impede or interfere with the lawful exercise of the local authorities' rights and responsibilities. Any person who knowingly and without lawful authority or reasonable excuse:

(a) fails to comply with a notice to return the child;

(b) harbours or conceals a child—

(i) in respect of whom a parental responsibilities order has been made; and
(ii) who has run away, or been taken away or whose return is required by such a notice; or

(c) induces, assists or incites a child in respect of whom any such order has been made to run away or stay away, from a place where he is looked after,

shall be guilty of an offence. Where found guilty a person may be liable on summary conviction for a fine up to level 5 on the summary scale and/or imprisonment for up to six months.

EMERGENCY PROTECTION OF CHILDREN

4.31 In many instances it becomes necessary to intervene in the child's interests through the provision of compulsory measures of supervision, primarily through the work of the children's hearing system operating in Scotland. In addition to this there are often situations where intervention is undertaken on an emergency basis to protect the child. It is a fact that child protection has been given greater prominence in the 1990s, primarily because of increased recognition of the incidence of child sex abuse and increasing emphasis on the rights of the child. Local authorities have a crucial role to play in prevention, support, detection, intervention, and sanction. As child abuse and neglect have implications for child welfare, criminal justice and other agencies' responsibilities, there is clearly a need for inter-agency co-operation.[1] In an effort to promote local co-operation there are in operation Child Protection Committees.[2] These local authority committees develop guidance as to the circumstances likely to be appropriate to initiate child protection procedures, the information required, and the recording of information and procedures for joint investigation with the police. Training is clearly central to properly discharged functions in relation to child protection.[3] It is also the case that a Child Protection Register is maintained by each local

[1] See *Protecting Children—A Shared Responsibility*, The Scottish Office (1998).
[2] See Circular No. SWSG 14/97.
[3] See Davies, Marshall and Robertson, *Child Abuse; Training Investigating Officers*, Police Research Series, paper 94, Home Office (1998).

authority, either alone or in conjunction with others. These registers will contain details of children considered to be at risk.

The child protection order[4]

Yet a further innovation of the Children (Scotland) Act 1995 is the Child Protection Order **4.32** (CPO) which replaces the old "place of safety orders" previously available under section 37 of the Social Work (Scotland) Act 1968.[5] The CPO is to be regarded as a serious step and not a routine response to allegations of child abuse. In contrast to other orders under the 1995 Act which only a local authority can seek, an application may be made to the sheriff court for a CPO by "any person". Where the applicant is someone other than the local authority that person must notify the local authority and the Principal Reporter to the children's hearing that the order has been made. Where **the sheriff is satisfied that there are reasonable grounds for believing** that the child is being so treated or neglected that he is suffering significant harm or that he will suffer such harm if he is not removed to a place of safety then, he may make an order to protect the child from the significant harm.

Notwithstanding that others may make an application under the foregoing provisions, it is envisaged that in most instances the applicant will be the local authority acting under slightly different provisions designed to permit the local authority to act in particular circumstances. A sheriff may make a CPO **if first, the local authority has reasonable grounds for believing** that the child is suffering or will suffer significant harm as a result of the way the child is being treated or neglected; secondly, the local authority is making enquiries to allow it to decide if it should act to safeguard the welfare of the child; and thirdly, those enquiries are being frustrated by access to the child being unreasonably denied and the authority has reasonable cause to believe that access is required as a matter of some urgency.

Unreasonable denial of access

It is difficult to offer definitive guidance on what a court will consider to be an unreasonable **4.33** denial of access. Guidance to the new order suggests that it might be unreasonable if the parent has had explained to him the reason for the enquiries and fails to respond positively to a reasonable request for access, perhaps by having the child seen by a medical practitioner. Of course the child himself may be in a position to refuse medical examination or treatment.[6] Such a voluntary response may make a refusal of access reasonable but only in circumstances where a prior voluntary agreement has not been reneged on.[7] Sheriffs will doubtless have their own views as to the question of the reasonableness of any refusal and each case will inevitably rest on its own circumstances. The imminence of the risk to the child is likely to diminish regard for the parents' rights to deny access but it should not be taken that any refusal must of consequence be deemed "unreasonable". The significant harm test assesses the current situation but also looks to the future. Moreover, where the applicant for the CPO is the local authority, the test under section 57(2) of the 1995 Act is that the applicant has reasonable cause to believe, whereas where the application is made by any person under section 57 (1) it is the court that must have reasonable cause to believe that the child is suffering or will suffer significant harm. There is doubtless a difficult balance to be struck

---

[4] See 1995 Act, s. 57.
[5] As discussed in Sutherland, "The Orkney Case", 1992 J.R. 93.
[6] Age of Legal (Capacity) Scotland Act 1991, s. 2(4).
[7] *Draft Guidance on Child Protection Order and Exclusion Orders*, The Scottish Office, para. 2.5.

between the rights of parents and the need to protect children.[8] Professionals face considerable problems in this regard, aptly alluded to in a speech by Lord Nicholls in *Re H (Minors)*[9] where he said,

"I am very conscious of the difficulties confronting social workers and others in obtaining hard evidence, which will stand up when challenged in court, of the maltreatment meted out to children behind closed doors. Cruelty and physical abuse are notoriously difficult to prove".

Lord Nicholls recognised that the law could be made unworkable by demanding unreasonable expectations as to proof. In Scotland the phraseology of the law errs on the side of the need to protect the child at the expense of the parental right to family autonomy.

Making an application for a CPO

4.34　In practice the arrangements for CPOs are that they are usually dealt with in the same day that the application is made. There is out of normal hours provision in Glasgow and Edinburgh where duty sheriffs will make themselves available to hear cases. In other areas it is possible for persons to attend at the sheriff's house where the emergency situation dictates. Sheriffs will consider evidence including hearsay in CPO applications. Anecdotal evidence suggests that hearings may take around an hour. Social workers may be put on oath though this is not necessary. Sheriffs may ask if the views of the children have been ascertained and, if so, what they are.[10]

Before making an application for a CPO a local authority will wish to assess alternative courses of action. They will also require to ascertain the wishes and feelings of the child having regard to his age and understanding. In addition to this there will require to be some consideration of what will happen to the child if the order is made. In practical terms there will be much to consider and plan for. Prior preparation may not only help determine whether to seek an order but will also ensure that the local authority is ready to fulfil its obligations following the granting of the CPO. Much of the preparatory work may arise from child protection case conferences where there is inter-agency consideration of children believed to be at risk. The case conference seeks to ensure that all information about the child is shared, to assess the degree of existing and likely future risk to the child, to identify the child's needs and to review any child protection plan. In the child protection case conference, professionals from a broad array of disciplines are brought together to discuss a child's case. The parents and the child will be fully involved in the process. A case conference may decide to put a child on the Child Protection Register, following which there will require to be periodic review conferences.[11]

8　　See Hayes, "Reconciling protection of Children With Justice for Parents in Cases of Alleged Child Abuse", 1997 *Legal Studies* Vol. 17, 1–21.

9　　[1996] 1 All E.R. 1 at p. 22; on the difficulty of proof see also Muram, "Child Sexual Abuse: Relationship Between Sexual Acts and Genital Findings" (1989) 13 Child Abuse and Neglect 211; Bays and Chadwick, "Medical Diagnosis of the Sexually Abused Child" (1993) 17 Child Abuse and Neglect 91; *Re G* [1987] 1 F.L.R. 310; *Re M (A Minor) (No. 2) (Appeal)* [1994] 1 F.L.R. 59; *Physical Signs of Sexual Abuse*, Royal College of Surgeons (1991); *Diagnosis of Child Sexual Abuse: Guidance for Doctors* DHSS Standing Medical Advisory Committee (1988); *Child Abuse and Neglect: Facing the Challenge*, Open University (1989); Waterhouse, Dobash and Carnie, *Child Sexual Abusers*, Scottish Office (1994).

10　　Kearney, "Children's Hearings, Child Protection and the Children (Scotland) Act 1995", 1996 SCOLAG 102 at p. 106.

11　　See *Protecting Children—A Shared Responsibility*, The Scottish Office (1998), pp. 31–39.

The application for a CPO must identify the applicant and where practicable the child. It **4.35** must also state the grounds on which the application is made and must be accompanied by supporting evidence.[12] In determining whether to make a CPO the sheriff must make the welfare of the child his paramount consideration.[13] The CPO may require any person in a position to do so to produce the child and to authorise the child's removal to a place of safety. It may also prevent the child being removed from the place he or she is currently accommodated in. In addition it may order that the place at which the child is being kept should not be disclosed to any person or persons.[14] In taking any action required by the CPO the applicant must only act in a way that he reasonably believes is necessary to safeguard or promote the welfare of the child.[15] Where they remove a child to a place of safety the local authority will have a duty to safeguard and promote the child's welfare and to take such steps to promote on a regular basis personal relations and direct contact between the child and any person with parental responsibilities towards the child.[16] Notwithstanding the local authority's obligations, section 58 makes specific provision for the sheriff to make a direction as to contact with the child. He may prohibit contact or allow it on certain conditions as he sees fit. Applicants for a CPO may at the same time seek a direction if they believe it is necessary to safeguard and promote the child's welfare on the issue of exercise or fulfilment of parental rights and responsibilities in relation to the child. It is suggested for example that a sheriff may direct a limit to the number of examinations a child may undergo.[17] A CPO may direct the authorisation of an examination of the child's physical and mental state, or some other assessment or interview and related treatment.[18] In implementing the order, local authorities are counselled to ensure that where siblings are removed from home they are kept together unless there are compelling reasons for not so doing. If siblings are separated they should be kept under regular review and permitted contact with each other. Children should be allowed to retain such personal possessions as they reasonably wish or require. Access to the child in the place of safety should be allowed by parents, friends, and relatives albeit on such restrictions as are necessary. In addition there should be attempts to secure the continued education of the child.[19]

Given the emergency nature of the order, the speed which is inherent in the legal process, and the fact that the initial application will be heard by the sheriff in private with only the applicant represented, the order will be served by the applicant on the child, any relevant person (usually parent or guardian) and, where the applicant is not the local authority, on it and the Principal Reporter for the area in which the child is resident. The order will be accompanied by a notice which will also inform of the right to seek a variation or discharge of the CPO.

The Reporter to the children's hearing has the power to discharge a CPO where, having regard to the welfare of the child and the change in circumstances of the case, or further information, he concludes that the conditions for making the CPO no longer exist.[20] He may likewise discharge a condition or direction of a CPO. CPOs are designed to last as short a

---

[12] 1995 Act, s. 57.
[13] *ibid.*, s. 16(1).
[14] On scope of CPO see 1995 Act, s. 57(4).
[15] 1995 Act, s. 57(6).
[16] *ibid.*, s. 57(7).
[17] *Draft Guidance, Child Protection Orders*, Scottish Office, para. 2.12.
[18] Subject to the proviso that a child with capacity under the Age of Legal Capacity (Scotland) Act 1991 may refuse to consent to medical treatment or examination: s. 90, 1995 Act.
[19] *Scotland's Children, Regulations and Guidance*, Vol. 1, "Support and Protection for Children and their Families", p. 63.
[20] 1995 Act, s. 60(3)(c).

time as possible. It is an emergency procedure to offer immediate protection of the child. The system of CPOs has a number of checks and balances as well as mechanisms for speedy recall. Professor Thomson has said of CPOs that they are:

"Paradigmatic of the tension inherent in any system of child protection law between the autonomy of the family and the obligation of the state to intervene in order to protect a child".[21]

The initial hearing[22]

4.36 Unless he discharges the referral or receives notification of an application to the sheriff to vary or discharge a CPO, the Reporter must arrange a reference to a children's hearing to determine whether or not, in the interests of the child, the CPO should continue. This hearing, known as the "initial hearing", must take place on the second working day after the order has been implemented. Where the initial hearing is satisfied that the conditions for making a CPO exist they may continue it, with or without variation, until a second children's hearing is arranged to decide whether compulsory measures of supervision are required.

If no attempt is made within 24 hours of the CPO being made by the sheriff to implement the order, it will cease to have effect. In circumstances where the Reporter has exercised his powers under the Act to discharge the CPO or vary the conditions attached to it, he must notify the sheriff.

Variation or discharge of a CPO[23]

4.37 Unhappiness at the decision of a sheriff to grant a CPO or a children's hearing to continue it, is not governed by any formal right of appeal to the sheriff principal.[24] However, as noted earlier there is a right to seek to have a CPO discharged or varied. An application for variation or discharge is again made to a sheriff and may be made immediately on receipt of the order.[25] Such an application must be made before the initial children's hearing organised by the Reporter. Applications may be made by the child, a person having parental rights over the child, a relevant person, anyone to whom notice of the application was given under the rules, or the person who made the original application. The applicant must give notice of the application to discharge or vary to the Reporter forthwith. The Reporter for his part may convene a children's hearing for the purposes of giving the sheriff appropriate advice to assist in the determination of the application. Where the application is for variation of the decision of the initial hearing to continue the CPO, it must be heard by the sheriff within two days of the hearing. The sheriff, after hearing the parties to the application and the Reporter (if he wishes to make representations), will determine whether the conditions for making a CPO are satisfied or whether any direction or condition should be varied or cancelled. He may thereafter vary any term or condition, confirm or vary any direction, and continue the order. He may, of course, decide to recall the order and cancel any direction.

---

[21] Thomson, *Family Law in Scotland* (3rd ed., 1996) at p. 278.
[22] See 1995 Act, ss. 59–60.
[23] See generally, 1995 Act, s. 60.
[24] 1995 Act, s. 51(15).
[25] Professor Thomson *op. cit.* at p. 275 presumes that this application will be made to a different sheriff from the one who determined the original application, but the basis of that assumption is unclear.

The second hearing

Where no application to vary or discharge is made to the sheriff, a second children's hearing **4.38** shall be convened to take place on the eighth working day after the order was implemented.[26] This hearing will have the same powers as a children's hearing convened to deal with a child thought to be in need of compulsory measures of care under section 52.[27] There may well be the need to issue a warrant to detain the child in a place of safety where the hearing is unable to dispose of the case and they believe that it is necessary to safeguard and promote the child's welfare.[28] Warrants last for 22 days and thereafter they lapse. There is scope for a warrant to be extended during that period, on cause shown by the Reporter, for further periods of 22 days but for no more than 66 days from the day the child was first taken into the place of safety. However, the Reporter can apply to the sheriff to keep the child in the place of safety after any warrant by a children's hearing has expired and he may grant it on cause shown.[29] Any warrant granted by the sheriff to detain the child in a place of safety must specify the date on which it expires. Further applications can be made to the sheriff for warrant at any time before the expiry of a warrant and there is no limit specified on the maximum duration that a child can be detained by a sheriff granting warrants. It is thought that a right of appeal against the sheriff's decision will lie to the sheriff principal though the Act makes no specific provision to that effect.[30] Children must be consulted in warrant proceedings.[31]

Other emergency measures[32]

There is scope under the legislation for any person to make an application to a Justice of the **4.39** Peace to remove a child to a place of safety or to prevent a child's removal from a place of safety in circumstances where it is not practical to make an application to the sheriff for a CPO. The Justice of the Peace must be satisfied that the conditions in section 57 (1) of the 1995 Act for the making of a CPO exist and it is likely that there would be a direction to remove the child to a place of safety, before giving the authorisation. Where the application is made by the local authority the Justice of the Peace must be satisfied that the grounds in section 57 (2) are met and that an authorisation to remove to a place of safety would be granted, before giving authorisation. The authorisation of the Justice of the Peace operates in similar fashion to that of the sheriff in that it requires any person to produce the child to the applicant; prevents anyone from removing the child from a place of safety; and authorises the removal of the child to the place of safety. This authorisation lasts for 12 hours if arrangements have been made to remove the child to, or to prevent the child's removal from, a place of safety. Where arrangements have been made the authorisation ceases after 24 hours or, if earlier, when an application for a CPO has been disposed of.

The Act also confers a power on the police to intervene and remove a child to a place of safety where a constable has cause to believe that the conditions for a CPO exist, it is not practicable to make an application to the sheriff and it is in order to protect the child from significant harm. Children can only be detained in a place of safety for up to 24 hours where

---

[26]   1995 Act, s. 65(2).
[27]   See below at para. 4.51.
[28]   See 1995 Act, s. 66.
[29]   1995 Act, s. 67.
[30]   See Thomson, *Family Law in Scotland* (3rd ed., 1996) at p. 278.
[31]   See 1995 Act, s. 16(2) and (4).
[32]   See 1995 Act, s. 61.

removed to such a place by the police. One can anticipate in such cases an application for a CPO being made to the sheriff within the 24 hours. The Principal Reporter, if he considers that the conditions for granting authorisation are not satisfied or that it is no longer in the best interests of the child, can authorise the release of the child from a place of safety.

THE CHILDREN'S HEARING SYSTEM

4.40 Part III of the Social Work (Scotland) Act 1968 introduced a system of children's hearings to Scotland. Both the scheme itself and the principles underpinning it were of huge significance.[33] The original scheme has undergone a process of modernisation and the new provisions are to be found in Part II of the Children (Scotland) Act 1995.

Criminal responsibility of children

4.41 Before the children's hearing system was introduced, children who offended were prosecuted before the ordinary criminal courts albeit that there were some specialist juvenile courts. Although the courts were charged with dealing with juvenile offenders in their best interests, there was clearly dissatisfaction with the way in which children who offended were being dealt with. The Kilbrandon Committee recognised that children who offended were just as likely to need support as those children who were offended against. Accordingly, the children's hearing system is imbued with a welfare-orientated approach. The scheme operates to divert most child offenders, victims of abuse and those threatened with abuse into the hearing system. It is of course the case that some children who offend are still dealt with in the criminal courts. Section 42 of the Criminal Procedure (Scotland) Act 1995 provides that:

> "No child under the age of 16 shall be prosecuted for any offence except on the instructions of the Lord Advocate, or at his instance; and no court other than the High Court and the sheriff court shall have jurisdiction over a child under the age of 16 years for an offence".

Such prosecutions are rare and will proceed only if it is absolutely necessary. If the prosecuting authorities consider an offence serious enough to proceed by solemn procedure, it is likely they will ensure that the case is not diverted into the hearing system.[34] Moreover, where a child commits an offence in conjunction with an adult and the prosecuting authorities believe that it will be prejudicial to separate the accused, the child may stand trial with his co-accused. It is not uncommon for young offenders jointly involved in the commission of an offence to fall either side of the dividing line of "childhood".[35] In addition, as the children's hearings have no power to confiscate weapons or disqualify from driving,[36] it may be that the prosecuting authorities will proceed in the criminal courts in order to facilitate confiscation or disqualification.

---

[33]   *Report of the Committee on Children and Young Persons, Scotland* (1964, Cmnd 2306), para. 1.
[34]   See para. 8.12 *et seq.*
[35]   In *X v. Sweeney*, 1982 J.C. 70 one finds an illustration of young offenders being prosecuted together.
[36]   Disqualification is possible even for those who have not legally held a licence because they are too young.

In Scots law children under eight years of age have no criminal responsibility whatsoever and will accordingly never be prosecuted in the court.[37] Such children who commit what would otherwise be a criminal offence will be referred into the hearing system. Because it only deals with very minor offences, no child will be prosecuted in the district court. If the matter is of such limited consequence, it is clearly inappropriate for the child to face prosecution. Where a child has committed an offence or is accused of an offence, or there is some other ground of referral, that matter will ordinarily be referred to the Reporter to the children's hearing in the first instance. In 1994 there were 42,934 referrals involving 25,232 children. Of the boys, 69 per cent referred were offence-related referrals whilst 31 per cent were care and protection referrals. Referrals of girls show a different pattern with only 26 per cent of girls referred for committing offences whilst 74 per cent were care and protection referrals.

Compulsory measures of supervision

Any person who has reasonable cause to believe that a child requires compulsory measures **4.42** of supervision may make a referral to the Reporter.[38] Those most likely to make a referral are social workers, school authorities, the police, a relative, or neighbour.[39] The police will notify the Reporter to the children's hearing as well as the procurator fiscal whenever an offence has been committed by a child. The law compels the police to give the Reporter such information as they have been able to discover and enables other persons to do so.[40] In circumstances where information is received by the social work department of the local authority that a child may be in need of compulsory measures of care, the local authority is under a statutory duty to "cause enquiries to be made into the case unless they are satisfied that such enquiries are unnecessary".[41] If after an investigation it believes that the child may be in need of such care then it is under a duty to pass to the Reporter such information as they have been able to discover. Additionally, under section 54(2) of the 1995 Act a court may refer a case to the Reporter if during "relevant proceedings" it is satisfied that one or more of the grounds of referral (except the ground that the child has committed an offence) are established. "Relevant proceedings" are defined as actions of divorce or separation, declarations of marriage, nullity, parentage or non-parentage, actions relating to parental rights and responsibilities, adoption proceedings or freeing for adoption proceedings, and proceedings against a parent for failing to secure regular attendance at school.[42] Given the strict construction of statutory provisions it is only in these cases that referrals from court may occur, although in other cases anyone including a judge is at liberty to pass information to the Reporter.[43] There are other ways in which a child or consideration of a child may come before a children's hearing. For example, there are referrals by the criminal courts for guidance and disposal in sentencing of children prosecuted before the criminal courts.[44] Moreover, children detained in a place of safety where prosecution does not follow will be the subject of a

---

[37]   Criminal Procedure (Scotland) Act 1995, s. 41.
[38]   1995 Act, s. 53(2)(b).
[39]   The police are thought to be the main source of referrals to the Reporter. See Hallet and Murray, *The Evaluation of Children's Hearings in Scotland: Deciding in Children's Interests* (1998, SOCRU), Vol. 1, p. iv.
[40]   1995 Act, s. 53(2) and (3).
[41]   1995 Act, s. 53(1).
[42]   *ibid.*, s. 54(2)(a)–(d).
[43]   Norrie, Annotations in Mays (ed.), *Scottish Social Work Legislation*, C207.3.
[44]   Discussed below at para. 4.70.

referral to a children's hearing by the Principal Reporter, unless he considers that compulsory measures of care are not required.[45] Any hearing organised under this latter provision must be held no later than the third day after the Principal Reporter receives the information.[46]

The Reporter to the children's hearing

4.43   The person who stands at the very centre of the children's hearing system from an administrative point of view is the Reporter. The Reporter is an officer of the Scottish Children's Reporter Administration and cannot without the Secretary of State's permission be employed by a local authority.[47] Many Reporters will be legally qualified but that is not an essential pre-requisite of the post holder. The 1995 Act empowers the Reporter to conduct proceedings in the sheriff court where that proves necessary irrespective of whether they are legally qualified or not.[48]

The Reporter has a varied role.[49] On the one hand he or she is responsible for ingathering information and arranging the hearing. In that sense they act as the administrator of the hearing. However, the Reporters also have a major decision-making role in that they will decide, following receipt of a referral, whether the matter should be referred to a hearing. In conjunction with the procurator fiscal they will have to determine whether a child offender should be dealt with by the hearing system or prosecuted in the criminal courts. Finally, the Reporter has the responsibility of arguing matters before the sheriff, particularly where the grounds of referral to the children's hearing are disputed.

On receipt of information which suggests that a child may be in need of compulsory measures of care the Reporter is required to undertake an initial investigation. In his capacity of gatherer of information, the Reporter may request a report from the local authority on any issue he thinks relevant. The local authority is obliged to supply this report. This report may be wide-ranging and far more extensive than any report made by them in originally referring the matter to the Reporter, if they are the source of the original reference. Reports are likely to come from social workers and/or the child's school.[50] A report at this stage is designed to assist the Reporter in his initial investigation. Once the Reporter has conducted his initial investigation and gathered any reports he requires, he may decide that a hearing does not require to be arranged. Research has disclosed that the main factors taken into account by Reporters in their initial decision-making role include families' co-operation (or lack of it), school-related issues, current social work input, evidential issues, the seriousness of any offence, any prior record of the child or young person offending, the attitude of the family, the age of the child or young person, risk to the child or young person, and aspects of family functioning (for example attitudes, relationships, presence of addiction, aggression).[51] The majority of decisions are relatively straightforward. A substantial proportion of decisions are taken within a month of receipt of notification. Reporters' decision-making has been described as:

---

[45]   1995 Act, s. 63(1), as amended by Criminal Procedure (Consequential Provisions) (Scotland) Act 1995.
[46]   1995 Act, s. 63(2).
[47]   *ibid.*, s. 40(2).
[48]   *ibid.*, s. 40(4)(a).
[49]   *ibid.*, s. 56.
[50]   Examples of *pro forma* reports are to be found in the now dated Moore, *Guide to the Children's Hearing System in Scotland* (1989).
[51]   See Hallet and Murray, *The Evaluation of Children's Hearings in Scotland: Deciding in Children's Interests*, (1998, SOCRU), Vol. 1, p. i.

"characterised by an individual and non-formulaic approach, the exercise of independent judgement, a wide amount of discretion, principles of diversion and minimal intervention, a degree of cultural relativism and, at times, the operation of form of a tariff".[52]

The decision to convene a hearing[53]

Where the Reporter decides that a hearing should not be convened, he must inform the child, any "relevant person", and the person who brought the case to his notice, and anyone else he considers should be informed. A relevant person is a parent or other person with parental rights or responsibilities, or someone who appears to be a person who ordinarily has charge of, or control over, the child in question.[54] The Reporter can if he considers it appropriate refer the matter to the local authority with a view to their providing advice, guidance and assistance to the child and his family. Once the Reporter has decided that a hearing need not be arranged and he has advised the parties accordingly, in the absence of new circumstances, he cannot revoke his decision and arrange a hearing on the basis of the information he obtained in his initial investigation.

4.44

Where on the basis of the information he has, it appears to the Reporter that the child may be in need of compulsory measures of care, the Reporter must arrange a hearing to consider and determine the child's case. Basically, the Reporter must be convinced that one of the grounds of referral in section 52 of the 1995 Act exist before making the referral to the hearing. Where he has not already done so he must arrange for reports from the local authority. Equally he may seek an additional report where a preliminary report has been made referring the child.

Composition and procedure

For every local government area in Scotland there is a children's panel. These panels are constituted and operate under the guidance of a Children's Panel Advisory Committee (CPAC) which every local authority is required to form.[55] Local authorities may band together and form joint Advisory Committees. It is the duty of the CPAC to submit names of possible panel members to the Secretary of State for Scotland and to advise on their suitability and on general matters of administration. The composition of the CPAC is 60 per cent nominated by the Secretary of State and 40 per cent nominated by the local authority. Each CPAC will seek to compile a panel of members for the children's hearings from amongst the locality. There is no gender bias nor need panel members be parents or be married. Once appointed the list of names and addresses of the members of the children's panel is published in each locality. It is from this list that the members of the actual hearing are drawn. Each hearing of a child's case will be constituted by three members of the panel. Hearings cannot consist solely of males or female members.[56] One of three will act as chairman of the hearing[57] but that person's voice carries no more authority than other panel members. In most cases the hearing members reach a unanimous decision.[58]

4.45

---

[52]   See Hallet and Murray, *op. cit.*, p. ii.
[53]   See 1995 Act, s. 56.
[54]   *ibid.*, s. 93(2)(b).
[55]   *ibid.*, Sched. 1.
[56]   *ibid.*, s. 39(5).
[57]   *ibid.*
[58]   See Hallet and Murray, *op. cit.*, p. ii.

Informality of proceedings

4.46   Children's hearings are designed to be as informal as possible.[59] With this in mind they are conducted in private. No other person than those whose presence is necessary for the proper consideration of the case or whom the chairman allows shall be present.[60] As if to reinforce this point section 43 (2) of the 1995 Act insists that the chairman should take all reasonable steps to ensure that the numbers are kept to a minimum. Research has shown that between seven and nine persons usually attend the hearing with between five and seven non-family members.[61] In the ordinary course of events one may find the panel members, the Reporter, the child, relevant persons and a social worker present, occasionally with other professionals in attendance.[62] Parties are not normally legally represented but any child who comes before a hearing and any relevant person who attends may each be accompanied by one person for the purpose of assisting the child, or as the case may be the relevant person, at the hearing. The same person may represent both the child and the relevant person though if they are a lawyer no legal aid will be made available.[63] Given the limitations on attendance it is impossible for even small groups of students to attend as observers but from time to time solitary students are allowed to attend. Bona fide members of a newspaper or news agency may attend the hearing although they may be excluded from the hearing or parts of it where the hearing is satisfied that it is necessary to do so in the interests of the child, to obtain the child's view of the case, or their presence is causing, or likely to cause, the child "significant distress".[64] In such situations where exclusion has taken place, the chairman may subsequently explain to the person excluded the substance of what has taken place in his absence.[65] In reporting the children's hearing the press are prohibited from publishing information which is intended or likely to identify any child[66] concerned in the proceedings, the child's address or school.[67] The Secretary of State has the power to lift such a ban in the case of a children's hearing where he considers it to be in the interest of justice.[68] Despite attempts to make the proceedings relatively informal, there is often an inescapable degree of formality in the hearings associated with ensuring their proper conduct and protecting the rights of families. Families have described feeling nervous and apprehensive about hearings. The majority of hearings last less than an hour.[69]

Attendance and notification[70]

4.47   Attendance at the hearing by the child and relevant persons prior to the 1995 Act was something of a controversial legal area.[71] The provisions in the 1995 Act now clarify the matter. As a general proposition of law a child has the right to attend all stages of the hearing and is obliged to do so. The child may be excused attendance where the hearing is satisfied

---

59   See *Rose*, 1994 S.L.T. (News) 137.
60   1995 Act, s. 43(1).
61   See Hallet and Murray, *op. cit.*, p. ii.
62   At one hearing the writer attended as a representative, a health visitor was in attendance.
63   See the Children's Hearings (Scotland) Rules 1996, constituted under 1995 Act, s. 42(2)(i).
64   1995 Act, s. 43(4).
65   *ibid.*, s. 43(5).
66   See *McArdle v. Orr*, 1994 S.L.T. 463.
67   1995 Act, s. 44.
68   *ibid.*, s. 44(5).
69   See Hallet and Murray, *op. cit.* pp. ii and iii.
70   See 1995 Act, ss. 45 and 46.
71   See Norrie, "Excluding Children from Children's Hearings", 1993 S.L.T. (News) 67; Wilkinson and Norrie, *Parent and Child* (1993) at pp. 464; *Sloan v. B*, 1991, S.L.T. 530.

in a Schedule 1 offence case (case of bodily injury or sexual abuse)[71a] that the attendance of the child is not necessary for a just hearing or in any type of case that it would be detrimental to the interests of the child to be in attendance. The Reporter is responsible for notifying the child of the hearing and ensuring their attendance. In the normal course of events the child will come along with his or her parents. In circumstances where the Reporter thinks it unlikely that the child will attend voluntarily he may apply to a children's hearing for a warrant to have the child detained in a place of safety and brought before a children's hearing.

Similarly, a "relevant person" has the right to attend all stages of the hearing and is obliged to attend.[72] If the hearing is satisfied that it would be unreasonable to require their attendance or their attendance is unnecessary for the proper consideration of the case they will not be compelled to attend. In fact, the hearing may exclude the relevant person (or his representative) if it is satisfied that in the interests of the child the presence of the person is causing or is likely to cause the child significant distress, or that it is necessary in order to obtain the views of the child. Where someone is so excluded the chairman must explain the substance of what has taken place in the person's absence. As Professor Norrie explains:

"It may frequently happen that a child is likely to speak more openly in the absence of the parent. This may be because there is a conflict of interest between the parent and the child, or because the child is embarrassed to talk about certain personal things in front of a parent".[73]

It is also thought that parents disrupting the hearing by continually interrupting or answering on behalf of the child may be properly excluded under this ground. Exclusion may be particularly relevant where the child has been the victim of parental abuse.

A major criticism aimed at the hearing process until quite recently was the inability of the parents or the child to be served with the reports before the hearing took place. In *McMichael v. United Kingdom*[74] the European Court of Human Rights held that the failure to give a parent full access to medical and social enquiry reports placed before the tribunal was an infringement of human rights. The position is now regulated by the Children's Hearing (Scotland) Rules 1996 which require relevant persons to receive identified documents which the chairman and members of the hearing themselves receive from the Principal Reporter.[75] The child will not be entitled to receive the documents though must be made familiar with the substance of relevant reports unless, in the opinion of the chairman, such a disclosure would be detrimental to the child.[76]

Appointing a safeguarder

A safeguarder may be appointed by the hearing to protect and represent the interests of the **4.48** child. He or she is entitled to the papers of the case and thereafter makes appropriate enquiries. He or she may decide to become a party to the action. If the safeguarder decides to do so he must lodge a report before the sheriff on the extent and findings of his enquiry and conclusions on the interests of the child. If the safeguarder is a legal practitioner he or she

---

[71a] See para. 4.55 below.
[72] *cf. L v. H*, 1996 S.L.T. 612.
[73] Norrie, Annotations in Mays (ed.), *Scottish Social Work Legislation*, C199.3.
[74] [1995] Fam. Law. 478.
[75] r. 5(3).
[76] rr. 20(4) and 22(4).

may appear before the sheriff for the child but not as the child's solicitor or advocate. Safeguarders are not very well remunerated and accordingly their appointments are not as extensive as they might be. In contrast curators *ad litem* can be funded from legal aid and as a consequence there is often dual appointment of safeguarder and curator *ad litem*.

Child's age

4.49 It is the duty of the hearing at the commencement of the proceedings to enquire as to the child's age. Only on being satisfied that the person is a child over whom they have jurisdiction may they proceed.[77] Any declaration or finding as to the child's age will be deemed to be the true age of the child and any decision of the hearing will not be invalidated by subsequent evidence that the person was not a child over which they had jurisdiction.[78] The hearing only has jurisdiction over persons under 16 years of age or a person under 18 who is already the subject of a supervision requirement of the children's hearing.

Stating the grounds of referral[79]

4.50 Having asked the child or his parent to state his age, the chairman of the hearing will explain the ground of referral stated by the Principal Reporter as the reason for the referral. The hearing can only proceed if the ground of referral is accepted. All relevant persons must accept the grounds of referral though if they are not present at the hearing this will not be necessary. If the ground of referral is accepted the role of the hearing will be to decide how the case should be disposed of. However, where the ground of referral is rejected by either, or both, the child or the relevant persons the hearing must direct the Principal Reporter to make an application to the sheriff for a finding as to whether such grounds of referral are established. Alternatively, the hearing may discharge the referral completely. These two options are also available where either the child or the relevant persons reject part of the ground of referral and the hearing does not consider it appropriate to continue with the hearing. Where there is part acceptance of the grounds of referral the hearing may proceed in respect of those grounds that are accepted. It will often be the case that there are numerous grounds of referral. In some circumstances only one or some of those grounds are accepted whilst others are rejected. It may also be the case that a ground of referral is broadly accepted. For example, the child may have committed an offence but deny the extent or magnitude of the offence. The hearing may proceed in these circumstances.

In situations where the child is incapable of understanding the ground of referral or any explanation by the chairman, the hearing may direct the Reporter to make an application to the sheriff to determine if the grounds of referral are established or it may discharge the hearing. The chairman is under a duty to explain to the child and the relevant persons the purpose of the application and to advise them that they must attend the hearing before the sheriff. Where the hearing is not able to dispose of a case because the matter has been referred to the sheriff, it may nevertheless grant a warrant to detain the child in a place of safety if it has reason to believe that the child is unlikely to attend any subsequent hearing or that it is necessary in order to safeguard or promote the child's welfare.

---

[77]   1995 Act, s. 47(1).
[78]   *ibid.*, s. 47(2) and (3).
[79]   *ibid.*, ss. 65 and 66.

REFERRING CHILDREN TO THE CHILDREN'S HEARING SYSTEM[80]

The grounds of referral of a child to a children's hearing have remained substantially the same throughout the past 30 years. There have been moderate amendments to cater for recognition of contemporary social problems as well as changes to update and refine the law in the light of experience. These grounds are of crucial importance in the hearing process, though it was held in *O v. Rae*[81] that hearings may take into account matters which are not contained within these specific grounds, including "disputed facts". That case involved an allegation of sexual abuse by the father of four children against one of those children, which he emphatically denied. On the basis of this assertion and another ground which had been accepted by the father, the four children were retained in local authority care while arrangements for foster care were made. The court overruled a previous decision that a hearing could only proceed where grounds were accepted or established.[82] In light of this decision Professor Norrie explains that: **4.51**

> "[T]he existence of the grounds of referral founds the jurisdiction of the children's hearing. When the children's hearing are deciding whether to impose compulsory measures of care a consideration of the grounds of referral is central, but it is open to them to take account of any other factor (including a disputed factor) that touches upon the child's welfare."[83]

Taking account of information other than that related to the ground of referral has been criticised by Sheriff Mitchell.[84] Notwithstanding, the ground or grounds of referral will set in context the extent of the child's need for compulsory care and for the most part will guide the solution to the child's need. Identification and acceptance of the problem will by definition tailor the solution in nearly all cases. The grounds of referral, previously set in out in the Social Work (Scotland) Act 1968, are now to be found in section 52 of the Children (Scotland) Act 1995.[85]

The grounds of referral

Section 52(2)(a): "is beyond the control of any relevant person"

A "relevant person" is described as any parent enjoying parental responsibilities or parental rights, or anyone in whom parental rights and responsibilities are vested or any person who appears to be someone who ordinarily has charge of or control over the child.[86] Professor Norrie[87] suggests that "control" must be viewed as subjective to the particular child and there will be a diminution of parental control as the child matures. Such a view offers support for the postulation advanced by Professor Thomson[88] and others prior to the advent of the 1995 Act, that parental rights diminish as the child matures and correspondingly the child's rights **4.52**

---

[80] See Statistical Bulletin: *Referrals of Children to Reporters and Children's Hearings* (1994 Scottish Office), referred to in Breustedt *et al.*, "The Evolution Of The Children's Hearings System Over The Last Twenty-Five Years", 1997 S.L.P.Q. 73 at p. 81.

[81] 1993 S.L.T. 570.

[82] *K v. Finlayson*, 1974 S.L.T. (Sh. Ct.) 51.

[83] Norrie "In Defence Of *O v. Rae*", 1995 S.L.T. 353 at p. 355.

[84] 1997 SCOLAG p. 13.

[85] In 1996, 27,000 children were referred to Reporters, 23 per cent more than 10 years previously. Source: Scottish Abstract of Statistics No. 26, 1998.

[86] 1995 Act, s. 93(2)(b).

[87] Norrie, Annotations in Mays (ed.), *Scottish Social Work Legislation*, C205.5.

[88] Thomson, *Family Law in Scotland* (2nd ed., 1991), pp. 179–182; *cf. Stewart v. Thain*, 1981 J.C. 13.

increase. One may of course read too much into this view. On a purely factual assessment generally "control" of a child weakens as that child matures and formulates his or her own independent thinking. Professor Norrie appears to suggest that a Reporter considering the circumstances of a particular child may reflect on the expectations of control over a child by a "relevant person".[89] Whilst it is difficult to hypothesise one may also imagine that the Reporter will dwell not just on the nature or quality of the lack of control, but rather more on the consequences of the failure to control. In so doing one of the other grounds of referral may come into consideration as a more suitable alternative basis for referral.

Section 52(2)(b): "is falling into bad associations or is exposed to moral danger"

4.53   This ground also previously existed in the 1968 Act. The continuing failure to define concepts such as "bad association" and "moral danger" leave a great deal of subjectivity to the assessment of the child's circumstances. The lack of definition ensures some linkage to varying standards of public decency and morality. Wilkinson and Norrie argue that "Moral danger is commonly equiperated with the risk of sexual corruption, but there is no warrant for restricting it to such cases." Some illustrations of the matters which will constitute evidence of falling into bad associations or exposure to moral danger may by their very nature offer the opportunity of pursuing a referral under a "better" and more precise ground. Solvent or drug abuse might for example offer considerable evidence of falling into bad associations as might a pattern of criminal conduct. In seeking to define the parameters of the aforementioned concepts there is much merit in Wilkinson and Norrie's view that "there are obvious hazards and difficulties in going beyond recognised categories such as sexual corruption and criminality".[90] Notwithstanding this in *Constanda v. M*[91] one finds an illustration of a Reporter utilising the "exposure to moral danger" based on the commission of a criminal act. The Court of Session took the view that exposure to moral danger should be approached in a "practical fashion" referring to the whole circumstances, but in this particular case where only criminal behaviour was alleged, it would require to be established before the sheriff using the criminal standard of proof and not the usual civil standard of proof ordinarily used when assessing whether a child has been exposed to moral danger. Professor Norrie has suggested that a child at threat from a visiting absent father may be referred under this ground[92] but with respect this must only be in the most unusual of circumstances.

Section 52(2)(c): "is likely (i) to suffer unnecessarily; or (ii) be impaired seriously in his health or development, due to lack of parental care"

4.54   The concept of parental care and parenting continues to be further defined in academic writings,[93] case law[94] and indeed the 1995 Act itself.[95] In exploring the terminology of the

---

[89]   Norrie, Annotations in Mays (ed.), *Scottish Social Work Legislation*, C205.5.
[90]   Wilkinson and Norrie, *Parent and Child* (1993), at p. 450.
[91]   1997 S.L.T. 1396.
[92]   Norrie, "The Meaning Of Household In Referrals To Children's Hearings", 1993 S.L.T. 192.
[93]   See *e.g.* Ross, "Reasonable Parenting—Borders Of Acceptability", 1994 Fam.L. B., Vol. 7, pp. 10–12.
[94]   See *e.g. Kennedy v. S*, 1986 S.L.T. 679 at 682.
[95]   1995 Act, s. 2.

paragraph certain matters require further explanation. First, the reason for the absence of parental care is of little importance[96] and emphasis is on the likelihood[97] that there will be unnecessary suffering or serious impairment to the health or development of the child rather than any attempt to attribute culpability to the parental conduct. On the face of things this ground might be established not just by reference to the nebulous concept of "normal" parenting but more properly by considering medical, psychological and other professional reports which might narrate the damage or impairment to the child in less emotive and more precise terms, particularly given that parental culpability is not an essential component of this ground. Sheriffs may of course discount professional advice. In *Kennedy v. M*[98] the child allegedly sustained bruising to his forehead after becoming involved in an altercation between the respondent and his estranged wife. A few days later the child's hand was burned after touching an iron. No medical help was sought and in a subsequent medical examination bruising was noticed to the boy's buttocks and his penis. The doctor's evidence was that these were not accidental injuries. After hearing a court-appointed safeguarder's report the sheriff was unable to support a finding that there was sufficient lack of parental care, and that many of the events simply reflected the "difficulties of looking after a lively toddler and no parent can be 100 per cent vigilant". In *D v. Kelly*[99] the sheriff held that the development of two adopted girls was being impaired by the overly protective regime imposed by their parents. The parents had sought professional help and according to the sheriff were acting responsibly. Nevertheless he found that the ground of referral was established in that the children's development was being impaired. This view was rejected by the Court of Session which contended that there had to be a lack of parental care in the first instance leading to the impairment of development.

Sheriffs must not simply decide that the child would be better off elsewhere but must apply the statutory test. In *H v. Harkness*,[1] a case considered under the analogous provisions of the 1968 Act, two children of an incestuous relationship were taken into care because of the lack of parental care. There was a supervision requirement in respect of the children which had been allowed to lapse due to an administrative error and the Reporter made a further referral. The mother successfully appealed to the Court of Session arguing that in the fresh application the statutory test must still be applied and that the sheriff should not simply reflect upon whether it would be better for the children to remain with the foster parents with whom they were now placed. The Court of Session also expressed the view that the lack of parental care must be such as is likely to cause serious harm or impairment to health and development of the child even where it might not be possible to be specific about what that harm might be. For an illustration where this ground of referral was upheld see *Finlayson Applicant*[2] where the parents of a haemophiliac child refused to consent to conventional treatment. A recent decision has also highlighted the fact that on this ground, as indeed in all others, one cannot appeal further from the sheriff court to the Inner House and seek to have new reports placed before the court.[3]

[96]   See the *obiter* comment in *D v. Kelly*, 1995 S.L.T. 1220 at p. 1224.
[97]   *H v. Lees*; *D v. Orr*, 1994 S.L.T. 908; Mays, "Home Alone, Left Alone", 1996 64 2 S.L.G. 94–96.
[98]   1989 S.L.T. 687; see also *Kennedy v. S*, 1986 S.L.T. 679.
[99]   1995 S.L.T. 1220.
[1]   1998 S.L.T. 1431.
[2]   1989 S.C.L.R. 601 (Sh. Ct.).
[3]   *Stirling v. R.R.*, 1996 S.C.L.R. 191.

Section 52(2)(d): "is a child in respect of whom any of the offences mentioned in Schedule 1 to the Criminal Procedure (Scotland) Act 1995 (offences against children to which special provisions apply) has been committed"

4.55   The offences referred to by Schedule 1 to the Criminal Procedure (Scotland) Act 1995 read as follows[4]:

1. Incest.

2. Intercourse with a step-child.

3. Intercourse of person in position of trust with child under 16.

4. Intercourse with girl under 16.

5. Indecent behaviour towards girl between 12 and 16.

6. Procuring.

7. Abduction and unlawful detention.

8. Permitting girl to use premises for intercourse.

9. Seduction, prostitution etc. of girl under 16.

10. Trading in prostitution and brothel-keeping.

11. Allowing child to be in brothel.

12. Homosexual offences.

13. Cruelty to persons under 16.

14. Causing or allowing persons under 16 to be used for begging.

15. Exposing children under seven to risk of burning.

16. Failing to provide for safety of children at entertainments.

17. Any other offence involving bodily injury to a child under the age of 17 years[5]

18. Any offence involving the use of lewd, indecent and libidinous practice or behaviour towards children under the age of 17 years.[6]

Evidence suggests that 99 per cent of child sex abusers are male. Frequently they are fathers or stepfathers of the children concerned, or friends of the family. There is also evidence that around three quarters of abused children are female and the majority of children were under 12 when abuse begins.[7] The standard of proof in establishing whether the child has been a victim of some form of physical or sexual abuse is the balance of probabilities[8] despite the allegation being a criminal offence. The Reporter is not concerned with proving guilt, rather that the child is in need of protection. In *M v. Kennedy* one finds a

---

4   See Criminal Law (Consolidation) (Scotland) Act 1995, ss. 1–13; Children and Young Persons (Scotland) Act 1937, ss. 12, 15, 22 and 23.

5   *e.g. B v. Harris*, 1990 S.L.T. 208; *Kennedy v. A*, 1993 S.L.T. 1134.

6   *e.g.* see *Harris v. E*, 1989 S.L.T. (Sh. Ct.) 42.

7   See Waterhouse, Dobash and Carnie, "Child Sex Abusers", 1994 Social Work and Research Findings No. 3, p. 1.

8   *B v. Kennedy*, 1987 S.L.T. 765; *Harris v. F*, 1991 S.L.T. 242.

reported illustration of a sheriff rejecting this ground of referral on the balance of probabilities.[9] The case is also authority for the proposition that a sheriff can hold the ground of referral not established on the basis that he cannot decide which particular offence had been committed. The original allegation was that the child had been the subject of penile penetration by a member of her own household. Medical evidence established that sexual penetration could have taken place at anytime between 12 and 15 years of age. Sex with a child under 13 is a different offence to that of sex with a female child over 13 years of age. Emphasis must be placed on the word "any" in the ground of referral.

There may be a referral where there has been no criminal conviction.[10] Where there has been a criminal complaint this will in no way inhibit the right of the Reporter to place evidence before the sheriff if the ground of referral is contested.[11] The conduct complained of need not have occurred in Scotland and the alleged offence need not be capable of being tried in Scotland.[12] The identity of the offender need not be established,[13] nor need the time and the place of the offence.[14] In establishing the ground of referral hearsay evidence is allowable[15] and corroboration is not necessary.[16] In assessing whether the ground of referral is established it can be argued that the interests of the child take primacy over the interests of natural justice.

The liberal and indeed purposive approach to construction of this ground of referral can be found in the statement of Lord Justice-Clerk Ross in *S v. Kennedy*[17] where he contended that:

> "Parliament has not stated expressly that the offences referred to must be offences which can be prosecuted in Scotland. In my opinion, it is doing no violence to the language used to construe 'offence' in its context as including conduct amounting to such an offence."[18]

Section 52(2)(e): "is, or is likely to become, a member of the same household as a child in respect of whom any of the offences referred to in paragraph (d) above has been committed"

Clearly it would be anomalous if only children who were the victims of Schedule 1 offences rather than being at risk of exposure to them were referred to the hearing system. The whole purpose of the hearing system is to provide for children in need of compulsory measures of care. The welfare concept of the system dictates that agencies and the system should be proactive as well as reactive. The fact that a child has not yet been a victim of the abusive conduct set out in Schedule 1 should not in any way detract from the obvious potential peril they face where they reside with someone who has already been the victim of such abuse. For the victim the system may act in the form of rescue from a hideous ordeal and, for the sibling or other child resident with the victim, the hearing system offers the prospect of prevention

4.56

---

9   1996 S.L.T. 434. Note however he upheld an alternative ground of referral.
10   See *M v. Kennedy, supra*; it may also arise that in subsequent criminal proceedings the alleged abuser is found not guilty and this will not necessarily interfere with the referral which proceeds on the lesser standard of proof: see *Kennedy v. DB*, 1992 S.C.L.R. 55 (IH).
11   *P v. Kennedy*, 1995 S.L.T. 476.
12   *S v. Kennedy*, 1996 S.L.T. 1087.
13   *McGregor v. K*, 1982 S.L.T. 293; *Kennedy v. F*, 1985 S.L.T. 22; *S v. Kennedy*, 1987 S.L.T. 667.
14   See *W v. Kennedy*, 1988 S.L.T. 563; *S v. Kennedy*, 1996 S.L.T. 1087.
15   *W v. Kennedy*, 1988 S.L.T. 583.
16   *Harris v. F*, 1991 S.L.T. 242.
17   1996 S.L.T. 1087; *cf. Merrin v. S*, 1987 S.L.T. 193 and Professor Thomson's comments in *Family Law in Scotland* (3rd ed., 1996) at p. 284.
18   1996 S.L.T. 1087 at p. 1090.

and safety. It seems almost trite that where one child has been the subject of abuse by a source of danger, that source is likely to pose a continuing threat to children that he or she has access to.[19]

An illustration of this type of referral is to be found in *Ferguson v. P.*[20] A referral of two children whose father was charged with the culpable homicide of a two year old child whom he had allegedly wilfully neglected by leaving her in a bath of water without adequate supervision, as a result of which she suffered injury leading to her death. In this case the father rejected the grounds of referral, and additionally sought (and was granted) an adjournment before the sheriff. The Inner House overturned the adjournment reaffirming that the primary concern was the welfare of the child and that the referrals would ordinarily be disposed of before criminal proceedings were concluded or, in some instances, commenced. The potential prejudice to the parent in pursuant criminal proceedings was of secondary importance. In *Templeton v. E*[21] the court distinguished between the continuing existence of family ties and continuing membership of the same household when the father of three children was alleged to have committed an offence under Schedule 1 during overnight contact. The fact that a contact order might be imminent did not suggest that the children were likely to become part of the same household as their father and this did not thereby constitute a ground of referral.

Section 52 (2)(f): "is, or is likely to become, a member of the same household as a person who has committed any of the offences referred to in paragraph (d) above"

4.57 Unlike the preceding ground of referral there is, it is submitted, a requirement to identify the offender who is part of the household or is to become part of the household. There is no requirement that the Schedule 1 offence has been committed against a child.[22] The term "household" in this (as well as the preceding and the following) ground of referral is of some interest. In the normal scheme of things one would imagine that it relates to a group of individuals living together. However in the context of the various grounds of referral its meaning is something more expansive than this. In *McGregor v. H*[23] Lord Emslie said:

"The word 'household' is plainly intended to connote a family unit or something akin to a family unit—a group of persons, held together with a particular kind of tie who normally live together, even if individual members of the group may be temporarily separated from it".

In *Kennedy v. R's Curator ad Litem*[24] Lord Hope argues that "the important question ... is whether the ties of affection and regular contact which hold the parties together as a group of persons will continue". Persons can be considered part of the same household even where they live apart. In Professor Norrie's view the requirement is that there has to be some living together either in the present or at some time in the past. This point is important in the context where a child is born into a "household" which has changed in composition. An

[19] Norrie, Annotations in Mays (ed.), *Scottish Social Work Legislation*, C205.6.
[20] 1989 S.L.T. 681.
[21] 1998 S.C.L.R. 672.
[22] Professor Thomson in *Family Law in Scotland* (3rd ed., 1996) at p. 283 offers the illustration of non-consensual homosexual intercourse against an adult.
[23] 1983 S.L.T. 626 at p. 628.
[24] 1993 S.L.T. 295 at p. 300.

illustration of such a case is to be found in *A v. Kennedy*[25] where a child was born some eight and a half years after the death of another child of the mother following that child's wilful ill-treatment. The mother objected to the referral on the basis that the household was immeasurably changed from that in which the dead child existed. The court disagreed pointing out that household membership may change but still continue. The question remains one of degree. In certain circumstances a child born into a household which has previously had a child referred, may be referred irrespective of the lapse in time between the original referral and the birth of the new child.[26] Moreover, a household may still be said to exist despite the fact that the original perpetrator of the offence has left that household. One would imagine that the hearing would simply dismiss the referral on the basis that the child no longer needed protection.

Section 52(2)(g): "is, or is likely to become a member of the same household as a person in respect of whom an offence under sections 1 to 3 of the Criminal Law (Consolidation) (Scotland) Act 1995 (incest and intercourse with a child by a step-parent or person in position of trust) has been committed by a member of that household"

Incest and related offences are now consolidated in the Criminal Law (Consolidation) (Scotland) Act 1995. The analogous provision in section 32 of the Social Work (Scotland) Act 1968 only provided for the referral of female children whereas the current provision creates parity between the sexes. There is a suggestion that this ground of referral is superfluous in that the offences to which it refers are all Schedule 1 offences and may be thought to be covered elsewhere.[27] Notwithstanding this there have been a few referrals on this specific ground.[28]   **4.58**

Section 52(2)(h): "has failed to attend school regularly without reasonable excuse"

The ground of referral in section 52 (2) (h) on the face of things represents one of the clearer grounds of referral. The current provision is a complete re-enactment of the earlier provision in the 1968 Act. Despite its evident clarity Wilkinson and Norrie[29] point to several uncertainties. First, they contend that the ground of referral can only be open to a parent who has chosen to have his child educated at school. Exclusion from school for an allegation of misconduct which is not admitted may amount to reasonable excuse.[30] The onus of establishing reasonable excuse undoubtedly rests with the parent.[31] Under the Education (Scotland) Act 1980 where a parent is charged with an offence in respect of the child not attending   **4.59**

---

[25]   1993 S.C.L.R. 107.
[26]   The writer has dealt in practice with one such referral where the lapse was 18 months.
[27]   Norrie, Annotations in Mays (ed.), *Scottish Social Work Legislation*, C205.6.
[28]   13 out of 13,395 females in 1993; Statistical Bulletin, Scottish Office.
[29]   Wilkinson and Norrie, *Parent and Child* (1993), p. 454.
[30]   *cf. D v. Kennedy*, 1988 S.L.T. 55.
[31]   The writer has represented one such parent who was able to satisfy the sheriff that the lack of attendance of her child at school was neither due to the child's unwillingness to attend or the parent's lack of desire to send the child but rather circumstances related to the parent's peripatetic lifestyle and administrative procedures in enrolling the child in school.

school regularly and the court is satisfied that the child has not attended school regularly, the court may direct that the ground of referral is established for the purposes of a referral to the children's hearing.[32]

Section 52(2)(i): "has committed an offence"

4.60   Despite the fact that the majority of grounds of referral are welfare-orientated, this particular provision remains of great importance especially in relation to male children where statistics point to over two-thirds of all referrals to be for offence-related matters.[33] In respect of female children the percentage drops to almost one-quarter.[34] Given the number of referrals in respect of both sexes, there must by definition be a high incidence of referrals for offending behaviour. Where the matter comes before a sheriff for a finding on this ground of referral the standard of proof, unlike other grounds, is the criminal standard of proof. No child under the age of eight may be referred under this ground.[35]

Section 52(2)(j): "has misused alcohol or any drug, whether or not a controlled drug within the meaning of the Misuse of Drugs Act 1971"

4.61   Growing concern surrounding the misuse of drugs by children undoubtedly influenced the inclusion of this new ground of referral.[36] The inclusion was primarily to bring Scots law into line with Article 33 of the United Nations Convention on the Rights of the Child.[37] A provision such as this may well have found intellectual merit with legislators irrespective of the Convention. Whilst drug or alcohol abuse are not new phenomena, there is growing public and governmental concern on these issues. In the past the manifestations of the problem would undoubtedly have led to the child being referred under some other heading. It is the nature of social and welfare problems that many of the issues addressed by the grounds of referral are not always found in isolation. For example truancy may be accompanied by offending behaviour. The absence of parental control may similarly be accompanied by drug or alcohol abuse. The permutations are manifold. Fortunately the issue of referral need not be overly concerned with the primary causative or dominant factor. That may of course be of great importance at the disposal stage. The inclusion of this new ground of referral, given its clarity, may offer a more simplistic route into the hearing system where the child can receive appropriate welfare-predicated measures.

---

[32]   Education (Scotland) Act 1980, s. 44(1).
[33]   Breustedt *et al.*, "The Evolution of The Children's Hearings System over the Last Twenty-five Years" 1997 S.L.P.Q. 73.
[34]   *ibid.*, at p. 82.
[35]   *Merrin v. S*, 1987 S.L.T. 193.
[36]   See *Use of Controlled Drugs in Scotland: Findings from the 1993 Scottish Crime Survey*, pp. 6–25; McKeagney, *Pre-teen Drug Users in Scotland*, Univ. of Glasgow, Unpublished; Miller and Plant, *Drinking, Smoking and Illicit Drug Use Among 15 and 16 Year Olds in the United Kingdom*', 1996 B.M.J. 31, 394–397; Parker, Bury and Egginton, *New Heroin Outbreaks Amongst Young People in England and Wales*, Police Research Group, Home Office Paper 92 (1998); Haw, *Drug Problems in Greater Glasgow*, (1985, SCODA); Russell, *Adolescent Drug Dependency and Its treatments* (1998); *Drugs and Young People in Scotland*, Scottish Health Education Group (1988); Perri, *The Substance of Youth: The Place of Drugs in Young People's lives Today* (1997); O'Connor, *Glue Sniffing and Solvent Abuse* (1986); Watson, *Solvent Abuse: The Adolescent Epidemic*? (1986); O'Connor, *Profiles of Glue Sniffing and Volatile Substance Abuse in Children and Adolescents* (1983); Ives (ed.), *Solvent Misuse in Context* (National Children's Bureau, 1986).
[37]   Norrie, Annotations in Mays (ed.), *Scottish Social Work Legislation*, C205.7.

Section 52(2)(k): "has misused a volatile substance by deliberately inhaling its vapour other than for medicinal purposes"

This particular ground of referral was introduced in 1983 by the Solvent (Abuse) Scotland **4.62** Act 1983, s. 1, in response to a perceived social problem. Despite being supplanted in the public consciousness by the arguable greater evil of "hard" drug abuse it remains a problem within Scottish society and as such the provision remains relevant.

Section 52(2)(l): "is being provided with accommodation by a local authority under section 25, or is the subject of a parental responsibilities order obtained under section 86 of this Act, and in either case, his behaviour is such that special measures are necessary for his adequate supervision in his interest or the interest of others"

This ground of referral permits a referral to a children's hearing where a child subject to one **4.63** of the aforementioned orders is behaving in such a way that special measures are required for his "adequate supervision". One slight modification to the analogous ground of referral in the 1968 Act is the inclusion of the words "or the interests of others". One can only speculate that those legislating perceived a situation where other persons in care, or perhaps even those looking after such children, may need the help of the children's hearing in identifying adequate measures of supervision.

Reference to the Sheriff[38]

Where the ground of referral is rejected or not accepted either in full or in part, the Reporter **4.64** may refer the matter to the sheriff court for a ruling as to whether the ground of referral is established. Referrals to the sheriff for proof have increased markedly, particularly in respect of cases referred on care and protection grounds.[39] Any application by a Reporter must be heard by the sheriff within 28 days of the referral being lodged. Reference will be made to the sheriff court which would have jurisdiction if the child had committed a criminal offence. The child has a right and a duty to attend. Notwithstanding this, the sheriff can release the child from the duty to attend if he is satisfied that in cases involving grounds 52(2)(d), (e), (f) or (g) above, the child's attendance is not necessary for the just hearing of the case or, on any ground of referral, that it would be detrimental to the interests of the child to be present.[40] If the child fails to attend the sheriff can make an order to have the child brought before him and for the child to be detained in a place of safety. The child and any relevant person has the right to be represented.[41] In all probability they will have legal representation; legal aid is available for this purpose where applicants qualify.

The Reporter must establish the ground or grounds or referral. If during the hearing the child and the relevant persons accept the grounds of referral the sheriff may dispense with evidence and refer the case back to the children's hearing. Similarly, evidence may be dispensed with if the referral arises because the child was incapable of understanding the ground of the referral and the sheriff becomes satisfied that he or she now understands. The

---

[38] See generally 1995 Act, s. 68.
[39] See Hallet and Murray, *The Evaluation of Children's' Hearings in Scotland: Deciding in Children's Interests* (1998, SOCRU), Vol. 1, p. iv.
[40] Thomson, *Family Law in Scotland* (3rd ed., 1996), p. 286, suggests that a child can be released from the obligation to attend even although it would not be detrimental to his interests to be present.
[41] See *S v. Lynch*, 1997 S.L.T. 1377.

standard of proof in cases other than that the child has committed an offence is the balance of probabilities.[42] As in analogous civil proceedings there is no need for corroboration.[43] Where the ground of referral alleges that the child has committed an offence the standard of proof is beyond a reasonable doubt and corroboration is required.

Section 68 (9) of the 1995 Act provides that

"Where a sheriff decides that none of the grounds of referral in respect of which the application has been made are established, he shall dismiss the application, discharge the referral to the children's hearing in respect of those grounds and recall, discharge or cancel any order or warrant or direction [under the Act] which relates to the child in respect of those grounds".

Occasionally, this will not be necessary for an evidential hearing to reach this point. It may be that in the intervening time between the original child's hearing and the referral to the sheriff new information has come to the Reporter's attention which obviates the need for evidence and allows the sheriff to pronounce such an order.[44]

In cases where the sheriff decides that the grounds of referral or any part of them are established, he will remit the case to the Reporter to arrange for a children's hearing to determine the child's case. If he thinks it necessary in the child's interests, he may make an order either keeping a child in a place of safety or, if he thinks it likely that the child may abscond before the hearing, he may issue an order directing that the child be kept in a place of safety until the sitting of the children's hearing. Any such order of the sheriff will only be valid for either three days or until consideration of the child's case by the children's hearing. The hearing may of course grant a fresh warrant to keep the child in a place of safety.[45]

4.65   The 1995 Act permits a procedure whereby a sheriff's finding that the grounds of referral are established can be reviewed in the light of new evidence.[46] This will only be possible where the applicant claims to have new evidence which was not considered by the sheriff on the original application, which might have materially affected the determination of the original application. In addition to this, the evidence must be likely to be credible and reliable as well as admissible in relation to the ground of referral which was established at the original referral. Moreover, there must be a reasonable explanation for the failure to lead such evidence at the original application. On satisfaction of these criteria the sheriff may proceed to consider the new evidence brought before him, failing which the application must be dismissed. On consideration of the new evidence, if the sheriff is satisfied that none of the grounds of referral are established he may proceed to discharge the referral, possibly terminating any supervision requirement immediately, or at some future date. Alternatively, he may find that the ground of referral is still established and remit the case to the Reporter. Appeals can be taken from any review decision to the sheriff principal or the Court of Session.[47] The deficiency in this new appeal procedure is that it does not allow review on the basis of the quality of evidence but only on the basis of new evidence.[48] It is also the case that the number of appeals is reasonably small.[49]

---

[42]   See *S v. Kennedy*, 1987 S.L.T. 667; *Harris v. F*, 1991 S.L.T. 242.
[43]   Civil Evidence (Scotland) Act 1988, s. 1.
[44]   The writer dealt with one such case where information came to hand that a child had been attending school.
[45]   1995 Act, s. 69(7).
[46]   *ibid.*, s. 85.
[47]   *ibid.*, s. 51(11)(a)(iii) and (b).
[48]   See Thomson, *Family Law in Scotland* (3rd ed., 1996) at pp. 292–3; *K v. Kennedy*, 1993 S.L.T. 1281.
[49]   See Hallet, and Murray, *op. cit.*, p. iv.

Where a ground of referral is established before a sheriff and evidence which assisted the sheriff is later retracted, it is for the children's hearing to consider the matter in the review process.[50]

DISPOSAL AND POWERS OF THE CHILDREN'S HEARING[51]

Where the grounds of referral are accepted by the child and the relevant persons or, where the grounds have been established before the sheriff, the children's hearing may proceed to dispose of the case. The hearing will have before it reports and other relevant information.[52] However, if it requires further information the hearing may continue a case to a subsequent hearing to allow further investigation. Where the hearing continues the case, it may require a child to attend or reside in any clinic, hospital or other establishment for a period not exceeding 22 days for the purposes of investigation. If the child fails to fulfil such a requirement the hearing may grant a warrant to find the child and to remove that child to a place of safety and possibly to take the child from the place of safety to a clinic or hospital or other such establishment. These warrants also expire after 22 days. As an alternative, the hearing may decide that it is in the child's interests to be detained in a place of safety and in such cases it may grant a warrant for such detention. These warrants allow detention for a maximum of 22 days and may contain conditions as to contact with the child as well as requiring the child to submit to a medical or other examination or treatment. Under section 2(4) of the Age of Legal Capacity (Scotland) Act 1991 children, in the opinion of the medical practitioner of sufficient knowledge and understanding, may refuse to consent to such treatment.[53] Section 16 requires the hearing to consult the child in making a warrant and to decide to grant a warrant only if it thinks to grant such an order is better than to grant no such order at all.[54] **4.66**

Supervision requirement

In proceeding with the child's case, the children's hearing must act in the child's best interest. In so doing it may simply discharge the referral after consideration of the child's case.[55] This course of action is likely if the hearing believes that the child's problem is being tackled at source. For example, a child not attending school is to be henceforth the subject of monitoring by parents and the school. Alternatively, the hearing may be convinced that the original problem which led to the referral has been resolved. However, in circumstances where the hearing is of a mind that the child needs a compulsory measure of supervision it can make a "supervision requirement".[56] Before making a supervision requirement the hearing must consult the child and be convinced that in making such an order it is better for the child than not making any order at all.[57] There is evidence that the contributions of children and young people to discussion at the hearings is limited.[58] In the majority of cases **4.67**

---

[50]   *H Petrs*, 1997 S.L.T. 3.
[51]   See generally 1995 Act, s. 69.
[52]   *O v. Rae*, 1993 S.L.T. 570 (allegations against a relevant person not previously used in the ground of referral accepted or established); Norrie, 1995 S.L.T. News 353; *cf. M v. Kennedy*, 1993 S.L.T. 431 (allegations rejected by the sheriff).
[53]   1995 Act, s. 90.
[54]   *ibid.*, s. 16(4)(a)(ii).
[55]   *ibid.*, s. 69(1)(b).
[56]   *ibid.*, s. 69(1)(c).
[57]   *ibid.*, s. 16(2), (3), (4)(a)(i).
[58]   See Hallet and Murray, *op. cit.*, p. ii.

the decision of the hearing usually conforms with the social worker's recommendation.[59] Accordingly, the extent of consultation and its genuineness must be left open to question.

A supervision requirement may require a child to reside at a particular place or places.[60] The supervision requirement will constitute authority for the person in charge of any place where the child is required to reside to restrict the child's liberty.[61] Moreover, the hearing may impose any condition to the supervision requirement it sees fit.[62] It may be, for example, that a condition will require a child to attend for a medical or some other examination or treatment.[63] In addition, the children's hearing may regulate contact with any other person or persons.[64] It is thought incompetent for a court to regulate contact during the existence of a supervision requirement.[65] In conjunction with this, it may be a part of the supervision requirement that the place where the child is required to reside should not be disclosed to certain persons.[66] Given the various grounds of referral, it is obvious that there may be circumstances where concealment of the child's whereabouts will be an essential prerequisite to the protection of the child. Where the hearing is satisfied that it is necessary for the child to be supervised in secure accommodation, they may order this on the basis that the child has previously absconded, is likely to abscond again, it; likely that his physical, mental or moral welfare will be at risk.[67] Secure accommodation may also be ordered where the child is likely to injure himself or someone else unless he is detained in such accommodation.[68] Under section 71 of the 1995 Act, a local authority is under a duty to provide a place in any specified residential establishment, and where the child is the subject of a supervision requirement staying with a parent, relatives or associated person or in any accommodation not provided by the local authority, that authority will nonetheless have a duty from time to time to check that the child is resident there and that the conditions of the supervision requirement are being observed.[69]

4.68   Some children who are subject to a supervision requirement may be required to live in accommodation provided by the local authority and this will impose further obligation on that authority.[70] However, the supervision requirement conditions must still be complied with. Where the local authority finds any requirement unduly burdensome and unnecessary, they may seek a variation of the supervision requirement by referring the matter back to the children's hearing.[71] Following the imposition of a supervision requirement parents do not lose parental rights and responsibilities, but to all intents and purposes the supervision requirement operates to limit severely the exercise of those rights, especially if the child is required to reside in a residential establishment. Thus, for example, the parent will have the right to give medical consent where that right is consistent with the rights of the child but the parent is unlikely to be able to dictate disciplinary or particular aspects of education.[72] In situations where the child remains with their family or relatives, parental rights and

---

[59]   Hallet and Murray, *op. cit.*, p. ii.
[60]   1995 Act, s. 70(3)(a); that place may be in England and Wales: see s. 70(4).
[61]   1995 Act, s. 70(4).
[62]   *ibid.*, s. 70(3)(b).
[63]   *ibid.*, s. 70(5)(a); again any child who has capacity under the Age of Legal Capacity (Scotland) Act 1991, s. 2(4), may refuse to consent to medical treatment.
[64]   1995 Act, s. 70(5)(b).
[65]   *A v. G and S.R.C.* 1996 S.C.L.R. 787.
[66]   1995 Act, s. 70(6).
[67]   *ibid.*, s. 70(10)(a).
[68]   *ibid.*, s. 70(10)(b).
[69]   *ibid.*, s. 71(2)(b); see also *Re J (Accommodation By a Local Authority)* [1995] 1 F.L.R. 159.
[70]   S. 17 principles will apply which include the duty to safeguard and promote the child's welfare which shall be their paramount concern.
[71]   See para. 4.69 below
[72]   See para. 3.33 above.

responsibilities will have more potency. It is obviously far easier to guide and direct from a custodial position than not.

Appeal and review[73]

Supervision requirements will endure for a period no longer than is necessary in the interests of promoting or safeguarding the welfare of the child. Unless reviewed or varied, a supervision requirement will not last longer than a year.[74] If nothing is done to continue it, the requirement automatically ceases. A supervision requirement will cease on the child attaining 18 years of age. The local authority through its social work department has the power to refer a case to the Reporter where they believe the requirement in respect of a child ought to cease to have effect or be varied. They may also refer a case to the Reporter if they apprehend that a condition of the requirement is not being complied with or they are of the opinion that it is right to seek a parental responsibilities order, or freeing for adoption order or that they are placing the child for adoption and intend to apply for such an order.[75] Likewise if the local authority is aware that an application for an adoption order has been made or is pending they must as soon as practicable notify the Reporter.

4.69

In addition to the right of the local authority to refer a case back to the children's hearing the child, or any relevant person, may also seek a review not less than three months after the supervision requirement has been made or at least three months after the most recent continuation or variance of the supervision requirement. Where it is proposed that the child be removed from Scotland other than as a condition of the supervision order, the person proposing to do so must report the matter to the Reporter and the children's hearing.

Once the matter has been referred to the Reporter for review it is his role to arrange for a children's hearing to review the child's case. The hearing for its part may order a further investigation into the child's situation, terminate the requirement, vary the requirement, impose further conditions, or simply continue the order without variation.

Referral back to the children's hearing via the Reporter is not the only means of redress which a child or relevant person has against the original decision of the children's hearing or for that matter any subsequent review decision. There is scope under the legislation for judicial redress. A child or a relevant person may, within three weeks of the children's hearing decision, appeal to the sheriff court against that decision.[76] It is the duty of the Reporter to ensure that all information and reports before the hearing are lodged with the sheriff clerk along with a report of the hearing's proceedings and decision.[77] It is competent to appeal not only against the decision but also any condition imposed by the hearing.[78] The sheriff may decide to hear evidence from or on behalf of the parties. He may also question the Reporter, the persons who wrote or compiled the reports or, alternatively, he may call for further reports.[79]

It is also the case that the sheriff may appoint a safeguarder to look after the child's interests.[80] If he rejects the appeal, the sheriff simply confirms the decision of the hearing.[81] Moreover, if the sheriff determines that the appeal was frivolous he may also decree that no

---

[73] See generally 1995 Act, s. 73.
[74] *Stirling v. D*, 1995 S.L.T. 1089.
[75] See para. 3.43 for discussion on adoption.
[76] 1995 Act, s. 51(1); *S. Appellants*, 1979 S.L.T. (Sh. Ct.) 37.
[77] 1995 Act, s. 51(2).
[78] *Kennedy v. A*, 1986 S.L.T. 358.
[79] 1995 Act, s. 51(3).
[80] See the 1995 Act, s. 41(1); *Catto v. Pearson*, 1990 S.L.T. (Sh. Ct.) 77; *Kennedy v. M*, 1989 S.L.T. 687.
[81] 1995 Act, s. 51(4).

further appeal against the decision of the hearing to continue a supervision requirement may be taken within 12 months of that decision.[82] On the other hand he may uphold the appeal and direct that any condition of the supervision requirement cease to have effect or he may remit the case, discharge the child from the referral or substitute a decision which the hearing itself would have imposed.[83] If the child or a relevant person lodges an appeal with the sheriff against supervision requirement they may also request that the hearing itself suspends the supervision requirement pending the outcome of the appeal.[84]

Further appeal from any decision of the sheriff can be taken by stated case to the sheriff principal[85] and to the Court of Session with leave of the sheriff principal.[86] It is open to the Reporter as well as the child and relevant persons to appeal.[87] There is no scope for appeal beyond the Court of Session.[88] Successful appeals to the sheriff principal or the Court of Session will result in the case being remitted back to the sheriff with or without guidance on disposal.[89]

CHILDREN'S HEARINGS AND THE CRIMINAL COURTS[90]

4.70 Where a child who is not the subject of a supervision requirement of a children's hearing pleads guilty to an offence, the court:

(a) instead of making an order on that plea or finding, may remit the case to the Principal Reporter to arrange for the disposal of the case by a children's hearing; or

(b) on that plea or finding may request the Principal Reporter to arrange a children's hearing for the purposes of obtaining their advice as to the treatment of the child.

Having sought the advice under paragraph (b) above the court may proceed to dispose of the case or remit the case back to the children's hearing for disposal.

In cases where the child who is the subject of a supervision requirement pleads guilty or is found guilty of an offence, the High Court **may** and the sheriff court **shall** request the Principal Reporter to arrange a children's hearing for the purpose of obtaining their advice as to the treatment of the child, and on consideration of that advice they may dispose of or remit the case back to the children's hearing for disposal. Once the case is remitted for disposal to the children's hearing it stands as a referral and the jurisdiction of the court in respect of the child ceases. There can be no remit to the children's hearing where the penalty is fixed by law. It is also the case that a court of summary jurisdiction can remit a person who is not subject to a supervision requirement, over 16 but not yet 17 years and six months old, where that person has pled guilty or been found guilty, for advice as to how the case should be disposed. Following receipt of that advice the matter may be remitted to the hearing for disposal.

---

[82]   1995 Act, s. 51(7).
[83]   1995 Act, s. 51(5); Professor Norrie is hostile to the idea that the sheriff should "trespass" into what should properly be the role of the children's hearing: see Norrie, *Children's Hearings in Scotland* (1997) at p. 188.
[84]   1995 Act, s. 51(9); the Reporter must arrange a hearing as soon as practicable: see s. 51(10).
[85]   Sheriff Mitchell criticises the right of appeal to the sheriff principal on the basis that the appeal should go to a tribunal and not a solitary judge: see 1997 SCOLAG, p. 16.
[86]   1995 Act, s. 51(11); see *e.g. D. G. v. Templeton*, 1998 S.C.L.R. 180; Act of Sederunt 1997, rr. 3.59–3.61.
[87]   See *e.g. Sloan v. B*, 1991 S.L.T. 53, where the Reporter took an appeal but on a point of principle only.
[88]   1995 Act, s. 51(11)(b).
[89]   1995 Act, s. 51(14).
[90]   See the 1995 Act, s. 49.

A certificate that the child has pled, or has been found, guilty acts as conclusive proof that the ground of referral is established in all such referrals to the children's hearing. The hearing will have before it social enquiry reports prepared by the local authority.

CHILDMINDING AND DAY CARE FOR YOUNG CHILDREN[91]

Though principally an English statute, the Children Act 1989 contains important provisions in respect of childcare which are applicable to Scotland. Every local authority is required to keep a register of childminders in their area and also persons who provide day care not on domestic premises for children under eight. A person is a childminder if he or she looks after one or more children under the age of eight for reward, and the period, or the total of the periods, which he spends looking after the children exceeds two hours. Parents, relatives, foster parents or anyone with parental responsibility for the child is not a childminder for the purposes of the legislation. Likewise there are exemptions for schools, hospitalised and residential homes.[92] Persons who provide daycare such as nurseries at separate establishments are required to register each separately. Nannies who look after children wholly or mainly in the child's own home do not require to be registered as a childminder. If someone is employed by two employers and looks after the children wholly or mainly in the home of either of his employers, he will be likewise exempt from the registration process.

4.71

The local authority may refuse to register an applicant for registration on the basis that he or anyone looking after (or likely to be looking after) the children is not a fit and proper person to look after children under eight years of age, or that anyone living (or likely to be living on the premises) or working (or likely to be working) on the premises is not a fit and proper person to be in proximity to children under eight. Alternatively, the local authority may refuse registration on the basis that the premises are unfit.

Following registration, the local authority must issue a certificate of fitness. Premises must be inspected once per year for which they can charge a fee. Persons authorised by the local authority may enter premises at any reasonable time.[93] The Secretary of State for Scotland also has a right to cause premises to be inspected.[94] In addition to its powers of inspection, the local authority may:

1. impose conditions as to the maximum number of children, or the maximum within specified groups, who may be looked after by the child minder;

2. require the premises to be secure and that the equipment is maintained and used; and

3. require the keeping of a record of the children looked after, the names of persons involved in the looking after of the children and any person living or likely to be living on the premises.[95]

A registration may be cancelled by the local authority where it appears to them that the circumstances are such that they would be justified in not registering the person as a childminder; that the care provided is seriously inadequate having regard to the needs of the child; or the person has contravened a requirement placed upon them.[96] Registration of a

---

[91]   See generally Children Act 1989, s. 71.
[92]   *ibid.*, Sched. 9, paras 3–5.
[93]   *ibid.*, s. 76(4).
[94]   *ibid.*, s. 80.
[95]   *ibid.*, s. 72(2) (for childminders) and s. 73(3) (for those providing day care facilities).
[96]   *ibid.*, s. 74(1).

particular place may be cancelled on similar grounds.[97] Registration of all premises operated by a person may be cancelled where the local authority would be justified in refusing registration of that person with respect to any place.[98] There is a right of appeal against cancellation to the sheriff court.[99] In exceptional circumstances the local authority has the power to seek a court order for the immediate cancellation of the registration of a childminder or daycarer where the court thinks that the child is suffering or is likely to suffer significant harm.[1] Such an order is sought by way of *ex parte* statements of the local authority but may be challenged by the person affected by the cancellation.

---

[97]   Children Act 1989, s. 74(2).
[98]   *ibid.*, s. 74(3).
[99]   *ibid.*, s. 77.
[1]   See Mays (ed.), *Scottish Social Work Legislation*, para. C120.2.

Chapter 5

EDUCATION LAW

INTRODUCTION

Educational and social needs are often interlinked, and increasingly inter-professional **5.01** liaison is being recognised as essential. Whilst the focus of this chapter is that of primary and secondary school education, it is acknowledged that important developments are occurring in relation to pre-school education and childcare, especially now that all authorities are required to have produced integrated plans for childcare and pre-school education by April 1999.[1]

Within Scotland there are currently four types of schools:

(a) Education authority schools—are financed directly by local authorities, the education authorities. Within around three-quarters of these schools, parents are represented on school boards.

(b) Self-governing schools—receive funding directly from central government. There are only two of these schools in Scotland, Dornoch Academy and St Mary's Primary, Dunblane, and it appears that Dornoch Academy is likely to return to educational authority control in the near future.

(c) Grant-aided schools—are run by Boards of Managers, mainly dealing with special needs pupils. Funding is received direct from central government.

(d) Independent schools—are independent of the education authority and receive their funding through school fees charged to parents. They receive no direct public funding, although some still participated in the assisted places scheme which is being phased out and should end around 2005.[2]

In addition new community school pilots are being established within Scotland, in recognition of the relationship between education and other social needs. The new community schools will be created in disadvantaged areas with the aim that the school will bring together in a single team professionals from a range of services dealing with education, family

---

[1] "Guidance On The Planning Of Pre-School Education And Childcare And The Establishment Of Childcare Partnerships", SOEID (October 1998).
[2] "The Assisted Places Scheme 1997–98", SOEID news release, June 2, 1998.

support and health education and promotion.[3] It is expected that up to 60 new community schools will be created from April 1999.[4]

However not all children attend school, perhaps due to long-term confinement in hospital or the choice of the parents to educate the child at home. In the week commencing September 15, 1997, 237 children were being educated in hospital; 297 children were being educated at home; 161 excluded children were receiving special temporary tutoring; and 27 excluded children were not receiving any education.[5]

In Scotland whilst there is not a statutory national curriculum, as there is in England & Wales, the Secretary of State may make national guidelines which require to be followed,[6] and within Gaelic speaking areas there is a requirement that Gaelic is taught.[7] Notwithstanding the apparent degree of flexibility within Scottish education, parents and local government have a clear legal duty to provide their children with appropriate education.

DUTY TO EDUCATE

Local education authorities

5.02   All children of school age, that is between the ages of five and 16, are required to receive appropriate education,[8] and in general this is achieved by parents sending their children to a school maintained and run by the local education authority. It is a duty of local education authorities "to secure that there is made for their area adequate and efficient provision of school education".[9] As with all statutory duties the local authority can be taken to court if they are in breach of this, although in Scotland such action is currently rare. In *Walker v. Strathclyde Regional Council (No. 1)*[10] the parents of pupils affected by strike action sought a court order against the council due to the interruption caused to their children's education, but were unsuccessful. However, in England and Wales the tendency to sue for inadequate education is growing and since the beginning of 1997 there have been over 70 cases raised by pupils against schools for damages due to inadequate education.[11] Such cases may become more commonplace in Scotland in the future.

Local education authorities have several statutory duties in relation to school education. Not only must they provide education in public schools, providing the necessary buildings and staffing thereof, the authorities are also responsible for ensuring attendance at schools,[12] providing special needs resources[13] and providing a careers service.[14] Furthermore, since the education reforms of the 1980s, the authority is responsible for operating the school placing request scheme as well as for liaising with school boards regarding financial information and

---

[3]   *New Community Schools—The Prospectus*, Scottish Office, Nov. 1998.
[4]   "Scotland Leads the Way with Radical Plan for New Community Schools", news release 2254/98, Scottish Office Nov. 4, 1998.
[5]   SOEID Statistical Return Form SC4.
[6]   Education (Scotland) Act 1980 ("1980 Act"), s. 2, as amended by the Self-Governing Schools etc. (Scotland) Act 1989, s. 69(1), and by the Education (Scotland) Act 1996, s. 36 and Sched. 6.
[7]   1980 Act, s. 1(5), as substituted by the Education (Scotland) Act 1981, s. 3(1) and Sched. 8.
[8]   1980 Act, s. 30.
[9]   *ibid.*, s. 1.
[10] 1986 S.L.T. 523.
[11] Gow, "Law in the Classroom", 1998 Fam. Law Bull., 32–2, at pp. 2–3.
[12] 1980 Act, ss. 38–44.
[13] *ibid.*, s. 1.
[14] *ibid.*, s. 126.

other matters.[15] Exactly how an authority discharges it's duties is a matter for their discretion, and as such, procedures do vary between authorities. Therefore in advising pupils or parents it is essential first to obtain copies of the local education authority's policies on the matter at issue.

The function of education is not just an interest of the local authority. Currently central government, through the office of the Secretary of State for Scotland, retains a number of important powers ranging from the inspection of schools to consenting to the closure of schools in certain circumstances.[16] Moreover, the current Government are concerned with raising the standards in schools, and have set targets for achievement in reading, writing and mathematics.[17] The central government function of education is to be devolved to the Scottish Parliament.[18]

Parental duties in relation to education

The prime duty of a parent in relation to education is to ensure that their child receives **5.03** appropriate education whilst they are of school age, which can either be at a fee paying school, at a local authority school or indeed at home.[19] Although this duty may seem to form part of the general responsibilities of parents under section 1 of the Children (Scotland) Act 1995 (the 1995 Act), in practice education problems are dealt with under the Education (Scotland) Acts. The definition of parent for the purposes of education law means more than the natural parent or the parent with custody of the child:

> "'parent' includes guardian and any person who is liable to maintain or has parental responsibilities within the meaning of section 1(3) of the Children (Scotland) Act 1995 in relation to, or has care of, a child or young person."[20]

Therefore even after divorce both parents have duties and therefore rights in relation to the education of their child. Where the relationship between the parents is such that no agreement can be reached between them regarding education issues, a specific issue order under section 11 of the 1995 Act would be appropriate.[21] A specific issue order can deprive a parent of their parental rights and responsibilities under the Act, such as access to information about the child's education.

If the local authority has assumed the parental responsibilities for a child, in other words the child is a "looked after" child in terms of section 17(6) of the 1995 Act, the local authority must comply with the duties of parents in respect to education. Furthermore the authority must comply with the general duties of the 1995 Act to seek the views of the child and in doing so "safeguard and promote his welfare (which shall, in the exercise of their duty to him, be their paramount concern)".[22]

It is important to note that in general the Act imposes duties and rights on parents, and it is only once a child attains the age of 16 that they have an independent right of action in terms

---

[15] School Boards (Scotland) Act 1988, s. 17; School Boards (Financial Information) (Scotland) Regulations 1990, (S.I. 1990 No. 1277).

[16] 1980 Act, s. 66.

[17] To date a number of support packs have been developed for schools to deal with the implications of "Setting Targets—Raising Standards in Schools", SOEID (March 1998).

[18] Scotland Act 1998, ss. 28, 29 and 30.

[19] 1980 Act, s. 30.

[20] 1980 Act, s. 135(1), as amended by Children (Scotland) Act 1995 ("1995 Act"), s. 105(4) and Sched. 4, para. 28(5).

[21] Edwards & Griffiths, *Family Law* (1997), para. 5.13.

[22] s. 17(1)(a).

of the Education (Scotland) Act 1980. Of course, they have a general ability from the age of 12 onwards to instruct a solicitor in connection with any civil matter, which would include education issues such as exclusion.[23]

Where parents send their child to a local education authority school, the education authority has a general duty to educate the child in accordance with the parents' wishes.[24] As part of this, parents now have a right to choose which local education authority school they would prefer their child to attend through the placing request system.[25] The principle of education in accordance with the parents' wishes has arguably been strengthened by the Human Rights Act 1998, which states that in providing education, "the state shall respect the rights of parents to ensure such education and teaching is in conformity with their own religious and philosophical convictions".[26]

PARENTAL CHOICE IN LOCAL AUTHORITY EDUCATION

General issues

5.04   Parental choice was one of the initiatives of the Conservative Government in the 1980s. Parents can acquire several Scottish Office publications which explain their right to choose the school to be attended by their child.[27]

Parental choice as defined by the legislation refers to the obligation on education authorities to ensure "... so far as is compatible with the provision of suitable instruction ... and the avoidance of unreasonable expenditure, pupils are to be educated in accordance with the wishes of their parents."[28]

This section gives to parents a general right to ensure that their child is educated in accordance with their wishes; however it does not give parents an overriding say in all matters relating to their child's education.[29]

Parents may either enrol their child at the local school allocated to their child by the education authority or the parent may make a placing request, where they reside outwith the catchment area of their preferred school.[30] Although the principle of education in accordance with the parents' wishes may suggest that the parents should have an ongoing right to determine how their child's education should progress, the ability of parents to challenge local authority decisions on the running of schools have been strictly limited by the courts. In the case of *Walker v. Strathclyde Regional Council*[31] a parent challenged the decision of the local authority to temporarily close their schools due to strike action, but his challenge was not successful, the courts adopting the view that:

> "The Act imposes a general duty to make education available. It may well be that in order to achieve this end it will be necessary in a state of emergency to close the schools for a while ... The council are entrusted with the duty of running the schools, and if what they

[23]   Age of Legal Capacity (Scotland) Act 1991, s. 4A as inserted by 1995 Act, Sched. 4, para. 53.
[24]   1980 Act, s. 28.
[25]   1980 Act, ss. 28A–28a, as amended by Education (Scotland) Act 1981 s. 1.
[26]   Art. 2 of the First Protocol, Human Rights Act 1998, s. 1 and Sched. 6.
[27]   "Choosing A School: A Guide for Parents", The Parents Charter (1995); "Information for Parents In Scotland", Circular No. 10/93.
[28]   1980 Act, s. 28.
[29]   1980 Act, s. 28A(3), as amended by Education (Scotland) Act 1996, s. 33.
[30]   Discussed at paras 5.05 and 5.06.
[31]   1986 S.L.T. 523.

do is directed to that end and is a legitimate choice of the various options they would not be in breach of duty."[32]

Furthermore, following the Scottish courts' approval[33] of the dictum of Lord Denning LJ. in *Watt v. Kesteven County Council*,[34] the courts have limited the scope of the principle of education in accordance with the wishes of parents. Denning LJ. held that the equivalent English law section applying to the County Council,

"does not say that pupils must in all cases be educated in accordance with the wishes of their parents. It only lays down a general principle to which the County Council must have regard. This leaves it open to the County Council to have regard to other things as well, and also to make exceptions to the general principle if it thinks it fit to do so".

As a result of this approach by the court, it is clear that parental wishes cannot be treated as enforceable parental rights. This position was not greatly changed by the recognition of the right of parents to have their child educated in accordance with their religious or philosophical conviction under the Human Rights Act 1998.[35]

The limitations of the rights of parents is evident in the disappointment experienced by those who are unsuccessful in saving their local school from closure or in getting their child into the school of their choice under the placing request system.[36] Nonetheless, whilst parents cannot challenge all decisions made by authorities, through the school board initiative[37] parents do have more of a say in how schools are run.

Placing requests

Education authorities divide their area into catchment areas for their schools. If a parent would prefer to send their child to another school (or in the case of children over school leaving age, they may exercise the right of choice for themselves) they must inform the education authority, often by a given date, normally in February, and they must put their request in writing. Simple guidance on choosing a school has been produced by the Scottish Office.[38] Where the child is already attending school and the parent wishes to change school, again they may make a placing request. However where change is suggested during a school year, the educational authority will need to consider the impact of the change on the child's education. As regards denominational education, it appears that even although the catchment area for a denominational and a non-denominational school overlap, a parent who wishes to transfer their child from one sector to the other must do so through the placing request system.[39]

Parents may make requests to place their child in a school run by a different education authority than that in which area they reside. However, a placing request in respect of a recorded child (one requiring education in a special school) may be for a private special

5.05

---

[32] 1986 S.L.T. 523 *per* Lord Davidson at 527C.

[33] *Keeney v. S.R.C.*, 1986 S.L.T. 490.

[34] [1955] 1 Q.B. 408 at 424.

[35] Art. 2 of the First Protocol, ss. 1,6 and 7 and Sched. 6, Human Rights Act 1998.

[36] *e.g.* in 1996–97 12.7 per cent of placing requests were unsuccessful: see *Statistical Bulletin—Education Series*, Scottish Office Edn/B6/1998/1, Feb. 1998.

[37] School Boards (Scotland) Act 1988.

[38] "Choosing a School: A Guide for Parents", The Parents Charter (1995); "Information for Parents in Scotland", Circular No. 10/93.

[39] *Regan v. City of Dundee D.C.*, 1997 S.L.T. 139.

school including such schools in England, Wales or Northern Ireland.[40] Note that parents of children with records of needs may not make a placing request for a school outwith the local education authority sector, even in Scotland, unless that school is a special school.[41]

The education authority is obliged to comply with the request made unless:

(a) placing the child in the specified school would—

    (i) make it necessary for the authority to take an additional teacher into employment;

    (ii) give rise to a significant expenditure on extending or otherwise altering the accommodation at or facilities provided in connection with the school;

    (iii) be seriously detrimental to the continuity of the child's education; or

    (iv) be likely to be seriously detrimental to order and discipline in the school or the educational well-being of pupils there;

(b) the education normally provided at the specified school is not suited to the age, ability or aptitude of the child;

(c) the education authority have already required the child to discontinue his education at the specified school;

(d) where the specified school is a special school, the child does not have special educational needs requiring the education or special facilities normally provided at that school; or

(e) the specified school is a single sex school (within the meaning given to that expression by section 26 of the Sex Discrimination Act 1975) and the child is not of the sex admitted or taken (under that section) to be admitted to the school.[42]

The exceptions listed above are either based on the nature of the education or educational establishment requested or on financial issues. In relation to the ground of refusal (b) above, it is important to note that due to the Disability Discrimination Act 1995 it is not acceptable for an authority to refuse entry to a school if reasonable expenditure would then render the school premises or facilities suitable for the disabled pupil.[43] Since 1996, a new ground of refusal has been introduced in relation to placing requests made by persons residing outwith the catchment area of the school, primarily to enable education authorities to reserve a few spare school places in order that they may accommodate any child who moves into their area during the school year.[44]

5.06   In the period 1996–97 the total number of placing requests received was 32,281, of which 87.3 per cent were granted, with the main ground for lack of success being accommodation restraints (61.7 per cent). One of the least granted requests was for early entry into primary school, only 33.7 per cent of which were successful.[45] The education authority must inform parents of the outcome of their placing request in writing, and if they are refusing the request must give reasons for the refusal. These reasons must relate to one or more of those listed above. Any parent not satisfied with the reasons for refusal can refer the matter to an education appeal committee within 28 days of the receipt by the parent of the education

[40]   1980 Act, Sched. A2, para. 3, as amended by Self-Governing Schools (Scotland) Act 1989, s. 71.
[41]   Marr and Marr, *Scots Education Law* (1995), para. 13.22.
[42]   1980 Act, s. 28A(3), as amended by Education (Scotland) Act 1981, s. 1(1).
[43]   *Children and Young Persons With Special Educational Needs (Assessment And Recording)*, SOEID Circular 4/96, para. 164.
[44]   1980 Act, s. 28A(3A)–(3E), as amended by Education (Scotland) Act 1996, s. 33.
[45]   "*Statistical Bulletin—Education Series*", The Scottish Office Edn/B6/1998/1, Feb. 1998.

authority's decision, provided that they have not already referred a previous refusal to the committee within the last 12 months.[46] In dealing with the appeal the education appeal committee should take into account the matters detailed in the refusal, which requires the authority to satisfy the appeal committee of the reason for refusal on the authority.[47]

The appeal committee is obliged to notify the parents of its decision in writing. If the committee refuses to confirm the decision of the authority to refuse the request, then the authority must immediately make the place requested available.[48] However, if the committee confirm the authority's refusal, then the parent has again 28 days to make a further appeal to the sheriff, although the sheriff, can on cause shown hear an appeal made outwith the 28 day period.[49] It is important to acknowledge that an appeal against refusal will only be successful if the education authority did not have sufficient reasons for their refusal.

RELIGIOUS AND DENOMINATIONAL EDUCATION

Within Scottish education, there has always been a tradition of religious education, and as such all public schools in Scotland will provide instruction in religion unless the withdrawal of such provision has been approved by the majority of electors in a ballot of electors in the area.[50] All schools under education authority management must include in the school handbook a statement of school policy in relation to the development of pupils' spiritual, moral, social and cultural values.[51] Notwithstanding the importance attached to religious education, parents can elect to have their child withdrawn from any religious instruction or observance, and that child must not be placed at a disadvantage as a result of their withdrawal from the religious education.[52] The right of parents in regard to the religious education of their child is now further entrenched by virtue of the Human Rights Act 1998.[53]

5.07

All public schools, grant-aided schools and self-governing schools require to be open to pupils of all denominations. Education authorities often run denominational schools, where the school is operated with regard to the religious beliefs of the majority of parents whose children are in attendance; nonetheless even these schools must be available to children of other religious beliefs. Whilst the majority of denominational schools in Scotland are Roman Catholic there is nothing in the legislation to prevent the establishment of denominational schools for different faiths, and indeed there are two Jewish primary schools in Scotland. Despite the closure of some schools by educational authorities, it is still possible for new denominational schools to be established where an authority has been satisfied that it is required to accomodate children whose parents are resident in the area of the authority.[54]

Special rules exist in relation to denominational schools which afford such schools further protection from local authority closure.

---

[46]   1980 Act, s. 28C, as amended by Education (Scotland) Act 1981, s. 1(1).
[47]   Convention of Scottish Local Authorities, Jan. 1988.
[48]   1980 Act, s. 28E(4), as amended by Education (Scotland) Act 1981, s. 1(1).
[49]   1980 Act, s. 28F(3), as amended by Education (Scotland) Act 1981, s. 1(1).
[50]   1980 Act, s. 8, as amended by Self-Governing Schools etc. (Scotland) Act 1989, s. 82 and Sched. 10, para. 8(3).
[51]   Education (School and Placing Information) (Scotland) Regulations 1982 Pt II, Sched. 1, para. 2 (888), inserted by the Education (School and Placing Information) (Scotland) Amendment etc. Regulations 1993, Sched., para. 2.
[52]   1980 Act, s. 8 and 9, as amended by Self-Governing Schools etc. (Scotland) Act 1989, s. 82 and Sched. 10, para. 8(3) and (4).
[53]   Art. 2 of the First Protocol, Human Rights Act 1998, s. 1 and Sched. 6.
[54]   1980 Act, s. 17(2), as substituted by Education (Scotland) Act 1981.

SPECIAL NEEDS EDUCATION

5.08   Special needs education applies to around one in five children,[55] and covers a wide range of requirements including classroom based learning support, the provision of special equipment such as for visual impairment, and attendance at a specialist centre or special school on either a full- or part-time basis. As at September 1997 there were some 7,650 pupils attending educational authority special schools in Scotland.[56] Other children with a record of needs may be hospitalised for prolonged periods, and as such the local authority is required to provide these children with appropriate education in hospital provided the child is well enough to receive education.[57]

The education authority has a duty to carry out an assessment of needs of any child brought to their attention as having special needs, and thereafter it has a duty to provide for the special needs of particular children.[58] This can be at the request of the parent, which request they cannot refuse unless they are satisfied that it is unreasonable,[59] or through identification by the school. There is no special obligation on the education authority to assess educational needs of children in hospital or those in local authority accommodation under the 1995 Act. If a child appears to be requiring special needs education the authority must assess the child to determine whether the child has special needs which are pronounced, specific or complex, and which require continuing review. The education authority can then determine the best form of assistance and monitoring. The process of getting this information is referred to as opening a record of needs in respect of the child. A record of needs can be opened for any child over two years of age, so for children with obvious severe disabilities help can be sought at a very early stage.

A record of needs is a very important document as once prepared it sets out where and how a child should be educated. The preparation of a record of needs requires the assessment of the child by an appropriate medical officer and psychologist.[60] There is however a variation in the process of identifying whom to record, where to place the pupil and indeed the mechanics of the process from one education authority to another within Scotland.[61] Once a child has been identified as appearing to be in special need, the parents must be invited by notice in writing to submit their child for assessment,[62] and the authority must state the name of an individual within the education authority who is available to give advice and information to the parents. The parents should have at least 21 days to make their views known to the authority regarding their child's special educational needs and what should be done about them.

5.09   At this point parents should make a request for their preferred school, if they have not already done so through the placing request system. Certainly if the parents have a legitimate reason for not being able to submit their child on the time and date specified they should contact the authority, as failure of the parents to submit their child on invitation will result in

55   *A Parents' Guide to Special Educational Needs*, Scottish Office, 1993, p. 5.
56   *Provisional Results of the 1997 School Census*, Scottish Office news release 1753/97.
57   *Children and Young Persons with Special Educational Needs (Assessment and Recording)*, SOEID Circular 4/96, para. 201.
58   Marr and Marr, *Scots Education Law* (1995), para. 13.04.
59   1980 Act, s. 61(6), as substituted and amended by the Disabled Persons (Services, Consultation and Representation) Act 1986, s. 14(3).
60   1980 Act, s. 61(1), as substituted and amended by the Disabled Persons (Services, Consultation and Representation) Act 1986, s. 14(3), and Self-Governing Schools etc. (Scotland) Act 1989.
61   *Criteria for Opening A Record of Needs*, Interchange No. 40, SOEID, 1996.
62   See generally 1980 Act, s. 61 as amended and substituted by the Education (Scotland) Act 1981, s. 4(1).

the authority serving a second notice requiring the child to be submitted for assessment. Failure to comply with the second notice will render the parent guilty of an offence and liable to summary prosecution,[63] and more crucially, will remove the obligation on the authority to carry out the special needs assessment.

Parents may attend the medical examination provided either they requested the assessment or they submitted the child for assessment when first invited. That is, parents who only bring their child for assessment when required to do so are not entitled to attend the examination.[64] However, psychological examinations may require that the parents are not present. In addition to these assessments, if the child has attended school, a report from the child's teacher or managers of the school will be sought. As a child with special education needs may also have social care needs, often the social work department will be directly involved with the process of opening a record of needs. There is expected to be co-operation between all the different professionals involved—medical, education and social work, and case conferences are not unusual[65].

Parents of children being assessed will be invited to identify a "named person" to give them support through the assessment process, although they are not obliged to do so.[66] The named person is often a close friend or neighbour. The idea is that the named person may help the parent ask questions more effectively, and more generally give the parent support. For the named person to make a valuable contribution it is important that the parent select someone who not only knows the strengths and weaknesses of the child, but is also willing to speak up for the best interests of the child and parent. The named person does not have the rights that a parent has in respect to the assessment, indeed their entitlement is limited to getting a copy of the record of needs, which copy the authority must update when the record of needs is altered.[67]

Once the assessment has been carried out, the authority will notify the parents in writing **5.10** as to their decision on whether to record the child and the terms in which they propose to record the child, together with the reasons for the decision. If they propose to record the child, they must include with their notification a draft record of needs which will set out:

1.   the child's abilities and problems;

2.   the educational needs of the child; and

3.   how the authority proposes to meet these needs.

The form which the record of needs is to take has been laid down in regulations.[68] Once the draft record of needs has been issued to the parents, they have 14 days to comment on the contents and make observations. Thereafter the record of needs will be prepared, and it will include the observations of the parents.

---

[63]   1980 Act, s. 61(3) and liable to a fine not exceeding level 2 on the standard scale.
[64]   1980 Act, s. 61(2), as amended by the Disabled Persons (Services, Consultation and Representation) Act 1986, s. 14(3).
[65]   *Children and Young Persons with Special Educational Needs (Assessment and Recording)*, SOEID Circular 4/96, para. 94–103.
[66]   1980 Act, as amended by the Disabled Persons (Services, Consultation and Representation) Act 1986, s. 14(4).
[67]   *Children and Young Persons with Special Educational Needs (Assessment and Recording)*, SOEID Circular 4/96, para. 121.
[68]   Education (Record of Needs) (Scotland) Regulations 1982 (S.I. 1982 No. 1222).

Any parent who either does not agree to the opening of a record of needs or does not agree with the content of a record of needs may appeal to the education appeal committee;[69] however the grounds of appeal are limited.[70] Interestingly, a young person who seeks to challenge a decision in their own right has even more limited grounds of appeal.[71]

The grounds for appeal include the refusal of a placing request. As discussed, the parent of a child with a records of needs may make a placing request of any independent, grant-aided or self-governing school which is a special school in Scotland, England, Wales or Northern Ireland.[72] In addition an education authority can also make financial assistance to enable a child with pronounced, specific or complex special educational needs to attend an establishment outwith the United Kingdom, such as the Peto Institute in Hungary. The education authority can not only pay all or part of the child's travelling, maintenance and other expenses, it can also pay the expenses of one or both parents or another person to accompany the child during their period of attendance at the establishment, if the authority is of the view that company would be an advantage to the child.[73]

5.11   A child with special educational needs will normally be a "child in need" in terms of sections 22, 23 and 93 of the 1995 Act. The importance of this is that as regards education, which is a service provided, the local authority must have "due regard to a child's religious persuasion, racial origin and cultural and linguistic background" as far as is practical. Moreover in terms of section 27 local authorities must provide after-school and holiday care for a child in need.

Perhaps one of the most important aspects of special needs pupils for social workers is that of the future provision for recorded children after they cease to be of school age. Within two years to nine months prior to a child ceasing to be of school age, the education authority must consider what future provision is required for the benefit of the child during their remaining time at school, and the authority must produce a report thereon.[74] In creating the report the authority will take account of the views of the parent, the child and those involved in the child's development, such as social workers, teachers and the medical profession. The authority may recommend that the child continue to receive education after they are of school leaving age, and if they so decide, they must then determine whether the child continues to be Recorded. The completed report must be sent to the parent, to the Health Board and to the social work department.[75] The social work department must then consider whether the young person is a disabled person, as if they are the social work department must determine what the young persons needs are under the welfare enactments.

A record of needs will come to an end where, on appeal or review, it is deemed no longer necessary or on the child leaving school. However, although the authority may decide to continue the record for as long as a child receives school education, in other words after school leaving age, it is possible for the child or parent (where the child is unable to express a view) to request that the Record be ended.[76]

---

[69]   *Code of Practice for the Constitution and Procedures of Education Appeal Committees in Scotland*, Convention of Scottish Local Authorities, Jan. 1988.

[70]   See 1980 Act, s. 63(1), as amended by Education (Scotland) Act 1981, s. 4(1) and Sched. 8, and Disabled Persons (Services, Consultation and Representation) Act 1986, s. 14(5).

[71]   See 1980 Act, s. 63(2), as amended by Education (Scotland) Act 1981, s. 4(1) and Sched. 8, and Disabled Persons (Services, Consultation and Representation) Act 1986, s. 14(5).

[72]   1980 Act, Sched. A2, para. 3, as amended by Self-Governing Schools etc. (Scotland) Act 1989, s. 71.

[73]   1980 Act, s. 65G, inserted by Self-Governing Schools etc. (Scotland) Act 1989, s. 71(2).

[74]   1980 Act, s. 65B(1) and (2), as substituted by Education (Scotland) Act 1981, s. 4(1), and Sched. 8.

[75]   1980 Act, s. 65B(6), as amended by the 1995 Act, s. 105(4) and Sched. 4, para. 28(4).

[76]   1980 Act, s. 65(c), as substituted by Education (Scotland) Act 1981, s. 4(1) and Sched. 8.

ASSISTED PLACES

The assisted places scheme first came into effect in Scotland in the school session 1981–82. **5.12**
The scheme provides financial assistance, depending on "relevant family income", to parents
who want their child to attend a fee-paying school, but who could not pay the full fees.
However by virtue of the Education (Schools) Act 1997 the assisted places scheme is being
phased out, with no new assisted places being created after the 1997–98 academic year. Those
children within an assisted places scheme for the academic year 1997–98 or before may
continue to receive assistance until they complete their education at that school—although in
the case of primary school pupils they may, with the consent of the Secretary of State,
continue to hold an assisted place during their secondary education.[77] However, it appears
that such continuation will be unlikely with Scottish Office projections stating that "all
assisted pupils will have left the scheme by the end of the 2004–05 school session."[78]

PROVISION FOR SCHOOL CHILDREN

The duty of the education authority to provide appropriate education is supplemented by **5.13**
other duties towards children of school age.
   Of these the five main duties are: the duty to provide guidance; the duty to provide
transport; the duty to provide clothing; the duty to provide school meals; and the duty to
provide medical and dental treatments.

Guidance

One of the most crucial services provided to school pupils is that of guidance. Guidance **5.14**
covers personal, curricular and vocational matters, and should not be confused with the
careers service which is operated under the Secretary of State and deals purely with careers
advice.[79] The fundamental objective is to ensure guidance provision for all pupils and to
provide a consistent relationship between the pupil and a teacher. Depending on the stage of
school the focus of guidance changes, for example for those pupils newly entering secondary
schools guidance will focus most likely on personal settling-in problems, whereas for those in
fifth year the focus will be on careers assistance. As the guidance teacher has the first hand
knowledge of the pupil, it is the guidance teacher who often updates the pupil progress
records, and who would be most appropriate to attend children's hearings and other
meetings. Therefore the guidance staff provide an important link to social work, although
often this link is not established effectively enough.[80]

Transport

The power of the educational authority to provide transport is set out in section 51(1) of the **5.15**
Education (Scotland) Act 1980 as amended which gives the authority a broad discretion as to
the form of the facilities they make available, although the authority is obliged to have regard
to the safety of pupils in so doing.[81]

---

[77]   1980 Act, s. 75A(1A)–(1B), as amended by Education (Schools) Act 1997, s. 5.
[78]   *The Assisted Places Scheme 1997–98*, SOEID news release, June 2, 1998.
[79]   For a discussion on the careers service see Marr and Marr, *Scots Education Law*, para. 04.16–04.17.
[80]   *Guidance in Secondary Schools*, Howieson & Semple Interchange No. 41, SOEID, 1996.
[81]   1980 Act, s. 51(2C), as amended by the Education (Scotland) Act 1996, Sched. 5, para. 2.

The key duty of the authority is to make transportation facilities available to those pupils who attend the school nominated by the education authority, where that school is more than walking distance (defined as being "in the case of a child who has not attained the age of eight years, two miles [3.218188 km],[82] and in the case of any other child, three miles [4.828032 km]"[83]) away from the pupils' home. If the authority has not made transportation available for a child to attend the nominated school (allocated by the authority) which is outwith walking distance, the parents will have a reasonable excuse for the non-attendance of their child at school,[84] although they would need to educate their child themselves.

Where a child lives within walking distance the onus is on the parents to make arrangements to ensure that the child attends school. Clearly the implication is that parents will supervise their children getting to and from school. In the older case of *Skeen v. Tunnah*[85] the parents were successful in defending the prosecution of them under the similar provision of the Education (Scotland) Act 1962, on the ground that, whilst they lived just over a mile from the school, due to the father's employment and the mother having to look after a younger child, the parents had a reasonable excuse for their child not attending school as such attendance would have required them to walk along a main road without pavements, unaccompanied. Therefore in certain circumstances such as the unavailability of public transport or a safe walking route, or indeed due to the medical condition of the pupil, the education authority may make transport available to such pupils regardless of the fact that they live within walking distance.[86]

Where the pupil attends a school other than that nominated by the authority, through a placing request for instance, the authority need not provide transport, even if the selected school is outwith walking distance. Although in such cases the authority can choose to provide that pupil with transport, in practice few authorities exercise this discretion. Furthermore, the authority is under no obligation to provide transport for a pupil who, although attending one of their schools, is a pupil who normally resides in another local authority area in Scotland, or indeed in England or Wales. Where transport is provided the education authority are liable for the safety of the pupils.[87]

Clothing grants

5.16 Education authorities can recommend that pupils attending their schools wear a school uniform, although they cannot legally enforce such a recommendation. Where a school board has been established, the headteacher will provide the board with a statement of the policy on uniform.[88] The authority is legally required to provide suitable clothing for all children who would not be able to participate fully in their education due to a lack of adequate clothing. Therefore, the authority may have to provide clothing for daily wear and clothing for physical exercise, etc. Again, whilst an authority must provide such clothing for pupils attending schools under their management, they have no obligation to provide clothing for pupils attending other schools in their area, although they have a discretion to so

[82] Metric given due to the adoption on Oct. 1, 1995 of metric units as the primary system of measurement in the U.K.
[83] 1980 Act, s. 42(4).
[84] 1980 Act, s. 42(1), as amended by Education (Scotland) Act 1981.
[85] 1970 S.L.T. (Sh. Ct.) 66.
[86] In the event of special circumstances the local education authority's policy should be consulted initially, *e.g.* in Aberdeen City the authority has produced a booklet *Notes for Parents* which details their transport policy, pp. 9–10.
[87] Marr and Marr, *Scots Education Law*, para 07.11–07.14.
[88] School Boards (Scotland) Act 1988, s. 10(2)(c).

do. In respect of a self-governing school the provision of special clothing may be made by the Board of Management and they may provide it free or at a charge[89] or they may come to an agreement with the local education authority for the authority to provide clothing in certain circumstances.[90] Although it is normal policy for authorities to make only one clothing grant per child per academic session, an education authority must consider whether an application for an additional grant may be justified in the circumstances of the child in question.[91]

It will always be open to schools to determine whether in the individual circumstances of a particular pupil, the clothing worn is completely unacceptable, for which the ultimate sanction would be exclusion. It is generally acknowledged that some items of clothing could be prohibited on the grounds of safety.

School meals

An education authority may make arrangements to provide milk, meals and other refresh- **5.17** ments for pupils.[92] When providing school meals the authority has a discretion as to charging, except where the pupil is entitled to free school meals. The authority must provide a school meal in the middle of the day free of charge for any pupil whose parents are in receipt of income support or income-based jobseeker's allowance, or for any pupil who is personally in receipt of either of those benefits.[93] However, it is the responsibility of the pupil or parent to bring their entitlement to the attention of the authority, although most authorities do make provision for this. As at April 1997, 22 per cent of nursery and primary pupils and 16 per cent of secondary pupils were entitled to free meals, although the actual uptake was slightly lower.[94]

Medical and dental care

The Secretary of State is primarily responsible for ensuring, under section 39 of the National **5.18** Health Services (Scotland) Act 1978,[95] the proper medical and dental inspection and treatment of children and young persons. In practice the Secretary of State has delegated this function to the local health boards. In consequence, arrangements are made for medical and dental inspections at school to which parents are required to submit their child for inspection. If the pupil fails to attend the examination the parent or young person (if the pupil is over 16 years of age) will be guilty of an offence.

In this respect there appears to be an anomaly between education law and the capacity of children under the age of 16 to consent to medical treatment where in the opinion of the medical practitioner they understand the nature and consequence of the treatment.[96] Therefore, good practice requires their consent to be taken and indeed, even if the medical or dental practitioner does not believe that the child can consent, they should take into account the wishes of the child.[97] Note that the child retains this capacity to consent even where they are a "looked after" child by the local authority. Consideration of the child's right

---

[89]   Self-Governing Schools etc. (Scotland) Act 1989, s. 11(3)(b).
[90]   1980 Act, s. 55(b), as amended.
[91]   *Shaw v. S.R.C.*, 1988 S.L.T. 313.
[92]   1980 Act, s. 53(1)(a), 1980 Act, as amended.
[93]   1980 Act, s. 53(3), 1980 Act, as amended.
[94]   "*School Meals In Education Authority Schools, 1996–97*", Scottish Office news release, Nov. 17, 1997.
[95]   As amended by the Health and Medicines Act 1988 and Self-Governing Schools (Scotland) Act 1989.
[96]   Age of Legal Capacity (Scotland) Act 1991, s. 2(4); see Edwards and Griffiths, *Family Law*, paras 2.18–2.3.
[97]   *A Guide To Consent To Examination, Investigation, Treatment Or Operation*, NHS in Scotland Management Executive, Oct. 1992.

to consent is also required by the UN Convention on the Rights of the Child,[98] Art. 12, which requires that children be given the opportunity to express their views about their own health and treatment, and Article 19 which gives children the right to ensure that examinations and treatments are necessary and do not interfere with the child's right to physical and personal integrity.

In addition to such power to provide for medical and dental examination, the education authority has powers to authorise a medical officer to carry out examinations of the clothing and/or bodies of all or any pupil where the medical officer considers such inspection necessary in the interests of cleanliness.[99] Moreover the schools have a general duty to promote good health by virtue of the Schools General (Scotland) Regulations 1975 (S.I. 1975 No. 1135), reg. 11, which states

"In the day to day conduct of every school under their management, an education authority shall ensure that care is taken to develop, in pupils in attendance at that school, reasonable and responsible social attitudes and relationships, to cultivate in such pupils consideration for others, and to encourage in such pupils the practice of good manners, good attitudes to work, initiative and self-reliance and habits of personal hygiene and cleanliness."

DISCIPLINARY ISSUES

5.19   Disciplinary issues involving pupils often focus on the tripartite relationship between parent, pupil and school. Certainly a child's poor performance or lack of attendance could be the result of problems at home. In this section the duty to ensure that a pupil attends school will be examined together with a review of the methods of punishment available to teaching staff, and of the procedures relating to the exclusion of pupils from school. All schools should have school behavioural policies which ought to encourage good behaviour, and which should include a range of sanctions of differing severity suited to different circumstances.[1]

Attendance

Enforcing attendance

5.20   The Education (Scotland) Act 1980, s. 30, places a very clear duty upon parents:

"It shall be the duty of the parent of every child of school age to provide efficient education for him suitable to his age, ability and aptitude either by causing him to attend a public school regularly or by other means."

The duty relates to parents of children who are of school age, which is defined as those children who have attained the age of five years but are under 16 years of age.[2] However, the education authority must discharge its duty of providing suitable education to those children who, although not five years of age at the school commencement date, will be of such an age by the "appropriate latest date" (normally by the end of February following the commencement date).[3]

---

98   Ratified by the U.K. in Dec. 1991.
99   1980 Act, s. 58.
1   *Guidance on Issues Concerning Exclusion from School*, SOEID Circular 2/98, s. 1, para. 2.
2   1980 Act, s. 31.
3   *ibid.*, s. 32.

Obviously a parent may elect to educate their child at home, and hence they are not obliged to send their child to school. However once a child has attended an education authority school at least once, the parent will be in breach of their duty if that child does not, without reasonable excuse, regularly attend the school.[4] The parents will in fact be committing an offence for which they may be prosecuted, and could be fined or imprisoned for up to one month.[5] In addition to the possibility of prosecution, the failure of a child to regularly attend school amounts to a ground of referral to the Reporter.[6]

The Act defines three categories of reasonable excuse for non-attendance, which comprise[7]:

1. where there is no school within walking distance that is prepared to receive the child, and either no transport arrangements have been made by the authority, or the transport arrangements made by the authority would require the pupil to walk more than the walking distance in getting to school;

2. where the child has been prevented by sickness from attending; or

3. where the circumstances in the view of the education authority or court amount to a reasonable excuse.

In relation to a child whose attendance at a school was the result of a placing request, the lack of transport would not amount to a reasonable excuse, provided the authority had made an alternative school available either within the walking distance, or if outwith had made suitable transport arrangements.[8] Moreover in determining what either the court or the authority would deem a reasonable excuse, it is interesting to note that in *Skeen v. Tunnah*[9] the sheriff accepted as a reasonable excuse the fact that the children would need to walk one mile along a main road with no pavement without supervision, as the father was prevented by his employment and the mother was prevented from other family commitments from accompanying the children. Even if a parent successfully defends a criminal prosecution for failing to ensure their child's attendance at school, they are still obliged to satisfy the courts that they are providing adequate education for their child. Where the pupil is absent due to illness, it should be noted that not all forms of illness will amount to a reasonable excuse. In *Kiely v. Lunn*[10] the court decided that a pupil who was 15 years of age and absent due to glue sniffing illnesses was not absent for a reasonable excuse, the illness being caused by the actions of the pupil.

As well as providing reasonable excuses for non-attendance, the Act also creates a limited exemption from the obligation to attend school which applies to children over 14 years of age where the authority is satisfied that in view of the home circumstances of the child, their attendance at school would cause an exceptional hardship.[11]

Enforcing Attendance Procedure

All education authorities will provide schools in their area with a detailed procedure on how **5.21** to deal with non-attendance by a pupil. Usually the procedure will commence somewhat

---

[4] 1980 Act, s. 35.
[5] *ibid.*, s. 43.
[6] Children (Scotland) Act 1995, s. 52(2)(h).
[7] 1980 Act, s. 42(1).
[8] *ibid.*, s. 42(1A), as amended by Education (Scotland) Act 1981, s. 2(1).
[9] 1970 S.L.T. (Sh. Ct.) 66.
[10] 1983 S.L.T. 207 (High Ct).
[11] 1980 Act, s. 34(1).

informally, such as the sending of a letter to the parents.[12] However if attendance does not improve the Home School Liaison Officer will become involved and eventually the statutory scheme will come into effect. Where a parent has failed to secure the regular attendance of their child at school the authority must issue a notice to the parent requiring them within a period of not less than 48 hours, but not more than seven days, to attend the authority and explain the reason for the absence. If the parents fail to satisfy the authority that the absence was due to a reasonable excuse, the authority will either move for prosecution of the parents or may warn the parent and defer the matter for a period of up to six weeks.[13] Should the parents be prosecuted, the court may also refer the matter to the Principal Reporter under section 54(1) of the 1995 Act. The Principal Reporter will carry out an investigation of the case, and if he or she thinks that compulsory measures of supervision are necessary, they will arrange a children's hearing to consider the case. Where the decision to prosecute has been postponed, the authority may make an attendance order, which will require the child to attend a specified school.

Equally, attendance orders are used where a child has been withdrawn from school and the authority are not satisfied that the child is receiving adequate appropriate education.[14] The order specifies the school to be attended, and therefore the authority is bound to take account of the wishes of the parent in preparing the order, and in particular, the authority cannot specify a fee paying school unless at the request of the parent. An attendance order can be made for a child for as long as they are of school age.[15] If a parent is aggrieved at the contents of an attendance order they have 14 days from their receipt of the copy order in which to appeal against it to the sheriff.[16]

Once made, an attendance order is served on the parent and thereafter the parent will be guilty of an offence if the child fails to attend the specified school without reasonable excuse.[17] However, the attendance order may be amended to change the name of the specified school, either due to a decision of the education authority or by the parent, if for example the family has moved house.[18] Where the change is due to a decision of the authority, the parent has 14 days to raise objections with the authority, which objections must be considered by the authority.

Indeed, the parents may have the order revoked if they have made arrangements for the child to receive efficient education at a school other than that named in the order or elsewhere than at school.[19] The authority should grant the request by the parents unless satisfied that the change of school is not in the best interests of the child or that the arrangements made are not satisfactory. Where the authority does not reach a decision on the parental request within one month, or where the authority refuse the request, the parent has the right to appeal to the sheriff, who has the power to make any direction he thinks fit.

Discipline

5.22   In November 1996 the "Promoting Positive Discipline in Scottish Schools" programme was set up to support schools and education authorities in instituting practical school-based

[12]   *e.g.* in Aberdeen City Council Circular PP/ASC/16/97.
[13]   1980 Act, s. 36.
[14]   1980 Act, s. 37.
[15]   1980 Act, s. 40, as amended by the Education (Scotland) Act 1981, Sched. 2, Pt. II, para. 6 and Sched. 8.
[16]   1980 Act, s. 38(5).
[17]   *ibid.*, s. 41.
[18]   *ibid.*, s. 39.
[19]   *ibid.*, s. 39(4).

developments and disseminating examples of positive approaches to establishing good discipline and relationships in schools.

In general, a school pupil may not be subjected to corporal punishment in school[20] but may be disciplined in other ways such as additional homework or a verbal reprimand. In the most serious cases a child may be excluded from school. If this happens the parent must be notified and they have the right to appeal.

Corporal punishment

Corporal punishment is defined as doing anything which without reasonable justification would amount to a physical assault on the pupil[21] which includes any intentional application of force, such as slapping, throwing missiles such as chalk, or rough handling.[22] The use of corporal punishment in Scottish schools was until the early 1980s commonplace. However, the decision in *Campbell v. United Kingdom*[23] found the use of corporal punishment in the United Kingdom contrary to the European Convention on Human Rights. As a result of this case, the law has been modified substantially and in general corporal punishment is prohibited in local education authority schools.[24] In independent fee paying schools corporal punishment is still allowed, provided it is not inhuman or degrading,[25] although publicly funded pupils at fee paying schools (under the assisted places scheme) may not be corporally punished nor may their exemption from such discipline be a factor in refusing their admission to the fee paying school.[26]

5.23

In assessing whether punishment amounts to inhuman or degrading treatment the court shall have regard to "all the circumstances of the case, including the reason for giving it, how soon after the event it is given, its nature, the manner and circumstances in which it is given, the persons involved and its mental and physical effects."[27]

The Act specifically excludes from the definition of corporal punishment anything done to avert an immediate danger to either a person or their property.[28] The type of situation which may provide justification for corporal punishment might include the breaking up of a fight between pupils.

Even where corporal punishment has been administered by a member of staff on grounds not justified by the Act, the member of staff will not have committed a criminal offence[29] provided always that the punishment inflicted is moderate and reasonable.[30] However, they would be capable of being sued in a civil action for damages. Moreover depending on the policy of the particular education authority, the member of staff would be likely to be subject to disciplinary proceedings.

---

[20] 1980 Act, s. 48A(1) as added and amended by Education (No. 2) Act 1986, s. 48, and Education (Scotland) Act 1996, s. 582(1).

[21] 1980 Act, s. 48A(2), as added by Education (No. 2) Act 1986, s. 48.

[22] *Education (No. 2) Act 1986: Corporal Punishment*, SED Circular 1155/1987, para. 3.

[23] (1982) 4 E.H.R.R. 293.

[24] 1980 Act, s. 48A(1A), as added and amended by Education (No. 2) Act 1986, s. 48, and Education (Scotland) Act 1996, s. 582(1).

[25] 1980 Act, s. 48A, as added and amended by Education (No. 2) Act 1986 and Education (Scotland) Act 1996.

[26] *Education (No. 2) Act 1986: Corporal Punishment, op. cit.*, paras 7 and 8

[27] 1980 Act, s. 48A(1A), as added and amended by Education (No. 2) Act 1986, s. 48, and Education (Scotland) Act 1996, s. 582(1).

[28] 1980 Act, s. 48A(3), as added by Education (No. 2) Act 1986, s. 48.

[29] 1980 Act, s. 48A(4), as added by Education (No. 2) Act 1986, s. 48; on whether punishment is done with cruel intent, see *Stewart v. Thain*, 1981 S.L.T. (Notes) 2.

[30] *Education (No. 2) Act 1986: Corporal Punishment op. cit.*, para. 5; see also Smith "Carefully Chastising a Child or Beating a Brat?—A v. UK, September 23, 1998", 1999 J.R. 131.

Other punishment

5.24   There is little statutory regulation on other forms of punishment, although it is generally accepted that punishment administered by teaching staff, such as writing lines, should have an educational value. Where a pupil is detained in school such detention should only be within school hours, such as the pupil missing a break.[31] Attempts to detain a child past the ordinary school hours could amount to an unjustified deprivation of liberty, a delictual wrong in Scotland.

Within the ambit of punishment by staff, it is important to remember that dealing with classroom problems often involves overlap with other areas of law. For instance if a member of staff discovers a child with a drug problem, they may initially choose to deal with that as a school matter and should follow the local education authority's policy on dealing with a drugs-related incident. Such action will involve the police, the parents and the pupil's guidance teacher. However, in addition, there is the potential to refer the matter to the Reporter to the Children's Panel for appropriate advice.[32]

Exclusion

5.25   The ultimate disciplinary action that can be taken against a pupil is to exclude the pupil from the school. Due to the severity of this action, and the detrimental effect on the pupil, the current Government's target is to reduce exclusions by one-third by the year 2002, and to ensure that education is provided for all pupils excluded for more than three weeks. It is now no longer possible for headteachers to suspend a pupil on an ad hoc basis for a few days. Scottish Office guidance identifies children excluded from school as being children in need.

The exclusion of a pupil by the education authority is only allowed where:

(a) they are of the opinion that the parent of the pupil refuses or fails to comply, or to allow the pupil to comply, with the rules, regulations, or disciplinary requirements of the school; or

(b) they consider that in all the circumstances to allow the pupil to continue his attendance at the school would be likely to be seriously detrimental to order and discipline in the school or the educational well-being of the pupils there.[33]

As regards the distinction between the two grounds of exclusion, the case *Wyatt v. Wilson*[34] well illustrates the point. The pupil had been excluded from school because of his violent behaviour. After his exclusion his parents attended the school but refused to co-operate in signing an undertaking that the pupil would comply with the rules, regulations and disciplinary requirements of the school, which the school had made a condition for the pupil to return to school. Further letters were sent to the parents and meetings scheduled, but to no avail. Eventually the pupil turned up at school without his parents and without the signed undertaking, so he was refused admission on that and subsequent days. The education authority thereafter raised criminal proceedings against the parent for contravention of

---

[31]   See "Education", *Stair Memorial Encyclopaedia*, Vol. 8. para. 904.
[32]   1995 Act, s. 52(2)(j).
[33]   Schools General (Scotland) Regulations 1975 (S.I. 1975 No. 1135), reg. 4, substituted by Schools General (Scotland) (Amendment) Regulations 1982 (S.I. 1982 No. 56), reg. 3, and amended by Schools General (Scotland) Amendment (No. 2) Regulations 1982 (S.I. 1982 No. 1735), reg. 3.
[34]   1994 S.L.T. 1135.

section 35 of the Education (Scotland) Act 1980, failure of a parent to secure regular attendance of a pupil at school. The court convicted the parent because the child was prevented from attending the school due to exclusion caused by the parents' refusal to comply with the rules and regulations of the school.

The grounds for exclusion naturally involve the school coming to a view as to the extent of either the parents' refusal to co-operate or the pupil's failure to behave. Research into the use of exclusion in the latter years of the two-tiered local government structure found a vast diversity in practice in relation to exclusion.[35] In consequence national guidance on the best practice in relation to exclusion was issued in April 1998, which guidelines recognised the home/school relationship and encouraged a multi-disciplined approach to exclusion and the need for cross-agency co-operation.[36] Where the child to be excluded is a pupil with a record of needs, exclusion is particularly problematic as the pupil may require facilities which are not available from any local school other than the original nominated school. In such cases the authority must balance the case for exclusion with the duty to provide appropriate provision for the pupil.

Exclusion can be either temporary exclusion or exclusion/removed from the register. The length of the period of exclusion should be proportional to the severity of the breach of discipline and the pupil's past school record. The term "temporary exclusion" is to be used where a pupil is excluded from the school but remains on the school register, as it is expected that the pupil will return to that school when the period of exclusion has ended. Exclusion/ removed from the register is where the school do not anticipate the pupil returning to that school—the term "permanent exclusion" which may have been previously used in such circumstances has been deemed inappropriate.[37] As the power to exclude rests with the education authority, each authority is required to develop policies to deal with exclusion.

Where it has been decided to exclude a pupil, the school must advise, either orally or in writing, the parents of the pupil, or in the case of a young person aged over 16, the young person, on the day of that decision. The notice must also include a date and time, within seven days of the date of exclusion, where the parent or young person can meet with either the Headteacher, another teacher at the school or an official of the educational authority to discuss the exclusion.[38] So although there is no right for the child to be heard prior to the decision to exclude, they have a right to be heard within seven days from the exclusion decision. If the child is looked after by the local authority, then the case social worker and the carer of the child will also need to be informed.

At the meeting the parent, or the young person, will have the opportunity to accept the decision to exclude. If the decision is accepted and the pupil re-admitted within the seven-day period no further action is necessary—although the education authority may provide the parent with any information that they consider appropriate. However if the pupil is not re-admitted within seven days or if the parent or the pupil, being a young person, does not accept the decision to exclude and does not inform the head teacher of the school, either orally or in writing, whether they intend to take the matter to appeal or not, then the education authority must intimate to the parent or young person the reasons for exclusion, the grounds for re-admission, the right to refer the decision to an education appeal committee and any other information that the authority consider appropriate. In the event of an appeal, the education appeal committee can either confirm or annul the decision to

5.26

---

[35]   *Exclusions and In-school Alternative*, Interchange No. 47, SOEID 1997.
[36]   *Guidance on Issues Concerning Exclusion from School*, SOEID Circular No. 2/98.
[37]   *Guidance on Issues Concerning Exclusion from School, op. cit.*, paras 14–16.
[38]   See generally, Schools General (Scotland) Regulations 1975 (S.I. 1975 No. 1135) reg. 4A, inserted by Schools General (Scotland) Amendment (No. 2) Regulations 1982 (S.I. 1982 No. 1735), reg. 4.

exclude, and moreover it may amend any conditions to be attached to re-admission. The education appeal committee should take account of those matters identified in Annex 2 of their Code of Guidance, such as the background to the exclusion.[39]

ACCESS TO EDUCATIONAL RECORDS

5.27   The education authority is required to keep a record of the progress of each pupil, which along with the pupil's personal details will contain the results of any testing, any factors affecting the child's performance, the pupil's health, and information relating to any decision to exclude the pupil.[40] Where the child has been excluded the education authority must advise the parent, or if the pupil is a young person, the young person, of the terms of the entry as soon as practicable after the entry has been made.[41] This could be very important, especially where the facts are disputed between the parent and the school. The school is obliged to keep the progress record for a period of five years from the date the child left the school.

The School Pupil Records (Scotland) Regulations[42] give the parents of the pupil, or the pupil if they are a young person over the age of 16, the right to apply to the school to see the pupil file. Provided the application to the school is in writing they must receive access, without any charge, to all information relating to the child's progress. However, they will not see all information, as some information, such as references prepared for employers, is protected.[43] The right to information relates to both parents, even if separated or divorced, unless one has lost their right due to a specific issue order.[44]

The confidentiality of school records may in some limited circumstances be overridden by the courts. In the case *McLeod v. British Railways Board*,[45] which was an action for damages resulting from the pupil falling on a power cable, a substantial change in the pupil's character resulting in behavioural problems and truancy was alleged. The court therefore allowed the school records to be disclosed to establish whether the behavioural problems and truancy pre-dated the accident.

INJURY TO PUPILS WHILST AT SCHOOL

5.28   At common law, an education authority has a legal duty of care towards pupils in its charge. Therefore the authority can be sued for damages where a pupil suffers injury as a result of the failure to provide reasonable care for the safety of the pupil. By contrast, in the private independent school sector it is ultimately the school governors who are responsible, and many take out liability insurance. Recently, due to concern amongst the governors about their potential liability in damages to injured pupils, the Governors of Dollar Academy had

---

[39]   *Code of Practice for the Constitution and Procedures of Education Appeal Committees in Scotland*, Convention of Scottish Local Authorities, Jan. 1988.
[40]   Schools General (Scotland) Regulations 1975, reg. 10, as amended by the Self-Governing Schools (Application and Amendment of Regulations) (Scotland) Regulations 1994 (S.I. 1994 No. 351), reg. 8; Testing in Primary Schools (Scotland) Regulations 1990 (S.I. 1990 No. 2104), reg. 6; Schools General (Scotland) Amendment (No. 2) Regulations 1982 (S.I. 1982 No. 1735), reg. 5.
[41]   Schools General (Scotland) Regulations 1975, reg. 10(1A)(b), as amended by the Self-Governing Schools (Application and Amendment of Regulations) (Scotland) Regulations 1994 (S.I. 1994 No. 351), reg. 8; Schools General (Scotland) Amendment (No. 2) Regulations 1982 (S.I. 1982 No. 1735), reg. 5.
[42]   S.I. 1990 No. 1551.
[43]   reg. 5.
[44]   1995 Act, s. 11.
[45]   1997 S.L.T. 434.

to raise a case in court to have the terms of their endowment fund altered to allow for the payment of liability insurance premiums.[46]

The common law duty of care extends to pupils whether in the playground or within the school building.[47] If an authority has failed to satisfy the duties placed upon it, the injured person would be entitled to damages for the authority's negligence. The duty of care requires the taking of reasonable measures to prevent foreseeable injury, so not every accident will mean that there has been a breach of the duty of care. For example, in the case *Taylor v. Fife Regional Council*[48] a sixth year schoolgirl was unsuccessful in claiming damages from the authority in respect of an acid burn received in school whilst working on her biology project, because in the circumstances the court was satisfied that the teacher had provided adequate supervision.

The duty to take reasonable care for the safety of pupils is not merely limited to accidents. The duty includes an obligation to put into place anti-bullying practices, since bullying at school not only affects the safety of pupils but also the benefit of the education being provided. The Scottish Office has produced two anti-bullying packs which have been issued to all schools. Certainly if a school has not attempted to implement the advice given then it could be liable in damages for their negligence should they be sued by a victim of school bullying.[49]

The general common law duty of care has been supplemented by specific statutory duties **5.29** under the Occupiers' Liability (Scotland) Act 1960 and Health and Safety at Work Act 1974. In addition, there are regulations which impose specific duties with which the authority must comply.[50]

The Occupiers' Liability (Scotland) Act 1960 creates a duty to persons who are lawfully on the premises.[51]

The importance of this Act is that the reasonableness of the care taken will be assessed by reference to the person injured, and in particular their right to be in the place where the injury took place. In schools, especially primary schools, the legal duty to take reasonable care for the safety of the pupils will be rather higher, and certainly a warning notice or similar is less likely to excuse the school from liability.

The duty applies to any failure by the authority to ensure that the premises are safe, both inside and out, so where playground equipment is fitted, the authority is under a duty to ensure that the equipment is safe, otherwise they will have failed in their duty. In the unreported English case *J (A Minor) v. Staffordshire C.C.*,[52] which involved a 13-year old pupil pushing open a glass door in the corridor, missing the push plate and putting her hand through a pane of glass, the authority was found to be in breach of its duty under the equivalent English legislation[53] for failing to comply with the British Standards Institute Code of Practice regarding glass thickness and glass toughening.

The duty on the authority requires that they ensure the ongoing safety of pupils in response to events such as bad weather. The court in such circumstances will be considering the adequacy of the system used to combat the danger. In another English case *Murphy v. Bradford MDC*[54] the court found the authority liable for injuries to a teacher who slipped on

[46] *Governors of Dollar Academy v. L.A.*, 1995 S.L.T. 596.
[47] For a general discussion of duty of care, see Thomson, *Delictual Liability* (1992) Chap. 3.
[48] 1991 S.L.T. 80.
[49] Clelland, "Education law—It's Time to Act", 1995 SCOLAG 172–175.
[50] Schools (Safety and Supervision of Pupils) (Scotland) Regulations 1990, (S.I. 1990 No. 295).
[51] Occupiers' Liability (Scotland) Act 1960, s. 2.
[52] Aug. 1, 1997, C.C. (Stafford).
[53] Occupiers' Liability Act 1957.
[54] [1992] P.I.Q.R. 68.

an icy path at 8.30 a.m. The path had been cleared and salted at 6.30 a.m.; however in view of the steepness of the path, and the fact that a handrail was installed after the incident, the authority were found to be in breach of their duty.

Where children have entered school premises out of hours then the duty owed to them will be lessened. In the case *Devlin v. Strathclyde Regional Council*[55] the parents of a 14-year old boy who died when, on a Saturday, he fell through a sky light on the roof of his former primary school whilst playing tig, were unsuccessful in claiming damages. The court decided that in all the circumstances the actions of the boy were outwith the reasonable foresight of the authority.

5.30   The Health and Safety at Work etc. Act 1974 places employers under a duty to ensure the health and safety of employees and others, which means that for education purposes the local education authority (or the Board of Management in respect of fee paying schools) owes this duty to teachers.[56] The teacher has a duty to take reasonable care for their own safety and for that of others likely to be affected by their actions. There are very few prosecutions under the Act involving schools, and indeed there are no special provisions in the Act exclusively aimed at schools. Guidance for schools is supplemented by training and information from the Scottish Office. In addition, minimum standards for premises have been set down by the Workplace (Health, Safety and Welfare) Regulations 1992, which apply to schools.[57]

Pupil safety is also covered by the Schools (Safety and Supervision of Pupils) (Scotland) Regulations 1990[58] which provide that every education authority will take reasonable care for pupils under their charge, and in particular as regards playground supervision they require that in every primary school with 50 or more pupils, and in every special school, there must be at least one adult in the playground at break time. If an education authority fails to provide the minimum level of supervision then they will be liable in damages for any injury to pupils.

Just as the education authority has a duty to take reasonable care for the health and safety of pupils whilst at school, they also have a duty of care where the pupils are taken on school transport and also on school trips. In relation to pupils attending activity centres, by virtue of the Activity Centres (Young Persons Safety) Act 1995, any centre providing adventure facilities and instruction for persons under 18 years of age must be licensed; failure to have a licence will result in criminal prosecution.

SCHOOL MANAGEMENT ISSUES

School boards

5.31   The School Board (Scotland) Act 1988 introduced a new obligation on education authorities, namely to facilitate the establishing of a school board for every school in its area.[59] The objective of the school board initiative is to provide a forum for the expression of parental views through their representatives on the board, and it is a requirement that the majority of members on the school board are parents of children attending the school. As at May 1998, 83 per cent of eligible education authority schools had a school board.[60] The school board share in the running of the school and are required to approve the spending proposals of the

55   1993 S.L.T. 699.
56   For a general discussion of this Act, see Craig & Miller, *Law of Health and Safety* (1995), Chap. 5.
57   Craig & Miller, *op. cit.*, para. 4.67.
58   S.I. 1990 No. 295.
59   s. 1(1).
60   SOEID press release 2505/98.

Headteacher. In addition, the board has the ability to control the use of school premises outwith school hours, to influence the appointment of teachers and to fundraise.[61]

Self-governing schools

Although the school board scheme gives parents more say in the running of local education authority schools, it is possible for schools to completely opt out of the control of the local educational authority and to become a self-governing school.[62] Such a move requires a vote by the majority of parents. A board of management must be established, which must include the head teacher and parent representatives and can include others co-opted onto the board. The effect of self-governing status is that the school will be directly financed by the Secretary of State. However, the self-governing school differs from independent schools as they are unable to charge fees for pupils to attend the school.

5.32

School closure

One of the principal questions which arises at the time of school closure is to what extent parents and indeed pupils have any rights to determine the range of educational facilities to be made available.

5.33

Even with the support of the majority of the parents, a parent may not be able to prevent the authority from closing a school. The leading Scottish case on this point is that of *Harvey v. Strathclyde Regional Council*.[63] The proposed closure of Stanley Green High School in Paisley along with John Neilson and Paisley Grammar sparked a great deal of public debate on school closure, resulting in the Education (Publication and Consultation etc.)(Scotland) Amendment Regulations 1988, which prevented the closure of Paisley Grammar but not Stanley Green. Despite the strong parental campaign, the court action by the parents was unsuccessful, parental wishes being only one of the relevant factors to which the authority had to have regard.

Undeniably one of the most sensitive aspects of school closure is the closure of denominational schools, especially in rural communities. The sensitivity of such proposals is emphasised by the protection afforded to denominational schools by sections 22A–D of the Education (Scotland) Act 1980,[64] which effectively require the Secretary of State's approval where the proposed school closure would result in the discontinuation of denominational education for the pupils of the school. The requirement to obtain approval was unsuccessfully challenged in *Scottish Hierarchy of the Roman Catholic Church v. Highland Regional Council*.[65]

Before an authority may close a school, regardless of denomination, consultation is required.[66] In terms of the legislation the authority must consult with those who "would be affected by that implementation or by an implementation of any part of the proposal and such a reference shall include a school to which pupils may be transferred".[67] At first sight the duty appears to be capable of very wide interpretation. However in *Regan v. City of Dundee*

---

[61] School Boards (Scotland) Act 1988 ss. 13, 14; for further discussion see Marr & Marr, *Scots Education Law* (1995), Chap. 20.
[62] Self-Governing Schools etc. (Scotland) Act 1989.
[63] 1989 S.L.T. 25.
[64] Inserted into the Education (Scotland) Act 1980 by Education (Scotland) Act 1981, Sched. 9.
[65] 1987 S.L.T. 708.
[66] 1980 Act, s. 22, being supplemented by the Education (Publication and Consultation) (Scotland) Regulations 1981.
[67] Education (Publication and Consultation) (Scotland) Regulations 1981, reg. 2(3).

Council[68] the court was reluctant to apply this duty too widely. As part of the consultation the neighbouring four non-denominational schools had been consulted but not the parents of those attending S.S. Peter and Paul Primary School, a denominational school with an overlapping catchment area. The court decided that the duty to consult was confined to those schools to which the authority proposed to relocate the pupils, not those schools to which placing requests would be made as a result of the proposed closure.

Parents challenging closures cannot rely automatically on receiving the remedy sought against a closure decision solely because a procedural irregularity has been proved. The court reserves the right to consider the practical effect of granting the reduction. In *King v. East Ayrshire*,[69] although the petitioner, an aggrieved parent, successfully proved that the authority had erred by not having regard to historic attendance figures in calculating whether the school they proposed closing exceeded a pupil capacity of 80 per cent (hence being a proposal requiring the approval of the Secretary of State), the court nonetheless refused to reduce the authority's decision because it was not satisfied that in any event the proposal would have had to go to the Secretary of State for approval.

WORK EXPERIENCE AND THE EMPLOYMENT OF SCHOOLCHILDREN

5.34 It is now a generally accepted part of secondary education that schoolchildren will participate in some work experience as part of their education. Generally education authority and self-governing schools are permitted to allow pupils to undertake work experience placements within the period from the May 1 in the calendar year before they reach 16 until the end of the year in which they reached 16.[70] Where work placements are arranged by the school the normal statutory prohibitions regarding the employment of children in particular types of employment will not apply. However pupils cannot be employed in any type of employment for which the employment of young persons is prohibited. Note that for the purpose of any enactment relating to the employment of children, child means a person under school-leaving age.[71]

As for the employment of schoolchildren in general, no child may be employed if they are under 13 years of age.[72] In addition, the employment of a child is now prohibited unless it is for either light work or work for the purposes of performance in cultural, artistic, sports or advertising activities.[73] Light work is defined as being work which is unlikely to be harmful to either the health, safety or development of the child or the child's attendance at school. Employers are now under a duty to carry out a risk assessment of work being undertaken by young persons, and to inform the parent of the child of the potential risks to the child and the protective/preventative measures being taken.[74] Currently the child cannot be employed before 7 a.m. or after 7 p.m. and, moreover, a child can only be employed for a maximum of two hours on any schoolday or Sunday. In addition, on a schoolday, the child cannot be employed during school hours. As well as these general statutory restrictions, the local authority may pass byelaws relating to the general employment of schoolchildren in their

---

[68] 1997 S.L.T. 139.
[69] 1998 S.C. 182.
[70] See generally 1980 Act, s. 123(4), as substituted by Self-Governing Schools etc. (Scotland) Act 1989, s. 82(1), and Sched. 10, para. 8(21).
[71] 1980 Act, s. 125.
[72] s. 28(1)(a), Children and Young Persons Act 1963, s. 28(1)(a), substituted by the Children Act 1972, s. 1(2); Craig & Miller, *Employment Law in Scotland* (2nd ed., 1996), paras 3.27–3.28.
[73] art. 3 of Council Directive 94/33/E.C. on the protection of young people at work.
[74] Health and Safety (Young Persons) Regulations 1997 (S.I. 1997 No. 135), reg. 5.

area. After June 22, 2000 the working time of a child at school will be restricted to a maximum of two hours on a school day and 12 hours per week for work performed outside hours fixed for school attendance.[75] Where the child is to be employed in performances the child will in many situation require a licence from the authority, and naturally the authority will refuse the licence if it is of the opinion that the child's education would suffer.[76]

There is now an increased recognition of the rights of parents in education of their child within the general legal framework applying to education. Nonetheless it is the education authority that retains the main control over educational decisions such as school closure or placing requests.   **5.35**

The link between education and other needs cannot be ignored. As mentioned in the process of the opening of a record of needs, there is expected to be co-operation between all the different professionals involved—medical, education and social work—and case conferences are not unusual.[77] Certainly, the development of the role of guidance teachers at schools as well as the new community schools signals an increasing acceptance of the need to bring social work and education into a closer relationship.

---

[75]   art. 8(1)(b) of Council Directive 94/33/E.C. on the protection of young people at work.
[76]   Children and Young Persons Act 1963, s. 37.
[77]   *Children and Young Persons with Special Educational Needs (Assessment and Recording)*, SOEID Circular 4/96, paras 94–103.

Chapter 6

MENTAL HEALTH LAW

Scots law provides for intervention in a whole range of ways in the lives of those who are **6.01** mentally incapacitated. The issues with which this chapter is concerned are the compulsory detention of mentally disordered individuals in hospital, mental health guardianship, medical treatment of mentally disordered persons, protection of the property rights of mentally disordered patients, the role of the Mental Welfare Commission, mental health and criminal justice, and the role of the State in safeguarding the interests of mentally disordered people and society as a whole. It does not cover the care in the community dimensions of mental health care, which are addressed in Chapter 7. There are many mentally disabled persons who with support and assistance from their families and agencies live relatively normal lives in the community. Like many mentally able citizens, the law will play an unintrusive role in their lives. There are, however, many others for whom the law that follows will be of considerable importance whether they are liable to be compulsorily detained in hospital, an offender with a mental disability, or incapable of managing their own welfare or financial affairs.

The law relating to mental health is governed principally by the Mental Health (Scotland) Act 1984 ("1984 Act") although for a complete picture of how the law treats mentally disordered people in society one must travel beyond that Act to other areas of law such as criminal justice. The 1984 Act did not in itself introduce new laws and so, fundamentally, is based on long-standing notions, albeit with subsequent piecemeal amendment. The absence of a fundamental overhaul has been a matter of some concern.[1]

Mental disorder[2]

Central to any understanding of the 1984 Act is an appreciation of the term "mental **6.02** disorder". A mental disorder is a mental illness or mental handicap however caused or manifested. There are two types of mental handicap. "Mental impairment" is a state of arrested or incomplete development of mind not amounting to severe mental impairment but which includes significant impairment of intelligence and social functioning and is associated with abnormally aggressive or seriously irresponsible conduct on the part of the person concerned. "Severe mental impairment" is a state of arrested or incomplete development of mind which includes severe impairment of intelligence and social functioning, and is associated with abnormally aggressive or seriously irresponsible conduct on the part of the

---

[1]   See Ward, "A Review of Mental Health Law—At Last", 1999 J.L.S.S. 20–22.
[2]   See generally Mental Health (Scotland) Act 1984 ("1984 Act"), s. 1.

person concerned. No person is to be treated as suffering from mental disorder simply because of promiscuity or other immoral conduct, sexual deviancy, or alcohol[3] or drug dependency, although it should be noted that one judge has said that sexual deviancy is only to be discounted when unaccompanied by mental disorder.[4] Defining the person's status impacts upon the reception, care and treatment of persons who suffer, or appear to suffer, from mental disorder, and to the management of their property and affairs.

Duties of local authorities

6.03 The local authority has a pivotal role in mental health with several important duties placed upon it. First, it has discretion to make arrangements for the provision, equipment and maintenance of residential accommodation which may be required by mentally disordered persons. It should also make provision for its duties under guardianship, for ancillary and other services, and for those suffering from mental handicap who are neither detained in hospital nor under guardianship.[5] A local authority must also provide after-care services for any persons who are or have been suffering from a mental disorder and also for those who are the subject of a community care order.[6]

In addition to these core duties, the local authority is required to appoint mental health officers—a category of specially trained social workers experienced in dealing with the mentally disordered.[7]

Local authorities have particular duties in respect of certain hospital patients suffering from mental disorder. Specifically in respect of children, they may have duties to cause visits to be made to them and to take such steps as may be expected of a parent.[8] There is a duty on local authorities to provide or secure the provision of suitable training or occupation for persons suffering from mental handicap who are over school age (unless they are in hospital).[9] The authorities often make provision themself in Adult Training Centres, or they may simply support community ventures. To this end the local authority has the statutory power to make payments to voluntary organisations who provide such facilities.[10] Linked to the duty to provide or secure suitable training and occupation, the local authority may provide "suitable" transport for the conveyance of persons to training and occupational facilities.[11]

A further duty of the local authority is to apply to the court for the appointment of a curator *bonis* where the authority is satisfied that any person in its area is incapable by reason of mental disorder of adequately managing and administering his property or affairs, that a

---

[3] See *e.g. Carver v. Fraser*, 1997 S.C.C.R. 653.

[4] *W v. Secretary of State for Scotland*, 1998 S.L.T. 841.

[5] 1984 Act, s. 7 (1)(a), (b), (c) and (d).

[6] 1984 Act, s. 8, as amended by the Mental Health (Patients in the Community) Act 1995 s. 4(2) and Sched. 2, para. 3.

[7] There is a detailed direction from the Secretary of State for Scotland on the precise qualifications expected of mental health officers. See Circular SWAG 5/88, Mar 3, 1988.

[8] 1984 Act, s. 10, as amended by the Children (Scotland) Act 1995, s. 105(4) and Sched. 4, para. 33(2). On the issue of prevention of mental disorder in children see Dulmus and Wordarski, "Prevention of Childhood Mental Disorders: a Literature Review Reflecting Hope and a Vision for the Future", 1997 *Child and Adolescent Social Work Journal* 14(3), pp. 181–198.

[9] 1984 Act, s. 11(1), as amended by the Further and Higher Education (Scotland) Act 1992, s. 62 and Sched. 9, para. 9.

[10] 1984 Act, s. 11(3).

[11] *ibid.*, s. 11(2).

curator *bonis* ought to be appointed, and that no arrangements have been made or are being made by anyone else in this regard.[12]

Duties of the Secretary of State

The Secretary of State is required to publish and keep up to date a Code of Practice on Mental Health.[13] In addition to this, the Secretary of State has a central role in appointments to the Mental Welfare Commission[14] as well as directing the activities of local authorities.[15] Moreover, he has important functions in relation to the registration and inspection of private hospitals which provide mental health care.[16] There is also a role in relation to restriction orders and directions,[17] transfers and transfer directions to hospital or guardianship of prisoners,[18] and the removal of mentally disordered patients in and around and from the United Kingdom.[19] Perhaps most significantly of all is the Secretary of State's power to make a considerable number of regulations affecting the operation of mental health law in Scotland.[20]

6.04

THE MENTAL WELFARE COMMISSION[21]

The Mental Welfare Commission for Scotland consists of 10 commissioners. At least three of the 10 must be women, at least three must be medical practitioners (known as "medical commissioners"), and one is compulsorily a member of the Faculty of Advocates, or the Law Society of Scotland of at least five years' standing. Commissioners are appointed by the Queen on recommendation of the Secretary of State for Scotland who is charged with a duty of consulting other appropriate bodies as to the appointments. Civil servants are not eligible for appointment to the Commission.

6.05

The Commission has the duty to exercise protective functions in respect of persons who may, by reason of mental disorder, be incapable of adequately protecting their person or their interests.[22] Principal among their powers is the power to discharge a mentally disordered patient who has been detained in a hospital under statutory powers. The Commission is under a duty to make enquiries in any case where they believe there may be ill-treatment or deficiency in the care of a mentally disordered patient, and in circumstances where they believe that the mentally disordered patient's property may be exposed to danger or damage as a result of the mental disorder. In exercise of their functions the Commission may appoint an advocate or solicitor of at least five years' standing to carry out an inquiry either by himself or as chairman of a committee of commissioners. Where there is such an inquiry, the Commission may, having given him written notice, require any person to attend

12   1984 Act, s. 92(1); see also *Information for Families of Persons Subject to Curatory*, Accountant of Court, Edinburgh.
13   1984 Act, s. 119, as amended by the Mental Health (Patients in the Community) Act 1995, s. 4(2). The Code was introduced in 1990: see SWSG 1/90, Mar. 30, 1990.
14   1984 Act, s. 2(4).
15   *ibid.*, s. 7(1).
16   *ibid.*, ss. 12(4) and 13.
17   1984 Act, ss. 62, 62A, 64(4) and (5), 65(1), (2)(a) and (b), 68,69.
18   1984 Act, ss. 70–75.
19   1984 Act, ss. 77,80,82,83, 87(2).
20   See 1984 Act, ss. 25(6),43(1),58,86, 96(2),97(1)(b), 97(6), 98(1)(a), (2) and (6), 115(8), 116(3).
21   See 1984 Act, ss. 2–4, generally for provisions on the powers, duties and functions of the Commission.
22   1984 Act, s. 3(1), as amended by the Mental Health (Patients in the Community) Act 1995, s. 4(2) and Sched. 2, para. 1.

and give evidence. Proceedings of any inquiry are given the same privilege as a court of law. Parties giving evidence may do so on oath although evidence on affirmation, or a written statement, may be admitted at the discretion of the chairman of the inquiry. Refusal to give evidence or to appear at the inquiry may result in criminal prosecution of the person concerned.

As part of its function it is the duty of the Commission to visit regularly patients who are detained in hospital or who are the subject of guardianship.[23] Where the patient so requests he must be given a private interview. Mentally disordered patients not detained may also seek a private interview. Although the scheme of visits is very much at the discretion of the Commission, there are circumstances where they must visit, namely where (1) authority for detention of the patient has been renewed for a period of one year and the patient has not within that period appealed against his detention to the sheriff, or has not been visited by the Commission, and (2) the authority for the patient's detention is renewed for a further period of one year. The patient must be visited before the end of the further period of detention unless he has previously been discharged. Visits to a patient must include a medical commissioner, or medical officer, who may examine the patient in private.

Where the Commission is alerted to any issue, it is under a general duty to bring to the attention of managers of any hospital or any local authority any action which it thinks is necessary to prevent the ill-treatment of a patient, to remedy any deficiency in their care or treatment, to terminate his improper detention, or to prevent or redress loss or damage to his property. Additionally, where a matter is referred to it by the Secretary of State, local authority, or health board, the Commission must offer advice on that matter.[24] In similar fashion, it is entitled to bring to the attention of the foregoing parties any matter concerning the welfare of anyone who is suffering from mental disorder. One of the other functions of the Commission is to advise the Secretary of State where it has formed the view that a patient detained, who is a restricted patient, should be discharged, and to recommend the discharge of that patient. The Commission publishes an annual report of its activities, copies of which must be submitted to the Secretary of State and laid before Parliament.

6.06   The Commission has the power to appoint one or more of its number to carry out its function in all matters except the discharge of patients. In all cases where there is a visit to a patient liable to be detained in hospital or the subject of guardianship, the visit must include a medical commissioner or medical officer of the commission who may inspect any medical records of the patient. The Commission may authorise the managers of a hospital to receive and hold valuables and/or money of any patient who is deemed by reason of his mental disorder to be incapable of managing or administering his property and affairs.[25] The Commission also has the power to petition the court for the appointment of a curator *bonis* to look after the property and finances of a mentally disordered patient.[26] Moreover, the Commission has the power to review and reverse any decision by the hospital to withhold correspondence to the patient because they consider that it is liable to cause distress or danger and it is necessary for the safety of others.[27] In respect of consent to treatment of detained patients the Commission has several key powers.[28]

[23]   1984 Act, s. 3(2)(b), as amended by the Mental Health (Patients in the Community) Act 1995, s. 4(2) and Sched. 2, para. 1.
[24]   1984 Act, s. 3(2)(e), as amended by the National Health Service and Community Care Act 1990, s. 66(1) and Sched. 9, para. 28(1).
[25]   1984 Act, s. 94(2).
[26]   *ibid.*, s. 93.
[27]   1984 Act, s. 116(1) and (2).
[28]   Discussed above, paras 6.18 *et seq.*

The Commission also receives a great deal of information designed to assist it in the discharge of its functions. It will receive reports from mental health officers of local authorities, or a medical officer of the hospital, on the patient's social circumstances and the need for further detention.[29] It will be notified of any admissions under emergency procedures,[30] as well as detentions by a nurse[31] or other short-term detentions under emergency procedures.[32] Other information which may be notified to the Commission includes addresses of patients granted leave of absence from the hospital, information on transfers between institutions and reports from medical officers on the need for renewal of detention.[33]

In respect of guardianship cases, the Commission receives from the local authority information on those received into guardianship, any change of address of the guardian or patient, and the termination of guardianship. It will also receive reports from mental health officers where those officers are of the opinion that the guardianship should be continued.[34] Where patients are removed to or from Scotland, the Secretary of State will notify the Commission accordingly.[35]

COMPULSORY ADMISSION TO HOSPITAL

There are many mentally disordered persons who are thought to require detention and treatment in hospital. This naturally raises human rights issues. It is thought, for example, that the power of conveyance may contravene article 5 of the European Convention on Human Rights: the right not to be deprived of one's liberty.[36] But conveyance is only one part of the prima facie infraction of the human rights of a mentally disordered person. Sadly, there have been occasions when mental health patients have been found to have been the subject of brutality, intimidation, inhuman and degrading treatment.[37] Whilst such instances are not thought to be commonplace, they do raise two general legal issues. First, those admitted to hospital are owed a duty of care by the hospital and the hospital staff.[38] This duty of care may extend to observation of the patient's movements[39] and making sure that a patient's mental disorder is treated properly. Thus, for example in, *Clunis v. Cambden and Islington Health Authority*[40] a patient who murdered a stranger was held entitled to sue the hospital for failing to treat him properly for a mental disorder.

Secondly, there is the question of criminal law. Notwithstanding the possibility of a deliberate physical attack, any professional who restrains[41] or carries out any unauthorised medical procedure prima facie commits an assault on a patient. The implications are that criminal charges may be brought, while a civil claim for damages against the professional and

6.07

---

[29] 1984 Act, s. 22.
[30] *ibid.*, s. 24(5).
[31] *ibid.*, s. 25(4).
[32] *ibid.*, s. 26(4).
[33] On this last point see *ibid.*, s. 30(3).
[34] *ibid.*, s. 47(3).
[35] *ibid.*, ss. 87(2) and 88(2).
[36] Hewitt, "The Supervised Discharge of Former Mental Patients: Part Two" (1997) *Litigation*, Vol.16, p. 204.
[37] See, for example, Committee of Inquiry into the Personality Disorder Unit, Ashworth Special Hospital, July 1999 (London, H.M.S.O.) (established Feb. 1997).
[38] It has been held in England that hospital wards in prison need not provide the same standard of care as psychiatric hospitals see *Knight v. Home Office* [1990] 3 All E.R. 237.
[39] See *G's Curator Bonis v. Grampian Health Board*, 1995 S.L.T. 652.
[40] *The Times*, Dec. 27, 1996.
[41] Smith and Humphreys, "Physical Restraint of Patients in a Psychiatric Hospital", *Medicine Science and the Law*, Vol. 37, No. 1, pp. 145–149.

his employer is a distinct possibility. Proper authorisation by obtaining proper consent is a prerequisite to ensuring that those who infringe a patient's bodily integrity remain free from legal sanction.[42]

6.08   There are approximately 30,000 admissions to hospital each year in Scotland.[43] The vast bulk of those admissions are on a voluntary basis, but frequently it is necessary for mentally disordered patients to be compulsorily detained in hospital. As a general proposition compulsory treatment cannot be given to anyone other than someone who is compulsorily detained.[44] A hospital has no common-law power of detention in the way that an individual can temporarily detain someone pending the arrival of help, or transfer than to the authorities for the urgent protection of that person.[45] Under statute, a person may be admitted to hospital and compulsorily detained where he is (1) suffering from a mental disorder of a nature or degree which makes it appropriate for him to receive treatment in hospital, and (2) it is necessary for the health and safety of that patient or for the protection of other persons that he should receive such treatment and that treatment cannot be provided unless he is detained in hospital.[46] If the mental disorder is a persistent one manifested by abnormally aggressive or seriously irresponsible conduct,[47] or if the mental disorder is a mental handicap comprising mental impairment, the patient cannot be compulsorily admitted or detained unless the treatment is likely to alleviate or prevent his condition.[48] In considering the issue of health and safety, it is not the case that there must be an immediate threat to life or limb. Severity of symptoms, or severity of distress, may be sufficient to justify admission, especially if the alternative is likely to be a worsening of an already distressing situation and effective treatment or care is available in hospital.[49] Medical treatment in this context includes nursing or therapeutic care under medical supervision.[50] Applications for compulsory admission are not subject to time limits although there are time limits attached to the medical recommendations which must underwrite compulsory admission.[51]

Irrespective of the foregoing provisions relative to compulsory admission, a patient may be admitted voluntarily on a private basis, or continue to remain in hospital on a voluntary basis after he no longer requires to be there on a compulsory basis.[52] In situations where a young person is competent under section 2 (4) of the Age of Legal Capacity (Scotland) Act 1991 and refuses to consent to voluntary treatment it seems likely that a parent cannot give consent to medical treatment on his behalf. Accordingly, if treatment is necessary, the child will require to be compulsorily detained.[53] However. in situations where the child is not competent to give consent to medical treatment either under the 1991 Act or because of some mental deficiency, the parent may exercise the right to consent to the child's voluntary admission in conformity with their parental rights and responsibilities, thus rendering compulsory detention unnecessary.

---

[42]   see para. 10.04.
[43]   Ward, "A Review of Mental Health law at Last" 1999 J.L.S.S. 20–22 at p. 20.
[44]   Patrick and Blackie, *Mental Health: A Guide to Law In Scotland* (1990), p. 32.
[45]   *B v. Forsey*, 1988 S.L.T. 572; *cf. R. v. Bournewood Community and Mental Health NHS Trust, ex p.L* [1998] 1 All E.R. 634.
[46]   1984 Act, s. 17(1).
[47]   See *R. v. Canons Park Mental Health Tribunal, ex p. A* [1994] 3 W.L.R. 630.
[48]   1984 Act, s. 17(1).
[49]   MWC Annual Report (1994–95), p. 125.
[50]   See 1984 Act, s. 125; *R. v. Secretary of State*, 1997 S.L.T. 555.
[51]   *J v. C*, 1990 S.C.L.R. 783, commentary by Sheriff Stewart.
[52]   1984 Act, s. 17(2).
[53]   *Houston, Applicant*, 1996 S.C.L.R. 943; *cf. V v. F*, 1991 S.C.L.R. 225 (Sh. Ct).

Procedure for admission

In order that a person may be detained under the Mental Health (Scotland) Act 1984 it is **6.09** necessary for three things to happen. First, there must be an application by an "interested party" addressed to the manager of the hospital to which admission is sought.[54] This application must be accompanied by two medical recommendations which state that the patient liable to be detained is a person requiring treatment under section 17 of the 1984 Act, and which identify the mental disorder from which the patient suffers. There is evidence from England that second opinion doctor support is often routine and it seems likely that this is also the case in Scotland.[55] In addition, the sheriff must approve the application.[56] Under a power of short-term detention, discussed below, it is possible for a person to be detained for up to 28 days (following emergency detention) on the recommendation of a consultant psychiatrist. Without the approval of the sheriff it is not possible for the person to be detained beyond 31 days (the emergency detention of three days plus the short-term detention of 28 days).[57]

Submitting an application for detention[58]

An application for admission may be made by the nearest relative or a mental health officer **6.10** of the local authority.[59] If the nearest relative is to make the application it will be necessary for him to have seen the patient within the 14 days preceding the application. If asked to do so by the nearest relative, the local authority must direct one of its mental health officers, as soon as practicable, to look into the person's case with a view to making an application for admission. If the mental health officer decides not to make an application he must inform the nearest relative. The mental health officer will make an application to admit

> "in any case where he is satisfied that such an application ought to be made and is of the opinion, having regard to any wishes expressed by relatives of the patient and to any circumstances that it is necessary or proper for the application to be made by him."

A mental health officer who proposes to make an application for admission must interview the patient in the 14 days prior to the making of the application. Additionally, he must satisfy the sheriff that detention in hospital is the most appropriate way of providing the care and medical treatment which the patient needs and he must inform the nearest relative of his decision and of that relative's right to object. In a situation where the mental health officer has received two medical recommendations for admission and one of those doctors requests the admission, he must make an application for admission. In making the application the mental health officer must state his opinion and the grounds for that opinion as to whether the application should be granted.

Relatives are often reluctant to be the ones to insist on admission or to make an application for compulsory detention. The Mental Welfare Commission (MWC) is of the opinion that no pressure should be put upon them to make applications. Certainly where a mental health officer is making the application he is required to have regard to the wishes of the relatives,

---

[54] 1984 Act, s. 18(1).
[55] Foley, *Human Rights, Human Wrongs* (1995) at p. 224.
[56] 1984 Act, s. 18(1).
[57] Although note 1984 Act, s. 21(3B), as inserted, which permits a 5-day extension where an application is made for detention.
[58] See, generally, 1984 Act, ss. 19 and 20.
[59] For a discussion of mental health officers, see para. 6.03.

but the 1984 Act does not define the parameters of exactly who is to be consulted. It is likely that he will take a commonsense view and deal with immediate family where possible.[60]

The medical recommendations required under the 1984 Act are required to be signed on or before the date of the application by two medical practitioners, neither being the applicant, who have examined the patient separately and not more than five days apart, or together where no objection has been raised by the patient or their nearest relative. One of the practitioners must be approved by the Health Board as having special experience in the diagnosis or treatment of mental disorder, and the other should be the patient's G.P. or some other doctor with previous acquaintance of him. If the hospital providing the accommodation is a private hospital, or the facility is a private one within the NHS, medical staff of the hospital to which the patient is to be admitted cannot make the recommendation.[61] It is a further requirement that the medical recommendation contain a statement as to whether the doctor is related to the patient or has any pecuniary interest in the admission of the person to hospital. These provisions seek to protect the mentally disordered person from unscrupulous medical practitioners who may abuse their power of recommendation of detention for their own ends. It is an unlikely scenario but one which the law nevertheless seeks to prevent and in the process ensures an absence of conflict in the recommendation process.

Application to the sheriff court

6.11   Applications must be made to the sheriff court of the sheriffdom in which the patient is resident, or where the hospital in which the person who is a patient is situated.[62] The sheriff has the power to make such enquiries and hear such persons (including the patient) as he thinks fit.[63] Furthermore, the sheriff must afford any relative and any witness the opportunity of being heard where the nearest relative objects to the patient being compulsory detained.[64] Where a mental health officer makes an application at the request of two doctors but he himself objects to the application, the mental health officer should be allowed the opportunity of being heard before the sheriff.[65] In other cases, the sheriff must first hear the applicant before deciding to reject the application.[66] There is a requirement that within five days of an application being made the sheriff must either approve the application or decide to hold a hearing to determine the application.[67] Where an application for short-term or interim admission is made[68] a patient may have their detention in hospital extended for a period of five days from the date on which the application was made.[69] Hearings on the issue of whether to compulsorily detain a patient may, if the patient or the applicant so desires or if the sheriff so decides, be conducted in private.[70] It is also possible that a hearing may be held in a hospital or some other place if the sheriff so directs. In conducting the hearing the sheriff has

---

[60]   See the English case of *Re S-C (Mental Patient: Habeus Corpus)* [1996] Q.B. 599 where the social worker erroneously consulted the mother rather than the father.

[61]   1984 Act, s. 20(1)(c), as amended by the National Health Service and Community Care Act 1990, s. 66(1) and Sched. 9, para. 28(3).

[62]   1984 Act, s. 21(1)(a) and (b), as amended by the Law Reform (Misc. Prov.) (Scotland) Act 1985, s. 51.

[63]   1984 Act, s. 21(2)(a), as amended by the Law Reform (Misc. Prov.) (Scotland) Act 1985, s. 51.

[64]   1984 Act, s. 21(2)(b), as amended by the Law Reform (Misc. Prov.) (Scotland) Act 1985, s. 51.

[65]   1984 Act, s. 21(2)(c), as amended by the Law Reform (Misc. Prov.) (Scotland) Act 1985, s. 51.

[66]   1984 Act, s. 21(3), as amended by the Law Reform (Misc. Prov.) (Scotland) Act 1985, s. 51.

[67]   1984 Act, s. 21(3)(A), as inserted by the Mental Health (Detention) (Scotland) Act 1991, s. 2.

[68]   Under 1984 Act, s. 26 or s. 26 A (inserted by the Mental Health (Detention) (Scotland) Act 1991, s. 1).

[69]   1984 Act, s. 21(3B), as inserted by the Mental Health (Detention) (Scotland) Act 1991, s. 2.

[70]   1984 Act, s. 21(4).

the power to summon and examine witnesses, award expenses, and conduct himself in all other regards as if he were sitting in exercise of his civil jurisdiction.[71]

A sheriff is required to give a patient an opportunity to be heard in person (unless excluded for cause) or by way of representation.[72] In proceedings before the sheriff, if a person is unable to speak on their own behalf and wishes to do so the sheriff must give his representative an opportunity to be heard. There is some confusion as to whether a representative needs to be legally qualified, and, on balance, opinion appears to be that a representative need not be so.[73] If the patient is not represented the sheriff may appoint a solicitor to represent the patient's interests.[74] Normally in civil proceedings a person will receive notice of those proceedings. However, in compulsory detention proceedings if a patient is in hospital and two doctors certify that it is prejudicial to the patient's health for him to receive such notice, the sheriff may dispense with the service and appoint a curator *ad litem* who will represent the person in all proceedings.[75] Although a person has a right to attend a hearing, he may be excluded if the sheriff is convinced that it is not in the interests of his health or treatment for him to attend.[76] Exclusion on health grounds may afford an opportunity to exclude a violent or disruptive patient. At no time can a patient's representative be excluded from proceedings.

Removal to hospital[77]

Where a sheriff has approved an application for admission then this approval is sufficient authority for removal of the patient to the hospital named in the application. It also acts as authority for the patient to be admitted to the hospital at any time within seven days of the order being granted by the sheriff. Once admitted to the hospital it is incumbent upon the managers of the hospital to notify the Mental Welfare Commission and also the local authority for the area in which the hospital is situated, unless the admission is at the behest of the mental health officer appointed by that local authority (in which case the local authority are presumed to already know). On being notified, the local authority shall arrange for one of its mental health officers, as soon as is practicable but not later than seven days before the expiry of the period of 28 days beginning with the date on which the patient was admitted to hospital, to (a) interview the patient whose admission has been notified to them, and (b) provide the patient's responsible medical officer and the Mental Welfare Commission with a report on the patient's social circumstances. Moreover, where a patient has been admitted, it is a requirement that a medical officer shall examine the patient or obtain from another medical practitioner a report on the condition of the patient and also consult such other person or persons who appear to him to be principally concerned with the patient's medical treatment. Having examined the patient, or obtained reports, if the medical officer is satisfied that the patient is not suffering from any mental disorder which makes it appropriate for him to be detained for medical treatment, or is not a danger to the health and safety either of himself or others, he should order a discharge of the patient. Following examination, if he does not discharge the patient he must inform the Mental Welfare

6.12

---

[71] *ibid.*, s. 21(5).
[72] *ibid.*, s. 113(1).
[73] See Patrick, Annotations to the Mental Health (Scotland) Act 1984, in Mays (ed.), *Scottish Social Work Legislation*, H.022.5.
[74] Act of Sederunt (Mental Health Rules) 1996 (S.I. 1996 No. 2149), para. 6.
[75] *ibid.*, para. 5.1.
[76] 1984 Act, s. 113(2)
[77] See generally 1984 Act, ss. 22 and 23.

Commission, the nearest relative of the patient, the local authority, and the managers of the hospital.

One immediately comprehends that one of the key aspects of the 1984 Act is to ensure there are adequate safeguards for the patient built into the procedures for compulsory admission. The patient alone may not be able to protect and enforce their rights (principally but not exclusively the right not to be unfairly or improperly detained), but by ensuring that others are notified of the position it is expected that the rights of the detainee can be adequately secured.

There are provisions within the 1984 Act for rectification of any decision made based upon an erroneous medical recommendation. If it is found that the medical recommendation is in any respect incorrect or defective it may, at any time within the 14 days after the patient has been admitted to hospital, be amended. Where it appears to the managers of the hospital that one of the two medical recommendations on which the application for admission is founded is insufficient to warrant the detention of a patient then they may give notice in writing to that effect to the applicant and to the sheriff. The patient may continue to be detained if a fresh medical recommendation complying with the relevant provisions is furnished to the managers and to the sheriff. The sheriff will require to be satisfied that the two reports that he now has are sufficient for compulsory detention.

Emergency admission to hospital[78]

6.13   There are many situations where it is urgently necessary for a patient to be admitted to hospital. Where a medical practitioner is of the opinion that it is urgently necessary for the health and safety of the patient or for the protection of other persons that a patient should be admitted, he may recommend admission of that patient. An emergency recommendation shall not be made unless, where practicable, the consent of a relative or mental health officer has first been obtained. The recommendation must be accompanied by a statement that such consent has been obtained or a statement as to why there has been a failure to obtain that consent. Where the medical practitioner makes an emergency recommendation this will be authority for the immediate removal of the patient to hospital any time within three days from the date on which it is made, and for the detention of that patient for up to 72 hours from the time of admission. An emergency recommendation can only be made by a medical practitioner who has examined the patient on the same day that he has signed the recommendation.[79] Where a patient is admitted under these provisions the hospital managers shall without delay inform the nearest relative and the Mental Welfare Commission, or some responsible person residing with the patient who is the subject of the detention. The fact that medical practitioners need not report any emergency medical treatment on the detainee to the Mental Welfare Commission has been severely criticised.[80] It is not possible to extend the 72 hours' detention with a further emergency detention after its expiry. It will be a requirement of those responsible, if they are of a mind that the patient should be further detained, to resort to some other form of detention, either the general power of detention or short-term detention.

Emergency detention is the most common form of detention. It is possible for any doctor to sign the form—it need not necessarily be a psychiatrist. It is commonplace for general practitioners to be signatories. There is no scope for appeal against emergency detention,

78   See generally 1984 Act, s. 24.
79   1984 Act, s. 24(1).
80   Patrick, Annotations, in Mays (ed.), *Scottish Social Work Legislation*, para. H.025.2.

although by providing notification to the Mental Welfare Commission it is possible that they may intervene to discharge the patient. However, it is a rather forlorn hope that the Mental Welfare Commission will be able to investigate every case of a patient detained for 72 hours within the time-frame of their detention. The human-rights dimension of the absence of appeal provisions are all too obvious.

Detaining in-patients[81]

It is possible for an emergency recommendation for admission to be made when the patient is already voluntarily in hospital. Where, in the case of a patient who is already in hospital receiving treatment for a mental disorder but not liable to be detained, it appears to a registered nurse[82] (a) that the patient is suffering from a mental disorder of such a degree that it is necessary for his health and safety or for the protection of other persons for him to be immediately restrained from leaving, and (b) that it is not practical to secure the immediate attendance of a medical practitioner for the purpose of making an emergency recommendation, the patient may be detained in hospital for a period of up to two hours or until the earlier arrival of a medical practitioner having the power to make an emergency recommendation. It is the requirement in this type of emergency detention that the nurse as soon as possible records in writing the fact that the patient has been detained, the facts surrounding the detention and the time at which the patient was first detained. The nurse must deliver the report in writing to the managers of the hospital and within 14 days of the record being made it should be sent by the managers to the Mental Welfare Commission. A patient who has been detained in hospital by a nurse under these emergency powers cannot be further detained under this power immediately after the expiry of the period of detention. However, in *R v. Lothian Health Board (No. 2)*[83] it was held that a patient who had been detained under the emergency detention procedures and thereafter had stayed a further day voluntarily could not argue that a subsequent detention was immediately after the first.

6.14

Short-term detention

The foregoing emergency detention procedures allowing for 72 hours' detention or two hours' detention facilitate an opportunity to assess the patient and determine whether further detention is necessary. There are provisions in section 26 of the Mental Health (Scotland) Act 1984 which provide for further short-term detention of the patient for a period of up to 28 days. Where a patient is admitted under the emergency procedures in section 24 and a report on the condition of the patient is furnished to the managers of the hospital, and where practical consent to the continued detention has been given by the nearest relative of the patient or a mental health officer, the report will act as authority for continued detention of the patient for 28 days following the expiry of the period of 72 hours.[84]

6.15

Again it is a requirement of the legislation that where a patient is detained under the short-term detention measures the managers of the hospital must inform the Mental Welfare Commission, the nearest relative of the patient (unless that person has consented to the continued detention), and the local authority (unless the mental health officer has consented). The requirement is that the hospital managers must notify the aforementioned

---

[81]   See generally 1984 Act, s. 25.
[82]   Mental Health (Prescription of Class of Nurses) (Scotland) Order 1984 (S. I. 1984 No. 1095).
[83]   1993 S.L.T. 1021.
[84]   See 1984 Act, ss. 26(1), (2) and (3).

parties not later than seven days after the patient was detained.[85] On being informed of the patient's detention the local authority shall arrange for a mental health officer, as soon as practical and in any event not later than seven days before the expiry of the period of 28 days, to interview the patient and to provide the responsible medical officer and the Mental Welfare Commission with a report on the patient's social circumstances.[86]

Consecutive use of detention measures

6.16   If a patient is detained under the short-term detention measures for 28 days it is not possible to immediately detain them again for a further 28 days or indeed to revert back to the emergency detention provisions.[87] In *CDR v. Hay*[88] a patient was admitted to hospital under an emergency recommendation under section 24 of the 1984 Act which authorised her detention for 72 hours. She was thereafter admitted under section 26 for 28 days. Two weeks into this detention the patient indicated that she would be prepared to stay as a voluntary patient at the end of the 28 days. A day after the expiry of the 28 days the patient sought to leave and was stopped by a psychiatrist. A new short-term detention was imposed of 28 days. In response to several questions raised in a judicial review action it was held that the computation of time of detention should be computed in such a way that the clock starts running the moment the patient is detained and the time concludes exactly at that time 28 days later. The court also held that it will always be a matter of impression as to whether one detention immediately follows another. Since the patient in this case had stayed voluntarily and 24 hours had elapsed, the second detention did not follow the other.

Only a patient who has been detained under section 24 (emergency admissions) can be the subject of short-term detention for 28 days. There is a right of appeal against the short-term detention period.[89] The original provisions of the 1984 Act contained a loophole whereby it was not possible for doctors to further extend the detention of patients detained under the short-term detention by invoking further emergency procedures. This was illustrated in *B v. F*[90] where the patient had during the short-term detention made good progress and as a consequence no further application was made for long-term detention. Immediately before the expiry of the 28-day period, the patient's condition deteriorated and it was not possible for the hospital to further detain him. As a consequence of this decision a new section 26A was inserted into the 1984 Act by the Mental Health Detention (Scotland) Act 1991, s. 1. It provides that, where a patient is detained in hospital under section 26, and a change in the condition of the patient makes it necessary in the interests of his own health and safety or with a view to the protection of others that the patient continue to be detained until the expiry of the 28-day period, where no application for admission has been submitted to the sheriff in respect of the patient, and it is not reasonably practical to submit such an application before the expiry of that period, it is possible for a relevant medical practitioner to lodge with the sheriff court a report on the condition of the patient which will constitute sufficient authority for the continued detention of the patient in hospital for a further three days from the day when the report was lodged.[91] It is a requirement that the relevant medical practitioner personally examine the patient. The medical practitioner should not lodge a

---

[85]   1984 Act, s. 26(4).
[86]   *ibid.*, s. 26(5)(a) and (b).
[87]   *ibid.*, s. 26(7), as amended by the Mental Health (Detention) (Scotland) Act 1991, s. 3(1).
[88]   1993 S.C.L.R. 112; *cf.* earlier hearing reported at *R. v. Lothian Health Board*, 1991 S.L.T. 282.
[89]   1984 Act, s. 35.
[90]   1987 S.L.T. 681.
[91]   See 1984 Act, s. 26A, as inserted by the Mental Health (Detention) (Scotland) Act 1991, s. 1.

report unless where practical the consent of the nearest relative of the patient or of a mental health officer has been obtained. The medical practitioner's report will state that the patient is suffering from a mental disorder which requires detention in hospital for a limited time and that the patient ought to be so detained in the interests of his own health or the health and safety of others. As with all detentions there is a notification requirement. In this case the relevant medical practitioner must forthwith notify the Mental Welfare Commission, where practical the nearest relative of the patient, and the local authority. The notification must inform the patient of his right of appeal and the period during which that right of appeal may be exercised. A patient detained under these provisions has the right of appeal to the sheriff. It is reported that since the modifications in 1991 there have roughly been 20 instances where section 26A has been invoked.[92]

CARE AND TREATMENT OF PATIENTS IN HOSPITAL

Care and treatment of mentally disordered persons is naturally important and controversial. **6.17** Hospitals and medical practitioners must navigate a fine line to ensure that they stay within their civil duties of care to the patient and at the same time ensure that their conduct is such that they do not transgress the criminal law. It is worth noting at the outset that a mentally disordered patient, notwithstanding his right of legal redress, has several avenues of complaint against NHS treatment other than a complaint to the Mental Welfare Commission. These include referring a complaint to the Review Procedure for the Exercise of Clinical Judgment, the Health Board Administration, the Health Service Commissioner and the Service Committee Complaints Procedure.[93] Not surprisingly, many detained patients seem unaware of their status and their rights and therefore accessing and enforcing those rights may be problematic.[94]

Consent to medical treatment of detained patients

As a general proposition adults of sound mind have the right to refuse medical treatment **6.18** even where that will imperil that adult.[95] However, implicit in the notion of detention in hospital is the view that the person requires some form of medical treatment. It has been held that mental health detention cannot be used to detain someone and compel treatment just because that person's thinking appeared irrational, unusual or contrary to public opinion.[96] It has been claimed, however, that there is often a minimal link between physical medical treatment and mental disorder.[97] What is clear is that mentally disordered people may not have sufficient capacity to protect their fundamental right to bodily integrity and as a consequence the 1984 Act sets down important provisions in respect of consent to medical treatment. There are different rules for different forms of treatment. There are some categories of patient who are specifically excluded from these provisions and whose consent must be obtained before treatment can be given. They are (a) patients who are liable to

---

[92] Patrick, Annotations, in Mays (ed.), *Scottish Social Work Legislation*, para. H.028.4.
[93] For a discussion of all of these routes, see Hall, "Mentally disordered patients—Complaints Procedures in the NHS", 1991 SCOLAG 122; note that the Government are currently consulting on a review of the service committee complaints procedure.
[94] See Goldbeck, MacKenzie and Bennie, "Detained Patient's Knowledge of their Legal Status and Rights" (1997) Vol. 8, No. 3, *Journal of Forensic Psychiatry*, pp. 562–572.
[95] See *Re C (Adult: refusal of medical treatment)* [1994] 1 All E.R. 819 where a person was suffering from an ulcerated foot which became gangrenous.
[96] See *St George's Healthcare NHS Trust v. S* [1998] 3 All E.R. 673.
[97] See Foley, *Human Rights, Human Wrongs* (1995) at p. 225.

detained in hospital by virtue of an emergency recommendation, (b) people taken into hospital under a place of safety order under section 117 or section 118 or section 58 (9) of the Criminal Procedure (Scotland) Act 1995, or (c) patients who have been conditionally discharged from hospital and not subsequently recalled to the hospital.[98]

Given the nature of some medical treatment for mental disorder it is not surprising that there are fairly strict provisions on the administering of treatment to detained patients. The requirement under section 97 is that a doctor appointed by the Mental Welfare Commission and two other persons (not medical practitioners)[99] must certify that the patient understands the nature, purpose and likely effects of the treatment and has consented to it.[1] In addition, the medical practitioner must certify in writing that having regard to the likelihood of the treatment alleviating, and preventing, a deterioration of the patient's condition, the treatment for mental disorder should be given.[2] Copies of the certification must be forwarded to the Mental Welfare Commission within seven days following the issue of the certificate.[3] There are currently only two treatments that are subject to regulation under section 97, these being psychosurgery and surgical implantation of hormones for the purposes of reducing male sex drive.[4]

6.19   There are also some treatments where consent of the patient, or a second medical opinion, is required before that treatment can be administered. In this respect drug treatment or electro-convulsive therapy (ECT) are examples of treatment which requires this special added approval.[5] The taking of blood itself is not thought to be a medical treatment which requires consent, or a second opinion, under section 98.[6] A patient should not be given any form of treatment unless he has consented, and either the patient's responsible medical officer, or a medical practitioner, has certified in writing that the patient is capable of understanding its nature, purpose and effects, and has consented to it.[7] Alternatively, a medical practitioner may certify in writing that the patient is not capable of understanding the nature, purpose and likely effects of that treatment, and has not consented to it, but having regard to the likelihood of alleviating or preventing a deterioration of the patient's condition the treatment should be given.[8] It should be noted that in the event of the latter scenario, the doctor concerned cannot be the patient's responsible medical officer. In other words, there must be a second opinion. Treatments like ECT are highly controversial. Where the provisions of section 98 are not applied properly, the patient or their relatives may have recourse to the law, perhaps referring a complaint for prosecution under criminal law, or alternatively raising proceedings for compensation in a delictual action or raising an action for judicial review.[9]

The provisions in section 98 provide a mechanism whereby doctors can treat a patient even where that person refuses treatment as it is likely to be in the patient's best interest. The second opinion doctors required by the Act are appointed by the Mental Welfare Commission. Ordinarily, he will be consultant psychiatrists of some standing. The second opinion doctor will meet with all those involved in the patient's medical care.[10] He will also examine

98   1984 Act, s. 96(1).
99   They are usually commissioners of the Mental Welfare Commission.
1   1984 Act, s. 97(2)(a).
2   *ibid.*, s. 97(2).
3   *ibid.*, s. 97(4).
4   See Patrick, Annotations in Mays (ed.), *Scottish Social Work Legislation*, at para. H. 113.2.
5   1984 Act, s. 98(1).
6   See Patrick, *op. cit.*, at para. H.114.2.
7   1984 Act, s. 98(3)(a).
8   *ibid.*, s. 98(3)(b).
9   See Patrick, *op. cit.*, at para. H.114.4.
10   Mental Health (Scotland) Act 1984, s. 98(4).

the patient's medical records and interview the patient's relatives. In any situation where it becomes apparent that the patient is prepared to consent, the opinion of the second medical doctor is no longer required. The Mental Welfare Commission insists that any treatment plan, approved for the patient under the auspices of second medical opinion, is reviewed after three years.[11] It is also a requirement that any plan of treatment given to the patient in the wake of second opinion should be reported to the Mental Welfare Commission along with a note on the patient's condition.[12] Such reports should be given on the next occasion when the responsible medical officer is making a report for renewal of detention of the patient.[13] It is possible for the Mental Welfare Commission to stop the treatment of the patient,[14] although such a direction from the Mental Welfare Commission may be overruled if the patient's responsible medical officer considers that this continuance of the treatment or treatment under the plan would cause serious suffering to the patient.[15]

A patient who has previously consented to medical treatment may withdraw his consent at any time.[16] Again if the doctor considers that discontinuance of the treatment under the plan would cause serious suffering to the patient, the patient's withdrawal of consent may be overruled.[17] In all other instances, the medical practitioners should seek to gain the consent of the patient once again, or in the absence of consent adopt the second opinion procedure as outlined above.

Irrespective of all the foregoing provisions in respect of medical treatment of a patient with a mental disorder, it is possible for a doctor to provide emergency medical treatment (a) where it is immediately necessary to save the patient's life, (b) which (not being irreversible) is immediately necessary to prevent a serious deterioration in his condition, (c) which (not being irreversible or hazardous) is necessary to alleviate serious suffering by the patient, or (d) which (not being irreversible or hazardous) is immediately necessary and represents the minimum interference necessary to prevent the patient from behaving violently or being a danger to himself or to others.[18] Treatment is to be deemed "irreversible" if it has unfavourable, irreversible, physical or psychological consequences, and "hazardous" if it entails significant physical hazards.[19] Where a patient is treated under these emergency provisions the consultant psychiatrist must report details of the treatment to the Mental Welfare Commission within seven days.[20] In all other forms of treatment, not being the special forms of treatment outlined in sections 97 and 98, the responsible medical officer has the general authority to treat the patient for their mental disorder including treatment of drugs for up to three months.[21] In *South West Hertfordshire Health Authority v. KB*[22] it was

6.20

[11]   See Report of Mental Welfare Commission, 1994–1995, at p. 65.
[12]   1984 Act, s. 99(1).
[13]   1984 Act, s. 99(1)(a), as amended by the Mental Health (Patients in the Community) Act 1995, s. 5(10).
[14]   1984 Act, s. 99(2).
[15]   *ibid.*, s. 102(2).
[16]   *ibid.*, s. 101(1).
[17]   *ibid.*, s. 102(2).
[18]   *ibid.*, s. 102(1).
[19]   *ibid.*, s. 102(3).
[20]   *ibid.*, s. 102(4).
[21]   *ibid.*, s. 103.
[22]   [1994] 2 F.C.R. 1051; see also *B v. Croydon Health Authority* [1995] 1 F.C.R. 332 where it was held that tube-feeding was "medical treatment given ... for the mental disorder" and thereby did not require the consent of the patient. However, in *Riverside Mental Health NHS Trust v. Fox* [1994] 2 F.C.R. 577 the Court of Appeal discharged an order, obtained by the trust subsequent to the making of an interim declaration, to authorise naso-gastric feeding without the consent of the patient. Her condition was critical. The decision was based on a point of law, that there was no such thing as an interim declaration which in turn disallowed the order for force-feeding. For further reading on this latter decision see Case Comment, *Medical Law Review*, 1994, Vol. 2, Pt 1, pp. 95–99.

found that anorexia nervosa constituted a mental disorder which endorsed the administration of medical treatment without the consent of the patient.[23] To date there is no equivalent judicial direction in Scotland.

Medical treatment of mentally incapable adults not compulsorily detained

6.21 There may be some persons who are not detained with a mental disorder but who are admitted to hospital temporarily or permanently mentally incapacitated. It is generally thought that patients in such situations may be given treatment on the basis of necessity and because treatment cannot reasonably be postponed.[24] The House of Lords ruled in *Re F (Mental Patient: Sterilisation)*[25] on the sterilisation of a 35-year-old resident in a mental hospital who was having a sexual relationship with a fellow patient. Lord Brandon stated that:

"A doctor can lawfully operate on, or give other treatment to, adult patients who are incapable, for one reason or another, of consenting to his doing so, provided that the operation or other treatment concerned is in the best interests of such patients. The operation or other treatment will be in the best interests if, but only if, it is carried out in order to save their lives or to ensure improvement or prevent deterioration in their physical or mental health".

In *Re Y (Mental Patient: Bone marrow Donation)*[26] it was held that it was in a mentally and physically handicapped adult's best interests to donate bone marrow to her sister who was suffering from leukaemia. The court reasoned that she would benefit from her sister's prolonged life. Whilst the view in *Re F* is thought to be the one that would be followed in Scotland, here there is the possibility of appointing a tutor *dative* who may give the consent on the patient's behalf.[27] In the Scottish Law Commission's *Report on Incapable Adults* they suggested a scheme of advance statement whereby a person's while competent may declare his or her wishes concerning future treatment.[28]

In one matter at least there has been recent clarification by the Scottish courts. In *Law Hospital NHS Trust v. Lord Advocate*[29] it was held that the Court of Session had jurisdiction to protect certain patients in a persistent vegetative state since they were not able to protect themselves. Thus, in exercising its role as *parens patriae* the court was able to authorise the

[23]   For further reading on this decision see Case Comment, *Medical Law Review*, (1994), Vol. 2, Pt 2, pp. 208–210 and on the law with respect to procedures for compulsory treatment and proposed changes in consent requirements in Ireland, see Connolly, "Consent and Involuntary Treatment in Anorexia Nervosa" 1996, *Medico-Legal Journal of Ireland*, 2(2), 55–56.

[24]   Mason and McCall-Smith, *Law and Medical Ethics* (5th ed., 1999) at p. 253; it is suggested that doctors adopt a three-fold test—Can the patient take in and retain the information? Does the patient believe the information? Can the patient make an informed choice? See *Re C (Adult: Refusal of Medical Treatment)* [1994] 1 All E.R. 819. For patients not compulsorily detained it now seems accepted medical practice that advance statements of the patient's desire not to have certain treatments will be given effect to: see *Airedale NHS Trust v. Bland* [1993] A.C. 789 which stipulates 3 criteria—clear instrcutions must be given; the patient must have been competent at the time of making the advance statement; and it must be clear that the advance statement was intended to apply to the situation which has arisen; see also *Advance Statements About Medical Treatment—Code Of Practice for Health Professionals*, BMA (1995); *Advance Statements About Future Medical Treatment—A Guide for Patients*, The Patients Association (1996); Davis, *Textbook on Medical Law* (2nd ed., 1998).

[25]   [1990] 2 A.C. 1; *cf. Re LC (Medical treatment Sterilisation)* [1997] 2 F.L.R. 258.

[26]   [1997] W.L.R. 556.

[27]   See SLC (1995) No. 151 at paras 5.3–5.4.

[28]   SLC (1995) No. 151 at para. 5.41ff.

[29]   1996 S.C. 301.

hospital to discontinue life-sustaining treatment where it was not in the best interests of the patient to continue it.[30]

Leave of absence

The consulting psychiatrist in charge of the patient has the power to grant a patient **6.22** permission to be absent from the hospital.[31] The leave of absence may be on specific occasions for a specified period of not more than six months but this may be extended. It is not permissible for initial leave of absence plus extensions to exceed 12 months.[32] The purpose of allowing such leave of absence is to facilitate the patient's rehabilitation into the community. Where leave of absence is granted to a patient it is the duty of the consulting psychiatrist to inform the Mental Welfare Commission within 14 days of the granting of leave or of any extension of it, of the address at which the patient is residing. Likewise that person must inform the Commission of the return of the patient within 14 days. The responsible medical officer may at any time where it appears to him to be in the interest of the health and safety of the patient, or for the protection of others, revoke the leave of absence and recall the patient to hospital. There was prior to the statutory amendment some concern that medical practitioners were using leave of absence as a long-term means of ensuring medical treatment in the community. The revised provisions now limit leave of absence to 12 months but this has not met with universal approval.[33] The Code of Practice suggests that the responsible medical officer should see the patient regularly while the patient is on leave of absence and should monitor the patient's progress.[34] There should be consultation by the medical officer with the patient's general practitioner and the general practitioner should be made aware that the patient is on leave of absence. It may also be necessary to advise social work departments in order that assistance can be given to the patient whilst in the community. The Mental Welfare Commission has been critical of the approach of some medical officers on the basis that inadequate planning has been put into place in respect of patients' leave of absence from hospital.[35]

Section 28 of the 1984 Act provides that where a patient is for the time being liable to be detained and:

(a) absents himself from hospital without leave;

(b) fails to return to hospital on any occasion on which, or at the expiration of any period for which, leave of absence was granted to him or upon being, recalled; or

(c) absents himself without permission from any place where he is required to reside in accordance with the conditions imposed on the grant of leave of absence,

---

[30] For further reading on this decision see Laurie, "*Parens Patriae* Jurisdiction in the Medico-Legal Context: The Vagaries of Judicial Acitivism", 1999 *Edinburgh Law Review*, Vol. 3, Pt 1, pp. 95–107; Crerar, "*Parens Patriae* Jurisdiction Applied", (1996) 41 J.L.S.S. 400–402; Gibb, "*Parens Patriae* Reviewed", 1996 Fam.L.B. 21–2; Lardy, "Euthanasia and Euphemism", 1997 *Edinburgh Law Review*, Vol. 1, Pt 2, pp. 227–234 and Case Comment, 1996 Fam.L.B. 26–670; Mason and Laurie, "The Management of Persistent Vegetative State in the British Isles", 1996 J.R. 263.

[31] See, generally, 1984 Act, s. 27.

[32] 1984 Act, s. 27(2A), as inserted by the Mental Health Patients in the Community Act 1995, s. 6(3).

[33] See Patrick, Annotations in Mays (ed.), *Scottish Social Work Legislation*, para. H.029.4.

[34] Code of Practice, para. 3.6.

[35] Mental Welfare Commission's Annual Report 1994/95 p. 18.

he may be taken into custody and returned to the hospital or place by any mental health officer, any officer on the staff of the hospital, any constable, or by any person authorised in writing by the managers of the hospital.

Transfer to another hospital

6.23   Section 29 makes provisions for the transfer of patients between hospitals. The patient may be transferred to another hospital with the consent of the managers of that hospital or into the guardianship of a local authority with the consent of the authority, or into the guardianship of any person approved by the local authority with the consent of that person.[36] It seems likely that courts will not interfere where a transfer between ordinary psychiatric hospitals is based on clinical judgment.[37] Any transfer should be intimated to the nearest relative and to the Mental Welfare Commission by the managers of the hospital to which the patient is transferred, or, if appropriate, by the local authority within seven days of the date of transfer.[38] Where a patient is transferred to the state hospital, he, or his nearest relative, may within 28 days of the transfer appeal against the decision to transfer by way of summary application to a sheriff of the sheriffdom within which the hospital from which the patient was transferred is situated. The sheriff may order the return of the patient to the hospital from which he was transferred unless he is satisfied on account of his dangerousness, violent or criminal propensities that the patient requires treatment under conditions of special security and cannot suitably be cared for in a hospital other than a state mental hospital.[39]

     For a patient to be transferred to the state mental hospital it must be shown that it is necessary for the patient to have treatment under arrangements of special security on account of the patient's violent, dangerous, or criminal propensities, and that he could not be suitably treated in another hospital.[40]

DURATION OF AUTHORITY FOR DETENTION AND DISCHARGE

6.24   Where an application is made to the sheriff and the patient is admitted to hospital he can be detained for a period not exceeding six months beginning with the day on which he was first admitted.[41] The patient can only be detained for longer than this if there is an application for renewal of the detention. Unless the patient has previously been discharged there is a possibility of authority for detention of the patient for a further period of six months.[42]

Renewal of detention

6.25   On expiry of the renewal, it is possible to further extend the detention for periods of one year at a time.[43] The consultant psychiatrist is required to examine the patient in the final two months of his detention or obtain from another medical practitioner a report on the

---

[36]   1984 Act, s. 29(1)(a), (b) and (c); discussed at para. 6.34 *et seq.* below.
[37]   See the English case of *R v. Inner London Education Authority, ex p. F (No. 2), The Times*, Nov. 28, 1988.
[38]   1984 Act, s. 29(2).
[39]   1984 Act, s. 28(4), as amended by the Mental Health (Detention) (Scotland) Act 1991 s. 3(2). *F v. Management Committee and Managers, Ravenscraig Hospital*, 1987 S.L.T. (Sh. Ct.) 76 at 80. The sheriff's decision may be subject to judicial review.
[40]   *C v. Greater Glasgow Community and Mental Health Services NHS Trust*, 1998 S.C.L.R. 214.
[41]   1984 Act, s. 30(1).
[42]   *ibid.*, s. 30(1) and (2)(a).
[43]   See, generally, 1984 Act, s. 30.

condition of the patient. He is also required to consult other persons who appear to be principally concerned with the patient's medical treatment. Thereafter, he must make an assessment of the need to further detain the patient and if it appears to him that the patient should be detained, he must make a report to the managers of the hospital in which the patient is currently detained and to the Mental Welfare Commission. Where the consultant psychiatrist makes such a report this will be enough for renewal of the detention. The managers of the hospital on receipt of a report from a consult psychiatrist are required, unless they discharge the patient, to inform the patient and their nearest relative. The patient has on receipt of such intimation a right of appeal to the sheriff.

Although section 30 has the facility for successive renewals of detention, there are a number of important safeguards built into the legislation. Not only is the responsible medical officer required to keep the patient's condition under review, and if necessary discharge the patient, but the patient may also apply to the Mental Welfare Commission for discharge. In order to justify the extension of detention, it has been held by one sheriff that the responsible medical officer must satisfy himself that actual detention and not just the liability to detention is appropriate and necessary.[44] However, in *K v. Murphy*,[45] Lord Marnoch supported the renewal of detention of a patient who had been on continuous leave of absence for a period of two years, indicating that "it would suffice ... if the patient's condition was such that it was generally appropriate for him to receive medical treatment in a hospital". He did not distinguish between the need for the actual detention and the need to be liable to detention.

The detention is not renewed until such times as the responsible medical officer has furnished the hospital management with his report. If by some mishap that report is not received until after the expiry of the original detention no renewal is possible. It has however been held that to place the report in the internal mail was sufficient intimation to hospital managers.[46] It is possible to extend a patient's detention where they are absent without leave but return to the hospital or are taken to custody within a week of the end of his or her detention. The extension of time is deemed to be sufficient to allow the doctors time to examine the patient and decide whether he or she should remain subject to detention.[47] Where a patient who is absent without leave returns to hospital, or is taken into custody within 28 days, the doctors may renew his or her detention as long as the patient continues to be liable to detention.[48] Where the patient is taken into custody, or returns after more than 28 days absence, different provisions apply. In such cases, the consultant psychiatrist, within one week of the patient returning, is required to examine the patient or obtain from another medical practitioner a report on the condition of the patient, and to consult with such other persons who appear to him to be principally concerned with the patient's medical treatment and the mental health officer of the local authority. The purpose of the examination and consultation is to assess whether the patient is in need of further detention and whether a ground of detention exists. If the consultant psychiatrist is of the opinion that grounds for detention exist, he must furnish the manager of the hospital, the patient liable to be detained, and the Mental Welfare Commission with the report to that effect.[49] On receipt of the report, unless the hospital decides to discharge the patient, they must inform the patient and the

---

44   *AB and CB v. E*, 1987 S.C.L.R. 419 at 427.
45   1997 S.L.T. 248.
46   See *Milborrow Applicant*, 1996 S.C.L.R. 314.
47   1984 Act, s. 31, as substituted by the Mental Health (Patients in the Community) Act 1995, s. 5(3).
48   1984 Act, s. 31A, as substituted by the Mental Health (Patients in the Community) Act 1995, s. 5(3).
49   See, generally, 1984 Act, s. 31B, as substituted by the Mental Health (Patients in the Community) Act 1995, s. 5(3).

nearest relative of the contents of the report. The furnishing of the report will renew the authority for the patient's detention. Where the authority for detention of the patient is renewed, the renewal shall take effect on the day on which the original detention would have expired. The net effect of these provisions is that where a patient returns after 28 days and is thought to be liable to detention they will have the detention extended by either six months or a year. In the event that there are no grounds for further detaining the patient following the assessment by the relevant practitioner, the patient will be discharged within seven days of his return to hospital.

Detention in a penal institution

6.26 There are also special provisions regarding patients sentenced to imprisonment. Where a patient is liable to be detained and is detained in custody in pursuance of any sentence or order passed by court in the United Kingdom (including an order committing or remanding him in custody), and is so detained for a period exceeding six months, he will cease to be liable for detention at the expiry of that six-month period.[50] Quite simply, a patient in custody following a court appearance is treated as if he is on unauthorised leave of absence from the first day of his or her release from custody, and may be taken back to hospital at any time within 28 days of his release.

DISCHARGE OF PATIENTS FROM HOSPITAL[51]

6.27 A patient may be discharged from detention in hospital by an order made by the responsible medical officer (usually a consultant) or by the Mental Welfare Commission, or where an appeal has been successfully taken to the sheriff.[52] The responsible medical officer cannot make an order discharging a patient in a state hospital without the consent of the managers of the hospital. A responsible medical officer, or the Mental Welfare Commission, can make an order for discharge of the patient where he is, or they are, satisfied that (a) he is not suffering from mental disorder of a nature or degree which makes it appropriate for him to be liable to be detained in hospital for medical treatment; or (b) it is not necessary for the health or safety of the patient or for the protection of other persons that the patient should receive such treatment.

It is also possible for an order for discharge to be made in respect of a patient by managers of the hospital or by the nearest relative. Where the order for discharge is being made by managers of the hospital with the consent of the responsible medical officer, it should take effect on the expiry of a period of seven days from the date on which the order was made. In the event that an application for detention is pending but has not been determined by the sheriff and an order for discharge is made, it is a requirement that a sheriff is notified of the making of the order for discharge.[53] Under these provisions the patient may be discharged from liability to detention even if the responsible medical officer or Mental Welfare Commission consider that the patient should remain in hospital if the patient agrees to stay as a voluntary patient.[54]

---

[50]   1984 Act, s. 32(1).
[51]   See, generally, 1984 Act, ss. 33 and 34.
[52]   1984 Act, s. 33(2), as amended by the Mental Health (Detention) (Scotland) Act 1991, s. 3(3).
[53]   1984 Act, s. 33(7), inserted by the Mental Health (Detention) (Scotland) Act 1991, s. 3(3).
[54]   See Patrick, Annotations in Mays (ed.), *Scottish Social Work Legislation*, at para. H.037.4.

Where an order for the discharge of a patient is sought by the patient's nearest relative, the relative must give seven days' notice in writing to the manager of the hospital. The order of the nearest relative will cease to have effect if the responsible medical officer delivers a report to the managers of the hospital that in his opinion the order of the nearest relatives should have no effect and that no further order for discharge of the patient should be made by that relative during the period of six months from the beginning of the report. In order that the responsible medical officer can keep the patient in hospital, there must be a requirement that the patient needs treatment in hospital, and accordingly, it is inappropriate to stop a discharge where the patient is on leave of absence.[55] Where the nearest relative makes an order and this is disputed by the responsible medical officer, the nearest relative must be notified by the managers of the hospital within 28 days. The nearest relative thereafter has a right of appeal to the sheriff. It is not possible for a relative to make an order for discharge in respect of a patient detained in the state mental hospital.

As part of its care in the community strategy, the Government have been keen to develop a care programme approach to managing mental health in the community.[56] The purpose behind the idea is to ensure that properly designed and managed individual packages of care are arranged for people with severe and enduring mental illness. Care programme management is appropriate for individuals already in the community and those about to be released from hospital detention. It is the Government's view that no-one should be discharged from hospital until suitable packages of health and social care and accommodation are available.[57]

APPEALS AGAINST DETENTION IN HOSPITAL

Where an appeal lies to the sheriff in respect of a report on a patient, the managers of the hospital have a duty to inform any person having a right to appeal recommending detention of their rights and the period upon or the period within which they may exercise their rights.[58] Those taking appeal are well advised to obtain independent medical evidence to help substantiate their case. There is scope within the law for a medical practitioner to visit any patient who is the subject of an appeal and for that medical practitioner to examine the patient in private.[59]

6.28

COMMUNITY CARE ORDERS

The Mental Health (Patients in the Community) Act 1995 ("1995 Act") introduced into the 1984 Act community care orders for those patients who suffer from serious mental illness but who after discharge from hospital failed to continue to take medication or to co-operate with a care plan prepared for them by the social work department.[60] The consequences of their failure to adhere to their care plan often results in their being repeatedly re-admitted to hospital and posing a risk both to themselves and the wider community.

6.29

---

[55] Patrick, Annotations in Mays (ed.), *Scottish Social Work Legislation*, at para. H.038.2.
[56] See *Caring for People* (1989, Cmnd 849), para. 10.26; "Community Care: Guidance on Care Programmes for People with Mental Illness Including Dementia", Circular SWSG 38/1996.
[57] See Circular SW 38/96 at pp. 3–4.
[58] 1984 Act, s. 35(1).
[59] 1984 Act, s. 35(3), as amended by the Mental Health (Detention) (Scotland) Act 1991, s. 3(4).
[60] See Eastman, "The Mental Health (Patients in the Community) Act 1995: A Critical Analysis" (1997), Vol. 170 *British Journal of Psychiatry*, 492–496.

In *AB and CB v. E*,[61] the sheriff expressed concern that leave of absence was being used for patients who did not require any degree of in-patient treatment. Until the law was revised it was the case that the patients who refused to take their medication while on leave of absence could be immediately recalled. It is suggested that this use of the law was dubious to say the least. Renewal of detention meant that there should be some need for in-patient treatment and in many instances this was clearly not the case. As an alternative to unlimited leave of absence with the power of recall, the Government decided to introduce community care orders. The introduction of such orders was not without some controversy.[62] Hilary Patrick suggests that the law which was finally introduced reflects several key issues:

(1) the importance of a multi-disciplinary approach;

(2) the need for a health lead power;

(3) the importance of gaining co-operation of the patient and the carers;

(4) the power to recall to hospital;

(5) greater powers to the Mental Welfare Commission;

(6) greater freedom to the sheriff to fix conditions of the community care order; and

(7) there is no power to take and convey a patient to another place as part of the community care order.[63]

However, it would be fair to say that there remain genuine concerns about some mentally disordered persons being treated in the community.[64]

A patient's responsible medical officer may make an application to the sheriff for a community care order with a view to ensuring that the patient receives medical treatment and aftercare services.[65] A community care order must specify the conditions to which the patient is subject; the name of the medical practitioner who will undertake the patient's medical treatment; and the name of the person who is responsible for co-ordinating the provision of aftercare services.[66] While the community care order application is under consideration, the patient may be liable to be detained in the hospital until such times as the

---

[61] 1987 S.C.L.R. 419.

[62] See Patrick, Annotations in Mays (ed.), *Scottish Social Work Legislation*, paras. H.040.2 to H.040.4.

[63] *ibid.* at para. H.040.4.

[64] Eastman, "Anti-therapeutic Community Mental Health Law" (1995) BMJ 310: 1081–1082, April 29. The 1995 Act has also been criticised as "clinically unworkable" and "medico-legally flawed".

[65] 1984 Act, s. 35A(1), inserted by the Mental Health (Patients in the Community) Act 1995, s. 4. Substituted (for the purposes of applying to a community care application made or to be made by virtue of s. 35K of the Act) by the Mental Health (Patients in the Community) (Transfer from England and Wales to Scotland) Regulations 1996 (S.I.1996 No. 742), reg. 3 and Sched., as follows:

"(1) As respects a patient who is subject to after care under supervision under the Mental Health Act 1983 and who intends to leave England and Wales in order to reside in Scotland, the applicant may in accordance with section 35B of this Act make an application to the sheriff for an order providing that the patient shall instead of being subject to after care supervision in England and Wales, be subject to the conditions specified in the order, being conditions imposed with a view to ensuring that he receives—(a) medical treatment; and (b) after care services provided for him under section 8 of this Act.

(1A) In the immediately foregoing subsection and in section 35B of this Act "applicant" means the medical practitioner who is to be the patient's special medical officer."

[66] 1984 Act, s. 35A(4)(a),(b) and (c), inserted by the Mental Health (Patients in the Community) Act 1995, s. 4.

application is determined.[67] In *K v. Craig*[68] a patient's responsible medical officer sought a community care order. In the responsible medical officer's report dated October 9, she recorded her opinion that the patient did not need to be detained in hospital. The application for a community care order was lodged on October 11 and granted on November 22. The patient sought a judicial review contending that she should have been released on October 9, as it was the responsible medical officer's view that it was no longer necessary for her to be in hospital. She had ceased to be a person "liable to detention". Moreover, as she had ceased to be liable to detention no application for a community care order could be made in respect of her. The Inner House of the Court of Session rejected these submissions on the basis that Parliament could not have intended it so, and that the duty to discharge a patient in section 33(3) did not apply where the responsible medical officer considered a community care order appropriate. In the House of Lords, Lord Hope, endorsing the Inner House's view of Parliament's intention, argued that the expression by a medical officer of the opinion required to be given in a recommendation for a community care order, which had to be made while the patient remained liable to detention, was tantamount to an *expression of opinion* that it was time to discharge the patient from that liability.[69]

The coming into force of the community care order has the effect of ending the patient's **6.30** liability to detention in hospital.[70] The community care order must be copied to the patient, the Mental Welfare Commission, the patient's special medical officer, and the patient's aftercare officer within seven days of the making of the order.[71] On receipt of a copy of the order the patient's aftercare officer must take such steps as are practical to explain to the patient both orally, and in writing, (a) the purpose and effect of the order and the conditions specified in it, (b) the patient's right of appeal to the sheriff, and (c) that the patient may make representations to the Mental Welfare Commission.[72]

A patient need not be resident in hospital at the time the application for a community care order is made. He may already be on leave of absence from hospital. Community care orders can also be made in respect of patients who are transferred to hospital under a hospital order[73] made under section 58 of the Criminal Procedure (Scotland) Act 1995. However, community care orders are not available in respect of patients who have a restriction order attached to their hospital order under section 59 of the Criminal Procedure (Scotland) Act 1995. Although the community care order seeks to ensure that the patient receives medical treatment, it is not the case that the patient can be forced to take medical treatment against his will.

An application for a community care order cannot be made until the patient has been **6.31** liable to detention for at least 28 days.[74] Before making a community care application, the responsible medical officer must consult the following persons:

---

[67] s. 35A(6): repealed (for the purposes of applying to a community care application made or to be made by virtue of s. 35K of the Act) by the Mental Health (Patients in the Community) (Transfer from England and Wales to Scotland) Regulations 1996 (S.I.1996 No. 742), reg. 3 and Sched.

[68] 1999 S.L.T. 219.

[69] See also *Krol*, 1997 S.C.L.R. 566.

[70] 1984 Act, s. 35A(8), substituted (for the purposes of applying to a community care application made or to be made by virtue of s. 35K of the Act) by the Mental Health (Patients in the Community) (Transfer from England and Wales to Scotland) Regulations 1996 (S.I.1996 No. 742), reg. 3 and Sched., as follows: "(8) A community care order made in respect of such a patient as is referred to in subsection (1) above shall come into force on the date on which the patient takes up residence in Scotland."

[71] 1984 Act, s. 35A(9), as inserted by the Mental Health (Patients in the Community) Act 1995, s. 4.

[72] 1984 Act, s. 35A(10), as inserted by the Mental Health (Patients in the Community) Act 1995, s. 4.

[73] See below at para. 6.53.

[74] 1984 Act, s. 35B(1), inserted by the Mental Health (Patients in the Community) Act 1995 s. 4.

(a) the patient and, if practicable and if the patient does not object, his nearest relative;

(b) the persons who have been principally concerned with the patient's medical treatment in hospital;

(c) the medical practitioner who is to be the patient's special medical officer and the other persons who are to be concerned with the patient's medical treatment once the community care order comes into force;

(d) the person who is to be the person's after care officer;[75]

(e) any other person who the responsible medical officer believes has a continuing professional involvement with any aspect of the aftercare services; and

(f) any person who the responsible medical officer believes will play a substantial part in the care of the patient after the order comes into force.[75a]

In addition to this, the responsible medical officer must consider the aftercare services to be provided to the patient, and any conditions which should be specified in the order which will ensure that the patient receives medical treatment and aftercare services.[75b] The order itself will set out the conditions relative to the community care, the name of the medical practitioner who is to be the patient's special medical officer, and the name of the person who is to be the patient's aftercare officer. The order will also state how long the responsible medical officer considers the order should have effect.[75c]

There must be two supporting medical recommendations for the community care application.[76] There must also be a report by the aftercare officer which details the patient's social circumstances, and the aftercare services and medical treatment to be provided to the patient.[77] Following the multi-disciplinary consultation by the responsible medical officer, the application is submitted to the sheriff along with the medical recommendations. It is essential that the medical recommendations indicate that the patient is not liable to be detained in hospital.

6.32   Community care orders can last for no longer than six months. However, it is possible to renew an order after the expiry of the period for a further period not exceeding six months. Renewals after the initial renewal are for periods of one year at a time.[78] Two months prior to the end of the community care order the patient's special medical officer should examine the patient and undertake consultation with a view to assessing whether the patient should have a renewal of the community care order.[79] If the patient has a propensity to violence, or dangerous behaviour, the responsible medical officer may consult the patient's nearest relative, even if the patient objects.[80] Following consultation, if the special medical officer

---

[75] who may be a mental health officer or a care manager.

[75a] 1984 Act, s. 35B(3), as inserted by the Mental Health (Patients in the Community) Act 1995, s. 4.

[75b] 1984 Act, s. 35B(5), as inserted by the Mental Health (Patients in the Community) Act 1995, s. 4.

[75c] 1984 Act, s. 35B(6)(d), amended (for the purposes of applying to a community care application made or to be made by virtue of s. 35K of the Act) by the Mental Health (Patients in the Community) (Transfer from England and Wales to Scotland) Regulations 1996 (S.I.1996 No. 742), reg. 3 and Sched., as follows: for "the responsible medical officer" there shall be substituted "the applicant".

[76] 1984 Act, s. 35B(7)(a), as inserted by the Mental Health (Patients in the Community) Act 1995, s. 4.

[77] 1984 Act, s. 35B (7)(b) and (9)(a) and (b) as inserted by the Mental Health (Patients in the Community) Act 1995, s. 4.

[78] 1984 Act, s. 35C(1)–(2), as inserted by the Mental Health (Patients in the Community) Act 1995, s. 4.

[79] 1984 Act, s. 35C(3), as inserted by the Mental Health (Patients in the Community) Act 1995, s. 4.

[80] 1984 Act, s. 35C(4), as inserted by the above Act, s.4. Amended (for the purposes of applying to a community care application made or to be made by virtue of s. 35K of the Act) by the Mental Health (Patients in the Community) (Transfer from England and Wales to Scotland) Regulations 1996 (S.I. 1996 No. 742), reg. 3 and Sched., as follows: for "the responsible medical officer" substitute "the special medical officer".

considers that there should be renewal of the community care order he may so order, always subject to the fact that he must notify the Mental Welfare Commission, the patient, and the patient's aftercare officer.[81] Naturally, the special medical officer may discharge the patient from the community care order at any time if he thinks it is no longer necessary.

There is scope within the law for variation of the conditions to be attached to a community care order.[82] The special medical officer may order a variation and notify the patient, the aftercare officer, and the sheriff of the proposal. In the event that the patient wishes to object to the variation, a hearing will be heard before the sheriff within seven days. In the absence of an objection, the sheriff will approve the variation without a hearing and the special medical officer will thereafter notify the patient, the Mental Welfare Commission, and the patient's aftercare officer. A new special aftercare officer may be appointed following a consultation process.

Appeals against Community Care Orders[83]

Any patient subject to a community care order may appeal to the sheriff for revocation of the order. The sheriff must revoke the order if

6.33

(1) he is satisfied that the patient does not require to be subject to a community care order with a view to ensuring he receives medical treatment and aftercare services, and

(2) he is satisfied that the patient does not require to be subject to such an order in the interest of his health or safety, or with the view to the protection of other persons.

The sheriff may otherwise affirm or vary the order. Where the sheriff revokes the community care order, he may order the revocation to have immediate effect or from a date not later than 28 days after his decision. It is the responsibility of the special medical officer to notify the patient's aftercare officer of any revocation or variation of the community care order.

In circumstances where the special medical officer believes after consulting various parties that the patient's mental health has deteriorated, he may re-admit the patient to hospital for some form of re-assessment. Whilst the patient is re-admitted to hospital, the community care order will continue to be effectual over him, but the conditions to which his treatment is subject shall not apply. On re-admission the patient will be examined by at least two doctors, one of whom must be a psychiatrist approved by the health board. If those doctors decide that the patient should be discharged the community care order and its conditions will be re-instated. In the event that the doctors decide that the patient should be re-admitted, the community care order ceases to have effect and the patient can be kept in hospital for up to 21 days. If no application for admission is made within seven days of the patient's return to hospital and the patient is not discharged, the community care order automatically lapses. Community care orders may be revoked either by the special medical officer or the Mental Welfare Commission.

---

[81] 1984 Act, s. 35C(5) and (6) as inserted by the Mental Health (Patients in the Community) Act 1995, s. 4.
[82] See, generally, 1984 Act, ss. 35D and 35E, as inserted by the Mental Health (Patients in the Community) Act 1995, s. 4.
[83] See, generally, 1984 Act, ss. 35F–35I, as inserted by the Mental Health (Patients in the Community) Act 1995, s. 4.

MENTAL HEALTH GUARDIANSHIP

6.34   As an alternative to detention or a community care order, there exists within the legislation a possibility of mental health guardianship.[84] The aim of this form of guardianship is to provide a level of supervision for those persons who need control and supervision under social care. A person may be received into guardianship, on the grounds that (a) he is suffering from a mental disorder of a nature or a degree which warrants his reception into guardianship, and (b) it is necessary and in the interests of the welfare of the patient that he should be so received.[85] Guardianship is used principally in three situations: first, to move people with dementia to residential care or nursing homes where they are unwilling or unable to consent to this themselves; secondly, to remove people with mental disorder from abusive or unsuitable living conditions; and thirdly, to provide a measure of supervision in the community for some people with a learning disability.[86] The person named as guardian on the guardianship application may be a local authority, a person chosen by that authority, or any other person accepted as suitable by the authority.[87] In practice, guardians are the social work department of the local authority or its chief social work officer. Guardianship has for some time proved to be unpopular and is often viewed as a last resort.[88]

Procedure for guardianship

6.35   Guardianship applications must be approved by the sheriff.[89] The application is founded on, and accompanied by, two medical recommendations and the recommendation of a mental health officer.[90] The medical recommendations must include a statement of the mental disorder from which the patient is suffering, this being mental illness or mental handicap or both. The mental health officer in his statement must offer the opinion that the patient is suffering from a mental disorder. Guardianship applications and orders are only applicable where the patient is over 16.[91]

A guardianship application may be made either by the nearest relative of the patient, or a mental health officer.[92] For applications from the nearest relative, it is necessary that the relative has personally seen the patient in the previous 14 days. The local authority may be required by the nearest relative to have a mental health officer visit the patient with a view to considering a guardianship application. Where the mental health officer proposes to make a guardianship application, he must interview the patient no later than 14 days prior to the making of the application, and take such steps as are reasonably practicable to inform the nearest relative of the patient of the proposed application and of their right to object. The accompanying medical recommendations must be given by medical practitioners who have personally examined the patient separately not more than five days apart, or together where no objection has been made. It is necessary for one of the medical recommendations to be a specialist psychiatrist.[93] It is is also necessary for the guardianship application to be submitted

84   See generally Richardson and McGregor, *Guardianship in Scotland* (1992).
85   1984 Act, s. 36.
86   See Patrick, Annotations in Mays (ed.), *Scottish Social Work Legislation*, para. H.051.3.
87   1984 Act, s. 37(2).
88   See Richardson and McGregor, *op. cit.* at pp 32–37; Weatherhead, "Why Isn't Guardianship More Popular in Scotland?" (1991) *Psychiatric Bulletin*, Vol. 15, No. 6.
89   1984 Act, s. 37(1).
90   *ibid.*, s. 37(3).
91   *ibid.*, s. 37(1).
92   *ibid.*, s. 38.
93   *ibid.*, s. 39(a) and (b).

to the sheriff no later than seven days after the last day on which the patient was examined.[94] In considering the application the sheriff may make such enquiries, or hear such persons, as he thinks fit and, if there is an objection from the nearest relative, he must hear him along with any witnesses he may wish to call.[95] Proceedings may be in private where the applicant or patient so desires, or the sheriff sees fit.[96]

Where a patient has been received into guardianship, the local authority must notify the **6.36** Mental Welfare Commission by serving a copy of the application and any recommendations relating to the person's reception within seven days of it taking place.[97] Where the sheriff has approved the guardianship application and the same has been forwarded to the local authority, the application can confer on the authority or any person named in the application, the following powers:

(a) power to require the patient to reside at a place specified by the authority or person named as guardian;

(b) power to require the patient to attend at places and times so specified for the purposes of medical treatment, occupation, education or training;

(c) power to require access to the patient to be given at any place where the patient is residing to any medical practitioner, mental health officer, or other persons so specified.[98]

The powers of guardianship are therefore fairly rigid. The guardian cannot detain a patient in a place against his wishes, nor is there any power conferred on the guardian to deal in any property of the patient.[99] Nor is it possible for the guardian to administer corporal punishment to the patient.[1] Where a person does administer corporal punishment he may be guilty of an offence and on conviction this must be reported by the court to the Mental Welfare Commission. The guardian cannot make medical decisions on behalf of the patient. In situations where there is a refusal to undertake medical treatment, it may be necessary for the court to apply for a tutor *dative* to be appointed.[2] The Scottish Law Commission are known to have suggested a new form of personal guardianship where guardians have limited but slightly more far-reaching power than those that currently exist under legislation. Under their model it is proposed that guardians would have powers to decide welfare matters including financial matters and also the powers to take a range of medical decisions.[3]

There are provisions in the 1984 Act for rectification of errors in guardianship applications and orders. Ordinarily, a defect in the medical recommendation may result in the guardianship application being discharged. It may, however, be possible to substitute a fresh medical recommendation which may be sufficient for the order to be confirmed when the sheriff is reviewing it.[4]

Where a patient who is subject to guardianship absconds without the leave of the guardian **6.37** from a place in which the patient is required by the guardian to reside, he may be taken into

---

[94] 1984 Act, s. 40(1), as amended by the Law Reform (Misc. Prov.) (Scotland) Act 1985, s. 51. See the Act of Sederunt (Mental Health Rules) 1996 (S.I. 1996 No. 2149).
[95] 1984 Act, s. 40(2).
[96] *ibid.*, s. 40(4).
[97] *ibid.*, s. 41(1).
[98] *ibid.*, s. 41(2).
[99] *ibid.*, s. 41(3).
[1] *ibid.*, s. 41(4).
[2] See para. 6.39.
[3] See S.L.C. Report No. 151, *Incapable Adults* (1995); see also below at para. 6.62 *et seq.*
[4] 1984 Act, s. 42(2).

custody and returned to that place by the guardian, or an officer on the staff of the local authority, or police officer, or any other person authorised in writing by the guardian or the local authority.[5] Notwithstanding, where a patient has been absent from his place of residence for a period in excess of six months, he cannot be returned to custody in this way. Nor is it possible to return him when the period of guardianship has expired.[6] It is, though, possible to transfer a patient who is subject to guardianship to the guardianship of another.[7] Any transfer of this nature must be notified to the Mental Welfare Commission within seven days of the date of transfer. Transfer of guardianship is only possible where the guardian himself consents and, in the absence of such consent, a fresh application must be made. It is possible for there to be transfer of guardianship where the guardian dies, or the guardian gives notice in writing to the local authority that he desires to relinquish the functions of guardian. In such circumstances, the guardianship vests in the local authority which has the power to transfer the patient into the guardianship of another.[8] Where the guardian proves to be unsuitable it may be necessary to make a fresh application to the sheriff to transfer the guardianship.

Guardianship orders last for a period of not more than six months beginning on the day on which the person is received into guardianship.[9] It is possible for the authority to renew a guardianship for a further period of six months and for succeeding periods of one year at a time.[10] It is essential that patients are examined by a responsible medical officer in the two-month period prior to the ending of the guardianship application.[11] The purpose of the examination is to assess whether they continue to require the benefits of guardianship and to report to the Mental Welfare Commission. In the event that the local authority decides to remove the guardianship, it must inform the nearest relative and the guardian.[12] Patients are able to appeal to the sheriff against a renewal decision.[13]

In the event that a person who is subject to a guardianship order is absent without leave and returns to custody within a week of the end of the guardianship, it is possible to extend the guardianship order with a view to examining the patient and deciding whether he should remain the object of guardianship.[14] Where a person has been absent without leave from guardianship and returns, or is returned, within 28 days of the initial absence, guardianship may be renewed as long as the grounds for guardianship are still valid.[15] Where a patient is absent for more than 28 days, the responsible medical officer is required to examine him and obtain a medical report from another medical officer no later than one week after their return. On receipt of such medical reports, the mental health officer can decide to extend the guardianship order for six months or a year. Following examination, if it appears that there are no grounds for continuation of the guardianship, the person will be discharged within seven days of his return to hospital.[16] Where the person who is the subject of a guardianship

---

[5] 1984 Act, s. 44(1).
[6] *ibid.*, s. 44(2), as substituted by the Mental Health (Patients in the Community) Act 1995, s. 5(5).
[7] *ibid.*, s. 45.
[8] *ibid.*, s. 46(1).
[9] *ibid.*, s. 47(1).
[10] *ibid.*, s. 47(2).
[11] *ibid.*, s. 47(3).
[12] *ibid.*, s. 47(5).
[13] 1984 Act, s. 47(6), as amended by the Mental Health (Patients in the Community) Act 1995, s. 5(6).
[14] 1984 Act, s. 48, as substituted (for former s. 48) by the Mental Health (Patients in the Community) Act 1995, s. 5(7).
[15] 1984 Act, s. 48A, as substituted (for former s. 48) by the Mental Health (Patients in the Community) Act 1995, s. 5(7).
[16] See 1984 Act, s. 48B, as substituted (for former s. 48) by the Mental Health (Patients in the Community) Act 1995, s. 5(7).

order is detained in custody in pursuance of any sentence or order passed by a court, including committal and remand, he is treated as if he were on unauthorised leave of absence from the first day of release from custody if the custodial sentence is less than six months.[17] In the event that the detention is for a period in excess of six months, the patient shall cease to be subject to the guardianship order.[18] It is possible that a person may be taken back into guardianship following the custody at any time within 28 days of the release.[19]

A person may be discharged from guardianship[20] by order of the Mental Welfare **6.38** Commission, or by order of a sheriff following an appeal. In addition to this the responsible medical officer may order the discharge of a patient where he is satisfied that he is not suffering from a mental disorder of a nature or degree which warrants him remaining under guardianship. The local authority, or the Mental Welfare Commission, may make an order for discharge where they are satisfied that it is not necessarily in the interests or welfare of the patient that he should remain under guardianship. In respect of appeals to the sheriff, the sheriff must order discharge where the patient is not at the time of the hearing suffering from mental disorder of a nature or degree which warrants his remaining under guardianship, or it is not in the interest of the welfare of the patient that he should remain under guardianship. It is possible for the nearest relative to also seek an order for discharge in respect of the patient. In the event that the sheriff grants an application for compulsory admission to hospital under the 1984 Act any guardianship order ceases to be applicable.

There are fairly complex rules in respect of who is to be deemed as the nearest relative.[21] In exceptional circumstances, the sheriff may appoint a person to act as the person's nearest relative.[22] Where there is no nearest relative, or it is not practical to find out who that person is (namely that the nearest person cannot act because of mental disorder or illness of their own, or the nearest relative is unwilling to continue to act), it is likely that the sheriff will exercise his powers to appoint a new nearest relative.

PROTECTION OF PROPERTY AND REGULATING THE FINANCIAL AFFAIRS OF MENTAL HEALTH PATIENTS

On attaining the age of 16 one attains autonomy over one's affairs.[23] This general proposition **6.39** is not automatically displaced when someone becomes mentally disabled but the law must make provision for those individuals so that another can assume the capacity to make decisions over their personal and financial affairs where that is necessary. It is fairly obvious that many people who have a mental disorder are often unable to deal with their own financial affairs permanently, or temporarily. It is to be hoped that when decision-making is transferred to another, the transferee will try to involve the mentally disabled person in any decisions.[24] In respect of non- financial matters it is possible to appoint either a **tutor dative**[25] or a **mental health guardian**.[26] A tutor dative can be appointed by the Court of Session to

---

[17]   1984 Act, s. 49(2).
[18]   *ibid.*, s. 49(1).
[19]   1984 Act, s. 49(2)(b), as amended by the Mental Health (Patients in the Community) Act 1995, s. 5(8).
[20]   On orders for discharge from guardianship, see generally 1984 Act, s. 50.
[21]   1984 Act, s. 53. See also Patrick's Annotations in Mays (ed.), *Scottish Social Work Legislation* at para. H.070.2 and also 1984 Act, ss. 54 and 55.
[22]   1984 Act, s. 56.
[23]   See para. 3.36.
[24]   Ward, *Power to Act* (1990) at p. 8.
[25]   For a full history to the tutor *dative* see Ward, *op. cit.*, pp. 12–16, Chaps V and VI.
[26]   Discussed above at paras 6.34–6.38; see also Richards and McGregor, *Guardianship in Scotland* (1992).

either have full powers or limited powers. There will often be more than one tutor dative.[27] The appointment of a tutor dative requires proof of the necessity of appointment and where an appointment is simply for the management of property a **curator *bonis*** should be appointed rather than a tutor dative.[28] However, where the purpose of the appointment is for the welfare and/or financial powers (including medical treatment) of the incapax an appointment of a tutor dative is appropriate.[29] Mental health guardians on the other hand, are appointed by the sheriff court and their powers are strictly limited.[30]

Appointing a curator *bonis*

6.40   There are approximately 400 curators *bonis* appointed each year. Any interested party may apply for the appointment of a curator *bonis* although, as noted earlier, local authorities must in some situations apply for the appointment of a curator *bonis*.[31] Applications must be supported by medical evidence. Appointment can be a relatively expensive procedure. Once appointed, curators have to prepare an inventory of the person's financial affairs and annual accounts which are supervised by the Accountant of Court in Edinburgh. The curator *bonis* is usually an accountant or a solicitor, who assumes all powers in respect of the patient's financial affairs. This has led to criticism that they are often "impersonal and insensitive".[32] The curator has no power when dealing with the welfare of the patient in respect of care and treatment.[33]

Under section 92 of the 1984 Act, if a local authority is satisfied that:

(a)   a person in their area is incapable, by reason of mental disorder, of adequately managing and administrating his property and affairs;

(b)   that a curator *bonis* ought to be appointed in respect of that person; and

(c)   that no arrangements have been made, or are being made to this end,

they may petition the court for the appointment of a curator *bonis*.[34] If the person is in hospital, or under a guardianship order, and the local authority is successful in having a curator *bonis* appointed, they should within 28 days advise the hospital managers. Given the expense involved in such appointments, it is suggested that only where patients have financial estate in excess of £20,000 are they to be recommended.[35]

There is also scope in the legislation for the Mental Welfare Commission to seek the appointment of a curator *bonis*. The appointment would be on the same grounds as if the local authority had sought the order.[36] It is more likely that the Mental Welfare Commission,

---

[27]   For a full discussion of the tutor *dative* see Ward, "Tutors to Adults: Developments", 1992 S.L.T. (News) 325; Ward, "Revival of Tutors Dative" 1987 S.L.T. (News) 69.
[28]   Ward, *Power to Act* (1990), Chap. X.
[29]   *Chapman, Petrs*, 1993 S.L.T. 955.
[30]   See para. 6.35.
[31]   See para. 6.03.
[32]   See McKay, *Whose Rights Are They Anyway*? (1991), p. 8.
[33]   *Cameron v. Carr* 1997 S.C.L.R. 1164, where a curator was held not to be entitled to authorise a blood test.
[34]   1984 Act, s. 92(1).
[35]   See the Mental Welfare Commission Annual Report 1992–1993, pp. 15–16.
[36]   1984 Act, s. 93.

prior to exercising their powers, will seek to convince the local authority that their intervention is appropriate.

Hospital managers[37]

Another possibility is that the hospital may take over the financial affairs of mentally   **6.41**
disabled patient where a doctor certifies that he is incapable of doing so. Managers of any
hospital may receive and hold money and valuables on behalf of any patient who is liable to
be detained in hospital, or who is receiving medical treatment for a mental disorder as a
patient within the hospital, where the medical officer in charge of this treatment has stated
that in his opinion that person is incapable by reason of his mental disorder of managing and
administrating his affairs. The hospital should issue receipts for any money or valuables
received. There are financial limits on the amount of money the hospital can receive and hold
without the consent of the Mental Welfare Commission. The current limit is £5,000. Where
the managers of the hospital hold money or valuables on behalf of the patient, they may
spend that money, or dispose of the valuables, for the benefit of the patient and in exercise
of powers conferred upon them. They should have regard to the sentimental value that any
article may have to the patient or would have but for his mental disorder. The hospital is not
allowed to receive or hold money or valuables in situations where another representative has
been appointed for the patient.[38] In the event that the hospital has made some expenditure
this should be accounted for to the representative. The power available to the hospital to
spend the patient's money and dispose of valuables for his benefit has been criticised as an
infraction of human rights on the basis that only one medical certificate is required.[39] It has
also been claimed that hospitals often allow the patient's money to accumulate or that they
spend money on things which would ordinarily be available on the NHS.[40]

Other appointees and *negotiorum gestio*

Two further options for the management of a mentally disabled person's financial affairs are   **6.42**
appointees to collect and manage social security benefits and those whose authority arises
under ***negotiorum gestio***.[41] In respect of the former the procedure is for an application to be
made to the Department of Social Security on a form. The appointee is entitled to uplift and
utilise the benefit money (and only the benefit money) on behalf of the mentally disabled
person. That person is personally liable for any errors he may make. Some care establishments lump the money together of all their residents.[42] *Negotiorum gestio* is a legal principle
applicable outside mental health law. It permits someone to act on behalf of another on an
assumption that person would consent were they able to do so.

In addition to these methods there is the possibility of two other general methods of
administering a person's financial affairs. These are by a **trust** or by **power of attorney**. The
creation of a trust fund permits the trustees to administer the finances of the mentally
disabled person. It requires the person to voluntarily transfer assets into the trust fund in
anticipation of some future problem. It will not be possible for an incapax to transfer funds

[37]   1984 Act, s. 94.
[38]   Curator *bonis*, judicial factor, tutor, committee, receiver or person having the powers of a receiver or
       guardian.
[39]   See Patrick, Annotations in Mays (ed.), *Scottish Social Work Legislation*, at para. H.110.2.
[40]   McKay, *Whose Rights Are They Anyway?* (1991) at p. 9.
[41]   Ward, *Power to Act* (1990), Chap. XI.
[42]   McKay, *op. cit.* at p. 8.

during the period of their incapacity. The power of attorney is a legal document drawn up by one person, appointing another to act on his or her behalf. The power of attorney can often be drawn very widely. Given the inability to predict the duration of the incapacity, many individuals will frame open-ended powers of attorney. The Law Society has counselled against wide drafting and open-ended powers of attorney and it is often the case that they will be for a fixed period of time. They are a method which requires forward planning as mental incapacity will preclude their formation and also once made, the withdrawal of the power of attorney.

The Scottish Law Commission in their report *Incapable Adults* have been very critical of the provision relative to management of the financial affairs of patients and have recommended wholesale reform.[43]

OFFENCES IN RESPECT OF MENTAL HEALTH PATIENTS

Ill-treatment and neglect

6.43 It is an offence for anyone who is an officer or a member of staff, who is employed in the hospital or nursing home, a manager of the hospital, or a person carrying on a nursing home, to (a) ill-treat or wilfully neglect a patient for the time being receiving treatment for mental disorder as an in-patient in hospital or a nursing home, or (b) ill-treat or wilfully neglect, on the premises of which the hospital or nursing home forms a part, a patient for the time being receiving treatment there as an out-patient.[44] It is also an offence for any individual to ill-treat or willfully neglect a patient who is the subject of a guardianship order in his custody or care.[45] In addition to all this, it is an offence for any individual to ill-treat, or wilfully neglect, a patient in respect of whom a community care order is for the time being in force.[46]

Sexual offences against mental health patients

6.44 There are also offences which seek to protect mentally handicapped females from predatory conduct. It is an offence for a man (including a man with learning disabilities) to have unlawful sexual intercourse with a woman who is protected by the provisions of the 1984 Act; for any person to procure or encourage any woman who is protected to have unlawful sexual intercourse; and for any owner or occupier of any premises or any person having or assisting in the management of control of premises to induce any woman who is protected to resort to or be upon such premises for the purpose of unlawful sexual intercourse with any man.[47] In one reported instance a sentence of six months was considered not excessive for an offence under section 106(1) where an assistant co-ordinator in a home for mentally defective people had an intimate relationship which spanned 13 months with a resident with a mental age of 12-13 years.[48] Following English statutory interpretation it would appear that "unlawful" sexual intercourse is sexual intercourse outwith marriage. It is thought that where a woman

---

43 See paras 4.33–4.41; see further, para. 6.62.
44 1984 Act, s. 105(1).
45 *ibid.*, s. 105(2).
46 1984 Act, s. 105(2)(a), as inserted by the Mental Health (Patients in the Community) Act 1995, s. 4(2) and Sched. 2, para. 6.
47 1984 Act, s. 106(1).
48 *Rhoden v. H.M. Advocate*, 1994 G.W.D. 23–1432.

has sufficient intelligence and understanding of relationships to genuinely make an informed choice to enter or continue a relationship it is unlikely that she would fall into the foregoing provisions whereby she required protection.[49] Whilst the need for protection is conceded there are those who are nevertheless critical of section 106 not least on the basis that the social work professional may be placed in an extremely invidious position. Enlightened views recognise that mentally disabled individuals often sexually mature in the same way that other young persons do. It may well be perfectly normal for the mentally disabled to develop into full sexual relationships. It certainly should not be for the rest of society to preclude this as a matter of course. Mentally disabled individuals may enlist the assistance of their social worker with a view to living together to further their relationship often against the wishes of their parents or relatives. The wording of section 106 is in this respect unhelpful. Hilary Patrick suggests that the provision could also inhibit the giving of sex education as this may be perceived as procuring or encouraging a woman to have unlawful sexual intercourse.[50] For all this, section 106 intends to address exploitative relationships and it is to be hoped that prosecutorial discretion will display common sense.[51] Males with learning disabilities are also protected from homosexual abuse.[52]

Further provisions in section 107 make it an offence for certain persons associated with the **6.45** care of mentally disordered people to have unlawful sexual intercourse with women who are mentally disordered. So, for example, it will be an offence for a man who is an officer on the staff, a manager of a hospital, a person otherwise employed in a hospital or nursing home, or a person who is carrying on a nursing home, to have unlawful sexual intercourse with a woman who is for the time being receiving treatment for mental disorder as an in-patient in the hospital or nursing home. Such a person is also committing a criminal offence where he has intercourse on the premises of which the hospital or nursing home forms part, with a woman who is for the time being receiving such treatment there as an out-patient. Furthermore, it will be an offence for a man to have unlawful sexual intercourse with a woman suffering from mental disorder who is subject to a guardianship order, or is otherwise in his custody or care or the care of a local authority, or is resident in a house that has been provided by the local authority. It would be a defence to such a charge for the man to prove that he did not know and had no reason to suspect that the person was suffering from a mental disorder. The foregoing offences also apply to homosexual sex and offer protection to male patients with mental disorders. The punishment for such offences on conviction on indictment is imprisonment not exceeding two years.

Absconding offences

Any person who induces, or knowingly assists, any other who is liable to be detained or **6.46** subject to a guardianship order to exempt themselves without leave, or to escape from legal custody is also guilty of an offence.[53] In addition to this, any person who knowingly harbours a patient who is absent without leave, or gives any assistance with intention to prevent or interfere with them being taken into custody and returned to hospital or other place, likewise

---

[49]   See Patrick, Annotations in Mays (ed.) *Scottish Social Work Legislation*, at para. H.122.3. See also Ward *The Power to Act*, and McKay, *Sex Laws and Red Tape* (1992).
[50]   See Patrick, *op. cit.* at para. H.122.4.
[51]   Ward, *Power to Act* (1990), Chap IX.
[52]   Criminal Law (Consolidation) Act 1995, s. 13(3).
[53]   1984 Act, s. 108(1).

is guilty of an offence.[54] Punishment on indictment can result in a person being jailed for up to two years.[55]

Refusing access to patients and premises

6.47   Any person who refuses to allow the inspection of any premises, or without reasonable cause refuses to allow the visiting, interviewing, or examination of the person by any authorised person or to allow access to a patient or any document or record pertaining thereto, or who otherwise obstructs persons in the exercise of their functions, shall commit an offence.[56] It is also an offence for someone to refuse to withdraw when asked to do so by someone who has a right to interview the patient in private.[57]

Correspondence[58]

6.48   There are provisions within the 1984 Act for the restriction of the receiving and delivering of mail by patients who are recognised as having a mental disorder. Letters addressed to Ministers of the Crown, M.P.'s, the Mental Welfare Commission, commissioners, the Ombudsman, various subsidiary Ombudsmen, a judge or a clerk, the Health Board, the local authority, managers of a hospital, a legally qualified person instructed to act as legal advisor, and the European Commission on Human Rights or the European Court of Human Rights, are excluded from these provisions. The managers of the hospital may open and inspect any postal packages (other than to those listed above) for determining whether it may be withheld. Where a postal packet is withheld by managers or hospital staff, the hospital must notify the Mental Welfare Commission of the date and the contents of the letter along with the name of the patient, the nature of the postal packets and the reason for withholding. The Mental Welfare Commission has the power to review any decision to withhold a postal package or anything contained in it.

MENTAL HEALTH AND CRIMINAL JUSTICE

6.49   There is a crucial relationship between mental health and criminal justice. Many of the offences known to Scots law require what is known as *mens rea*—the criminal mind. Where individuals with mental disability interact with the criminal justice system inevitably there requires to be a re-appraisal of the status and position of that person. Do they have the requisite mental capacity to commit the crime? Do they sufficiently understand the criminal justice process? Do they have sufficient mental capacity to instruct a defence? These questions and others are of crucial significance in how the criminal justice system deals with mentally disabled people. An assessment of the nature and extent of the mental incapacity of the individual is vitally important. Some mentally disabled persons will be immediately diverted from the criminal justice system into medical treatment; others will continue to be dealt with by it. For the sane, mental health might simply be a mitigating factor which affects

---

[54]   1984 Act, s. 108(2).
[55]   *ibid.*, s. 108(3).
[56]   1984 Act, s. 109(1), as amended by the Mental Health (Patients in the Community) Act 1995, s. 4(2) and Sched. 2, para. 7.
[57]   1984 Act, s. 109(2).
[58]   See generally 1984 Act, ss. 115–116.

sentence[59] and although the system generally attempts to preclude it, many mentally disordered people will still find their way into prison.[60] Sadly, for many mentally disordered persons in society, a court appearance may be the first time their needs become apparent.[61]

The pre-trial position

Where it appears to the prosecutor in any criminal proceedings that the person charged with the offence may be suffering from a mental disorder, it is his duty to bring that to the attention of the court.[62] It will always be a question of medical evidence whether the person is suffering from a "mental disorder"[63] and the prosecutor is likely to place before the court a medical report. Some such reports have attracted controversy by referring to the offence in what the defence may assert is a prejudicial way.[64] The judge and the prosecution are expected to ignore references to the offence in any report and it should not be founded upon in later proceedings. Where a court remands or commits for trial a person charged with any offence who appears to be suffering from a mental disorder, and they are satisfied that a suitable hospital is available, they may commit him to that hospital.[65] Even in circumstances where the trial is to be deserted *pro loco et tempore* (for the time being), the court may still consider that the accused is "charged with" the offence.[66] The committal to hospital must be supported by the opinion of a registered medical practitioner.[67] Where the accused is committed to hospital, and the responsible medical officer is satisfied that he is suffering from a mental disorder which warrants his detention in hospital,[68] the accused will be detained for the duration of the period he is remanded or committed unless he is liberated before that.[69] In effect, this means that the accused can only be committed for a maximum of 40 days on a summary offence and 110 days on an indictable offence.[70] Once the accused is examined by the responsible medical officer that officer must report his findings to the court.[71] Any detention in hospital must be taken account of in any final sentencing disposal.[72] If the medical officer finds that the accused is not suffering from a mental disorder of such a nature or degree as to warrant detention in hospital, the court may commit the person to prison or other institution, or deal with him in some other fashion according to law.[73] The court has the power to review any interim order made in the light of changed circumstances.[74]

6.50

---

[59] See *Wilson v. H.M.Advocate*, 1998 S.C.C.R. 437 where a first offender was sentenced to 12 months' imprisonment for producing cannabis, which was subsequently replaced by 18 months' probation.
[60] Fennel, "Diversion of Mentally Disordered Offenders from Custody", [1991] Crim.L.R. 333–348.
[61] Burney and Pearson, "Mentally Disordered Offenders: Finding a Focus for Diversion" (1995) *Howard Journal of Criminal Justice* 34(4) 291 at p. 309.
[62] Criminal Procedure (Scotland) Act 1995, s. 52(1).
[63] *Allan v. H.M.Advocate*, 1983 S.C.C.R. 183; *Jessop v. Robertson*, 1989 S.C.C.R. 600.
[64] See *Macdonald v. Munro*, 1996 S.C.C.R. 595; *Sloan v. Crowe* 1996 S.C.C.R. 200.
[65] Criminal Procedure (Scotland) Act 1995, s. 52(2).
[66] *Herron v. McCrimmon*, 1969 S.L.T. (Sh. Ct.) 37.
[67] Criminal Procedure (Scotland) Act 1995, s. 52(5).
[68] Under the 1984 Act, Pt V.
[69] Criminal Procedure (Scotland) Act 1995, s. 52(3).
[70] For time limits in the criminal justice system see para. 8.15.
[71] Criminal Procedure (Scotland) Act 1995, s. 52(4).
[72] Criminal Procedure (Scotland) Act 1995, s. 210, as amended by Crime and Punishment (Scotland) Act 1997, s. 12.
[73] Criminal Procedure (Scotland) Act 1995, s. 52(4).
[74] *ibid.*, s. 52(6).

Insanity in bar of trial

6.51 If the accused is insane[75] at the time of trial this will render him unfit to plead or instruct a defence.[76] Ordinarily, it will be the defence who bring this to the attention of the court as a special defence.[77] Although mental disorder is often difficult to detect and notwithstanding the problem of ignorance in the detection of mental disorder,[78] it will often be apparent before the trial that the accused is suffering from some form of mental disorder. At a preliminary investigative stage, the police may alert the prosecution to the dubious mental state of the accused.[79] Since 1990, when guidelines were issued to the police on the interviewing of mentally handicapped or mentally ill persons, such interviews take place in the presence of an "appropriate adult".[80] The role of an appropriate adult in police questioning is to be actively involved in advising the mentally disabled person and to facilitate communication with the police.[81] However, there is no statutory protection for the mentally disabled adult and one can find instances even where mental incapacity is apparent of evidence taken from that person still being admissible in court. For example, in *Higgins v. H.M.Advocate*[82] a statement made to the police by a person who suffered from delusions and who was suggestible was held admissible. It is also the case that the appearance of mental disorder will not preclude preliminary police activity such as the taking of a breath test.[83]

The defence will often see the accused before the case calls in court and the client's physical appearance, demeanour, or general inability to give instructions will often belie his mental state. The normal procedure is for the defence to contact the prosecution and invite them to instruct medical reports. Notwithstanding the undoubted role of the defence, it is also open to the prosecution, or the judge, to raise the issue. If the issue is raised, there will be an inquiry with medical evidence being led by two or more psychiatrists who have examined the accused. Usually, the local psychiatric hospital is contacted to provide the service of compiling reports. The judge will decide whether it is established that the accused is insane in bar of trial.[84] Not surprisingly, the medical evidence holds considerable sway.[85] In *McLachlan v. Brown*[86] the accused appeared on three separate summary complaints. A plea in bar of trial was taken in respect of each based on "mental disorder—accused handicapped". The accused was examined by two psychiatrists on behalf of the Crown and certified sane and fit to plead. The defence had a psychologist examine the accused who contended that he was unable to understand and deal properly with the legal process at every stage. It was held that pleas in bar of trial were to be dealt with under statute where the opinions of the medical practitioners were the determinants. Other professionals could form

---

[75] Insanity is given a fairly high test and amounts to a complete alienation of reason. Many serious criminals have been found fit to stand trial, *e.g.* Peter Sutcliffe, the so-called Yorkshire Ripper in England, and Mone and McCulloch who escaped from Carstairs State Mental Hospital in the mid-1970s, murdering three persons in the process: McCall-Smith and Sheldon, *Scots Criminal Law* (2nd ed. 1997), pp. 136ff.

[76] See Gordon, *Criminal Law* (2nd ed., 1978), paras 10–42 *et seq.*; Connelly, "Insanity and Unfitness To Plead", 1996 J.R. 206.

[77] See *e.g. Ross v. H.M.Advocate*, 1991 S.L.T. 564; *HMA v. Brown* (1907) 5 Adam 312.

[78] McKay, "Criminal Justice and Mentally Disabled People", 1992 SCOLAG 182.

[79] *Health, Social Work and Related Services for Mentally Disordered Offenders in Scotland*, Consulation Paper (1999), Scottish Office.

[80] See McKay, 1990 SCOLAG 134.

[81] See Foley, *Human Rights, Human Wrongs* (1995) at p. 233.

[82] *Higgins v. H.M.Advocate*, 1993 S.C.C.R. 542.

[83] See *Francis v. DPP* [1997] R.T.R. 113.

[84] *Stewart v. H.M.Advocate* (No.2), 1997 S.C.C.R. 457.

[85] *Health, Social Work and Related Services for Mentally Disordered Offenders in Scotland*, Consulation Paper (1999), Scottish Office.

[86] 1997 S.L.T. 1059.

part of the process perhaps giving evidence upon which the medical practitioners could comment. Where a person is found insane in bar of trial and recovers his insanity, he may stand trial subsequently.[87]

Insanity at the time of the offence

Where evidence comes before the court that the accused was insane[88] at the time of doing the act, or making the omission which constitutes the offence, he cannot be convicted on the basis that he was incapable of having the necessary criminal mind.[89] If an accused intends to found upon insanity at the time of the act or omission as a special defence, he must give the prosecutor notice before the calling of the first witness. Upon such notice being given, the prosecutor will seek to adjourn the case for inquiry.[90] On indictment proceedings the judge must direct the jury to find whether the accused was insane or not and, if so, to declare whether he is acquitted on account of his insanity.[91] In summary proceedings the judge will make a finding to the effect that the person is insane, acquit the accused and record that he was acquitted on the ground of his insanity.[92]

6.52

Temporary hospital order[93]

If the court is satisfied, on the evidence of two medical practitioners, that the person is insane and the trial cannot proceed, the court must:

6.53

(a) make a finding to that effect and give reasons;

(b) discharge the trial diet and organise an examination of the facts diet; and

(c) remand the person on bail or in custody, or if satisfied on the written or oral evidence of two medical practitioners that he is suffering from a mental disorder sufficient to warrant detention, they may make a temporary hospital order.

Before making a temporary hospital order, the court may adjourn a case to carry out an investigation of the accused's mental state. Where it appears to the court that the accused is in no fit state to be brought before the court to determine whether he is insane, if there is no objection from the accused, the court may decide to proceed with the case. The court who made the temporary hospital order may review it at any time, and may confirm, revoke, or vary the order.

Examination of facts

What is interesting about the current system is the ability to continue to examine the evidence in a case by way of an examination of facts procedure.[94] At the examination of facts, the court, on the basis of any evidence already given at the trial or further evidence, may

6.54

---

87   *H.M.Advocate v. Bickerstaff*, 1926 J.C. 65.
88   See McCall-Smith and Sheldon, *Scots Criminal Law* (2nd ed., 1997), pp. 136.
89   Criminal Procedure (Scotland) Act 1995, s. 54(6).
90   *ibid.*, s. 54(7).
91   *ibid.*, s. 54(6).
92   *ibid.*, s. 54(6)(b).
93   *ibid.*, s. 54(1), (3) and (4).
94   Recommended by the second *Thomson Report on Criminal Procedure* (Cmnd 6218 (1975)).

determine whether it is satisfied (a) beyond a reasonable doubt that the accused committed the act, or made the omission constituting the offence; and (b) on the balance of probabilities, that there are no grounds for acquitting him. If the court is not so satisfied it must acquit the person of the charge.[95] The examination of facts hearing may also make a finding that the person was at the time of the offence insane and that is the reason for his acquittal.[96] The examination of facts may proceed in the absence of the accused if it appears to the court that it is not practical or appropriate that the accused attend, and he raises no objection.[97] In practical terms, the examination of facts might not be wholly dislocated from the original trial proceedings especially where the issue of insanity arises in the course of the trial.[98] In situations where the accused recovers his sanity and subsequently stands trial for the same matter, any order made arising out of the examination of facts is negated.[99]

Disposals of the court after the examination of facts

6.55   A court has a number of disposals available to it after examination of the facts in summary and solemn proceedings, and where the accused is acquitted by reason of being insane at the time of commission of the act or the making of the omission. The court may impose:

(a)   a hospital order with or without a restriction;

(b)   a guardianship order;

(c)   a supervision and treatment order[1];

(d)   no order at all.[2]

Hospital orders and guardianship orders

6.56   Where a person is convicted of an offence in either the High Court or the sheriff court, the court may impose a hospital order or a guardianship order if the following conditions are satisfied:

(a)   the grounds set out in section 17(1) (the grounds for admission to hospital following mental disorder) of the 1984 Act are satisfied;

(b)   the court is of the opinion having regard to all the circumstances including the nature of the offence and the character and antecedents of the offender, and to other available methods of dealing with him, that the most suitable method of disposing of the case is by means of an order.[3]

Some offences will have a fixed sentence of imprisonment and in those cases an order will not be appropriate. Otherwise, the court must be satisfied on the basis of the oral or written evidence of two medical practitioners, one of whom must be a doctor at the hospital which is

---

[95]   1995 Act, s. 55(1) and (3).
[96]   *ibid.*, s. 55(4).
[97]   *ibid.*, s. 55(5).
[98]   See Patrick, Annotations in Mays (ed.), *Scottish Social Work Legislation*, para. H. 162.2.
[99]   1995 Act, s. 56(7).
[1]   See para. 8.57.
[2]   1995 Act, s. 57(2).
[3]   *ibid.*, s. 58(1).

to be specified in the order.[4] Where a person is charged on summary complaint with an act or omission and the court has the power of convicting, if it is satisfied that the accused did the act or made the omission, they may make the order without convicting him.[5] Moreover, in respect of such a person, the court cannot make a hospital order unless satisfied that the hospital can take the accused within seven days of the making of the order.[6] If the court wishes the hospital order to be effective in the state mental hospital it must be satisfied that the offender, on account of his dangerous, violent or criminal propensities, requires treatment under conditions of special security, and cannot suitably be cared for in a hospital other than a state hospital.[7]

A hospital order may also be subsequently imposed when it becomes apparent that the offender was suffering from a mental disorder at the time of the commission of the offence. In *Jackson v. H.M.Advocate*[8] the appellant had been sentenced in 1984 to life imprisonment for attempted murder and assault with intent to rape. In 1993, a doctor certified that he was no longer a danger to the public following treatment in 1989. The evidence of psychiatrists was that the offender was mentally ill at the time of the offence and that the mental illness was of such severity to warrant a hospital order. The life sentence was quashed and a hospital order substituted.[9]

A guardianship order should not be made unless after considering the evidence of a mental health officer it is deemed necessary in the interests of the welfare of the person that he be placed under guardianship. The local authority must also be willing to receive that person into guardianship.[10]

In making a hospital order or a guardianship order, it is necessary for the court to find that the patient is suffering from mental disorder, and accordingly both medical opinions must state that the patient is suffering from the same mental disorder, albeit they may state that he is suffering from any additional disorder.[11] In making a hospital order or guardianship order the court may not additionally impose imprisonment, a fine, probation or community service, but may impose anything else the court has the power to impose, for example a compensation order, disqualification or forfeiture.[12]

A court making a hospital order may give directions as it thinks fit for the conveyance of the patient to a place of safety and detention there pending admission within the seven days provided the authority is willing to accept the patient.[13]

Restriction order

It is possible for a court to impose a restriction order along with any hospital order where, **6.57** having regard to the nature of the offence with which the accused is charged, the antecedents of the person, and the risk that as a result of his mental disorder he would commit offences if set at large, it is thought necessary for the protection of the public from serious harm.[14]

[4] 1995 Act, ss. 58(1) and 61(1A), as amended by the Crime and Punishment (Scotland) Act 1997, s. 10(2).
[5] 1995 Act, s. 58(3).
[6] 1995 Act, s. 58(4), as amended by the Crime and Punishment (Scotland) Act 1997, s. 62 and Sched. 1, para. 21(6).
[7] 1995 Act, s. 58(5).
[8] 1998 S.C.C.R. 539.
[9] See also some English examples in *R v. Crozier* (1990) 12 Cr. App. R. 206; *R v. Fairhurst* [1996] 1 Cr. App. R. 242.
[10] 1995 Act, s. 58(6).
[11] *ibid.*, s. 58(7).
[12] *ibid.*, s. 58(8).
[13] 1995 Act, s. 58(9), as amended by the Crime and Punishment Act 1997, s. 62 and Sched. 1, para. 21(6).
[14] 1995 Act, s. 59(1).

Where the charge is one of murder the court must impose a hospital order and a restriction order without limit of time.[15] It is not possible to have a restriction order attached to a guardianship order.[16] Where a restriction order is made the patient will be hospitalised in the state mental hospital without limit of time. It is possible to seek a discharge of a restriction order under sections 64 and 65 of the 1984 Act. In the recent case of *R. v. Secretary of State for Scotland*[17] a patient who had been detained in the state mental hospital since he had committed culpable homicide in 1967 appealed for a discharge of his restriction order in terms of section 64(1) (a) of the 1984 Act. Section 64 states: (1) where an appeal to the sheriff is made by a restricted patient who is subject to a restriction order, the sheriff shall direct the absolute discharge of the patient if he is satisfied:

(a) that the patient is not, at the time of the hearing of the appeal, suffering from mental disorder of a nature and degree which makes it appropriate for him to be liable to be detained in a hospital for medical treatment; or

(b) that it is not necessary for the health and safety of the patient or for the protection of other persons that he should receive such treatment[18]; and (in either case)

(c) that it is not appropriate for the patient to remain liable to be recalled to hospital for further treatment.

It was established that the patient was suffering from an untreatable mental deficiency which manifested itself by abnormally aggressive, or seriously irresponsible behaviour. In determining the issue of liability for detention, Lord Justice-Clerk Cullen sitting in the Inner House of the Court of Session said that the issue fell to be determined by reference to section 17, that liability to detention was not to be equated with "treatability", and that because the patient's abnormality was not one which rendered him liable to detention in hospital for treatment he met the criteria set down in section 64(1) (a) and accordingly should be absolutely discharged. However, in the subsequent House of Lords ruling[19] where the Inner House judgment was overruled, it was held that the treatment of a patient was an inherent part of the appropriateness test in section 64(1) (a). In this case the treatability test was wide enough to cover treatment other than medication and psychiatric. The structure and controlled environment of the hospital resulted in improvement in Mr Reid's anger management and this could be part of the treatability test.[20]

Hospital direction

6.58 There has from time to time been concern expressed at the fact that many individuals suffering from a mental disorder are fit to stand trial.[21] Leaving such controversy aside, it is the law in Scotland that where a person is convicted on indictment in either the High Court, or in the sheriff court, of an offence punishable by imprisonment, the court may in addition

15   1995 Act, s. 57(3).
16   *ibid.*, s. 59(3).
17   1998 S.L.T. 162.
18   For an example of where release was refused on this ground, see *JB v. Secretary of State for Scotland*, 1989 S.C.L.R. 774.
19   1999 S.L.T. 279; see also *W v. Secretary of State*, 1998 S.L.T. 841.
20   Note the release of restricted patients is currently the subject of urgent proposals before the Scottish Parliament following the release of a Mr Ruddle under those provisions. See emergency amending legislation: Mental Health (Public Safety and Appeals (Scotland) Act 1999 (Sept. 1999).
21   See, *e.g.* Henham, "Dangerous Trends in the Sentencing of Mentally Abnormal Offenders", 1995 *Howard Journal of Criminal Justice*, vol. 34, No. 1, p. 10.

to any sentence of imprisonment impose a hospital direction which authorises the offender's admission and detention in hospital.[22] This permits a specialised disposal for those thought well enough to stand trial but nevertheless suffering from a mental disorder. It is a custodial disposal combined with hospitalisation for treatment. A hospital direction cannot be made in respect of a child. Before the hospital direction can be made, two medical practitioners must provide the court with oral or written evidence that the offender is suffering from a mental disorder and that the grounds of detention in section 17(1) of the Mental Health (Scotland) Act 1984 apply. The court must be satisfied that the hospital is prepared to take the offender within seven days of making the direction. A hospital direction will only specify the state mental hospital if the offender needs treatment under conditions of security, and he cannot suitably be cared for in any other hospital. Any court making a hospital direction may make additional directions as to the offender's conveyance to a place of safety pending admission. The court may not, however, make additional directions as to conveyance to a place of safety which is a residential establishment unless it is satisfied that the managers of the establishment are willing to receive the offender.

Interim hospital orders

Where a court is satisfied (on the written or oral evidence of two medical practitioners) **6.59** that:

(a) the offender is suffering from a mental disorder; and

(b) the mental disorder from which the offender is suffering is such that it may be appropriate for a hospital order to be made; and

(c) having regard to the circumstances the hospital may be the state mental hospital;

the court may, before making a hospital order or dealing with an offender in some other way, make an interim hospital order.[23] Again, the court must be satisfied that the hospital specified in the interim hospital order is able to take the person within seven days of making the order.[24] The court may make directions as to the offender's conveyance to a place of safety pending admission to hospital.[25]

Interim hospital orders will be in force for a period not exceeding 12 weeks and may be renewed for 28 days at a time where written or oral medical evidence support this, though subject to the fact that an interim hospital order cannot last longer than 12 months in total.[26] The interim hospital order ceases on the making of a hospital order, or when the court decides to deal with the offender in some other way. Interim hospital orders may be renewed without the offender being present in court as long as they are represented and that representative has had the opportunity of being heard.[27] Where the offender absconds from hospital while under an interim hospital order or while being conveyed there, he may be

---

[22] See generally 1995 Act, s. 59A, as inserted by the Crime and Punishment (Scotland) Act 1997, s. 6(1).

[23] 1995 Act, s. 53(1), as amended by the Crime and Punishment (Scotland) Act 1997, ss. 10(1), 62, Sched. 1, para. 21(5) and Sched. 3.

[24] 1995 Act, s. 53(3), as amended by the Crime and Punishment (Scotland) Act 1997, s. 62(1) and Sched. 1, para. 21(5).

[25] 1995 Act, s. 53(5), as amended by the Crime and Punishment (Scotland) Act 1997, s. 62(1) and Sched. 1, para. 21(5).

[26] 1995 Act, s. 53(6), as amended by the Crime and Punishment (Scotland) Act 1997, ss. 11, 62(1) and Sched. 1, para. 21(5).

[27] 1995 Act, s. 53(7).

arrested without warrant, and thereafter brought before the court. The court may terminate the interim hospital order and substitute some other competent disposal.[28] The interim hospital order does not in any way prejudice the court's power to remand for medical enquiry reports.[29] The real benefit of the order is its capacity to permit a thorough assessment of the offender's mental condition.

Appeals against orders and findings

6.60   Where a hospital order, interim hospital order (but not a renewal), guardianship order, restriction order or hospital direction is made by a court, the person affected has the right of appeal notwithstanding any other rights of appeal he may have in respect of the particular instance, such as conviction or sentence.[30] Prosecutors also have a right of appeal where it appears to them that the order, decision or direction was inappropriate, or on a point of law.[31]

A person may appeal to the High Court against any finding, or a refusal to find, that he is insane. There are specific time limits for the lodging of such appeals.[32] Following a recent amendment to the law, the prosecution now also have the right of appeal against a finding of insanity, or the refusal of such a finding, in bar of trial, a trial verdict of acquittal by reason of insanity, and against an acquittal after an examination of the facts.[33]

PROPOSALS FOR CHANGES TO MENTAL HEALTH LAW AND ITS APPLICATION

A new framework for Mental Health Services

6.61   In recent times, one of the major tasks undertaken by the Secretary of State for Scotland was to facilitate and implement *A New Framework for Mental Health Services in Scotland*.[34] The framework represented a response to the Scottish Affairs Committee's *Report on The Closure of Psychiatric Hospitals in Scotland* (1995). The purpose behind the framework is to foster an inter-agency approach to the planning, commissioning, and provision of integrated mental health services.[35] It does not create new policy, but seeks to invigorate the implementation of existing policy. In addition to the framework, the Secretary of State implemented a package of initiatives:

   (a) a mental health development fund of £3 million per annum for the three years 1998–2001, designed to give pump priming money for health boards to find new ways of working in partnership with other agencies for those with mental health problems; also the creation of the Scottish Development Centre for Mental Health Services to provide development assistance, advice and support for agencies in the field including research and training;

---

[28]   1995 Act, s. 53(8).
[29]   1995 Act, s. 53(10).
[30]   1995 Act, s. 60, as amended by the Crime and Punishment (Scotland) Act 1997, s. 6(2).
[31]   1995 Act, s. 60A, as inserted by the Crime and Punishment (Scotland) Act 1997, s. 22.
[32]   1995 Act, s. 62(1) and (2).
[33]   1995 Act, s. 63, as amended by the Crime and Punishment Act 1997, s. 62 and Sched. 1, para. 21.
[34]   Launched on Sept. 19, 1997.
[35]   SWSG Circular 30/97; on the issue of integration see Hodge and Howenstine, "Administrative Update: Organizational Development Strategies for Integrating Mental Health Services" (1997) *Community Mental Health Journal* 33(3) 175–187.

(b) local care partnerships to promote integrated health, housing and social care services;

(c) a guide to the new framework of mental health services;

(d) a guide to good practice on advocacy; and

(e) Scottish Needs Assessment Programme Reports to be made widely available to assist in the development of local mental health strategies.

The framework and associated measures are clearly designed to impact upon mental health provision and practice well into the next century.

The Incapable Adults Bill

The Scottish Law Commission *Report on Incapable Adults*[36] recommends significant changes **6.62** to the law relating to the looking after of mentally disabled persons' welfare, property, and financial affairs. The existing arrangements for appointment of representatives to look after the interests of the mentally disabled person and the limitations on those persons' powers have been heavily criticised.[37] The Scottish Law Commission have recommended that there be an integrated scheme whereby those appointed to look after the interests of mentally disabled people have both personal welfare and financial powers. In addition, the Law Commission foresaw a situation whereby individuals would plan ahead and make arrangements for possible future incapacity.[38] Any intervention must be for the benefit of the incapable adult and be the least restrictive to achieve that benefit.[39] Guardianship would be undertaken by relatives and friends rather than professionals, particularly where finances were modest or for matters of personal welfare.

Adrian Ward has said that what is required is:

"a modern statutory code governing all aspects of personal decision making and management of affairs by and for mentally disabled adults. In the meantime, practitioners will continue to test the limits of what can be achieved with the existing law and with existing procedures in order to meet the legitimate needs of mentally disabled people."[40]

Furthermore,

"The structure must be planned and built with care. Not only will it serve a very important function, but we and our descendants will probably have to live within it for a very long time ... We simply cannot afford to get it wrong. We cannot afford to omit anything or overlook anything. We must meet all present needs and any future predictable needs. We must try to give room to adapt to future needs which cannot exactly be predicted, without having to dismantle and rebuild."[41]

The draft Bill annexed to the Report of the Scottish Law Commission foresees the appointment of a Public Guardian who would approve hospitals and home carers acting in

[36] SLC No. 151 (1995).
[37] See Marshall, *Report on Incapable Adults* (S.L.C. No. 151) 1995 S.L.G. 169.
[38] SLC No. 151 (1995), para. 1.28; *Mentally Disabled Adults: Legal Arrangements for Managing their Welfare and Finances*, Discussion Paper No. 94 (1991); see *also Mentally Disordered and Vulnerable Adults: Public Authority Powers*, No. 96 (1993).
[39] SLC No. 151 (1995), para. 1.27.
[40] Ward, "Tutors to Adults: Developments", 1992 S.L.T. (News) 325 at p. 329.
[41] Ward, *Power to Act* (1990), pp. 172–173.

the financial affairs of patients. In addition, the Public Guardian would have investigatory powers and deal with complaints. The Public Guardian might also act in small estates where the cost of professional representation may be prohibitive.[42] The Bill also seeks to address the thorny issue of doctors dispensing medical treatment and to set down a system which will permit them to give or withhold treatment where it is in the interests of the patient. A mechanism for enlisting the approval of the Court of Session in problematic cases is envisaged. There will also be a role for sheriffs to intervene by way of an intervention order or a guardianship order to deal with specific problems in the patient's life. The Law Commission stated that this would provide an integrated system whereby personal welfare and financial issues could be dealt with in the same proceedings.[43] It is anticipated that the long-awaited Incapable Adults Bill will be implemented by the Scottish Parliament in the not too distant future.

A review of mental health law

6.63   The Scottish health minister announced on December 18, 1998 a review of mental health law in Scotland. A committee under the chairmanship of former Secretary of State for Scotland Bruce Millan is due to report in the summer of 2000. There is to be a separate review of serious violent and sexual offenders under Lord McLean also due to report in the year 2000.

[42]   SLC No. 151 (1995), para. 1.29.
[43]   SLC No. 151 (1995), para. 1.30.

Chapter 7

Community Care

Introduction

Background

Community care, in the simplest of terms it exists to offer combined support and services to people with health and social care needs who are living in their own homes, with a view to preserving and sustaining their position within the community.[1] The legislation which was introduced to enforce this policy was accompanied by a transfer of earmarked resources from the NHS to local authorities.[2] Social work departments were to become the custodians of various client-care groups and were to ensure that social care could be effectively provided and managed in their area. The community care remit is generally understood to embrace people who are elderly, physically or mentally disabled, or suffering in some manner from a limiting illness. This includes people suffering from AIDS and HIV.[3]

    The vision at the outset, which has subsisted until the present day, was of an enabling service whereby users could support themselves on a daily basis if an adequate range of services could be accessed by them. As a result, some people would be better off cared for in their own homes. Community care is essentially non-medical in nature as the object is principally one of social care. However, specific health needs are present in many of its users and where feasible they will receive medical treatment in the community setting, usually in their own homes.

    Community care was extant for a number of years before legislative reform was undertaken on the basis of a formal set of objectives. Since the 1970s it has met with some mixed reactions though has continued to provide a model for performance within social work

7.01

7.02

---

[1] For further reading on community care generally see Lewis and Glennerster, *Implementing the New Community Care* (1996, Oxford University Press); Scottish Affairs Committee *Implementation of Community Care in Scotland a 2nd Report* (1996/97, London, HMSO); Legg (ed.), *Care in the Community: Illusion or Reality?* (1997, Chichester, John Wiley & Sons); Baldwin, *Needs Assessment and Community Care: Clinical Practice and Policy-Making* (1997, Oxford, Butterworth-Heineman); Smith and Means, *Community Care: Policy and Practice* (1998, Basingstoke, Macmillan); Priestley, *Disability Politics and Community Care* (1998, London); Kingsley, *Modernising Community Care: An Action Plan* (1998, Edinburgh, HMSO).

[2] By virtue of s. 16A of the National Health Service (Scotland) Act 1978 health boards are empowered to transfer money to social work and housing departments, housing associations, Scottish Homes and independent voluntary non-profit making organisations providing housing or social care.

[3] The definition of "persons in need" under s. 94 of the Social Work (Scotland) Act 1968 ("1968 Act") is generally used to determine who is entitled to community care services.

practice.[4] In 1986 the Audit Commission Report *Making a Reality out of Community Care* stressed that the growing emphasis on residential and nursing home care was detracting severely from the development of services for people living in their own homes.[5] While there was confirmed support for care in the community, resources were conversely being directed at institutional care. The Report insisted that progress was only to be achieved by bringing services to people, not people to services.[6] It proved to be the impetus required for immediate action and in 1988 the Griffiths Report, *Community Care—An Agenda for Action*[7] and the Wagner Report, *Residential Care: A Positive Choice*, together formed a response to the reproach of the Audit Commission.[8] Griffiths' recommendations were to become the rudiments of the prospective White Paper *Caring for People—Community Care in the Next Decade and Beyond*,[9] which in turn formed the basis of the NHS and Community Care Bill published one week later. The substance of the Griffiths Report was that systems should be in place within social service and social work departments which could fully support community care and the assessment of community care needs. These components are now central to the present legislative provisions which regulate community care.

The objectives of the White Paper were laid down as follows[10]:

1.   To promote the development of domiciliary, day and respite services to enable people to live in their own homes wherever feasible and sensible.

2.   To ensure that service providers make practical support for carers a high priority.

3.   To make proper assessment of need and good case management the cornerstone of high quality care. Packages of care should then be designed in line with individual needs and preferences.

4.   To promote the development of a flourishing independent sector alongside good quality public services.

5.   To clarify the responsibilities of agencies and so make it easier to hold them to account for their performance.

6.   To secure better value for taxpayers' money by introducing a new funding structure for social care.

---

[4]   One initial concern was that community care had not developed beyond a "catch-all phrase" and thus had little to give it the intended effect (see HCSS, *Community Care* (1985)) though much of the more recent criticism has been based on the idea that community care is progressively becoming a "resource-led" exercise in the sense that arrangements are based around local authority budgets, often at the expense of prevailing individual needs. This is a point which the courts have sought to clarify but which continues to be much of an issue in social work generally. See paras 7.29–7.31 below on local authority resources.

[5]   The Report promised that community care would increase the quality of life for the thousands of people located in residential care and for the millions of Britain's carers. Despite these aspirations it seemed that progress was slow and funds with which to bridge the transition of responsibility from NHS to local social work departments limited. The response to community care across Britain had been mixed, with copious examples of both good and bad practice amongst local social work and social services departments: Audit Commission for Local Authorities in England and Wales, *Making a Reality of Community Care* (1986, London, HMSO), pp. 2–3.

[6]   *ibid.*, p. 10.

[7]   A Report to the Secretary of State for Social Services, Department of Health and Social Security (Griffiths Report) (London; HMSO).

[8]   The Report of the Independent Review of Residential Care (Wagner Report) (London, HMSO) was based principally on promoting good practice in residential care and was not concerned with promoting community care to the same extent as the report produced by Sir Roy Griffiths.

[9]   Department of Health, Cmnd. 849 (1989, London, HMSO).

[10]   Local authorities are told in guidance on community care to refine their arrangements in accordance with the principles of the White Paper: SWSG11/91, para. 22.2.

The NHS and Community Care Bill which followed aimed to transpose these objectives into a workable statutory framework. The legal structure which now forms the backbone of community care practice has emerged as the result of protracted and piecemeal efforts to realise a fairly tolerant set of objectives. Despite cries for statutory coherence the result has been a somewhat fragmented legal representation of community care rights. Alongside, an unrelenting string of government circulars have sought to translate the legal framework into more practical social work terms.

Statutory framework

The legislation ultimately regulates the operations of local government so as to ensure that community care clients can benefit from maximum levels of social welfare dispensed through their local authorities. Social work departments and often housing authorities are their primary source of assistance. Voluntary organisations are prompted by their own particular objectives and not by the law. **7.03**

The activities of local government are governed by legislative duties and powers. Where a local authority is under a duty to discharge its functions, it is impelled to do so and is not granted the liberty of exercising a discretion. A failure to observe such a term may render an authority in breach of its statutory obligations. A statutory empowerment, on the other hand, authorises or enables the local authority to act. It can exercise a discretion in doing so, and will make a decision based on the individual circumstances of the case in hand. There is more limited recourse against an authority which is lawfully exercising a discretion. The outcome of any legal action which is taken will rest upon the actual manner in which the decision was made, and not its legality as such.[11]

The legal provisions which are presently of interest to us are contained within a range of social work statutes. There may be a number of valid reasons for this. Firstly, "care" as we know it is multi-faceted and carries quite diverse objectives: support services seek to ensure that daily needs are met at home and in the wider community setting; housing services aim to meet physical disability and infirmity with the most suitable type of accommodation; residential and nursing care is designed for people with maximum care needs who cannot cope in their own homes, either alone or with domiciliary support. It would be impossible to confine these distinct elements of social work within an aggregate piece of legislation. Nevertheless, the need for one comprehensive Act has been highlighted by writers in the field.[12] Secondly, the area is a dynamic one which continually undergoes reform, often in the form of Private Members' Bills. Time and again the most critical of community care legislation has emerged from the parliamentary backbenches where the struggle for recognition can sometimes be most heartfelt.[13] And thirdly, the law has evolved in something of a piecemeal manner as new initiatives have come to fruition at irregular intervals. This alone makes a clear framework of the relevant provisions quite difficult to produce. It is for students simply to note that "community care law" is an umbrella term for an amalgam of social work statutes examined individually below.

The Social Work (Scotland) Act 1968 ("1968 Act") was largely responsible for the growth of a contemporary social work structure in Scotland. Section 12 placed an obligation for the **7.04**

---

[11] See Chap. 2.

[12] See *e.g.*, Clements, "Community Care—Towards a Workable Statute" (1997) Liverpool Law Review, Vol. 19 no. 2 pp. 181–191.

[13] Chronically Sick and Disabled Persons Act 1970 ("1970 Act"), the Disabled Persons (Services, Consultation and Representation) Act 1986 ("1986 Act") and the Carers (Recognition and Services) Act 1995 ("1995 Act") were each Private Members Bills in turn.

organisation and provision of "welfare services" with social work departments throughout Scotland, and fundamentally defined a client base, namely "persons in need", upon which all future activity in this field would eventually turn. The definition incorporates both disabled and elderly people, as well as those with mental health problems and long-term health problems.[14] The Act has undergone a number of critical revisions in the years since its implementation with the result that its original content has been substantially modified.[15] It is largely the 1968 Act which regulates community care, incorporating the amendments of the NHS and Community Care Act 1990.[16]

Almost immediately following the 1968 Act, the Chronically Sick and Disabled Persons Act 1970 ("1970 Act") placed a further duty on local authorities to make arrangements for the provision of the welfare services which had been identified in section 12 of the 1968 Act, once it was satisfied that a need for them existed within a given individual.[16a] This hinted at the need to undertake an assessment of needs but was not quite that specific. In addition, the 1970 Act produced a list of possible services which could be read alongside the more standard terms of section 12 and thus specifically guided service-users towards named facilities. Of course this was to apply in respect of people who were chronically sick or disabled and not those who were elderly or suffering from mental health problems.

The Disabled Persons (Services, Consultation and Representations) Act 1986 ("1986 Act") allowed disabled people, their carers or their representatives to actually request an assessment of need for the services outlined in section 2 of the 1970 Act.[17] As a result the local authority is bound to carry out an assessment, and to make the necessary arrangements thereafter. This Act was also the first evidence that carers of disabled people were valued in their role since local authorities were to undertake a carer's assessment where substantial amounts of care were being provided to a disabled person on a regular basis.[18]

7.05   Notwithstanding these fragmentary efforts to ensure comprehensive service provision, gaps in the law remained, as did the lack of co-ordinated planning. It was in light of these difficulties that the NHS and Community Care Act 1990 was introduced, undertaking to supplement Part II of the 1968 Act which relates to welfare services. Amongst other things it placed a duty on local authorities to assess the need for "community care services." This enhanced the duty of local authorities to secure the provision of welfare services under section 12. Furthermore, it applied to people who were elderly, disabled, or suffering from mental or physical health problems, and thus improved the position for those who were omitted by the provisions of the 1970 Act. Its primary goal was to increase both the range and amount of services which were available to people in their own homes.

More recent legislation has tried to extend this sort of recognition beyond the client to those directly and regularly involved with his or her welfare. The Carers (Recognition and Services) Act 1995 highlights the fundamental role which is played by carers and entitles them to an assessment of their own. It thereby amplifies the provisions of the 1986 Act which

---

[14]   1968 Act, s. 94.
[15]   For instance the NHS and Community Care Act 1990 ("1990 Act"), the Children (Scotland) Act 1995 which removed many of the provisions of the 1968 Act and placed them in a format specifically for children, the Local Government (Scotland) Act 1994 which gave effect to local government reorganisation, the Health and Social Services and Social Security Adjudications Act 1983, the 1995 Act and the Community Care (Direct Payments) Act 1996.
[16]   The 1968 Act repealed many of the provisions of the National Assistance Act 1948 which had represented the first recognition of the need to make welfare provision for people who were disabled or of pensionable age. Some of it still operates in England and it continues to co-ordinate the funding arrangements for residential care in Scotland.
[16a] 1970 Act, s. 2.
[17]   1986 Act, s. 4.
[18]   *ibid.*, s. 8.

relate to carers. In addition, the provisions of the Community Care (Direct Payments) Act 1996 authorise local authorities to make cash payments in lieu of community care services. Individuals will then purchase the services and facilities which they require.

Guidance and direction

This piecemeal growth in legislation has impelled a catalogue of government guidance and direction stretching back for a number of years on the practical operation of social work, and more specifically community care law. In terms of their social work duties under the 1968 Act, local authorities are required to perform their duties in accordance with guidance issued by the Secretary of State. To all intents and purposes this serves as a source of advice to local authorities on how to implement the rather vague terms of the legislation. Guidance is issued under section 5(1) of the 1968 Act.[19] However, while "policy" guidance issued under section 5(1) must be followed, "practice" guidance is an indication of good practice alone. Respectively, local authorities are told what to do and how to do it. It seems likely that a failure to observe guidance will render the body in question open to judicial review.

    An oversight of practice guidance might constitute grounds for setting the decision of the local authority aside.[20] A breach of policy guidance would appear to carry more certain ramifications for the offending authority. In *R. v. North Yorkshire County Council, ex p. Hargreaves*[21] the applicant sought judicial review of a decision by his local authority to offer respite care to his sister on the grounds that the arrangements did not accord with her particular wishes. The court referred in its judgment to policy guidance which expressly stated the need to allow the user to participate actively in the assessment and in making any subsequent choices regarding the care package.[22] Failure to adhere to this policy guidance gave the court grounds to set the decision aside.[23]

    In 1991 the Scottish Office issued *Community Care in Scotland: Assessment and Care Management* to prepare local authorities for their new and emerging duties under the 1990 Act.[24] This provides essential practice guidance on the conduct of all bodies involved in community care and stresses the lead role to be played by social work departments in deciding how assessment and care management are to operate.

    Quite distinctly, directions issued by the Secretary of State place an obligation on the local authority to fulfil a legal duty supplementary to that defined in statutory provisions and carry more weight than the government circulars referred to above. For instance, the Social Work (Scotland) Act 1968 (Choice of Accommodation) Directions 1993 retain a resident's right to choose his or her residential accommodation. This carries the same force as the provisions of the 1968 Act itself. Directions are enforceable under section 5(1A).

7.06

---

[19]   Guidance is sometimes referred to as quasi-legislation in the sense that it is designed to have a regulatory effect on the appropriate bodies, supplementary to the legislative provisions which ultimately govern them. An instance of such guidance, often referred to as a government circular, is *Community Care in Scotland: Assessment and Care Management*, SWSG11/91 which is heavily relied upon in community care.

[20]   In *R. v. Islington LBC, ex p. Rixon, The Times*, April 17, 1996 it was the opinion of the court that Parliament had intended local authorities to follow the path charted by the Secretary of State's guidance, with liberty to deviate arising only with good reason judged on admissible grounds by the authority itself. However, this does not confer a general freedom to take a substantially different course from that contained in the guidance unless cogent reasons exist for doing so.

[21]   *The Times*, Nov. 9, 1994.

[22]   *Community Care Into the Next Decade and Beyond: Policy Guidance* (1990), Dept of Health, paras 3.9, 3.16 and 3.25.

[23]   Though this decision was based on policy guidance issued in England and Wales it is likely that Scottish courts would follow the reasoning.

[24]   SWSG11/91.

COMMUNITY CARE SERVICES

7.07 At the core of community care is the provision of services which enable clients to remain in their own homes. The statutory provisions which govern this process are principally located within the 1968 Act.

Welfare services

7.08 Section 12 of the 1968 Act in a large sense forms the basis of social work operations in Scotland and seeks to specify the broad duty to provide social work services for adults. Similar obligations towards children are contained in the Children (Scotland) Act 1995.[25] The duty in respect of adults is to provide "advice, guidance and assistance" and in turn to secure the provision of facilities, including residential and other establishments.[26] However, in avoiding a definition of what may or may not constitute a "welfare service", the Act seemed to recognise the potentially broad nature of care and assistance which was required. In this sense, it undertook to encourage needs-led service provision. It is for each local authority to specify the support services available in its area. However, the 1968 Act does expressly recognise the need which exists for a number of services:

1. Domiciliary services

Section 14 obliges local authorities to make arrangements for persons in need to receive domestic assistance in their own homes. This includes homehelp and laundry facilities. Before amendment by the 1990 Act this section referred to homehelp specifically but has been broadened to incorporate

> "any services, being services provided in the home, which appear to the local authority to be necessary for the purpose of enabling a person to maintain as independent an existence as is practicable in his home."[27]

These provisions overlap with those contained in section 2 of the Chronically Sick and Disabled Persons Act 1970 to provide assistance in the home for chronically sick and disabled people.[28]

2. Care and aftercare

Under section 13B of the 1968 Act local authorities are authorised to make arrangements for the prevention of illness, and for both the care and aftercare of those suffering from illness. This is essentially a NHS function under section 37 of the National Health Service (Scotland) Act 1978, which places an onus on the Secretary of State to ensure that those arrangements are in place. However, local authorities are in a position to assist by virtue of this enabling section. The boundaries between NHS and social work responsibilities are quite often unclear, especially so in the region of community care where health and social care needs can easily seem to constitute the same thing. Guidance has sought to clarify the distinction and to

---

[25]   See para. 7.25 below.
[26]   See paras 7.37–7.41 for a fuller discussion of the law relating to residential and nursing establishments.
[27]   1990 Act, s. 66(1), Sched. 9, para. 10(6).
[28]   See para. 7.09 below.

predetermine the circumstances which will guarantee NHS intervention.[29] The Social Work (Provision of Social Work Services in the Scottish Health Service) (Scotland) Regulations 1991 seek to ensure that those receiving both NHS treatment and social work care benefit from collaboration between the relevant bodies.

3. Burial and cremation of the dead

Section 28 provides local authorities with a function towards people who have died while receiving their care or assistance, namely to bury or cremate the deceased in accordance with any religious persuasion. Local authorities are not responsible for subsidising the said arrangements though an application may be made to the Social Fund for assistance with funeral costs.[30] However, where it appears that no suitable arrangements have been or are being made for the disposal of a body, the local authority is compelled to intervene and to bury or cremate the deceased whether or not the individual was in receipt of its services.[31]

Services under the 1970 Act

These are services provided specifically for people who are chronically sick or disabled. Section 2 of the 1970 Act is quite specific regarding the types of service which are to be available in meeting the needs of applicants, and in this sense serves to augment the more general content of section 12 of the 1968 Act. The services available are as follows:

7.09

(a) practical assistance in the home;

(b) a radio, television, books or similar recreational facilities in the home;

(c) recreational facilities outside the home such as lectures, games and outings, and services which promote the use of educational facilities;

(d) assistance travelling to and from local authority services, or similar services run by other bodies;

(e) assistance arranging adaptation to the home in which a disabled person lives with a view to securing his greater safety, comfort or convenience[32];

(f) holidays;

(g) meals at home; and

(h) telephone and related equipment.

The scope for social work intervention is clearly quite broad. Nevertheless, guidance on the 1970 Act states that the local authority should not only look at the need for things expressly mentioned in section 2, but at all relevant needs. In other words, this is not intended to be an exhaustive list of options.[33]

---

[29] *NHS Responsibility for Continuing Health Care* (1996), MEL 22.
[30] See Chap. 9.
[31] National Assistance Act 1948, s. 50.
[32] See below for a full discussion on adaptations to the home.
[33] Dept of Health Circular 12/70, *The Chronically Sick and Disabled Persons Act 1970*, para. 7.

Community care services

7.10 The 1968 Act expanded the network of support services available to persons in need. Supplementary provisions have since developed the range of services so as to facilitate the assessment process and subsequent care management. The NHS and Community Care Act 1990 appended to the social work provisions contained at section 12 of the 1968 Act a new section 12A requiring local authorities to assess the needs of anyone thought to be in need of a "community care service", defined as any service which a local authority has a duty or power to provide or secure the provision of under Part II of the 1968 Act and sections 7, 8 and 11 of the Mental Health (Scotland) Act 1984.[34] This essentially incorporates all of the services examined above with the effect that they can be classed as community care services.

It is now well established through case law in England and Wales that community care services incorporate the services listed under section 2 of the 1970 Act and that in inserting a duty to assess the need for community care services Parliament had intended that the obligation apply equally to services under section 2.[35]

Voluntary and private bodies

7.11 When local authorities are obliged to make arrangements for service provision they are free to operate a tendering process whereby they purchase services and facilities from other bodies who may be in a better position to provide them. While the independent and voluntary sectors are encouraged to play an active role in service provision, contracting-out by local authorities has yet to be developed to its full potential. It seems that the services offered by the private sector are presently complementing rather than substituting those provided by local authorities.[36]

Voluntary organisations, "the sole or primary object of which is to promote social welfare", are often funded by local authorities.[37] The Secretary of State is further enabled by virtue of the same statutory discretion to make grants and loans to bodies or persons, including local and national charities, so that they can assist local authorities in exercising their social work functions under the 1968 Act. Supplementary to this provision is a discretion on local authorities to make arrangements with voluntary organisations for the provision of assistance in meeting their responsibilities under the Act.[38]

Information needs

7.12 The duty to inform potential clients of the services available was originally introduced by section 1(2) of the Chronically Sick and Disabled Persons Act 1970 which placed a general obligation on local authorities to distribute information on services available from the

---

[34] 1968 Act, s. 5A(4). Services for children are expressly excluded from the definition.

[35] *R. v. Kirklees MBC, ex p. Daykin*, Queen's Bench Division, November 26, 1996; *R. v. Gloucestershire C.C., ex p. Barry* [1997] 2 All E.R. 1 where Lord Clyde stated "What is significant is that s. 2(1) is clearly embodied in the whole of the community care regime, distinct only in its particular procedure and the importing of an express duty of performance once the local authority has been satisfied regarding the necessity to make the arrangements" at 18b.

[36] Social Work Research Findings No. 11, "The Range and Availability of Domiciliary Services in Scotland", (1998) The Scottish Office, Home Department, CRU. The study also noted that Scottish local authorities were more willing to contract with the voluntary rather than the private sector, entering into block and spot contracts respectively. The study suggested that the independent sector was being utilised in more of a specialist manner.

[37] 1968 Act, s. 10.

[38] *ibid.*, s. 4.

authority itself or from any other statutory or voluntary body.[39] Local authorities are now compelled by section 5A of the 1968 Act[40] to publish, and review at regular periods thereafter, a community care plan with which to advise client groups on the availability of community care services.[41] Services for children are not to be written into the plan since childrens' services are excluded from the definition of community care services.[42] A separate duty exists in respect of children under the Children (Scotland) Act 1995.[43] Local authorities should, however, give details of all services which they have a duty to secure under Part II of the 1968 Act, namely welfare services under section 12, homehelp and laundry facilities, residential accommodation, respite care, care and aftercare, and the services contained within section 2(1) of the Chronically Sick and Disabled Persons Act 1970. There should also be some reference to facilities provided under the Mental Health Act 1984. While section 5A is not overly specific about what is to be incorporated into the plan it does specify the need for local authorities to consult health boards, relevant voluntary organisations representing community care client groups, and housing providers. This is reiterated in guidance on Community Care Planning published in 1994 which strongly urges social work departments to produce their plans together with health boards, thereby allowing them to distribute one comprehensive plan and to keep confusion amongst potential service-users to a minimum.[44] Critically, it implored local authorities to produce plans which were both accessible and concise, and which targeted the appropriate groups and fully informed them of their various rights and options.

Directions produced since the 1990 Act under section 5(1A) specify that the volume and cost of local authority services and those purchased from the voluntary and private sectors should be detailed in the plans.[45] More recent directions have required that the comparative costs of residential care homes in the public and independent sectors are removed from community care plans when the budget is being set and made public.[46]

Complaints procedure

Each local authority is bound to implement and publish details of a complaints procedure,[47] **7.13** though more fundamentally perhaps service-users should be directly provided with details of the complaints procedure in place within their local authority.[48] The procedure should allow a person to make representations concerning the discharge of local authority functions under the 1968 Act.[49] For instance if an assessment has not been carried out, or if the outcome is substantially different from the expectations of the service-user, the authority may be at fault. The complaints procedure is intended to rectify anomalies in decision-making without involving the courts. The person making the complaint may be represented by somebody else, usually someone with an established interest in the welfare of the individual, for

[39]   DHSS 12/70, para. 5, suggested that those who might benefit by help, and their families, should know what help is available to them and that this is to be secured both by general publicity and by personal explanations.
[40]   Inserted by the NHS and Community Care Act 1990.
[41]   SWSG11/91 requires new plans to be produced every three years and reviewed on an annual basis. Scottish authorities were detained in their fulfilment of this duty by the reorganisation of local government in 1994.
[42]   1968 Act, s. 5A(4).
[43]   See para. 7.25 below.
[44]   SWSG 14/94, *Community Care Planning*, para. 6.
[45]   Community Care (Purchasing) Directions 1994.
[46]   Community Care Plans (Information) Directions 1997.
[47]   Social Work (Representations Procedure) (Scotland) Order 1990 (S.I. 1990 No. 2519), constituted under s. 5B of the 1968 Act.
[48]   SWSG 11/91, para. 5.10.
[49]   1968 Act, s. 5B(1).

instance a relative, friend or carer. Only those to whom a local authority owes a duty to provide services, and whose need or possible need has been noted by the authority, are allowed to access the complaints procedure.[50]

Assessment and Care Management

The duty to assess

7.14   Assessing need is the starting point of service provision, constituting both a key element in the wider context of community care and a prelude to longer-term care management. However, the statutory provisions which govern its operation are admittedly piecemeal. While section 12(1) of the Social Work (Scotland) Act 1968 engages local authorities in a duty to secure the provision of social work services, it does not actually compel the authority to make an assessment of the need for those services:

> "It shall be the duty of every local authority to promote social welfare by making available advice, guidance and assistance on such scale as may be appropriate for their area, and in that behalf to make arrangements and to provide or secure the provision of such facilities as they may consider suitable and adequate."

Section 2 of the Chronically Sick and Disabled Persons Act 1970 embellishes the more general terms of section 12(1) by requiring local authorities which are "satisfied" that services are necessary to meet needs, to make suitable arrangements in that pursuit. However, while bringing to the attention of social work departments the potential needs of one particular group of persons in need, the 1970 Act was not very specific regarding the obligation to actually assess that need. Though section 1 did place a duty on local authorities to establish a register of disabled people and to "inform themselves" of the need for arranging social welfare on their behalf, the Act did not in so many words direct councils to undertake assessments. In *R. v. Bexley LBC, ex p B.*[51] the court observed that section 2(1) may well give rise to an action for damages since Parliament had provided no statutory remedy for a breach. The reality was that few authorities were observing their obligations under the 1970 Act notwithstanding that a failure to comply with a request for an assessment was unlawful.[52]

The Disabled Persons (Services, Consultation and Representation) Act 1986 makes some provision for needs assessment and allows either a disabled person, his authorised representative or private carer to request the local authority to assess the need for any of the services contained in section 2 of the 1970 Act. In other words, they are entitled to request an assessment which the local authority must subsequently carry out.[53] These provisions were in part designed to remind local authorities of their obligation to make arrangements to meet

[50]   1968 Act, s. 5B(2).

[51]   July 31, 1995, unreported.

[52]   ss. 1 and 2 were brought to Scotland by the Chronically Sick and Disabled Persons (Scotland) Act 1972. The initial hesitation to incorporate them into Scots law arose from concerns that the provisions of the 1968 Act already placed a duty on local authorities to make suitable and adequate provision for an umbrella group of persons in need, a definition which expressly included chronically sick and disabled people. The client-group specific duties of the 1970 Act introduced a risk that service provision would become dependent on a statutory status. It was only following a recognition of the imprecise and largely indiscriminate nature of s. 12 that ss. 1 and 2 were extended to Scotland by virtue of the Chronically Sick and Disabled Persons (Scotland) Act 1972.

[53]   1986 Act, s. 4.

needs under the 1970 Act, and in part to provide a statutory impetus for the assessment of those needs.

However, under these arrangements the duty to carry out an assessment of needs was **7.15** triggered only by the disabled person himself, or by a carer or representative acting on his behalf. The scope existed for social work departments to rely largely on other people or bodies to be alerted to a social work need. In order to remedy this problem and so as to encourage pro-activity across Scottish local authorities, the NHS and Community Care Act 1990 ("1990 Act") introduced section 12A of the 1968 Act:

"(1) Subject to the provisions of this section, where it appears to a local authority that any person for whom they are under a duty or have a power to provide, or to secure the provision of, community care services may be in need of any such services, the authority

    (a) shall make an assessment of the needs of that person for those services, and

    (b) having regard to the results of that assessment, shall then decide whether the needs of that person call for the provision of any such services".

This firmly engages social work departments in a twofold duty to assess need for the wide range of community care services and to decide whether services are necessary to meet the assessed need. Though the provisions do not seem to impel authorities to make arrangements once they are satisfied that services are necessary, recent case law indicates that this will be an inclusive part of the obligation.[54]

It is essential to clarify during the assessment that a community care and not a NHS remit exists. There may be a need for advice and assistance alone, or for a further specialist assessment of specific needs. It may be possible to identify that an urgent need exists.[55] Community care services can be provided without an assessment where need is urgent though it should be undertaken as soon as possible thereafter.[56] Both the individual service-user and his carer if there is one should participate in the assessment, which it should be noted is not only concerned with the physical needs of the user, but with his mental and social functioning also.[57]

The provisions of the 1970 and 1986 Acts still carry force. If during a community care assessment a local authority becomes aware that the person is disabled, it is referred to the 1986 Act.[58] This in turn allows the disabled person to insist that an assessment is undertaken of their need for the specific services contained within section 2 of the 1970 Act. It is thereby a feature of section 12A that disabled people are guaranteed an assessment of their disability needs specifically, and of their community care needs more generally. While these are distinct statutory duties they will usually amalgamate to form one comprehensive assessment in practice. It should be noted however that there are two assessment duties encumbent on the local authority in respect of disabled people and

"potentially, any community care assessment of a disabled person which does not make it clear that the local authority specifically addressed the possible need for services under section 2 could be open to legal challenge."[59]

---

[54]   *R. v. Gloucestershire C.C., ex p. Barry* [1997] 2 All E.R. 1.
[55]   SWSG11/91, para. 5.2.
[56]   1968 Act, s. 12A(5) and (6).
[57]   SWSG11/91 para. 5.3.
[58]   1968 Act, s. 12A(4).
[59]   McKay, Annotations in Mays (ed.), *Scottish Social Work Legislation*, E.085.3.

Accordingly, for a person who is chronically sick or disabled, access to a comprehensive assessment of needs is secured through one of three statutory routes. First, a local authority may independently make an assessment of the need for the services offered in section 2 of the 1970 Act. Secondly, it may be compelled to do so by virtue of a request under the 1986 legislation. Thirdly, it may be required to assess community care needs under section 12A of the 1968 Act concurrently with an assessment of disability needs under section 2 of the 1970 Act. People with needs arising out of old age or mental disorder will only be entitled to a "community care assessment" under section 12A.

7.16   Other agencies may need to become involved in an assessment, for instance if housing adaptations are required, or if residential care is thought to be appropriate.[60] Any need for housing or health services which comes to the attention of the social work department in the course of an assessment must be conveyed to the relevant statutory body.[61] The guidance stresses the need for collaboration in community care between social work departments, housing authorities, health boards and the voluntary and private sectors.[62] This embellishes the duties placed on local authorities, health boards, NHS trusts, and education authorities to co-operate in securing health services[63] and to undertake joint planning and development of services for disabled and elderly people.[64] Integral to this latter duty is consultation with any voluntary organisations who are expected to make a substantial contribution to the process.

Needs differ in all users of community care. In 1991 the Department of Health issued a Manager's Guide which suggested that need should be equated with the requirements of individuals to enable them to achieve, maintain or restore an acceptable level of social independence or quality of life as defined by the particular care agency or authority.[65] Need has been found to include psychological as well as physical need,[66] and in considering the provision of respite care the preferences of a mentally disabled patient may well be relevant.[67] In *R. v. Haringey LBC, ex p. Norton*[68] the care plan of a multiple sclerosis sufferer was amended further to a reassessment by the local authority so as to meet his personal care needs though not his social, recreational and leisure needs. This had the effect of reducing his care from 24 to five hours a day. The court found that in differentiating between these various needs and rendering some subordinate to others, the local authority had failed to produce a multi-faceted care package in accordance with the legislative requirements. It was subsequently ordered to undertake a reassessment of needs.[69]

An assessment of need for services is not contingent upon those services being presently available from the local authority. This was confirmed by the court in *R. v. Royal County of Berkshire, ex p. Parke*.[70] The local authority supposed that the duty to assess need was conditional upon it being shown that it had in place existing arrangements to provide services of a kind which, in light of an assessment, the disabled person might need. The court clarified

---

[60]   1968 Act, s. 12A(2) and (3).
[61]   SWSG 11/91, para. 12.2.
[62]   *ibid.*, para. 1.4.
[63]   National Health Service (Scotland) Act 1978, s. 13.
[64]   National Health Service (Scotland) Act 1978, s. 13A, inserted by the 1986 Act.
[65]   Dept of Health, *Care Management and Assessment: Manager's Guide* (1991, London, HMSO)
[66]   *R. v. Avon C.C., ex p. Mahfood* [1994] 2 F.C.R. 259.
[67]   *R. v. North Yorkshire C.C., ex p. Hargreaves, The Times*, Nov. 9, 1994.
[68]   (1998) 1 C.C.L. Rep. 168.
[69]   In light of the difficulties which surround community care assessments there are calls to concentrate on the definition of need to facilitate and clarify the process. see Preston-Shoot, "Contesting the Contradictions: Needs, Resources and Community Care Decisions" (1996) *Journal of Social Welfare and Family Law*, Vol. 18, pp. 307–325 at p. 317.
[70]   (1997) 33 B.M.L.R. 71; (1998) 1 C.C.L. Rep. 141; *Times Law Reports*, Aug. 15, 1996.

that a duty to assess arises where the local authority has the legal power to provide community care services to an individual and there is no condition that the duty to assess is dependent upon the physical availability of resources.

The assessment is an opportunity for the local authority to form opinions on the type of **7.17** care which is required, not simply the type of services. What appears at first to be a demand for homehelp and laundry facilities, may in fact be a more profound need. Local authorities are alerted to the different levels of care which may reveal themselves during an assessment:

> "The aim should be to provide support for the person in their own home, which might include periods of respite care, or the provision of equipment or physical adaptations. A move to more suitable accommodation, possibly in the form of supported accommodation or sheltered housing, together with social support, might be an alternative possibility. Admission to residential care, nursing home care and long-stay hospital care should only be considered where the person's particular dependency needs require the kind of intensive care available in that kind of setting."[71]

Local authorities are urged that service provision should be needs-led and not service-led.[72] The disparity of need existing across community care client groups as a whole, as well as the vast potential for alternative service provision within different local authorities, is such that needs are best met through an assessment which does not seek to identify the client's suitability for a particular service or another. Instead the assessment should seek to identify what the disability, illness or condition demands and the social work authority should subsequently undertake to provide a service which meets that demand. Prior to the introduction of community care a social worker making an assessment may have referred to a menu of services which were available and the eligibility criteria for each.[73] Identifying a need requires the local authority first to establish the difficulties encountered by an individual. Unless the need is accurately detected from the start, the response may be entirely unsuited to the particular needs of the service-user and furthermore a waste of public resources.

Ordinary residence

In order to determine which local authority is responsible for the provision of services, **7.18** facilities or accommodation, the test is one of "ordinary residence". In other words, an individual who is ordinarily resident in a given local authority area shall be entitled to assistance by that local authority.[74] Scottish Office guidance issued in 1996 should be used where the area of ordinary residence is uncertain.[75] As a general note it states that "if there is a dispute about the ordinary residence of a person in need of services it should be debated after the care assessment and any provision of service".[76]

"Ordinary residence" is to be construed according to its ordinary and natural meaning subject to any interpretation which may be applied by the courts in individual circumstances.[77] The construction given by the courts to date indicates some quite varied notions of ordinary residence, including in one instance, voluntary settlement for a settled purpose as

71 SWSG 11/91, para. 6.2.
72 *ibid.*, para. 5.1.
73 See Morris, *Community Care: Working with Service Users* (1997) at p. 33.
74 1968 Act, s. 86(1).
75 SWSG 11/96, *Ordinary Residence.*
76 *ibid.*, para. 10.
77 See *Shah v. LBC of Barnet* [1983] 1 All E.R. 226 at 232j–233g.

part of the regular order of life for the time being.[78] An applicant may have permanent
residence outside the United Kingdom, or might fully expect that he will eventually live
outside the United Kingdom, and still have ordinary residence therein. Furthermore, a
settled purpose might be a specific and limited purpose such as education.[79] A person who has
been resident in a place with some degree of continuity and apart from accidental or
temporary absences may be deemed ordinarily resident there.[80] In *R. v. Waltham Forest
London Borough Council, ex p. Vale*[81] the individual concerned was an adult with severe
learning disabilities who was totally dependent on his parents. The court deemed that as his
position was comparable to that of a small child who is unable to choose where he or she lives,
his ordinary residence was the same as that of his parents. In some situations, there is a
likelihood that another person or body will act in *loco parentis*.[82] When undertaking to
establish ordinary residence, the local authority must discount certain periods of time,
primarily, periods spent in hospital care in another local authority area.[83]

Ordinary residence should not be confused with the term "local connection" which binds
housing authorities in homelessness issues.[84] If a local connection exists in another area, a
person may become the responsibility of the housing authority in that area. However, it will
not be possible for a social work authority which is being requested to assess and provide
services for a person with no or with unknown ordinary residence, to suggest that the possible
existence of a local connection elsewhere means the possible existence of ordinary residence
elsewhere also. If responsibility is actually transferred to another housing authority, the
social work department may only at that stage consider whether ordinary residence is in the
same area.[85]

Where a person requires health care, the health authority which holds responsibility for
him is the one in which he or she is "usually resident".[86] Again, this is distinct from ordinary
residence. Guidance suggests that if there is any doubt as to where a person is usually
resident, he is to be treated as usually resident at the address which he gives as being where
he usually resides. In a limited number of cases, usual residence will be in the area where the
person is found to be in need of treatment. It follows therefore that ordinary residence for the
purposes of social work care, and usual residence for the purposes of health care, will
normally run concurrently.[87]

Managing care

7.19   Guidance issued by the Scottish Office translates care management as a process of relating
services to needs. Duties under the community care provisions begin with identifying the
group of people who have community care needs, assessing the care needs of the individual,
planning and arranging for the delivery of care, monitoring the quality of care provided, and

---

[78]   *Shah v. LBC of Barnet, supra.*
[79]   *ibid.*
[80]   *Levene v. IRC* [1928] A.C. 217.
[81]   *The Times,* Feb. 25, 1985.
[82]   *R. v. Redbridge LBC, ex p. East Sussex C.C.* [1993] C.O.D. 256 Q.B.D.
[83]   1968 Act, s. 86(3).
[84]   See para. 7.62 below and Chapter 9 on housing.
[85]   SWSG 1/96, para. 18.
[86]   The NHS Scotland—the Function of the Health Boards (Scotland) Order 1991 establishes a process for health
        boards working out where a person is usually resident.
[87]   SWSG 1/96, para. 20.

undertaking systematic reviews of needs and the services provided to meet them. Care management is distinct from service provision and is concerned with obtaining for individuals the most suitable and cost-effective services from the statutory, voluntary and private sectors through the execution of the tasks identified above.[88]

A care plan should be comprised following an assessment of needs, outlining any services which are to be provided or arranged, by whom they are to be provided, and of course, by which means they are to be provided.[89] The plan will usually comprise a variety of services which will combine in meeting the assessed needs. The obligation to follow up a care assessment with a care plan is as onerous as the obligation to carry out an assessment. In *R. v. Sutton LBC, ex p. Tucker*[90] the local authority was compelled to provide a care plan for an individual who had been assessed as needing to be removed from hospital and placed in shared residential accommodation in the community. It was found that in failing to devise a plan the council was in breach of its obligations under the 1990 Act to provide services and furthermore was in breach of community care guidance. Similarly, in *R. v. Islington LBC, ex p. Rixon*[91] a care plan produced under the community care legislation failed to incorporate a set of overall objectives including the long-term obligations of both service-providers and carers. The plan was found to be defective.

Once an assessment has been carried out and a care plan has been devised it is imperative **7.20** that service provision for each individual is managed on an ongoing basis. In order that the care plan works to its full potential in meeting the care needs of the user, reviews should be undertaken at regular intervals and reassessments may also be required. Clearly it will be the intention of the local authority to ensure that the objectives identified in the original plan have been met. Thus further to a reassessment, services should be adjusted to meet any additional needs or to remove facilities which are no longer required. The review should therefore concern all those originally involved in planning services, namely the user, carers, social work departments, housing authorities and providers if a housing need formed or forms part of the overall need, and possibly representatives from the private and voluntary sectors.[92]

A care package cannot be altered without a reassessment of needs. In *R. v. Gloucestershire County Council, ex p. Mahfood*[93] the local authority had removed services from 1,000 clients without undertaking or offering to undertake individual reassessments. Its decision to withdraw assistance was deemed unlawful and it was compelled by the court to write to each individual service-user offering reassessments. Only 273 responded and in respect of the three remaining quarters, the local authority was of the opinion that no further duty existed since an offer for reassessment had been imparted. As a separate action Royal Association for Disability and Rehabilitation (RADAR) challenged this decision in the High Court[94] which found that an offer to reassess was inadequate. The duty to the service-users was one to actually undertake a reassessment. This did not depend upon a request by the service-user, but upon an appearance of need. Since the initial duty to assess the need for community care services was not triggered by a request or the acceptance of an offer, reassessment must be on the same terms.

---

[88]   SWSG 11/91 paras 4.1–4.5.
[89]   *ibid.*, para. 6.
[90]   (1998) 40 B.M.L.R. 137.
[91]   *The Times*, April 17, 1996.
[92]   SWSG 11/91 paras 19.1–19.3.
[93]   *The Times*, June 21, 1995.
[94]   *R. v. Gloucestershire C.C., ex p. RADAR* [1996] C.O.D. 253, Q.B.D.

Guidance suggests that local authorities appoint care managers with a remit to oversee both care management and service delivery within their area, specifically, to secure the most appropriate services within available resources. It is often more suitable to select an individual from the voluntary sector who has professional knowledge of specialist needs.[95]

Assessment of carers

7.21   The shift from institutional to community care has engendered more widespread reliance on the imperative contribution of "community carers"—for instance, people who care for their older relatives, husbands and wives suffering from illness, or their disabled children. In many instances, this is a burden which is assumed progressively over some time and which is not always voluntary. As more people are encouraged to remain within their own homes, someone new must shoulder the responsibilities previously accepted by professional carers in professional settings.

The 1990 Act does not contain any specific reference to the need of carers in the community to be assessed although the White Paper *Caring for People* alluded to the cardinal role played by them.[96] In fact, it was to be a "high priority" to provide them with practical support in light of a certain shift in emphasis from "care *in* the community" to "care *by* the community" throughout the 1980s.[97] The growing profile of carers is clearly demonstrated in guidance prepared for local authorities on the operation of respite care,[98] while the Carers' National Association exists to support the growing number of carers in Britain.[99] However, this type of informal care should be backed up with services which are appropriate to the needs of both the carer and the individual being cared for.[1]

7.22   In 1995 the Carers (Recognition and Services) Act undertook further amendment to the new section 12A of the 1968 Act, which as a result now incorporates in the assessment process an assessment of anyone providing a substantial amount of care on a regular basis to the service-user.[2] This seeks to ensure that carers are fully involved in planning service provision, and that their abilities to go on caring are ultimately reflected in the final care plan.[3] If they do not foresee their confirmed future involvement, the local authority may have to find alternative means of support for the service-user.[4]

Carers of disabled people were previously entitled to an assessment under the Disabled Persons (Services, Consultations and Representation) Act 1986 during an assessment of a disabled person.[5] The new provisions are essentially a mirror of those contained in the 1986 Act though they apply to all users of community care. Once an assessment of the carer has

---

[95]   SWSG 11/91, paras 4.3 and 4.4.
[96]   See para. 7.02.
[97]   See DHSS, *Growing Older* Cmnd.8173 (1981, London, HMSO).
[98]   *Respite Care*, SWSG 10/96.
[99]   Estimates in 1990 revealed 1.56 million carers in Britain caring for 20 hours or more per week: General Household Survey, Carers in 1990, OPCS.
[1]   For further reading on all aspects of caring see Bolton (ed.) "Carers Voices: A Report from Carer's Day 1996—A Conference for Informal Carers and Professional Workers in Aberdeen and Aberdeenshire" (1996).
[2]   1968 Act, s. 12A(3A), (3B), (3C).
[3]   Final decisions should involve both user and carer so that each is aware of how any services to be provided will assist the user, and conceivably how they will assist the carer: SWSG 11/91, paras 5.3 and 6.1.
[4]   For further reading see Clements, "The Rights Created by the New Carers Act" (1996) 93 L.S. Gaz. 21; Edis, "Community Care Update" (1997) E.C.A. Vol. 1, pp. 4–5; Bates and Clements, "New Rights for Carers" (1996) Legal Action (Feb.), pp. 19–21.
[5]   1968 Act, s. 8.

been carried out under section 12A the local authority is relieved of its duties under the 1986 Act.[6]

The provisions do not extend to an assessment of paid carers or those which are working for a voluntary organisation,[7] though guidance does indicate that a "carer" may include a person who may or may not be a relative, and who may or may not be living with the person for whom they are caring.[8] Furthermore, an assessment under the new Act is not automatic and must be requested by the carer.[9] If the carer wishes an assessment to be carried out, he can request an assessment of the service-user under section 4 of the 1986 Act during which the carer will also be assessed. If services and facilities are already in place, the carer's need to be assessed may be revealed during a reassessment of the care package.

To qualify for an assessment the carer should provide a substantial amount of care on a regular basis. This criteria was first introduced in the 1986 Act and has been reproduced in the Carers (Recognition and Services) Act 1995 ("1995 Act"). Policy guidance suggests that these terms are to be interpreted in their everyday sense.[10] In seeking to establish whether someone is providing the requisite level of care to demand an assessment, the authority will wish to look at the type of tasks in which the carer is involved, the amount of time spent with the service-user, the amount of supervision required by the user and whether the carer has made or intends to make a "continuing commitment" to the individual concerned.[11] It will not be appropriate to assume that the carer is able, let alone willing, to continue providing a substantial, regular amount of care and to reflect this policy, his age, circumstances, views and preferences should form part of the assessment.[12]

Other than organised periods of respite care,[13] carers will not receive services directly. In *R. v. Kirklees MBC, ex p. Good*[14] the applicants sought a housing improvement grant in respect of their own first floor flat on the grounds that they were caring for an elderly and disabled couple on the floor beneath them. The council refused to award the grant and legal proceedings were instigated. The court dismissed the application for a review of the decision. Not only was the Carers Act irrelevant to their claim since it does not confer a right to services *per se*, but so too was the 1970 Act under which they were alleging an entitlement to an adaptation of accommodation.[15] Their only entitlement was to an assessment of their ability to care which might subsequently be reflected in the services provided for the couple living downstairs. However, the carer often has community care needs of his own, especially where he is caring for a spouse in the same home. The local authority will then need to assess that person's own need for social work support as well as his ability to continue caring for the original service-user.

While the measures introduced by the 1995 Act are no doubt welcomed by both service-users and carers, the extent to which it can be fully implemented may be impeded by the

7.23

---

[6]   1968 Act, s. 12A(3C). It will be retained for assessments undertaken independently of s. 12A, namely under the 1970 and 1986 Acts concurrently.
[7]   1968 Act, s. 12A(3B).
[8]   *Carers (Recognition and Services) Act 1995 Policy and Practice Guidance*, SWSG 11/96, Policy Guidance, para. 5.
[9]   1968 Act, s. 12A(3A).
[10] SWSG 11/96, Policy Guidance, para. 8.
[11] SWSG 11/96, Practice Guidance, para. 6.
[12] SWSG 11/96, Policy Guidance, para. 19.
[13] See *R. v. North Yorkshire C.C., ex p. Hargreaves, The Times,* June 12, 1997.
[14] Q.B.D. CO/436/96.
[15] Under s. 2(1)(e) local authorities are under a duty to assist people who are chronically sick and disabled in making adaptations to their home with a view to ensuring their greater safety, comfort or convenience. This entitlement only arises when the applicant is chronically sick or disabled or living in the same house: see paras 7.53–7.56 below on house adaptation.

constraint of finite local government resources. Local authorities have already voiced their concerns as to the allocation of funds for the realisation of their obligations under the Act.[16] However, there are some promising signs. In *R. v. Secretary of State for the Home Department, ex p. Zackrocki*[17] the applicants sought judicial review of the decision of their local authority to refuse to extend their leave to remain in the United Kingdom so that they could continue providing care for an elderly relative. The court found in their favour noting that their plans were in accordance with the general policy of community care, the objective of which was to promote domiciliary support. Since the applicants were helping their relative to remain in her home, any action which resisted this was ultimately unreasonable.

Young carers

Carers of young children are provided with a corresponding right to an assessment under the terms of the Children (Scotland) Act 1995,[18] though it would seem that "young carers" are not actually covered by the terms of the 1995 Act.[19] Carers under the age of 16 in Scotland have no right to request an assessment under the 1995 Act in light of their incapacity to contract under the terms of the Age of Legal Capacity (Scotland) Act 1991. Children who have not yet reached the age of 16 are only entitled to enter into transactions which a person of their age and circumstance would normally enter into.[20] Contracting with a local authority in receiving an assessment is not included within this remit.[21]

Though both the health and education of children in these circumstances is liable to suffer, the Children (Scotland) Act 1995 is also silent on the entitlement of young carers to receive assessments. Policy guidance does suggest a number of options.[22] Legislative reform would remove the inconsistency in the law. Alternatively, a young carer might constitute a "child in need" under the terms of the Children (Scotland) Act 1995 and be embraced by the obligations of the local authority to promote upbringing and welfare.[23] Otherwise, the vested interest on the part of a parent or guardian might be able to substitute that of the child.[24]

Community care for disabled children

7.24   The endeavours of the Chronically Sick and Disabled Persons Act 1970 and the Disabled Persons (Services, Consultation and Recognition) Act 1986 to meet the needs of disabled people were inclusive of children though the anomalies in the statutory framework were

---

[16]   *In on the Act? Social Services' Experience of the First Year of the Carers Act*, October 1997. The survey revealed a large variance in the interpretation of "regular and substantial care" in local authorities across Scotland, while diversity in levels of support, allocated funds, procedure, and the ability of carers to access their rights under the Act were amongst other reported concerns. A large majority of local authorities in Scotland felt that there should be National Standards for carers' assessments and services: paras 12.7 and 12.13.

[17]   (1996) 32 B.M.L.R. 108; (1998) C.C.L. Rep. 374.

[18]   Children (Scotland) Act 1995, s. 24: see paras 7.24–7.26 below.

[19]   For a fuller discussion of the legislative provisions which might be used to protect "young carers" in England and Wales, see Dearden and Becker, "Protecting young carers: legislative tensions and opportunities in Britain" (1997) *Journal of Social Welfare and Family Law*, Vol. 19, pp. 123–138.

[20]   Age of Legal Capacity (Scotland) Act 1991, s. 2.

[21]   See Chap. 4 on caring for children.

[22]   SWSG 11/96, Policy Guidance, para. 11.

[23]   Children (Scotland) Act 1995, s. 22.

[24]   More recently, social services departments in England have been alerted to what is clearly a growing problem: Social Services Inspectorate (1995a) Letter to all Directors of Social Services, 28 April, and Social Services Inspectorate (1995b), *Young Carers: Something to Think About*, Papers presented at four SSI Workshops, May–July 1995, London: Dept of Health.

frustrating to younger as well as older segments of the population.[25] The Kilbrandon Report which in 1964 hinted at specialist support for families with disabled children in the community was one of two White Papers to inform the contents and structure of the Social Work (Scotland) Bill. There was some confidence that disabled children would at long last benefit from express legal recognition.[26] The general social work provisions contained in the Social Work (Scotland) Act 1968 were extended to children and their families though how much this impressed upon disabled children in their own right is unclear.

Children (Scotland) Act 1995

Amendments made to the 1968 Act in 1990 finally distinguished child from adult in the framework of community care,[27] though most fundamentally the Children (Scotland) Act 1995 made a specific commitment to disabled children. In the terms of the White Paper *Scotland's Children* which formed the basis of the Act, "services ha[d] continued to concentrate largely on the disability rather than on the child."[28] Until that time, statutory provisions for disabled adults had accommodated the needs of disabled children based principally on the assumption that disability was a stronger bond than childhood itself.[29] A training programme commissioned by the Scottish Office on the Children (Scotland) Act 1995 notes:

> "The provision of services to children with or affected by disability and their families is an area which has largely been neglected by social work as child care workers struggle to manage workloads dominated by child protection issues. The community care legislation has led to some improvement in service and it is to be hoped that the provisions of the Children (Scotland) Act 1995 can build on these so that the needs of these children and young people and their families are addressed in ways which are more comprehensive and responsive to individual circumstances than at present."

Chapter I of Part II of the Children (Scotland) Act 1995 seeks to provide support for children and their families and is underpinned, like the rest of the Act, with Kilbrandon's welfare principle.[30] Local authorities are under a general duty to promote the upbringing and welfare of "children in need" under section 22. This is comparable to the section 12 duty to "persons in need" under the 1968 Act. The term includes children who are disabled, or whose health will be further impaired without adequate service provision.[31] Services which seek to promote the welfare of children in need must therefore be designed in light of this specific client group and will need to take account of their special needs. More specifically, section 23A binds local authorities in a duty towards children affected by disability, to minimise the effects of the disability which features in their lives, and to provide them with an opportunity to lead lives which are as normal as possible.[32] "Disability" incorporates chronic sickness, disability or mental disorder.[33] Unlike previous legal provisions the 1995

7.25

[25] See paras 7.14–7.15 above.
[26] See Chap. 4.
[27] With the introduction of the 1995 Act, the general duties under s. 12 of the 1968 Act were amended to remove a social work duty towards children.
[28] *Scotland's Children: Proposals for Child Care Policy and Law*, Cm.2286, (1993, Edinburgh, HMSO), para. 4.1.
[29] *ibid.*
[30] See Chap. 4.
[31] Children (Scotland) Act 1995, s. 93(4)(a).
[32] *ibid.*, s. 23(1).
[33] *ibid.*, s. 23(2).

Act extends the duties of local authorities beyond disabled children alone, to children who are affected by the disability of a family member. This is designed to support the position of any child living with disability, whether or not the impairment is his own.[34]

The general provisions of section 22 of the 1995 Act do not incorporate a duty to make an assessment of needs, merely to provide a range and level of services appropriate to the child's needs. An assessment of a child is triggered only by a request from a parent or guardian.[35] These requirements are in some sense subordinate to the more forceful community care provisions which make up section 12A of the 1968 Act, whereby the duty to assess any adult who appears to have a need creates more impetus for independent social work intervention.[36] The services to which section 22 refers are those contained within Part II of the Children (Scotland) Act 1995, including the provision of accommodation under sections 25 and 26, the provision of daycare under section 27, aftercare under section 28, financial assistance towards education or training under section 30, and a profusion of supplementary assistance.

7.26   It is uncommon for disabled children to be confined to residential establishments except where the most severe of impairments render the parents simply unable to cope.[37] The White Paper for the 1995 Act was quite animated on this issue, stressing that childcare is almost always provided from somewhere within the confines of the family unit. Care for disabled children, it seems, is no exception:

> "The bulk of child care is given through families and not through outside services . . . Many families would prefer services to reinforce their caring capacity and not to offer a substitute for it."[38]

The provisions of the Carers (Recognition and Services) Act 1995 are written into the Children (Scotland) Act 1995 at section 24 so as not to overlook the imperative role which is played by those caring for disabled children. When undertaking an assessment of a child who is presently or foreseeably cared for to a substantial degree and on a regular basis by a carer, that carer may place a request with the local authority for an assessment of his or her capacity to continue, not as parent, guardian or family member, but specifically as carer.[39] In seeking to interpret the qualification of substantial and regular care, commentary on the Children (Scotland) Act suggests the targeting of the main, or one of the main, carers of the child, without whose care the development or welfare of the child would be prejudiced.[40] These provisions are framed in the same light as those which apply to adult service-users and it is their inclusive aim that the local authority will devise a care plan based on the need for services, which takes account of the carer's ability to continue caring. Furthermore, anyone providing care for children under a contract of employment or in the capacity of a volunteer for a voluntary organisation is excluded from an assessment of this nature.

The importance of planning for services is underpinned by the need for families to make informed choices regarding their children and their needs. In this pursuit the local authority is required to publish plans for childrens' services similar to those which are produced for

---

[34]   Guidance has been produced to advise local authorities on all aspects of the Children (Scotland) Act 1995, including procedures for the assessment of children affected by disabilities: *The Children (Scotland) Act 1995: Regulations and Guidance* (1997, Edinburgh, Scottish Office Stationery Office).

[35]   see Children (Scotland) Act 1995, s. 23(3).

[36]   See para. 7.15 above.

[37]   OPCS (1988) revealed that 33,000 disabled children were living in the community and 771 in communal establishments.

[38]   *Scotland's Children,* Proposals for Child Policy and Law, Cm.2286, para. 4.2.

[39]   Children (Scotland) Act 1995, s. 24(1).

[40]   See Norrie, *The Children (Scotland) Act 1995* (2nd ed.).

adults, and to review them periodically thereafter.[41] This duty extends to services referred to in Part II of the 1995 Act and section 5(1B) of the 1968 Act thereby incorporating services provided under the Chronically Sick and Disabled Persons Act 1970. In the production of care plans for children local authorities are required to consult wherever appropriate with bodies providing health services, voluntary organisations and housing bodies in the area.[42] In other words, plans should identify foremost the type of assistance which is actually available and the form in which it is to be received. Again, this largely duplicates the terms of the 1968 Act which relate to adult service-users. Supplementary to the duty to publish plans is a duty to publish information on services provided by the authority and other authorities, and where appropriate those supplied by voluntary organisations which, as always, play an active role in overall service provision.[43]

The 1995 Act as a whole is heavily flavoured with the notion of building and sustaining a fruitful partnership between local authority, parent and child, from which the child will ultimately benefit, a concept which applies to no less an extent in the provisions promoting the welfare of children affected by disability. It is essential as a result that services and facilities are effectively broadcast to those wishing to access them. The *Managers Handbook* impresses upon local authorities the need to stress, in the information they publish about available services, their wish to be proactive, the need for co-ordinated liaison and the inclusion of family members in that liaison.[44]

COMMUNITY CARE RESOURCES

Charging for services

Local authorities are under a duty to assess the need which exists for home care services and to make arrangements to provide them.[45] However there is no attending obligation on councils to support these arrangements through their own budgets.[46] Under section 87 of the 1968 Act local authorities may recover from the service-user the cost of services provided under the 1968 Act, sections of the Mental Health Act 1984, and Part II of the Children (Scotland) Act 1995.[47] These provisions do not apply to residential and nursing care.[48]

7.27

If a service-user has insufficient means to contribute towards the facilities he is receiving he cannot be compelled to pay.[49] "Means" has been recently construed as meaning the financial resources of a person: his assets, his sources of income, his liabilities and expenses.[50] However, it will be necessary for the service-user to persuade the authority that his means are

---

[41] Children (Scotland) Act 1995, s. 19.

[42] *ibid.*, s. 19(5)(e).

[43] *ibid.*, s. 20.

[44] *The Managers Handbook* (1996) at p. 81.

[45] 1968 Act, s. 12A and 1970 Act, s. 2.

[46] A study of local authorities providing domiciliary care services indicated that around half of social work providers charged for some or all of their services. see n. 35 above (SWRF 11 1998).

[47] Since a local authority is exercising its functions under the 1968 Act when it provides services under the 1970 Act it will also be possible for charges to be made for the provision of s. 2(1) services: *R. v. Powys C. C., ex p. Hambidge* (1998) 1 C.C.L. Rep. 182.

[48] See paras 7.42–7.47 below.

[49] 1968 Act, s. 87(1A).

[50] "If he has a reasonable asset, that is part of his means; he has the means to pay . . . If he has an asset which he can reasonably be expected to realise and which will (after taking into account any other relevant factor) enable him to pay, his means make it practicable for him to pay": *Avon C. C. v. Hooper* [1997] 1 All E.R. 532 at 537.

not adequate.[51] The local authority is not entitled to charge him more than it is reasonably practicable for him to pay.[52] In other words, it is sanctioned to make a "reasonable" charge. The legislation does not seek to qualify this term and it would seem that the final decision would rest heavily upon the circumstances of the individual case. In particular, each local authority will have regard to what has become its own common practice, and equally perhaps to its current budgetary constraints. Community care guidance does however suggest that the assessment of financial means should be undertaken subsequent to the assessment of need and decisions about service provision so that the final care package is not diluted to reflect the inability of the user to pay for his services.[53] In *Avon County Council v. Hooper*[54] a local authority sued the mother of a severely disabled child for the costs which it had incurred in maintaining her son. Although he had suffered some degree of brain damage at birth, she had been responsible for his physical and mental impairments in the period since. The court's construction of the English provisions, equivalent to those which apply in Scotland,[55] was that the local authority must have relevant and reasonable grounds for choosing to exercise what is essentially a discretionary power, and may waive that power in the absence of reasonableness. This would seem to be the only bar to enforcing a charge.

It will not be a sufficient or appropriate defence to claim that charges are being made some time after the services were provided. However,

> "if the claim is first made some time after the provision of the services, the local authority must be prepared to justify the reasonableness of making the claim notwithstanding the delay."[56]

Some useful comments were made in *Avon County Council v. Hooper* regarding the ability of the service-user to meet a delayed payment. The individual in question will be required to demonstrate that his means are insufficient only at the time when the charges are being made, not at the point of service provision some time earlier when he may well have had the necessary means to meet the charges. However, he will be entitled to use a defence of reduced means in limited circumstances, namely where the reduction in income came about as a result of the injury or disability with which the services are linked.

Inevitably, community care assessments, including those carried out under the 1970 Act, must be provided free of charge, as must advice or guidance regarding the availability of services. While the legislation is indiscriminate about which categories of persons in need might be more or less liable to charging, the guidance does go as far as to suggest that people who are terminally ill should be exempt, though this will of course depend upon the particular circumstances of the carer.[57]

Independent living fund

7.28   Recipients of a disability living allowance who are under threat of entry into residential care may be entitled to receive further financial assistance from the Independent Living (1993)

[51]   "It is for the recipient of the services to discharge this burden of persuasion. He must show that he has insufficient means"; *Avon C. C. v. Hooper, supra* at 537(CA)g.

[52]   1968 Act, s. 87(1A).

[53]   SWSG 11/91 para. 11.

[54]   [1997] 1 All E.R. 532.

[55]   Health and Social Services and Social Security Adjudication Act 1983, s. 17.

[56]   *Avon C. C. v. Hooper, supra* at 537d–f.

[57]   SWSG 11/91, *Community Care in Scotland: Assessment and Care Management*.

Fund.[58] Assistance is available only further to a local authority community care contribution and accordingly the Fund operates in partnership with local authorities, administering funds to disabled people understood to require some degree of domestic or personal assistance. Once the local authority has provided services or an equivalent cash sum of up to £200 per week, the 1993 Fund may be required to supplement that initial allocation to a total of £500. The applicant can receive no more than £300 from the 1993 Fund. If need is assessed as exceeding a weekly total of £500 the trust withdraws from negotiations and the local authority must meet the calculated sum of the care package regardless of its total. This removes any possibility of an assessed need being overlooked. To qualify for an award, the applicant must be aged between 16 and 66. Discrepancies between the income levels of disabled and able-bodied people were found to be more prevalent amongst people below pensionable age.[59]

In a move to target those under the greatest financial pressure the applicant must be in receipt of the highest rate of a disability living allowance, live alone or with people who cannot fully meet their care needs, and be at risk of entering residential care, while having savings which total less than £8,000. Assessment is undertaken by the local social work authority and a social worker from the Fund. The aim is to reach a settlement in conjunction with the applicant. Guidance issued in 1993 details the process involved in making an award.[60]

Local authority resources

The community care arrangements introduced by the NHS and Community Care Act 1990 placed an increasing emphasis on service provision in the home, and in the period since, resources have become a difficult and sensitive issue. Individual service-users are seldom in a position to pay for home care services in full and must rely quite heavily on their local authority to meet their costs.
7.29

Both the 1968 and 1970 Acts are silent on the role which resources are to play in local authority decision-making. As a starting point however, guidance on community care suggests that resources will be relevant at some stage during the proceedings, probably when services are being agreed upon. Local authorities are advised that in drawing up a care plan, the availability of resources and services for meeting needs will have to be taken into account.[61] Furthermore, in deciding what packages of care should be provided, account should be taken of the costs of service options and budgeting information.[62] A circular published in 1970 stated that "criteria of need are matters for the authorities to determine in light of resources."[63] What appears to be an established principle is reinforced in policy guidance issued on the 1990 Act, and is seemingly entrenched in social work law for the time being:

"local authorities will also have a responsibility to meet needs within the resources available and this will sometimes involve difficult decisions where it will be necessary to

---

58 The 1993 Fund was introduced to replace the Independent Living Fund which operated prior to the community care arrangements. The Independent Living (Extension) Fund manages all applications processed at the time the ILF was wound up while the 1993 Fund handles all new applications.
59 *Hansard*, H.C., Vol. 221, col. 40.
60 *Independent Living Arrangements from April 1993: Replacement of the Independent Living Fund*, SWSG 7/93.
61 SWSG 11/91, para. 6.1.
62 *ibid.*, para. 6.3.
63 DHSS 12/70, para. 7.

strike a balance between meeting the needs identified within available resources and meeting the care preferences of the individual."[64]

A series of decisions emerging from the English courts have since sought to dispel the ambiguity, and in this pursuit have provided firm guidance to the Scottish courts for future challenges to local authority spending. In *R. v. Avon County Council, ex p. M*[65] the strong wishes of a service-user to be accommodated in a particular residential care home were upheld by the court notwithstanding the resulting increase in cost incurred by the local authority. The applicant's psychological needs were such as to justify provision over and above services which the council felt would meet his basic needs. This did seem to be a positive result for service-users generally. However, indications that this was not to be a decision upon which future considerations would be based emerged shortly after. Recent case law suggests that a lack of resources will be a reliable defence when local government budgets fall short in meeting the demands of service-users. The particular stage at which resources might legitimately be taken into consideration, however, is something which requires a closer look.

7.30 Under the terms of the 1970 Act the local authority is required to decide first whether services are necessary to meet need, and secondly to make the necessary arrangements. Quite distinctly, under section 12A of the 1968 Act the local authority is required first of all to assess needs, and secondly to decide whether those needs call for the provision of services. In this latter instance there is no absolute duty that identified needs must be met and it is this omission which has caused judicial adversity and growing concern amongst service-users, their carers and their representatives.

In *R. v. Gloucestershire County Council, ex p. Mahfood*,[66] home care provision was removed from over 1,000 disabled service-users without a reassessment of their needs. Following a review of the decision, the High Court found that local authorities were entitled to take their resources into account at the stage of assessing a person's need for community care services under the 1990 Act, and when deciding whether it was necessary to make arrangements to meet the assessed needs under section 2 of the 1970 Act. However, once the authority had deemed it necessary to make arrangements to meet the assessed needs, it would be under an absolute duty to do so and could not claim that insufficient resources existed to meet what it had confirmed to be a need for services. In other words, in deciding *how* services were to be provided there could be no reference to inadequate funds, though in deciding *whether* services were necessary, resources were relevant.

R. v. London Borough of Islington, ex p. McMillan, was considered alongside *Mahfood*. In this instance, homehelp services had been removed from the applicant. It was the opinion of the court that the council had properly carried out a balancing exercise, considering on the one hand the comparative needs of disabled people in its area, and available resources on the other hand. If home care assistance was not available while the carer was on leave, an interruption to services would be legitimate. In these particular circumstances the needs of the user were not such that a disruption to service provision would be considered too harmful.

The court once more supported this inclination in *R. v. Lancashire County Council, ex p. Ingham and Whalley*[67] where the user in question required full-time home support so as to

---

[64] SWSG 11/91, para. 3.25.
[65] [1994] 2 F.L.R. 259.
[66] *The Times*, June 21, 1995, QBD. This was a joint action with *Barry, Grinham, Dartnell* and *McMillan*. *McMillan* and *Barry* are each considered below.
[67] [1995] CO/774/95.

avoid an admission to institutional care. Following a reassessment by the local authority domiciliary care was removed and the service-user was allocated a place in a residential care home. The court found that the local authority was fully entitled to take its resources into account both when assessing need and when subsequently deciding whether services were necessary in order to meet that need. Resources were relevant because of the comparative needs of other service-users in the area to whom an equivalent duty was owed. Residential care was clearly a cheaper option than home care support.

Gloucestershire

In *R. v. Gloucestershire County Council, ex p. Barry*[68] Barry was a service-user whose   **7.31**
cleaning provision had been withdrawn and laundry services reduced on financial grounds. His application for judicial review was part of the multiple action considered at paragraph 7.30. He appealed the decision to the Court of Appeal where it was overturned. Resources were deemed to be neither relevant at the point of assessing need, nor in deciding *whether* services were necessary in order to meet those needs. However, they might be a relevant factor in deciding *how* to meet need.[69]

The House of Lords proceeded to overturn the decision of the Court of Appeal and restore the original order of the High Court, confirming that resources might be a relevant consideration only at the point of deciding *whether* to make arrangements to meet a need and not at any time thereafter, including decisions as to *how* that need will be met.[70] As a consequence the services which are to be made available under section 2 of the 1970 Act will reflect the resources available to a given authority at a given point in time. Determining whether arrangements are necessary to meet a need, or simply desired, requires the application of criteria which the local authority must formulate and uniformly apply in all subsequent cases requiring an assessment of need.[71]

Specifically, the degree of necessity will be ascertained by matching the severity of the particular condition—the nature and extent of the disability and the manner in which and extent to which quality of life would be improved by the provision of a particular service—against the availability of resources. The more limited the resources, the greater the need must be in order to make the resulting expenditure a necessity. Lord Clyde drew a parallel between this process and the daily domestic experience:

"If my resources are limited I have to need the thing very badly before I am satisfied that it is necessary to purchase it . . . It is not necessary to hold that cost and resources are always an element in determining necessity. It is enough for the purposes of the present case to

---

68   [1996] 4 All E.R. 421.

69   For a fuller discussion of the potential implications of the initial Court of Appeal decision, see Guthrie, "The Significance of Resources in Community Care Assessments", 1997 S.L.P.Q. Vol. 2, no.2, pp. 149–154; Schwehr, "The Legal Relevance of Resources—or a Lack of Resources—in Community Care", 1995 *Journal of Social Welfare and Family Law*, Vol.17, no. 2, pp. 179–198; and Cragg, "The Court of Appeal gets to the Heart of the Matter" (1996) SCOLAG, Vol. 245, pp. 121–123. Also see *R. v. Essex C. C., ex p. Bucke* [1997] C.O.D. 66, where resources were held to be relevant at the point of deciding how to meet need.

70   *R. v. Gloucestershire C. C., ex p. Barry* [1997] 2 All E.R. 1.

71   However it is disputed that "operating blanket provision policies in community care services would breach the duty to assess an individual's need for services. It would fetter discretion by failing to consider all the issues relevant to an individual case, thereby failing to consider the possibility that this case may require departure from agreed eligibility criteria" Preston-Shoot, M. "Contesting the Contradictions: Needs, Resources and Community Care Decisions", 1996 *Journal of Social Welfare and Family Law*, Vol. 18, pp. 307–325 at p. 313.

recognise that they may be a proper consideration. I have not been persuaded that they must always and necessarily be excluded from consideration".[72]

It was not the majority opinion of the House of Lords, therefore, that Parliament had intended the extensive list of services contained in section 2(1) be provided regardless of the cost involved.[73] It is now entirely possible as a result that in deciding whether arrangements are necessary to meet needs, resources will be a principal determinant. As a consequence, an unmet need may be lawful in light of the criteria developed by local authorities to determine whether services are a necessity. However, in taking this to its logical conclusion, "whereby the necessity is measured by the appropriate criteria, what is necessary to be met will in fact be met and in the strict sense of the words no unmet need will exist."[74] Effectively, real need could be hidden under the guise of predetermined eligibility criteria.[75] The decision essentially creates a Scottish precedent in so far as the provisions of the 1970 Act apply uniformly across Britain.

This ruling would appear to be partially consistent with guidance on both the 1970 and 1990 Acts indicating that resources cannot always be overlooked. However, there is legitimate fear that it is retrogressive to notions of community care[76] and furthermore that resources may not be a relevant factor to local authorities making decisions outside of community care, for instance in relation to childcare and education.[77] Despite efforts to reverse the decision,[78] the Court of Appeal in England has already sought to apply the *Gloucestershire* precedent.[79] In summary the effect of the decision is that while local authorities are bound by a statutory duty of some significance, they are not equally bound to enforce it if they cannot meet the costs of doing so.[80]

Financial assistance

7.32   Local authorities are entitled to some assistance from health boards under the National Health Service (Scotland) Act 1978. Under the terms of section 15 of that Act, the local

---

[72]   *Barry, supra, per* Lord Clyde at 17a–b.
[73]   Though the decision is concerned with an assessment for services under s. 2 of the 1970 Act, it is likely that the same principles will apply in a community care assessment under s. 12A of the 1968 Act: see Lord Clyde in *Barry, supra,* at 18b.
[74]   *Barry, supra, per* Lord Clyde at 17c.
[75]   However, guidance does suggest that "where it is not possible to meet all assessed needs for community care services, information about the nature and extent of the *unmet* needs should be fed into the authority's community care planning process": SWSG11/91, para. 6.5.
[76]   "The [*Gloucestershire*] ruling has opened up a series of new questions about community care law and definitions of need within the community. In practice, it legitimises tighter eligibility criteria for assessments which could, in turn, impact on the number of carers eligible to ask for an assessment": *In On the Act? Social Services' Experience of the First Year of the Carers Act,* October 1997, p. 8, para. 1.18.
[77]   Preston-Shoot, *op. cit.,* pp. 307–325. In *R. v. Essex C. C., ex p. Tandy* [1998] 2 All E.R. 769 the House of Lords ruled in favour of an applicant whose home tuition had been reduced from five hours to three hours per week by a local education authority in England on the basis that its resources were insufficient to continue meeting the original costs. Resources could only be legitimately taken into account when there was more than one way of providing the mandatory "suitable education".
[78]   The Chronically Sick and Disabled Persons (Amendment) Bill sought to preclude allusions to limited resources at any stage in the process of assessment and service provision. The financial constraints of a local authority were to have no significance when assessing either need or the necessity to make arrangements to meet that need. The Bill did not succeed.
[79]   See para. 7.45 below for *R. v. Sefton B.C., ex p. Help the Aged.*
[80]   See Schwehr, "A Study in Fairness in the Field of Community Care Law", 1997 *Journal of Social Welfare and Family Law,* Vol.19, pp. 159–172, and Guthrie, "The House of Lords and Community Care Assessments", 1997 S.L.P.Q., Vol.2 pp. 225–229.

authority might receive equipment, goods, materials, administrative and professional services, vehicles, plants or apparatus from the health board, or a third party though arranged by the Board. The Board is further enabled to undertake maintenance work in buildings or land which are the responsibility of the local authority. Financial support is also available when the health board deems appropriate, to allow the local authority to perform its functions which relate to social work, housing and education.[81]

Direct payments

Augmenting the provisions contained in section 12(4) of the 1968 Act which authorise **7.33** emergency cash payments to people in need of social welfare, the Community Care (Direct Payments) Act 1996 inserted a new section 12B and 12C into the 1968 Act to enable direct cash payments to be made by local authorities to individuals who can subsequently procure services themselves. Cash payments can either supplement community care services or substitute them in full.[82] Regulations produced under section 12B(6) of the 1968 Act expand upon the terms of the Act.[83] Guidance on the 1968 Act and its Regulations has been issued and under the terms of section 5(1) of the 1968 Act, local authorities will be required to act in accordance with its policy content.[84] Initially, local authorities will be seeking to rely quite heavily on advice dispensed to them from central government.[85]

Under a direct payments scheme the cash recipient effectively assumes responsibility for himself and seeks to make his own arrangements for the acquisition of community care services. While carers may help to manage payments the user must remain in ultimate control of the service arrangements so as to prevent a situation in which a third party assumes what was previously the role of the local authority.[86] It may be that the service-user is able to individually manage his payments once he has become accustomed to securing services without the assistance of an independent party. The decision to dispense a direct payment is at the discretion of the local authority and will depend upon the results of a community care assessment.[87] The Regulations clearly stipulate that recipients should be capable of managing a direct payment.[88] If a carer's assessment is undertaken its results may be relevant to the final decision regarding services.[89]

People who are already in receipt of community care services may wish to start receiving direct payments. If the local authority does not suggest the possibility of substituting payment for service the individual should do so themselves either at, or in between, reviews.[90] It will be up to the authority in question to determine an appropriate sum though it will obviously need to reflect the estimate of securing the relevant community care services were no cash payment to be made. However, the guidance suggests that direct payments may be

[81] National Health Service (Scotland) Act 1978, s. 16A.
[82] SWSG 3/97, para. 7.
[83] Community Care (Direct Payments) (Scotland) Regulations 1997 (S.I. 1197 No. 693), established under s. 12B(6) of the 1968 Act.
[84] See para. 7.06 above.
[85] *Community Care (Direct Payments) Act 1996: Policy and Practice Guidance*, SWSG 3/97.
[86] SWSG 3/97, Policy Guidance para. 24.
[87] "Authorities have the discretion to refuse direct payments to any one who they judge would not be able to manage them, but should avoid making blanket assumptions that whole groups of people will necessarily be unable to do so": SWSG 3/97, Policy Guidance para. 23.
[88] Community Care (Direct Payments) (Scotland) Regulations 1997, reg. 2(1)(a)(b).
[89] Guidance stresses: "This duty is not affected by the possibility that the user may be offered direct payments instead of services, or that the user may receive direct payments for services which specifically reflect the results of the carer's assessment": SWSG 3/97, Policy Guidance, para. 33.
[90] SWSG 3/97, Policy Guidance, para. 21.

administered at a greater cost than the cost of arranging the equivalent services, provided the local authority is satisfied of the cost-effectiveness of this approach. An allowance over and above what might otherwise be necessary may have longer-term benefits for the person who is managing his or her own services and this in itself may provide a rationale.[91]

Direct payments will be subject to the rules which regulate charging for services with the effect that the assessed amount may be reduced to reflect the user's own contribution to the care package.[92] If the payment is less than reflective of the reasonable cost of securing services and the individual is unable to supplement it to the degree required, the local authority will be under a duty to make up the difference.[93] Local authorities are under no obligation to devise a scheme for making direct payments to its service-users. Consequently, entitlement will initially depend upon whether arrangements are in place within the area of residence. However where a local authority has established a scheme, it will be obliged to give due consideration to each applicant. Once payment has been made the local authority is immediately relieved of its duty to arrange services for the recipient, though only in respect of services to which the payment relates.[94] The local authority can still provide emergency cash to an individual who is receiving direct payments under the separate provisions of section 12 of the 1968 Act.[95]

7.34   The suitability of a user for direct payments will depend upon his own expectations and wishes. In other words, he must give his consent and be fully satisfied with the arrangements made. In procuring his own services he may become contractually bound, for instance in a relationship of employment or agency, and the possibilities for assuming full legal responsibility must be brought to his attention before his consent is taken as given. Where people are eager to have their services arranged by the local authority on their behalf, direct payments should not be administered. While legislation ostensibly seeks to ensure the local authority's satisfaction with the arrangements, the guidance specifically refers to the two-way nature of the arrangements. Recipients will be subject to the checks and balances of the local authority which can request a repayment where money is spent inappropriately or not spent at all, or where conditions attached to the payment have been breached.[95] Guidance stresses that this condition is not intended to penalise honest mistakes.[96]

The Regulations expressly exclude certain groups of people from entitlement to direct payments. Specifically, people aged over 65 are not entitled to a cash payment unless one has been made to them in the 12 months before they reached the age of 65.[97] It is noted in commentary on the Regulations that "[t]he exclusion of elderly people is simply a result of the Government's wish to see how the scheme operates before considering its extension".[98] People receiving criminal justice or mental health services are also excluded from the scheme though this does not automatically dismiss those suffering from mental health problems so

---

[91]   SWSG 3/97, Policy Guidance, para. 40.
[92]   s. 87(1) empowers local authorities to levy charges on the provision of services provided under the 1968 Act.
[93]   However, making provision over and above a reasonable amount will be at the discretion of the authority concerned: SWSG 3/97, Policy Guidance, para. 42.
[94]   1968 Act, s. 12C.
[94]   *ibid.*
[95]   1968 Act, s. 12B(5). Guidance states that authorities have discretion over the flexibility they allow people over their direct payments though later advises against the setting of excessive conditions in order to avoid frustrating the aims of the Act to give people more choice and control over their services: SWSG 3/97, Policy Guidance, paras 34, 37.
[96]   SWSG 3/97, Policy Guidance, para. 52.
[97]   Community Care (Direct Payments) (Scotland) Regulations 1997, reg. 2.
[98]   Annotations by McKay in Mays (ed.), *Scottish Social Work Legislation*, E-59, E-086.3. One of the wide-ranging recommendations of the Royal Commission on Long-Term Care for the Elderly is an extension of the system of direct payments to persons aged over 65 "subject to proper safeguards and monitoring" (*With Respect to Old Age: Long Term Care—Rights and Responsibilities*, Chap. 9): see paras 7.46–7.47 below.

long as they have the legal capacity to enter into the arrangement.[99] Direct payments are not available to anyone aged under 18, either directly or through an adult.[1] Furthermore, the Regulations are designed so as to prevent direct payments being used to procure services from relatives or people living in the same home as the service-user,[2] though a local authority may decide to make an exception where it is satisfied that this is the only appropriate way of securing the relevant services.[3]

Direct payments can be used to purchase short-term stays in residential care, though cannot be used to purchase more than four weeks' accommodation in a 12-month period.[4] Where periods in residential care are more than four weeks apart they are not added together and never reach the four-week limit. For instance, for someone who purchases a week in care every six weeks, the cumulative total is only ever one week. On the other hand, three weeks in residential care, followed by three weeks at home, followed in turn by one week in residential care, makes a cumulative total of four weeks and represents the maximum amount of accommodation which can be purchased. If the local authority feels that more residential care is required once direct payments have been depleted, it can arrange funding under the normal arrangements.[5]

RESIDENTIAL CARE

General duty

With the introduction of community care the emphasis on residential care has shifted. **7.35** Understandably, it is not heavily endorsed as a community care enhancement. However, intensive care needs often demand an additional dimension of care in a residential setting. This serves in some sense as a compromise between institutional and community living.

The basic right to residential care falls under the general terms of section 12 of the 1968 Act which requires local authorities to provide "residential and other establishments".

"[T]he local authority may feel it necessary to make provision, and may in fact make provision under s.12 of the 1968 Act, to have a disabled person accommodated in an 'establishment' in the sense of an institution or other place where he would benefit from supervision and control when he could not without danger or extreme discomfort live in his own home."[6]

A person will be assessed in terms of their need for residential care during a community care assessment.[7] If the social work department feels that needs cannot fully be met at home, relocation in residential accommodation may be deemed appropriate. Provisions written into the National Assistance Act 1948 allow people in need of care and attention to be removed to premises more suited to their needs though in practice this power is rarely

---

[99] reg. 2(2). For a fuller discussion of the implications for mental health, see Chap. 6.
[1] SWSG 3/97, Policy Guidance, para. 10.
[2] Specifically, a spouse, cohabitee, parents, children, in-laws, siblings, aunts, uncles or grandparents: 1968 Act, s. 12B(3) and reg. 3.
[3] SWSG 3/97, Policy Guidance, para. 36.
[4] reg. 4.
[5] SWSG 3/97 Policy Guidance, paras 16–17. For a fuller discussion of the funding arrangements for residential care, see paras 7.42–7.47 below.
[6] *Assessor for Edinburgh v. Brodie*, 1976 S.L.T. 234 at 238 *per* Lord Thomson.
[7] 1968 Act, s. 12A.

exercised.[8] Once residential care has been approved the resident must usually secure the financial means with which to fund their care and accommodation. Once an assessment has confirmed that residential or nursing care is required, the individual concerned will be at liberty to choose a home which they feel is the most agreeable.[9]

Section 59 of the 1968 Act places a duty on local authorities to provide and maintain residential establishments and embellishes the broader duty which is found in section 12. Residential care homes may be provided jointly between local authorities or in conjunction with the independent sector. Similar English provisions were examined by the court in *R. v. Wandsworth LBC, ex p. Beckwith*.[10] The council in question had sought to transfer three of its four elderly care homes over to the private sector and to close the remaining one. The question placed by the applicant was whether the local authority was under an obligation to provide residential care of its own or whether it was entitled to transfer its responsibilities in whole to the private sector. The court held that a local authority is entitled to discharge its statutory duty to arrange residential accommodation entirely by means of arrangements made with third parties. Furthermore, it was not bound to maintain some accommodation in its own premises for those for whom alternative arrangements had already been made. Lord Hoffman considered the "mixed economy of care" to which the guidance on community care refers,[11] and understood from such a phrase that a complete shift of provision from the public to the private sector was not outside the powers of local authorities seeking to discharge their community care obligations. In fact, while the Government had not expected that this would be undertaken with immediate effect, this did not construe as a reason for local authorities to retain some residential care provision for themselves.[12] As yet, there has been no equivalent challenge in the Scottish courts though the number of residential care homes managed by the private sector is on the increase.[13]

7.36   The duty to provide residential care is quite distinct from the duty in respect of nursing homes where qualified nursing care is provided. Local authorities are required to purchase places in nursing homes though are not actually sanctioned to supply them.[14] Prior to the NHS and Community Care Act 1990 local authority powers were restricted to providing residential care alone. Removing this constraint and expanding the options with which to keep people out of hospital was central to community care. Homes may be jointly registered as nursing and residential homes so as to allow a transition between levels of care as a condition improves or deteriorates without the disruption of "moving home".[15] Dual registration has become more commonplace in recent years as the line between nursing and residential care has become increasingly unclear. At least some medical attention is required in most residential care homes and caring staff will often be trained in minimal nursing duties. Detailed provisions governing the inspection, management and registration of residential establishments comprise Part IV of the 1968 Act.[16]

---

[8]   National Assistance Act 1948, s. 47. s. 48 provides for the protection of that person's property in the event of an exercise of the powers contained in s. 47.

[9]   Under the Social Work (Scotland) 1968 Act (Choice of Accommodation) Directions 1993 a person is entitled to choose any home which is available, suitable and affordable.

[10]   [1998] 1 All E.R. 129 (HL).

[11]   *Caring for People: Community Care into the Next Decade and Beyond* (1989, Cm.849).

[12]   [1998] 1 All E.R. 129 (HL) at 132 e–g.

[13]   In 1990 22 per cent of places in care homes for elderly people were managed by the private sector. This rose to 28 per cent in 1997. For physically disabled people, the figure rose from 0 to 3 per cent in the same timescale: see Community Care Scotland Statistical Bulletin (1997), Nov. 1998.

[14]   1968 Act, s. 13A.

[15]   Nursing Homes Registration (Scotland) Act 1938, s. 2A and 1968 Act, s. 63B.

[16]   Pt IV was substantially amended by the Registered Establishments (Scotland) Act 1987.

Residential care homes

A residential establishment or care home is defined as one which provides "personal care **7.37** and support" as a whole or substantial part of its functions.[17] Depending on the particular needs of an individual, care may be provided on a daily or longer-term basis, commonly for periods of respite.[18] Care in a residential home is available for people who are assessed as being unable to cope in their own homes but who are not in need of nursing care.[19] "Personal care" is defined in section 61(1A) of the 1968 Act as the provision of appropriate help with physical and social needs. Guidance issued in pursuance of the Registered Establishments (Scotland) Act 1987 offered an extension of this remit, namely the provision of "welfare and active help with dressing, eating, washing, and bathing; it might also extend to help with emotional problems and with the development of social skills".[20] "Support" is defined by the legislation as counselling or other help provided as part of a planned programme of care though the guidance indicates that residents are entitled to a less direct service,[21] and support might therefore be construed in its most ordinary sense as encouragement and motivation.

Registration[22]

All residential establishments providing personal care and support must register with the **7.38** local social work department. Failure to register carries a criminal penalty. Under the present provisions, homes run by local authorities do not need to be registered. Nursing homes are also exempt from these provisions since their registration is governed by the Nursing Homes Registration Act 1938.[23] An application for registration should be made to the local authority in the area where the establishment is to be located.[24]

Local authorities are responsible for ensuring by virtue of the conditions of registration that all registered homes meet with certain stipulated standards. In this pursuit it should determine the maximum number of people to be accommodated at any one time, as well as categories of people which the home is authorised to admit. The local authority may not register homes which it perceives to be unfit by virtue of their situation, construction, state of repair, accommodation, staffing or equipment, or which are to be run by a person who is unfit by reason of age or otherwise. Neither can homes which do not appear to the local authority to be offering services and facilities appropriate for meeting the needs of potential residents, be registered with the local authority.

The conditions of registration are subject to modification at any time. A procedure relating to appeals against such conditions is set out in section 63A[25] whilst appeals against refusal or cancellation of registration are regulated in detail by section 64 of the 1968 Act. In each instance, there are two rungs of appeal so that the case may eventually be considered by an appeal tribunal.[26]

---

[17]   1968 Act, s. 61(1).
[18]   See paras 7.48–7.50 below.
[19]   See the *Stair Memorial Encyclopaedia*, Vol.22, para. 24.
[20]   *The Registered Establishments (Scotland) Act 1987 and Associated Subordinate Legislation*, SWSG 16/88, para. 8.
[21]   *ibid.*
[22]   See generally ss 61 and 62, 1968 Act.
[23]   see paras 7.40–7.41 below.
[24]   The Registration of Establishments (Application Form) (Scotland) Order 1988, made under s. 62(2) of the 1968 Act, prescribes the type of application form to be used for these purposes.
[25]   Inserted by the Registered Establishments (Scotland) Act 1987.
[26]   The procedure and constitution of the appeal tribunal is regulated by the Registration of Establishments (Appeal Tribunal) (Scotland) Rules 1983 (S.I. 1983 No. 71) established under s. 64(4) of the 1968 Act.

In *R. v. Durham County Council, ex p. Curtis*[27] residents of a residential home for elderly people had been given only five days' notice of plans to close the home. The decision to do so was later overturned on the basis that the applicants who were residents of the home had a legitimate expectation to be fully consulted. Similar circumstances arose in *R. v. Devon County Council, ex p. Baker*[28] although over a month's notice had been given to the residents who were aware some time before the final decision that closure was imminent. While the closure of residential accommodation obligated the local authority responsible for the change in circumstances to consult the residents, allow their objections, and in turn to consider those objections, each of these requirements had in fact been satisfied and there were no subsisting grounds for an appeal against the decision of the council.

Residential establishments which are not granted registration or which have been informed of a cancellation of registration will become subject to the powers of the local authority under section 65 of the 1968 Act to remove residents immediately, though this power is rarely exercised and will be retained for the most extreme circumstances.[29] A breach of the conditions of registration also carries a criminal penalty.

Inspection

7.39 Local authorities are empowered to examine the state and management of residential establishments which are registered, or equally, which it suspects ought to be registered.[30] In this pursuit the local authority, or a person empowered by it, is authorised to inspect the conditions and treatment of the residents, and of any records and registers which pertain to the running of the home. Inspections may in turn be recorded within those registers.[31] This is in addition to the more general powers of inspection under section 6 of the 1968 Act according to which anyone authorised by the Secretary of State is empowered to examine local authority-run or privately-run residential establishments.

In contrast to this discretionary power of inspection, local authorities are more strictly regulated by a mandatory duty to visit residents in establishments both within and outside their area, with a view to ensuring that the well-being of those residents is secure. Though it is not explicitly stated in the 1968 Act, this translates as a social work function and applies whether or not the period in residence was arranged by the social work department in question.[32] This means that those who voluntarily admitted themselves to residential care are still owed what is essentially a duty of care by the authority. This obligation would appear to extend to private sector homes as well as those under the control of the local authority.

Nursing homes

7.40 Individual needs quite often demand an additional dimension of medical care and in given cases nursing assistance in a residential setting will be required. If a community care assessment reveals a suspected or possible need for nursing care the local authority must

---

[27] [1995] 1 All E.R. 73.
[28] [1998] 1 All E.R. 73.
[29] For further reading on registration and the extent to which these provisions serve in a practical sense to maintain standards in residential homes, see Mackay and Patrick, *The Care Maze—The Law and Your Rights to Community Care in Scotland*, p. 39, and Mitchell, "*Registration and Raising Standards*"; (1995, Glasgow, Enable and SAMH), 1996 *Solicitors Journal*, vol. 140, pp. 968–970.
[30] 1968 Act, s. 67.
[31] 1968 Act, s. 62(10).
[32] 1968 Act, s. 68.

consult with a medical practitioner before any further action is taken,[33] and guidance suggests that an agreement over nursing care must be reached between health boards and local authorities about which specific services are to be provided.[34] Urgent admissions to both nursing and residential care may be provided without consultation with a medical practitioner though an assessment must be carried out as soon as possible after admission.[35]

Though local authorities are themselves barred from running nursing homes they are required to contract with companies, voluntary organisations or charities, and private individuals, as a means of purchasing places in homes to ensure appropriate and adequate provision of nursing care for persons in need in their area.[36] As a result, nursing homes are regulated by the health board rather than the local authority. Section 13A of the 1968 Act empowers local authorities to contract with nursing homes registered under Scottish legislation alone and in an endeavour to overcome this predicament the Scottish Office issued guidance in 1994 suggesting that social work departments extend the choice beyond homes which are situated in Scotland.[37]

All nursing homes must be registered with the local health board under the Nursing **7.41** Homes Registration (Scotland) Act 1938 or will be liable to criminal prosecution.[38] While the process for the registration of nursing homes is not written into the 1968 Act, it is not dissimilar from that which applies to residential care homes. The 1938 Act has been heavily augmented since its implementation[39] and provides the main statutory framework for the registration of nursing homes in Scotland. A contravention of the conditions of registration will constitute a criminal offence under section 1 of the 1938 Act. The only grounds which exist for a cancellation of registration are that an offence has been committed under the Act, or that there exists a ground which would have prevented registration from being initially conferred.[40] In *McDermott v. Highland Health Board*[41] the Health Board sought to cancel the registration of a nursing home on the grounds that its staffing levels were inadequate, and that medical records were not being properly maintained. There was also concern regarding the recording, handling and disposal of drugs on the premises. The decision was later overturned by the court on the basis that these were not competent grounds on which to cancel a registration in light of section 2 of the 1938 Act.

All registered homes must be under the charge of a registered medical practitioner or qualified nurse though the health board may refuse registration where the home itself by virtue of its general condition, or the applicant through age, conduct or some other factor, is improper or unsuitable for the intended purposes.[42] The board is to stipulate for its area the requisite nursing qualifications and number of qualified nurses to be employed within a home.[43] The Nursing Homes Registration (Scotland) Regulations 1990[44] co-ordinate the conduct and inspection of nursing homes[45] and set the appropriate registration fees.[46] Nursing

---

[33] 1968 Act, s. 12A(4).
[34] SWSG 11/91, para. 13.2.
[35] *ibid.*, para. 14.
[36] 1968 Act, s. 13A, as inserted by s. 56 of the NHS and Community Care Act 1990.
[37] SWSG 6/1994, *Choice of Accommodation: Cross Border Placements.*
[38] Nursing Homes Registration (Scotland) Act 1938 ("1938 Act"), s. 1(1).
[39] Registered Establishments (Scotland) Act 1987 and the Nursing Homes Registration (Scotland) Regulations 1990 have been foremost in amending the 1938 Act.
[40] 1938 Act, s. 2.
[41] 1993 S.L.T. (Sh. Ct.) 34.
[42] 1938 Act, s. 1(3).
[43] *ibid.*, s. 1(3A).
[44] S.I. 1990 No. 1310, constituted under s. 4 of the 1938 Act.
[45] Nursing Homes Registration (Scotland) Regulations 1990, reg. 4–13.
[46] Nursing Homes Registration (Scotland) Regulations 1990, reg. 3 and Sched. 2.

homes may also be inspected under section 6 of the 1968 Act which authorises anyone approved by the Secretary of State to inspect establishments providing accommodation. By virtue of section 13A this includes nursing homes funded by local authorities.

Funding

7.42 Charges for residential care are distinct from those made in respect of home care services. In most situations, the local authority and the resident will share the cost between them. The average weekly charge for a place in a residential home depends upon the particular care needs of the individual, and the area in which the home is located. Prices vary in homes across Scotland though people with physical disabilities do tend to pay in excess of the average weekly cost for an elderly person. Furthermore, local authority homes by and large carry higher prices than those which are run by either the private or voluntary sector.[47]

The funding of places in residential care is largely regulated by the National Assistance Act 1948 ("1948 Act"). While this is principally an English Act, the provisions which relate to charging for accommodation are specifically incorporated into Part IV of the 1968 Act.[48] In simple terms, the local authority is required to apply charges for residential care which it has provided or arranged and which exceeds a period of eight weeks.[49] This is underpinned by the general principle that those needing residential accommodation should pay for it themselves if they are able to do so.[50]

The provisions which relate to funding incorporate both care in residential care homes which the local authority provides and maintains, and care in nursing homes within which it has purchased places and which it thereby arranges. The maximum amount payable is the standard rate. This will reflect the expense incurred by the local authority.[51] In other words the resident may be required to meet the full costs of care and accommodation. The expense which accompanies a stay in residential care has meant that financial responsibility quite often falls exclusively on the resident. However, where he or she urges the local authority that there are insufficient resources to meet the costs of a residential establishment, that authority will undertake an assessment and an amount will be agreed upon which is a proportion of the standard rate and a reflection of the applicant's income and capital. By virtue of the Community Care (Residential Accommodation) Act 1998, local authorities are restricted in the amount of capital which they can take into account in determining the extent to which individuals with savings are able to contribute towards residential accommodation.

7.43 The means test is regulated in detail between section 22 of the 1948 Act and the National Assistance (Assessment of Resources) Regulations 1992 which are themselves established under section 22(5).[52] There is also consistent reference to the Income Support (General) Regulations 1987.[53] The area is in fact extremely complex. Calculation of income, capital and the liability of relatives all form part of the means test. Income is estimated on a weekly basis,

---

[47] See Community Care Statistical Bulletin Scotland (1997), Nov. 1998, Table 7.2.
[48] 1968 Act, s. 87(3).
[49] National Assistance Act 1948, s. 22 and 26.
[50] See *R. v. Somerset C. C., ex p. Harcombe* (1997) 37 B.M.L.R. 1 where it was said that the courts should be slow to interfere with funding arrangements when it was clear that careful consideration had been given to all the relevant material circumstances.
[51] National Assistance Act 1948, s. 22(2).
[52] S.I. 1992 No. 2977. Guidance issued by the SWSG on the assessment process has been amended from its original form and can be found in *Community Care: National Assistance (Assessment of Resources) (Amendment No. 2) Regulations 1993: Regulations and Guidance*, issued on Jan. 21, 1994.
[53] S.I. 1987 No. 1967.

while a capital in excess of £16,000 will render the resident liable to pay the standard rate in full.[54] Where capital is below £10,000 the local authority will not be in a position to apply charges to the resident. Under the present arrangements, if capital falls between these thresholds, some contribution towards care and accommodation will be required. From every £250 of capital held, a sum of £1 will be charged each week.[55] A liable relative is one which is the spouse or former spouse of the resident in question. Liability to the local authority for the costs of residential care may arise when he or she makes payments to that resident.[56]

There is no stipulated maximum or minimum sum payable, though even those on income support will usually be required to make some contribution towards their residential care. The local authority is empowered by section 22(5A) of the 1948 Act to apply charging costs independently of the Regulations for the first eight weeks of a stay in residential care, and to begin charging the resident according to the terms of the Regulations thereafter. The local authority will not be entitled to include in the resources of the client the sum of his personal requirements. These are set by the National Assistance (Sums for Personal Requirements) Regulations 1998 and presently stand at £14.45 per week.[57] This provision is inserted with a view to ensuring that everyone in residential accommodation has at least some income which cannot be exhausted on their care. If special circumstances prevail the local authority may allocate a larger personal allowance than that which is stipulated in the Regulations.[58]

In calculating the amount which an applicant can contribute, certain sums of money are to be disregarded.[59] These are contained in some detail in Schedules 2 and 3 to the 1992 Regulations. In some cases the resident's home will be included as an asset in the financial assessment and sold to help pay for the costs of residential care. This will of course depend on whether the period in residential care is permanent or temporary. If the resident intends returning to the home within 52 weeks it will not constitute an asset.[60] Similarly, where the house continues to be occupied by a partner or relative who is aged over 60, a child aged under 16, or an incapacitated relative, financial assessment will not incorporate the home.[61]

The health board will intervene in a limited number of cases, namely where the resident has been in long-term hospital care and is being discharged into a residential or nursing home. However, under section 16A of the National Health Service (Scotland) Act 1978, health boards are empowered to transfer to social work departments the funds which they would previously have used for subsidising long-term stays in hospital. Prior to the NHS and Community Care Act 1990 the bulk of residential care costs could be met with income support payments made by the DSS. Financially speaking, people were often "better off" in residential care. For those who have been in care since before April 1, 1993 costs will usually continue to be met by the DSS.[62]

---

[54] reg. 20.
[55] reg. 28.
[56] Pt IV of the 1998 Regulations.
[57] Established under s. 22(4) of the National Assistance Act 1948. Regulations are introduced on an annual basis so that the sum of personal requirements reflects the current rate of inflation.
[58] National Assistance Act 1948, s. 22(4).
[59] reg. 11(3) excludes certain sums from the net profit of self-employed earners, reg. 14(2) excludes the same sums from the net earnings of employed earners and reg. 15(2) excludes certain sums from income other than earnings.
[60] reg. 2(1).
[61] Income Support (General) Regulations, Sched. 10, para. 4; National Assistance (Assessment of Resources) Regulations 1992, Sched. 4, para. 2; National Assistance Act 1948, s. 42.
[62] For a fuller and more detailed discussion of the funding arrangements for people who have been in residential care since before April 1993 see McKay and Patrick, *Care Maze* (1992), at pp. 61–64.

Disposal of income and capital

7.44 A person will be treated as in fact possessing *income* which he has disposed of for the purpose of decreasing the amount which he may be liable to pay for his accommodation.[63] This is a mandatory requirement in the sense that the local authority will not have a discretion to allow the income disposed of to be discounted from calculations of the costs of residential care. On the other hand, a person will not necessarily be treated as possessing *capital* which he has sought to dispose of for the same reasons.[64] This is referred to as "notional capital". Where a person disposes of assets within six months prior to admission to residential accommodation, knowingly, and with the intention of avoiding charges for that accommodation, the person to whom the assets are transferred will be liable to pay the difference between the actual costs of the care provided, and the amount which the service-user is assessed as being liable to pay, were the disposed asset initially retained by him.[65] This provision is one means of redeeming a recoverable sum. In other cases, assets disposed of so as to allow reduced charges for residential accommodation may not be recoverable. In *Yule v. South Lanarkshire Council*[66] a resident in a nursing home disposed of her heritage "for love, favour and affection" some 16 months prior to her admission. Since the disposal was outwith the six-month limit, the local authority was not entitled to recover the sum from the third party involved. Notwithstanding that, the council was still entitled to take into account the sum disposed of in calculating the amount which the resident was liable to pay, so long as it was disposed of for the purpose of decreasing the amount for which the resident would be liable, under the terms of the 1992 Regulations.[67]

Application of Gloucestershire[68]

7.45 The House of Lords decision in *Gloucestershire* that resources may be relevant in deciding whether arrangements are necessary to meet need will no doubt impact upon the funding arrangements for residential accommodation. The decision has already started to filter through to social work practice. In *R. v. Sefton MBC, ex p. Help the Aged*[69] an elderly woman was assessed by her local authority and found to be in need of nursing care in a residential setting. Local authority resources were such that the applicant was asked to continue to meet the costs of her care notwithstanding the results of the assessment that she was a "person in need". The court applied the House of Lords ruling in *Gloucestershire*. In deciding whether the applicant was a person in need the local authority was entitled to have regard to its own limited resources "as there was a limited subjective element in determining whether an elderly person was in need of care and attention".[70] However, if the authority had decided that the person was in such need, it was under a duty to fulfil its statutory obligation, namely to make arrangements for accommodation to be made available. A lack of resources would not relieve the authority of that obligation.

---

[63] National Assistance (Assessment of Resources) Regulations 1992, reg. 17.
[64] *ibid.*, reg. 25(1).
[65] Health and Social Services and Social Security Adjudication Act 1983, s. 21.
[66] 1998 S.L.T. 490.
[67] For further reading on funding see Spiers, "Nursing and Residential Homes: Paying for Care" 1997 S. J., Vol. 141, pp. 453–455 and McKay and Patrick, *Care Maze* (1992).
[68] see para. 7.31 above.
[69] [1997] 4 All E.R. 532.
[70] The National Assistance Act 1948, s. 21(1)—provision of residential accommodation.

Royal Commission

A Royal Commission was set up in December 1997 by the Secretary of State for Health to **7.46** examine the system of funding of long-term care for elderly people.[71] Its official remit was to examine both the short- and long-term options for a sustainable system for funding long-term care for elderly people, both in their own homes and in other settings, recommending how and in which circumstances the cost of such care should be apportioned between public funds and individuals. In this pursuit it was to have regard to the following:

(a) the number of people likely to require various kinds of long-term care both in the present and through the first half of the next century, and their likely income and capital over their lifetime;

(b) the expectations of elderly people for dignity and security in the way in which their long-term care needs are met, taking account of the need for this to be secured in the most effective manner;

(c) the strengths and weaknesses of the current arrangements;

(d) fair and efficient ways for individuals to make any contribution required of them;

(e) constraints on public funds and;

(f) earlier work done by various bodies on this issue.

Less officially perhaps, the final report was expected to allay growing fears that residential care was of huge financial consequence in later life, in particular for those who had foreseen the ramifications and accordingly sought to invest wisely in anticipation of the costs. The irony that health care was available free of charge to hospital patients but not to those without such demanding medical requirements was expected to benefit from a considerable degree of reflection.

With Respect to Old Age: Long-Term Care—Rights and Responsibilities[72] was published in **7.47** March 1999 and made a number of far-reaching and innovative recommendations. Principally, it advocated free nursing care for all elderly people, whether it be provided in their own homes, nursing homes or in residential care. Nursing care should in this sense be referred to as "personal care" and include both health care and social care. The report defines personal care as including all direct care relating to: personal toilet; eating and drinking; managing urinary and bowel functions; managing problems associated with immobility; management of prescribed treatment; behaviour management and ensuring personal safety, though drawing the line at cleaning and housework; laundry; shopping services; specialist transport services; and sitting services for company or companionship on the basis that these are in fact "living costs" and should therefore be means-tested.

Accommodation should remain means-tested though the Commission recommended that the current £16,000 threshold, referred to in para. 7.43 above, be raised to £60,000. It is further suggested that elderly people be permitted to stay in care for three months before their home is counted as an asset against the costs of residential care. This would allow them to return to their home if they no longer wished or needed to remain in care. The report further suggests the introduction of loans from local authorities to assist people in adapting their own homes and calls for greater integration of budgets for aids and adaptations. It is thought that these costs might be met from a single accessible budget pool.

---

[71] The Commission was chaired by Professor Sir Stewart Sutherland, vice-chancellor of Edinburgh University.
[72] A Report by the Royal Commission on long-term care, Cm. 4192, Mar. 1999, London: HMSO.

To complement these core recommendations, the Commission has suggested that the system be overseen by a National Care Commission with a view to enforcing minimum standards and monitoring costs. Carers are also high on the agenda with a national carer support package hoping to help people stay in their own homes with the support of others. It is foreseen by the Commission that the sum allocated to this particular initiative will increase by £220 million to £700 million by 2050. The report is underpinned by concepts of long-term regeneration and highlights the opportunities for programmes of rehabilitation in the objectives of an elderly person's care plan. Furthermore, it stresses the need for health education and preventative medicine to delay the onset of long-term illnesses and henceforth the need for long-term care. In this respect, at least, it has given some careful consideration to the long-term implications of the recommendations. Underpinning these recommendations, the report suggests measures to ensure increased efficiency and a "client-centred" approach, with budgets being shared between health, social services and other statutory bodies.

As expected, the recommendations have met with some mixed reactions. Clearly, national and local support organisations have welcomed the underlying themes of the Report and the measures intended to realise its central propositions. However, the implications for the taxpayer are expected to sustain opposition to the proposals. It is now for the Government to decide how it will respond to the valuable and comprehensive work of the Commission which has made a number of suggestions regarding the long-term costs of renewed care for the elderly. While social work, housing and health implications will be dealt with by the Scottish Parliament, social security matters will remain in the hands of Westminster.

Respite care

7.48   Respite care is a service which targets both users and their carers, and involves an individual spending a period of time either away from the home in a hospital, residential or nursing home, or remaining in the home but receiving care from someone other than the routine carer on a one-off or regular basis. Hospital care is usually limited to circumstances which involve compulsory medical care ancillary to the social care objectives of respite. Day centres are a popular choice for people wishing to join others sharing the same interests.

While this service is not expressly found within the legislative framework it has developed as part of the more general social welfare services under section 12 of the 1968 Act which incorporate residential care generally. The need to make adequate legal provision for respite care was alluded to in the White Paper to the 1990 Act though the 1968 Act has remained essentially the same. Section 2(1) of the Chronically Sick and Disabled (Persons) Act 1970 refers, in the comprehensive list of welfare services which local authorities are under a duty to arrange, to holidays in holiday homes or otherwise. It is the responsibility of the local social work department to make the appropriate arrangements for respite care though of course it may contract-out to the voluntary or private sector.

The duty under section 12A to assess the need for community care services embraces an assessment of the need for respite care and the rules detailed above relating to community care assessments apply in this context.[73] A local authority may respond to a request from a service-user, or may target the recipient on its own initiative. Alternatively, the need for respite care may be brought to its attention through a request for an assessment of the carer's ability to continue caring under section 12A(3A).[74]

[73]   See paras 7.14–7.17 above.
[74]   Inserted by the Carers (Recognition and Services) Act 1995: see para. 7.22 above.

Holidays or short breaks need not necessarily be taken without the carer. In *R v. North* **7.49**
Yorkshire County Council, ex p. Hargreaves[75] the High Court in England compelled the local
authority to cover the holiday costs of both a disabled person and the carer. The local
authority concerned had sought to pay for the board and travel costs of the disabled
applicant, and to make a further contribution to the overall travel costs. This implicitly
excluded the carer from the financial assistance it was providing. The council argued that it
had not been Parliament's intention under section 2 of the 1970 Act to relieve poverty, but
merely to assist as far as possible with the extra expense incurred as a result of a disability.
The court found in favour of the applicant and said that once the local authority had
determined that the need for a holiday was the result of the disability, the cost of that holiday
must be seen and understood to be an additional cost resulting from the disability. Furthermore, the obligation to "facilitate" the taking of holidays under section 2 of the 1970 Act
did not oblige the council to meet the basic costs of the holiday, but conferred upon it a
discretion to do so. By limiting its consideration to additional costs it had unlawfully fettered
that discretion.

The duty to make respite care arrangements includes holidays which have been arranged
by someone other than the local authority. In *R. v. Ealing London Borough Council, ex p.
Leaman*[76] a carer orchestrated a holiday for a disabled person without seeking the help of the
social work department. In seeking to secure the assistance of the authority at a later stage
under the terms of section 2(1) of the 1970 Act the carer was met with some resistance on the
grounds that the arrangements had not involved the local authority from the start. Interpreting the terms of the 1970 Act the court rejected these contentions ruling that social
services support in this form was a right, notwithstanding the relatively late involvement of
the local authority.

Most people will need to make a contribution towards the cost of their respite care though **7.50**
a short-term break in hospital will usually be paid for by the NHS.[77] Care provided in a
residential establishment or at home is not free of charge. The National Assistance (Assessment of Resources) Regulations 1992 allow the local authority to make reasonable charges
for the first eight weeks spent in short-term care. For any longer period of time it will enforce
a charge which reflects the means of the individual to pay for services further to a financial
assessment like one undertaken for periods spent in residential care.[78]

Guidance issued by the Scottish Office on respite care submits that it will often be part of
a wider package of health and social care services provided on an on-going basis and that
decisions should be reached in light of discussions which take place between user, carer and
service providers.[79] Arrangements will need to be kept under regular review, though it will
not be necessary to conduct a new assessment before each care episode.[80] Local authorities
will need to take account of the preferences which an applicant has.[81] To ensure that the

---

[75] *The Times*, June 12, 1997.
[76] *The Times*, Feb. 10, 1984.
[77] However, guidance on respite care notes that "the scope which the NHS has to meet a local need for social
respite care in the margins of its provision of long-stay will reduce and will, in time, cease as services are re-
provided and firmly established in the community": SWSG 10/96, para. 27.
[78] See paras. 7.42–7.45 above.
[79] *Respite Care*, SWSG 10/96.
[80] *ibid.*, para. 38.
[81] In *R. v. North Yorkshire C. C., ex p. Hargreaves, The Times*, Nov. 9, 1994, the local authority had rightly taken
account of the wishes of both the service-user and the carer though had failed to consider that their individual
preferences might differ. Physical and mental handicap did not in this instance preclude the service-user from
expressing a preference which was distinct from that of her carer: see para. 7.06, no. 21.

health needs of the service-user are adequately met during any periods in respite care, arrangements should also involve purchasers of health care.[82]

The extent to which service-users are ensured a positive experience in respite care depends largely on the local authority putting arrangements in place. A study of the processes of local authorities across Scotland in 1993 revealed a lack of uniformity in the provision of respite care and a need for clarity in the roles played by the respective agencies involved.[83] A number of key recommendations were made in light of these results though indications one year later were that these had not been taken forward and that services were still relatively patchy. The lack of a strategic framework for authorities across Scotland to apply has impeded co-ordinated implementation and the guidance issued in 1996 called upon local authorities to review their present arrangements for community care with a view to eliminating the inconsistencies which persist in respite care provision.

HOUSING AND COMMUNITY CARE

7.51   Housing tailored to meet specific needs is a precondition to the successful operation of community care.[84] The central role to be played by housing bodies was reflected in the £40 million allocated to local housing authorities in 1995 and earmarked for fulfilling community care obligations.[85] However, the reforms introduced by the 1990 Act were somewhat minimal in respect of housing as a specific facility to enable community living.[86] Social work departments were simply compelled to refer cases to the relevant housing authority where a community care assessment revealed a housing need.[87] The present position is summarised as follows:

"Community care in itself creates no new category of entitlement to housing, and housing needs which are identified by community care planning and individual assessments should be considered alongside processes and local priorities".[88]

In response to concerns that housing was not receiving enough emphasis in community care, the Scottish Office issued guidance entitled *Community Care: The Housing Dimension*[89]

---

[82]   See SWSG 10/96, paras 20–21 on collaboration between health boards and social work departments over respite care. Guidance issued to the NHS in 1996 referred to the continuing role of health purchasers in arranging respite care: *NHS Responsibility for Continuing Health Care*, MEL (1996) 22.

[83]   Lindsay, Khols and Collins, *The Patchwork Quilt: A Study of Respite Care Services in Scotland* (1993, Edinburgh, Scottish Office).

[84]   See Cowan, "Accommodating Community Care" (1995) *Journal of Law and Society*, vol. 22, pp. 212–233 for a full discussion of the intersection between community care legislation and homelessness legislation and the paradox which emanates from the failure to co-ordinate statutory provisions.

[85]   A census in 1991 placed the mobility problems of disabled people fully in context when it revealed that a quarter of households in Scotland were accommodating a member with a limiting, long-term illness. Of that total 100,000 were in housing with no accommodation at ground level: see Walker, *The OPCS Surveys of Disability in Britain: An Overall Analysis* (1991, London, Disability Alliance).

[86]   This was notwithstanding that the Report of the Social Services Committee which, along with the Audit Commission report which provided the foundation for the White Paper *Caring for People*, made explicit reference to the need to provide "ordinary domestic housing" and underlined the obligations of housing departments in the provision of community care.

[87]   s. 12A(3). Similarly, if a housing department is itself undertaking an assessment and becomes aware of non-housing problems, it is deemed good practice to alert the appropriate bodies, particularly if it is clear that a community care assessment is required to be made by the social work department: Code of Guidance on Homelessness, para. 5.15.

[88]   SWSG 7/94, para. 15.

[89]   SWSG 7/94.

with the intention that it would heavily influence all future activity in this field.[90] Until that time the involvement of housing bodies had been sporadic, and co-operation between health, housing and social work sectors wanting. The guidance drew attention to the need for inter-agency care and reminded all those involved that their own contribution would be made most effective by increasing their involvement with each of the other relevant bodies.[91] Health, housing and social work bodies were urged to co-ordinate their operations and, to this end, to establish housing forums which were housing-led, though drawing representation from other relevant sectors.[92] Social work authorities were reminded of the housing component contained within the community care assessment, and of the duty to involve housing bodies in several aspects of the assessment process.

Housing for community care client groups is regulated by two pieces of legislation. In the first instance the Social Work (Scotland) Act 1968 Act stresses the need for social work departments to involve housing departments in community care assessments,[93] while the Housing (Scotland) Act 1987 lays down the rights of homeless people who are either elderly, disabled or chronically sick, and the rights of home owners and home occupiers to adaptation and improvement within their homes.[94]

Local housing authorities are compelled by a general duty under section 1(4) of the Housing (Scotland) Act 1987 ("1987 Act") to have regard to the special needs of people who are chronically sick and disabled when considering the needs for further housing accommodation in the area. This was reinforced in *Assessor for Edinburgh v. Brodie*[95] when the court concluded that

7.52

"if a local authority wishes to supply as a home for a disabled person a house which makes special provision for the needs of that disabled person, the local authority has power to do so under the Housing Acts and not under the Social Work (Scotland) Act 1968."

In undertaking an assessment of those housing needs it must take account of housing provided by other housing providers, including housing associations and other voluntary providers and the public and private sectors.[96] If it appears that a greater degree of care is

---

[90] Draft guidance entitled *Modernising Community Care Guidance on the Housing Contribution* was issued for consultation in December 1998 with a view to supplementing and complementing the 1994 Guidance. Consultation was due to end on Feb. 28, 1999. At time of writing the guidance outlines good practice for senior and fieldwork staff in the areas of strategic planning, implementation, assessment, hospital discharge arrangements, home- based options, housing management arrangements and monitoring and evaluation. The guidance is again aimed at housing, health and social work agencies with a view to ensuring their continued collaboration in community care and is said to constitute "the latest piece of a much larger jigsaw" which "maintains the momentum of recent initiatives aimed at improving quality of life for people with community care requirements". Callum MacDonald, Dec. 9, 1998.

[91] "Health will benefit since housing is an essential component of the programme for shifting the balance of care from institutional to community care. Social work will benefit since most people in need of community care live, or should live, in their own homes, and suitable housing is required to allow social work authorities to fulfil their duty to secure the provision of community care. Finally, housing will benefit since it needs the support of social work and health services in providing for customers with community care needs. In short, within the field of community care the three sectors are *mutually dependent*, and must co-operate to succeed." SWSG 7/94 (emphasis added).

[92] SWSG 7/94, para. 3.7.

[93] 1968 Act, s. 12A(3)(b).

[94] The general duties contained in s. 12 of the 1968 Act do not incorporate a duty to provide housing, as clarified in *Assessor for Edinburgh v. Brodie*, 1976 S.L.T. (Lands Tr.) 234. The question in this instance was whether the reference in that section to the duty to provide "residential and other establishments" extended to a duty to provide housing. On the basis that the definition of both "establishments" and "residential establishments" in s. 94 of the 1968 Act began "an establishment managed by a local authority", s. 12 was deemed by the court to refer to something other than a private house.

[95] 1976 S.L.T. (Lands Tr.) 234.

[96] SWSG 7/94, para. 3.18.

required, the social work department may find a place in residential accommodation.[97] The nature of this process stresses the need for co-operation between housing and social work departments.

Responsibility for housing in Scotland is shared between local housing authorities, Scottish Homes, housing associations, and both the voluntary and private sectors.[98] While each body has an individual role to play there is a considerable degree of overlap and co-operation in securing housing for both disabled and non-disabled residents. Both the young and elderly segments of the disabled population are more likely to live in public rented accommodation and account for a small proportion of owner occupiers. They will usually be exempt from the right to buy their own local authority homes.[99]

Adaptation and improvement

7.53 Housing can be specifically designed so as to manage the needs of people with mobility problems, though to the extent that it is also suitable for people without special needs. On the other hand, housing which is designed for able-bodied people cannot always accommodate those who are physically disabled. Emphasis is increasingly placed on the need to build flexibility into mainstream housing so as to ensure that care groups are absorbed into the community at maximum level.[1] In 1974 the Department of the Environment distinguished between wheelchair and mobility type housing. Wheelchair housing is designed to give people who need to use a wheelchair full time, access to all main rooms, whilst mobility housing allows disabled people to move around freely within their homes and is just as suitable for non-disabled tenants.[2] The Scottish Office recommendation in terms of total housing stock presently stands at 1 per cent built to wheelchair standard and 10 per cent to mobility standard.[3]

Local authorities play a crucial role in the adaptation of homes given the large stock of existing homes under their control.[4] Funding for the adaptation of housing association property is provided by Scottish Homes, and by central government for the conversion of local government and owner-occupied property. The occupational therapist plays a key role in decision-making on adaptations in each of these instances. The law which relates to housing adaptations in Scotland is principally contained within Part XIII of the 1987 Act.

If, during a community care assessment, it becomes apparent that a client is disabled, he or she will be entitled to an assessment under the 1970 Act. Section 2 qualifies the type of assistance which may be given to disabled people in their homes and includes practical assistance in the home, assistance in making arrangements for adaptation of the home, and the provision of additional facilities designed to secure greater safety, comfort or convenience.[5] However, since the 1970 Act the rights of disabled people to have their homes adapted have been further extended. The 1987 Act empowers, and in some instances obligates, local authorities to allocate repair and improvement grants to disabled people to assist in the

[97] 1968 Act, s. 59. Code of Guidance on Homelessness, para. 4.14.
[98] See Chap. 9 on Housing.
[99] see para. 7.54 below on sheltered housing.
[1] SWSG 7/94, para. 3.26.
[2] *Disability Rights Handbook 1997–98*, Disability Alliance, ERA.
[3] *Scottish Housing Handbook No.6 (Housing for the Disabled)*. Further guidance to local authorities on how to estimate aggregate housing and support needs for the main community care client groups, incorporating those with physical and multiple disabilities, is forthcoming at the time of writing.
[4] *The Ewing Inquiry*, p. 21.
[5] See para. 7.09 above.

alteration of their homes to meet their own specific needs. Assistance under the 1970 Act is distinct from and supplementary to that provided under the 1987 Act.

Sheltered housing

In an endeavour to preserve housing stock which has been specially adapted for the needs of people who are disabled and elderly, homes in that bracket are exempt from the provisions of "right to buy" under section 61 of the 1987 Act. Specifically, housing which has been fitted with a call system and the services of a warden cannot be purchased by the occupier.[6] Furthermore, where 50 per cent of a group of no more than 14 houses owned by a housing association in the same neighbourhood are let for the purposes of community care, their occupants are unable to purchase their own homes.[7] This is what is referred to as sheltered housing.[8] It is primarily provided by local authorities and housing associations, though Scottish Homes do make some provision.[9] The amount of sheltered housing in Scotland is rising, a trend which may well reflect the growth of elderly and disabled people who occupy their own homes in the community instead of places in institutional care.[10] In many instances, sheltered housing serves as a popular compromise between residential and community care.

7.54

It is enough to exempt a house from the tenant's right to purchase, that it is designed and equipped to accommodate a warden who is resident in a group of houses provided with a call system and warden services. In *Moonie v. Dundee District Council*[11] the tenant was excluded from the right to purchase a home which had been adapted according to these terms, despite the fact that she herself was neither of pensionable age nor disabled. The court was of the opinion that the provisions applied to the house, not the tenant, who could not be allowed to deplete the stock of specially adapted homes.

In *Houston v. East Kilbride Development Corporation*[12] the tenant was the resident warden in a sheltered housing complex and sought to purchase the home on the basis of her secure tenancy. The house did not itself contain a call system, though it had been designed to accommodate a warden and contained receiving equipment connected to the call system. It was also joined to the neighbouring house occupied by another warden, with a communicating door. Further to an appeal against the refusal of the application, the applicant was found to be entitled to purchase the house. It did not constitute sheltered housing for the purposes of section 61 unless it had been specifically provided with a call system and warden services, which it had not. Similarly, an applicant had a right to buy a house which was not fitted with a call system but which was in one of three tower blocks fitted with emergency lighting and wired to provide for the installation of a call system. In order to be excluded from the right

---

[6]   Housing (Scotland) Act 1987 ("1987 Act"), s. 61(4)(a).
[7]   *ibid.*, s. 61(4)(f).
[8]   Housing may be sheltered, very sheltered, or sheltered wheelchair housing. In the first instance dwellings are located at ground or first floor, or above when a lift has been fitted, and will have additional safety features and a warden service. Very sheltered housing will, in addition to these amenities, have special bathroom facilities and meals provided, as well as an added dimension of care from carers and extra wardens. Finally, sheltered wheelchair housing is designed to accommodate elderly wheelchair users and carries the above features in addition: see *Community Care Scotland Statistical Bulletin 1997*, Nov. 1998.
[9]   In March 1997, 51 per cent of all sheltered housing was provided by local authorities, and 46 per cent by housing associations: see *Community Care Scotland Statistical Bulletin 1997*, Nov. 1998.
[10] Between 1996 and 1998 there was a 4 per cent increase in the number of public sector sheltered housing dwellings. This was a 26 per cent increase in the period since 1990.
[11] 1992 S.L.T. (Lands Tr.) 103.
[12] 1995 S.L.T. (Lands Tr.) 12.

to buy under section 61 it was not sufficient, in light of the lack of facilities, that the house was included in a block which was adapted to the needs of elderly and disabled people.[13]

Improvement grants

7.55 A local authority is regulated by both a discretion and an obligation to confer an improvement grant depending upon whether the improvement is standard or non-standard in nature. Improvement grants will usually be made to assist in the alteration or enlargement of a house, or in the completion of works which will make the house suitable for the accommodation, welfare or employment of the disabled person, and includes repair and replacement work.[14] Grants can be made to improve housing which is a disabled person's only or main residence, or housing which will become so within a reasonable time after the relevant works are completed.[15] It is not relevant that other non-disabled people are residing in the home in question. An application must be submitted to the local authority from whom the grant is being sought, and must detail both plans and costs for the proposed works.[16]

Grants which relate exclusively to standard amenities are guaranteed, though works on completion must meet the tolerable standard.[17] Standard amenities are specified in Schedule 18 to the 1987 Act.[18] The house must also have a life expectancy of at least 10 years before a grant is awarded.[19] A disabled occupant may be entitled to install a standard amenity even if one is already in place, if it is deemed essential to meet their needs.[20] For instance, if a toilet has already been installed on one floor and the person cannot reach it, another grant may be available to put a toilet on another floor so that it becomes more accessible to the disabled person.[21]

An application may be made to assist with the improvement of a house through the installation of a non-standard amenity, in other words, one which is not specified in Schedule 18 to the 1987 Act. In this instance there is no guarantee of financial assistance from the local authority.[22] The owner of any land on which non-standard improvement works are to be carried out must give written consent. A local authority will not issue an improvement grant for a non-standard amenity where the house in question has a life expectancy of less than 30 years after the work has been completed, and in any case no less than 10, or where improvements will prevent other houses in the same building from being improved themselves.[23]

---

13 *Holloran v. Dumbarton D. C.*, 1992 S.L.T. (Lands Tr.) 73.
14 1987 Act, s. 236(2).
15 *ibid.*, s. 236(3).
16 1987 Act, s. 237. The application form itself is prescribed by the Housing (Forms) (Scotland) Regulations 1980 (S.I. 1980 No.1647) as amended by the Housing (Forms) (Scotland) Amendment Regulations 1996 (S.I. 1996 No. 632) to account for the change from using rateable values to using council tax valuation bands as a means of imposing valuation limits above which applications for improvements and repair grants in respect of certain houses will not be approved.
17 1987 Act, s. 244(1). The definition of a tolerable standard is contained at s. 86 of the Act. In short, it must be structurally stable and free from damp, with satisfactory heating, ventilation, water and drainage provision, facilities for cooking and access to external doors and outbuildings.
18 Fixed bath, hot and cold water supply at a fixed bath or shower, wash-hand basin, hot and cold water at a wash-hand basin, sink, hot and cold water supply at a sink, water closet.
19 1987 Act, s. 244(4).
20 *ibid.*, s. 244(3).
21 Under s. 244(2) of the 1987 Act, works which propose to prevent the improvement of any other house in the same building will not be assisted by the local authority.
22 1987 Act, s. 240.
23 1987 Act, s. 240(2)(a) and the Scottish Development Department Circular 21/1988, para. 3.

The maximum grant payable to the applicant for standard or non-standard improvements **7.56** is prescribed by the Housing (Percentage of Approved Expense for Improvement Grants) (Disabled Occupants) (Scotland) Order 1982[24] and presently stands at 75 per cent of the approved costs of the adaptations, though this must not exceed £12,600.[25] A grant may be retrospectively increased where works exceed the amount originally contained in the estimate, though the local authority must be satisfied that the circumstances were outwith the control or influence of the applicant.[26] Where a house is owned and situated in a housing action area or subject to an improvement order, the percentage payable may be increased from 75 per cent to 90 per cent where the housing authority is satisfied that the applicant will suffer undue hardship in meeting the remaining costs once the initial grant has been paid.[27] Grants may be made within one month of completion or by instalments as the work progresses.[28] Works must be completed within 12 months of making the grant or any sums paid will be redeemed by the local authority.[29] Grants can also be sought for replacement and repair works in addition to the original improvement or adaptation. The local authority may fund repairs which cost up to 50 per cent of the original work.[30] For instance, Mr B requests an improvement grant for the installation of a stair lift. The existing stairwell is in a state of disrepair and requires restoration before it can take the weight of the new lift. The lift will cost £4,000 and the wall repair will cost £2,500. The maximum grant payable for the installation of the lift is 75 per cent—£3,000. The extra grant payable is 50 per cent of the cost of £4,000 and so £2,000 is added to the original £3,000.[31] It is foreseeable that 50 per cent of the cost of the original work does not adequately cover the repair work which is necessary for the original work to completed. A disabled person will generally be in a position to receive another grant for new adaptations.[32]

Duties under the Chronically Sick and Disabled Persons Act 1970 are supplementary to those of the local housing department and any sums outstanding for works to adapt the home once the improvement grant has been paid may be met by the social work department.[33]

THE EWING INQUIRY[34]

The Ewing Inquiry was an initiative of Disability Scotland in light of the growing concerns **7.57** expressed through its members that a lack of choice and growing shortages in suitable accommodation was inhibiting care in the community for disabled people. The Committee of Inquiry undertook to investigate the state of housing in Scotland for people with physical disabilities. Following a survey of the policies of both housing associations and local authorities, and in addition of the experiences of a small sample of disabled people located in Scotland's central belt, the Committee identified what it perceived to be the primary

[24] 1987 Act, s. 242(7), (8) and (9).
[25] Under s. 242(4)(a) of the 1987 Act the Secretary of State may be requested to increase the limit where there is good reason for him to do so.
[26] 1987 Act, s. 242(2).
[27] *ibid.*, s. 250(1)–(5).
[28] *ibid.*, s. 243(1).
[29] *ibid.*, s. 243(3).
[30] *ibid.*, ss. 236(2)(b) and 242(3).
[31] *Access to Housing in Scotland: Rights for Disabled People*, Scottish Homes (1995).
[32] 1987 Act, s. 282(5).
[33] Scottish Office Circular SDD 40/1985 *Provision of Aids, Equipment and House Adaptations for Disabled People Living at Home*, para. 2. Grants are also available from Scottish Homes for disabled people in exceptional circumstances, to help them purchase a new house under a Special Needs Capital Grant Scheme.
[34] *The Ewing Inquiry* (1994, Edinburgh, Disability Scotland).

impediments to a comprehensive and supportive system of housing rights for disabled people:

(a) planning information on the numbers and locations of accessible housing and on the location of suitable homes for conversion was at times poor, as were processes for recording adaptations giving rise to a lack of co-ordination between housing providers; a number of joint planning initiatives were identified and, while they showed potential, were at times of surface reparation value, failing to get to the root of the difficulties encumbent in planning housing for disabled people;

(b) gaps in the extent to which housing providers across Scotland were giving full effect to barrier-free housing, especially private house builders who lack both the interest and the inclination to build houses sensitive to the needs of disabled;[35]

(c) dissatisfaction with the management services of local housing authorities in terms of housing allocations, nominations to housing associations and house adaptations; policies and resources did not fully reflect the responsibility on housing authorities in relation to adaptations; there was a lack of housing services for disabled people;

(d) the bewildering scene which often faces disabled people looking for accommodation is the result of inadequate advice and information on the services and help available notwithstanding the statutory responsibility of local authorities to inform disabled people of their rights to assistance[36]; there was corresponding lack of consultation with disabled people and the groups representing them on housing policies and wider housing issues.

Accordingly the Committee sought to redress these anomalies in the key recommendations contained at the close of the final Report, appealing initially to the Scottish Office to strengthen the requirements for barrier-free housing through amendment of the Building Regulations.[37] It also recommended that the Scottish Housing Handbooks incorporate barrier-free standards and suggested that responsibility for these handbooks might be passed to Scottish Homes. In an effort to avoid any further deficit in housing provision for disabled people, the Scottish Office was asked to issue guidelines to Scottish Homes and local housing authorities on conditions of transfers of housing stock to other landlords with a view to ensuring that the property transferred from the public sector was available for both renting and for adaptation and conversion should a disabled tenant choose to occupy it. The Committee was clearly keen to expand the choice of tenure available to disabled people and in this pursuit stressed the need to provide for choice, including shared ownership. In response to problems of housing management, local authorities were urged to appoint disability housing managers to co-ordinate and improve services, and were further encouraged to develop initiatives for matching individual needs to available housing.[38]

7.58   In the period since the Ewing Inquiry a number of initiatives have sought to gratify its recommendations. The Scottish Office has endorsed barrier-free design as the preferred standard for mainstream housing to the extent that housing funded by Scottish Homes will be

---

[35] Barrier-free housing is defined as housing "designed as new, or adapted in the course of refurbishment, to allow access to the less able-bodied and internally allow for wheelchair manoeuvre and step free access to a WC. Also switches, controls etc. should be easily reached from a wheelchair or by someone who has difficulty stretching or bending": Scottish Homes, *Consultation Paper on Barrier-free Housing* (August 1993).

[36] s. 1 of the 1970 Act places a duty on local authorities to publish information on services provided by it under s. 12 of the 1968 Act: see para. 7.12 above.

[37] It was also urged to enter into discussions with the Royal Incorporation of Architects in Scotland: p. 32.

[38] *The Ewing Inquiry*, p. 33.

built to barrier-free standards unless there are good reasons to justify a failure to do so. Both the private sector and local authorities will seek to comply with similar expectations. Notwithstanding, barrier-free standards will not at present be incorporated into forthcoming amendments to the Building Standards (Scotland) Regulations 1990 in terms of access to all new dwellings. Guidance on a number of aspects of disabled housing needs is imminent and at the time of writing awaits consultation and subsequent responses.[39] Some other independent schemes have complemented these developments.[40]

HOMELESSNESS[41]

Council house allocation is regulated by section 20 of the 1987 Act which stresses that reasonable preference is to be given to homeless people. Allocations should be based on need and urgency of need. Consequently, "unintentionally homeless people in priority need should always be included in a local authority's mainstream allocation system as from the date of the application rather than at a later date."[42] Housing authorities have duties under Part II of the 1987 Act to secure that accommodation becomes available to disabled people who are homeless and are deemed automatically to be in priority need.[43] Section 37(1) of the Act requires local authorities to have regard to guidance which is issued by the Secretary of State in the exercise of their homelessness functions and in some sense are bound by its contents to a lesser extent than social work departments under section 51(A) of the Social Work (Scotland) Act 1968.[44] While local authorities have a discretion to deal with each application on its merits, a failure to have regard to the material considerations of the guidance may give grounds for judicial review of a local authority's decision.[45]

A person may be homeless when they have accommodation but it is not sufficient for the entire household, carers included, it is overcrowded and consequently presenting a danger to health, it is a mobile home, or perhaps most crucially for a disabled person, where the current accommodation is not reasonable for the person to continue living there.[46] Whether a home is reasonable will be considered in the wider context of the local authority area and its general housing circumstances.[47] A home which is deficient in meeting the physical needs of a disabled person, for instance where a wheelchair cannot be accommodated, will not be a reasonable home for that person. If adaptation cannot be undertaken, the person may be

7.59

---

[39] This includes Prevalence Guidance on how to estimate aggregate housing and support needs for community care client groups, and the guidance which supplements SWSG 7/94: see p. 244 n. 89 above.

[40] For instance, a Disabled Persons Housing Service was established in 1996 which has since developed a database system operating in and around Edinburgh. Information on both the housing needs of disabled people in the area, and on the full range of housing options available from local landlords in the public, private and voluntary sectors is fed into the database and used to construct Personal Housing Plans: see *Personal Housing Plans for People with Physical Disabilities* (1996, Edinburgh, Scottish Homes). Further to a study of housing and advice services for disabled people which revealed a shortage of suitable housing in Scotland to meet their needs and a huge information deficit, Scottish Homes produced comprehensive advice on both housing adaptation and homelessness: *Access to Housing in Scotland: Rights for Disabled People* (1995, Edinburgh, Scottish Homes).

[41] For core reading on homelessness provisions generally, see Chap. 7, paras 9.20 *et seq.*

[42] Code of Guidance on Homelessness (1997 Scottish Office Development Department, para. 10.25.

[43] 1987 Act, s. 31.

[44] Code of Guidance on Homelessness (1997).

[45] See *R. v. Wandsworth LBC, ex p. Hawthorne* [1995] All E.R. 331; *R. v. Tower Hamlets LBC, ex p. Mouna Mahmood*, Mar. 1993, *Legal Action* 12 (QBD); *R. v. Shrewsbury and Atcham B.C., ex p. Griffiths* (1993) 25 H.L.R. 613, (QBD); *R. v. West Dorset D.C. ex p. Phillips* (1985) 17 H.L.R. 336, (QBD); *R. v. Newham LBC, ex p. Bones* (1991) 23 H.L.R. 35 (QBD) for examples of judicial review of decisions by local housing authorities which failed to take account of guidance on homelessness.

[46] 1987 Act, s. 24.

[47] *ibid.*, s. 24(2B).

entitled to be rehoused under this provision. To date there is no authoritative definition of what makes accommodation unreasonable to the extent that a person cannot be expected to continue to occupy it. There are suggestions as to what might justify a refusal to continue living in a home.[48] Furthermore, a sudden or gradual deterioration in the applicant's health, perhaps accompanied by a spell in residential or hospital care, or an awareness that a person's house does not meet his needs further to a community care assessment, will constitute changed circumstances which render an application possible. Likewise, if the applicant's spouse is no longer able to help him or her manage the house it may no longer be reasonable to continue to occupy the accommodation.

Priority need

7.60 Where an applicant is homeless or threatened with homelessness[49] the housing department will have to decide whether that person is a priority need person and will have to establish that they became homeless unintentionally. Once satisfied as to these requirements it is compelled to provide accommodation for the person in need.[50] A person who is vulnerable as a result of old age, mental illness or handicap, physical disability or other special reason, is contained within the category of priority need.[51] Furthermore, someone with whom such a person resides or might reasonably be expected to reside, falls within the definition. Guidance states that chronically sick people, including people with AIDS and HIV-related illnesses, may well constitute people who are vulnerable for a special reason, not only because their illness has progressed to the point of physical or mental disability, but because the manifestations of their illness, or common attitudes towards it, make it very difficult for them to find stable or suitable accommodation, and they may also become subject to harassment.[52]

However in *Re Desmond McAulay*[53] the Court of Session chose to support the decision of a local housing authority to refuse to rehouse an applicant when homelessness was alleged to have resulted from the effects of a long-term illness. The petitioner, by virtue of his impediment, was predisposed to abnormalities of behaviour which manifested themselves in confrontational disputes with his neighbours. Specialist medical opinion advised that he was suffering from Gilles de la Tourette Syndrome and had been since the age of seven, giving rise to uncontrollable vocalisations, commonly taking the form of swear words, intermittent twitching of the face and shoulders and obsessional and compulsive symptoms. His contention was the tendency of neighbouring residents to verbally and physically threaten him and his family. The petitioners had a history of such altercations and were at the time of their application residing in their sixth council property. No consideration was given to the possibility that they were a priority need unit as a result of the illness suffered and its

[48] For instance, a lack of space to store a wheelchair; lack of central heating where illness necessitates that a particular body temperature is maintained; a home which is outwith walking distance of a disabled applicant's family which provides help on a regular basis; a home which is situated in an area with steep gradients or excessive distance from shops and amenities if a manual wheelchair is the only means of mobility: HomePoint, Scottish Homes.
[49] A person is threatened with homelessness if it is likely he will become homeless within 28 days: 1987 Act, s. 24(4).
[50] 1987 Act, s. 31(2).
[51] *ibid.*, s. 25(1)(c).
[52] Code of Guidance on Homelessness (1997), para. 7.3.
[53] 1996 S.L.T. (Notes) 318.

unfortunate displays. This application was in fact refused on the grounds that no other suitable property was available in the local authority area which was substantially different from that in which they were already residing.

Permanent accommodation must be able to contain the applicant and any other persons **7.61** who it is reasonable to expect will reside with him.[54] If a disabled person is offered accommodation without room for a carer, he or she will be entitled to refuse it on the grounds that it is not technically available to him. In *R. v. Hackney LBC, ex p. Tonnicodi*[55] a decision taken by a local authority to provide accommodation for a disabled person in priority need though not for his carer was quashed when the local authority was deemed to have applied the wrong test in deciding whether that person was someone who might reasonably be expected to reside with the homeless person. The carer in question had lived with the applicant for three years before the two entered the United Kingdom together and sought to continue that arrangement. Further to an application to their local housing authority, accommodation was provided which did not make requisite provision for the carer. The local authority had reached its decision on the basis that to cope with a disability the applicant did not actually need a live-in carer. The court refuted this approach and redirected the local authority to consider whether the carer in question was someone who might reasonably be expected to live with the individual concerned rather than making an assessment of the applicant's need for care. In drawing its conclusions a local authority was required to make reference to the contents of a Code of Guidance which the respondents had overlooked. In particular it underlined the need to include in the assessment "persons who normally live with the applicant but who are unable to do so for no other reason than that there is no accommodation in which they can live together." This English case was decided on the basis of provisions which replicate section 41 of the 1987 Act.[56] Furthermore, accommodation which is overcrowded or which might endanger the health of the occupants can also be refused on the grounds that it is not actually accommodation.[57] However, there is no legal requirement that it must be either suitable or reasonable.[58]

Disabled people should not be discharged from hospital without an assessment of their **7.62** needs as they will almost always need help to settle back into the community.[59] If that assessment determines that accommodation is necessary, it should be provided before discharge.[60] Where emergency accommodation is required it may be good practice for housing and social work departments to delegate authority to decide on immediate admissions to voluntary and other bodies running emergency accommodation.[61] Section 39 of the 1987 Act serves to encourage the role of voluntary organisations in accommodating homeless people and allows local authorities to make available to such organisations local authority premises, furniture and goods and services by local authority staff. The Code of Guidance suggests that people being discharged from institutions will require extra care to ensure that

---

[54] 1987 Act, s. 41.
[55] Dec. 4, 1997 (QBD).
[56] Housing Act 1985, s. 75.
[57] 1987 Act, s. 32(5).
[58] In *Bradley v. Motherwell D. C.*, 1994 S.L.T. 739 an applicant in priority need was offered accommodation under s. 31(2). While it was neither overcrowded nor causing a danger to her health under the terms of s. 32(5), she sought to refuse it on the grounds that it was "unreasonable" for her to occupy it. The court was not sympathetic to this notion and did not feel that additional words could be added to the relevant statutory provisions to qualify accommodation.
[59] This may include an assessment of any carers who are to assist the individual. See paras 7.21–7.23 above.
[60] SWSG 11/91, para. 15.2.
[61] Code of Guidance on Homelessness (1997), para. 5.16.

they are not discharged to a homelessness service. Pre-discharge discussions should eliminate fears that housing difficulties might impair the chances of discharge.[62]

If an applicant has a "local connection" with the local authority area in which he is seeking to be housed, this will assist in the subsequent provision of accommodation. Such a connection will exist where he is or was normally resident in the area by choice, has a job or family there, or has some other special circumstances,[63] for instance if he receives medical treatment in that area. This is quite separate from the test of "ordinary residence" in deciding which local authority has responsibility for meeting community care needs.[64]

---

[62] "Advance planning will be required to ensure accommodation is available for long-stay patients who are discharged from hospital, sometimes several years in advance where new accommodation has to be provided, particularly specialist accommodation": Code of Guidance on Homelessness, para. 3.36.

[63] 1987 Act, s. 27.

[64] See para. 7.18 above. The significance of this lack of legislative co-ordination was outlined by the Health Committee in its 1992–93 Report Community Care: The Way Forward: "Currently it is perfectly possible for a homeless person with community care needs to be eligible for community care services such as domiciliary support because they are "ordinarily resident" but for there to be no responsibility on the housing authority to provide accommodation because they have no "local connection": 482–I, para. 106–7.

Chapter 8

SOCIAL WORK AND THE CRIMINAL JUSTICE SYSTEM

INTRODUCTION

It is a regrettable fact that many of the client groups which social work embraces will **8.01** interface with the criminal justice system. Elsewhere in this book (particularly in Chapter 4 in respect of children, and Chapter 7 in respect of the mentally disordered), one will have noted particular rules, processes and procedures for certain sections of the community. This chapter seeks to discuss the criminal justice system in its broader application to the whole community.

The criminal justice system represents a major component of social work provision. Following the merging of probationary services into singular social work departments in the late 1960s, the nature and extent of social work provision to the criminal justice system has considerably expanded.[1] In 1991 the Government decided to wholly fund social work provision to the criminal justice system. At the time it was said that:

"The Government's objective in refunding to local authorities the full approved cost of funding social work services for the criminal justice system is to ensure that the services which the courts require for dealing with offenders in the community are available in the right quantity and at the right quality ... The provision of community disposals of sufficient quality and quantity will enable sentencers to use them in cases where otherwise they might have imposed a custodial sentence. The overall aim is to create a situation in which it is practicable to use prisons as sparingly as possible through providing community based disposals which contain and reduce offending behaviour, assist social integration, have the confidence of the courts and the wider public, and make efficient and effective use of sentencing resources".[2]

Reorganisation along specialist lines and government funding gave much cause for optimism[3] and while there have been many tangible benefits attached to the new arrangements, the price paid for funding has been more centralised control. This is illustrated by the

---

[1] See McIvor, "Social Work and Criminal Justice in Scotland : Developments in Policy and Practice" (1994) 24 *British Journal of Social Work* 429–448 at pp. 429–30.

[2] SWSG National Objectives and Standards for Social Work Services in the Criminal Justice System (1991), Scottish Office, paras 4 and 5.

[3] McIvor, *op. cit.* at p. 443.

full system of inspection by the Social Work Services Group in 1992–93 of arrangements put in place by local authorities.[4]

The Role of the Police and Police Powers

Organisation of the police

8.02 The modern legal framework for the police is contained in the Police (Scotland) Act 1967. Certain important matters are also dealt with in the Police (Scotland) Regulations 1976. Historically, in Scotland at least, police forces have been localised organisations linked primarily to local government. There are now eight Scottish police forces. They are maintained by separate police authorities. Police authorities in Scotland have the power to appoint their senior officers, the Chief Constable and his deputy and assistants, subject to the approval of the Secretary of State for Scotland. In practice, at the time of appointment, the police authority draws up a shortlist which is then submitted to the Secretary of State for approval. Thereafter, any appointment is ratified by him. The police authority has the power to dismiss or retire these senior officers in the interests of the efficiency of the force, though the consent of the Secretary of State must be sought.[5] The police authority is also under a duty to provide necessary premises and equipment, though central government may also do this.

The police authority receives an annual report from its Chief Constable. In practice there are usually several meetings of the police authority to discuss matters throughout the year. In reality, whilst the police authority appears to oversee the workings of the local police force, two major factors militate against outright control. First, the power of the Chief Constable once appointed, and second the powers conferred on the Secretary of State. For operational purposes the police force is under the control of the Chief Constable and he is not accountable to the police authority for his operational actions. This has in the past provoked division between some police authorities and their senior police officer.

The Secretary of State has the following powers:

- power to consent to senior appointments;

- powers in appeals in disciplinary, dismissal and compulsory retirement cases;

- power to make regulations in relation to pay, discipline, organisation, training;

- power to require reports from Chief Constables;

- power to give grants to police authorities (50 per cent of funding is given by central government);

- power through the police inspectorate to inspect individual forces or to hold inquiries into these forces;

- power relating to the amalgamation of forces;

- power to provide central services including the supply of guns or C.S. gas.

These powers are quite considerable leaving limited scope for the police authority to influence in any major way the operation of the police force which it maintains.

4   SWSI, *Social Work Services in the Criminal Justice System: Achieving National Standards* (1993).
5   White, "Disciplining Chief Constables", 1998 S.L.T. (News) 77.

Complaints against the police

At common law a police constable is personally liable to be sued for damages in respect of **8.03** any wrongful or unlawful acts which he commits in the course of his duties. He may also be liable for a wilful neglect of duty and thus a crime at common law.[6] Prior to the passing of the main Acts governing the police in the 1960's there was no vicarious liability attaching to the police authority in respect of wrongful acts of a policeman. However, with the passing of the 1967 Act, the Chief Constable is vicariously liable for the wrongful acts committed by constables in the course of their duty.[7] The police authority also has a discretionary power to pay damages awarded against a policeman. Suing the police is no easy matter, especially where a failure of duty is alleged.[8]

The issue of complaints against the police has been the subject of considerable controversy. In Scotland the system is fairly simple but nevertheless imperfect. Someone may complain to the Chief Constable or directly to the procurator fiscal who has the power to prefer criminal charges.

Where a crime is alleged against a police officer the procurator fiscal has a duty to investigate. If a complaint is made direct to the police of criminal conduct by a police officer, the assistant chief constable is required to refer the complaint to the procurator fiscal. It may be that the matter is one of misconduct stopping short of criminal conduct and as such it will be referred back to the police to be dealt with. On receipt of a referral a regional procurator fiscal may investigate the matter himself, instruct the procurator fiscal for the district, or instruct a fiscal from another part of the region to investigate and report to him. Complaints against the police are often associated with pending criminal proceedings against the complainer and the regional procurator fiscal has the power to discontinue the relevant current proceedings or delay the trial. The procurator fiscal staff will interview the complainer and any other material witness. In this respect if criminal proceedings are still pending, the complainer will be cautioned that he does not require to answer any question which relates to the outstanding charges against him. It is an offence to make a false and malicious complaint against a police officer.[9] The statements of the complainer and the witnesses are not to be made available to the procurator fiscal who will take the complainer's trial. The regional fiscal is under a duty not to withhold any evidence which may be beneficial to the complainer's subsequent defence.

If the regional procurator fiscal decides there is no substance to the complaint he will inform the complainer, the assistant chief constable, and, if appropriate, the district procurator fiscal. If there is substance to the allegation, the regional procurator fiscal will submit a report of the evidence to the Crown Office in Edinburgh for an assessment and recommendation. All reports submitted are considered by a Law Officer—the Lord Advocate or the Solicitor-General. Investigations are expected to be concluded within four months of receipt of a report from the assistant chief constable. In cases where there is insufficient proof to proceed to prosecute an officer but there are grounds for concern that conduct has fallen below accepted standards, the procurator fiscal may refer the matter back to the assistant chief constable in the belief that the police officer may fall within the scope of police misconduct regulations.[10]

---

[6] *Wilson v. Smith*, 1997 S.L.T. (Sh.Ct) 91.
[7] Police (Scotland) Act 1967, s. 39.
[8] See Brodie, "Pursuing The Police", 1995 J.R. 292; see also Brodie, "Public Authorities and the Duty of Care", 1996 J.R. 127.
[9] Moreover it is possible that one may be sued in civil law for defamation: see Crichton-Styles, "Two Flaws in the Law of Defamation", 1991 S.L.T. (News) 31–36.
[10] See Report of Crown Office and Procurator Fiscal Service 1997/98, Annex 1.

Powers of the police

8.04   Police powers are for most part contained in the Criminal Procedure (Scotland) Act 1995. They can be sub-classified into arrest, detention, search and seizure.

Arrest, detention, and questioning

8.05   Arrests may be made on order of a warrant issued by a justice of the peace, sheriff or a senior judge. Equally, arrests may be made without a warrant. Only the persons *afore*mentioned can continue a detention of an arrest without warrant and anyone arrested must be taken before a court. At common law, it is generally accepted that an arrest may be made without a warrant where a constable apprehends someone in the commission of a crime or reasonably suspects someone of committing a crime. The lawfulness of arrest without warrant at common law is generally weighed up in the circumstances. Notwithstanding, statute has conferred in many instances the power to arrest without warrant. An arrested person has the right immediately to have intimation sent to a solicitor and in addition that person has the right to a private interview with their solicitor.[11]

Section 13(1) of the Criminal Procedure (Scotland) Act 1995 ("1995 Act") states that,

> "where a constable has reasonable grounds for suspecting that a person has committed or is committing an offence at any place [a constable] may require (a) that person, if found at that place or any place where the constable is entitled to be, to give his name and address and may ask him for an explanation of the circumstances which have given rise to the constable's suspicion".

Equally, anyone else found at the scene who the constable believes has information relating to the suspected offence can be required to give his name and address. Suspects may also be required to remain with the constable until such time as the address given can be verified or any explanation noted.[12] A constable may exercise reasonable force to detain the person suspected but not any witness.[13] On detention, the constable shall inform the person of the nature of the offence suspected, the reason for requiring his or her address, and that failure to comply may constitute an offence.[14] It is an offence not, without reasonable excuse, to give the details requested, for a which a person may be arrested without a warrant.[15] The Act does not offer any guidance on what amounts to "reasonable suspicion" and courts have demonstrated that they are prepared to give considerable latitude to police officers. In *Dryburgh v. Galt*[16] it was said:

> "the fact that the information on which the police officer formed his suspicion turns out to be ill-founded does not necessarily establish that the police officer's suspicion was unfounded. The circumstances known to the police officer at the time he formed his suspicion constitute the criterion, not the facts as subsequently ascertained".

Where the constable has reasonable grounds for suspecting that a person has committed or is committing an offence punishable by imprisonment, he may detain him for the purposes of carrying out his investigations, and as soon as reasonably practicable take him to a police

---

[11]   Criminal Procedure (Scotland) Act 1995 ("1995 Act"), s. 17.
[12]   *ibid.*, s. 13(2).
[13]   *ibid.*, s. 13(4).
[14]   *ibid.*, s. 13(5).
[15]   *ibid.*, s. 13(6) and (7).
[16]   1981 S.C.C.R. 27 at 29, *per* Lord Wheatley.

station or other premises.[17] Detention may last for only six hours or until the subject is arrested, whichever is the earlier. A person must be informed immediately once his detention ends. That person shall not be detained again on the same grounds, or on any grounds arising out of the same circumstances. However, it is possible to be detained and released for a period of less than six hours and be subsequently detained for a period which, taken with the earlier detention, does not exceed six hours. At the time of detention the police officer will inform the suspect of the general nature of the offence and the reason for his detention.[18] Records require to be kept of the place of detention, the time at which it began, when the person was informed of his rights, and the time of release from detention. If a suspect is detained in England and transported to Scotland, there is an allowable four-hour period for the accused to be transported north before the six-hour detention begins.[19]

A person has the right to have his solicitor and another reasonable person named by him **8.06** notified of his detention or his arrest without delay. However, the police may delay the notification where it is necessary in the interests of the investigation or the prevention of crime, or the apprehension of offenders.[20] If the person detained or arrested appears to the police officer to be a child under 16 years of age he is required to notify the person's custodial parent. "Parent" is defined as a parent or guardian, or someone who has actual custody of the child. If the parent is suspected of being involved in the crime the police have a discretion to allow access but in all other cases must grant access to the child by the parent.[21] In *H.M. Advocate v. GB and DJM*[22] there was a denial of parental access and a confession obtained from the child was subsequently held inadmissible. In addition where it is in the interests of the child's welfare or of furthering the investigation access may be restricted.[23] It is usual for children to be released on an undertaking by the child or the parent to appear in court at a later date.[24] A child will not be released if he is charged with a homicide offence, or if it is necessary to remove him from association with any criminal or prostitute, or where the police officer believes that the child's liberation may defeat the ends of justice.[25] If the child is not released he will be detained in a place of safety unless a police officer of the rank of inspector or above certifies that (a) it is impracticable to do so; (b) he is of such unruly character that he cannot safely be detained; or (c) by reason of his state of health or of his mental or bodily condition it is inadvisable to detain him.[26] There is power to take a detained or arrested drunken person to a specially designated clinic for treatment of alcohol abuse.[27] The provision is rarely used due to absence of designated premises.[28]

Powers of search and gathering evidence

A person may not be searched to obtain evidence to justify arrest but an arrested suspect may **8.07** be searched.[29] A police officer must have reasonable grounds for undertaking a search, for

---

[17] See generally 1995 Act, s. 14.
[18] See *Ucak v. H.M. Advocate*, 1998 S.C.C.R. 517 for an instance of the detention of a person unable to speak English.
[19] Criminal Justice and Public Order Act 1994, s. 138(6)(a).
[20] 1995 Act, s. 15(1).
[21] *ibid.*, s. 15(4).
[22] 1991 S.C.C.R. 533.
[23] 1995 Act, s. 15(5).
[24] *ibid.*, s. 43(1).
[25] *ibid.*, s. 43(3).
[26] *ibid.*, s. 43(4).
[27] *ibid.*, s. 16.
[28] See Shiels and Bradley, *Criminal Procedure Act 1995* (2nd ed., 1999), p. 35, s. 16.
[29] *Jackson v. Stevenson*, 1897 2 Adam 255; *Bell v. Leadbetter*, 1934 J.C. 74.

instance that the accused is at risk of harming himself.[30] In cases of urgency where evidence might otherwise be lost, the police may without warrant search premises and a person not arrested.[31] Search and the gathering of evidence may, like arrest, be carried out with a warrant.[32] Many Acts confer the power of search without warrant.[33]

Where a person is arrested, or is detained, a constable may take fingerprints, palm prints, and such another prints and impressions of any external part of the body, as having regard to the circumstances the constable reasonably considers to be appropriate.[34] All such records should be destroyed following a decision not to institute criminal proceedings or if no conviction follows a prosecution.

A constable on the authority of an officer no lower than the rank of inspector may take from a person a sample of hair or other material by combing or plucking an external part of the body; a sample of nail or other material from the fingernails or toenails; a sample of blood or other body fluid or tissue or other material from the external part of the body by means of a swab; and again by means of a swab from inside the mouth a sample of saliva or other material. The foregoing procedures are thought to be non-invasive. If the prosecution authorities require evidence which can only be obtained by invasive techniques they will require a warrant from the sheriff. The sheriff will take account of the method proposed, the degree of physical invasion, the public interest in the detection of crime and whether there is a need for the procedure at this stage of the proceedings.[35] The police have the power to check prints, samples and impressions against any others held by them in connection with any other offence.[36]

THE PROSECUTION SYSTEM

8.08 Ordinarily, prosecution of crime in Scotland is undertaken by the State. The person nominally in charge of all State prosecution of crime is the Lord Advocate. The Lord Advocate is a political appointee. The Lord Advocate is assisted by the Solicitor-General who is also a political appointee. He, or the Solicitor-General, may appear for the Crown in extremely important cases. The Lord Advocate has sole discretion and direction of the prosecution of crimes in Scotland. In respect of his prosecutorial function the Lord Advocate adopts a politically neutral approach. Naturally, given the extent of criminal activity within Scotland he requires individuals to assist him in the day-to-day matter of prosecution. In respect of the High Court, the Lord Advocate appoints a number of advocates-depute. They may be either senior or junior counsel who sacrifice their own personal workload to act for the Crown in State prosecutions for a determined period of time. They are not permitted to engage in other aspects of legal practice work. In aspects of prosecution in the High Court they will often be assisted by the local procurator fiscal.

In respect of the lower courts—the sheriff court and the district courts—prosecution is undertaken by the procurator fiscal service. Procurators fiscal can be solicitors or advocates employed as civil servants and located at various sheriff courts throughout Scotland. There is a regional procurator fiscal for each sheriffdom. They and their officers are responsible for

[30] *Gellatly v. Heywood*, 1997 S.C.C.R. 300.
[31] *H.M. Advocate v. McGuigan*, 1936 J.C. 16.
[32] *Hay v. H.M. Advocate*, 1968 J.C. 40.
[33] See *e.g.* Misuse of Drugs Act 1971, s. 23.
[34] See 1995 Act, s. 18.
[35] See *Hay v. H.M. Advocate*, 1968 S.L.T. 334; *H.M. Advocate v. Milford*, 1973 S.L.T. 12; *McGlennon v. Kelly*, 1989 S.L.T. 832; *Smith v. Cardle*, 1993 S.C.C.R. 609; *Hughes v. Normand*, 1993 S.L.T. 113.
[36] 1995 Act, s. 20.

investigating and instituting criminal proceedings and for prosecuting cases in the lower criminal courts. More serious crimes are reported to the Crown Office in Edinburgh and for further instruction of Crown counsel located there. It will often be the case that the procurator fiscal will receive reports from police officers and, on the basis of those reports, decide to initiate a prosecution. It is also the case that the procurator fiscal may require the police to investigate a particular matter to decide if a prosecution should be brought.[37] The police have no prosecutorial role in the Scottish legal system. They mainly act under the auspices of the procurator fiscal and once they have referred a matter to him it is a matter for his discretion as to whether or not to prosecute. It will often be the case that in petty matters the procurator fiscal will decide not to initiate prosecutions, and indeed, in this respect, greater discretion has been given to the fiscal in modern times. This is illustrated in the most recent figures which show that of 291,383 reports received in 1997–98 there were no proceedings in 36,701 cases, warnings were issued in 22,421 cases, conditional offers were issued in 7,599 cases, fiscal fines were issued in 18,961 cases (up 25 per cent on previous year), diversions in 1,209 cases (down 1.23 per cent on previous year) referrals to the reporter in 9,153 cases (up 109 per cent).

As an adjunct to the criminal prosecution system the Crown Office acts as a central nexus for the entire prosecution system. Under the control of the Crown Agent, the Crown Office receives referrals from procurators fiscal while Crown counsel tender advice on all aspects of prosecution. It is they who may guide the procurator fiscal to initiate a prosecution in particular circumstances. It is through this office that policy advice of the Lord Advocate is tendered to the procurator fiscal service.

Although possible, private prosecution in Scotland is extremely rare. The last such **8.09** prosecution occurred in 1982.[38] Following that prosecution, clear guidance has now been given which would appear to severely restrict the possibility for further occurrences. Before a person can bring an action for private prosecution they must be able to show that the alleged crime amounts to a wrong against them personally. The person who seeks private prosecution must apply to the Lord Advocate for his concurrence in the prosecution. In the event that the Lord Advocate refuses, the High Court may authorise the private prosecution to proceed. The fact that the Crown has abandoned prosecution does not act as a bar to the bringing of a private prosecution. A person who brings a private prosecution and is unsuccessful may be found liable in expenses. Private prosecution is only brought under solemn procedure.

ALTERNATIVES TO PROSECUTION

Whilst it has always been open to the procurator fiscal (and prosecutors generally) not to **8.10** bring proceedings where prosecution is not in the public interest, the 1990s have seen some new initiatives which have expanded the alternatives open to the prosecution. The Stewart Committee Report in 1983[39] noted the pressure on the prosecution service and the high cost of prosecution on the public purse. The Committee recommended non-formalised diversion for appropriate cases whereby a person would have no formal action taken but perhaps the issuance of a fiscal warning, or the accused agreeing to seek medical help or social work intervention or the making of reparation.[40]

---

[37] See Ferguson, "Disclosure: the Prosecutor's Duties", 1998 S.L.T. (News) 233.
[38] *X v. Sweeney*, 1982 J.C. 70; see also *J. & P. Coats Ltd v. Brown*, 1909 6 Adam 19.
[39] *Keeping Offenders Out of Court: Further Alternatives to Prosecution*, (1983) Cmnd 8958.
[40] McIvor, *op. cit.*, at p. 441.

One of the interesting new initiatives prompted by the Stewart Committee is the fiscal fine.[41] The fiscal fine has been expanded to encompass statutory offences, and there is now a sliding scale of fiscal fines for various offences. In paying the fiscal fine, the transgressor is not prosecuted and nor does the transgression count as a criminal conviction. There has recently been some disquiet over the use of official fines with suggestions that these have been expanded to the point where some people who properly should be prosecuted are not. Nevertheless despite some criticism it seems clear that the fiscal fine will continue to be a prominent feature of the criminal justice system.

Following another recommendation of the Stewart Committee, social work diversions from prosecution began in early 1982. Persons accepted onto a diversion scheme become voluntary clients of the social work department for a minimum of six months. Some schemes work on the basis of waived prosecution while others simply defer a decision to prosecute.[42] Social work diversion is not yet encompassed in the full funding arrangements for criminal justice services, and the absence of funds is hampering its development. Cases which are often diverted from prosecution are ones involving family disputes.[43] Another feature of diversion is that high incidence of women and elderly persons are diverted from prosecution in comparison to other offending groups.[44]

CRIMINAL PROCEDURE

8.11 There are two forms of criminal procedure in Scotland—solemn procedure and summary procedure. As the name implies solemn procedure is somewhat more formal and, as a consequence, it is the more serious criminal matters that are taken on solemn procedure. "Summary" implies a measure of speed, and although there is less formality involved in summary procedure, it nevertheless is imbued with various technicalities. Solemn procedure operates in the High Court of Justiciary and the sheriff court (solemn), whereas summary procedure operates in the sheriff court (summary) and in the district court.

Solemn procedure

8.12 All solemn procedure prosecutions are initiated by the serving of a document known as an indictment. The indictment is a full written statement of the charges that the person will face at the trial. Indictments are authorised and initiated by, and proceed in the name of, the Lord Advocate. No case will proceed on indictment unless authorised and approved by Crown counsel in the Crown Office. The part of the indictment which contains the charges is known as the libel. As well as the libel the indictment will contain a list of evidence productions and labels as well as a list of names and addresses of all prosecution witnesses. It is in this way that the accused knows the rudiments of the case he has to face.

Where someone is arrested in respect of what is viewed as a very serious matter, and one likely to proceed by way of indictment, the prosecuting authorities are likely to initially serve

---

[41] See Duff, "The Fiscal Fine: How far Can It Be Extended" 1996 S.L.T. 167; Meechan, "Extra-Judicial Punishment and Procurator Fiscal Fines", 1991 S.L.T. (News) 1.

[42] See Middleton, "Community Alternatives Reconsidered" (1995) 34(1) *Howard Journal of Criminal Justice* 1.

[43] See Moody, *Diversion From the Criminal Justice Process: Report on the Diversion Scheme in Ayr* (Scottish Office, CRU, 1983).

[44] Stedward and Millar, *Diversion From Prosecution: Vol. 1—Diversion to Social Work* (Scottish Office, CRU, 1989).

the person with a petition.[45] Alternatively, the prosecution may petition the court for a warrant permitting the arrest of the accused, the search of his home or other premises, the citation of witnesses and production of documentary and other productions. A person detained will be brought before the court on petition and is dealt with in private. Even in respect of the most serious offences, the person will appear on petition before a sheriff, albeit that they may subsequently be tried in the High Court of Justiciary.

Judicial examination and committal

Under the Criminal Procedure (Scotland) Act 1995 Act, ss. 35 to 39, there is scope for judicial examination of those accused of serious crimes. The purpose of judicial examination is to have the accused state a defence at an early part of the proceedings. Under judicial examination, the prosecutor is not allowed to ask questions which (a) are designed to challenge the truth of anything said by the accused, (b) reiterate any question which the accused has refused to answer, and (c) put questions to the accused which are leading.[46] The accused may emit a declaration but this is highly unlikely. The accused does not take the oath, nor can he be cross-examined. The process of judicial examination gives the procurator fiscal the right to question the accused as far as such questioning is directed towards releasing any admission, denial, explanation, justification, or comment which the accused may have.[47] It is an investigative procedure where questions are put. The sheriff will endeavour to ensure that proceedings are conducted fairly.[48] The accused's solicitor has the right to be present at the examination[49] but is restricted to advising his client, or raising issues with the sheriff.[50] The accused is not required to answer any questions put to him by the fiscal.[51] In consequence, many accused are advised by their solicitors not to answer any questions at judicial examination stage. Judicial examinations are ordinarily recorded and transcribed.[52] They take place in private with any co-accused and his representatives excluded.[53] The failure to answer any question may be commented on later at any trial by the prosecution but not by a co-accused.[54] Where a defence is disclosed in any statement by the accused the prosecutor is under a duty to investigate it.[55]

8.13

Either at the first appearance, or after further judicial examination, the accused person will be committed for trial. The fiscal will undertake all preparatory work including obtaining witness precognitions and the gathering of evidence and will submit a report to the Crown Office.

8.14

Following any judicial examination, the Crown will proceed to prepare the case by precognosing all their witnesses and submitting the same along with productions to Crown counsel at the Crown Office. If there is a decision to indict the accused in the High Court, indictment will be prepared in the Crown Office and signed by an advocate depute.[56] If it is

---

[45]   1995 Act, s. 34.
[46]   *ibid.*, s. 36(5).
[47]   *ibid.*, s. 36(1).
[48]   *ibid.*, s. 36(5).
[49]   *ibid.*, s. 35(1).
[50]   *ibid.*, s. 36(7).
[51]   *ibid.*, s. 36(8).
[52]   *ibid.*, s. 37(4). A copy of the transcript is then served on the accused's solicitor if he has one: s. 37(6). The transcript of the judicial examination is then penned to the list of productions for the trial.
[53]   1995 Act, s. 35(7).
[54]   *ibid.*, s. 36(8) though the trial judge should also make known to jurors that no oath is administered nor need an accused answer: see *Morrison v. H.M. Advocate*, 1990 S.C.C.R. 235.
[55]   1995 Act, s. 36(10).
[56]   1995 Act, s. 64(3).

decided to indict in the sheriff court, the precognitions and other documents are returned to the procurator fiscal, and it is he who will prepare the indictment.[57] An indictment should name the accused, state the time and place where the crime was committed, and it should set forth the way in which the crime was committed. It should not mention any previous convictions nor should these be referred to in any list of productions annexed to the indictment.[58]

In preparing for the trial in a solemn case the defence is entitled to precognose the Crown witnesses. Witnesses will be approached by the defence and in the event they refuse, the defence may apply to the court to have a witness cited for precognition on oath.[59] The accused may also apply to hold an identification parade with the accused in it.[60] The defence shall ordinarily receive copies of any documentary productions that the Crown intend to rely on, and in addition to this, they are entitled to examine and inspect the productions which have been lodged by the Crown.[61] The defence are required to give notice of any witnesses they intend to call at least 10 clear days before the day in which the jury is first sworn to try the case.[62] The defence will also require to lodge productions on which they intend to found. There are a number of special defences of which the accused must give advance notice to the Crown. These include alibi, incrimination, self-defence and insanity. In addition to this, automatism and coercion must be previously notified to the prosecution.[63]

Time limits in solemn trials

8.15   Various safeguards are incorporated into solemn procedure to protect an accused person who is committed for trial. In the first instance there is the 110-day rule designed to ensure that no person is detained in custody for more than 110 days awaiting the commencement of the trial.[63a] An application may be made for an extension of this period to a single judge of the High Court of Justiciary where the delay is due to the illness of the accused or the judge, the absence or illness of any necessary witness or any other fault which is not attributable to any fault on the part of the prosecutor.[64]

There is also the year-and-a-day rule which stipulates that no accused person shall be tried on indictment unless the trial commences within 12 months of his or her first appearance on petition.[65] Not only is the accused liberated in such circumstances, but shall be discharged forthwith from any indictment in respect of the offence and shall not at any time be proceeded against on indictment with respect to that offence. This terminology prevents any problems where cases are reduced from solemn procedure to summary procedure. In practice 61 per cent of all solemn cases were completed within nine months of first appearance in 1997–98.[66] A person cannot be detained for any more than 80 days unless within that period an indictment is served upon him.[67] An application can be made to a single judge of the High Court of Justiciary for an extension but will not be entertained if the fault

---

[57]   *ibid.*, s. 64(4).
[58]   *ibid.*, s. 69(1).
[59]   *ibid.*, s. 291.
[60]   *ibid.*, s. 290.
[61]   *ibid.*, s. 68(2).
[62]   *ibid.*, s. 78(4)(a).
[63]   s. 78(1) and (2), 1995 Act; prior intimation of a defence of incrimination of a co-accused is not necessary: see *McShane v. H.M. Advocate*, 1989 S.C.C.R. 687.
[63a]   1995 Act, s. 65(4)(b). As an example see *X v. H.M. Advocate*, 1996 J.C. 129.
[64]   1995 Act, s. 65(7).
[65]   In *Main v. H.M. Advocate*, 1998 S.C.C.R. 694 the 12-month period was extended due to a missing witness.
[66]   Crown Office Annual Report 1998.
[67]   1995 Act, s. 65(4)(a).

lies with the prosecution.[68] If the indictment is not served within 80 days the accused should be liberated forthwith but he is not free from all process. In *H.M. Advocate v. Swift*.[69] important clarification about granting of extensions was offered. It is clear that fault on the part of the prosecution is not in itself a bar to an extension being granted, although the nature and extent of their failing may be relevant. Moreover, the gravity of the charge is not in itself sufficient reason for granting an extension.[70]

Under the 1995 Act where an accused person wishes to speed up the process, there are **8.16** provisions for them to plead guilty by letter allowing the matter to be disposed of relatively speedily.[71] A person is served with an indictment. It will simply dictate the charges that the accused faces and the court at which he should appear and when. In normal circumstances the accused will simply appear at that diet, plead guilty, and the case will be disposed of at that stage. The accused must plead guilty in open court and sign a minute to that effect which is countersigned by the judge.[72] In the event that the accused appears at the arranged diet and tenders a plea of not guilty, or is not prepared to plead guilty to the charges which the prosecutor finds acceptable, then the prosecutor simply deserts that diet and puts the case off for the time being (*pro loco et tempore*). The accused person still remains committed for trial and the normal procedure is simply re-initiated.[73]

Solemn procedure trials

Where the accused maintains a plea of not guilty from the outset, he will simply proceed **8.17** through to a trial which will be heard in the case of the sheriff court (solemn) before a sheriff and a jury of 15 persons and, in the case of the High Court of Justiciary, a Lord Commissioner of Justiciary and again a jury of 15 persons. The judge, or sheriff, has the role of directing the jury in all legal matters and rules on any questions of law. In addition to this he will impose sentence upon conviction. The jury's role is one simply of determining the accused's guilt or otherwise. In Scotland it is the case that there are three possible verdicts: not guilty, guilty, and not proven.[74] The not proven verdict is a unique and controversial feature of the Scottish legal system and there are no current plans to undertake a review of the three-verdict system.

All solemn criminal trials are recorded either by tape recorder or verbatim by a shorthand **8.18** writer.[75] At the trial itself the accused will be asked at the outset to confirm his identity. It is a requirement of solemn trials that the accused be present although there is a mechanism for removal of an accused who misconducts himself.[76]

Juries for solemn trial are selected from local residents whose names appear on the **8.19** electoral register. A substantial number are summoned for jury service but in the event only 15 serve on each jury. They are selected by ballot.[77] There is no legislative procedure for jury

---

[68]   *ibid.*, s. 65(5) and (6).
[69]   1984 J.C. 83.
[70]   For a discussion on the 12-month rule see Stewart, *The Scottish Criminal Courts and Action* (2nd ed., 1997), pp. 117–118.
[71]   1995 Act, s. 76(1).
[72]   *ibid.*, s. 77(1).
[73]   See *Frost v. McGlennan*, 1998 S.C.C.R. 573.
[74]   The not proven verdict has been the subject of some criticism: see Duff, "The Not Proven Verdict—Jury Mythology and 'Moral Panics'", 1996 J.R. 1.
[75]   1995 Act, s. 93; see *McLaughlin v. H.M. Advocate*, 1996 S.L.T. 304, for an instance where conviction was quashed because proceedings had not been recorded.
[76]   1995 Act, s. 92(1).
[77]   1995 Act, s. 88(2).

vetting in Scotland. It is possible for any party to object to a juror on cause shown.[78] However, it is possible, where all the parties to the trial agree, that a juror may be objected to without any reason being stated.[79] Following selection of the jury, the clerk to the court will read the indictment to the jurors.[80] Jurors will be provided with the indictment and lists of witnesses and productions.[81] Where the accused has lodged a special defence this will also be read to the jury.[82] There are circumstances where the jury reduces in number from 15. Jurors may fall ill, or for other reasons become unfit to continue to serve as a juror. It is possible for the trial to continue so long as the number of jurors does not fall below 12.[83] In circumstances where the number of jurors falls below 15 it is still a requirement that at least eight support any majority verdict.[84] Once a jury is sworn in, the judge will doubtless make some introductory remarks to the jury and then the prosecution will proceed with their case. Evidence is always given on oath or after a solemn affirmation.[85]

8.20   There may be an attempt at the end of the Crown case to suggest that there is no case to answer.[86] The judge will hear both parties on the question of sufficiency of the Crown's evidence. If satisfied that the evidence is inadequate he will acquit the accused on any charge which is not supported with sufficient evidence. The trial will proceed on any remaining charges.

Following closure of the Crown's case the defence may or may not lead evidence of their own. There is no requirement for an accused to give evidence.[87] If the accused does give evidence, he must do so on oath or affirmation and may be cross-examined by the prosecution or counsel for any co-accused. Following closure of the defence case, there are speeches by the prosecution and the defence. The defence is always entitled to speak last.[88] Principally, these speeches are designed to take the jury through the evidence they have heard, and to suggest on the basis of what they heard that the person should either be convicted or acquitted. It is the presiding judge's job to submit a charge to the jury which advises them on the law. The judge may make reference to certain aspects of the evidence. For example, there may be a certain piece of evidence absolutely vital to the Crown case, and the judge may simply direct the jury that if they do not accept that evidence, they must acquit the accused.[89] Following the charge to the jury, the jury will ordinarily retire to consider their verdict.[90] On their return their spokesperson will be asked whether they have reached a verdict and whether the verdict is unanimous or by majority.[91] Where the accused has been found guilty the prosecutor will move for sentence and will submit to the judge a note of the accused's previous convictions. The defence will probably offer a plea in mitigation. It is likely that social enquiry reports will be before the court and the court will simply proceed to pass sentence. Following sentence, the jury will be discharged.

---

[78]   *ibid.*, s. 86(2).
[79]   *ibid.*, s. 86(1).
[80]   *ibid.*, s. 88(5).
[81]   *ibid.*, s. 88(5).
[82]   *ibid.*, s. 89(1).
[83]   *ibid.*, s. 90(1).
[84]   *ibid.*, s. 90(2).
[85]   Oaths Act 1978, s. 5(1).
[86]   1995 Act, s. 97.
[87]   *ibid.*, s. 266(2).
[88]   *ibid.*, s. 98.
[89]   For discussion of the judge's charge to the jury see Stewart, *The Scottish Criminal Courts in Action* (2nd ed., 1997), pp. 179–182.
[90]   See 1995 Act, s. 99 of seclusion of the jury.
[91]   1995 Act, s. 100.

Summary criminal procedure

Discretion as to which court the case is taken in under summary procedure is primarily a **8.21** matter for the procurator fiscal. The severity of the offence, and the past record of the accused, will often determine the court in which the case is brought. Charges in summary procedure proceed by way of a complaint.[92] Complaints against the accused are in standard form.[93] The accused's name and address will be stated, as will his or her date of birth. Complaints are normally initiated in the name of the procurator fiscal, and the principal complaint must be signed by the procurator fiscal or one of his deputies.[94] Attached to the complaint will be a list of the previous convictions of the accused. The complaint will also have guidance on the action the accused may or may not take. They may plead guilty by letter, or appear in court, or arrange for representation in court. Persons detained in connection with a criminal offence may be detained in custody and will appear in court on the next lawful day. This requires that those arrested on a Friday evening will not appear in court until Monday morning at the earliest. Police may arrest individuals and release them on an undertaking to appear in court at a certain time on a specified day. In the normal course of events the accused must simply be served with a citation indicating the diet of the hearing.[95] Roughly, three-quarters of summary complaints are issued by the procurator fiscal within six weeks of receiving a report from the police. Over the last two years the average number of summary cases appearing before sheriff courts has fallen slightly as new alternatives to prosecution take effect, and less serious cases are directed to the district courts.[96]

Summary procedure has a first diet at which the accused may plead guilty or not guilty, or **8.22** may ask for the matter to be continued without plea. The matter might also be continued for investigation.[97] Roughly half of all cases are disposed of at a first appearance in sheriff court, whereas just over three-quarters of cases are disposed of at first appearance in district court.

If the accused pleads guilty, then the matter may be disposed of immediately. The prosecutor will offer a narrative of the events surrounding the offence, and the accused and/ or his representative will be invited to say anything by way of mitigation. Thereafter the presiding judge will pass sentence. In the event that the accused pleads not guilty, the matter will be remitted for trial. The average waiting period between pleading and the trial diet is approximately 10 weeks.[98] In some circumstances the accused will plead guilty by letter, or a guilty plea is tendered on the accused's behalf by their legal representative. The matter may be disposed of in the accused's absence, or the court may continue the case for a personal appearance by the accused.[99]

Summary procedure also has an intermediate diet which takes place prior to the trial diet to ascertain whether the accused is prepared to go to trial and whether they are maintaining their plea of not guilty.[1] The accused is required to appear unless he is legally represented or

---

[92] 1995 Act, s. 138(1).
[93] 1995 Act, s. 138(2). It will state the court in which the case has been brought and that the complaint is at the instance of the procurator fiscal.
[94] *Lowe v. Bee*, 1989 S.C.C.R. 476.
[95] 1995 Act, ss. 140 and 141.
[96] *Criminal Justice Information Bulletin*, The Scottish Office: http://www.scotland.gov.uk/library/documents-w/cj-05.html.
[97] 1995 Act, s. 145.
[98] *Criminal Justice Information Bulletin*, The Scottish Office: http://www.scotland.gov.uk/library/documents-w/cj-05.html.
[99] 1995 Act, s. 144.
[1] 1995 Act, s. 148.

there are exceptional circumstances justifying non-attendance. The whole purpose of intermediate diet is to save court time. Of those summary cases which are actually called for trial, only one-quarter actually proceed to evidence on the day. Of the remainder, most fall because of a plea of guilty at the trial diet or because the accused or a key witness fails to attend.[2]

8.23   Although prosecution may be taken against an accused who has been detained in custody, or has been released on an undertaking, the majority of cases are those in which the accused has simply been told by the police that the matter will be reported to the fiscal, after which they subsequently receive a complaint and citation to attend court. The original police report sent to the fiscal usually contains only a summary of the case with draft charges and a note of the accused's criminal record. On receipt of the report, the fiscal may decide to offer the accused the opportunity to pay a fixed penalty instead of facing prosecution.[3]

Where the accused is in custody or appearing on undertaking, he will almost certainly be served with the complaint by a police officer. In other cases, the accused will be served with a citation which will be accompanied by the complaint. In addition to this there will be a form of reply to complaint which will detail how the accused must proceed. An accused must be cited at least 48 hours before he is due to appear in court.[4] An accused may be cited by having the citation delivered to him personally, or left at his dwellinghouse or place of business with some person resident or employed there, or at some other place where he is resident at the time.[5] As an alternative to citation by an officer of law, the prosecutor may post, by registered or recorded delivery, the citation to the accused's house or place of business.[6]

In many statutory summary offences a time will be stipulated within which proceedings for the offence must be commenced. If there is no time limit imposed by the statute, a general time limit of six months applies after the date of the contravention, or the date of the last contravention in respect of a continuous event.[7]

8.24   Whether from custody, or as an undertaking, or in response to citation, the accused will have his case called at a first diet. If someone who is the subject of an undertaking refuses to attend they are guilty of an offence.[8] A person who has simply been cited to attend need not attend in person. There is a possibility for him to respond in writing, or he may simply be represented by a solicitor or some other person who satisfies the court that they are authorised to act for the accused.[9] At the first diet, any preliminary objections, either to the competency or relevancy of the complaint, must be stated prior to any plea being tendered. The objection may be dealt with at the first diet, but more usually is set down for a further preliminary hearing to resolve the issue at some future date. If there is no preliminary objection or the preliminary objection has been disposed of, it will then be up to the accused or his representative to tender a plea, or to seek to have the first diet continued without

2   *Criminal Justice Information Bulletin*, The Scottish Office.
3   1995 Act, s. 302(1); where the offence is appropriate and the fixed penalty is offered unpaid no conviction is recorded against the accused.
4   1995 Act, s. 140(2).
5   *ibid.*, s. 141(1).
6   1995 Act, s. 141(3); if the postal citation is returned "not known at this address" then there is no proper citation: *Keily v. Tudhope*, 1987 S.L.T. 99.
7   1995 Act, s. 136(1): if there is undue delay in commencing prosecution there may be substantial prejudice to the accused. See *Connachan v. Douglas*, 1990 J.C. 244.
8   1995 Act, s. 22(2). Those appearing on undertaking and those in custody are entitled to legal representation from the duty solicitor. The duty solicitor will be a local practitioner who has agreed to provide service in that court for a given period of time (usually a week). Although clients obtained in this way may remain with the duty solicitor throughout the process many may subsequently revert to other practitioners with whom they may be better acquainted.
9   1995 Act, s. 144(2)(a) and (b).

plea.[10] A case cannot be adjourned for longer than 28 days if the accused is on bail at any one time.[11] If the accused is in custody no continuation can be granted for any longer than seven days at a time, and the total period must not exceed 21 days.[12] If the accused, or his representative, tenders a plea of guilty the matter will ordinarily be disposed of there and then. There are a number of situations when the matter must be continued. For example, in road traffic cases it is necessary for the accused's driving licence to be produced in court. In addition to this, there may be circumstances where the judge wishes to ordain the accused to appear for the passing of sentence. In passing sentence, the court will consider the accused's prior convictions.[13] Only convictions which have been served in a notice to the accused may be taken into account.[14] If the offender has pled guilty by letter he is presumed to have admitted the convictions unless he expressly disputes them.[15] Disposal usually takes the form of the prosecutor narrating the circumstances of the offence. The accused, or his representative, thereafter makes a plea in mitigation. If the accused has responded in writing then the court will simply consider the terms of the letter. The court proceeds to sentence. In some circumstances it may simply continue the case in order to obtain reports, or a personal appearance of the accused.[16]

A plea of not guilty will result in a trial diet being fixed and in many instances an intermediate diet.

In summary criminal trials, the Crown will usually rely upon police statements and, although there is no obligation to make witness statements available to the defence, as a common courtesy they will, on request, provide a list of witnesses. In addition, the fiscal will be prepared to discuss with the defence solicitor the possibility of agreeing evidence, and will undoubtedly be willing to let the defence know the line of evidence that the prosecution intends to lead. The defence may apply to the sheriff for an order to hold an identification parade.[17] They will also doubtless make every effort to precognose witnesses that the Crown intend to call. In the event that a witness is unwilling to comply the defence may seek an order to precognose a witness on oath on behalf of the accused before the sheriff.[18] Witnesses for the defence are cited either by postal citation or by sheriff officer. **8.25**

On the day of the trial, there are likely to be a number of trials set down to be dealt with in the court. These will be "called over" and it may be at this stage that an accused decides to plead guilty. If so, the case will probably be disposed of or, in the event that the accused does not appear, a warrant for his arrest may be issued. There is also the possibility that cases may be adjourned. Following a call-over, in the absence of a change of heart on the part of the accused, the trial will proceed. There are no opening speeches at the trial and the prosecution will lead their evidence first. All witnesses who appear will be required to take an oath or affirmation. At the end of the Crown case, there is the possibility of a "no case to answer" submission.[19] The judge is required to determine whether there is sufficient evidence to convict but he is not at this stage required to rule on the quality of the evidence.[20] **8.26**

---

[10]   1995 Act, s. 144(1).
[11]   *ibid.*, s. 145(3).
[12]   *ibid.*, s. 145(2).
[13]   See, 1995 Act, s. 166.
[14]   1995 Act, s. 166(2); see also *Adair v. Hill*, 1943 J.C. 9. Note that other convictions may be referred to in a social enquiry report and these may be taken into account in the sentencing disposal but only after the offender has been afforded the opportunity of admitting or denying them.
[15]   1995 Act, s. 166(4)(a).
[16]   *ibid.*, s. 144(3)(b).
[17]   *ibid.*, s. 290.
[18]   *ibid.*, s. 291(1).
[19]   1995 Act, s. 160.
[20]   See *Williamson v. Wither*, 1981 S.C.C.R. 214.

Thereafter if the no-case submission is repelled, the defence may or may not lead evidence on behalf of the accused. There are closing speeches and thereafter the sheriff or the justice of the peace or stipendiary magistrate will reflect upon the evidence, and determine the accused's guilt or innocence. The accused or his representative has the right to speak last.[21] If the accused is found guilty there will be a short plea in mitigation by the defence, and the presiding judge will then proceed to pass sentence or defer for further reports. Prior to the passing of sentence the court will of course consider any previous convictions of the accused.

Bail[22]

8.27   Any person accused on petition of a crime which is bailable is entitled on being brought before the sheriff prior to committal to apply to the sheriff for bail. The prosecutor may hear any such application and in practice their view carries considerable weight. The sheriff can clearly refuse the application and is likely to do so where he has concerns about the accused's previous record, perhaps a breach of earlier bail, the seriousness of the offence or the attitude of the prosecution to bail being granted. If an accused is granted bail prior to committal, there is no need to commit him and an indictment can simply be served at a later date. If bail is refused, an application can be renewed after committal. Similarly, if an application is refused, an accused is entitled to appeal against the decision of the sheriff.[23]

Where the accused is charged on summary complaint the sheriff may similarly grant bail after having heard the prosecutor. If the application for bail follows committal or relates to a summary complaint it must be heard within 24 hours.

It is no longer possible to grant bail on pledge or deposit of money although in special circumstances as a further condition, money may be deposited.[24] The court may impose standard conditions and any further conditions upon the order. The standard conditions are that the accused:

(a)   appears at the appointed time at every diet relating to the offence with which he is charged for which he is given due notice;

(b)   does not commit an offence while on bail;

(c)   does not interfere with witnesses or otherwise obstruct the course of justice whether in relation to himself or any other person; and

(d)   makes himself available for the purpose of enabling enquiries or a report to be made to assist the court in dealing with him for the offence with which he is charged.

Certain offences are not bailable, namely murder, attempted murder, culpable homicide, rape or attempted rape. Where the accused has been convicted previously of one of the foregoing offences, or of murder or manslaughter in England or Wales, they will be denied bail. That denial of bail will be mandatory if the culpable homicide or manslaughter conviction resulted in the offender being imprisoned or detained (if a young offender), or in a hospital order being imposed.

8.28   It is an offence to breach bail conditions. If the breach is constituted by the commission of a further offence, the fact that this offence occurred while on bail will act as an aggravating

21   1995 Act, s. 161.
22   See generally 1995 Act, ss. 23, 24 and 26–32.
23   1995 Act, s. 32(1), *Love, Petr*, 1998 S.L.T. 461.
24   *Adam v. Kirichenko*, 1995 G.W.D. 26–1373.

factor. If a police officer has reasonable grounds for suspecting that an accused on bail has broken, is breaking, or is likely to break a bail condition, he may arrest him without warrant. The accused arrested in this way will be brought before the court who heard the bail application on the next available court day. The court has the power to revoke bail, release the accused, continue the bail or vary the bail imposing further conditions. Any money deposited may be forfeited, although the court has the power to return it if it wishes.

A court has the power to review bail. Where a review is sought by the accused after the initial decision, that review cannot take place until five days have elapsed, and if it relates to a subsequent decision this period extends to 15 days. The prosecutor has the power to seek review of a decision to grant bail. Notwithstanding the accused's opportunity to seek variation or to make a fresh application, there is also the opportunity for both the accused and the prosecution to appeal against a sheriff's refusal or grant of bail.

It has become possible by virtue of the 1995 Act for bail to be granted after the accused has been convicted, though only while he awaits the outcome of an appeal.[25] This may only be granted by the High Court of Justiciary when it has been satisfied by the appellant that cause for bail has been shown to exist.[26] As in the case of bail granted in the earlier stages of criminal proceedings, if the appellant has previously been convicted of murder, culpable homicide, rape, attempted murder or attempted rape, and his conviction in the current instance is for one of these offences, bail will not be granted. In *H.M. Advocate v. Renicks*[27] the decision of a single judge sitting in the High Court to grant bail to an appellant convicted of murder was deemed incompetent.

THE NATIONAL OBJECTIVES AND STANDARDS FOR SOCIAL WORK SERVICES WITHIN THE CRIMINAL JUSTICE SYSTEM

The National Objectives and Standards for Social Work Services within the Criminal Justice System were drawn up and implemented in 1991 after wide consultation with COSLA and other bodies. In 1996 further revision of the National Objectives and Standards took place. The supposition is that by setting national standards, a uniformly high standard of service might be secured on a national basis. The National Objectives and Standards were accompanied by the full funding by central government of social work services to the criminal justice system. As the solitary source of funds to the service it is hardly surprising that the Government would seek to shape and influence how those services should operate.

The objectives of social work practice in the criminal justice system are:

8.29

13.1 to enable a reduction in the incidence of custody, whether on remand, at sentence, or in default of a financial penalty, where it is used for lack of a suitable, available community-based social work disposal;

13.2 to promote and enhance the range and quality of community-based social work disposals available to the courts and ensure that they are managed and supervised in such a manner that they have the confidence of the courts, the police and the public at large;

---

[25] 1995 Act, s. 112; see also *Ogilvie v. H.M. Advocate* 1998 S.C.C.R. 187.
[26] *Young v. H.M. Advocate*, 1946 J.C. 5.
[27] 1999 S.L.T. 407.

13.3 to ensure that the social work disposals are provided to the courts or other agencies in such a way that the full range of disposals is available when required so that the most appropriate one can be used, particularly with the persistent offender;

13.4 to give priority to the development of community-based social work disposals and other services to young adult offenders;

13.5 to promote the development of schemes to enable the courts to grant bail in an increased number of cases;

13.6 to provide and facilitate services for prisoners, and their families, to help them prepare for release from custody and to assist them to resettle in the community on release;

13.7 to help offenders tackle their offending behaviour, assist them to live socially responsible lives within the law, and, whenever appropriate, further their social integration through the involvement and support of their families, friends and other resources in their community;

13.8 to assist the families of offenders where family life suffers as a consequence of offending behaviour;

13.9 to promote, provide and facilitate the development of schemes for diverting accused persons from prosecution to social work in those cases where there is sufficient evidence to prosecute but it is not deemed necessary to do so in the public interest;

13.10 to promote and assist the development of services to the victims of crime; and

13.11 to promote and assist action to reduce and prevent crime.[28]

The National Objectives and Standards, as their name implies, guide and direct the work of the social worker in the criminal justice system. And whilst there has been criticism that a large proportion of social enquiry reports prepared by social workers still do not meet the desired standard,[29] they are intended as benchmark standards against which ordinarily the performance of the social worker in the criminal justice system will be measured. Professional discretion may dictate departure from the standards, but the onus will be on those departing to establish a justification for doing so.

SOCIAL ENQUIRY REPORTS

8.30   A key feature of the social worker's role in the criminal justice system is in the preparation of social enquiry reports ("SER").[30] The courts have the power to adjourn a case to enable enquiries to be made or to determine the most suitable method for dealing with the case. The relationship between disposal and the report is at times unclear.[31] The law says little as to the content of the report. Social workers are asked about community service but there is a lack of clarity on exactly what should be in the report. It will be a matter of degree as to how far the social worker can go before they intrude into the domain of the judge. Certainly given the

---

28   National Objectives and Standards, Pt 1, para. 13.
29   SWSI, *Helping the Court Decide* (1996).
30   Social Work (Scotland) Act 1968, s. 27(1).
31   See *H.M. Advocate v. M*, 1997 S.L.T. 359 where the High Court allowed an appeal against the decision of a sheriff to reject the conclusions of a social enquiry report and to sentence a probation order and community service order to a sexual offender who had committed a number of offences within the family unit.

terminology in the National Objectives and Standards, it is expected that the report will provide illumination of the offender's circumstances which bear on his offending. One aspect of this is whether the offender accepts responsibility for his behaviour. Reports will comment on the offender's view of the impact of the offending on the victim and may offer a view on the issue of reparation to that victim. The report will state the writer's preferred community-based disposal (if he has one), and where the recommendation is for probation the report should include a plan of action of what the offender will be required to do during the probationary period.

Reports are not about averting custody *per se* but to give the court an informed appraisal of the possibility of a community-based punishment as an alternative to imprisonment. Local authorities (and their officers) are to pursue the following objectives in framing SERs:

(a) engage with the offender and seek to motivate and encourage active participation in facing up to his or her behaviour and in considering its consequences;

(b) carry out an assessment which may provide a basis for future social work action;

(c) begin to negotiate a specific course of action to address problems and issues associated with offending behaviour;

(d) explain to the offender what will be involved in any action plan which may be put to the court and seek his informal consent;

(e) explain to the offender the range of uses to which a SER may be put and the boundaries of confidentiality; and

(f) explain that the final decision rests with the court.[32]

The SER is a service for the court not the offender. It has been said that: **8.31**

"Reports should be seen as limited exercises, intended solely to help decide what should happen to an offender as a consequence of committing a particular offence. They should be aimed at negotiating the least restrictive sanction commensurate with the seriousness of the offence. They are aids to administering or managing the criminal justice system in relation to an individual offender. They do not cover everything in the offender's life and they do not cover all considerations which the court may take into account".[33]

The areas it might cover are the age of the offender, the family circumstances, financial circumstances, accommodation, employment, education and training, physical and mental health, use of alcohol or drugs and current emotional problems, information about the current offence, previous offending and the subject's attitude to the current offence and previous offending.[34] There is a mixed view as to whether a report should conclude with a clear recommendation as to disposal or simply confine itself to an examination of the merits and demerits of particular disposals.[35] Research suggests that 40 per cent of reports are compiled after one interview with the offender. If it is necessary to speak to others to compile a report on an offender, consent will normally be obtained before contacting a third party.

The cost of SERs represents about 25 per cent of the total time spent on social work criminal justice services. The average cost of a report is in excess of £200.[36] A workload

---

[32] SWSI, *Helping the Court Decide* (1996), p. 6.
[33] Worral, *Punishment in the Community* (1992) at p. 85.
[34] SWSI, *Helping the Court Decide* (1996), pp. 13–20.
[35] See Mays (ed.), *Scottish Social Work Legislation*, para. I.006.5.
[36] SWSI, *Helping the Court Decide* (1996), p. 1.

measures study initiated in 1991 found that the average time spent on a SER was six hours and 24 minutes. Whilst there has been criticism, principally in England[37] of the nature of SERs one will often hear Scottish judges pay tribute to the assistance offered to them by such reports. Notwithstanding this the court is not obliged to accept any recommendation contained in a SER.[38]

Once prepared the SER should be lodged in court the day before the court hearing. In certain rare circumstances the social worker may have to attend court to answer any question regarding unusual aspects of any report or subsequent to the lodging of the report if any matter requires clarification.

SENTENCING OF OFFENDERS

8.32   Sheriff Alistair Stewart suggests sentencing is the most difficult task that the judge ever has to face.[39] It is a facet of the judicial role which at times attracts considerable controversy.[40] Sheriff Stewart suggests three reasons why difficulty arises. First, the judges are very often given little training in sentencing disposals; secondly, there is a wide range of disposals; and thirdly, there are a number of competing interests in the sentencing equation which makes the task inherently difficult. Others too have commented on the problem of sentencing[41] and to Sheriff Stewart's list must be added the absence of clear guidelines. Certainly, the Appeal Court has shown great reluctance to intervene in the undoubted discretion offered to trial courts.[42] although the 1995 Act encourages the High Court in solemn and summary appeals to pronounce an opinion on sentence or other disposal which would be appropriate in a similar case.[43] Section 197 of the 1995 Act provides that a court in passing sentence should have regard to any relevant opinion pronounced by the High Court of Justiciary sitting as a Court of Appeal. Irrespective of whether guidance is given or not it is the case that a court is always restricted by the powers set for that particular court.[44]

Custodial sentences

8.33   Although there are a number of custodial disposals for those under 21, imprisonment is the only form of custodial sentence for a person over 21.[45] It is not possible for a summary court to send anyone to prison for less than five days.[46] In an effort to ensure that no-one goes to prison unnecessarily, the convicted person who has not previously been sentenced to imprisonment or detention in a United Kingdom court may not be sentenced to imprisonment unless the court considers that there is no alternative. It is the case that where the court is considering sending an offender to prison for the first time, they must obtain social enquiry

---

37   Harris (1992) in Worral (n. 33, above): "Empirical research into the quality, content, consistency and impartiality of SER's found them wanting and probably incomprehensible to their subjects, disappointingly few of whom possessed the social science degree which would have enabled them to have understood the more linguistically and conceptually complex of these documents" (p. 146).
38   See *Kyle v. Cruikshank*, 1961 J.C. 1 *per* Lord Justice-General Clyde at p. 4.
39   See Stewart, *The Scottish Criminal Courts in Action* (2nd ed., 1997), p. 221.
40   *e.g.* Hough, "People talking About Punishment" (1996) 35(3) *The Howard Journal* 191–214.
41   Nicholson, *Sentencing* (2nd ed., 1992); Hutton and Tata "Some Options for Sentencing Reform in Scotland", 1993 S.L.T. (News) 89; McLean, "Judicial Discretion In Sentencing", 1995 S.L.T. 331 and 1995 S.L.T. 339.
42   See *H.M. Advocate v. Lee*, 1996 S.C.C.R. 205, *per* Lord Justice-General Hope at p. 212; *H.M. Advocate v. McKay*, 1996 S.L.T. 697.
43   1995 Act, ss. 118(7) and 189(7).
44   See paras 2.11–2.26.
45   1995 Act, s. 207(1).
46   *ibid.*, s. 206(1).

reports which look into the offender's circumstances and also provide evidence and information about the offender's character, and physical and mental condition.[47] Where a court of summary jurisdiction considers that imprisonment is necessary, it must state its reasons why and these must be recorded.[48] There are further restrictions on the sending of persons to imprisonment where they are not represented. Only where the person convicted has applied for legal aid and been refused or having been informed of the right to apply has not done so, may he be sent to jail.[49]

Under section 196 of the 1995 Act, a court may take into account the stage of the proceedings at which the accused indicated his intention to plead guilty.

In other respects, the length of sentence depends upon the gravity of the crime, the accused's previous convictions, and his circumstances. A judge may decide to backdate a sentence to when the accused was taken into custody.[50] One of the issues the court often has to determine in cases where the accused is already serving a sentence or appears on a number of charges is whether the sentences should be consecutive or concurrent. As a basic rule, where an accused appears on a number of charges, they should be sentenced separately for each charge. Following the decision in *Nicholson v. Lees*,[51] a number of general propositions are now accepted as guiding the dilemma posed to the judge. The first of these is that the highest custodial sentence is that which may be the maximum imposed for the charge which carries the highest sentence on the complaint or indictment. Where the charges have been separated out for convenience, the court should not impose a sentence which added together exceeds the maximum that could be imposed in respect of one complaint or indictment. In other circumstances, the court should decide whether the sentences should be concurrent or consecutive. If an accused is sentenced to life imprisonment, any other sentence imposed at the same time or later should be concurrent and not consecutive.[52]

Where the accused is serving a sentence and is subsequently sentenced for another matter **8.34** it is entirely up to the judge's discretion whether it should be consecutive or concurrent.[53] In passing a custodial sentence, the court should have regard to any time the accused spent in custody on remand awaiting trial or sentence.[54] The court may or may not impose a backdating of the sentence. Generally, it is not desirable to impose a sentence of imprisonment in conjunction with another non-custodial sentence. Imprisonment cannot be imposed along with a probation order. A person who is serving a custodial sentence of less than four years is a short-term prisoner and will be released unconditionally after serving one-half of their sentence.[55] When the offender is serving two unrelated sentences concurrently he becomes eligible for parole only once a sufficient proportion of each sentence has been served.[56]

Where a person is in prison for a period in excess of one year but less than four, the court may impose a Supervised Release Order designed to protect the public from serious harm from the offender on release (see para. 8.56 below).

---

[47]   1995 Act, s. 204(2).
[48]   *ibid.*, s. 204(3).
[49]   *ibid.*, s. 204(1).
[50]   "Backdating—Recent Developments", 1991 S.L.T. (News) 93.
[51]   1996 S.L.T. 706.
[52]   See *McPhee v. H.M. Advocate*, 1990 S.C.C.R. 313.
[53]   1995 Act, s. 167(7).
[54]   *ibid.*, s. 210(1)(a).
[55]   Prisoners and Criminal Proceedings (Scotland) Act 1993, s. 1(1).
[56]   Prisoners and Criminal Proceedings (Scotland) Act 1993, s. 1A, as inserted by Crime and Disorder Act 1998, s. 111.

Long-term prisoners are those serving four years or more.[57] It is possible for a long-term prisoner to be released on licence, having served two-thirds of his sentence. Moreover, it is possible for a long-term prisoner to be released having served only half of his sentence if the Parole Board for Scotland recommends release and the Secretary of State accepts the recommendation.[58] Where a long-term prisoner is released on licence they must comply with any conditions specified by the Secretary of State.[59] The licence subsists for the whole period of the sentence.[60] Where the licence is revoked, then the prisoner is recalled to prison, and serves the remainder of his or her sentence.[61] It is the case that in practice the Secretary of State only revokes the licence on the recommendation of the Parole Board. Where a prisoner released on licence commits an offence punishable by imprisonment before what would be the official end of his sentence, he may be returned to prison to serve a period equivalent to the balance of his sentence.[62] The court will look at the prisoner's entire circumstances and not simply the circumstances of the new offence.[63]

The mandatory sentence for murder in respect of a person over 21 is life imprisonment.[64] The judge may or may not make a minimum recommendation as to how long the prisoner should be detained before being released on licence.[65] In normal circumstances the judge will indicate that he is considering doing this, and allow defence counsel to address him on the matter.[66] Recommendations should not normally be for any less than 12 years.[67] A person convicted of murder may be released on licence at any time by the Secretary of State on the recommendation of the Parole Board.[68] The licence endures for the rest of the prisoner's life, and as a consequence he may be recalled to prison at any time in situations where the release on the licence is revoked.

8.35   There are a number of prisoners known as discretionary life prisoners who have been given life imprisonment for an offence for which a penalty is not fixed.[69] In these cases the court will have specified the period that should elapse before the person will be considered for release. The court is required to take into account the seriousness of the offence, and other offences associated with it, and the previous convictions of the offender, in setting the period of time that must elapse before the prisoner may be considered for release. If the Parole Board is satisfied that the prisoner is no longer a danger to the public and that the prisoner should be released, they may direct the Secretary of State to release him. Matters of this nature come before the Parole Board because the Secretary of State has referred the prisoner's case to it, or because the prisoner has required the Secretary of State to refer his case to the Parole Board. In some unusual circumstances the court will propose a life sentence for an offence where life is not mandatory but also fail to recommend the period that should expire before the prisoner is released. The court is required to state reasons for imposing a sentence of this nature. A prisoner who has such a sentence imposed may be released on licence by the Secretary of State on the recommendation of the Parole Board but

---

57   Prisoners and Criminal Proceedings (Scotland) Act 1993, s. 27(1).
58   *ibid.*, s. 1(2) and (3).
59   *ibid.*, s. 12(1).
60   *ibid.*, s. 11(1).
61   *ibid.*, s. 17(1)(a).
62   *ibid.*, s. 16(1) and (2)(a).
63   *Lynch v. Normand*, 1995 S.C.C.R. 404.
64   1995 Act, s. 205(1).
65   *ibid.*, s. 205(4).
66   See *Murphy v. H.M. Advocate*, 1995 S.C.C.R. 55.
67   See *Casey v. H.M. Advocate*, 1993 J.C. 102.
68   Prisoners and Criminal Proceedings (Scotland) Act 1993, s. 1(4).
69   See generally *ibid.*, s. 2.

only after the Secretary of State has consulted the Lord Justice-General or the Lord Justice-Clerk and the trial judge.[70]

When an offender is under 21 but over 16, a custodial sentence will be served in a Young Offenders Institution.[71] A court may not impose a custodial sentence on a young offender unless it is convinced that there is no other appropriate method of dealing with the offender. In helping to determine this issue, the court will order a social enquiry report. The court must also take into account the accused's character and physical and mental condition. In sentencing the young offender the court must state its reasons why it is imposing a custodial sentence. As the sentence imposed on the young offender is the same as with an adult going to prison, the normal rules in respect of release apply.[72] In cases where a person under 18 is convicted of murder, he is sentenced to be detained without a limit of time, and detained in such a place and under such conditions as the Secretary of State may direct.[73] Where the murderer is over 18 but under 21, they will be detained in a Young Offenders Institution. The judge may recommend a minimum period that the young offender should be detained for before being released on licence.[74]

Scotland has a high incidence of imprisonment with 110 per 100,000 of the population in prison against a western European average of 80. Roughly, 15 per cent of all court disposals result in imprisonment.[75] There are no suspended sentences in Scotland.

Where children are prosecuted in court notwithstanding the possibility of referral to the children's hearing for advice and/or disposal, the court has the power to impose a period of residential care not exceeding one year. The local authority will determine the place, conditions and duration of the care.[76]

Fines

Fines are the most common disposal of criminal offences.[77] A number of issues are assessed in determining the quantum of the fine. For example, one can anticipate that the accused's past record, the gravity of the offence and the means of the offender are taken into account.[78] It is not competent to impose both a fine and a custodial sentence for the same common law offence. In addition a fine should not be imposed in respect of one charge where the court is deferring sentence on another charge.

As a means of laying down maximum fines for statutory offences, the standard scale was introduced.[79] The standard scale sets out five levels of fine. These are currently level 1—£200, level 2—£500, level 3—£1,000, level 4—£2,500 and level 5—£5,000. There is a mechanism in the 1995 Act for these figures to be altered as and when the Secretary of State determines that they should be. In the event that a statute makes no provision for a fine but simply states that the punishment may be imprisonment, the court nevertheless has the power to impose a fine.[80] Where the statutory offence is a summary offence, the maximum fine will normally be stated in the Act as a level on the standard scale.

8.36

---

[70]   Prisoners and Criminal Proceedings (Scotland) Act 1993, s. 1(4).
[71]   See 1995 Act, s. 207.
[72]   Prisoners and Criminal Proceedings (Scotland) Act 1993, s. 6(1)(a).
[73]   1995 Act, s. 205(2).
[74]   *ibid.*, s. 205(3) and (4).
[75]   Patterson and Tombs, *Social Work and Criminal Justice: The Impact of Policy*, Scottish Office, 1998.
[76]   1995 Act, s. 44(1) and (3).
[77]   Black, "Fine Tuning", 1986 S.L.T. (News) 185.
[78]   1995 Act, see also *Paterson v. McGlennan*, 1991 J.C. 141; *Reynolds v. Hamilton*, 1994 S.C.C.R. 760; *Forsyth v. Cardle*, 1994 S.C.C.R. 769.
[79]   See 1995 Act, s. 225.
[80]   *ibid.*, s. 199(2).

Ordinarily in the criminal courts where the accused has a fine imposed following sentence, he or his representation will ask for time to pay or to be allowed to pay in instalments.[81] In the event that the accused does not ask for either of these, then the court is within their powers to demand that payment be made immediately. Payment by cheque is acceptable but in such circumstances the court will ordinarily allow seven days in order for the cheque to clear. The defender must be allowed at least seven days to pay either the whole fine or the first instalment unless

(a) he appears to the court to possess sufficient means to enable him to pay forthwith; or

(b) he states to the court that he does not wish time to pay; or

(c) fails to satisfy the court that he has a fixed abode; or

(d) the court is satisfied for any other special reason that no time should be allowed.[82]

Where the offender is allowed time to pay or to pay by instalments, the judge may at the same time impose an alternative imprisonment in the event of default of payment, if he considers that having regard to the gravity of the offence, the character of the offender or any other special reason, that the offender should be imprisoned with expedience and without further inquiry.[83] It is competent to impose an alternative of imprisonment even where the offence itself is not punishable by imprisonment.[84]

It is possible for an offender to apply to court for further time to pay.[85] The application will ordinarily go to the court which imposed the fine.[86] The court is required to allow further time unless it is satisfied that the offender's failure to pay has been wilful or that the offender has no reasonable prospects of being able to pay if further time is allowed.[87] A court can also vary instalments of a fine, and allow further time for payment of instalments.[88] An offender who has been allowed to pay by instalments can be placed under the supervision of a social worker, either at the time of the imposition of the penalty or at any time thereafter.[89] Such supervision is known as a Fine Supervision Order and lasts until the fine is paid. Fine Supervision Orders are particularly appropriate for young offenders or for offenders who suffer from some disability.[90]

8.37   Where the offender has been fined and no alternative has been imposed at the same time, it is not possible to imprison the offender for non-payment unless the offender attends court. The purpose of the attendance in court is to enquire into any reason why the offender has not paid the fine.[91] The offender will ordinarily be cited to attend a special Fines Enquiry Court, but in circumstances where his whereabouts are unknown, or he fails to appear following citation, a warrant for his arrest may be issued. If a Fine Supervision Order is in place, it is likely that a report from the social worker will be available to the court, and indeed imprisonment cannot be imposed as an alternative unless the court has taken steps to obtain such a report. In respect of offenders under 21, imprisonment cannot be imposed as an

[81]   *ibid.*, s. 214(1) and (8).
[82]   *ibid.*, s. 214(2).
[83]   1995 Act; see *Stephen v. McKay*, 1998 S.L.T. 280.
[84]   See *Kausen v. Walkingshaw*, 1990 S.C.C.R. 553.
[85]   1995 Act, s. 214(7).
[86]   *ibid.*, s. 215(1).
[87]   *ibid.*, s. 215(3).
[88]   *ibid.*, s. 214(9).
[89]   *ibid.*, s. 217(1).
[90]   See *Muirhead v. Normand*, 1995 S.C.C.R. 632.
[91]   1995 Act, s. 216.

alternative unless a Fine Supervision Order has first been attempted, or it is not practical to place the young offender under such supervision.[92] At the Fines Enquiry Court it is likely that having heard the offender, the court may allow further time to pay and perhaps add that imprisonment will be an alternative if there is any future default. It is also possible for a Supervised Attendance Order to be imposed (see below). The 1995 Act contains a table of alternatives of imprisonment for certain levels of fine. For example, it is suggested that seven days be imposed for a fine of less than £200. If part of the fine is paid, only a proportion of the alternative is appropriate.[93] Where the court does impose an alternative to imprisonment for non-payment and the offender does not pay, the court simply grants a warrant for his arrest and imprisonment or detention. The warrant will specify the period for which the offender must be detained.[94] If the offender is able to pay the full balance of the fine to the arresting officer, the warrant is not enforced. The arresting officer simply then remits the money gathered to the clerk of court who issued the warrant.[95]

It is open to the court to order that a fine on an individual offender be recovered by civil diligence.[96] Civil diligence is not competent after the offender has been imprisoned or detained for default of the fine.[97]

Supervised Attendance Order[98]

In response to the growing concern about people going to prison for defaulting on payments of fine,[99] an order called a Supervised Attendance Order was introduced in 1990.[1] The supervised attendance order is aimed at reducing the number and proportion of offenders who are imprisoned for being in default of a fine. It has the objectives of: **8.38**

(a) providing courts with a credible community-based alternative to custody for fine-defaulters;

(b) providing defaulters with an opportunity to receive a community-based penalty instead of serving a custodial sentence;

(c) imposing discipline, firm and reliable supervision, and constructive activities.

Supervised Attendance Orders are only available in certain courts throughout Scotland although it is anticipated that they will soon be universally available. The Supervised Attendance Order requires the offender to attend a place of supervision for a stated period which must be not less than 10 hours. Where the fine does not exceed level 1 of the standard scale, the maximum number of hours is 50. In any other circumstances, the maximum number of hours is 100. On attending the place of supervision, the offender is required to carry out instructions given to him by the supervising officer. A Supervised Attendance Order is available if

(a) the offender is over 18 years of age;

[92]   1995 Act, s. 217(4).
[93]   *ibid.*, s. 219(4).
[94]   *ibid.*, s. 224.
[95]   *ibid.*, s. 218(3).
[96]   *ibid.*, s. 214(6).
[97]   *ibid.*, s. 221(3).
[98]   See generally ss. 235 and 237, and Sched. 7, paras 1, 3, 4, 5 of the 1995 Act.
[99]   8,339 receptions into prison in 1992 were for fine default.
[1]   Law Reform (Miscellaneous Provisions) (Scotland) Act 1990, s. 62.

(b) he has failed to pay a fine or a part thereof, and the court would imprison him if they did not make the Supervised Attendance Order; and

(c) the court considers the Supervised Attendance Order more appropriate than a custodial sentence.

The order is not appropriate if the offender is already in prison. The court will explain to the offender in ordinary language the purpose and effect of the order, the consequences of breach, and that the order can be reviewed on the application of the offender, or by the supervising officer. The order should ordinarily be completed within 12 months of being made. However, there are provisions for extension of that time. Where the court receives a report that the offender is in breach of the Supervised Attendance Order, or is failing to comply with any of its conditions, it may grant a warrant for the arrest of the offender or cite him to appear before the court. Such reports are likely to come from the supervising officer of the establishment concerned. If the breach is proved, the court may revoke the order and impose a custodial sentence or vary the number of hours specified in the order. These alternatives represent a fairly restricted discretion on the part of the court. Imposing a Supervised Attendance Order means the original fine has been discharged and accordingly it can not be reinstated. If the court decides following a breach of a Supervised Attendance Order to impose a period of imprisonment, it may exercise this discretion up to the maximum imposed by the particular court. It is possible to have an order take effect in the event of future default in the same way that imprisonment can be imposed in the event of fine-default. In these circumstances the order comes into effect the day after a failure in respect of a payment. In circumstances where part of the fine has been paid, a calculation will be made which will be proportionate to the hours that the offender requires to attend. These will be rounded up to the nearest 10 hours but may not be reduced to less than 10 hours.

8.39   The order is intended to be a low cost order requiring minimum assessment and participation in group activity. Successful completion of the order discharges the fine. Potential attendees are not assessed for suitability pre-sentence but their consent is required. The Supervised Attendance Order is intended to provide a time penalty in substitution for a fine. Disciplinary procedures are instigated for failure to comply with requirements, including lack of punctuality, failure to attend and failure to perform an activity satisfactorily.[2]

Between 1989 and January 1993, 100 Supervised Attendance Orders were made by the courts. The majority of orders (62 per cent) were imposed for periods of 30 hours or less; 26 per cent of orders were for 20 hours; 23 per cent were for 30 hours; and 21 per cent were for 60 hours. In the Dundee and Highland courts, orders of 20 hours were most common; in Ayr, 30-hour orders were most frequently given; whilst in the Perth courts, 60 hours was the most common length of order. Sentencers in most courts operated a tariff system for orders of about one hour for each £5 of outstanding fine.[3]

Supervised Attendance Orders for 16- and 17-year-olds[4]

8.40   The 1995 legislation makes provision for Supervised Attendance Orders for young offenders but these are not universally in operation. At the moment there is a pilot scheme in operation for 16- and 17-year-olds. The court is required to assess whether the 16- or 17-year-old is

2   See Brown, *A Fine on Time: The Monitoring and Evaluation of the Pilot Supervised Attendance Order Schemes* (1994), Crime and Criminal Justice Research Findings No. 2, p. 2.
3   See Brown, *op. cit.*, p. 3.
4   See 1995 Act, s. 236.

likely to pay a fine within 28 days, if a fine is the appropriate sentence. In the event that the court does consider that the offender is likely to pay then it should impose the fine and make a Supervised Attendance Order in default of payment of the fine within that period. Obviously, if the fine is not paid the Supervised Attendance Order comes into effect on a specified date which must be not less than 28 days after the making of the order. There are similar provisions for proportionate reductions in the hours required where part of the fine has been paid.

In circumstances where the court considers that the offender is not able to pay within 28 days then it should make a Supervised Attendance Order immediately. There is concern that by imposing supervised attendance orders on 16- and 17-year-olds, the possibility of a young offender having a custodial sentence is increased on the basis that the court has very little discretion where a Supervised Attendance Order has been breached.[5]

Caution

Although a relatively rare disposal of a case, there is the possibility that the court may order   **8.41**
an offender to find caution, whereby a sum of money is deposited as a guarantee that the offender will be of good behaviour over a certain period of time. The district court has power to order an offender to find caution in a sum not exceeding level 4 on the standard scale and for a period not exceeding six months.[6] The sheriff summary court has the power to order the offender to find caution for a maximum period of 12 months.[7] Caution cannot be paid in instalments, nor can the Supervised Attendance Order be imposed for default. If the offender is of good behaviour throughout the period for which he is required to be, he is entitled to recover the sum paid together with any interest that has accrued.

Compensation Orders[8]

A court may impose a Compensation Order on an offender. Under section 249(1) of the 1995   **8.42**
Act, a Compensation Order requires a person convicted of an offence to pay compensation for any personal injury, loss or damage caused, directly or indirectly, by the acts which constituted an offence. A Compensation Order is not made where the loss arises from the consequence of the death of any person. Moreover, a Compensation Order may not be made in respect of injury, loss or damage due to an accident arising out of the presence of a motor vehicle on the road, except where the motor vehicle has been stolen or taken away without authority and is recovered damaged. A court may impose a Compensation Order instead of, or in addition to, any other sentence, but not where it gives an absolute discharge, or where it defers sentence for good behaviour or some other condition. Moreover, a court cannot impose a Compensation Order at the same time as making a Probation Order. However, compensation may be a condition of probation.[9] It was observed in *Sullivan v. McLeod*[10] that it would rarely be appropriate to impose a Compensation Order while deferring sentence on another charge, but that each case will turn on its own merits. The most common usage is for a Compensation Order to be conjoined with a fine.[11] Compensation Orders are often

---

[5]   See Stewart, *The Scottish Criminal Courts in Action* (2nd ed., 1997) at p. 240.
[6]   1995 Act, Sched. 7(6)(c).
[7]   1995 Act, Sched. 5(2)(b).
[8]   See generally ss. 249, 250, 252 and 253 of the 1995 Act.
[9]   1995 Act, s. 229(6).
[10] 1998 S.L.T. 552.
[11] Hamilton and Wisniewski, *The Use of the Compensation Order in Scotland* (SO CRU, 1996).

relatively small but nevertheless play an important role in convincing the victim that his loss is addressed in the criminal justice system.

In solemn jurisdiction courts the amount of compensation which may be ordered is unlimited. In the summary courts, the amount which may be imposed has the same maximum as the amount of fine that the court may impose for common law offences. The court must take into consideration the offender's means in determining whether to make a Compensation Order and the amount of that order. There is no statutory guidance on how compensation is to be calculated. In practice, the prosecutor will obtain information from the police as to the loss suffered by the victims and this will be either led in evidence at a trial or narrated in the prosecutor's summary of facts. A judge is not entitled to make a Compensation Order in the absence of evidence as to the loss or damage being led before the court.[12] It is not thought that corroboration of the amount of loss is required.[13] In assessing the amount of compensation, the conduct of the victim may be taken into account. Any contribution he has made to his own loss will result in the compensation being reduced. If his behaviour is of such culpability that he would not obtain an award from the Criminal Injuries Compensation Board, then likewise, he should not receive a Compensation Order.[14]

8.43   The system of compensation is such that payment is made by the offender to the clerk of court who in turn accounts it to the victim. Compensation Orders take priority over fines and in circumstances where the accused is unable to pay both the fine and the Compensation Order, the court should impose the Compensation Order. Moreover, where an order and fine are made and some payment is made, payment should first be set off against the Compensation Order and to the fine only after the Compensation Order has been paid. The court may review a Compensation Order and remit it in entirety, or in part.[15] Such a circumstance would be appropriate where the victim's loss has turned out to be much less than was first thought.

Although the Compensation Order is designed to be for the benefit of the victim, that person has no power to enforce the Compensation Order. It is the court who will enforce such an order. It is not possible to impose, as an alternative, imprisonment or detention in anticipation of default on the Compensation Order. Anyone in default of a Compensation Order must be brought before a Fines Enquiry Court who may then impose an alternative punishment. Where the offender has been ordered to pay a fine and a Compensation Order, the court may impose imprisonment or detention in respect of the default of the fine. If the offender defaults on both the fine and the Compensation Order, it is possible to aggregate the two sums payable for the purpose of calculating the period of custody which may be imposed. Any award by way of a Compensation Order will be deducted from any civil damages that the victim may have claimed.

Probation[16]

8.44   A Probation Order requires the offender to be under the supervision of a social worker[17] for a period of no less than six months and no more than three years. Probation requires the offender to work towards an acknowledgement of responsibility for offending behaviour and seeks to reduce the risk of re-offending by combining supervision and control with help,

12   *Bruce v. McLeod*, 1998, S.L.T. 173.
13   See Docherty & Maher, "Corroboration and Compensation Orders", 1984 S.L.T. (News) 125.
14   See *Brown v. Normand*, 1988, S.C.C.R. 229.
15   1995 Act, s. 256(2).
16   See generally 1995 Act, ss. 228–233 and Sched. 6.
17   See Moore and Wood, "The Power of Positive Sentencing", 1988 S.L.T. 52.

encouragement and challenge[18] The purpose of a Probation Order is to place the offender in a situation where they can obtain advice and guidance. Following conviction, the court may adjourn sentencing for the purpose of obtaining a social enquiry report into the circumstances and character of the offender. Such adjournment should be no longer than three weeks if the offender is in custody. In circumstances where the convicted person is not remanded in custody but is on bail and ordained to appear, the adjournment may be for a maximum of four weeks or, on cause shown, eight weeks.[19] Once the social enquiry report has been prepared, it will be sent to the clerk of court who in turn will pass a copy to the offender or his solicitor.[20] Where a judge requires further information about the contents of the report, he may question a social worker in open court in the presence of the accused or ask for a further report to be prepared by the social worker.[21]

Like other orders, when a Probation Order has been imposed by a judge, he is required to explain in ordinary language the effect and nature of the Probation Order and also what is likely to happen if the offender fails to comply with the order or commits a further offence. One of the unusual features about probation is that the offender must agree to being placed on probation.

Probation Orders are in a set form. The order will ordain the local authority area in which the offender will be living, and will also provide for the offender to be under supervision of a social worker employed by that local authority. All Probation Orders require the offender to (1) be of good behaviour, (2) conform to the directions of his supervising officer, and (3) inform the supervising officer at once of any change of residence or place of employment. The court also has the power to impose individual conditions to be attached to the Probation Order, for instance, that the offender participate in or rehabilitation programmes to address any underlying problems which he may have. The court has the power to impose a requirement that the offender live in a particular place for a given period of time but not exceeding 12 months. There is also the opportunity of requiring an offender who is subject to a Probation Order to undertake a prescribed number of hours of unpaid work. Offenders may be required to pay compensation as a condition of probation. In order that the court can regulate matters, payment of compensation should be completed no later than 18 months from the making of the Probation Order or two months before the end of the probation, whichever is the earlier. It is also possible that a person who is suffering from a mental disorder may be required to undergo medical treatment as part of their probation for a period not exceeding 12 months.

8.45

The Probation Order represents a conviction and may be referred to in future cases as a previous conviction. In addition to this, a Probation Order does not prevent an offender having their licence endorsed or being disqualified from driving.[22]

It is possible to have a Probation Order transferred to another court. This is done by either the probationer or supervising social worker making an application to the appropriate court. Legislation also provides for flexibility in respect of Probation Orders, and in certain circumstances applications can be made for cancellation or addition of requirements to be attached to the Probation Order. The court may alter the length of the Probation Order but may not reduce it or extend it beyond the maximum limit of three years. Moreover, a condition requiring medical treatment for a mental condition can only be added within the first three months of the making of the Probation Order.

---

[18] SWSG National Standards, para. 7.1.
[19] 1995 Act, s. 201(3)(a) and (b).
[20] *ibid.*, s. 203(3).
[21] See *W v. H.M.Advocate*, 1989, S.C.C.R. 461.
[22] Road Traffic Offenders Act 1988, s. 46(3).

It is open to either the probationer or the social worker to apply to the court to have a Probation Order discharged. It will only be brought by the social worker where he considers that the probation has achieved its purpose, or in circumstances where the probationer has committed another offence and receives a long-term prison sentence.

8.46   In the not uncommon situation where a probationer fails to adhere to the requirement of a Probation Order, the social worker may apply to the court for breach proceedings. The social worker submits a report to the court alleging the breach and recommending whether or not proceedings should be taken. The court may either cite the offender to attend, or grant a warrant for his arrest. In other cases, the judge may discuss the case with the social worker before deciding whether to take breach proceedings. If cited or arrested and brought before the court, the offender appears and addresses the alleged failure to comply. If the offender denies he has been in breach of the Probation Order, evidence will be taken in court to confirm or deny the alleged breach. The evidence of only one witness is sufficient to prove a breach of probation conditions. In circumstances where the alleged breach is proved the court may continue the Probation Order and additionally impose a fine, not exceeding level 3 in the standard scale (except in cases where the breach represents a failure to pay compensation). Alternatively, the court may simply sentence the offender for the original offence which in effect terminates the Probation Order. As a further alternative, the court may amend the Probation Order, extending it but not beyond the maximum three years. The court may also, as a variation, impose a Community Service Order in addition to the Probation Order.

Where the convicted person commits a further offence, the supervising social worker will report this matter to the court. The probationer will be cited to attend court or have a warrant for his arrest issued. The Probation Order may be continued or the court may sentence him for the original offence. Ordinarily the further offence will be dealt with in the same court as the one the original Probation Order was imposed in. In such circumstances, the court may deal with the offender for both the offence and the original offence. The court is likely to look more severely at any situation where the offender commits an offence on or around premises whilst performing unpaid work as a condition of probation.[23]

8.47   Probation orders are used less frequently in Scotland partly because it is not often recommended by social workers in their social enquiry reports.[24] This in part may be explained by the transition *from* specialised probation officers to generic social workers.[25]

As a final alternative, the court has the power to impose probation with the condition that the offender submit himself to treatment for any mental conditions. This will require the consent of the probationer. The court must be satisfied that there is evidence from one doctor that the mental condition of the offender requires and is susceptible to treatment but not so bad as to warrant detention under the hospital order. The probation order must specify whether the treatment is to be as an in-patient or an out-patient in the named hospital, and who will provide the medical treatment. Treatment under the Probation Order must be for a specific period not exceeding 12 months. There is the power to vary the conditions of treatment, subject to agreement by the probationer and the supervising social worker, without a requirement that the matter return to court. The National Objectives and

---

23   See Stewart, *The Scottish Criminal Courts in Action* (2nd ed., 1997) at p. 250.
24   See Curran and Chalmers, *Social Enquiry Reports in Scotland* (1982); Williams, Creamer and Hartley, "Probation as an alternative to custody" in Adler and Millar (eds), *Socio-legal Research in the Scottish Courts* Scottish Office (1991) Vol. 2.
25   See McIvor, "Social Work and Criminal Justice in Scotland: Developments in Policy and Practice" (1994) 24 *British Journal of Social Work*, at pp. 433–434.

Standards regulate the frequency of contact between probationer and supervisor, and stipulate the type of offender for whom probation is suitable.

Community Service Orders[26]

In any offence, except murder, where the offender is over 16 and the offence is punishable **8.48** with a custodial sentence, the court has the discretion to impose a Community Service Order. The order requires the offender to perform unpaid work for a specified number of hours which may not be less than 80 and not more than 240 in a summary case, or 300 in a solemn procedure case.[27] The Community Service Order is imposed as an alternative to imprisonment and therefore must be seen as the last resort action. It is likely that breach of an order will result in imprisonment.[28] In making a Community Service Order the court must be satisfied that the offender consents; that the community service is available in the area in which the offender resides; and that the court is satisfied following a report from a social worker that the offender is a suitable person for community service and that suitable work is available. Community service assessments are carried out by social enquiry report authors in consultation with community service officers. The court is required to explain in ordinary language the nature and effect of the order. In addition, the court is required to warn the offender of the likely consequences were he to breach the order and to apply some of his obligation to perform the number of hours under the direction of a supervising social worker. Ordinarily, community service is the solitary punishment imposed, although there is power for the court to additionally disqualify an offender, make an order for forfeiture, have the defender find caution, or pay a Compensation Order. A fine cannot be imposed at the same time as a Community Service Order for the same offence. The order itself will specify the locality in which the offender resides. It will require the local authority to appoint or assign a social worker to supervise the order, and it will state the number of hours that the offender must perform. Community Service Orders may run concurrently, or consecutively, with other Community Service Orders, or with any period of unpaid work as a condition of probation. The only restriction on this is that the outstanding number of hours' work must not exceed 240 in summary cases or 300 in solemn cases. The offender is always supplied with a copy of the Community Service Order.

The required work must be completed within 12 months of the date of the order unless that period is extended. The hours of work must not conflict with the offender's religious beliefs, or any time which he would normally work or attend any educational establishment. Any absence for sickness reasons will require an offender to produce a medical certificate. The cost of obtaining a medical report may be refunded to the offender. The certificate will be retained on file until the offender completes the order or breach proceedings are complete.[29] In circumstances where there is an alleged breach of the Community Service Order, the supervising social worker will submit a breach report to the appropriate court describing failure to comply, and recommending whether breach proceedings should be commenced or not. In the event that the court decides to commence such proceedings, the offender will be either cited to attend at court, or a warrant will be granted for his or her arrest. The offender will appear in court and will either admit or deny the failure to comply. In circumstances where there is a denial, evidence must be led which will prove a failure or otherwise. The

---

[26]   See generally 1995 Act, ss. 238–241.
[27]   1995 Act, s. 238(1), as amended by the Community Service by Offenders (Hours of Work) (Scotland) Order 1996, (S.I. 1996, No. 1938).
[28]   See, however, Stewart, *The Scottish Criminal Courts in Action* (2nd ed., 1997) at p. 251.
[29]   See SWSG Circular 102/89.

evidence of one witness is sufficient to prove breach of community service. Where the court is satisfied that a breach has taken place, it may impose a fine not exceeding level 3 on the standard scale. It may alternatively revoke the order and deal with the offender for the original offence as if the order had not been made. As a further alternative, it may vary the number of hours provided that the total does not exceed 240 or 300 as may be appropriate. The commission of a further offence whilst the subject of a Community Service Order is not in itself breach of the order. Nevertheless, it is likely to be aggravation of an offence where it is committed on premises where the accused has been performing the community service.[30]

8.49   There is scope within the legislation for either the offender or the supervising social worker to apply to the appropriate court to have the Community Service Order amended, either with a view to extending the period of 12 months during which the hours are to be completed, or varying the number of hours, albeit that no variation beyond the upper and lower limits can be entertained. The court has sole discretion in this matter, and will determine the issue in the interests of justice.

Similarly, the offender or the supervising social worker may make an application for revocation of a Community Service Order. The Community Service Order may be revoked by the court without any further action being taken. Alternatively, it may revoke the order and deal with the offender as if an order had never been made. There are a number of circumstances where revocation may be appropriate: the offender may have become seriously ill, or it has become clear that he is not a suitable person for community service. Another possibility is that the offender has since been sentenced to a long prison sentence.

In cases where the offender is sentenced to complete more than one community service order, the hours worked in total each day/week should be attributed to completion of the first order made, and thereafter the following orders made on a consecutive basis. Moreover, where a number of orders are made by the court on the same occasion in relation to the same offender, and the court does not specify that they are to run concurrently, these orders should be treated as consecutive orders. Should a breach occur it will relate only to the order under supervision at that time.[31]

8.50   Community service has proved popular with the courts.[32] SWSG assumed full funding of community service in 1989.[33] There is evidence that community service was, in its earlier years, displacing other non-custodial sentences rather than imprisonment.[34] There is at evidence of a gender bias in the referral of offenders for community service assessment, with young male offenders most likely to receive community service.[35] Revised standards for the orders were issued in 1995 and it is expected that where the courts choose community service the penalty should be seen to be a suitably rigorous and challenging one. The Government has previously announced a desire for greater emphasis to be placed on physically challenging placements and encouraged local authorities to ensure there were adequate placements of this kind, particularly environmental improvement projects.[36]

[30]   See Stewart, *The Scottish Criminal Courts in Action* (2nd ed., 1997) at pp. 253–254.
[31]   SWSG Circular, *Breach Procedures and the Status of Consecutive Order*, No. 107/91, Oct. 10, 1991.
[32]   McIvor, "Social Work and Criminal Justice in Scotland: Developments in Policy and Practice" (1994) 24 B.J. Social Work at p. 431.
[33]   McIvor, *op. cit.* (1994) at p. 432.
[34]   McIvor, "Community Service and custody in Scotland", (1990) *The Howard Journal of Criminal Justice* 29, pp. 101–113; see also McIvor and Tulle-Winton, *The Use of Community Service by Scottish Courts* (1993), SOCRU.
[35]   McIvor, "Jobs for the Boys?: Gender Differences in Referral to Community Service" (1998) 37(3) *The Howard Journal of Criminal Justice* 280–290.
[36]   SWSG Circular *Public Awareness, Environmental Work and Hours*, 12/96, April 1996.

Local authorities are expected to involve victim support agencies in planning community service placements. In addition the Government are fully supportive of the idea that community service schemes should be publicised.[37] Following the SWSI Report *Realistic and Rigorous*, the Government issued guidance to local authorities on the management and monitoring of community service schemes. In the process they modified two of the National Objectives and Standards and in the process inserted a timescale of five days for submission of applications of breach to the courts.[38] There have been calls for social work intervention in community service to assist offenders in meeting of any order requirements.[39]

Admonition

All courts have the power to admonish a convicted person.[40] Admonition is in effect a   **8.51**
warning but is a conviction nevertheless. It is therefore only appropriate if the offence is very minor, or there are highly mitigating circumstances. It is often a form of disposal where the person has had their sentence deferred and bound over to good behaviour and the offender has complied.

Absolute discharge

Where it appears to the court to be inexpedient to inflict punishment, it is open to the court   **8.52**
to impose an absolute discharge.[41] In summary cases the absolute discharge will occur prior to conviction, whereas in solemn cases the absolute discharge will follow conviction. An absolute discharge cannot be imposed after conviction in summary cases where the accused has been bound over to be of good behaviour and sentence has been deferred. It is an extremely mild form of sanction.[42] It is possible to have an absolute discharge and have one's licence endorsed or be disqualified from driving. It is not however competent to additionally impose a Compensation Order.[43]

Deferred sentence

The court may defer sentence following a conviction.[44] Sentence may be deferred for any   **8.53**
period and on any condition, although in most circumstances sentence is deferred so that the accused can exhibit a period of good behaviour. It is likely that if the accused is of good behaviour during that period then he can anticipate the court imposing a more lenient sentence such as an admonition. Although this is well known, it is not appropriate for the judge to promise a particular disposal if the accused behaves for a period of time.[45] If the accused faces multiple charges it is not appropriate to impose a custodial sentence on one and

---

[37] *ibid.*, as modified by SWSG Circular 5/98, March 1998, including marked sign posts at projects and local media advertisement but not marked protective clothing and vehicles.

[38] See SWSG Circular, *Community Service By Offenders: Follow Up to SWSI Report on Discipline and Enforcement of Community Service Orders*, 31/97, Oct. 1997.

[39] McIvor, "Social Work Intervention in Community Service" (1991) 24 *British Journal of Social Work* 591–609.

[40] 1995 Act, s. 246(1).

[41] *ibid.*, s. 246(2) and (3).

[42] See, *e.g. Galloway v. Mackenzie*, 1991 S.C.C.R. 548; *Kheda v. Lees*, 1995 S.C.C.R. 63.

[43] 1995 Act, s. 249(2)(a).

[44] 1995 Act, s. 202(1); see Smith, "Deferred Sentence in Scotland", 1968 S.L.T. (News) 153; Nicholson, "Deferment of Sentence in Scotland", 1993 S.L.T. (News) 1.

[45] See *Cassidy v. Wilson*, 1989 S.C.C.R. 6.

defer sentence on another.[46] Similarly, again in respect of multiple charges, a fine should not be imposed on one charge and sentence deferred on the other. It is desirable that the sheriff who deferred sentence should hear the recalled case if at all possible. In circumstances where the offender commits a further offence during the period of the deferred sentence, he may be immediately brought before the court either by citation, or an arrest warrant.[47] In circumstances where the offence is committed and dealt with by another court, that matter will be reported to the original court. Where the offence is in the same court as imposed the deferred sentence, the court may, in considering the disposal for the case at hand, also dispose of the original conviction as though sentence had not been deferred. Research in Scotland has disclosed that female offenders and offenders under the age of 21 were the most common groups to have their sentences deferred.[48] Crimes of dishonesty are the most common crimes for which sentence is deferred. Social workers are often involved in the deferment process, and it is commonly recommended in a social enquiry report as a possible disposal. After deferral, the most common form of disposal is a fine and/or a compensation order. Although there is no statutory requirement to supervise the deferred sentence, social workers are often required to complete a social enquiry report following deferment. Many of those reports contained recommendations for ultimate disposal of the case.

Forfeiture and confiscation

8.54   Many statutes provide for forfeiture of certain items following conviction.[49] In addition to this, under Part 2 of the Proceeds of Crime (Scotland) Act 1995, it is open to the court to order confiscation of any property of the accused which the court is satisfied (a) has been used for the purposes of committing or facilitating the commission of any offence; or (b) was intended by him to be used for that purpose.[50] Confiscation and forfeiture may be additional to any other sentence imposed.[51]

Under Part 1 of the Proceeds of Crime (Scotland) Act 1995 the courts have the power to order confiscation of property which represents the proceeds of crime. The Act distinguishes drug-trafficking offences and other offences. In respect of other offences, the court can only impose a Confiscation Order where they are convinced that the accused has benefited from the commission of the offence.[52] In respect of drug-trafficking proceeds, the court will seek to assess the value of the proceeds of the accused's drug trafficking.[53] The court may postpone the making of a Confiscation Order for up to six months after the date of conviction in order to obtain further information, either to determine whether or not to make an order, or to determine the extent of the order.[54]

Where the court orders a Confiscation Order or a Suspended Forfeiture Order, the court may also make a Restraint Order which prohibits the person named in the order from dealing with certain property.[55]

---

[46]   See *Lennon v. Copeland*, 1972 S.L.T. (Notes) 68.
[47]   1995 Act, s. 202(2).
[48]   See Nicholson, *The Deferred Sentence in Scotland* (1992) Scottish Office, CRU.
[49]   See, *e.g.* the Road Traffic Offenders Act 1998, s. 33A, which provides for confiscation of vehicles.
[50]   Proceeds of Crime (Scotland) Act 1995, s. 21(2).
[51]   See Kelly, *Criminal Sentencing* (1993), Chap. 7.
[52]   Proceeds of Crime (Scotland) Act 1995, s. 1(4).
[53]   *ibid.*, s. 1(5).
[54]   *ibid.*, s. 10.
[55]   Proceeds of Crime (Scotland) Act 1995, s. 28(1).

Disqualification and deportation

A further possibility open to the court is disqualification. In respect of road traffic offences, **8.55** the court may impose endorsements or disqualifications from driving. Disqualification might also be appropriate where the accused has been cruel to an animal,[56] or where the accused is engaged in some corrupt practice whilst serving on a public body. In the modern era a further area where disqualification might serve as a punishment is in respect of company directors under the Company Director's Disqualification Act 1986. In respect of any offender over 17 who is not a British subject, the court may in certain circumstances order the deportation of that person. If the offender commits an offence punishable with imprisonment, the sheriff court or the High Court may exercise their discretion to recommend deportation.[57] The decision to deport is taken by the Home Secretary.[58] Where a court makes a recommendation to deport, this may be appealed to the High Court of Judiciary sitting as the Scottish Court of Criminal Appeal.

Supervised Release Order

Under a Supervised Release Order the offender is required to report to a supervising officer **8.56** in a manner and at intervals specified by the supervising officer, and to notify that officer without delay of any change of address.[59] They arise where the offender has been sentenced for a period greater than one year but less than four years, and where the court is of the opinion that it is necessary to protect the public from serious harm by the offender on his release. The offender will be under the supervision of a supervising officer or a probation officer. The supervised offender must also comply with any reasonable requirements as specified by the supervising officer. The court at the time of imposing the order may specify further conditions such as treatment for addiction or a requirement to stay away from the victim.

Supervision and Treatment Order[60]

These orders are closely modelled on orders of the same name which have operated in **8.57** England for some time.[61] The purpose of the order is to secure access to supervision and treatment (including medical treatment) in the community for those who are unfit to stand trial but who are found to have committed the act constituting the offence following an examination of the facts, or who were insane at the time of committing the act constituting the offence.[62] Before making an order, the court must be satisfied, on the basis of evidence of two medical practitioners approved for the purposes of sections 20 or 39 of the Mental Health (Scotland) Act 1984, that the mental condition of the person requires, and may be susceptible to, treatment but not such as to warrant a hospital order.[63] The court may only make an order if it is satisfied that it is the most suitable means of dealing with the person, that arrangements can be made for the treatment, and that a supervising officer is willing to

---

[56] Protection of Animals (Amendment) Act 1954, s. 1(1).
[57] Immigration Act 1971, s. 6(1).
[58] *ibid.*, s. 5(1).
[59] Criminal Justice and Public Order Act 1994 s. 132; Act of Adjournal (S.I. 1995 No. 1875).
[60] See generally 1995 Act, Sched. 4, paras 2–8.
[61] See Criminal Procedure (Insanity and Unfitness to Plead) Act 1991.
[62] 1995 Act, s. 57 and Sched. 4.
[63] On hospital orders, see para. 6.56.

undertake the supervision. The court is required to explain to the offender the effect of the order, and thereafter provide the offender with a copy of the order. Suitability assessment and supervision will be carried out by a social worker with mental health experience, usually a mental health officer. It is anticipated that the local authority report as to the suitability of the offender for a supervision and treatment order should be submitted at the same time as the medical recommendations.[64] The factors to be considered in assessing suitability are the risk the person poses; whether the person is likely to comply with the conditions of the order; the home surroundings of the offender; and whether a condition of residence may be necessary.

A person who is the subject of a Supervision and Treatment Order must submit to treatment by a named specialist psychiatric medical practitioner. Wherever possible, this will be one of the recommending doctors. Where the doctor is of the opinion that treatment might be better or more convenient at a hospital, he may, with the consent of the supervised person, make the necessary arrangements.

The order must last longer than three years. It also possible for the court to impose a residence requirement on to the Supervision and Treatment Order. The supervising officer is likely to draw up a care plan for the person being supervised. The offender or the supervising officer may apply to the sheriff to have the order revoked having regard to circumstances which have arisen, and which make revocation in the interests of the supervised person's health and welfare. There is scope to seek a variation of the order for reasons of change of residence, by request or in pursuance of a medical report.

If arrangements under the order have broken down, the supervising officer should inform the court at once. However, it should be noted that a Supervision and Treatment Order is not enforceable in the same way that a probation order or community service is. If compulsory medical treatment is thought necessary, then resort must be had to the compulsory detention measures in the mental health legislation.[65] If a person insane in bar of trial subsequently becomes mentally fit, the Supervision and Treatment Order automatically falls on the person being served with a complaint, or an indictment. Where the supervised person is found guilty of another offence, before passing sentence the court must obtain a social enquiry report, usually from the supervising officer, which will amongst other things address the person's attitude to the order.

Drug Treatment and Testing Order[66]

8.58   Following an amendment to 1995 Act by the Crime and Disorder Act 1998 the court may make a Drug Treatment and Testing Order when it has been satisfied of three conditions:

1.   that the offender is dependent on, or has a propensity to misuse, drugs;

2.   that his dependency or propensity is such as requires and is susceptible to treatment; and

3.   that he is a suitable person to be subject to such an order.[67]

In seeking to satsify the final condition, the court is authorised to retrieve samples from the individual concerned, though his consent must first be obtained. Before making the order the

---

[64]   Supervision and Treatment Order Guidance, SWSG 4/98.
[65]   On which see paras 6.07–6.16.
[66]   See, generally, 1995 Act, ss. 234B, 234C and 234E–234G.
[67]   1995 Act, s. 234B(3)(c), as inserted by Crime and Disorder Act 1998, s. 89.

court must receive a report from the social work department confirming that the aforesaid conditions have been met. It must therefore be fully alerted to the individual circumstances of the offender before taking any decisions on drug testing and treatment. Whether or not a court may make such an order will depend on whether arrangements exist within the local authority area to give it the necessary effect. In addition, such an order is only available when the offender is aged 16 or above and when he has committed an offence to which an indeterminate sentence is attached.[68] Once more, his consent is central to the making of an order.

The "treatment and testing period" shall be not less than six months and no more than three years in duration. However, the Secretary of State is empowered to substitute these two periods thereby increasing or decreasing the period over which the order stretches. In a attempt to regulate the operation of this discretionary power, he may only do so by introducing a statutory instrument which requires to be laid before Parliament.

The purpose of the order is clearly to rehabilitate the offender instead of enforcing a punishment, though clearly the adversity which results from its conditions is expected to serve as some means of formal discipline. The stated aim of the order is the reduction or the elimination of the offender's dependency on, or propensity to misuse, drugs. The treatment may involve residency for some or all of the total period specified by the order in an appropriate institution. On the other hand, the individual may be treated at non-residential premises as an out-patient of that institution. In either case he will be required to allow samples to be taken from his body during the treatment and testing period to ascertain whether or not he is continuing to use drugs. The extent to which the treatment provider is authorised to draw samples is specified in the order made by the court, which must make known the minimum number of samples to be provided each month.

While the order is in force the offender will be placed under the supervision of a **8.59** supervising officer with whom he must, as a condition of the order, maintain regular contact in accordance with the particular details of the order itself. The statute details the role which is to be played by the supervising officer, namely, that he will report on the offender's progress to the appropriate court, including the results of all drug tests undertaken, and inform that court if the offender fails to comply with the requirements of the order. It is also the responsibility of the officer in charge of the individual to recognise circumstances which demand that the order should be revoked or varied in any way.

Since the duration of the order must comply with the statutory requirements, there must be some measures to allow the order to be varied or revoked within this period. If the supervising officer is satisfied that requirements need to be amended, deleted or inserted, that the order should be entirely revoked, or that it should be increased or decreased in duration within the period authorised by statute, he will need to make an application to the court before which the offender will subsequently have to appear. The court is empowered to amend the order if it is in the interests of justice to do so. If the offender is required to appear in court in these circumstances and fails to do so, the court may issue a warrant for his arrest. As a further means of regulation, each order must arrange for monthly reviews to be undertaken, at which the offender must himself be present. This provides another opportunity for the terms of the order to be varied, though in this instance an amendment cannot be undertaken without the consent of the offender. Once more, a failure to appear at a periodic review of the order may result in the arrest of the offender.

---

[68]   This order is not available in respect of offences committed before the Crime and Disorder Act 1998 came into force.

Finally, a failure to comply with the order will amount to an offence punishable by a fine, or may result in the variation or revocation of the order. It is likely in the event of these circumstances that the court will pass another disposal with which the offender is more likely to comply. Clearly, the Drug Treatment and Testing Order will not be appropriate for all individuals with drug problems.

The Restriction of Liberty Order and electronic tagging[69]

8.60   The Crime and Punishment (Scotland) Act 1997 introduced a new non- custodial sentence called the Restriction of Liberty Order (RLO) into Scots criminal law. On January 26, 1998 the Scottish Office announced the introduction of a pilot project for electronic tagging. This scheme will operate in Aberdeen, Peterhead and Hamilton Sheriff Courts until March 2000.

A RLO can be made in respect of any person aged 16 years or more who is convicted of an offence, where the offence does not carry a fixed sentence by law, and the court considers it the most appropriate method of disposal.[70] The aim of a RLO is to restrict the offender's movements to such an extent as the court thinks fit which may include the offender being restricted to, or excluded from, a specified place at specified times during each day or week. The offender cannot be restricted to a specific place for more than 12 hours in any one day, and the RLO itself cannot exceed 12 months.

The Secretary of State is responsible for making the arrangements, including contractual arrangements, for the remote monitoring of RLO's and these arrangements may vary in different areas and for different forms of monitoring. The Secretary of State, by statutory instrument, determines the method of monitoring compliance, the classes of offenders and which courts may make a RLO. He may also vary the maximum hours and duration of a RLO. The court is then notified of the person, class or description of persons who may be chosen to monitor the offender's compliance and any changes to the chosen person results in the RLO being varied and the offender notified.

When making the RLO, the court must consider information about the place of restriction and attitudes of people affected by the offender's restriction. The court then has to explain to the offender the effect of the RLO, the consequences if breached, and that the order may be reviewed on application from either the offender or the monitoring company. The offender's consent is needed before the order is made. A copy of the order is sent to the offender and the monitoring company. The period in which the offender has to wear a "tag" will be specified in the order.

It is also possible for both a RLO and a probation order to be made together if the court thinks it is fitting in the circumstances. Factors to be taken into account are the nature of the offence, and the character of the offender. Where both orders are made, the clerk of the court sends a copy of each order to both the person monitoring the electronic tagging and the local authority officer supervising the probationer.

8.61   It is possible for the offender or the person responsible for monitoring the offender's compliance with the order to apply to the court to have the order reviewed. The court, after hearing the offender and the person responsible for monitoring, may in the interests of justice vary the order by amending or deleting any of its requirements, insert new requirements, increase the period for which the order has to run, or revoke the order.

---

[69]   See generally ss. 245A–245I, as inserted by s. 5 of the Crime and Punishment (Scotland) Act 1997. See also Crichton and Mays, "Electronic Tagging of Offenders—Scotland Joins in", 1999 S.L.P.Q. (forthcoming October issue).

[70]   A RLO is classed as a sentence for the purposes of this Act: s. 245A (7).

If a person other than the offender applies to vary the order (other than by deleting a requirement), the court will issue a citation requiring the offender to appear before the court,[71] so as to explain the effect and consequences of the varied order. Failure to appear may lead to the issue of a warrant for arrest.

If the court suspects the offender has failed to comply with any requirement of the RLO, it may issue a citation requiring the offender to appear before the court or, if appropriate, the court may issue a warrant for his arrest. If the court is satisfied that the offender has, without reasonable excuse, failed to comply with all the requirements of the RLO, the court may impose a fine, vary or revoke the order. If a fine is imposed, it is deemed to be paid in respect of a conviction or a penalty imposed on a person summarily convicted. Variation of an order is dealt with as above, and if the order is to be revoked, the court may dispose of the offender in the way that would have been competent had the RLO not been made, but must take into consideration the length of time the order has been in operation. If the offender is also subject to a Probation Order, the Probation Order will also be discharged.

In cases where both a RLO and a Probation Order have been made, a breach of a requirement in the Probation Order may result in any requirement of the Probation Order being varied by the court,[72] and in addition the court may vary the RLO. Similarly, if the breach relates to a requirement in the RLO, the court, in addition to varying the requirements of the RLO, may vary the requirements in the Probation Order. If the offender, by act or omission, fails to comply with a requirement in *both* orders the court may vary the requirements of the Probation Order, impose a fine,[73] vary or revoke the RLO, but the offender shall not be liable to be otherwise dealt with in respect of the act or omission. When a RLO is varied or revoked, the person responsible for monitoring the offender's compliance is given a copy of the amended order and is responsible for giving a copy to the offender.

DEALING WITH CHILD OFFENDERS IN THE CRIMINAL JUSTICE SYSTEM

Most child offenders will be dealt with by the children's hearing system.[74] However, some will require to be dealt with in the court for reasons already set out elsewhere in this book. Children accused of a crime must be kept apart from all other adults accused of crimes, except those with whom they are co-accused.[75] If in custody, the child must be kept separate from ordinary remand prisoners, and if not in custody the child must be kept in a separate room from other defendants while awaiting a court appearance. A female child must at all times be under the care of a woman.[76]

8.62

Unless the child has been removed from the parent or guardian's custody or care under a court order, the parent or guardian has an obligation to attend any court hearing. The local social work department will be notified of the intention to bring a child before the court and will in the fullness of time prepare a social enquiry report.[77] The press and media generally are restricted in their reporting of a case where a child is involved.[78] They may not disclose his name, address, school or any particulars likely to lead to the child concerned being identified.

---

[71] The offender is also required to appear before the court if the order is to be revoked: s. 245E (3)(b) as inserted by the Crime and Punishment (Scotland) Act 1997, s. 5.
[72] 1995 Act, s. 232(2)(c).
[73] *ibid.*, s. 232(2).
[74] See Chap. 4, paras 4.40 *et seq.*
[75] See 1995 Act, s. 142 for children charged with summary offences.
[76] 1995 Act, s. 42(10).
[77] 1995 Act, s. 42(7).
[78] *ibid.*, s. 47(1), (2) and (3).

They may not publish any picture including the child. Where the child is simply a witness the restriction only applies if the courts so directs. The court has the power to lift the restriction at any time where it thinks it is in the public interest to do so.[79] It is an offence to infringe reporting restrictions.[80]

Where a child appears in a summary criminal case the sheriff is required to sit in a different court or building from that which he would ordinarily conduct criminal business.[81] The numbers attending the court will be strictly controlled and the public will not be admitted.

If the child is remanded awaiting trial or pending conviction he should be committed to the care of the local authority if the court directs, in secure accommodation or a place of safety chosen by the local authority.[82] In circumstances where the child is unruly or depraved and the court is advised that a remand centre is available, the child will be committed there or to prison.[83] Children initially committed to the care of the local authority may, if their behaviour so warrants, have their committal to the local authority revoked and substituted with a committal to a remand centre or prison.[84]

SEXUAL OFFENDERS

8.63   On September 1, 1997 the Government implemented the Sex Offenders Act 1997 designed to register all known sexual offenders.[85] It is intended that the information provided to the police is used for the prevention of crime and the protection of children and vulnerable adults. Part I of the Act requires persons convicted of specified sexual offences to notify the police of their name, home address and date of birth and any subsequent changes to these details.[86] These offences are listed in Schedule I to the Act. The offender will do this at the time of conviction. Notification is not a punishment in itself and should not be taken account of by a court which is considering an appropriate sentence.[87]

The offender is further required to notify the police in the home area of any premises in which he stays for a period of 14 days or more, or two or more periods within a period of 12 months which, taken together, amount to 14 days or more. If the offender has no fixed abode or is homeless he must give the police details of any place he visits regularly and where he may be contacted.[88] Failure to notify the police or to give false information is an offence punishable on summary conviction with a fine and/or imprisonment for up to six months.[89] An offender under 18 years of age when convicted cannot be imprisoned for failure to notify the police. There are different notification periods (period during which the sexual offender must comply with the requirement to notify) attached to different disposals and those under 18 years of age when convicted will have their notification periods halved.[90] For example, an 11-year-old offender who indecently assaulted his two-year-old cousin was recently required

---

[79]   The Secretary of State for Scotland can lift reporting restrictions after the trial on similar grounds: see 1995 Act, s. 47(3)(c).

[80]   See Moody, "Publicity in Criminal Cases Involving Children", 1999 J.R. 1.

[81]   1995 Act, s. 142(1); *Heywood v. B*, 1994 S.C.C.R. 554.

[82]   1995 Act, s. 51(1)(a).

[83]   *ibid.*, s. 51(1)(b).

[84]   *ibid.*, s. 51(3).

[85]   The idea of registration is based on American schemes: see Hebenton and Thomas, *Keeping Track?: Observations on Sex Offender Registers in the US*, Paper 83, Home Office (1997).

[86]   Sex Offenders Act 1997 ("1997 Act"), s. 2(1), (2) and (3).

[87]   *Re Att. Gen. Ref. (No. 50 of 1997)* [1998] 2 Cr.App.R.(S.) 155.

[88]   1997 Act, s. 2(7).

[89]   *ibid.*, s. 3(1).

[90]   1997 Act, s. 4(2).

to register for a period of two and a half years.[91] British citizens who commit their offences outside the United Kingdom may nevertheless be dealt with by the Scottish courts.[92]

The people affected by the notification requirements are those persons who are convicted   **8.64**
of a specified sexual offence, and those who have been found not guilty of such an offence by reason of insanity. It is incumbent on the convicting court to notify the police of the imposition of a notification requirement. Various categories of offenders already within the criminal justice system were subjected to the notification requirements at the time of the Act's implementation. The police hold computerised records of all those subject to notification requirements.

The following notification requirements apply:

Sentence	Notification period
Life imprisonment	Indefinite
Imprisonment of 30 months or more	Indefinite
Admission to hospital subject to a restriction order	Indefinite
Imprisonment of less than 30 months but more than 6 months	10 years
Imprisonment of less than 6 months	7 years
Admitted to hospital but no restriction order	7 years
Non-custodial order (including guardianship order)	5 years[93]

Where a sentence is adjourned or deferred the police are still expected to be notified of the conviction even although the registration period will not be known. In practice they will allot the minimum five-year period pending final disposal of the case. Even offenders who are given an absolute discharge will still be the subject of notification requirements. Notification periods start from the date of sentencing, or in the case of mentally disordered persons, the date of the finding that the person committed the offence with which he was charged.[94]

It is envisaged that local authorities will have an important role in the supervision of sexual   **8.65**
offenders who have community-based sentences but more than this they will have aftercare responsibilities for up to 12 months, namely to provide guidance and assistance to sexual offenders released from prison. There are particular arrangements for local authorities to be notified by prison social work departments of the release of prisoners who have been convicted of offences against children at least four months prior to the offender's release.[95] Because of the various general duties to children (see Chapter 4) local authorities are required to make enquiries, protect from risk, assess the need for compulsory measures of supervision and generally promote the welfare of children. In this respect, local authorities are to be regarded as corporate entities whereby all appropriate parts of that authority must investigate the case of a child known to be at risk of exposure to a sex offender.

While local authorities have a key role in ensuring relevant offenders register with the police, it is the responsibility of the offender to register. With the provision of a certificate by the convicting court the offender should be in no doubts as to the requirement.[96] Local

---

[91]   Mar. 25, 1999 in Newcastle, reported in *The Scotsman*, Mar. 26, 1999.
[92]   1997 Act, s. 8.
[93]   *ibid.*, s. 1(4).
[94]   *ibid.*, s. 1(2), (3) and (7).
[95]   See SWSG Circular 14/94.
[96]   1997 Act, s. 5.

arrangements will be made with the police for the disclosure of details of any person on the register to the social work department.[97] Obviously in fulfilling their role in protecting children the social work department will from time to time require to know the whereabouts of a sex offender. The information supplied by the police is to be treated in the strictest confidence. The guidance issued to local authority social work departments states that:

"When the local authority receives information from the police about a sex offender in their area they should collate available information to try to identify the likely level of risk which the offender may present to previous or potential victims, and thereafter take appropriate steps to reduce risk to children, or other vulnerable people in the area. The local authority should check whether the offender is known to local criminal justice services, whether he is under the supervision of a social worker, and whether there is any information about him held by any other social work services with whom he may have been in contact".[98]

Once the information is received, there will naturally require to be an assessment of the risk posed. Information may be required to be shared with agencies outside the local authority, but this should only be done on a restricted basis. In circumstances where a child is thought to be at risk of exposure to a sex offender the panoply of powers canvassed in Chapter 4 of this book can be applied to protect the child.

8.66   In assessing risk to children or others, the police may decide to disclose information about a registered sex offender to a third party such as the victim, the victim's family, the offender's new partner, or a headteacher or playgroup organiser. Information is limited to that which is necessary and will be disclosed in person by a police officer. Guidance dictates that they should only do so after taking account of the nature and pattern of the offender's previous offending; his compliance with previous sentences or court orders; any predatory behaviour which indicates a likelihood of re-offending; the probability that a further offence will be committed; the likely harm that behaviour may cause; the extent to which potential victims are vulnerable; the potential consequences of disclosure to the offender and his family; and the potential disclosure for other aspects of law and order. In *R. v. Chief Constable of North Wales, ex p. AB*[99] a married couple released from prison following convictions for serious sexual offences against children attempted to settle at a caravan site in North Wales. Following a report compiled by Northumbria Police, the local police were of the opinion that a substantial risk was present since many children were likely to frequent the caravan park during an imminent school holiday. They asked the couple to move and when they refused they disclosed information to the park owner who asked them to leave. Although they left, an action for judicial review was raised on their behalf. In dismissing the application the court held that in reaching the decision to disclose the details of the offences to the park owner, North Wales Police had not acted irrationally, nor was the policy on which this decision was based unlawful. Furthermore, the identity of former sex offenders should only be disclosed to the public when there was a pressing need to do so and once the police had accumulated as much information on the case in hand. Though the applicants should have been given the opportunity to respond to the contents of the report, their representations would have had no bearing on the decision to disclose its details.

In this respect the police have an unenviable task. In several instances around Scotland there has been community unrest when the presence of sex offenders has been disclosed. The

---

[97]   SWSG 11/97, para. 19.
[98]   *ibid.*, para. 20.
[99]   [1998] 3 W.L.R. 57.

police have the alternative of giving the offender a warning as to areas he should avoid, and it is also possible for the police to enjoin the assistance of social work criminal justice services where the offender is under statutory supervision.

Sex Offender Orders[1]

Introduced by the Crime and Disorder Act 1998, the Sex Offender Order seeks to take the monitoring of sex offenders beyond registration alone. Sex offenders who are of or over the age of 16 and who give reasonable cause for the police to believe that an order is necessary may become subject to its provisions. Its purpose is to actually regulate the offender's behaviour. The legislation is not specific about how this might be achieved though it is likely that the order might seek to restrict the movements of the offender, and define the areas to which he might be confined. Furthermore, there is no indication in the Act of what a valid and likely duration for an order would be.   **8.67**

An application is submitted to the sheriff by the Chief Constable in whose area the offender is present. The sheriff will place prohibitions on the person in question with a view to protecting the public from serious harm. It will not be sufficient that the individual is merely present in a police force area—he will have to give actual cause for concern.

Where an order is made, the provisions of Part I of the Sex Offenders Act 1997 will take effect, thus requiring persons convicted of certain specified sexual offences to notify the police of their name, address and date of birth, and to inform the police of any changes made to those details. A power of arrest is attached to any order made and will be exercised when a police constable reasonably suspects that the person who is the subject of the order has done or is doing an act which is prohibited by the order.

It is thought that this initiative was largely a response to the actions of a convicted paedophile in Aberdeen in 1997 which culminated in the death of a young boy.[2] The conduct of the local social work department and the Chief Constable were placed under intense scrutiny as a result of these events. Of course, since that time the Sex Offenders Act 1997 has also taken effect. Together, it is hoped that these various provisions will alert social work departments to the presence of sex offenders in their area.

Extended sentences

Section 86 of the Crime and Disorder Act 1998 confers a discretion on courts to pass extended sentences in respect of sex offenders where they are of the opinion that passing a determinate sentence of imprisonment would not be adequate for the purpose of protecting the public from serious harm.[3] This power only exists in respect of offences committed after the commencement of this section of the 1998 Act and is not to be applied to persons serving indeterminate sentences, in other words, life sentences. The provisions of this section are extended to children and young offenders.   **8.68**

The aggregate sentence is the original term of imprisonment, referred to as the "custodial term", and a further period for which the offender is to be subject to a licence, namely the "extended period". Its length will be determined by the court passing sentence though it should not exceed 10 years in respect of sex offenders, and five years in respect of violent

---

[1]   See, generally, Crime and Disorder Act 1998, s. 20.

[2]   See *Renton and Brown's Criminal Procedure Legislation*, Annotations to Crime and Disorder Act 1998 by Iain Bradley, para. A6.08.

[3]   1995 Act, s. 210A, as amended by Crime and Disorder Act 1998, s. 86.

offenders. In this latter instance, the extended period may be substituted for a longer period, though one which does not exceed 10 years, only by order of the Secretary of State. In respect of statutory offences, the extended period must not exceed the maximum custodial term which the Act attaches to a particular offence. The extended period begins on the day following the date on which, had there been no extension period, the prisoner would have been released on licence in respect of the custodial term. In other words, on the day after the custodial term ends.[4]

The section refers to an extensive catalogue of sexual offences in seeking to define the limits of this discretionary power. Any attempt, conspiracy or incitement to commit one of those offences is to be construed as if the offence had actually been committed by the accused. In respect of the statutory offences listed, aiding, abetting, counselling or procuring the commission of the offence will again amount to a violation for the purposes of these provisions. A violent offence is simply to be construed as one involving personal violence of some nature.

A prisoner released from an extended sentence will be released on licence which shall remain in force until the end of the extension period and which allows the individual in question to be recalled to prison.[5] It is possible for any prisoner in these circumstances to require the Secretary of State to refer his case to the Parole Board not less than one year after it last disposed of his case.[6] However, if the prisoner is serving another sentence which is not running concurrently with the extended sentence, the prisoner will be required to serve one-half of that sentence before the Parole Board becomes involved in his case.[7] The Board must be satisfied that the prisoner is no longer a serious threat to the public before he is released on licence.[8] Where a prisoner receives two extended sentences they will run concurrently.[9]

PRISONS AND SOCIAL WORK

8.69 Whilst there is considerable involvement for the social worker in the criminal justice system leading to the sentencing of offenders, supervision obviously does not end once a disposal has been made. As has been noted elsewhere in this chapter, there remains a social work role in the supervision of several sentences which entail punishment in the community. In addition to this there is a significant requirement for social work services for those on whom a custodial disposal has been imposed and for those remanded in custody awaiting trial or sentence. There is a relatively high rate in Scotland of remand for persons awaiting trial or sentencing following conviction, with roughly 20 per cent of the prison population being remand prisoners at any one time.[10]

---

[4] Prisoners and Criminal Proceedings (Scotland) Act 1993, s. 25A(5), as inserted by Crime and Disorder Act 1998, s. 87.

[5] Prisoners and Criminal Proceedings (Scotland) Act 1993, s. 26A(4), as inserted by Crime and Disorder Act 1998, s. 87.

[6] Prisoners and Criminal Proceedings (Scotland) Act 1993, s. 3A(2), as inserted by Crime and Disorder Act 1998, s. 88.

[7] Prisoners and Criminal Proceedings (Scotland) Act 1993, s. 3A(3), as inserted by Crime and Disorder Act 1998, s. 88.

[8] *ibid.*, s. 3A(4), as inserted by Crime and Disorder Act 1998, s. 88.

[9] *ibid.*, s. 26A(6), as inserted by Crime and Disorder Act 1998, s. 87.

[10] The average period of remand was 23.7 days in 1992 and there were 13,548 remands that year: see McManus *Prisons, Prisoners and the Law* (1995), p. 18. A Scottish Association for the Care and Resettlement of Offenders Working Party in 1987 recommended bail supervision officers be appointed to the principal courts in Scotland. The Grant for Bail Services (Scotland) Order 1993 provided for 100 per cent funding of bail services and in the process allowed for pre-trial bail services to be expanded nationally: see McIvor "Social Work and Criminal Justice in Scotland: Developments in Policy and Practice" (1994) 24 B.J. Social Work (1994) at p. 440.

This requirement for throughcare and aftercare is central to the criminal justice system achieving its aims of protecting the community and rehabilitating the offender. In contemporary Scotland, there has been greater emphasis on the supervision of offenders following release, particularly those who have offended against children or who are sex offenders,[11] and throughcare could be seen to be the least developed of the criminal justice social work services.[12] However, there is evidence that throughcare, as well as aftercare, is belatedly becoming increasingly important.[13]

Although principal responsibility for throughcare and aftercare falls upon the local authority, there is voluntary sector provision designed to fill gaps in mainstream provision. SACRO, Barony Housing Association and APEX are the three key voluntary sector organisations operating with offenders.

Social work provision in prison is a service level agreement between local authorities and the Scottish Prison Service. Prison social workers are provided by the local authority of the area in which the prison is located. Prison authorities need not provide social work though prison governors need to ensure reasonable assistance so that prisoners can maintain and develop relationships with family and friends and other persons and agencies outwith the prison during the period of imprisonment and in preparation for their release.[14] There is an obvious need for a close relationship between the Scottish Prison Service and social workers.[15]

The objectives of social work in prisons can be summarised as follows: **8.70**

(a) to offer prisoners access to a range and level of social work services similar to those in the community;

(b) to contribute to public safety by making available a range of individual and group work programmes to address offending behaviour; and

(c) to provide support and assistance to help prisoners resettle and re-integrate into society following release.

The key roles that social workers fulfil can likewise be stated as:

(a) assessment—of risk and dangerousness, personal and social need, and re-offending and preparing action plans;

(b) programme provision—individual and group;

(c) programme co-ordination—with other agencies;

(d) monitoring and evaluation—of social work programmes;

(e) consultancy—with prison staff and management;

(f) sentence planning; and

(g) family work—to assist re-integration.[16]

11   Moore and Whyte, *Moore and Wood's Social Work and Criminal Law in Scotland* (3rd ed., 1998), p. 278.
12   McIvor and Barry, "Community Based Throughcare", *Social Work and Criminal Justice*, (1998), Vol. 1.
13   Moore and Whyte, *op. cit.*, Chap. 11.
14   McManus *Prisons, Prisoners and the Law* (1995) at p. 47.
15   Moore and Whyte, *op. cit.*, at pp. 293ff.
16   Moore and Whyte, *Moore and Woods, Social Work and the Criminal Law in Scotland* (3rd ed., 1998) p. 294.

Offenders face a multitude of problems on release, not least the problem of finding accommodation.[17] The role of the social worker is to work with the prisoner to develop and achieve a realistic release plan, especially near the time of release. Home circumstance reports will be prepared by community-based social workers for those being considered for release. They will ordinarily be disclosed to the prisoner.[18]

8.71   There are special practical arrangements made for prisoners who commit what are known as Schedule 1 offences against children (lewd and libidinous offences or offences of personal injury). The social work unit in prison will be notified and supplied with the social enquiry report prepared for the case prior to disposal. The court may forward further information such as psychiatric and other reports. Within two days of arrival, the social work unit in the prison must advise the prisoner as to the prison arrangements, a likely timescale for release, the social work help available and generally begin the process of engagement which will allow an assessment of risk at or near the time of release. There are arrangements in place for the local authority to be informed if a prisoner is being considered for release. There are forms for the process of notification and response as well as a procedure for notification of the intention to release. In this way community-based social workers are aware of the imminent release of an offender and can prepare to provide support services and appropriate supervision if that is required.

8.72   Local authorities have a statutory duty to provide aftercare services to offenders on their release from prison.[19] The National Standards which envisage more than the simple provision of material aid for the released offender. There must be provision of advice, guidance and assistance for persons in the area of the local authority who within 12 months of their release from prison, or another form of detention, request such advice, guidance, or assistance.[20] The objectives of this voluntary care are:

(a) to provide and facilitate a range of services for prisoners and ex-prisoners and where appropriate, their families, to assist them to deal with any problems they may face, particularly following release;

(b) to assist offenders to reduce risk of their re-offending through the provision of a range of services to meet identified needs;

(c) to seek to limit and redress the damaging consequences of imprisonment including the dislocation of family and community ties, the loss of personal choice, and the resultant stigma;

(d) to help prisoners and their families to develop their ability to tackle their own problems;

(e) to help prisoners and their families, on request, to prepare for release;

(f) to assist the families of released prisoners to adjust to the changed circumstances arising from the prisoner's return, where such service is needed and requested; and

(g) to assist ex-prisoners to re-integrate successfully into the community and thus reduce the incidence of crime.

---

[17]   See Corden, Kuipers and Wilson, "Accommodation and Homelessness on Release From Prison", *British Journal of Social Work*, 1979, Vol. 9, pp. 71–86.

[18]   Moore and Whyte, *op. cit.*, pp. 300–301.

[19]   Social Work (Scotland) Act 1968, s. 27(1)(b)(ii) as amended.

[20]   *ibid.*, s. 27(1)(c).

Short-term prisoners are released after serving half of their sentence.[21] There is no statutory scheme of supervision of such released offenders though they may apply for voluntary supervision.[22]

THE REHABILITATION OF OFFENDERS

The preamble to the Rehabilitation of Offenders Act 1974 states that it is an Act to   **8.73**

"rehabilitate offenders who have not been re-convicted of any serious offences for periods of years, to penalise the unauthorised disclosure of the previous convictions, to amend the law of defamation and for the purposes connected therewith."

The principal purpose behind the legislation is to allow those who have been convicted of offences to put first convictions behind them, and in that way allow them to attempt to re-establish their lives. Central to the re-establishment of citizenship within the community is the ability to secure employment. In this respect and others, the legislation aims to circumvent any discrimination or prejudice that an offender may face in years subsequent to their convictions. The legislation is based on proposals set out in a document called *Living it Down: Problem of Old Convictions*, a report of the committee set up by Justice, the Howard League for Penal Reform, and the National Association for Care and Re-settlement of Offenders (NACRO) under the chairmanship of Lord Gardner.

The legislation allows the person who has been convicted of an offence and who has not been convicted of a subsequent offence, within a particular period of time, to treat the conviction as spent.[23] Where the offender is convicted of a second offence of a particular type the rehabilitation period may be extended and it will be considerably longer than the normal periods before the first conviction can be treated as spent. The 1974 provisions also apply to children who have committed an offence but have been dealt with by the children's hearing system in Scotland.[24] This will even be so where the disposal of the hearing was to discharge the referral.

A person who has become a rehabilitated person shall be treated by the law as a person   **8.74** who has not committed, been charged with, prosecuted for, convicted of, or sentenced for, the offence or offences which were the subject of that conviction.[25] It is thought that the rehabilitated person is not required to disclose his convictions when filling in forms, for instance, when applying for jobs. Nor need he disclose spent convictions in questions at job interviews. In *Property Guards Ltd v. Taylor and Kershaw*[26] two employees were both employed by the appellant company as security guards. On entering employment they were both required to sign a statement to the effect that neither they, nor any member of their family, had been convicted of a criminal or civil offence. When it subsequently emerged that they had in fact both been convicted of minor offences of dishonesty, they were dismissed. In both cases because of the nature of the offences and the length of time that had elapsed since conviction, the convictions were regarded as spent within the meaning of the Act. Section

---

[21] Prisoners and Criminal Proceedings (Scotland) Act 1993, s. 1(1).
[22] Social Work (Scotland) Act 1968, s. 27(1)(c), as amended by the Law Reform (Misc. Prov.) (Scotland) Act 1990, s. 64(4)(a).
[23] See Rehabilitation of Offenders Act 1974 ("1974 Act"), s. 1(1).
[24] 1974 Act, s. 3, as amended by the Children (Scotland) Act 1995, s. 105(4) and Sched. 4, para. 23(2).
[25] 1974 Act, s. 4(1).
[26] (1982) I.R.L.R. 175.

4(3)(b) also specifically provides that "a conviction which has become spent or any circumstances ancillary thereto, or any failure to disclose a spent conviction or any such, shall not be a proper ground for dismissing or excluding a person from any office, profession, occupation or employment". An employment appeal tribunal found that the industrial tribunal were right to decide that the employees had been unfairly dismissed. A rehabilitated person need not disclose spent convictions in making an agreement for hire purchase or insurance,[27] or when giving evidence in civil proceedings.[28]

8.75 It must always be borne in mind that certain occupations such as doctors, solicitors, social workers, teachers, lecturers and those working with children or older people are exempt from the provisions of the legislation and as such convictions must always be disclosed.[29] Moreover, where a person appears in criminal proceedings after the first conviction either as a witness, or as the accused, he is not at liberty to deny the existence of his convictions, or treat them as spent.[30]

It is also the case that certain offences are excluded from rehabilitation. The following sentences can never be spent: (a) a sentence of imprisonment for life, (b) a sentence of imprisonment or detention for a period exceeding 30 months, (c) a sentence of detention in excess of 30 months passed on a child by the court, and (d) a sentence of detention that has run without limit of time imposed on young offenders who have committed murder.[31] Where an accused has more than one sentence imposed in respect of a conviction and none of the sentences excludes him for rehabilitation, the applicable period for rehabilitation shall be the longer or the longest of those periods of rehabilitation applicable to the offences.[32] The rehabilitation period set down for particular offences whereby they will be considered spent must be halved if the person is under 18 at the time of conviction.[33]

8.76 Where a sentence of imprisonment, youth custody or detention for a term exceeding six months but not exceeding 30 months is imposed the **rehabilitation period** before the conviction is considered spent is 10 years. In respect of sentences of imprisonment, youth custody or detention in a young offenders institution for a term not exceeding six months the **rehabilitation period is seven years**. A fine or other sentence subject to rehabilitation (for example supervised attendance or a compensation order or admonition) has a **rehabilitation period for five years**. The rehabilitation period for a Probation Order is five years from the date of conviction. Where the person is under 18 years of age, the rehabilitation period is two and a half years from the date of conviction for a period beginning with the date of conviction and ending when the Probation Order ceases or ceased to have effect, whichever is the longer.[34] Where an offender is diverted from prosecution there is no conviction, therefore even where the person is applying for a job which is exempt from the 1974 Act, he need not disclose the diversion from prosecution. Under section 9(2) of the 1974 Act it is an offence to disclose details of previous convictions without authorisation.[35] It is not an offence where the disclosure is to: (a) a rehabilitated person, (b) a person reasonably believed to be a rehabilitated person, or (c) another person at the express request of the rehabilitated person

---

27   *Arif v. Excess Insurance Group Ltd*, 1982 S.L.T. 183.
28   1974 Act, s. 4(1); see Moore and Whyte, *op. cit.* (see p. 300, n. 16) at p. 351. However, note that it has been held that a judge could admit evidence of spent convictions if justice could not be done otherwise: see *Thomas v. Commissioner of the Police of the Metropolis* [1997] 1 All E.R. 747.
29   See Rehabilitation of Offenders 1974 Act, Exceptions (Order) 1975 (S.I. 1975 No. 1023).
30   1974 Act, s. 4(2).
31   1974 Act, s. 5(1) as amended by the Criminal Justice Act 1982, s. 78 and Scheds.
32   1974 Act, s. 6(2).
33   See 1974 Act, s. 5, as amended by the Criminal Justice Act 1991, s. 68 and Sched. 8, para. 5.
34   1974 Act, s. 5(4A)(a) and (b), inserted by the Criminal Justice and Public Order Act 1994, s. 168 (1) and Sched. 9, para. 11.
35   1974 Act, s. 9(2).

or one whom the person disclosing reasonably believed to be such a person.[36] In addition to criminal sanction, a person who maliciously discloses a spent conviction will not be able to defend an action for defamation on the basis that their statement is true.[37]

It is an offence for anyone who in the course of his official duties has or at any time has had custody of or access to any official record or the information contained therein, to knowingly or having reasonable cause to suspect that any specified information he has obtained in the course of his duties is specified information, disclose it otherwise than in the course of his duties.[38] It is also an offence to obtain specified information from official records by means of fraud, dishonesty or bribe. Both of these offences may be particularly pertinent to staff in the social care services.[39] Specified information is defined as information that a named or otherwise identifiable rehabilitated living person has committed, or has been charged with, prosecuted for, or convicted of, any offence which is the subject of a spent conviction.[40] Disclosure in the following circumstances will not constitute an offence:

(1) disclosure in accordance with statutory duty;

(2) disclosure to persons or authorities who by virtue of exceptions provided by order of the Secretary of State, have a lawful use for information about spent convictions;

(3) disclosure to persons or authorities who though not exempted may continue to have a proper use for such information; and

(4) disclosure for official purposes between officers of the same organisation.

As previously stated, persons employed in aspects of social work must disclose previous **8.77** convictions. Schedule 1 to the 1974 Act provides that any employment by a local authority or by any other body in connection with the provision of social services, being employment which is of a kind to enable the holder to have access to any of the following classes of persons in the course of his normal duties, falls within the scope of the considerations above: over the age of 65; suffering from serious illness or mental disorder of any description; addicted to alcohol or drugs; who are blind, dumb or deaf; who are substantially handicapped; who are under the age of 18; and in any employment which is concerned with the administration of, or is normally carried out wholly or partly within the precincts of, female institutions.

Nothing in the Act affects:

(a) the rights of the Queen to grant a royal pardon to quash any conviction or sentence or to commute any sentence;

(b) the enforcement by any process of proceedings of any fine or other sum adjudged to be paid by or imposed on a spent conviction;

(c) the issue of any process for the purpose of proceedings in respect of any breach of a condition or requirement applicable to a sentence imposed in respect of a spent conviction; or

(d) the operation of any enactment which disqualifies, disables, prohibits or imposes some other penalty the period of which extends beyond the rehabilitation period.[41]

---

[36] 1974 Act, s. 9(3).
[37] See McManus and Russell, *Delict* (1997), p. 305; *Herbage v. Pressdam Ltd* [1984] 2 All E.R. 769; see also 1974 Act, s. 8.
[38] 1974 Act, s. 9(2).
[39] See Moore and Whyte, *op. cit.*, (see p. 300, n. 16) p. 358.
[40] See 1974 Act, s. 9(1).
[41] 1974 Act, s. 7(1).

Moreover, where a judicial authority is satisfied in the light of any considerations which appear to be relevant that justice cannot be done in the case in hand except by admitting or requiring evidence related to the person's spent convictions, that judicial authority may admit or require evidence on those convictions.[42] This allows judges in particular proceedings (perhaps actions under the Children (Scotland) Act 1995 for parental rights and responsibilities) to look at the accused's previous record.

---

[42]   1974 Act, s. 7(3); in *Francey v. Cunningham D.C.*, 1987 S.C.L.R. 6 and *Morton v. City of Dundee Council*, 1992 S.L.T. (Sh. Ct.) 2, it was held that a licensing committee was a judicial authority.

Chapter 9

Housing, Benefits and Debt

Introduction

Housing or financial problems are commonplace, especially amongst those in social need, **9.01** regardless of whether they are home owners or tenants, employed or not. An understanding of the law relating to housing, to state benefits and to debt is essential for the social worker. Whilst all three of these areas, in particular that of state benefit, are frequently the subject of legislative change, nonetheless the current legislative framework does provide general rules and principles that are likely to remain. For the provisions relating to specific adaptations required for those who are chronically sick or disabled, reference should be made to Chapter 7.

Housing in Scotland

In Scotland housing generally falls into three categories: **9.02**

1. Owner-occupied.
2. Rented from the public sector.
3. Rented from a private landlord (which now includes housing associations).

At the end of 1996 approximately 59 per cent of housing was owner-occupied, 30 per cent was rented from public sector bodies, 4 per cent from housing associations and 7 per cent from private landlords.[1] The number of persons in owner-occupation has greatly increased over the last decade largely due to the introduction of the tenant's right to buy in the public sector, and the ending of local authorities building new rented stock of their own. Inevitably, the availability of good quality local authority housing has declined. Despite this, the local authority remains the key player in public sector housing as it is the housing authority which has the prime responsibility to perform various statutory duties, including the housing of homeless persons. The change in emphasis of the role of housing is echoed in the housing expenditure figures: "In the last 20 years, there has been a substantial shift in the way government supports rented housing, away from 'bricks and mortar' subsidies to personal subsidies through housing benefit."[2] In addition some of the other key bodies involved in housing in Scotland, of which the social worker should be aware, include:

[1] Memo. submitted by the Scottish Office to Select Committee on Scottish Affairs, June 3, 1998.
[2] 1998 Green Paper on Welfare Reform, Chap. 5.

1. Scottish Homes

9.03   Scottish Homes was established in April 1989 and replaced the Scottish Special Housing Association and the Scottish element of the Housing Corporation. Scottish Homes is directly accountable to the Secretary of State, providing the Scottish Office and government Ministers with information and advice on housing issues. For tenants, perhaps the most important function of Scottish Homes is the funding, supervision and control of registered housing associations. For 1998–99 Scottish Homes has a development programme of £194 million, of which the bulk will be expended on new socially-rented housing to be provided by housing associations.[3] In addition, it is responsible for the management of its own stock, including the sale of housing to individuals and the transfer of stock to non-profit making organisations

2. Housing associations

9.04   In Scotland the majority of housing associations are community-based, and as such have formed an important link between community involvement and private investment. Whereas in the 1980s housing associations received over 90 per cent in grants from central government towards building costs, these were reduced to 70 per cent in 1997–98.[4] The consequence of this is that tenants have to pay higher rents, which has effectively increased the demands on housing benefit payments. Since the Housing (Scotland) Act 1988 ("1988 Act") housing association tenancies are treated as private sector tenancies, which is important as it means that new tenants of housing associations will not benefit from the right to buy provisions. Therefore it is important to establish when a person became a tenant of a housing association.

3. Voluntary organisations

9.05   Within the voluntary sector perhaps the most prominent provider of housing information is Shelter. Shelter produce numerous housing titles, run events and conferences, and commission and produce housing reports. It is therefore a very useful source of information and advice in respect of the majority of housing queries that are likely to be encountered by the social work profession.

OWNERSHIP, TENANCIES AND RIGHT TO BUY

Owner-occupation

9.06   In Scotland, owner-occupied housing is generally held in feudal tenure, which means that the owner has the right to use the property subject to certain conditions specified in the title deed. Normally these conditions are for the benefit of the area, such as the restriction on height of walls or fences, or prohibiting the keeping of certain animals such as bees or ducks. Perhaps more importantly an owner's freedom of use is limited by the legal obligation that they will respect the rights of their neighbours.[5]

It is important to acknowledge that owner-occupation of housing does not remove problems such as debt or repairs both of which will be examined later in this chapter.

---

[3]   Memo. submitted by the Scottish Office (June 3, 1998) to Select Committee on Scottish Affairs, para. 20.
[4]   *Paying for Housing—October 1998*, Scottish Poverty Information Unit.
[5]   *Fleming v. Hislop* (1886) 13R. 304.

Private rented sector

In the private rented sector the rights and duties of the landlord and tenant are set out in the lease, the contractual agreement between the parties. However even in the private sector the lease will not always be a full measure of the rights of tenants. If the tenant was in occupation before January 1989, it is possible that they could have additional rights as a protected tenant under the Rent Acts. Also, they may have an assured tenancy which gives them additional protection against a landlord seeking to repossess the house. **9.07**

Regulated tenancy

Until January 2, 1989[6] it was possible in the private sector to create a protected, regulated tenancy provided the property being let was a separate dwelling with a rateable value below the prescribed maximum.[7] Regulated tenancies were introduced by the Rent Act 1965 (later incorporated by the Rent (Scotland) Act 1984) and are either "protected tenancy" where the tenant occupies under a lease, or "statutory tenancy", where the lease has been validly terminated but the tenant remains in possession since regulated tenancies can only be brought to an end by a court order.[8] In addition to the limitations on the landlord bringing the tenancy to an end a further benefit of a regulated tenancy is that the rent chargeable by the landlord is restricted, through the registration of a fair rent (as opposed to a market rent) for the property, which cannot be exceeded. Both the landlord and the tenant may have the rent reviewed by making an application to the local authority rent officer. Once the rent officer has notified the parties of his decision, either party can appeal the new rent within 28 days to a rent assessment committee. **9.08**

A regulated tenancy in existence before 1989 may still continue, but no new tenancies can be created except in special circumstances such as a new lease between the same tenant and landlord to prevent landlords circumventing the legislation.[9] Where the tenant of a regulated tenancy dies, then their spouse or the person with whom they lived as husband and wife will be entitled to succeed to the regulated tenancy.[10] If they have no spouse then any person who was a member of the tenant's family and resided with him for a period of two years immediately prior to their death will be entitled to succeed to the property, but only as an assured tenancy; they cannot get a regulated tenancy.

Assured tenancy

The assured tenancy is designed to afford tenants protection in giving them more security of tenure. However, unlike regulated tenancies, there is no provision for the setting of fair rents. Rent is left for the market to dictate, which tends to produce higher rents. To create an assured tenancy the lease must be of a house let as a separate dwelling to a person or persons for occupation as their only or principal home, provided that the house does not come within the statutory exceptions[11] which include: lets to students by educational institutions or others specified by the Secretary of State; tenancies under shared ownership agreements (where the **9.09**

---

[6]   Housing (Scotland) Act 1988 ("1988 Act"), s. 42.
[7]   Rent (Scotland) Act 1984, s. 19(1) and (2); Protected Tenancies and Part VII Contracts (Rateable Value Limits) (Scotland) Order 1985 (S.I. 1985 No. 314).
[8]   Rent (Scotland) Act 1984, s. 11 and Sched. 2, Pt II.
[9]   1988 Act, s. 42(1)(b).
[10] Rent (Scotland) Act 1984, s. 3A, and Sched. 3A, para. 2(1) and (2), as substituted by 1988 Act, s. 46.
[11] 1988 Act, s. 12, Sched. 4.

tenant purchases a percentage of the property and rents the other percentage) within the meaning of the Housing Associations Act 1985; and local authority and other public sector tenancies.

Where an assured tenancy exists the landlord is required to issue the tenant with the terms of the tenancy in writing and to provide a rent book if the rent is to be paid weekly.[12]

Where the assured tenancy is terminated by the landlord issuing a notice to quit, if the tenant remains in possession of the house, a statutory assured tenancy is created. It is not possible for the landlord to repossess the house except by applying to the court.[13] The court must grant the repossession order where any of the grounds set out in Part 1 of and Schedule 5 to the 1988 Act are satisfied, including where the landlord seeks repossession for his own occupation of the premises, or where the landlord has defaulted on his heritable security payments (mortgage), or perhaps more importantly where the tenant is at least three months in arrears with his rent payments.

The court may also order repossession on other grounds which relate to the tenant's habits such as persistent delay in rent payment, rent being due, deterioration of the premises or furniture, and the use of the premises for illegal or immoral purposes.[14]

With a statutory assured tenancy the landlord may serve on the tenant a notice proposing a new rent; if the tenant does not agree with it, it may be referred to the rent assessment committee.[15]

Short assured tenancy

9.10   This is a special type of assured tenancy which must be for at least six months in length. The tenancy is a "short" tenancy because unlike the assured tenancy, provided the landlord serves notice in the prescribed form before the tenancy commences, the landlord can end the tenancy by notice. Should the tenant not remove, the landlord will, providing he has followed the correct procedure, be automatically entitled to a court order. The other key difference is that the tenant of a short assured tenancy can apply to the rent assessment committee for a determination of the rent that "the landlord might reasonably be expected to obtain under the short assured tenancy",[16] that is the market rent. The rent assessment committee will only make such a determination if they are of the opinion that the rent paid by the tenant is significantly higher than what the landlord could reasonably expect in relation to other rents in the locality, and where there are a significant number of properties in the area also leased on assured or short assured tenancies.[17]

Tenancies in the public sector

9.11   Until the 1980s tenants in the public sector did not have any special protection and unlike private sector tenants they could not become protected tenants under the Rent Acts. The logic for the distinction between the sectors perhaps reflected the view that the public sector would inevitably treat tenants better than private landlords. However regulation and extra rights for tenants, including the right to purchase, now apply to the public sector.

---

[12]   1988 Act, s. 30.
[13]   *ibid.*, s. 16.
[14]   *ibid.*, Sched. 5, Pt 11.
[15]   *ibid.*, s. 24.
[16]   *ibid.*, s. 34(1).
[17]   *ibid.*, s. 34(4).

Secure tenancy

Secure tenancies were introduced by the Tenants' Rights Etc. (Scotland) Act 1980,[18] **9.12** providing public sector tenants not only with more security of tenure than they had had under the contractual lease, but in addition with the right to purchase their home. In July 1997 the Chartered Institute of Housing in Scotland produced a Model Secure Tenancy Agreement (MoSTA) which has been adopted by many local authorities. Similarly the Scottish Federation of Housing Associations has also produced a model tenancy for use by housing associations—Model Assured Tenancy Agreement (MATA). It is therefore important to be able to identify those tenants that are "secure tenants". Essentially there are three tests to be met:

1.   the house must be let as a separate dwelling;

2.   the tenant must occupy the house as an individual (not in the course of a business, etc.) and must occupy the house as their principal home; where there is more than one tenant, it is sufficient that at least one occupies the house as their main home;

3.   the landlord must be one of the those listed in section 61(2) of the Housing (Scotland) Act 1987 ("1987 Act"), which comprises:

   (a)   a local authority in Scotland;
   (b)   a development corporation;
   (c)   Scottish Homes; and
   (d)   a police or fire authority in Scotland.

Tenants of housing associations are not public sector tenants and cannot become secure **9.13** tenants unless they became a secure tenant in the period up to January 2, 1989.[19] Where a housing association tenant has a secure tenancy, they remain a secure tenant provided they continue to rent from the same landlord, even if they change house. This happened in *Milnbank Housing Association Ltd v. Murdoch*[20], where the housing association contended that the tenant who had moved house within their stock had lost their secure tenancy. The court decided that the tenant retained the secure tenancy and was entitled to a determination of a fair rent.

Even where a tenant appears to satisfy the three general tests, they will not have a secure tenancy if their lease is one of those specified in Schedule 2 to the 1987 Act, which comprises:

(a)   premises which the tenant occupies but which are the property of their employer to enable better performance of their employment;

(b)   premises let on a temporary basis to persons moving to the area for employment reasons;

(c)   temporary letting to a homeless person under Part II of the 1987 Act.

A secure tenancy may only be terminated in limited circumstances,[21] for example by written agreement of the tenant and landlord, or by four weeks' notice given by the tenant to

---

[18]   Now consolidated in the 1988 Act.
[19]   1988 Act, s. 43(3) (b); but see also Dailly, "Can Stock Transferees Remain Secure Tenants?" 1998 SCOLAG 104.
[20]   1995 S.L.T. (Sh. Ct.) 11.
[21]   Housing (Scotland) Act 1987 ("1987 Act"), s. 46.

the landlord, and most importantly by the landlord giving notice that he intends to recover possession on one of the 16 grounds laid down in Schedule 3 to the 1987 Act, which include, in relation to the occupation by the tenant (grounds 1–8), (a) non-payment of rent or breach of any other duty under the lease, or (b) deterioration of the house, common parts or furniture due to acts of waste or neglect by the tenant; in relation to the landlord (grounds 9–15) (a) that the house has been specially designed, adapted or is close to facilities for persons in need of special social support and there is no such person with such needs occupying the house and the landlord requires the house for a person with such special needs, or (b) that the house is overcrowded within the meaning of section 135 and as such renders the occupier guilty of an offence; and in relation to a change of tenancy on divorce or separation (ground 16), that the landlord wishes to transfer the tenancy to the tenant's spouse or person with whom the tenant resided as husband and wife, where the spouse or person has so requested, and either the tenant, their spouse or the person no longer wish to live together with the other in the same house.

Where the reason for the recovery of possession is a landlord reason (grounds 9–15) the landlord must make available suitable alternative accommodation for the tenant.[22] Suitable accommodation is defined as being a separate dwelling which is suitable for occupation by the tenant and his family taking into account factors such as proximity to places of employment, etc.[23]

9.14   The procedure for the recovery of possession must be strictly followed. The process is begun by the landlord serving a notice on the tenant in the form prescribed.[24] The purpose of the notice is to make the tenant aware that the landlord is going to start proceedings no earlier than the date specified in the notice, which date must be four weeks later than the date of the notice, but no later than six months from the date of the notice. The notice will identify which of the 16 grounds set out in Part 1 of and Schedule 3 to the 1987 Act the landlord seeks possession under.

If the landlord decides to proceed with the repossession of the property he will raise a summary cause action in the sheriff court. The court may decide to adjourn the matter before considering the order on various conditions, such as the payment of rent in instalments by the tenant, the idea being that such an adjournment may allow the tenant the opportunity to rectify his bad conduct, as the case may be. If the court does not adjourn the proceedings then it must make an order for repossession where:

(a)   repossession is sought on a tenant-conduct ground and the court is satisfied that it is reasonable to make the order;

(b)   repossession is sought on a management ground and it appears to the court that other suitable accommodation will be available to the tenant; or

(c)   repossession is sought on ground of a matrimonial breakdown and it appears to the court that it is both reasonable to make the order and that alternative suitable accommodation will be available.

Right to buy

9.15   The Tenants Rights, Etc. (Scotland) Act 1980 ("1980 Act") introduced a specific right to enable a qualifying secure tenant to purchase the dwellinghouse let to him by islands and

---

[22]   1987 Act, s. 48.
[23]   1987 Act, Sched. 3, Pt II.
[24]   Secured Tenancies (Proceedings for Possession) Order 1980, (S.I. 1980 No. 1389).

district councils as well as other bodies such as Scottish Homes. The rules are now set out in the 1987 Act.[25]

The tenant must be a public sector secure tenant and must be so at the date of the application to purchase. To be a secure tenant the dwelling must satisfy the conditions described above.[26] In addition, the tenant's landlord must be one of the specified landlords listed in section 61(2) of the 1987 Act, which list has been greatly expanded from that included in the 1980 Act by the Housing (Scotland) Act 1986. For example, prior to 1986 the tenants of islands or district councils had the right to buy; however the tenants of regional councils did not. This distinction between the councils resulted in the first case to be brought against a notice of refusal by a landlord disputing the tenant's right to purchase *Hill v. Orkney Islands Council*.[27] In this case the council sought to refuse to sell a school house on the ground that they held the house as education authority and if they had been a regional council exercising that function they would not be obliged to sell. The court however found in favour of the tenant, deciding that the tenant of an islands council did have the right to buy, regardless of the function under which the islands council held the house.

Even where the landlord is one of the specified landlords they may still be entitled to refuse to sell the house if one of the conditions in section 61(4) applies, which excepts houses such as those

"which form part of a group which has been provided with facilities (including a call system and the services of a warden) specially designed or adapted for the needs of persons of pensionable age or disabled persons".

This exception is however strictly interpreted and in the case *Houston v. East Kilbride Development Corporation*[28] the tenant was held to be entitled to buy a warden flat within a group of houses which had been equipped with special facilities, since the warden flat apart from containing receiving equipment for the call system was not itself provided with special facilities. In determining whether the house has been specially adapted, reference must be made to the facilities in the house at the date of the service of the application to purchase. In *Kennedy v. Hamilton District Council*[29] the tenant was not entitled to buy the house even although the call system and the services of a warden were not provided when the tenancy was entered into, rather being added later, albeit that the house was designed for use by a wheelchair-user.

Having established that the tenant is a secure tenant, in order to exercise the right to purchase the tenant must have so been for a period of two years prior to the date of application. In calculating the two-year period account will be taken of time where the property has been occupied as the spouse of a secure tenant or as a child/ member of a secure tenant's family,[30] thereby enabling recently widowed spouses to exercise rights attributed to their late spouse's period of occupation. **9.16**

The advantage of the right to purchase is that it is linked to a right to a discount and indeed a right to a loan from the district or islands council or Scottish Homes.[31] The amount of the discount is based on the time in occupation of the dwelling, with the maximum amount of

---

[25] For fuller discussion, see Robson and Halliday, *Residential Tenancies* (2nd ed., W. Green, 1998), Chap. 7.
[26] See para. 9.12; see also Himsworth, *Housing Law in Scotland* (4th ed., Butterworths/The Planning Exchange, 1994), pp. 101–110.
[27] 1983 S.L.T. (Lands Tr.) 2.
[28] 1995 S.L.T. 12.
[29] 1996 S.L.T. 1276.
[30] 1987 Act, s. 61(10).
[31] *ibid.*, s. 216.

discount being achieved after 30 years' occupation.[32] If the tenant were to sell the property within three years of the purchase they must repay a proportion of the discount granted.[33] When selling the property the public sector landlord is entitled to add to the offer of sale "such conditions as are reasonable."[34] In other words it is quite appropriate for the landlord to include obligations to contribute to the maintenance of common parts such as the roof, as well as including other title conditions relating to the amenity of the area such as restrictions on the number of pets, which restrictions are common in tenancy agreements. However, the landlord is specifically prohibited from adding any condition which has the effect of requiring the tenant to pay the landlord expenses[35] or which gives the landlord a right of pre-emption, that is a requirement that if the tenant decides to sell they must first offer the house for sale back to the landlord or a named third party.[36] The principle behind the legislation is to put the tenant in the position of owner in respect of the same subjects which he rented, and on the same conditions. In *City of Glasgow District Council v. Doyle*[37] the tenant was successful in challenging an offer of sale which did not include all the garden ground which he occupied under his tenancy. The council are in general not entitled to redefine boundaries on applications to purchase.

Procedure for purchase

9.17 The process for the purchase of the house is begun by the tenant serving on the landlord an application to purchase which must be in the prescribed form[38] and will include details of the tenant's period of ownership and any joint purchaser.

Once the application to purchase has been received the landlord has two months to either serve a notice of refusal or to serve on the tenant an "offer to sell". The landlord will refuse the application if the tenant is not a secure tenant, does not have sufficient length of tenancy or where the house forms part of an excluded category such as houses provided for the special needs of persons over pensionable age[39] or houses required for educational purposes.[40] The offer to sell is required to include the important details including the market value of the house, the discount calculated, and the conditions to be attached to the sale.[41]

By this stage, if the tenant wishes to proceed with the purchase they should consult either a solicitor or a licensed conveyancing practitioner. The tenant will have to pay his own legal fees for the purchase. The tenant has two months to serve a notice of acceptance on the landlord, thereby completing the contract for the purchase,[42] or alternatively the tenant may wish to dispute the terms of the offer and will have to serve a notice for the variation of conditions under section 65 of the 1987 Act or to refer the matter to the Lands Tribunal under section 71(1)(d) alleging that the offer of sale does not conform to the requirements about offer conditions discussed above.[43] Once the applications under sections 65 or 71 have been resolved the tenant will have two months to accept the offer of sale. Once the offer of sale is accepted the contract for purchase is completed.

[32]   See Himsworth, *Housing Law in Scotland* (4th ed., Butterworths/The Planning Exchange, 1994), pp. 110–114.
[33]   1987 Act, ss. 72–73.
[34]   *ibid.*, s. 64(1).
[35]   *ibid.*, s. 64(3).
[36]   *ibid.*, s. 64(4).
[37]   1993 S.L.T. 604.
[38]   1987 Act, s. 63(1); Right To Purchase (Application Form) (Scotland) Order 1993 (S.I. 1993, No. 2182).
[39]   1987 Act, s. 69.
[40]   *ibid.*, s. 70.
[41]   *ibid.*, s. 63(2).
[42]   *ibid.*, s. 66.
[43]   Requirements of s. 63; see para. 9.16.

ALLOCATIONS, HOMELESSNESS AND THE DUTY TO HOUSE

Allocation of housing

In creating housing waiting lists all relevant organisations are "providing services" and are **9.18** therefore covered by the sex and race discrimination legislation.[44] A person must not be treated less favourably in the allocation of housing by reason of their sex or race. There are also special duties in relation to the housing of chronically sick, disabled or elderly persons which are explained in Chapter 7.[45] Apart from the obligation not to discriminate on these grounds the matter of selection criteria is largely left to the local housing authority, although vetting and restricting access to housing should only be used as a last resort since local housing authorities often are the last hope of housing for some households. Housing should be allocated on an objective and non-discriminatory assessment of housing need.[46]

By virtue of section 21 of the 1987 Act, landlords in the public sector and in housing associations must publish their rules relating to the allocation of housing, comprising

(a) admission of applicants to any housing list;

(b) priority of allocation of houses;

(c) transfer of tenants from houses owned by the association or landlord; and to houses owned by other bodies; and

(d) exchange of houses.

The obligation of the authority to make the rules available effectively bars the authority from relying on a ground not specified in the rules. In *Pirie v. City of Aberdeen District Council*[47] the authority refused to admit Mr Pirie to the housing list on the ground that his wife, with whom he lived, had been evicted from her previous house for arrears of rent and unsatisfactory conduct. The summary of the rules published by the authority included a ground of unsatisfactory conduct on the part of the applicant, but did not mention unsatisfactory conduct by any other member of the applicant's family. The court decided that in the circumstances, as the ground was not one specified in the summary of rules, the council could not refuse Mr Pirie admittance to the housing list.

In the event of the authority altering the rules, the alterations must be published within six **9.19** months. As to the content of the rules, these vary at the discretion of the authority landlord, although some control on the nature of rules applied by local authorities are contained in sections 19 and 20 of the 1987 Act. Section 19(1) prevents an authority taking account of

(a) the age of the applicant provided they are over 16 years of age;

(b) the income of the applicant and his family;

(c) whether the applicant or his family own heritable or moveable property and the value thereof;

(d) any outstanding debt, such as rent, which relates to a house for which the applicant is not and was not the tenant when the debt was incurred: see *Pirie v. City of Aberdeen District Council*, above[48]; and

[44] See Discrimination Acts 1975 and 1986 and the Race Relations Act 1976.
[45] See para. 7.51.
[46] *Housing and Neighbourhood Problems*, SODD Circular 16/98, para. 5.7.
[47] 1993 S.L.T. 1155.
[48] See para. 9. 18.

(e)   whether the tenant is married or is living with someone as husband and wife.

In addition, the authority is not entitled to take into account the place of residence of the applicant where the applicant is either employed in the area or is seeking work in the area, nor where the applicant is over 60 and wishes to move into the area to be near younger relations or where the applicant has some other special social or medical need requiring them to move into the area.[49] Such applicants must not be treated less favourably than those residing within the local authority area. As well as determining matters that must not be taken into account, the authority is also required to give a priority to those with large families and those in occupation of housing that does not meet tolerable standard, overcrowded housing or in housing which provides unsatisfactory living conditions.[50]

Furthermore, local authorities are prohibited from imposing housing conditions on applicants which require the applicant to obtain a divorce or judicial separation from their spouse or that the applicant ceases to reside with or in the same house as a specified person.[51]

The obligations to house placed on local authorities do not rest with the creation of a waiting list. Local authorities have a duty to provide accommodation or assistance in obtaining accommodation to persons who are homeless or threatened with homelessness.

Homelessness

9.20   The Housing (Homeless Persons) Act 1977 (now consolidated in Part II of the 1987 Act) introduced statutory duties on housing authorities to assist those who are homeless or threatened with homelessness. In the period 1996–97 41,000 households in Scotland applied to local authorities in terms of the homelessness legislation, of which 30,900 were assessed as being homeless or potentially homeless, with 16,500 assessed as being in priority need.[52] The issue of homelessness is a target for the Government, who have stated that one of their housing objectives is to "ensure that appropriate housing is available for the roofless and the unintentionally homeless, for community care groups and for any others who are vulnerable and disadvantaged".[53] In order to promote uniformity in housing across the country, the legislation is explained further in the Code of Guidance on Homelessness. The Code should in general be followed otherwise the decision may be set aside by the court.[54] However as it is not legislation, authorities may be justified in some occasions from not strictly implementing the Code.[55] In particular, although the Code recommends that housing authorities consult with the social work department in ascertaining the vulnerability of a particular applicant (failure to do so amounting to a failure to take account of material decisions[56]) the housing authority may nonetheless take a different view than that of the social work department.[57]

The duty owed by the housing authority will depend on a number of factors:

1.   Is the person homeless or potentially homeless?

2.   Is the person in priority need?

---

[49]   1987 Act, s. 19(2).
[50]   *ibid.*, s. 20(1).
[51]   *ibid.*, s. 20(2)(b).
[52]   *Operation of the Homeless Person Legislation in Scotland 1986–87 to 1996–97*, The Scottish Office, HSG/Mar. 1, 1998.
[53]   Memo. submitted by the Scottish Office to the Select Committee on Scottish Affairs, Minutes of Evidence, para. 12.
[54]   *R. v. Wandsworth LBC, ex p. Hawthorne* [1995] 2 All E.R. 331.
[55]   *Mazzaccherini v. Argyll and Bute D.C.*, 1987 S.C.L.R. 475.
[56]   *Kelly v. Monklands D.C.*, 1986 S.L.T. 169.
[57]   *Stevenson v. Monklands D.C.*, 1987 G.W.D. 15–576; 1992 S.L.T. 690.

3.   Are they homeless intentionally?

4.   Do they have a local connection?

The chart on page 316 illustrates the full decision-making process that the housing authority must follow.

Homeless or potentially homeless

Homelessness as defined by section 24 of the 1987 Act means more than not having **9.21** accommodation within Scotland, England or Wales. Even where accommodation is available, the person may still be homeless where the accommodation is not such that the person may occupy it with any member of their family who normally resides with them,[58] where the accommodation is overcrowded[59] or where occupation of the accommodation will probably lead to violence or threats of violence which are likely to be carried out either by someone residing in the property or by someone with whom the person used to reside.[60]

A person is potentially homeless if it is likely that they will become homeless within 28 days. Moreover according to the Code, bed and breakfast or hostel accommodation should be treated as being temporary accommodation only.

Priority need

Unless an applicant is in priority need, the housing authority need only provide that person **9.22** with housing advice and assistance. Therefore the definition of priority need is fundamental to housing law. Section 25 of the 1987 Act defines those in priority need as:

(a)   a pregnant woman or a person with whom a pregnant woman resides or might reasonably be expected to reside;

(b)   a person with whom dependent children reside or might reasonably be expected to reside;

(c)   a person who is vulnerable as a result of old age, mental illness, handicap, physical disability or other special reason, or with whom such a person resides or might reasonably be expected to reside;

(d)   a person who is homeless or threatened with homelessness, as a result of an emergency such as flood, fire or any other disaster.

The Act does not define the meaning of other special reasons and therefore the categories of priority need are not closed: it will always depend on the actual circumstances of the applicant. However there are some trends. In the year 1996–97, 56 per cent of those applications deemed to be in priority need were deemed to be so due to dependent children, whilst 23 per cent were deemed to be so due to other special reasons.[61]

The categories above are further explained in the Code of Guidance which in general **9.23** encourages authorities to exercise common sense and to adopt a sympathetic approach.[62]

---

[58]   1987 Act, s. 24(2).
[59]   *ibid.*, s. 24(3)(d).
[60]   1987 Act, s. 24(3)(b) and (bb), as amended by the (Misc. Prov.) (Scotland) Act 1990, s. 65.
[61]   *Operation of the Homeless Person Legislation in Scotland 1986–87 to 1996–97*, The Scottish Office HSG/Mar. 1, 1998.
[62]   Code of Guidance on Homelessness (1997), SODD.

Decision-Making Process for Housing the Homeless

Application for Housing

Applicant Homeless

- Priority Need
  - Applicant Unintentionally Homeless
    - Where the applicant has a Local connection with the local authority
      - Secure Accomodation must be found
    - Where the applicant has a Local connection elsewhere
      - Where there is a threat of violence
        - Secure Accomodation must be found
      - Where there is no threat of violence
        - Refered to authority with whom they have a local connection
  - Applicant Intentionally Homeless
    - Temporary Secured Accomodation and Advice and Assistance is given
- Non-Priority Need
  - Local Authorities must provide advice and assistance

Applicant Potentially Homeless

- Priority Need
  - Applicant Unintentionally Homeless
    - Applicant must take reasonable measures to retain their accomodation
  - Applicant Intentionally Homeless
    - Local authority must provide advice and assistance
- Non-Priority Need
  - Local authority must provide advice and assitance

Applicant neither Homeless or Potentially Homeless

- Local Authorities have no statutory responsibility

Two categories that deserve particular comment here are those of women and children, the special provisions for those chronically sick or disabled being discussed in Chapter 7.[63] The Code recommends that women who are suffering or are in fear of domestic violence may be vulnerable even if they have no children. Again the Code recommends that in addition to providing housing support the authority should arrange for social work support if required.[64] In addition the Code has introduced a new category of vulnerability, namely that of a woman who has suffered a miscarriage or an abortion, since such a woman may be vulnerable due to the ensuing distress.[65]

As regards young persons Chapter 7 of the Code requires local authorities in discharging their duties to take into consideration the obligations imposed by the Children (Scotland) Act 1995. In particular it recommends that social work advice should be sought on all homeless applications by persons under 16 years of age because young persons of 16 or 17 years of age or younger are likely to be at risk of sexual or financial exploitation or involvement with drug or alcohol abuse. In addition to those classes specified by section 25, the Homeless Persons (Priority Need) (Scotland) Order 1997 has added a person who:

(a) has not yet attained the age of 21;

(b) at the time they ceased to be of school age or any subsequent time was

    (i) looked after by a local authority (within the meaning of section 17(6) of the Children (Scotland) Act 1995);

    (ii) in the care of a local authority by virtue of section 15 or 16 of the Social Work (Scotland) Act 1968; or

    (iii) subject to a supervision requirement; and

(c) is no longer being so looked after in such care or subject to such a requirement.

The duties of local authorities to accommodate children are further discussed in Chapter 4.[66]

A case that demonstrates the use of other special reasons is that of *Wilson v. Nithsdale District Council*.[67] In this case the applicant was an 18-year-old girl who had left her college course, been unable to return home and who had been sexually assaulted. Unrelated to the assault, a month later she suffered an ectopic pregnancy. She applied for housing but did not mention the assault or any of the consequences of it, and was refused housing. She was referred to a hostel by Women's Aid (which organisation also provided counselling to her) but she was expelled from the hostel due to suspected theft. Again she applied for housing and after inquiries was refused. Nithsdale Council voluntary service advice strongly contradicted this decision, raising the sexual assault and its effects. However, as the girl in a future interview answered "no" when asked if she thought she would be at great risk if not offered accommodation, she was again refused housing. The decision was referred to the court. In reaching the decision that the girl was vulnerable due to special reasons, Lord Prosser explained his view as to how the test for vulnerability should be carried out:

"The comparison must in my view be with some assumed average or normal or run-of-the-mill homeless person. But if there is a lesser ability to fend for oneself, against that comparison, in a housing context, so that injury or detriment would result when such an

[63] See paras 7.59–7.62.
[64] Code of Guidance on Homelessness, *supra*, Chap. 5, para. 5–13.
[65] *ibid.*, Chap. 7, para. 7.3.
[66] See para. 4.15.
[67] 1992 S.L.T. 1131.

ordinary homeless person would be able to cope without harmful effects, then in my opinion vulnerability for special reasons is established for the purposes of the Act, and nothing more special (far less, anything odd or exceptional) is required."[68]

This decision is most useful as it removes the need to establish anything odd or exceptional, and encourages an individually-based approach.

Intentionally homeless

9.24 If a person is deemed to be in priority need then the next issue to be considered is whether the homelessness was intentional. The consequences of being homeless intentionally are dramatic since for those in priority need the duty to house is reduced from securing permanent accommodation to providing temporary accommodation. In terms of section 26 of the 1987 Act

"A person becomes homeless intentionally if he deliberately does or fails to do anything in consequence of which he ceases to occupy accommodation which is available for his occupation and which it would have been reasonable for him to continue to occupy".

In determining whether the applicant has deliberately done or failed to do anything the authority must make further enquiries to determine whether the applicant has been made homeless intentionally.[69] In the case of *Speck v. Kyle and Carrick District Council*[70] the applicant had to leave his accommodation as a result of being dismissed from his employment as area manager with a leisure company, due to his misconduct. The exact misconduct was not specified by the employers. Although the applicant had received warnings relating to stock and staff level deficiencies, and although he had allowed his wife, children and indeed a girlfriend to stay without authorisation, the court held that the authority had not made sufficient investigations to determine whether the applicant had acted deliberately. The authority had to be satisfied that he had deliberately acted in the knowledge that the loss of his job and the accommodation was probable.

Moreover the accommodation has to be available for the occupation of the applicant and this means for the applicant and his family. To be "available" requires the applicant to have a legal right to occupy the accommodation. Further the authority has to consider whether it would have been reasonable for the applicant to have continued to occupy the accommodation. According to the Code of Guidance if persons have vacated their home due to anti-social behaviour towards them, particularly if amounting to violence or harassment, then they should be treated as not intentionally homeless. Moreover in placing the person the authority should take into account their need to escape the perpetrator of the violence. Equally if a person has been evicted for carrying out anti-social behaviour they should be treated as intentionally homeless.

Local connection

9.25 The local connection test originates in an attempt to prevent some local authorities, such as in the large cities, from having to house those homeless persons that have recently moved there, attracted by the city potential. A person has a local connection with a local authority

[68]   1992 S.L.J. 1131, at 1134A.
[69]   1987 Act, s. 28(2).
[70]   1994 S.L.T. 1007.

district if they normally reside there, if they have a family connection such as their parents or siblings or an adult child of theirs residing there or if they are employed there.[71] Where the applicant has left the area with which they had a local connection due to domestic violence and has applied to their new local authority for housing the Code emphasises that the applicant cannot be transferred back to the original authority if there is a risk of domestic violence. Moreover the Code advises that if the local authority is unable to confirm evidence of the violence or threat of violence the applicant's fears should be considered sufficient.[72]

Accommodation secured

Where an applicant is in priority need and is not intentionally homeless the authority must secure accommodation.[73] The accommodation should be permanent. Paragraph 10.9 of the Code of Guidance reminds authorities that if they secure short-term accommodation they will still need to secure further accommodation when the accommodation initially secured ceases to be available and the person becomes homeless as a consequence. The accommodation secured must be such that it is not overcrowded within the meaning of section 35 of the 1987 Act or be such that it may endanger the health of the occupants.[74] However provided both these tests are satisfied, there is no other general test of reasonableness to be applied.[75]

9.26

ANTI-SOCIAL NEIGHBOURS

Anti-social behaviour ranging from noise and other inconsiderate behaviour to harassment and violence may be seriously detrimental to the quality of life of neighbours. It is a cross-tenure problem, affecting both home owners and tenants. It is recommended that in selling property under the right to buy legislation, public sector landlords should incorporate conditions to combat anti-social behaviour. Tenure is important as it directly affects the remedies available: a tenant's landlord may be able to take action against another problem tenant, but cannot take action against a problem owner-occupier, although the tenant could raise an action of interdict.

9.27

In response to a Scottish Affairs Committee Report on *Housing and Anti-social Behaviour*, the Scottish Office issued guidance on dealing with anti-social behaviour to public sector landlords in 1998.[76] In addition to this guidance, new legislative measures introduced by the Protection From Harassment Act 1997 and the Crime and Disorder Act 1998, will serve to enable housing authorities to deal with anti-social behaviour in a way that will minimise evictions. One of the key recognitions of housing strategy is the need for housing departments to liaise with social work as well as the police and environmental health. The involvement of social work relates to the various social work duties in respect of social welfare, protection of children and community care—as well as those responsibilities under the criminal justice system such as the supervision of offenders or the support of victims of crime.

It is in the interests of the housing authority to resolve disputes at an early stage. Where a dispute has arisen then depending on its nature various courses of action are possible. Where

---

[71]   1987 Act, s. 27.
[72]   Code of Guidance on Homelessness, *supra*, Chap. 5, para. 5.13.
[73]   1987 Act, s. 31.
[74]   *ibid.*, s. 32(5).
[75]   *Bradley v. Motherwell D.C.*, 1994 S.L.T. 739.
[76]   *Housing and Neighbourhood Problems*, Circular 16/98.

the dispute is a low level one due to non-communication or misunderstanding, it may be resolved through community mediation.[77] If mediation does not result in agreement then provided that neither party appears at fault the housing authority may effect a management transfer, whereby one family, with their full co-operation, are moved to comparable housing in an area suitable to their needs.[78]

Where however there is an irresolvable dispute caused by one party then the housing authority should take action against that party, as opposed to persuading the victimised family to move. Where management approaches have failed, the remedies available to the local authority landlord for anti-social behaviour such as noise and disturbance include anti-social behaviour orders introduced by the Crime and Disorder Act 1998.[79] These orders are raised in the sheriff court by the local authority not the victims of the anti-social behaviour, hence the complainers need not be present. These orders may be sought against any person over the age of 16 whose conduct, on at least two occasions, has caused or was likely to cause alarm or distress to persons not of the same household.[80] The effect of these orders is to prevent the person from doing anything described in the order, thus giving the sheriff some discretion in dealing with the offender.[81]

9.28   In addition to the anti-social orders, the Crime and Disorder Act empowers the police to seize sound-producing equipment which is disturbing neighbouring households, without the need of a warrant, where the occupier has failed to stop the noise when asked to do so by the police.[82] The ultimate sanction for anti-social neighbours remains that of eviction, and the grounds for eviction due to anti-social behaviour have been extended so that the actions of the tenant, any persons residing with them and indeed visitors at the house or in its vicinity may be taken into account once a course of misconduct has been established.[83]

In the event that the anti-social behaviour complained of amounts to the harassment of another, the appropriate recourse would be to either raise the matter with the police as both intimidation and harassment are common law criminal offences or to raise an action under the Protection from Harassment Act 1997. Under this Act a person who is the victim of a course of harassment may seek damages and either interdict including interim interdict or a non-harassment order.[84] A non-harassment order will require the defender to refrain from specified conduct for a specified period, which can be an indeterminate period. Any person who breaches a non-harassment order is guilty of a criminal offence.[85] Racially aggravated harassment has now also been transformed into a criminal offence.[86]

HOUSING REPAIRS

9.29   Housing repairs and improvements are of central concern to many of those in social need. For example, according to the Scottish Housing Condition Survey[87] one in four homes in

---

[77]   See Mays and Clark, " 'It's Good To Talk': Community Mediation In Scotland", 1998 *The Police Journal* 4, and Dignan and Sorsby, *Resolving Neighbour Disputes Through Mediation In Scotland* (1999), SOCRU.

[78]   1987 Act, s. 47 and Sched. 3, para. 8; 1988 Act, s. 18 and Sched. 5, ground 9.

[79]   Crime and Disorder Act 1998 ("1998 Act"), s. 19.

[80]   *ibid.*, s. 19(1).

[81]   *ibid.*, s. 19(3).

[82]   1998 Act, s. 24, amending the Civic Government (Scotland) Act 1982, ss. 54, 60 and Sched. 2.

[83]   1998 Act, s. 23, amending 1987 Act, Sched. 3 and 1988 Act, Sched. 5.

[84]   Protection from Harassment Act 1997, s. 8(5); Mays, Middlemiss and Watson, *"Every Breath You Take … Every Move You Make—Scots Law, The Protection From Harassment Act 1997 And The Problem Of Stalking"*, 1997, J.R. 331.

[85]   Protection from Harassment Act 1997, s. 9.

[86]   1998 Act, ss. 33 and 96.

[87]   3rd survey, 1997.

Scotland suffer from dampness. The methods that are available to deal with problem housing depend on the nature of tenure, *i.e.* whether the property is rented or owner-occupied. The additional provisions for adapting and modifying premises to the special needs of the chronically sick and disabled are discussed in Chapter 7.[88]

The rented sector

In the rented sector, the issue of repair is important in two respects—establishing whether **9.30** the landlord is liable to have the repair carried out, and determining whether the tenant is entitled to carry out repairs, or improvements, on their own initiative. Dealing first with the landlord's obligations, apart from those specifically provided in the lease, there is at common law an obligation that the property will be fit for the purpose it is let for[89] and this obligation covers all major defects including condensation dampness.[90] In addition, under legislation there is implied into all lettings of a house for human habitation, where the rent is less than £300 per week and the lease not more than three years,[91] a condition that the house is at the commencement of the tenancy and will be kept by the landlord during the tenancy in all respects reasonably fit for human habitation.[92] Where the landlord has failed to maintain the house in a reasonably fit state for human habitation the tenant can resort to court action such as seeking a declarator of the landlord's duties under the tenancy agreement or the 1987 Act or seeking damages for injury caused due to the failure to repair. The court must be satisfied that due to the defect complained of the house was not in all respects reasonably fit for human habitation.[93] In assessing whether the house is reasonably fit for human habitation issues such as disrepair and sanitary defects as well as non-compliance with building regulations are relevant.[94] Furthermore where the lease is for a period of under seven years[95] the landlord has a duty to keep in repair not only the structure and exterior of the house but also the installations such as water and gas supplies, although the landlord is not responsible to maintain the fixtures, fittings and appliances which use these supplies.[96]

A further remedy is for the court to serve a nuisance order on the landlord under the Environmental Protection Act 1990—which can be served on either public or private sector landlords.[97] A nuisance order is competent for any person who is an aggrieved person[98] due to the existence of a statutory nuisance under section 79 of the 1990 Act, which includes "any premises in such a state as to be prejudicial to health or a nuisance."[99] The difficulty with this test was demonstrated in the first case on condensation dampness to be raised under this provision, *Alison Anderson v. Dundee City Council*.[1] In that case the court adopted the view that to be a nuisance the complaint must relate to something substantial and intolerable to the ordinary person; not merely to something that may cause discomfort.

---

88 See paras 7.53–7.58.
89 For fuller discussion see Robson and Halliday, *op. cit.*, Chap. 3.
90 *McArdle v. Glasgow D.C.*, 1986, S.C.L.R. 19.
91 Landlord's Repairing Obligations (Specified Rent) (Scotland) (No. 2) Order 1988 (S.I. 1988 No. 2155).
92 1987 Act, s. 113 and Sched. 10, para. 1(1) and (2), as amended by the 1988 Act, s. 72 and Sched. 8, para. 9.
93 *Haggarty v. Glasgow Corporation*, 1964 S.L.T. (Notes) 95.
94 1987 Act, Sched. 10, para. 1(4).
95 1987 Act, Sched. 10, para. 4.
96 1987 Act, Sched. 10, para. 3, as amended by the 1988 Act, s. 72 and Sched. 8, para. 9.
97 See Dailly, "Enforcing Housing Repairs in Scotland", 1998 SCOLAG 67.
98 Environmental Protection Act 1990, s. 82.
99 Environmental Protection Act 1990, s. 79(1)(a).
1 1998 SCOLAG 149.

Alternatively the tenant may pursue a non-court route such as withholding rent (provided that is not specifically excluded under the lease) or complaining to the local authority ombudsman.[2] Where the tenant withholds rent, this rent is liable to be paid once the defect has been fixed.[3]

With regard to improvements to the property made by tenants in the public sector, section 57 of the 1987 Act provides that "the tenant shall not carry out work, other than interior decoration, in relation to the house without the consent in writing of the landlord, which shall not be unreasonably withheld". Therefore tenants do have the power to carry out decoration to suit their taste without the landlord's consent. Where the work is more substantial amounting to repair or improvement, and the consent of the landlord has been given, if the tenant's work has materially added to the value of the house the tenant is entitled to compensation,[4] and more importantly is protected from being charged additional rent in consequence of the improvements which they have made.[5]

The owner-occupier sector

9.31 As housing authority the local authority has a duty to ensure that all houses in its area meet a tolerable standard. To meet a tolerable standard houses must satisfy those conditions specified in section 86 of the 1987 Act, which include the conditions that the house be structurally stable, substantially free from rising and penetrating damp, have an adequate supply of piped water, and have satisfactory facilities for the cooking of food within the house. In relation to sub-standard housing the authority has two powers: to force house improvement such as by issuing a repairs notice, and to assist improvement through the provision of housing grants.

Dealing first with the enforced improvement of properties where houses fail to meet this standard, the authority can deal with either the houses individually or, if a large number of houses in a particular area do not meet the standard, as part of a Housing Action Area.[6] The orders that may be made in respect of an individual property comprise closing and demolition orders, improvement orders and repair notices. Closing and demolition orders are used to secure the demolition of a building comprising housing all of which is below tolerable standard, whereas closing is used to prohibit human habitation of housing which forms part of a building in which not all the housing is below tolerable standard.[7] Improvement orders are used where the house fails to meet a tolerable standard and require the owner to bring the property up to tolerable standard within 180 days,[8] whereas repair notices are used where the house is in serious disrepair and require the owner to carry out the repairs specified.[9] The other power of the local authority is to provide grants for improvements and repairs. In general where the work is to provide standard amenities, such as to provide a hot and cold water supply at a fixed bath or shower, to bring the house up to tolerable standard the authority must provide a grant, otherwise the authority has a discretion as to whether to provide these amenities.[10]

---

[2]　Commissioner for Local Administration; for discussion see Chap. 2.
[3]　*City of Glasgow D.C. v. McCrone*, Jan. 3, 1985; (1991) 1 S.H.L.R. 54.
[4]　1987 Act, s. 58, as amended by the Leasehold Reform, Housing and Urban Development Act 1993, s. 146.
[5]　1987 Act, s. 59.
[6]　See Himsworth, *op. cit.*, Chap. 11.
[7]　1987 Act, ss. 114–130.
[8]　*ibid.*, s. 88.
[9]　*ibid.*, ss. 108–112.
[10]　*ibid.*, Pt XIII.

STATE BENEFITS

Introduction

The vast majority of persons in social need have welfare rights. It is essential to ensure that such persons receive the full range of social security benefits to which they are entitled, especially as, for many, social security benefits will be their only source of income. Whilst welfare rights are of great importance to social work clients, nonetheless social workers have no formal role in the social security system, and their involvement will often be limited to personal or authority-based decisions as to good practice. It is suggested that the role for the social worker is to ensure that clients apply for and receive all appropriate benefits. In welfare law the receipt of some benefits may entitle the claimant to other assistance, for example where a person is in receipt of income support or income-based jobseeker's allowance their children are entitled to free school meals. Consequently the social worker requires both a knowledge of the range of benefits available to different client groups and an appreciation of the need to encourage timely applications for all of such benefits, making use of other professions such as welfare rights officers if employed by the local authority. **9.32**

General issues

Benefits are classified in various ways and some of these distinctions are of crucial importance. Where a benefit is classed as a contributory benefit this means that entitlement to that benefit is dependent on the claimant having paid sufficient and appropriate national insurance contributions, whereas a non-contributory benefit is not so dependent. The other most important classification is that of means tested or non-means tested benefits. In order to qualify for a means tested benefit the financial circumstances (income and capital) of the claimant and their family must be such that they fall below a particular threshold figure, whilst for a non-means tested benefit the financial circumstances of the claimant are largely irrelevant. For the purpose of means tested benefits a family is defined as including both a married or unmarried couple (or a person who is not a member of such a couple) and a member of their household who is a child for which one of them is responsible or a prescribed person for which one of them is responsible.[11] In other words, the income of an unmarried couple is looked at if it appears that the couple live together as husband and wife—such an inference will be drawn from a number of factors such as the relationship of the couple regarding money, the sexual relationship of the couple and whether they have any children together.[12] **9.33**

As suggested above, the role of the social worker includes ensuring that their client lodges a claim timeously. For all benefits, including payments from the social fund, statutory time limits apply to applications and failure to claim may result in complete disentitlement or at least the loss of some benefit. A claim should be made within the prescribed time[13] which, for jobseeker's allowance, income support, new claims for family credit and disability working allowance, is the day the claim reaches the appropriate office. Therefore if a client wants to claim for an earlier period they will need to specify this and, depending on the reason for failure to claim, the time limit may be extended for up to three months, allowing the payment of the benefit to be backdated by the period of extension. Where a client is seeking child benefit or guardian's allowance, invalid care allowance, maternity allowance, or a retirement

---

[11] Social Security Contributions and Benefits Act 1992 ("1992 Act"), s. 137.
[12] *Adjudication Officers Guide*, para. 15021; *Robson v. Secretary of State for Social Services* [1982] F.L.R. 232.
[13] Social Security (Claims and Payments) Regulations 1987 (S.I. 1987 No. 1968), reg. 19.

pension, the claim should be made within three months of any day of entitlement. The three-month period is the maximum period that the benefit will be backdated, and as there is no provision for the time limit to be extended the client simply loses the benefit for any days of potential entitlement prior to three-month period.

9.34 In making a claim the client has a duty to disclose all material facts relevant to the assessment of the benefit. A material fact is one which makes a difference to how much benefit a person should be paid. If a claimant, whether fraudulently or not, misrepresents or fails to disclose a material fact which results in them being overpaid benefit, the Secretary of State may recover the overpayment.[14] It does not matter that the claimant did not intend to act dishonestly; what is important is whether the claimant either misrepresented or failed to disclose a fact which was material to the decision as to their entitlement. Whether a claimant has not done all that could reasonably be expected of them to disclose a material fact which was within their knowledge will depend on the individual circumstances of the claim.[15]

The benefit system operates at a local level with the initial decision on a claim being made by an adjudication officer working within the Benefits Agency. The majority of these decisions can be appealed to a Social Security Appeals Tribunal (SSAT) or a Disability Appeal Tribunal (DAT). From there leave may be granted to further appeal to the Social Security Commissioners, and further leave may permit appeal to the Court of Session. Finally matters may even go to the House of Lords. In applying the legislation official guidance is provided in the *Adjudication Officer's Guide* which is published by the Stationery Office. Other guidance can be obtained from the Child Poverty Action Group Publications.[16]

Benefits which provide for those on a low income or no income at all apply across the diverse range of client groups of the social worker, and hence knowledge of then is essential for all. Moreover as well as the benefit payments available the social worker needs to be aware of the social fund payments that can be obtained for low income groups in particular circumstances such as for maternity expenses or in an emergency. In addition to the general low income benefits there is range of benefits available to particular client groups, namely persons who are expecting or bringing up children; the disabled; and pensioners.

Low income benefits

Income support[17]

9.35 This is the basic benefit for those on either a low income or none at all who are not entitled to jobseeker's allowance. A person in Great Britain is entitled to income support only if they satisfy all of the following[18].

(a) they must be over the age of 16 (special rules apply to 16/17-year-olds, so in effect a claimant must be 18 years old or over);

(b) they must have no income or income does not exceed the applicable amount (the applicable amount relates to the individual or the family unit, whichever is appropriate);

---

[14] Social Security Administration Act 1992, s. 71, as amended by the Social Security (Overpayments) Act 1996.
[15] See commentary on s. 71: Mesher and Wood, *CPAG's Income Related Benefits: The Legislation* (annually updated).
[16] *e.g. National Welfare Benefits Handbook: Jobseeker's Allowance Handbook.*
[17] Leaflet IS20, *A Guide to Income Support.*
[18] 1992 Act, s. 124(1), as amended by Jobseekers Act 1995, Sched. 2, para. 30.

(c) they must not be engaged in remunerative work and, if a member of a married or unmarried couple, the other member must not be so engaged;

(d) except in such circumstances as may be prescribed, they must not be receiving relevant education; and

(e) they fall within a prescribed category of persons, which includes lone parents, persons temporarily looking after another person and persons incapable of work.[19]

The amount of benefit payable will be the result of deducting from the applicable amount of benefit the claimant's income,[20] which is calculated under regulations 17 to 22 of the Income Support (General) Regulations 1987.[21] In assessing the applicant's income the income of the applicant's family is taken into account.[22] Any person with capital exceeding £8,000 loses their entitlement to income support.[23] Moreover for every £250 (or part thereof) over £3,000 which an applicant has, they are deemed to receive a weekly income of £1, which will affect the amount of benefit payable to them.[24]

In claiming for income support it is important that the applicant claims all the premiums to which they may be entitled. The premiums to consider are[25]:

The family premium—this can be claimed if there is a dependent child in the household. If the parent was a lone parent as at April 5, 1998 the premium may be paid at a higher rate, unless the lone parent qualifies for a pensioner or disability premium.

Pensioner premiums—there are three different premiums payable depending generally on the age of the claimant and their partner, namely for persons over 60 but under 75; 75 or over but under 80; and lastly, higher pensioner premium for those over 80 or alternatively for those whom although they are 60 or over but under 80 they either satisfy the disability premium test or were in receipt of disability premium within eight weeks of their 60th birthday.

Disability premium—this is applicable to a person under 60 who is in receipt of specified benefits such as attendance allowance or is registered blind or is provided with an invalid carriage or other vehicle under section 5(2) of the National Health Service Act 1977. In the cases of severely disabled persons they may be entitled to the severe disability premium.

Disabled child premium—this is appropriate where a child of the household for which the claimant is responsible is either receiving disability living allowance (or only not receiving it by virtue of being in hospital) or is registered blind or treated as blind. If the child has capital exceeding £3,000 no premium will be awarded.

Carer premium—This is payable to a person who is in receipt of invalid care allowance or who is treated as receiving it.

Jobseeker's allowance[26]

This benefit is for unemployed jobseekers who are actively seeking work. Jobseeker's **9.36** allowance was introduced from October 7, 1996[27] to replace unemployment benefit and

---

[19] Income Support (General) Regulations 1987, Sched. 1B, para. 4ZA.
[20] 1992 Act, s. 124(4).
[21] For details on calculations consult the *CPAG National Welfare Benefits Handbook*.
[22] 1992 Act, s. 136.
[23] 1992 Act, s. 134; Income Support (General) Regulations 1987, reg. 45.
[24] Income Support (General) Regulations 1987, reg. 53, as amended by the Income-Related Benefits Schemes (Miscellaneous Amendments) Regulations 1996, (S.I. 1996, No. 462), reg. 12.
[25] Income Support (General) Regulations 1987, Sched. 2, Pts II and III.
[26] See leaflets JSAL5, *Jobseeker's Allowance—helping you back to work*; JSAL10, *Be Better off Working*.
[27] Jobseeker's Act 1995 ("1995 Act").

income support for those claimants who for benefit purposes require to be actively seeking employment. To qualify for jobseeker's allowance the claimant is required to be available for employment, to enter a jobseeker's agreement, and has to be actively seeking employment.[28] Income support remains available for those who do not require to be available for work such as lone parents, those incapable of work[29]—although a person incapable of work for up to two weeks may, subject to a limit of two such periods in any 12 months, still receive jobseeker's allowance[30]—and those over 60 years of age.

Jobseeker's allowance is composed of two elements: a contribution-based element, based on national insurance contributions, which varies depending on age and can only be claimed for a period of six months, and an income-based element, which is means tested.[31] The method of calculating the components of the benefit is detailed in section 4 of the Jobseekers Act 1995. A person may lose entitlement to jobseeker's allowance if they are voluntarily unemployed or if they fail without good cause to carry out a reasonable jobseeker's direction.[32] Those who receive income-based jobseeker's allowance can claim the same additional premiums as are available to income support claimants, namely family, pensioner, enhanced pensioner, higher pensioner, disability, severe disability, disabled child and carers premiums.

Family credit[33]

9.37 A further benefit for those on low incomes is family credit. Family credit is paid to couples or single parents with children who are in low paid work.[34] To qualify as remunerative the work must be for at least 16 hours a week, excluding holidays and time off due to illness.[35] As with income support the benefit is means tested, requiring a comparison of the family income with the applicable amount of benefit,[36] and capital over £8,000 prevents benefit.[37] When family credit is awarded it is initially for a spell of 26 weeks, after which the claimant may re-apply if in their circumstances they would still qualify—since, for example, their earnings may have risen over the applicable amount or on the other hand they may now be unemployed.[38]

From October 1999, family credit will be replaced by "Working Families Tax Credit", although claimants receiving their 26 weeks allocation of family credit will be transitionally protected. No new claims of family credit will be awarded from October 1999.

The social fund[39]

9.38 Where those on a low income or no income require to make a large expenditure they may receive a payment from the social fund. The social fund provides two different types of payments:

---

[28]   1995 Act, ss. 1(2)(a), (b), (c) and 6–11; Jobseeker's Allowance Regulations 1996 (S.I. 1996 No. 207), regs 5–22 and 31–45.
[29]   Contributions and Benefits Act 1992, Sched. 1, para. 2.
[30]   Jobseeker's Allowance Regulations 1996 (S.I. 1996 No. 207), reg. 55.
[31]   1995 Act, ss. 2 and 3.
[32]   1995 Act, s. 19; Jobseeker's Allowance Regulations 1996, regs 69 and 70 as amended by the Social Security Amendment (New Deal) Regulations 1997 (S.I. 1997 No. 2863).
[33]   See leaflets NI261, *A Guide to Family Credit*, and FC47, *Adviser Briefing*.
[34]   1992 Act, s. 128.
[35]   Family Credit (General) Regulations 1987 (S.I. 1987 No. 1973), reg. 4.
[36]   See regs 46–48 of the Family Credit (General) Regulations 1987.
[37]   1992 Act, s. 134(1).
[38]   See Bryson and Marsh, *Leaving Family Credit* (1996), DSS Research Report No. 48, HMSO.
[39]   See leaflet SB16, *A Guide To The Social Fund*.

(1) regulated social fund payment comprising those payments to which claimants are legally entitled, namely maternity and funeral expenses[40] as well as cold weather payments[41]; and

(2) discretionary social fund payments being those payments such as community care grants, budgeting loans and crisis loans,[42] which may be made at the discretion of the adjudication officer.

In respect of social fund maternity expenses payments[43] and funeral expenses the general qualifying criteria is whether the claimant is in receipt of qualifying benefits which include income support and income-based jobseeker's allowance, and whether the claimant's capital is under £500 for those under 60 or under £1,000 for those over 60.[44] The social fund cold weather payments are automatically made to those in receipt of a qualifying benefit[45] (namely income support or income-based jobseeker's allowance where the benefit includes one of the following premiums: pensioner's; disability; higher pensioner; severe disability or disabled child; or the claimant has a child under five years of age) when the average temperature at the weather station for the area in which they reside is either forecasted or actually recorded as being under 0°C for a period of seven consecutive days.[46] These social fund cold weather payments are distinct from the winter fuel allowance which was paid to all pensioners regardless of income for the first time in 1998,[47] which is an additional payment to the general social fund cold weather payments for pensioners in receipt of benefit.

The discretionary payments are far more complicated. Crisis loans and budgeting loans are repayable,[48] although there is no provision for interest to be charged[49]; however the community care grants will not be repayable.[50] As from April 1999 there will be a new scheme for applications to the discretionary social fund. Separate application forms are to be introduced for budget loans, community care grants and crisis loans; they will no longer be considered as applications to the social fund as a whole.

Budgeting loans are provided to enable claimants to meet special expenses which they cannot meet out of their weekly budget.[51] To qualify the claimant must be receiving income support or income-based jobseeker's allowance with capital of under £500 (£1,000 if over 60), although a loan will not be made in respect of certain expenses which can be met elsewhere, such as the cost of school clothing.[52]

---

[40] 1992 Act, s. 138(1)(a).
[41] *ibid.*, s. 138(2).
[42] *ibid.*, s. 138(1)(b).
[43] See section on maternity and child benefits, paras 9.41–9.42.
[44] See Social Fund Maternity and Funeral Expenses (General) Regulations 1987 (S.I. 1987 No. 481), as amended.
[45] Social Fund Cold Weather Payments (General) Regulations 1988 (S.I. 1988 No. 1724) reg. 1A, as amended by the Social Fund Cold Weather Payments (General) Amendment Regulations 1996 (S.I. 1996 No. 2544), reg. 3.
[46] Social Fund Cold Weather Payments (General) Regulations 1988, reg. 2 and Sched. 1, as amended by the Social Fund Cold Weather Payments (General) Amendment Regulations 1992, 1996 and 1997.
[47] Social Fund Winter Fuel Payments Regulations 1998 (S.I. 1998 No. 19).
[48] Social Fund Directions, direction 5, issued by the Secretary of State for Social Security under ss. 138(1)(b) and 140(2), (3) and (4) of the 1992 Act, and ss. 66(7), (8)(a) and (b) and 168(5) of the Social Security Administration Act 1992.
[49] 1992 Act, s. 139(3).
[50] Social Fund Directions, direction 6, *supra*, n. 48.
[51] Social Fund Directions, directions 8–12, *supra*, n. 48.
[52] Education (Scotland) Act 1980, s. 54(1), as amended by the Self-Governing Schools, Etc. (Scotland) Act 1989, s. 25(3) and Sched. 6, para. 1(3)(a); and see Chap. 3.

Crisis loans[53] are made to assist with an immediate short-term need of the claimant or their family which they could not meet as they have no savings and no alternative means of meeting the need. It does not cover housing costs, holidays, televisions or licences.

Community care grants[54] are designed to facilitate community care either by helping a person leave an institution or enabling them to avoid entering an institution. They can also help a family avoid exceptional pressure or stress. To qualify the claimant must be receiving either income support or income-based jobseeker's allowance and must not have capital of more than £500 (£1,000 if the claimant is over 60).

A real problem with the discretionary payment scheme is that the social fund officers will always be limited by the budget of the social fund.[55] Due to the discretionary nature of the latter category there is no right of appeal to a SSAT if a claimant is refused or otherwise dissatisfied, although the claimant is entitled to have a review of the decision by a social fund officer within 28 days of the decision.[56] If the claimant is dissatisfied with a review decision, they have the right to request a further review by a social fund inspector. Here the chances of success are generally higher than with the social fund officer review.

Housing benefit[57]

9.39 Distinct from the Benefits Agency, the local councils administer housing benefit for those who need help with their rent. Housing benefit does not cover mortgage interest payments, fuel costs and certain other service costs.[58] It is means tested and will not be available to any claimant who, together with their partner, has more than £16,000 in savings. Whilst the level of benefit will vary depending on the circumstances of the claimant, in general those in receipt of income support and income-based jobseeker's allowance may get all their eligible rent paid.

The local councils also administer council tax benefit. Again, the availability of this benefit is determined by means testing, however persons in receipt of income support or income-based jobseeker's allowance may get all their council tax liability paid. Note that the assessed benefit entitlement is deducted directly from the council tax bill rather than being paid to the claimant.

In addition to council tax benefit there is a council tax discount scheme administered by the local council which applies to certain disabled persons and their carers.

Extended payment scheme

9.40 Where a person who has been unemployed for more than six months leaves income support or income-based jobseeker's allowance due to either an increase in their own or their partner's earnings, they are likely to experience a gap in their income due to the move from benefits to earnings. This scheme is designed to bridge that gap in income by continuing housing benefit and council tax benefit for a period of four weeks.

---

[53]   Social Fund Directions, directions 14–23, *supra*, n. 48.
[54]   Social Fund Directions, directions 25–29, *supra*, n. 48.
[55]   See Vernon, *Social Work and the Law* (2nd ed., Butterworths, London, 1993).
[56]   Social Fund (Application For Review) Regulations 1988; *Murray v. Social Fund Inspector*, 1996 S.L.T. 38.
[57]   See Findlay and Ward, *CPAG's Housing Benefit And Council Tax Benefit Legislation*.
[58]   1992 Act, s. 130, as amended.

Child and maternity benefits

Maternity

Statutory maternity pay[59] is paid for a maximum of 18 weeks by an employer to qualifying **9.41** pregnant employees. Where a woman fails to qualify for statutory maternity pay because she is self-employed or because she recently changed or left her job, she may be entitled to maternity allowance. Maternity allowance is a contributory benefit and will depend on the amount of recent employment.[60] An expectant woman who is not entitled to statutory maternity pay or maternity allowance may nonetheless be entitled to incapacity benefit. This is only available for weeks when the mother is not working during the period from six weeks before the baby is due until 14 days after the baby is born.

In addition to the above payments, those in receipt of income support, income-based jobseeker's allowance, family credit or disability working allowance may be entitled to a social fund maternity expenses payment.[61] This is a one-off, non-repayable benefit which is made to help with the costs of things for a new baby. It is a means-tested benefit and will be affected by savings over £500 (or £1000 in respect of people over 60). A claim can be made for this benefit from 11 weeks before the expected week of confinement, until three months after the baby is born. The claim may be by the pregnant woman herself (regardless of age), her spouse or a member of the family of which the pregnant women forms part. It is also available for persons adopting a baby under 12 months of age and in cases of surrogacy, and the claim should be made within three months of the adoption. The amount of the payment is currently £100, as it has not been increased since 1990.

Child benefit

Child Benefit[62] is a non-contributory and non-means-tested benefit claimable by almost any **9.42** person who is responsible for the upbringing of a child under the age of 16, for a child under 19 in full-time, non-advanced education and for a child under 18 registered on a skillseeker programme. The claimant receives a payment for each qualifying child, although the amount paid for the eldest qualifying child is paid at a higher rate. Although child benefit had been paid at a higher rate for lone parents, this has been abolished for claims since April 1998.[63]

As well as child benefit, any person who is bringing up a child whose parents are dead, or in circumstances where one parent has died and either the parents were divorced or the other parent is missing or in prison, may also be entitled to guardian's allowance.[64] As with child benefit a payment is made for each child, although the payment for the eldest qualifying child is at a lower rate than that for subsequent children.

The payment of child benefit is important in respect of the home responsibilities protection scheme ("HRP") which is designed to protect the retirement pension of a person who has not paid enough national insurance contributions because of their caring responsibilities at

---

[59]   See leaflets NI17A, *A Guide to Maternity Benefits*, and PL958, *Maternity Rights*; Pt XII, 1992 Act, as amended.

[60]   1992 Act, s. 35, as amended.

[61]   Social Fund Maternity And Funeral (General) Regulations 1987, regs 5 and 6, as amended by the Social Fund Maternity And Funeral (General) Amendment Regulations 1988, 1992, 1996 and 1997, and Disability Living Allowance and Disability Working Allowance (Consequential Provisions) Regulations 1991 (S.I. 1991 No. 2742).

[62]   See leaflets CH1, *Child Benefit* and CH8, *About Child Benefit*.

[63]   Child Benefit and Social Security (Fixing and Adjustment of Rates) (Amendment) Regulations 1998 (S.I. 1998 No. 1581).

[64]   See leaflet NI14, *Guardian's Allowance*.

home. Usually HRP is paid to the person who claims child benefit, so it is important to ensure that clients claim child benefit in the name of the person staying at home to provide the care.

In addition to these benefits it is important that clients on no income, claim the appropriate family premiums, or that family credit[65] (or working families' tax credit) is claimed by those families on a low income who work on average 16 hours a week or more and bring up a child or children. Moreover, where the child being cared for has special needs the parent may also be entitled to disability living allowance or severe disablement allowance, discussed below.

Child support maintenance[66]

9.43   The Child Support Agency (CSA) which was established by the Child Support Act 1991 is responsible for child support maintenance. Child support maintenance is an amount of money that absent parents pay regularly as a contribution to the financial support of their children[67] and is discussed in detail in Chapter 3.[68] Where the other parent of the child is living elsewhere in the United Kingdom, the parent bringing up the child may apply to have child support assessed and collected by the CSA. Parents, or their partners, who claim income support; income-based jobseeker's allowance, family credit or disability working allowance, are required to apply for child support maintenance if asked to do so by the CSA.

If a claimant leaves income support or income-based jobseeker's allowance then they may be entitled to claim a child maintenance bonus[69] provided maintenance has been paid in respect of any child that they are bringing up. The bonus accumulates at a rate of £5 per week whilst benefit is being claimed and child maintenance is being paid. The maximum bonus is £1,000.

Widowed mother's allowance

9.44   This is a contributory benefit which can be claimed by widows bringing up at least one child of their late husband for whom they are entitled or treated as entitled to child benefit. It will also be paid to women expecting a child by their late husband or as a result of artificial insemination or *in vitro* fertilisation carried out before his death. Women widowed prior to April 11, 1988 may be entitled to widowed mother's allowance even if they are not entitled to child benefit but only if a child under the age of 19 resides with them. Once entitlement to this benefit ceases the woman may be entitled to a widow's pension.

Benefits for those with disabilities

9.45   In principle the benefit to which a client with a disability is entitled will depend on the extent of their disability, their age and whether the disability was caused by a particular incident such as an industrial injury. For those who require personal care or assistance with mobility the principal benefit is either disability living allowance or disability working allowance for those aged under 65 years and attendance allowance for those aged 65 years or over.

---

[65]   See para. 3.42.
[66]   See leaflet CSA2001, *For Parents who Live Apart.*
[67]   See Knights, Blackwell, Cox and Garnham, *Child Support Handbook* (6th ed, 1998, Child Poverty Action Group, London).
[68]   See para. 3.42.
[69]   See leaflet CMB20, *Child Maintenance Bonus.*

Disability living allowance[70]

Should a client require help either with personal care or with mobility due to illness or **9.46** disability then they may be entitled to disability living allowance (as with attendance allowance this may include those blind or deaf).[71] This can be claimed in respect of a child under the age of 16 but over three months, if the child requires more help or looking after than other children of the same age due to disability or illness, or for a child under 16 but over five years who has difficulty in walking or needs extra help in getting around. However this benefit is not payable to those over 65 unless their disability or illness began before their 65th birthday—those over 65 are entitled to attendance allowance discussed below. Provided the person meets the 65-year threshold and has been in need of assistance with personal care or mobility or both for at least three months and is expected to remain in need of such care for at least the next six months, then the amount of benefit payable will depend on the person's care and mobility requirements—for example the highest level of personal care entitles the claimant to a payment of £52.95 for the 1999/2000 tax year, whereas the lowest level for the same tax year entitles them to only £14.05. Where the claimant is terminally ill, that is not expected to live six months or more, special rules operate to ensure that they receive the benefit quickly and easily. Disability living allowance is not affected by savings nor is it usually affected by income. However claimants are not entitled to this allowance if they are in hospital or residential care.

Disability working allowance[72]

First introduced by the Disability Living Allowance and Disability Working Allowance Act **9.47** 1991, this benefit was designed to support those partially able to work. It is available to those who worked at least 16 hours a week in remunerative work[73] but their earning capacity has been limited due to an illness or disability.[74] However as from October 1999, disability working allowance will be replaced by disabled persons tax credit, although claimants already in receipt of a 26-week allocation of disability working allowance will be transitionally protected.

The benefit is payable to those over 16 and in receipt of a qualifying benefit such as the higher rate short-term incapacity benefit or disability living allowance or severe disablement allowance.[75] Although this is a non- contributory benefit, it is however means tested with an upper capital limit of £16,000.[76] Where a client could claim either family credit or disability working allowance, they will be generally better off on disability working allowance as they will be entitled to a disability or higher pension premium for housing benefit and council tax benefit. In addition, a disabled child's allowance has been introduced for disability working allowance. However a recipient of disability working allowance who has capital of under £8,000 is entitled to exemptions from prescription and dental and optical charges.

---

[70] See leaflet DS704, *Disability Living Allowance* and HB5, *A Guide to Non-Contributory Benefits for Disabled People.*

[71] *Mallison v. Secretary of State for Social Security* [1994] 1 W.L.R. 630 (HL); *Cockburn v. Chief Adjudication Officer; Secretary of State for Social Security v. Halliday; Secretary of State for Social Security v. Fairey* [1997] 1 W.L.R. 799.

[72] See leaflet DS703, *Disability Working Allowance*, and HB5, *A Guide to Non-Contributory Benefits for Disabled People.*

[73] Disability Working Allowance (General) Regulations 1991, reg. 6.

[74] *ibid.*, Sched. 1.

[75] 1992 Act, s. 129(2), (2A) and (2B), as amended by Social Security (Incapacity for Work) Act 1994, s. 10 and Sched. 1 and 1995 Act, Sched. 2, para. 34.

[76] Disability Working Allowance (General) Regulations 1991, reg. 31.

Attendance allowance[77]

9.48 This non-contributory benefit provides support to those aged 65 or over who need help with personal care because of their illness or disability.[78] The House of Lords have decided that being blind or deaf could amount to a need for attention in connection with bodily functions.[79] Normally the help must have been needed for at least six months, although as with disability living allowance there are special rules to ensure that those who are terminally ill, that is those not expected to live six months or more, can receive the benefit quickly and easily. This benefit can be claimed even if no one is actually providing the care required, although it cannot be claimed by a person in hospital or residential care.

Benefits for those unable to work

Statutory sick pay

9.49 Statutory sick pay is paid to employed people who are sick for four or more days in a row provided they earn at least £66 gross on average per week. It is currently paid at a rate of £59.55 per week, and payment is made in the same way as wages for a maximum of 28 weeks.

Where a person is employed but incapable of work and cannot get statutory sick pay from their employer, or is self-employed, unemployed or non-employed, they may be entitled to incapacity benefit (see below).

Incapacity benefit[80]

9.50 Incapacity benefit is contribution-based, and as such entitlement depends on whether the claimant has paid sufficient national insurance. Whereas the benefit is paid at a fixed rate for those over pension age, the benefit paid to those under pension age increases after 28 weeks and again after 52 weeks. After 52 weeks the person receives long-term incapacity benefit. If the claimant is also getting the highest level of disability living allowance they will go onto the long-term incapacity benefit after 28 weeks. In the event that incapacity benefit is not available as the claimant has not paid enough national insurance they may be entitled to severe disablement allowance (see below).

Severe disablement allowance[81]

9.51 Severe disablement allowance is available for persons between 16 and 65 who have been unable to work for at least 28 consecutive weeks due to illness or disability. Once a claimant receives this benefit they will continue to receive payment even after they reach the age of 65. However whilst a claimant will qualify automatically if they are under 20 years of age, unless they are in full time education for 21 hours a week or more, if the incapacity began after the claimant reached 20, they must be assessed as at least 80 per cent disabled for at least 28 weeks to qualify.

---

[77]   See leaflets DS702, *Attendance Allowance*, and HB5, *A Guide to Non-Contributory Benefits for Disabled People.*

[78]   1992 Act, s. 64.

[79]   *Mallison v. Secretary of State for Social Security* [1994] 1 W.L.R. 630 (HL); *Cockburn v. Secretary of State for Social Security v. Halliday; Secretary of State for Social Security v. Fairey* [1997] 1 W.L.R. 799.

[80]   See leaflet IB202, *Incapacity Benefit—Information for New Customers.*

[81]   See leaflet NI252, *Severe Disablement Allowance.*

Industrial and other injuries and diseases

Disablement benefit

Disablement benefit, formerly known as industrial injuries disablement benefit[82] is paid to those who are disabled due to either an accident at work or through the contraction of a prescribed occupational disease,[83] although it is not available to those who are self-employed. A person entitled to this benefit may also be entitled to constant attendance allowance (CAA) where their disablement is assessed as 95 per cent or more, and where the CAA is at the exceptional or intermediate rate and the claimant requires permanent attention they may also get exceptionally severe disablement allowance. In addition if the accident or the date of contraction of the disease was prior to October 1, 1990, the person may also be entitled to reduced earnings allowance if as a result they cannot return to the same job or perform work of the same standard. The amount of benefit that will be paid depends on the extent of the disability.   **9.52**

Pneumoconiosis, Byssinosis, Diffuse Mesothelioma, Diffuse Pleural Thickening and Miscellaneous Diseases Benefit Scheme

This scheme applies to those who contracted the named diseases or certain other prescribed diseases prior to July 5, 1948.

Workmen's Compensation (Supplementation) Scheme

This Scheme provides a supplement to the payments made by employers under the Workmen's Compensation Acts in respect of illness or disability resulting from an accident or disease which occurred prior to July 5, 1948.

Vaccine damage

A vaccine damage payment is made where a person has become severely disabled as a result of a specified vaccination. The payment is made as a lump sum, tax-free payment of £30,000. The scheme is administered by the Vaccine Damages Payment Unit.[84]   **9.53**

Benefits for carers

Invalid care allowance[85]

This may be claimed by those between the ages of 16 and 65 who are spending at least 35 hours a week caring for a severely disabled person who is in receipt of the middle or highest rate of disability living allowance care component, attendance allowance; and in some cases those getting constant attendance allowance under the industrial injuries or war pensions scheme, provided the carer does not earn more than £50 after deduction of allowable   **9.54**

---

82 See leaflet N16, *Industrial Injuries Disablement Benefit*.
83 Social Security (Industrial Injuries) (Prescribed Diseases) Regulations 1985.
84 Palatine House, Lancaster Road, Preston PR1 1HB.
85 See leaflet FB31, *Caring for someone?*

expenses and is not in full-time education. Note that the benefit must be claimed prior to the carer reaching 65 years of age, but can continue to be received after the carer has reached 65. Where the carer is in receipt of other benefits, these may be increased or decreased by the invalid care allowance.

Benefits for pensioners[86] and widows

9.55   Those over retirement age may be entitled not only to low income or disability benefits but also to a state pension. Currently the pension age for women is 60, whereas for men it is 65. However, it is to be made equal by virtue of the Pensions Act 1995, which will come into effect through a staged scheme running for a 10-year period from 2010. Effectively the state retirement age for women born on or after April 6, 1955 is now also 65 years of age.

Retirement pension

9.56   The basic retirement pension is paid to those who have reached pension age and have made sufficient national insurance contributions. The pension received by a woman may be based on her own or indeed solely on her late husband's contributions, although in the latter case the amount paid may be less.

Where the claimant is aged over 80 years, if they receive state retirement pension of less than the amount payable on a spouse contribution or indeed no state pension at all, they will receive an over-80 pension, provided they satisfy certain residency conditions. The over-80 pension is paid at a flat rate. A pensioner, whether in receipt of the basic retirement pension or not, may have their pension increased by virtue of either an additional pension or graduated retirement benefit. The additional pension refers to the SERPS scheme, being the earnings-related part of retirement pension. It is based on the level of class 1 national insurance contributions paid by an employee since April 1978. The graduated retirement pension is independent of basic retirement or additional pension and relates entirely to the amount of graduated contributions paid between April 1961 and April 1975.

War pensions

9.57   Where the claimant is unable to work due to injury incurred in military service[87] the claimant may be entitled to a war disablement pension.[88] Additionally a special scheme exists to providing for war widows pension.[89] Information and claims should be sought from the War Pensions Agency Distribution Unit.[90]

Widows[91]

9.58   The benefits available to a widow comprise the tax-free, lump sum benefit, widow's payment, and either the taxable weekly benefits of widowed mothers allowance or widow's pension.

---

[86]   See leaflets FB6, *Retiring?*, NP46, *A Guide to Retirement Pensions*.
[87]   Naval, Military and Air Forces, etc. (Disablement & Death) Service Pensions Order 1983; *Secretary of State for Social Security v. K.M.*, 1998 SCOLAG 256, 175–179.
[88]   See "War Pensioners Benefit Rights", 1997 W.B. 2(2) 4–5.
[89]   Grove, "Cruel Trap for War Widows", *The Times*, April 12, 1997 p. 33.
[90]   Room 403A, Norcross, Blackpool.
[91]   See leaflets D49, *What to do After a Death in Scotland* (Scottish Office leaflet); D49S, *Social Security Supplement*, and NP45, *A Guide to Widows' Benefits*.

Widow's payment is a lump sum payment of £1,000 for widows whose husbands were not entitled to a category A retirement pension when they died, or where the widow is under 60 at the date of widowhood and her late husband had paid sufficient national insurance in any one year prior to his death.

As for the weekly benefits, widowed mother's allowance is paid to widows with at least one qualifying child under 19 who lives with them.[92] Once entitlement to widowed mother's allowance ends or alternatively where the widow was aged 45 or over when their husband died, they may be entitled to widow's pension.

DEBT

Advising on debt

One of the major problems facing households within Scotland is that of debt. Debt problems are the most common matter referred to the Citizen Advice Bureaux. The reasons for debt problems are various; perhaps the multitude of apparently willing lenders, from shop purchase card companies and credit card companies to bank lenders, to name but a few, and the advertising pressures to own certain commodities, are the major factors in feeding this growing difficulty. In addition, where a person has had previous debt problems, or simply lives in an area where debt repayment is poor, they may well discover that despite the apparent availability of credit, they cannot obtain credit from the traditional sources. For those with no credit rating or those black listed, credit may only be available from family, friends or illegal money lenders, often referred to as "loan sharks". Such borrowing should be avoided.

9.59

Most debts arise out of contract, for example through purchase of goods from a shop or from a mortgage used to purchase a house. In advising a person with a debt problem, it is necessary to review the following:

1.   What type of debt contract has the debtor entered?

2.   Was the person legally able to make the purported contract of debt?

3.   How much is the debt for?

4.   What is the date and terms of repayment?

5.   What can be done when a debtor begins to have difficulties in meeting payments?

6.   What are the penalties for non-payment?

Nature of the debt

Basically lending can be divided into two forms. First there is lender credit, where the debtor receives a loan to make a purchase, for example using an overdraft facility on a current account or obtaining a personal loan from a bank. Alternatively, the credit may take the form of vendor credit, that is where the seller provides a credit facility, for example hire purchase. Hire purchase is a mechanism whereby the instalments paid by the debtor are rental payments for an agreed period of hire. At the end of the period of hire the debtor will have an option to purchase the goods from the creditor. Similar to hire purchase is conditional

9.60

---

[92]   See para. 9.44.

sale: the debtor is to make certain instalments payments, and once the last instalment has been paid, the debtor will become the owner of the goods. The important difference between the two types of credit, lender credit and vendor credit, is that in vendor credit, the debtor does not own the goods on receipt of them: the seller owns the property until all payments due are made; whereas in lender credit, the debtor owns the goods once purchased. Whether the debtor is the owner or the hirer of goods is very important, especially when looking at the recovery of debt.

Capacity to enter a contract of debt

9.61 Whilst the majority of issues are determined from the contract itself, the question as to the ability of the parties to enter into the transaction requires consideration in respect of the following special cases:

Children

9.62 The contractual capacity for children to incur a debt is governed by the Age of Legal Capacity (Scotland) Act 1991.[93] The general position is that persons under the age of 16 cannot enter into any transaction[94] except in the limited circumstances provided for in section 2 of the 1991 Act, which include those contracts which are usual for persons of that age. As incurring a debt would not appear to be usual for a person under 16, in general, any such contracts are likely to be void, making it impossible to sue the child for the unpaid debt. Between the ages of 16 and 18 the young person has full contractual capacity and can be sued for a debt arising out of a transaction,[95] unless the transaction was a prejudicial transaction. A prejudicial transaction may be set aside by the court before the young person's 21st birthday, and is defined as being a transaction which a reasonable and prudent person would not have made if they had been in the circumstances of the young person. However a transaction will not be deemed a prejudicial transaction, where the young person was acting in the course of their trade, business or profession, where the young person has misrepresented their age, or where the young person has, after attaining 18 years of age, ratified the transaction.[96] Section 4 of the 1991 Act provides a mechanism for any person seeking to contract with a person over 16 but under 18 years of age to apply to the court to have any purported transaction ratified.

Mentally incapax

9.63 Once a person has become insane they have no contractual capacity,[97] and any alleged contracts by them are null and void, hence an action of debt will not be enforced. Whether a person is insane and lacks the capacity to understand the contract is a question of fact, the court needing to establish that the party is not able to consent rather than merely being more easy to be persuaded, for example due to intoxication.[98] A curator *bonis* is often appointed to an insane person and the curator has the capacity to contract on behalf of the insane person.

---

[93] As amended by the Children (Scotland) Act 1995; see para. 3.36.
[94] Age of Legal Capacity (Scotland) Act 1991, s. 1(1)(a).
[95] *ibid.*, s. 1(1)(b).
[96] *ibid.*, s. 3(3).
[97] Stair, *Institutes*, I, x, 3., See paras 6.39–6.42.
[98] *Taylor v. Provan* (1864) 2M. 1226.

DEBT   337

However, disputes can still arise especially in relation to purported transactions prior to appointment. In the case *John Loudon & Co. v. Elder's Curator Bonis*[99] a wholesale merchant, Elder, ordered goods from Loudon & Co. However before any of the goods were delivered Elder was certified insane, and therefore Loudon & Co. were advised that the contracts had to be cancelled. Loudon & Co. sued Elder's curator *bonis* for damages but were unsuccessful as Elder was proved to have been insane at the time when the orders were made, and in consequence there could be no liability for breach of contract.

However there is an important exception to this: in terms of section 3 of the Sale of Goods Act 1979, where necessities are sold to a person of unsound mind they must pay a reasonable price for them. Necessities means goods suitable to the condition in life of the person and their actual requirements at the time of sale and delivery. The English case of *Nash v. Inman*[1] is a good example of the limitations of the definition of necessities. In this case a Savile Row tailor brought an action for £145 10s. 3d., the price of clothing including 11 fancy waistcoats which he had sold to an undergraduate at Cambridge University. The court decided against the tailor, requiring him to prove that the goods were suitable to the student's condition in life, and that the student was not sufficiently supplied with goods of that class at that time.

Amount of debt[2]

In general, creditors are free to lend whatever amount of money they wish, although normally for larger debts, such as mortgage debts, the creditor will require these to be secured over the debtor's heritable property or other assets. Whilst a contract for a loan need not be in writing to be effective special provisions apply to consumer transactions for the provision of credit or hire for sums less than £15,000. Such agreements are regulated by the Consumer Credit Act 1974 ("1974 Act") unless they come within section 74 of the Act, which excludes the provision of credit in certain transactions including transactions of under £50 and current account overdrafts. All credit cards, shops' own credit cards and hire purchase agreements are covered by these provisions. The significance of the 1974 Act is that all consumer credit agreements have to follow specified procedures using statutory forms and crucially the debtor must be allowed a cooling off period where he is entitled to decide not to enter into the agreement. In addition any advertising of these credit facilities must include the APR, annual percentage charge for the credit, as well as most other charges, and should alert the borrower to the risks of non-payment.

However, unless the transaction comes under the 1974 Act or either the Bankruptcy (Scotland) Act 1985, s. 61 (extortionate credit transaction), or the Insolvency Act 1986, s. 244, the parties may contract on whatever payment terms they wish. Whilst lenders such as banks have their own self regulatory codes,[3] with the right to take a complaint to an ombudsman, many other lenders do not.

9.64

Date and terms of repayment

The agreement will specify the date or dates when payment is to be made, the rate of interest to be paid and normally the additional interest applicable in the event of a delay in payment. Indeed even if there is no provision for additional interest on delay in payment, should the

9.65

---

[99]   1923 S.L.T. 266(OH).
[1]   [1908] 2K.B. 1(CA).
[2]   See Cowan and Ervine, *Consumer Law in Scotland* (W. Green/Sweet & Maxwell, 1995), Chap. 9, "Buying on Credit".
[3]   Produced by the British Banking Association.

creditor be forced to bring the debtor to court to enforce the overdue payment, the creditor will probably seek judicial interest.[4] Not only is it common for the agreement to require additional interest for delays in payment, it is also possible for the agreement to require an early redemption payment in the event that the debtor seeks to pay off the debt early.

Another important issue for a debtor is whether the debt is to be secured on some of their property.[5] Pawnbroking is one such method whereby an item of the debtor's is held by the broker until the debtor has repaid the debt and interest. Failure of the debtor to redeem the property entitles the pawnbroker to sell the item. Any profit over the debt and interest should be returned to the debtor. Another method of attaching property to debts is the granting by the debtor of a standard security over their heritable property, usually the debtor's home, in favour of the creditor. It is now very common for banks and building societies to require the standard security to be for "all sums due" by the debtor, thereby securing not only the lending for the purchase of the house but in addition any other lending made by them to the debtor. Such a clause therefore has serious implications for the self-employed if their business accounts are with the same lender as their mortgage. The standard security ensures that in the event of default by the debtor in making payment, the creditor may serve a notice of default on the debtor, and unless this achieves compliance, the creditor will then move to serving a calling-up notice. Thereafter the creditor would be able to raise a summary cause action in the sheriff court and may seek a number of remedies including the taking of possession of the debtor's home or obtaining the power to sell the property to recover the outstanding debt. If the power of sale is granted, any surplus on sale is to be repaid to the debtor. Lastly, security for debt can be obtained over property of the debtor's such as life assurance policies through the process of assignation. Effectively the debtor transfers the right to the policy to the lender in security for a specified debt. On repayment of the debt the creditor will transfer, retrocess, the right to the policy back to the debtor.

Difficulties in meeting payments

9.66   As soon as a debtor experiences problems in paying all the instalments due by them to their creditors on time, they should seek debt counselling from a registered source.[6] Solicitors and Citizen Advice Bureaux provide debt counselling services and have group licences from the Director General of Fair Trading to perform such work. Effectively, the debt counsellor will attempt to renegotiate with the creditors the debtor's various borrowing agreements in order to reduce the amount of instalment payments, usually by spreading the borrowing over a longer term. The process of replacing one debt arrangement with a new debt arrangement is referred to as novation.[7]

Penalties for non-payment

9.67   Where a debtor has failed to make payment, the contract may, as discussed above, provide for additional interest to be paid. Even then, however, if the debt is not paid within a reasonable time the creditor may be compelled to consider what other options are available to them to obtain repayment. Depending on the circumstances the creditor may be able to force payment through the non-court remedies of retention or lien, or may opt to raise court

4   Wilson, *The Scottish Law of Debt* (2nd ed., W. Green/Sweet & Maxwell, 1991), para. 11.7.
5   Grier, *Debt* (W. Green/Sweet & Maxwell, 1998), Chap. 7.
6   Consumer Credit Act 1974, s. 147.
7   Wilson, *op cit.*, para. 14.1.

action against the debtor. Alternatively, if the creditor has secured the loan on the debtor's property, such as by taking a standard security in respect of heritable property, the creditor would be entitled to recover their debt through the property secured by seeking repossession and sale of the heritage.

Non-court remedies

Retention is appropriate where the debtor has failed to pay a debt, whereas lien is appropriate if the debtor has refused to deliver a particular thing. The retention of money is allowable where both parties have liquid debts owed to the other.[8] The retention of goods belonging to the other is more properly referred to as a right of lien.[9] In some special areas the law also recognises a general right of lien. A general right of lien means a right to withhold a possession under a contract in security for debts that arise from any previous contracts of the same general character between the parties, within the same scope of business. It will normally only arise by either the custom of a trade or profession, such as solicitors, stockbrokers and bankers, or if it is expressly contracted for. Moreover, the right is a right to withhold only and does not entitle the holder to use or sell the goods, although where retention is not compelling the party to pay the holder could apply to the court for the power to sell.

9.68

Court remedies

In the event of continued non-payment, the creditor may elect to raise court action against the debtor, normally in the sheriff court but occasionally in the Court of Session. The creditor will raise an action for payment, seeking payment of the outstanding debt, interest and the expenses of the court action. The appropriate court and procedure will depend on the amount of the principal debt outstanding (that is excluding interest and expenses):

9.69

• below £750	small claims action	sheriff court
• £750–£1500	summary cause	sheriff court
• over £1500	ordinary cause	sheriff court or Court of Session

If a debtor is to be brought to court, they will receive a summons. The majority of debt actions are not defended, and decree in favour of the creditor is normally passed. However, it is important for the debtor to seek advice at this stage, by contacting either a solicitor or an appropriate welfare rights organisation, such as SHELTER in relation to housing matters, since there are options available to them even if they admit the debt. Exactly how the case proceeds depends on the procedure being used. Essentially there are similarities in the three types of court procedure, the major differences relating to the formality of the proceedings. In a court action the successful party will likely be awarded their legal expenses against the unsuccessful party, so if the creditor were to be successful, the debtor would be liable for the creditor's court expenses in addition to the debt.

---

[8]   Wilson, *The Scottish Law of Debt*, (2nd ed., W. Green/Sweet & Maxwell, 1991), para. 13.9.
[9]   *ibid.*, paras 7.7–7.11.

Small claims[10]

9.70   The small claims action for payment is commenced by a summons, by the creditor completing a form in the style of form 1 of the Appendix to the Small Claims Rules.[11] The completed summons is prepared together with a service copy summons, and is thereafter signed by the sheriff clerk and served on the debtor. Service is usually by first class recorded delivery post. The debtor/defender will be given 21 days' notice (or 42 days where they are resident outside Europe) to return the response form to the sheriff clerk. In response the debtor may:

(i)   Admit the claim and make payment. The claim will then end.

(ii)   Admit the claim and apply for a time to pay direction. Time to pay directions were introduced by the Debtors (Scotland) Act 1987 to enable the payment of the debt either by specified instalments or as a lump sum at the end of a specified period. Provided the proposals are acceptable to the creditor, decree will be granted in favour of the creditor with payment being ordered in accordance with the agreed instalments/lump sum payments. However if the proposals are not acceptable to the creditor then a preliminary hearing will take place.[12]

(iii) Admit the claim and intimate an intention to appear to make an oral application for a time to pay direction. Should the debtor fail to attend the preliminary hearing, decree will pass against them.

(iv)   Not admit the claim and indicate that they will defend the action. The debtor is then obliged to attend the preliminary hearing, and make representations to the court.

(v)   Make no response. Provided the claim has been properly set out decree will be granted against the debtor.

As mentioned above, where the matter has progressed to a preliminary hearing, the hearing will be heard seven days after the return date.[13] In the event of neither the debtor nor the creditor attending court or being represented, the sheriff shall dismiss the small claim, unless there is sufficient reason for him to do otherwise.[14] For instance, where the creditor has set out a sufficient claim yet the debtor has not lodged defences, the sheriff may grant decree in favour of the creditor.[15] If the debtor attends or is represented but the creditor does not, then provided no defence has been lodged the debtor will be absolved. However if a defence has been lodged the sheriff shall set a special hearing to take place not earlier than 14 days from the preliminary hearing date. A further failure by the creditor to appear at that date would lead to a decree of absolvitor being granted in favour of the debtor. It is odd that a defender who has lodged defences has to progress through an extra stage of procedure; nonetheless that is what the rules clearly state.[16]

9.71   The preliminary hearing can be conducted in any manner that the sheriff feels is best suited to identifying the issues at hand. In some courts the sheriff and occasionally the solicitors are encouraged to wear everyday dress to make the proceedings less daunting for the lay persons

---

[10]   Ervine, *Small Claims Handbook* (W. Green/Sweet & Maxwell, 1991), Chap. 4.
[11]   Act of Sederunt (Small Claims Rules) 1988 ("1988 Rules").
[12]   1988 Rules, r. 12(5).
[13]   *ibid.*, r. 12(4).
[14]   *ibid.*, r. 23(5).
[15]   *ibid.*, r. 13(1) and (2).
[16]   Ervine, *op. cit.*, pp. 37–38.

representing themselves. Provided the matters are sufficiently clear, the sheriff may be able to decide the case without requiring a further hearing.[17]

If a further hearing is required this is referred to as either a full hearing or proof. Both parties are required to attend the hearing or to be represented. The debtor will have the opportunity to make their defences and to make either a written or an oral application for a time to pay direction.[18] Again the sheriff has a discretion as to procedure and the the strict procedural rules of evidence are not applied. Either party may give evidence on their own behalf and may lead other evidence. However, should the debtor wish to lead a witness it is their responsibility to ensure that the witness attends the hearing, and to pay the witness's expenses. Once the parties have been heard the sheriff shall if practicable give both his decision and his reasons for it. If he cannot issue a decision at that time, he must do so within 28 days.[19] After 14 days since the making of the decision, an extract decree shall be issued. The extract decree is the final decree, and it is this that the creditor requires in order to commence enforcement action, referred to as diligence, against the debtor.[20]

The decision by the sheriff may include an award of expenses in favour of the successful party, the unsuccessful party having therefore to bear not only their own expenses but also those of the successful party. However, as small claims are designed to be accessible to the lay person, with legal aid not being available, expenses will not be awarded in an action for a claim of less than £200. For claims over £200, the amount of expenses is limited to £75.[21]

Summary Cause[22]

As with small claims actions the summary cause action is begun by the creditor preparing a summons which normally involves completing the relevant form[23] and attaching to it a statement of claim—the details of the creditor's case. In summary cause actions there are two key dates: the return date and the calling date. The creditor is obliged to ensure that the summons and certificate of citation are returned to the court by the return date, otherwise the cause, the court action, may be dismissed. The call date is the date that the action will begin in court, referred to as the first calling. Unlike small claims, in response to a summary cause summons unless the defender has made an offer to the creditor which is acceptable the debtor/defender will need to appear in court either to seek a time to pay direction or to defend the cause.[24] If the debtor has made an acceptable offer the appropriate procedure is for the creditor to enter a minute in the book of summary cause intimating that they do not object, which will then allow the court simply to grant decree accordingly.[25]

To ensure speed in the summary cause process, the issues in dispute will be decided at the first calling unless a continuation has been granted.[26] At the first hearing, the sheriff shall either grant decree against the defender,[27] dismiss the cause,[28] or fix a proof.[29]

9.72

---

[17] 1988 Rules, r. 13(b).
[18] *ibid.*, r. 24.
[19] *ibid.*, r. 25.
[20] See para. 9.74.
[21] Small Claims (Scotland) Order 1988 (S.I. 1988 No. 1999).
[22] See Mays, *Summary Cause Procedure in the Sheriff Court* (Butterworths, 1995), Chap. 2.
[23] form Aa is the relevant form for the payment of money: Act of Sederunt (Summary Cause Rules) 1976 (S.I. 1976 No. 476) ("1976 Rules"), r. 50(2).
[24] *ibid.*, r. 53(3).
[25] *ibid.*, r. 54.
[26] *ibid.*, r. 18(3).
[27] *ibid.*, r. 18(6).
[28] *ibid.*, r. 18(4).
[29] *ibid.*, r. 18(7).

At the proof[30] both parties are entitled to present their own evidence and to lead witnesses. However, as with small claims actions, the party calling a witness is personally liable to ensure attendance of the witness and to pay their travelling expenses. The proof in summary cause actions is more formal, the parties must lead evidence of any facts crucial to their case, and the normal rules of evidence apply.[31]

The sheriff normally will give his or her decision together with reasons at the end of the hearing, although they may reserve judgment, in which instance their decision is to be given within 28 days. Once the decision has been given the issue of expenses will be assessed,[32] and it is only after this assessment has been carried out by the sheriff clerk that the decree becomes final, enabling the creditor to take further enforcement action, diligence.[33]

Ordinary Cause

9.73 The rules for ordinary cause actions vary depending on whether the matter is raised in the Court of Session or in the sheriff court, although there exists a degree of similarity. The marked distinction between ordinary cause and either small claims or summary cause is that ordinary cause actions depend heavily on the written pleadings of the parties. Rather than the proceedings being initiated by a summons on a prescribed pre-printed form, the cause is commenced by an initial writ (sometimes referred to as a petition or summons), prepared by the creditor's legal agents. The formalities of ordinary cause action are such that legal representation should be sought by the debtor on receipt of the initial writ, since if the debtor wishes to defend the action they will need to lodge in court a notice of intention to defend, and enter an appearance. As with the other procedures failure of the debtor to take action will lead to a decree in absence being pronounced against him. After a period of the parties adjusting their written pleadings, the cause will move to an options hearing which decides whether a debate, where the parties are arguing on the legal issues of the case only, is to be held, or to a proof, where evidence may be lead. As with the other procedures, it is necessary for the creditor to take further action to enforce the court decree in their favour.[34]

RECOVERING DEBTS

Diligence

9.74 The legal procedure by which a creditor enforces a court decree in their favour and recovers the outstanding debt is referred to as diligence in execution of an action. It is also possible for a creditor to seek diligence on the dependence of an action where, having raised a court action against the debtor, the creditor wishes to protect against the debtor absconding, becoming insolvent or otherwise disposing of assets. However the forms of diligence on dependence of an action are limited to arrestment and inhibition. In addition to diligence which is instigated by the creditor, a debtor may, after decree has passed against him and the creditor has begun diligence, apply to the court for a time to pay order,[35] which is similar to a time to pay direction.

---

[30] See Mays, *Summary Cause Procedure in the Sheriff Court* (Butterworths, 1995), Chap. 2.
[31] See paras 2.27–2.37.
[32] 1976 Rules, r. 88.
[33] See section on diligence, paras 9.74–9.79.
[34] See section on diligence, paras 9.74–9.79.
[35] Debtors (Scotland) Act 1987, s. 5–11.

The use of diligence against the person of the debtor, namely civil imprisonment, is generally rare, being limited by statute to the non-payment of fines for contempt of court[36] or for the refusal to payment aliment (maintenance of spouse and children) when in a position to do so.[37] Diligence against the property of the debtor is the most common, and it may usefully be sub-divided into diligence against their heritable property (house, land, buildings) and their moveable property.

Diligence against moveable property

Arrestment

The main form of diligence against the debtor's moveable property is arrestment. Arrest-   **9.75**
ment means the attaching of the debtor's moveable property which is in the custody of, *i.e.* held by, a third party, in order to prevent the third party dealing with the property to the prejudice of the creditor. A schedule of arrestment is prepared which is served on the third party and thereafter, if the third party subsequently deals with the property, for example by returning it to the debtor, the third party will be liable to the creditor for any resulting loss to the creditor[38] and indeed is guilty of contempt of court. However not all items may be arrested; some items such as those necessary for the well-being of the debtor or their family are protected by section 16 of the Debtors (Scotland) Act 1987 and further, items jointly owned by the debtor and another are also excluded.

Similar in nature to arrestment is the arrestment of earnings introduced under the Debtors (Scotland) Act 1987. This Act created two types of arrestments: earnings arrestments[39] which relate to ordinary debts and court fines; and current maintenance arrestments[40] used for enforcing the payment of aliment or periodic allowance on divorce. This entitles the creditor to a direct payment of a statutory prescribed proportion of the debtor's earnings.[41] A debtor may be subject to a maximum of one earnings arrestment and one current maintenance arrestment only, therefore there is a mechanism for the creation of a conjoined arrestment order[42] where more than one creditor is entitled to proceed against the debtor. In such circumstances the payment from the debtor's wages is made to the sheriff clerk for distribution amongst the creditors.

Poinding

The other major diligence against the moveable property of the debtor is poinding. Personal   **9.76**
poinding is what is more colloquially referred to as a warrant sale. It is used to secure the debtor's moveable property which is in his own possession. The procedure is commenced by a formal request known as a charge for payment. A schedule of charge is delivered to the debtor's home or business address either by post or in person by an officer of the court (sheriff officer or messenger-at-arms). This requires the debtor to make payment within the specified period, the "induciae", namely 14 days for those residing within the United Kingdom, and 28 days for those outside the United Kingdom. If payment is not made within the induciae, poinding may be executed.

---

[36]   Debtors (Scotland) Act 1880, s. 4.
[37]   Civil Imprisonment (Scotland) Act 1882, s. 4.
[38]   *McSkimming v. Royal Bank of Scotland* 1996 S.C.L.R. 547.
[39]   Debtors (Scotland) Act 1987, ss. 47–50.
[40]   *ibid.*, ss. 51–56.
[41]   *ibid.*, Sched. 2.
[42]   *ibid.*, ss. 60–66.

A sheriff officer and a witness will attend the debtor's home or work premises, demand payment and if no payment is made, they will poind articles to the value of the debt by drawing up a schedule of articles and their value.[43] At this stage the poinded articles remain in the possession of the debtor, although the debtor may not interfere with those articles otherwise they will be in contempt of court. The debtor may within the next 14 days recover any of the articles poinded by paying over to the creditor the value specified for that article.

However not all items are poindable and the debtor should, within 14 days of the poinding, apply to the sheriff if any of the articles on the schedule of poinding should be exempt, for example because the article belongs to a third party, although the sheriff will require proof of ownership. The major exemption is found in section 16 of the Debtors (Scotland) Act 1987. This exempts essential items of furniture, clothing, tools of trade, toys and educational equipment reasonably required by the debtor and members of his family. For many debtors there may be little that can actually be poinded, since what is not protected is likely to be on hire purchase or rented.

Once the poinding has occurred, the sheriff officer reports the effect of poinding to the sheriff[44] and the next stage is for the creditor to move for a warrant of sale.[45] However the sheriff may on an application by the debtor prior to the application for warrant sale, recall the poinding if:

(a) it would be unduly harsh in the circumstances;

(b) the aggregate of values on the poinded articles is substantially below that which they would fetch on the open market; and

(c) the likely aggregate proceeds of sale would not exceed the expenses likely to be incurred in the application for warrant sale.[46]

Clearly the purpose of this section would be to offer protection to debtors against a warrant sale where such a sale, after expenses, would not reduce the overall debt to the creditor. However, sheriffs are not always sympathetic towards debtors.[47]

Where a warrant of sale has been granted, then provided the poinded goods have a value over £1,000 an auctioneer must carry out the sale, otherwise the sale will be carried out by the sheriff officer.[48] If there is a surplus after the sale it will be paid over to the debtor. If however the total sum recovered from the sale does not amount to the full debt, the creditor can uplift any articles unsold within a specified time for the value specified in the poinding schedule.[49]

Diligence against heritable property

9.77 Where a debtor owns heritable property there are two types of diligence available.

---

[43] Debtors (Scotland) Act 1987, s. 20.
[44] *ibid.*, s. 22.
[45] *ibid.*, s. 30.
[46] *ibid.*, s. 24(3).
[47] Findlay and Walker, *"Creditors Squeeze Blood From Debtors At Glasgow Sheriff Court"*, 1998 SCOLAG 84.
[48] Debtors (Scotland) Act 1987, s. 31.
[49] *ibid.*, s. 38.

Inhibition

The main diligence against an owner of heritable property is inhibition. Inhibition is a **9.78** personal prohibition which has the effect of preventing the debtor from dealing with any of the property owned by him at the date the inhibition takes effect. Inhibition proceedings are commenced by letters of inhibition or a summons being served on the debtor and a notice is then registered in the Register of Inhibitions and Adjudication. At that point the debtor cannot deal with his property: he may not sell, nor grant standard securities, in relation to new loans. Once the debtor has made payment to the creditor, the creditor shall record, at the debtor's expense, a discharge of the inhibition in the Register of Inhibitions and Adjudication. Otherwise, if not discharged an inhibition prescribes five years after registration.

Adjudication

The diligence of adjudication is used to attach the debtor's heritable property in payment or **9.79** security of debt, although this is rarely done. The process is commenced by a summons of adjudication and thereafter a notice of adjudication is registered in the Register of Inhibitions and Adjudications. Once the creditor obtains decree in the court action, and registers this in either the Land Register or Register of Sasines the property is transferred to the creditor, although it may be redeemed if the debtor makes payment within 10 years.

BANKRUPTCY

Whilst creditors may use diligence to recover their outstanding debts, no diligence may be **9.80** begun after a debtor has been adjudged bankrupt, that is sequestrated. Indeed no arrestment, poinding or inhibition carried out within 60 days prior to the date of sequestration will allow that creditor to gain a preference over other creditors, regardless of whether they were aware of the sequestration proceedings. The effect of sequestration is to pass control of the debtor's estate at the date of sequestration to a trustee in sequestration, normally either a solicitor or accountant specialising in insolvency. The duty of the trustee in sequestration is to safeguard the estate of the debtor for the benefit of the creditors, and the trustee is obliged to annually account to the Accountant in Bankruptcy, a civil service official.

Sequestration proceedings are commenced by a petition to the court from a creditor, an executor of a deceased debtor, a trustee under a trust deed[50] or the debtor himself. After the first order has been made appointing the interim trustee in sequestration, the sheriff clerk will advise the Registers of Inhibitions and Adjudications of the sequestration,[51] thereby inhibiting the debtor from dealing with his property. Moreover the interim trustee in sequestration will undertake advertising to invite creditors to intimate their claims against the debtor.[52] Thereafter the interim trustee will call a meeting of all creditors within 60 days of the date of sequestration at which they will elect a permanent trustee in sequestration.

Once the permanent trustee is appointed, he may dispose of the debtor's assets. However as with poinding those items protected by section 16 of the Debtors (Scotland) Act 1987, being items required for the general upkeep of the debtor and his family, cannot be sold by him. Assets acquired after the date of sequestration, *acquirenda*, vest in the permanent

---

[50] Grier, *Debt* (1998), para. 11.2–11.9.
[51] Bankruptcy (Scotland) Act 1985, s. 14.
[52] *ibid.*, s. 15(6).

trustee, although income received by the debtor after sequestration does not. The permanent trustee may however require the debtor to make a contribution to the debts from his income, provided sufficient remains for the aliment of the debtor and his family, including maintenance for any ex-spouse.

The permanent trustee is only entitled to deal with the assets of the debtor, although the legislation allows the court to reduce gratuitous alienations, *i.e.* transactions made by the debtor to family, friends or third parties for less than market value up to five years before the date of sequestration.[53]

Once the permanent trustee has ingathered the estate of the debtor he will distribute it amongst the creditors.[54] Three years after the date of sequestration the debtor will be discharged, except where the creditors have written to the Accountant of Bankruptcy giving reasons for not discharging the bankrupt.[55] A discharged bankrupt is free to embark on new business adventures, although it will be more difficult for them to obtain credit as they will be blacklisted.

---

[53]   Bankruptcy (Scotland) Act 1985, s. 34(3).
[54]   *ibid.*, s. 51.
[55]   *ibid.*, s. 54.

Chapter 10

THE SOCIAL WORKER AND THE LAW

In the foregoing chapters an attempt has been made to bring together the law as it applies to recipients of social work services. It is this law which the social worker requires knowledge of in dealing with his or her constituent groups; but there are other aspects of the law important to the social worker as a practitioner. In this chapter, subjects range from the social worker and sexual and violent crime, to discrimination, aspects of civil liability and social work practice, and confidentiality. This selection is by no means exhaustive of the areas which the social worker as an employee or as part of a professional service will wish to know, but rather an attempt to cover what, in the opinion of the writers, are key issues for social workers and social care professionals in their workplace environment. These issues are of course important for client groups too, which makes their inclusion and discussion all the more relevant.

10.01

THE SOCIAL WORKER AND VIOLENT AND SEXUAL CRIME

Given the nature of the occupation of social work, the social worker is often thrust into situations where physical danger follows. It is not uncommon for social workers to be victims of crimes of personal violence, some of which tragically result in fatality. Physical violence, threats and abuse of staff are sadly commonplace in social work practice.[1] The evidence of violence is not simply anecdotal. Strathclyde Social Work Department conducted a two-month monitoring exercise on violence during 1985 and found a high number of attacks and other violent incidents against their social work staff.[2] Furthermore, it has been suggested in studies in England that as many as a third of workers have experienced violence in their

10.02

---

[1] On the issue of violence towards social workers see Brown, Bute, and Ford, *Social Workers at Risk: The Prevention and Management of Violence*, (1986); Bute, *Staff Guidelines on the Management of Violence* (Hampshire Social Service, 1980); Brown, Bute, and Ford, *The Management and Prevention of Violence* (University of Southampton and Hampshire Social Service, 1982); Bute, "An Indictment Upon us Failing to Learn", 1979 *Social Work Today*, 6 Feb.; Bute, "The Threat of Violence in Close Encounters with Clients", 1979 *Social Work Today*, 4 Dec.; Rowett, *Violence in Social Work* (Cambridge, University of Cambridge Institute of Criminology 1987); Bute, "Violence and the Social Worker", 1986 *New Society*, 26 Sep.; Association of Directors of Social Services, *Guidelines and Recommendations to Employers on Violence Against Employees* (1987); Crate, "Social Workers and Violent Clients: Management Response", 1986 *Social Work Today*, 10 Nov.; "MP Tells Workers: 'Speak out on Violence', 1986 *Social Work Today*, 20 Oct.; Littlechild, "I needed to be told that I Hadn't Failed: Experiences of Violence Against Probation Staff and of Agency Support" (1997) 27 Br. J. Social Work 219–240.

[2] See Laurence, "Social Work and Self-Defence", 1986 *New Society*, 5 Dec.

current job, and that most staff at some time have been threatened or abused.[3] Attacks come from all user groups.[4] And whilst it is true that most social work clients are not violent towards social workers, it is also true that the incidence of violence against social work staff has in recent years given growing cause for concern.[5] Research studies, although still limited in number, have begun to highlight the very real dangers faced by social workers.[6]

The reasons for violence are relatively obvious. Social work clients are amongst society's most disadvantaged people, often living in poverty and often having an inability to provide for and to articulate their own needs. They are often physically and emotionally damaged individuals, a high proportion of whom may be disturbed, mentally ill, or exhibit challenging behaviour. Some will also have criminal convictions for violence.[7] Furthermore, people who work in social work spend considerable time in direct contact with these clients.[8] Thus, it may be expected that they will be likely to experience physical attacks, threats of violence, and verbal abuse. It is a fact that violence often takes place in the client's own home[9] where the social worker is often isolated from other members of the community and their colleagues. Other people who work with similar members of the community, such as police officers, are perhaps better prepared to cope with the physical dangers they may face, and would consider the arrangements often in place for the solitary social worker to be somewhat foolhardy.

However, it is not only field social workers who face the threat of violence. Those frontline counter staff located in social work offices are particularly vulnerable, whereas managers, with the exception of residential officers in charge, work in offices, having little contact with clients, and may be less at risk of attack primarily because of their isolation from the client and also because they may have a level of protection from the physical presence of their colleagues.

What is even more troubling is that there are often repeat incidents of violence.[10] It also seems likely that there is under-counting of the exact incidence of violence.[11] It has been claimed that the high level of danger faced by social workers in the United Kingdom is found to be a direct consequence of their growing role as agents of social control.[12] Whether that is so or not, it is an ironic paradox indeed that the social worker faces a considerable threat of violence from those whom they ultimately seek to serve.

10.03   Over the past few years some social work departments have set up systems for dealing with violence and many have issued guidelines.[13] Nevertheless, in some places, there is some way to go in providing structural help to social work staff for whom violence is a part of working life.[14] Inevitably, with the level of demand for social work provision and the constraint on resources, not every mechanism and procedure can be put in place to protect social work staff. Staff and their employers naturally look to the criminal law as a vehicle of protection,

---

[3]   "Working in the Social Services", National Institute for Social Work Policy Briefing, No.10, May 1995: < http:/ /www.nisw.org.uk/polb/fulltext/niswp10.html >; see McLean, "The Experience Of Working In The Social Services" in Balloch, Andrew, Ginn, McLean, Pahl and Williams, *Working in the Social Services* (1995, National Institute of Social Work), p. 59.
[4]   "Working in the Social Services", *op. cit.*
[5]   See Norris, *Violence Against Social Workers—The Implications for Practice* (1990), p.15.
[6]   *ibid.*
[7]   See McLean, *op. cit.*, pp. 58–59.
[8]   See McLean, *op. cit.*, p. 57.
[9]   Brown, Bute, and Ford, *Social Workers at Risk: The Prevention and Management of Violence* (1986).
[10]   Wiener and Crosby, *Handling Violence and Aggression* (National Council for Voluntary Child Care Organisations, 1986).
[11]   See Norris, *op. cit.*, p. 36.
[12]   *ibid.*, p. 22.
[13]   "Violence Against Staff in the Social Services", National Institute for Social Work Noticeboard, Autumn 1995, < http://www.nisw.org.uk/notice/not/aut952.html >
[14]   *ibid.*

but it must always be borne in mind that the criminal law operates after the event and in that sense offers little practical protection, although it might operate as a deterrent and a mechanism for control of repeat offending. In looking to the criminal law, it must be recognised that it is no substitute for effective policies and practices designed to limit staff exposure to violence and danger.

In the social worker/client relationship it is not always the social worker who is the victim. Violent and sexual crime by social work staff against those in their charge is rare although the breach of trust that it entails is always particularly shocking. Given the interface between the social worker and the client, it is not unsurprising that the social worker may from time to time be accused by a client of perpetrating a crime of physical or sexual violence against him or her. What follows is an attempt to draw out the salient features of the criminal law on sexual and violent crime, applicable in situations where the social work employee is the victim or the perpetrator.

Violent crimes

Assault

In Scots law assault is committed when one person makes an attack upon the other with the intention of effecting the immediate bodily injury of that person, or producing the fear of immediate bodily injury in his mind.[15] Although the concept of attack is very widely drawn in Scots law, mere words alone cannot constitute an assault.[16] Whilst in the normal course of events an assault will be constituted by physical violence, the concept of attack is much broader than this. **10.04**

Physically restraining someone may amount to assault, as will holding his head under water.[17] It is also the case that blocking the air supply to a critically ill patient is an attack on that person.[18] As has been noted in Chapter 6, various invasive medical procedures without proper consent may similarly constitute an assault.[19] It makes no difference whether the victim is conscious at the time of attack or not.[20] Although purely verbal attacks do not constitute assaults, threatening gestures which put the victim in bodily fear do.[21] Presenting a weapon will constitute assault even if the accused himself knows that no actual injury can be caused by it.[22] The extent of the injury on the victim is not determinant as to whether an attack has taken place although it will impact upon the prosecution of the offence and any consequent punishment.

As is plain, the exercise of force upon another may in many circumstances amount to an assault, but nevertheless there are a number of professionals, including social workers, who as an integral part of their duties from time to time have to physically restrain, or exercise reasonable force against, persons with whom they come into contact with as part of their professional duty. The law recognises this and provides some sensible protection from being accused of the crime of assault in these situations. As long as the professional does not exercise any more than reasonable force and there is no evil intent, such individuals will escape prosecution for assault, primarily because they do not exhibit the necessary criminal

[15] See Jones and Christie, *Criminal Law* (2nd ed., 1996), p. 181.
[16] See MacDonald, *Criminal Law* (1949), p. 115.
[17] See *Kepple v. H.M. Advocate*, 1936 S.L.T. 294.
[18] See *Atkins v. LWT Ltd*, 1978 J.C. 48.
[19] See para. 6.18.
[20] See *Charles Sweenie* (1858) 3 Irv. 109.
[21] See *Atkinson v. H.M. Advocate*, 1987 S.C.C.R. 534.
[22] See *Gilmour v. McLennan*, 1993 S.C.C.R. 837; Lord Advocate's Ref. (No. 2 of 1992), 1993 J.C. 43.

mind ("*mens rea*") for commission of the offence of assault.[23] The *mens rea* necessary is intention.[24] Assault cannot be committed accidentally, nor can it be committed recklessly or negligently.[25] Assault can be aggravated and thus treated as far more serious by prosecutors and courts. There are a number of factors known to aggravate assault including the age of the victim, where the assault takes place, the impact of the assault, and any relationship of trust between the victim and the assailant.[26] The social worker who assaults a very young or elderly client may well find that any assault is considered aggravated.

Consent may be a defence to an assault. An honest belief on the part of an accused that the victim consented may be sufficient.[27] There will be many situations in social care where consent is an appropriate counter to any accusation of assault. Although there is some confusion, provocation is not thought to offer a defence to a charge of assault.[28] Provocation will simply act as a mitigating factor and will have a bearing on the eventual punishment.

Where the motivation behind the social worker's actions is to prevent injury to their client, himself, or others, he may argue self-defence to any criminal charge of assault.[29] For self-defence to be argued in criminal courts it is necessary that there must be imminent danger to life or limb, and also that the conduct used was that which was necessary for the protection of oneself or another.[30] As a third requirement, where it is at all possible, the person who is in danger of assault is required to escape or retreat.[31] The questions of necessity and proportionality of response are always matters of fact and require some fine judgment.[32] The social worker or any employee working in a social care capacity facing a threat of assault from an assailant will be required to assess carefully their response. The law suggests that where possible they should flee and when that is not a possibility they should only exhibit force necessary to defend themselves and that force should be in proportion to the attack. Even in circumstances where the accused has the opportunity of retreating, he may nevertheless plead self-defence if he becomes involved in trying to protect another.[33]

Homicide

10.05 Although rare in the social care/client relationship homicides do happen. Scots law recognises two common law homicide crimes—murder and culpable homicide.

The requisite *mens rea* for murder is intention or wicked recklessness. The criminal mind is often inferred from the nature and quality of the conduct of the perpetrator. In respect of murder, the intention must be the intention to kill. Wicked recklessness is something more than simple recklessness.[34] According to Hume, the accused should mean to perpetrate some great or outrageous bodily harm, the harm should be such as might well result in death, and the harm must show an absolute and utter indifference as to whether the victim lived or

---

23   See *e.g. Skinner v. Robertson*, 1980 S.L.T. (Sh. Ct.) 43, compared with *Norman v. Smith*, 1983 S.C.C.R. 100.
24   See Jones and Christie, *Criminal Law* (2nd ed.), p. 186.
25   See Gordon, *Criminal Law* (2nd ed., 1998), paras 29–30; L. A.'s Ref. (No. 2 of 1992), *supra, per* L.J.C. Ross; however see Jones and Christie, *Criminal Law* (2nd ed.), paras 9–16 and 9–12, pp. 186–190.
26   McCall-Smith and Sheldon, *Scots Criminal Law* (2nd ed., 1997) at pp. 162–163; there is also the new provisions of racial aggravation discussed at para. 10.19.
27   See Jones and Christie, *op. cit.*, p. 191; *Meek v. H.M. Advocate*, 1983 S.L.T. 280; *Jamieson v. H.M. Advocate*, 1994 S.L.T. 537.
28   See Jones and Christie, *op. cit.*, pp. 193–194.
29   *ibid.*, pp. 152–159.
30   *Pollock v. H.M. Advocate*, 1998 S.L.T. 880.
31   See *H.M. Advocate v. Doherty* 1954 J.C. 1 at pp. 4–5 *per* Lord Keith.
32   *Pollock v. H.M. Advocate*, 1998 S.L.T. 880.
33   See *Fitzpatrick v. H.M. Advocate*, 1992 S.L.T. 796.
34   See Jones and Christie, *op. cit.*, paras 9–45 and 9–50, pp. 209–213.

died.[35] Even in circumstances where the accused had not intended death, but has acted in such a way as to **show total disregard for the life of another**, the charge of murder may be validly brought.[36]

Culpable homicide covers any killing of a human being brought about by another in circumstances where that other should be held criminally responsible for it.[37] Culpable homicide can be split into voluntary and involuntary culpable homicide.[38] Voluntary culpable homicide is essentially murder under mitigating circumstances. Principally, the law recognises two types of mitigating circumstances—provocation and diminished responsibility. Where the accused is provoked the response must be immediate to reduce any charge of murder to culpable homicide: if there is a considerable time gap between the provocation and the homicidal act then there is no mitigation. Scots law dictates that there should be some final provocative act in instances where there has been cumulative provocation.[39] The types of provocative act which are generally recognised in Scots law are acts of violence and sexual infidelity.[40] The acts of retaliatory violence must be reasonably proportionate to the provocation.[41]

Diminished responsibility represents some mental weakness which can be generally recognised. Uncontrollable temper[42] and the temporary effects of voluntary intoxication[43] are thought to be excluded. It is also the case that severe personality disorder is not sufficient to constitute diminished responsibility.[44]

Involuntary culpable homicide covers a range of circumstances. One form of it is where the perpetrator intends simply to assault the victim, and as a result of the assault the victim dies: there is no intention to kill and therefore a charge of murder is not appropriate. Nevertheless, a death has ensued and a simple charge of assault is equally not an appropriate charge. Some attacks are so serious that the charge of murder might be appropriate, especially those where the assault is of such severity that it can be inferred that the accused displayed the requisite wicked recklessness.

A further form of involuntary culpable homicide is unlawful act culpable homicide.[45] This is where the accused is involved in some illegal activity other than assault which might reasonably involve personal injury which ultimately ends in death. In the modern era two cases provide adequate illustration. In *Mathieson v. H.M. Advocate*[46] the accused committed the crime of reckless fire-raising by setting fire to some cans of paint. The paint, however, was stored at the rear entrance of a building which caught fire, resulting in the deaths of four people. The court had no difficulty in finding that the accused was guilty of culpable homicide. Similarly, in *Sutherland v. H.M. Advocate*[47] the accused, in an attempt to defraud his insurers, set fire to his property and again death ensued. Given the circumstances the court was prepared to consider that his conduct amounted to unlawful act culpable homicide.

10.06

---

[35]   See Hume, vol. i, pp. 238 and 256.
[36]   See *John McCallum and William Corner* (1853) 1 Irv. 259.
[37]   See Jones and Christie, *Criminal Law* (2nd ed., 1996), p. 213.
[38]   See Gordon, *Criminal Law* (2nd ed., 1978), p. 764.
[39]   See *Thomson v. H.M. Advocate*, 1986 S.L.T. 281; *Graham v. H.M. Advocate*, 1987 S.C.C.R. 20; *Parr v. H.M. Advocate*, 1991 J.C. 39.
[40]   *Rutherford v. H.M. Advocate*, 1998 S.L.T. 740.
[41]   See *Low v. H.M. Advocate*, 1994 S.L.T. 277, *per* L.J.-C. Ross at p. 286
[42]   *Braithwaite v. H.M. Advocate*, 1945 J.C. 55.
[43]   *Brennan v. H.M. Advocate*, 1977 J.C. 38.
[44]   See *Williamson v. H.M. Advocate*, 1994 J.C. 149, *per* L.J.-C. Ross at p. 153.
[45]   Ross, "Unlawful Act Culpable Homicide: A Suitable Case For Reappraisal", 1996 S.L.T. 75.
[46]   1981 S.C.C.R. 196.
[47]   1994 S.L.T. 634.

Finally, there are a number of types of homicide which fulfil the requirements for murder but are charged as culpable homicide. These are termed discretionary culpable homicides. They include euthanasia and suicide pacts. Scots law has recently had to address the issue of doctors withdrawing life-sustaining treatment in patients who are in a "persistent vegetative state". In the normal course of events such action could render a doctor or other person guilty of one of the homicide crimes. However, following the decision *Law Hospital National Health Service Trust v. Lord Advocate*,[48] doctors will be immune from prosecution in respect of such actions where they first sought prior approval of the Court of Session.

Sexual crimes

Rape

10.07   Whilst the threat of sexual assault against the social worker is clear, it is also not uncommon within the dynamics of the relationship of client and social carer that an allegation of sexual impropriety on the part of the social worker arises. The most serious sexual offence under the law of Scotland is that of rape. This consists of a male having vaginal intercourse with a female person against her will.[49] Unlike the law in England,[50] rape in Scotland is a gender-specific crime and can only be committed by males upon females. The penetration need be no more than slight, and there need be no ejaculation. Oral sex and anal sex do not constitute rape, but may nevertheless amount to indecent assaults. Anal sex by one man forcibly against another man in Scots law will require to be charged as indecent assault and not rape.[51]

There is a basic premise of law that for rape to be established the sexual will of the woman requires to be overcome. Accordingly, if a man has sex with a women who is, for example, unconscious or sleeping, then in the normal course of events this will not constitute the offence of rape but a separate Scottish offence known as clandestine injury to woman.[52] The will of the woman may be overcome in many ways either by physical force or by threat of injury to her or another. A girl under the age of 12 is deemed not to have developed sufficient mental capacity to have formed a will capable of being overcome. It follows therefore that sexual intercourse with a girl under 12 years of age is rape whether she consented or not. If a female is plied with drink or drugs to overcome her will then that too is rape. Where a female is unconscious by reason of drink, drugs or anaesthetics, etc., it is necessary for the prosecution to show that she was unwilling to have sexual intercourse immediately prior to her insensibility. In addition to this it is necessary to show that her will was overcome by the administering of drugs or drink to her. According to Jones and Christie, where the accused,

> "has no hand at all in producing her state of insensibility, where he happens upon her by chance and has sexual intercourse with her when she is totally unaware of his presence or intentions, then it cannot be established that she demonstrated unwillingness. It obviously cannot be shown that any force was used to overcome unwillingness which never existed in fact; and therefore, there is no rape."[53]

[48]   1996 S.C.L.R. 491.
[49]   See Jones and Christie, *Criminal Law* (2nd ed., 1996), pp. 225–226.
[50]   See Criminal Justice and Public Order Act 1994, s. 142 and s. 143.
[51]   See *Barbour v. H.M. Advocate*, 1982 S.C.C.R. 195.
[52]   McCall-Smith and Sheldon, *Scots Criminal Law* (2nd ed., 1997) at pp. 199–200.
[53]   Jones and Christie, *op. cit.*, at p. 230.

This may have some relevance in the social care environment. There has recently been a case where a patient in a persistent vegetative state was impregnated, and there was a suggestion that the person responsible was in fact one of her carers. Were such a situation to arise in Scotland, this would not amount to rape but would require to be prosecuted as the alternative charge of clandestine injury to a woman. The Scottish position can be contrasted with the English position where integral to the crime of rape is the issue of non-consent and where the absence of consent *per se* to sexual relations could result in a successful prosecution for rape.

The *mens rea* of rape was stated in *Jamieson v. H.M. Advocate*[54] by Lord Justice-General Hope as including

"the intention to have intercourse with the woman without her consent. The absence of a belief that she was consenting is an essential element in it. If a man has intercourse with a woman and believes that she is consenting to this, he cannot be guilty of rape."

Lord Hope went on to suggest it would be sufficient for rape if the man acted without thinking or was indifferent as to whether or not he had the female's consent.[55] Where the accused believes that the woman is consenting, there can be no argument that the accused has the requisite criminal mind either of intention or recklessness. If he can convince the jury of his belief he will be acquitted.

Statutory sexual offences

Scots common law does not treat mentally ill females any differently from females of normal **10.08** mental capacity.[56] Whilst this seems a glaring anomaly, what is in place to protect such persons are a number of statutory offences. Section 106(5) of the Mental Health (Scotland) Act 1984 renders it an offence to have sexual intercourse with a woman suffering from a state of arrested or incomplete development of mind.

There are other statutory sexual offences which are possible alternatives to the charge of rape, and there are alternatives open to a jury considering a rape charge, who do not consider that the essentials of rape have been established. For example, there is an offence of procuring a woman or girl to have intercourse with a man by threats, false pretences or drugging.[57]

It is an offence for a person to have sexual intercourse with a girl under the age of 13 years of age and any person who has such intercourse is liable to conviction on indictment and can be imprisoned for life.[58] Any person who attempts to have intercourse with a girl under 13 years of age is liable on indictment to be imprisoned for a maximum of up to two years or on summary conviction up to three months.[59] Anyone who has sex or attempts to have sex with a girl over 13 but under 16 is liable on conviction on indictment to imprisonment not exceeding a term of two years or on summary conviction to a term not exceeding three months. No prosecution for sexual intercourse with girls between 13 and 16 shall be commenced after more than one year after the commission of the offence.[60] A person charged with such an offence can defend himself on the basis that (a) he had reason to believe

---

54 1994 J.C. 88.
55 See *Jamieson v. H.M. Advocate*, 1994 J.C. 88 at p. 92.
56 See Gordon, *Criminal Law* (2nd ed., 1978), para. 33–16.
57 See Criminal Law (Consolidation) (Scotland) Act 1995 ("1995 Act"), s. 7(2).
58 *ibid.*, s. 5(1).
59 *ibid.*, s. 5(2).
60 *ibid.*, s. 5(4).

the girl was his wife; or (b) being a man under the age of 24 years who had not previously been charged with a like offence, he had reasonable cause to believe that the girl was of or over the age of 16 years.[61] It is not sufficient for a man to merely rely on the appearance of the girl and indeed he must point to some other evidence. Although it is common law rape to have sexual intercourse with a child under 12, in situations where a girl is between 12 and 13 the statutory offence will be used. Any person who uses, towards a girl on or over 12 years of age but under 16, any lewd and indecent practices or behaviour which, if used towards a girl under the age of 12, would have constituted an offence at common law, shall, whether the girl consented to such practice or behaviour or not, be liable on conviction on indictment to imprisonment for a term not exceeding two years or on summary conviction to imprisonment not exceeding three months.[62]

Homosexual offences[63]

10.09　A homosexual act in private shall not be an offence should the parties consent and have attained the age of 18. In any act where more than two persons take part, the incident is not to be considered as private. A male person who is suffering from mental deficiency which is of such a nature that he is incapable of living an independent life, or of guarding himself against serious exploitation, cannot in law give any consent which would prevent a homosexual act from being an offence. A person shall not be convicted on account of the incapacity of such a male person to consent of an offence if he proves he did not know or had no reason to suspect that the male person was suffering from a mental deficiency. It is an offence to procure or attempt to procure a commission of a homosexual act other than in private, without the consent of both parties to the act or if the person is under the age of 18. It is also an offence to attempt to procure or to procure a homosexual act between two other male persons. If the person is convicted on indictment in respect of such matters they are liable to imprisonment for up to a maximum of two years, or on summary conviction up to a maximum of three months.

THE SOCIAL WORKER AND DISCRIMINATION

10.10　Social work professionals are regularly exhorted to adopt anti-discriminatory practice. As one commentator has argued,

> "the social work practice which does not take account of oppression and discrimination cannot be seen as good practice no matter how high [those] standards may be in other respects."[64]

Discrimination appears in many guises throughout society. The discussion in this chapter concentrates on three areas thought particularly relevant to the practice of social work in Scotland — sex discrimination, race discrimination and disability discrimination.

---

[61]　1995 Act, s. 5(5).
[62]　*ibid.*, s. 6.
[63]　See generally 1995 Act, s. 13.
[64]　See Thomson, *Anti-discriminatory Practice* (1993), pp. 10–11.

SEX DISCRIMINATION

The Equal Opportunities Commission

The Equal Opportunities Commission was established in 1975. It is comprised of between **10.11** eight and 15 members each appointed by the Secretary of State on a full-time or part-time basis. The Commission is charged with the following duties:

(a) to work towards the elimination of discrimination;

(b) to promote equality of opportunity between men and women generally; and

(c) to keep under review the working of the Sex Discrimination Act 1975 and the Equal Pay Act 1970 and, when so required by the Secretary of State or otherwise think it necessary, draw up and submit to the Secretary of State proposals for amending them.[65]

The Commission may undertake or assist financially research and other educational activities designed to fulfil its objectives.[66] In addition the Commission are empowered to keep under review health and safety provisions in so far as they require men and women to be treated separately and to report to the Secretary of State if so required. It makes an annual report to the Secretary of State.[67]

The Commission is empowered to issue codes of practice containing guidance on the elimination of discrimination in employment, and the promotion of equal opportunity in employment between men and women.[68]

Another important power which the Commission has, if it sees fit or is required to do so by the Secretary of State, is the ability to conduct a formal investigation.[69] Terms of reference must be drawn up for such investigations and these must be notified to those affected by the investigation.[70] Persons named in the terms of reference have the right to make representations to the Commission.[71] Where it conducts a formal investigation the Commission can compel the delivery of written information and also the attendance of persons to give oral evidence to the investigation.[72] Following the conclusion of an investigation it will make a report of its investigation and may make recommendations to those investigated and to the Secretary of State.[73] The report can be made public. As an added power it can issue an employer with a non-discrimination notice requiring that employer not to commit discriminatory acts, to change certain practices and to advise the Commission what changes have been effected.[74] Where there is evidence of persistent discrimination, the Commission may seek an interdict in the sheriff court restraining the guilty party from engaging in discriminatory acts.[75]

---

[65] Sex Discrimination Act 1975 ("1975 Act"), s. 53.
[66] 1975 Act, s. 54(1).
[67] *ibid.*, s. 56.
[68] See generally the 1975 Act, s. 56A, as inserted by the Race Relations Act 1976, s. 79(4), Sched. 4, para. 1. See also Code of Practice, "For the Elimination of Sex and Marriage Discrimination and the Promotion of Equality of opportunity in employment", for a copy of this see Selwyn, *Selwyn's Law of Employment*, (10th ed., 1998), App. I(d), pp. 556–561.
[69] 1975 Act, s. 57(1).
[70] *ibid.*, s. 58(2) and (3).
[71] 1975 Act, s. 58(3A), as inserted by Race Relations Act 1976, s. 79(4) and Sched. 4, para. 2.
[72] 1975 Act, s. 59(1).
[73] *ibid.*, s. 60(1) and (2).
[74] *ibid.*, s. 67.
[75] *ibid.*, s. 71(1).

The Commission also has the power of direct intervention, and may bring proceedings at an employment tribunal, where discriminatory adverts are placed, or there are instructions or pressure to discriminate.[76] In addition persons may apply to the Commission for financial assistance in bringing a claim before an employment tribunal and this may be granted if:

(a) the case raises a question of principle;

(b) it is unreasonable having regard to the complexity of the case or the applicant's position to expect the applicant to deal with the case unaided; or

(c) there is any other special consideration.[77]

The assistance which the Commission may provide may include:

(a) giving advice;

(b) procuring or attempting to procure the settlement of any matter in dispute;

(c) arranging for the giving of advice or assistance by a solicitor or counsel;

(d) arranging for representation by any person, including all such assistance as is usually given by a solicitor or counsel in the steps preliminary or incidental to the proceedings or in arriving at or giving effect to a compromise to avoid or bring to an end any proceedings; or

(e) any other form of assistance which the Commission may consider appropriate.[78]

Sex discrimination law

10.12 The law on sex discrimination is to be found principally in the Sex Discrimination Act 1975 ("1975 Act") as modified by the Sex Discrimination Act 1986. The 1975 Act states that a person discriminates against a woman directly when he treats her less favourably than he treats a man on the grounds of her sex,[79] or indirectly when he applies a requirement or condition (1) which is such that the proportion of women who are able to comply with it is considerably smaller than the proportion of men in comparison, and (2) that cannot be shown to be justified in respect of the sex of the person to whom it is applied, and (3) which is to the detriment of that person in that she cannot comply with it.[80] It is equally unlawful to discriminate directly or indirectly against men, or against a married person of either sex on the grounds of that person's marital status.[81] Similarly, it is possible to discriminate against single persons of either sex in favour of married persons.[82] Positive discrimination in favour of either sex is unlawful.[83]

Because direct discrimination occurs where a person is treated less favourably than a person of the other sex on the grounds of that person's sex, to discriminate against someone

---

[76] 1975 Act, s. 72.
[77] *ibid.*, s. 75(1).
[78] *ibid.*, s. 75(2).
[79] *ibid.*, s. 1(1)(a).
[80] See *Home Office v. Holmes* [1984] I.C.R. 678; *Price v. Civil Service Commission* [1978] I.C.R. 27; *Jones v. University of Manchester* [1993] I.R.L.R. 218, *per* Gibson L.J.
[81] 1975 Act, s. 1(2)(b).
[82] See Selwyn, *Selwyn's Law of Employment* (10th ed., 1998), p. 88.
[83] See *Kalanke v. Freie Hansestadt Bremen* [1996] All E.R. 66 (EC); *cf. Marschall v. Land Nordrhein-Westfalen* [1997] All E.R. 865 (EC).

who is a transsexual because they are a transsexual amounts to direct discrimination.[84] Less favourable treatment is determined by an objective assessment by the tribunal or the court.[85]

In an attempt to counter any evasive ingenuity in respect of direct discrimination, the Act also provides for indirect discrimination explained above. An employer will be required to satisfy a tribunal that any requirement or condition which it places upon a man or a woman is necessary.[86] The tribunal or court will assess whether the requirement or condition is justified on an objective basis in determining whether the man or woman can comply with the condition. The tribunal should not consider the matter as an exercise in theoretical possibilities but rather one of reality and practice.[87] The compliance test is determined on the basis of whether an employee can comply rather than whether they wish or do not wish to.[88]

The third form of discrimination identified by the 1975 Act is discrimination by way of victimisation. Section 4(1) of the Act suggests that a person is victimised where he or she gets treated less favourably because he or she has brought proceedings under the 1975 Act or Equal Pay Act 1970, or has given evidence or information in connection with proceedings under either Act, or done anything (in relation to either Act) to the discriminator or another person, or has made allegations of a contravention of either Act, unless the allegation was false and not made in good faith.

Sex discrimination in employment

In social work services women comprise a majority of the workforce.[89] Not unlike other occupations, there is often disparity between those who have supervisory, managerial or leading policy roles and those who form the majority of the workers.[90] The large workforce also comprises a substantial block of part-time workers (most of whom are female). **10.13**

Whilst recognising that amongst professional social workers there are moves towards uniform qualifications and greater emphasis on enhancing professional status, it is a fact that a large segment of the social workforce are not social workers but operate in some other care capacity. It is in these groups that one is most likely to find occupational segregation. The nature of the workforce and the nature of the work make sex discrimination a very real issue for social work employees both in their own workplace environment and in furthering the aspirations of many of the clients they seek to serve as they too confront discrimination in their workplaces and elsewhere in society.

Part II of the 1975 Act prohibits unlawful discrimination in employment, not just between the employee and employer but also toward anyone working under a contract to execute any work or labour. It is unlawful to discriminate in respect of the arrangements a person makes for the purposes of telling who shall be employed.[91]

As noted above, the Equal Opportunities Commission has the power to bring an action against an employer who places a discriminatory advert for employment.[92] However, the law

[84] See Selwyn *Selwyn's Law of Employment* (10th ed., 1998) p. 89, para 4.5; E.C. Directive 76/207/EEC.
[85] See Selwyn *op. cit.*, p. 89, para. 4.7; *Schmidt v. Austicks Bookshops Ltd* [1978] I.C.R. 85; *Burrett v. West Birmingham Health Authority* [1994] I.R.L.R. 7, EAT; *Stewart v. Cleveland Guest (Engineering) Ltd.* [1994] I.C.R. 535; *Smith v. Safeway plc* [1996] I.C.R. 868.
[86] *Steel v. Union of Post Office Workers* [1978] 2 All E.R. 504.
[87] *Price v. Civil Service Commission* [1978] 1 All E.R. 1228.
[88] *Turner v. Labour Party and Labour Party Superannuation Society* [1987] I.R.L.R. 101.
[89] See Pahl, "*Men and Women In Social Services*", in Balloch, Andrew, Ginn, McLean, Pahl, and Williams, *Working In The Social Services* (National Institute for Social Work, 1995), p. 147.
[90] *ibid.*
[91] 1975 Act, s. 6(1)(a).
[92] 1975 Act, s. 38; see also para. 10.12.

does not simply regulate adverts. It is unlawful discrimination to put in place procedures or adopt policies and attitudes which make clear the intention to discriminate even after the placing of a non-discriminatory advert.[93] The nature of questions asked at the interview may also show that the employer's intention or arrangements are discriminatory.[94] It is not automatically discriminatory to put certain questions to female employees which are not put to male employees: many employers put in place application forms which ask a number of questions regarding the person's sex, marital status, and children. This in itself is not discriminatory.

10.14   The second basis on which there may be unlawful discrimination in the employment field is where the employer offers terms of employment to a person which are different from these offered to another employee of the opposite sex in the same circumstances of employment.[95] The employer may have a lawful reason for this, and if he can show that there is a genuine material difference between the two applicants which had nothing to do with their sex, it will not be unlawful to offer terms that are different. Where women are offered terms which are deemed to be chivalrous, for example starting late or finishing early, men must be likewise offered the same terms of employment.

A third variation of unlawful discrimination in employment is by refusing or deliberately omitting to offer employment to someone because of that person's sex.[96] It can be unlawful discrimination not to appoint someone to a post because the employer believes it is work undertaken properly by someone of the opposite sex, even in situations where no one is appointed to the post.[97] It is unlawful discrimination for an employee not to be offered opportunities of promotion, transfer or training, or access to any other benefits, facilities or services, or for an employer to refuse or deliberately omit to afford an employee access to them.[98] Moreover, it is unlawful discrimination for an employer to dismiss a person or subject him or her to any other detriment on the grounds of sex.[99] It is no defence on the part of the employer to argue that the dismissal took place because of pressure from other employees.[1] Nor is it lawful for an employer to discriminate by requiring employees of a certain sex to do unusual or inconvenient work and not require members of the opposite sex to do the same, even in situations where they pay additional monies to those undertaking such work.[2] Women should not be dismissed from employment on the basis that a man needs the job more where a redundancy situation arises.[3]

10.15   Sexual harassment may amount to unlawful discrimination under section 1(1)(a) of the 1975 Act on the basis that a person is being treated less favourably in regard of their sex. This may also amount in the employment field to subjection to a detriment under section 6(2)(b). In the leading Scottish case of *Porcelli v. Strathclyde Regional Council*,[4] the applicant was able to show that she had been sexually harassed to the point where she was obliged to seek a transfer from her employment. The conduct was designed to get her to leave. However, it was the conduct that was important and not the actual motive. A solitary incident of sexual

---

[93]   See *Brennan v. Dewhurst Ltd* [1984] I.C.R. 52 where the manager made it clear he intended to employ a man in the post of butchery assistant.
[94]   See *Saunders v. Richmond upon Thames Borough Council* [1977] I.R.L.R. 362.
[95]   1975 Act, s. 6(1)(b).
[96]   *ibid.*, s. 6(1)(c).
[97]   See *Roadburg v. Lothian R.C.* [1976] I.R.L.R. 283.
[98]   1975 Act, s. 6(2)(a).
[99]   *ibid.*, s. 6(2)(b).
[1]   See *Munro v. Allied Suppliers* [1977] I.R.L.I.R. (unreported).
[2]   *Jeremiah v. Ministry of Defence* [1979] I.R.L.R. 436.
[3]   See *Gubala v. Crompton Parkinson* [1977] I.R.L.R. 10.
[4]   [1986] I.C.R. 564.

harassment can amount to a detriment under the 1975 Act.[5] Compensation for sexual harassment cases can be quite considerable and must reflect the degree of detriment. Employers may be vicariously liable for the sexual harassment of an employee by another employee. The employer may have recourse to a defence that the sexual harassment was undertaken by a fellow employee but not within the course of his employment.[6] However, the employer is required to show that he takes such steps as are reasonably practicable to prevent employees sexually harassing another employee.

There is nothing in the 1975 Act which prevents discrimination on the grounds of sexual orientation.[7] However, the status of transsexuals is somewhat different to that of homosexuals. The European Court of Justice in *P v. S and Cornwall County Council*[8] decided that the applicant was treated unfavourably in comparison with persons of the sex to which he or she used to belong before undergoing gender reassignment. It is understood that the United Kingdom Government is seeking to pass legislation in the very near future which will offer protection from discrimination to transsexual employees.[9]

The 1975 Act permits discrimination in certain circumstances. First it is lawful to discriminate on the grounds of sex on health grounds,[10] for example it is permissible to discriminate against pregnant women in order to protect them against health risks which are specific to them alone. Moreover, discrimination is permitted by an employee where it is a genuine occupational requirement that a person of a particular sex is required.[11] There is a genuine occupational requirement where (a) the nature of the job calls for authentic male or female characteristics, perhaps in the field of acting or dramatic arts; (b) the job requires to be held by a person of a particular sex in order to preserve decency or privacy because (1) it is likely to involve physical contact with a person in circumstances where that person might reasonably object to it being carried out by a person of the opposite sex, (2) persons of one sex might reasonably object to the presence of the opposite sex because of their state of undress or the using of sanitary facilities, (3) the job is likely to involve the holder doing his work, or living, in a private home and needs to be held by a person of one sex because objection might reasonably be taken to allowing a person of the other sex (i) such a degree of physical or social contact with a person living in the home or (ii) the knowledge of intimate details of such person's life which would be allowed to, or available to, the holder of the job; (c) the employee is required to live in premises provided by the employer, and those which are available are not equipped with separate sleeping accommodation and sanitary facilities and it is not reasonable to expect the employer to equip these premises or provide those facilities; (d) the job has to be done by a person in a hospital, prison or a staff professional for people who need special care, supervision or attention; (e) the holder's job provides personal services promoting welfare or education which can be most effectively provided by one sex; (f) the job is likely to involve performance of duties outside the United Kingdom in a country whose laws or customs are such that duties could not be effectively performed by someone of the opposite sex; or (g) the job is one of two held by a married couple.

In social services there are a number of situations that may give rise to genuine occupational requirement. The situations detailed in (b) (c) (d) and (e), above, seem particularly relevant. It is not uncommon for social care and social service jobs to be advertised which will

10.16

---

[5]   See *Bracebridge Engineering Ltd v. Darby* [1990] I.R.L.R. 3.
[6]   See *Tower Boot Co. Ltd v. Jones* [1995] I.R.L.R. 529.
[7]   See *R. v. Ministry of Defence, ex p. Smith* [1996] Q.B. 517; *Smith v. Gardner Merchant Ltd* [1996] I.R.L.R. 342.
[8]   [1996] All E.R. (EC) 397.
[9]   See position of transsexuals in Selwyn, *Selwyn's Law of Employment* (10th ed., 1998) pp. 103–105.
[10] 1975 Act, s. 51(1).
[11] *ibid.*, s. 7.

only be filled by persons of a particular sex and because of the foregoing provisions, no claim of discrimination can be made.

Where unlawful discrimination takes place, an employment tribunal will have a right to make a declaration as to the parties' rights and the victim will have a claim for compensation.[12]

RACE DISCRIMINATION

The Commission for Racial Equality

10.17 The Commission for Racial Equality ("CRE") was established in 1976 under the Race Relations Act 1976 ("1976 Act").[13] It is comprised of between eight and 15 members each appointed by the Secretary of State on a full-time or part-time basis. The CRE is charged with the following duties:

(a) to work towards the elimination of discrimination;

(b) to promote equality of opportunity and good relations between persons of different racial groups generally; and

(c) to keep under review the working of the 1976 Act and, when they are so required by the Secretary of State or otherwise think it necessary, draw up and submit to the Secretary of State proposals for amending it.[14]

The CRE may, with the approval of the Secretary of State, give financial assistance to any organisation concerned in the promotion of equality of opportunity, and good relations, between persons of different racial groups.[15] In addition to this, it may also undertake or finance research and other educational activities designed to fulfil its objectives.[16] It is empowered to issue codes of practice containing guidance on the elimination of discrimination in employment, the promotion of equal opportunity in employment between persons of different racial groups, the elimination of discrimination in housing and the promotion of equality in the field of housing between persons of different racial groups.[17] In this respect it issued Code of Practice, *For the Elimination of Racial Discrimination and the Promotion of Equality or Opportunity in Employment*.[18]

Another important power which the CRE has, if it sees fit or is required to do so by the Secretary of State, is the ability to conduct a formal investigation.[19] Terms of reference must be drawn up for such investigations and these must be notified to those affected by the investigation.[20] Persons named in the terms of reference have the right to make representations to the Commission.[21] Where it conducts a formal investigation the CRE can compel the delivery of written information and also the attendance of persons to give oral evidence to

---

12 1975 Act, s. 65.
13 Race Relations Act 1976 ("1976 Act"), s. 43.
14 *ibid.*, s. 43(1).
15 *ibid.*, s. 44(1).
16 *ibid.*, s. 45(1).
17 See generally 1976 Act, s. 47.
18 For a copy of this Code of Practice see Selwyn, *Selwyn's Law of Employment* (10th ed., 1998), App. I.
19 1976 Act, s. 48(1).
20 *ibid.*, s. 49(2) and (3).
21 *ibid.*, s. 49(4).

the investigation.[22] Following the conclusion of an investigation the CRE will make a report of their investigation and may make recommendations to those investigated and to the Secretary of State.[23] The report can be made public. As an added power the CRE can issue an employer with a non-discrimination notice requiring that employer not to commit discriminatory acts, to change certain practices and to advise the Commission what changes have been effected.[24] Where there is evidence of persistent discrimination, the CRE may seek an interdict in the sheriff court restraining the guilty party from engaging in discriminatory acts.[25]

The CRE also has the power of direct intervention and may bring proceedings at an employment tribunal where discriminatory adverts for employment are placed, or there are instructions or pressures to discriminate.[26] In addition a person may apply to the CRE for financial assistance in bringing a claim before an employment tribunal and this may be granted if:

(a) the case raises a question of principle;

(b) it is unreasonable having regard to the complexity of the case, or the applicant's position, to expect the applicant to deal with the case unaided; or

(c) there is any other special consideration.[27]

The assistance which the CRE may provide may include:

(a) giving advice;

(b) procuring or attempting to procure the settlement of any matter in dispute;

(c) arranging for the giving of advice or assistance by a solicitor or counsel;

(d) arranging for representation by any person, including all such assistance as is usually given by a solicitor or counsel in the steps preliminary or incidental to the proceedings, or in arriving at or giving effect to a compromise to avoid or bring to an end any proceedings; or

(e) any other form of assistance which the Commission may consider appropriate.[28]

Racial discrimination law

The 1976 Act contains very similar provisions to the Sex Discrimination Act 1975. It seeks to prevent discrimination on racial grounds which are related to colour, race, nationality or ethnic national origins.[29] Like the Sex Discrimination Act, the Race Relations Act 1976 **10.18**

---

[22] 1976 Act, s. 50.
[23] *ibid.*, s. 51(1) and (2).
[24] *ibid.*, s. 58(2).
[25] *ibid.*, s. 62.
[26] *ibid.*, s. 63.
[27] *ibid.*, s. 66.
[28] *ibid.*, s. 66(2).
[29] See s. 3(1) of the 1976 Act for definition of racial grounds.

provides for direct and indirect discrimination[30] and victimisation.[31] It is direct racial discrimination to treat one person less favourably on racial grounds than another.[32] The discrimination need not necessarily be related to the racial characteristics of the particular person. Different treatment is not necessarily discrimination providing it is not due to race, although the employer may have some problems in satisfying the court or tribunal of this.[33] Segregating a person from other persons on racial grounds is to be considered as treating that person less favourably than another.[34]

The word "ethnic" is to be given a broader meaning than race. The factors to be considered are: a long shared history of which the group is conscious as distinguishing it from other groups; a cultural tradition including social customs and manners; a common geographical origin or descent from common ancestors; a common language; a common literature; a common religion different from that of neighbouring groups; and being a minority or being an oppressed or a dominant group in a large community.[35] Religion is not in itself considered a racial ground though it is suggested by one commentator that it may be covered by race, ethnic, or national origins.[36] In Scotland it will be particularly difficult to establish that any particular religious domination can be associated with characteristics of being Scottish. Accordingly, to advertise or discriminate on the grounds of Catholicism or Protestantism in Scotland may be perfectly lawful.[37] For the purposes of racial grounds, Scotland and England are to be considered places of national origin and, accordingly, to discriminate against persons from one nation or the other is unlawful discrimination.[38]

Unlike in England where there have been studies,[39] it is difficult to gauge the extent of racial discrimination in the field of social work in Scotland. It would however be naive to presume that it is not an issue at all. Whether or not there is institutional racism in Scottish social work structures, it seems likely that ethnic minority employees may face racism as they go about their everyday tasks.

Racial discrimination in employment

10.19   It is unlawful to discriminate on racial grounds in respect of employment. In particular it is unlawful to discriminate on racial grounds in the arrangements for determining who shall be offered employment; the terms that are offered; or by refusing or deliberately omitting to offer employment.[40] Following employment, it is unlawful to discriminate against an employee in the terms of employment which are given to that employee; in the way in which the employee is afforded opportunities of promotion, transfer and training, or access to

---

[30]   1976 Act, s. 1(1)(a) and (b).

[31]   *ibid.*, s. 2.

[32]   1975 Act s. 1(1)(a); see *Glasgow City Council v. Zafar*, 1998 S.C. (H.L.) 27.

[33]   *Barclays Bank plc v. Kapur* [1989] I.R.L.R. 387; *Weathersfield Ltd v. Sargent* [1998] I.R.L.R. 14.

[34]   1976 Act, s. 1(2); *Pel Ltd v. Modgill* [1980] I.R.L.R. 142.

[35]   *Mandla v. Dowell Lee* [1982] 3 All E.R. 1108.

[36]   See Selwyn, *Selwyn's Law of Employment* (10th ed., 1998), para. 4.107.

[37]   There was an attempt in 1998 to seek to remedy this gap in the law in the form of the Religious Discrimination and Remedies Bill.

[38]   *Northern Joint Police Board v. Power* [1997] I.R.L.R. 610 EAT.

[39]   Davey, "Services still suffer Racism at Work" (National Institute for Social Work Noticeboard, Autumn 1997), < http://www.nisw.org.uk/notice/not/97aut8.html >; "Working in the Social Services" (National Institute for Social Work Policy Briefing, No.10, May 1995), < http://www.nisw.org.uk/polb/fulltext/niswp10.html >; see Pahl, *op. cit.*, p. 149.

[40]   1976 Act, s. 4(1).

benefits, facilities or services; or in dismissing the employee or subjecting them to any other detriment.[41]

The employers must not only be careful about their own racial discrimination towards their employees, but must also be mindful that they may be liable under the concept of vicarious liability for racial harassment perpetrated by their employee.[42] Such vicarious liability of employers for harassment by employees may only arise in a situation where the employer can control it.[43]

Again in similar fashion to the 1975 Act, the 1976 Act lays down certain genuine occupational qualifications where it is permissible to engage what would otherwise be considered discriminatory practices. There may be a genuine occupational qualification that (a) the job involves participation in dramatic performance or entertainment, and for reasons of authenticity the person requires to belong to a particular racial group; (b) the job involves participation as an artist or photographic model and again a person of a particular racial group is required for reasons of authenticity; (c) the job involves working in a place where food and drink is provided and consumed by members of the public in a particular setting for which a personal or partnership group is required for reasons of authenticity; (d) the holder of the job provides persons of a racial group with personal services promoting their welfare, and those services or most of them should be provided by persons of that racial group.[44] Obviously paragraph (d) may well be relevant in the field of social services. However, an employer seeking to discriminate in the employment field will require to be fairly careful. In *Tottenham Green Under-Fives Centre v. Marshall*[45] the phrase promoting welfare was held to have a wide meaning. Notwithstanding this, in *Lambeth London Borough Council v. Commission for Racial Equality*[46] the local authority was held to be discriminating in seeking to engage only Afro-Caribbean and Asian community members for jobs in the housing benefits department. It appears the word genuine is instructive in this matter. It is likely that if one can show that there is a real need that the person be of a particular racial grouping or origin then that will escape sanction.

It is unlawful to instruct someone to racially discriminate.[47] Equally, it is unlawful to induce or attempt to induce or pressurise anyone to do anything which amounts to unlawful discrimination.[48] The Crime and Disorder Act 1998 also sought to tackle racism in society by introducing specific provisions for conduct involving racism. First there is a new offence of racially aggravated harassment.[49] Secondly, there is scope for any offence to become "racially aggravated".[50] Where, at any time of committing the offence, or immediately before or after doing so, the offender evinces towards the victim (if any) of the offence malice and ill-will based on the victim's 'membership (or presumed membership) of a racial group, or the offence is motivated wholly or partly by malice or ill-will towards members of a racial group based on their membership of that group, an offence will be deemed to have been racially

---

[41] 1976 Act, s. 4(2).
[42] *ibid.*, s. 32.
[43] See *Burton v. De Vere Hotels Ltd* [1996] I.R.L.R. 596; Middlemiss and Mays, "The Common Law and Statutory Concepts of Vicarious Liability—The Parting of Ways", 1997 S.L.T. (News) 95; *Harrods Ltd v. Remick* [1998] 1 All E.R. 52.
[44] 1976 Act, s. 5.
[45] [1989] I.R.L.R. 147.
[46] [1990] I.R.L.R. 231.
[47] 1976 Act, s. 30.
[48] *ibid.*, s. 31.
[49] Criminal Law (Consolidation) (Scotland) Act 1995 s. 50A, as inserted by Crime and Disorder Act 1998, s. 33.
[50] Crime and Disorder Act 1998, s. 96.

aggravated.[51] Evidence from a solitary instance will be sufficient to establish the aggravation.

DISABILITY DISCRIMINATION

10.20 It was not until the mid-1990's that attempts by the Government were made to outlaw discrimination against disabled persons. Provisions are now contained in the Disability Discrimination Act 1995 ("1995 Act") and there is in addition a Code of Practice.[52] The 1995 Act has similar provisions to the Sexual Discrimination Act 1975 and the Race Relations Act 1976. A person has a disability for the purposes of the 1995 Act if he has a physical or mental impairment which has a substantial and long-term adverse affect on his ability to carry out normal day-to-day activities.[53] In respect of education, service provision, and employment, provisions of the 1995 Act are to extend to those who have in the past had a disability but now no longer have it.[54] The intention behind these provisions is to ensure that there is no discrimination against those who have had a history of mental illness in the past and can be subject to discrimination on account of it. It is unlawful for an employer to discriminate against a disabled person (a) in the arrangements which he makes for the purposes of determining to whom he should offer employment; (b) in the terms in which he offers that person employment; or (c) by refusing to offer or deliberately not offering him employment.[55] It is also unlawful for an employer to discriminate against a disabled person in his employment (a) in terms of the employment which he affords him; (b) in the opportunity which he affords him for promotion, a transfer, training, or receiving any benefits; (c) in refusing to afford him, or deliberately not affording him, any such opportunity; or (d) by dismissing him, or subjecting him to any other detriment.[56]

10.21 An employer discriminates against a disabled person if (a) for a reason which relates to a disabled person's disability he treats him less favourably than he treats or would treat others for whom that reason does not or would not apply; and (b) he cannot show that the treatment in question is justified.[57] An employer discriminates against a disabled person if he fails to comply with one of the duties in section 6 of the 1995 Act imposed upon him in relation to that disabled person; and (b) he cannot show that his failure to comply with that duty is justified.[58] Under the Disability Discrimination (Employment) Regulations 1996 it would be possible to treat a disabled person less favourably where pay is linked to performance; where there are uniform rates of contribution to occupational pension schemes regardless of the benefits received and the cost of providing those benefits are likely to be substantially greater than would be for a comparable person without a disability; and where building works comply with the Building Regulations in relation to access to facilities for disabled persons at the time the work was carried out.

Under section 6 of the 1995 Act, where any arrangements made by, or on behalf of, an employer, or any physical feature of the premises occupied by the employer, place the

---

[51] Crime and Disorder Act 1998, s. 96(2).
[52] See Lardy, "The Disability Discrimination Act 1995", 1997 S.L.P.Q. 2(1), 24–29; for the Code of Practice, "For the elimination of the discrimination in the field of employment against disabled persons or persons who have a disability", see Selwyn, *Selwyn's Law of Employment* (10th ed., 1998) App. I(i), pp. 624–665.
[53] Disability Discrimination Act 1995 ("1995 Act"), s. 1(1); see also Sched. 1, para. 4 to the Act.
[54] 1995 Act, s. 2.
[55] *ibid.*, s. 4(1)(a), (b) and (c).
[56] *ibid.*, s. 4(2)(a), (b), (c) and (d).
[57] *ibid.*, s. 5(1)(a) and (b).
[58] 1995 Act, s. 5(2)(a) and (b); note the distinction between this provision and the indirect discrimination provisions in the Sex Discrimination Act 1975 and the Race Relations Act 1976.

disabled person concerned at a substantial disadvantage in comparison with persons who are not disabled, it is the duty of the employer to take such steps as are reasonable in all the circumstances of the case in order to prevent the arrangements or feature having that effect.[59] Examples of the steps an employer may have to take include making adjustments to premises; allocating some of the disabled person's duties to another person; transferring him to fill an existing vacancy; altering his working hours; assigning him to a different place of work; allowing him to be absent during working hours for rehabilitation, assessment or treatment; giving him, or arranging for him to be given, training; acquiring or modifying equipment; modifying instructions or reference manuals; modifying procedures for testing or assessment; providing a reader or interpreter; and providing supervision.[60] In deciding whether it is reasonable for an employer to take any of the foregoing steps, regard should be had to (a) the extent to which the step would prevent the effect in question; (b) the extent to which it is practical for the employer to take the step, *i.e.* the financial and other costs that would be incurred by the employer in taking the steps and the extent to which it would disrupt any of his activities; (d) the extent of the employer's financial and other resources; (e) the availability to the employer of financial or other assistance with respect to taking the steps.[61] The foregoing provisions are designed to indicate whether the employer has discriminated against a disabled person and not to be used as a basis of an action based on statutory duty.[62] Employers with less than 15 employees are exempt from these provisions,[63] which in effect exempts some 96 per cent of all employers.[64] It is estimated that only 65 per cent of the entire workforce are covered by the new provisions.[65]

A person who has a complaint regarding disability discrimination can take their case to an employment tribunal.[66] That tribunal may award a person discriminated against compensation or it may well lead to a declaration or a recommendation that the employer take such action as is necessary for obviating or reducing the adverse effect of the discrimination. A tribunal is to assume that where an employer places what amounts to a discriminatory advert for employment, indicating that they do not intend to appoint someone with a disability or that they are unwilling to make any reasonable adjustment, and a disabled person applies and is not successful, the reason for the lack of success is unlawful discrimination.[67] It is unlawful for trade organisations such as trade unions or other professional bodies to discriminate against a disabled person in respect of the terms on which they are prepared to admit them to membership or by refusing to accept or deliberately not accept his or her application for membership.[68]

LIABILITY FOR NEGLIGENCE AND MISFEASANCE IN SOCIAL WORK

As a basic proposition of law, a person who causes harm to another in the course of trade, business or profession can be liable for damages.[69] Where the professional relationship is a contractual one, naturally the person who is damaged by the wrongdoing of the professional **10.22**

[59]   1995 Act, s. 6(1).
[60]   *ibid.*, s. 6(3).
[61]   *ibid.*, s. 6(4).
[62]   *ibid.*, s. 6(12).
[63]   1995 Act, s. 7(1), amended from 20 to 15: see *Industrial Relations Law Bulletin* 602, Oct. 1998.
[64]   See Annotations by Thomas, to the Disability Discrimination Act 1995, Mays (ed.), *Scottish Social Work Legislation*.
[65]   Prescott-Clarke, *Employment Law and Handicapped* (1990).
[66]   1995 Act, s. 8.
[67]   *ibid.*, s. 11(1) and (2).
[68]   *ibid.*, s. 13(1).
[69]   See Thomson, *Delictual Liability* (1994) at p. 131.

will have remedies under contract law. So, for example, if a person has contracted for services in a private or for that matter public residential establishment then any failing may be breach of contract entitling the injured party to seek damages. In many situations there will be no such contract, and it will be to the general law of delict that the injured party must resort. In order to successfully pursue a delictual claim against a professional or employee, it will be necessary to show that the pursuer's injury or harm was caused intentionally or through negligence, as a result of a breach of a duty of care owed by that person to the pursuer.[70]

In pursuing a claim based on negligence against another, a person must establish that a duty of care exists towards him (*i.e.* it is reasonably, foreseeable that they will be injured by the negligent acts or omissions of the defender that there has been a breach of that duty of care; and that there is a link between the breach of the duty of care and and injury, damage or harm sustained by the pursuer. A pursuer of a delict claim is required to quantify his loss and damage and under the basic rules of delict is required to minimise his loss. Suffice it to say that the Scottish system of reparation is a compensatory system. Awards are not intended as punishments on those who perpetrated the wrongs.

10.23 While the individual is always liable for their own delicts, it is often the case that that person represents an unsuitable target for the party who has suffered at his hands. Delictual liability recognises the concept of vicarious liability whereby liability transmits through the original wrongdoer to another party who could be seen as being responsible for that person's actions. In the field of social work and social care, the most likely party to be held vicariously liable for the actions of a social worker or social carer is the employer, *i.e.* the local authority, a private organisation, or a voluntary organisation. The employer represents the more appropriate target for the litigant because they have sufficient funding and almost certainly employers' liability insurance.

The concept of vicarious liability arises out of the nature and proximity of the relationship that exists between the parties. In the employment field there is clearly a relationship between employee and employer. It is accepted that if an employer has expressly or impliedly authorised the delictual conduct, then the employee will be deemed to be acting within the scope of their employment. Moreover, if the employee is doing work which he is authorised to do, but is doing it in a way that is not authorised, the employer will nevertheless be vicariously liable.[71] Where the employee is employed to undertake a particular type of work or task, the employer will not be vicariously liable for actions undertaken by the employee which are outside this remit. Often this will be a question of fact and circumstances and will simply be a matter of degree.[72] Even in circumstances where the employee is using his employer's equipment and working in the employer's time, it will not necessarily be the case that he is acting within the scope of his employment. An employee may, even in such circumstances, be acting in what is known as a "frolic of his own".

In practical terms, it is likely that anyone aggrieved by the wrongdoing of a professional involved in the social work field is likely to seek to sue both the individual as the perpetrator of the wrong, and, through the concept of vicarious liability, his employer.

10.24 A range of potential delicted wrongings may arise in the social work context. For example, the wrongful disclosure of information may result in parties seeking legal recourse the negligent preparation of reports which results in some harm or damage, or the failure to provide appropriate services. However, when one turns to the exercise by public authorities

---

[70]   See *Donoghue v. Stevenson*, 1932 S.C. (H.I.) 31.
[71]   See *Rose v. Plenty* [1976] 1 All E.R. 97.
[72]   See *Williams v. Hemphill*, 1966 S.C. (H.L.) 31.

of their statutory duties, and in particular social work departments, and the duties owed by the social worker, one encounters a major legal hurdle. For the most part, the ordinary law of negligence simply does not apply.

There are four categories of private law claims for damages against public authorities: (i) actions for breach of statutory duty; (ii) actions based solely on the careless performance of a statutory duty in the absence of any other common law right of action; (iii) actions based on a common law duty of care arising from the imposition of a statutory duty or from performance of it; and (iv) misfeasance in public office; *i.e.* the failure to exercise, or the exercise of, statutory powers either with the intention to injure or in the knowledge that the conduct was unlawful. Breach of statutory duty does not give rise to a private law claim unless the statute explicitly confers this on the limited class of people covered by the statute. Neither does the careless exercise of a statutory duty give rise to a private remedy in damages. There is no common law duty of care in policy matters. The prospect of finding a justiciable situation is relatively remote and the rules have operated rather harshly against some persons who, in any assessment of the reported case law, can feel genuinely aggrieved by the actions of the local authority and their staff.

If it is to be at all possible to sue a public authority for a breach of statutory duty it will be necessary to show that the statute founded upon creates a private law cause of action in delict.[73] The general attitude of the courts is that it would be contrary to the public interest to impose a duty of care on a local authority in respect of decisions taken for the welfare and protection reasons.[74] The simple exercise of discretion which a local authority has will not amount to negligence. Several cases illustrate how complex the law is and sometimes how harshly it operates. **10.25**

For example, in *W v. Essex County Council*[75] a family agreed in writing to foster G, a 15-year-old boy, in reliance on the oral assurances of the council and a social worker in their employment that a suspected or known abuser would not be fostered with them and, in answer to the parents' specific question, that G was not known nor suspected. In fact the council knew that three years previously G had received a caution for indecent assault on his sister. During the month that G stayed with the family, their children were all sexually abused. The children suffered psychiatric illness and the parents claimed to have suffered psychiatric shock. An action was raised against the council claiming damages for negligence through breach of the duty of care owed to them, and for negligent mis-statement due to the denial of G's prior caution. The plaintiffs further claimed that the council were in breach of an express or implied term of the fostering agreement and that the council were vicariously liable for their employee's misfeasance in a public office. On appeal it was held that although no claim in damages lay in respect of decisions by a local authority in the exercise of a statutory discretion, if the decision complained of was so unreasonable that it fell outside the ambit of the discretion conferred, there was no reason for excluding liability. However in this case, having regard to the fact that a common law duty of care would cut across the whole statutory set up for the protection of children at risk, that the task of the local authority and its servants in dealing with such children was extraordinarily difficult and delicate, that local authorities might adopt a more defensive approach to their duties if liability in damages were imposed, that the relationship between parents and social workers was frequently one of

---

[73] *Clunis v. Camden and Islington Health Authority* [1998] 3 All E.R. 180.

[74] *Barrett v. Enfield LBC* [1997] 3 All E.R. 171, where a plaintiff alleged failure to provide a proper standard of care by the local authority who had a care order over a child and who was moved 9 times between placements and developed a psychiatric illness.

[75] [1998] 3 All E.R. 111.

conflict, and that the plaintiff children's injuries were compensatable under the Criminal Injuries Compensation Scheme, it was held not to be just and reasonable to attach liability to the council.

In *X (Minors) v. Bedfordshire County Council*[76] claims for damages based on a breach of statutory duty of the local authority, a breach of common law duty owed by the local authority, and a breach of a duty of care by the social worker for whom the local authority was vicariously liable, were raised in connection with cases where a local authority had failed to take children into care and conversely a case where they had taken a child into care. It was again re-iterated that in relying on a breach of statutory duty it is first necessary to show that the statute intends to confer rights on a limited group of people and that a right to claim damages is implicit in the statute terms. In these conjoined cases it was held that the wording of the statute was not such that an inference could be taken that one should be able to claim damages. The House of Lords *again* made it clear that policy decisions would not amount to breach of statutory duty and also that a duty would not be imposed if it discouraged the local authority from fulfilling its statutory duties. It would only be possible to sue for a wrongful exercise of discretion where that exercise of discretion was such that no reasonable authority would have taken it. In this case (as in *W v. Essex*, above) the court adopted a public policy approach, holding that acceptance of a duty would be detrimental to the statutory framework of child protection, recognising that the matter was delicate and the making of decisions extremely difficult. If a duty were to be imposed it would lead to local authorities being far more restrictive in their activities. Also it was likely that the courts would be inundated with claims against local authorities who would have valuable resources deflected away from their key statutory duties of child protection.[77]

In *T (A Minor) v. Surrey County Council*[78] a mother contacted a local authority with a view to engaging a childminder. She subsequently saw an advert for someone and contacted the local authority who confirmed that the person was a registered childminder and that there was no reason why she could not employ the woman. It subsequently transpired that some three months earlier a child in the care of the childminder had sustained a violent injury. Although there had been case conferences no action was taken to de-register the childminder. After engaging the childminder, a child of the mother sustained a non-accidental injury involving serious brain damage. The injury was similar to that sustained by the other child previously in the care of the childminder. The mother sued the local authority for breach of statutory duty, a breach of common law duty and negligence on the part of the local authority officer. It was held following a line of authority that only where the statute imposed liability for statutory duty could such an action be raised.

10.26	Although it was suggested by the English Court of Appeal in *Barrett v. Enfield London Borough Council*[79] that a local authority could be vicariously liable for the operational negligence of a social worker, the House of Lords in *X (Minors) v. Bedfordshire County Council*, above, decided that the duty which a social worker owes in deciding to take a child into care is to the local authority and not directly to the client.[80] This distinction between discretionary judgment and operational conduct severely limits the possibility of utilising the

---

76	[1995] 3 All E.R. 353.
77	Two of the conjoined cases under *X (Minors)* above are now before the European Court of Human Rights having been declared admissible by the Commission: *KL v. U.K.* and *TP and KM v. U.K.* (unreported).
78	[1994] 4 All E.R. 577.
79	[1997] 3 All E.R. 171.
80	See *M v. Newham LBC* [1994] 4 All E.R. 602, p. 630; *X. (Minors) v. Bedfordshire C.C.* [1995] 3 All E.R. 353 at p. 384; see also *Phelps v. Hillingdon LBC* [1999] 1 All E.R. 421 (CA).

law of negligence against a social worker and the social work department in many situations.[81] However, it is clear that not every action of a social worker is devoid of any duty to a third party.[82] Infliction of harm while undertaking such activities as driving within the scope of their employment will give rise to a negligence claim. In their professional capacity deliberate abuse is another instance where delictual liability may arise.

While it is possible to use judicial review to attack an authority's decision and actions and **10.27** hold the authority accountable,[83] it remains in many respects an unsatisfactory remedy. Notwithstanding this, there are some illustrations where it has proved useful. In *R. v. Norfolk County Council, ex p. M*[84] a man against whom sexual impropriety had been alleged by a 13-year-old girl and against whom the police decided to take no further action, was placed on the authority's child abuse register. The man sought judicial review of the council's case conference. The authority for their part contended that there could be no judicial review as the decision was part of their internal administrative procedures. The court rejected the council's view of the matter, holding that the rights of the alleged abuser were affected. The case conference was required to act fairly, reasonably and in accordance with natural justice. This it had failed to do and accordingly the court quashed the council's decision. This case can be contrasted with the case of *R. v. Harrow London Borough Council, ex p. D*,[85] a case concerning the physical abuse of two children by their mother. In this case the mother requested to attend the case conference but this was denied, although she was informed she could make written submissions. Because she had been afforded this opportunity, the court took the view that the authority had not acted unfairly, unreasonably or contrary to natural justice. The court did however make the point that judicial review of such cases should be rare because the welfare of the child is paramount and unbridled resort to judicial review could frustrate attempts to protect children. Accordingly criticism of aspects of procedure should not be entertained; only cases involving points of principle should be raised. Another good illustration of judicial review is *R. v. Gloucestershire County Council, ex p. Barry* where a successful challenge was mounted to a local authority's approach to care assessment.[86]

Ultimately, the law on this issue is unsatisfactory for those families desirous of a remedy which may compensate them for loss arising out of the negligence of social work staff and social work departments, and also for social work as a whole, for as one writer has claimed, imposing liability could be used to encourage good practice.[87]

The duty of care owed by the employer to the social work employee

The principles of delict operate to the employee's benefit in situations where he sustains **10.28** injury arising out of his employer's negligence.[88] It is an implied term of any contract of employment that an employer will take reasonable care for the health, safety and welfare of

---

[81] For a discussion and critique of the underlying policy issues of the social worker not having a duty of care see Guthrie "Legal Liability and Accountability For Child Care Decisions", (1998) 28 Br. J. Social Work 403–422.

[82] *Vicar of Writtle v. Essex C. C.* [1979] 77 L.G.R. 656.

[83] *T (A Minor) v. Surrey C. C.* [1994] 4 All E.R. 577.

[84] [1989] 2 All E.R. 359.

[85] [1990] 3 All E.R. 12.

[86] [1997] 2 All E.R. 1; see discussion on this case in para. 7.31.

[87] Guthrie, "Legal Liability and Accountability for Child Care Decisions" (1998) 28 Br. J. Soc. Wk. 403–422 at pp. 419–20.

[88] It might also be the case that the social worker can make a criminal injuries compensation claim; see *Re Burrows*, Mar. 1, 1993, unreported, where a female residential social worker who sustained a fracture after a child with behavioural problems kicked her on the arms obtained over £55,000.

his employees.[89] This common law duty has a threefold dimension. First, the employer must provide safe equipment to the employee.[90] Secondly, the employer must provide a safe system of work.[91] And thirdly, the employer must employ competent fellow employees.[92] In addition to the implied contractual obligations of the employer, there is also the basic delictual duty of care to prevent physical injury or harm to the employees.[93] An employee therefore has the opportunity of utilising the law of either contract or delict[94] in seeking damages for injury arising out of the employer's breach of duty.[95] In the past, it has been imagined that the most likely injury that an employee would sustain would be physical injury. Given all that has been said earlier in this chapter, there are many situations where those social services will sustain physical harm or injury partially or primarily because of the employer's negligence. In addition to this, there is now increasing recognition that an employer can be liable for any damage to the mental health or welfare of an employee. The leading case on employer's liability for workplace stress is that of *Walker v. Northumberland County Council*[96] which coincidentally involves a social worker. Mr Walker saw a marked increase in his work level as an area social services officer responsible for four teams of field social workers. As a consequence of his increased work place pressures, he suffered a nervous breakdown. He had already advised his superiors of the pressures on him. He was off work for a period of some four months. Before returning to work, Mr Walker was assured of seconded support to reduce his work levels. After a month the assistance was removed. Mr Walker went on to sustain a second breakdown of his mental health and was subsequently dismissed on the ground of permanent ill health. The English High Court found little difficulty in the circumstances in finding that the authority had breached their duty of care to Mr Walker.[97]

The employer's duty to provide a safe system of work for employees is a subjective duty and is variable depending on the employee. Where an employee has a known infirmity the employer must take account of this. Likewise, an employer must take greater care of younger employees, or in certain situations, older employees.[98]

The employer's duty is to take reasonable care of their employee. The question of reasonableness is always a matter of fact, circumstance and degree. The cost in limiting danger is a relevant factor.[99] The employer's duty of care to their employees either under contract or delict is not to be confused with the employer's obligations under the Health and Safety at Work Act 1974, which uses substantially the same terminology as these common law duties, but is an Act which provides offences with which the employer can be charged.[1] It will often be the case that there will be both a prosecution and a civil action and whilst there

---

[89]   Craig and Miller, *Law of Health and Safety at Work In Scotland* (1995), pp. 23ff; see also *Colclough v. Staffordshire C.C.*, June 30, 1994, unreported, where it was held that a social worker in an Elderly Care Team might foreseeably have dealt with emergency lifting situations and that the employer could be liable for a lumber spine injury where they had not warned their employee of the dangers of lifting or provided training.

[90]   Craig and Miller, *Law of Health and Safety at Work In Scotland* (1995) at pp. 37–39.

[91]   *ibid.* at pp. 33–37.

[92]   *ibid.*, p. 39.

[93]   See *Donoghue v. Stevenson*, 1932 S.C. (H.L.) 31.

[94]   See Hogg, "Concurrent Liability in the Scots law of Contract and Delict", 1998 J.R. 1.

[95]   See *Walker v. Northumberland C.C.* [1995] I.R.L.R. 35; and *Johnstone v. Bloomsbury Health Authority* [1991] I.R.L.R. 118; see Gregor and Mays, "Health and Safety—The Employer's Common Law Duty of Care Redefined", 1995 S.L.T. 323.

[96]   [1995] I.R.L.R. 35.

[97]   Discussed in Gregor and Mays, *op. cit.* Mr Walker subsequently accepted a substantial out of court settlement, prior to an appeal hearing, believed to be in the region of £75,000.

[98]   *Paris v. Stepney B.C.* [1951] A.C. 367.

[99]   See *Latimer v. AEC Ltd* [1953] A.C. 643.

[1]   See Health and Safety at Work Act 1974, s. 2.

is in practical terms often a link between the two, there is no direct legal link; one case will not be determined by the other. Both types of case are conceptually different and have differing standards of proof. The duties in the Health and Safety at Work Act are not to be used as providing a basis for a breach of statutory duty civil action.[2] Duties in other health and safety legislation may provide a basis for an action based on statutory duty.[3]

CONFIDENTIALITY

Information is central to the effective operation of any public authority and social work is no exception. What is significant about social work is that a great deal of the information that is required is of a personal and confidential nature. There is therefore a need for the development of policies, strategies and procedures which will ensure that information is managed effectively.[4] This may be important for organisational reasons, but also it is integral to the retention of client confidence both in the social worker and the practice of social work.   **10.29**

Scots law does recognise breach of confidence as a delict.[5] This delict is designed to provide a remedy against someone deriving a benefit from disclosing information which was given to him in confidence. The disclosure of the information need not be in bad faith but may be done negligently. There is no absolute right to confidentiality; often disclosure will be in the public interest. Thus for example the police may disclose information about sex offenders.[6] There must be an obligation of confidence between the owner of the secret information and the person who discloses it. Such obligations may arise in contract but clearly in the social work context of social worker and client there is unlikely to be a contractual obligation. When it comes to social workers and their employer, the social worker as an employee is under an obligation to keep the employer's information confidential. This legal obligation arises as an implied term of the contract of employment[7] and occasionally by express inclusion of a term in the contract. As well as a possible delictual claim against him, the employee who discloses confidential information is liable to dismissal for breach of contract.[8] The social worker who unlawfully discloses confidential information can expect the severest of sanctions from their employer given all that has been said as to the importance of confidentiality in social work. Employees may continue to be bound by confidentiality after they have left employment.[9]

A major caveat to the delict of breach of confidence lies in the fact that where disclosure is in the public interest the disclosing party will have an absolute defence.[10] The Scottish Law Commission have proposed (and it seems likely that courts will adopt this approach) that public interest should cover the purposes of preventing, detecting or exposing a crime or   **10.30**

---

[2]   See Health and Safety at Work Act 1974, s. 47.

[3]   See Craig and Miller, *Law of Health and Safety at Work In Scotland* (1995) at pp. 93–99; *e.g.* Workplace (Health, Safety and Welfare) Regulations 1992; Manual Handling Operations Regulations 1992.

[4]   "The Social Services Information Agenda", (*National Institute for Social Work Briefing*, No. 17, July 1996), < http://www.nisw.org.uk/polb/fulltext/niswb17.httr >.

[5]   See McManus and Russell, *Delict* (1998), Chap. 23; MacQueen, *"Breach of Confidence"*, *Stair Memorial Encyclopaedia* (1993); Walker, *The Law of Delict in Scotland* (2nd ed., 1981), Chap. 21.

[6]   See para. 8.66.

[7]   See *Liverpool Victoria Friendly Society v. Houston* (1900) 3 F. 42; for the duty of confidence of employees to employers, see Smith and Thomas, *Smith and Wood's Industrial Law* (6th ed., 1996), pp. 112 113.

[8]   Although the employer will require to have a fair hearing: see *Dietman v. Brent LBC* [1987] I.C.R. 737.

[9]   *Roger Bullivant Ltd v. Ellis* [1987] I.C.R. 464; see also (C110/84) *Gemeente Hillegom v. Hillenius, The Times*, Jan. 2, 1986.

[10]   Gurry, *Breach of Confidence* (1984) at pp. 325–352; see also SLC, *Breach of Confidence* (No. 90), Cmnd 9385 (1984).

seriously anti-social conduct; preventing the public being misled by some public statement or action of the individual concerned; or informing the public about matters directly affecting the discharge of any public function of the individual concerned or for the protection of public health and safety.[11] However, the court will act to restrict a claim of public interest where the interests of justice so require. In *Parks v. Tayside Regional Council*[12] a foster mother who claimed she had contracted hepatitis B from a child placed in her care sought social work records relating to the child and his birth mother. The court took the view that the public interest in seeing that justice was done would far outweigh any public interest in confidentiality. The Outer House of the Court of Session expressed the opinion that public interest only extended to national interest put forward by the Lord Advocate or a Minister of the Crown and existed to protect information the recovery of which was essential to the proper working of government.[13] Such a view of the public interest is probably too restrictive. In *R. v. Higgins*[14] it was held that a local authority could refuse to disclose files containing information about a boy's special educational needs under public interest immunity.[15]

Where a party is able to establish a duty of confidence and a breach of it, the remedies are interdict, which restrains the unauthorised disclosure (if it has not already taken place), or damages (where it has and there is a loss or injury to the person whose information it is).

Social work departments take their moral obligation as to confidentiality very seriously indeed. A Code of Guidance issued under section 5 of the Social Work (Scotland) Act 1968 on *Confidentiality of Social Work Records* was produced by the Social Work Services Group in 1989 applicable to local authorities but not voluntary or private organisations.[16] The Code of Guidance identified four general principles:

(1) All information should be regarded as confidential. Mutual trust between social work departments and those for whom they provide a service is essential to effective service delivery. The development of this trust will be assisted by making available clear guidelines on the circumstances in which relevant personal information may be shared both within social work departments and with other agencies.

(2) Information supplied by donors for one purpose should not be used for another purpose; the purpose, or purposes, for which the information may be used should be established with the donor at the outset.

(3) Information supplied by donors should not be disclosed without the donor's consent in other than exceptional circumstances. Social work departments should give an undertaking to donors to this effect, and explain where exceptional circumstances may apply. The timing and manner of any disclosure is a matter of professional judgment, taking into account statutory requirement and whatever relevant guidance may be available.

(4) Where information has been supplied by another agency, disclosure should be made in accordance with the policy and procedures agreed with that agency or with any wider group of agencies (which might include education authorities, health boards

11   See also *SLC Breach of Confidence* (No 90) Cmnd 9385 (1984).
12   1989 S.L.T. 345.
13   See also *R. v. Poole B.C., ex p. Cooper* (1995) 27 H.L.R. 605.
14   [1996] 1 F.L.R. 137.
15   See also *Re C (Disclosure)* [1997] 2 W.L.R. 322; *Oxfordshire C.C. v. L and F* [1997] 1 F.L.R. 235; *Re M (A Minor: Disclosure)* [1998] 1 F.L.R. 734; *Re R (Disclosure)* [1998] 1 F.L.R. 433; *Re W (Disclosure : Adoption Details)* [1998] 2 F.L.R. 625; *Re M (Disclosure)* [1998] 2 F.L.R. 1028; *Re L (Care: Confidentiality)* [1999] F.L.R. 165.
16   SWSG Circular 1/89, *Code of Confidentiality of Social Work Records*.

and relevant voluntary bodies). Responsibility for the establishment and review of procedures, and for the use of information in such circumstances, rests with the local authority.[17]

Personal information should normally be available only to staff in social work directly **10.31** involved with the service-user and to a limited range of others who may need personal information to carry out their duties, including:

- social work finance staff for assessment purposes;

- legal advisers;

- other agencies, particularly if providing services on behalf of the authority or working in partnership with them;

- senior staff in their supervisory or management roles;

- social work students, their field work teachers and tutors while undertaking direct work with service-users;

- researchers engaged in evaluative studies and other investigations relative to service provision;

- informal carers working with a social work department on a voluntary basis;

- members of a committee of inquiry, the local government ombudsman, or officers of the Secretary of State.

Exceptionally disclosure may be required by law or in the public interest, overriding a person's right to have information kept confidential. Professional legal advice should be sought in each case and information disclosed should be the minimum necessary to meet the requirements of the situation. Particular requirements of this kind may include:

- statutory requirements—where there is a statutory right to information, local authorities are not required to obtain consent, but should notify the donor, where practicable;

- requirement by a court—for example social enquiry reports: donors should be notified;

- children's hearing requirements;

- disclosure to appointees such as safeguarders, curators *ad litem* or reporting officers;

- disclosure to police—to prevent, detect or prosecute serious crime; there is no definition of what constitutes a serious crime and accordingly advice should be sought from senior colleagues on the issue of disclosure; the police have the power to seek a court order compelling disclosure;

---

[17]   SWSG Circular 1/89, para. 10.

- risk to personal and public health—medical advice should be sought as to the necessity and manner of disclosure;

- disclosure through the media: this should not take place without consent unless the welfare or other interests of the subject may be served by making personal information publicly available or by advertisement.[18]

10.32   Local authorities are expected to have clear policies and procedures on the issue of disclosure. It is expected that those policies will specifically deal with children and young persons. Sensitive information should not be disclosed without the consent of the child or, where that child is, for reasons of age, lack of maturity or mental capacity, incapable of giving informed consent, the child's parent or guardian or other person with parental rights and responsibilities.[19] Where a person is incapable of managing their own affairs because of mental illness or handicap, the consent to the disclosure of the curator *bonis*, nearest relative, or other person acting as a legal representative of the subject, should be sought when considering a request for disclosure of information.[20]

There is of course a dilemma between the public authority's role as a repository of societal rights and its need to discharge functions on behalf of citizens. The use and processing of private information is an important aspect of that function but it is one that must be carried out with care.

Where disclosure of information held is sought by the person whose information it is, it has been held by the European Court of Human Rights in *Gaskin v. United Kingdom*[21] that a refusal to allow access to case records based solely on a refusal of the compiler of the information without any independent method of determining whether such a refusal is reasonable, is a breach of human rights.

Several key Acts and regulations seek to ensure that data is carefully and appropriately stored, processed, disclosed, and used. It must nevertheless be conceded that data protection law represents only part of the strategy to ensure the proper use of confidential data.[22]

DATA PROTECTION LAW

Data Protection Act 1998[23]

10.33   The Data Protection Act 1998 ("1998 Act") modifies an earlier 1984 Act of the same name and is designed to implement European Council Directive 95/46 which protects individuals

---

[18] See Moore and Whyte, Moore and Woods, *Social Work and the Criminal Law in Scotland* (3rd ed., 1998), pp. 364–365; see also SWSG Circular 1/89, para. 13.

[19] SWSG Circular 1/89, para. 18.

[20] *ibid.*, para. 19.

[21] [1990] 1 F.L.R. 167.

[22] Blume, "*The Citizens Data Protection*", 1998 (1) *The Journal Of Information, Law and Technology* < http://Relj.warwick.ac.uk/jilt/infosoc/98_1blum/ >.

[23] The Act will repeal the Data Protection Act 1984, the Access to Personal Files Act 1987 and the Access to Personal Files (Social Work) (Scotland) Regulations 1989. Although the Act was due to come into force in October 1998, its implementation has been delayed until 1999. There are two transitional dates in 2001 and 2007. Eligible automated data already being processed will be exempt from the new provisions until 24/10/2001. Any exemptions under the 1984 Act will continue to apply until 2001. Eligible manual data already held on files will be exempt until 2001 but subject to existing regulation (Access to Personal Files Act 1987). Other manual data may be given exemption until 2007.

with regard to the processing of personal data and regulates the free movement of such data. The 1998 Act is a much more substantial piece of legislation and considerably more complex than its predecessor. The legislation contains a number of data protection principles. There is also a new Data Protection Commissioner who has considerable powers over investigation enforcement. It is individuals who enforce their rights under the 1998 Act, but the Commissioner can assist them in this respect. Individuals enforce their rights by direct application to the courts. The new Data Protection Act not only covers computerised records but also covers manual records held in relevant filing systems. This inclusion will result in an amendment to other analogous legislation like the Access to Health Records Act 1990.

There are new provisions in respect of sensitive personal data relating to race, ethnic origin, political persuasion, trade union membership, sexuality, religious views, information about criminal offences and health. Under the old system, data-users were required to register. With the 1998 Act this is replaced with a system of notification. It will be no longer possible for employers or insurers to require the applicant to make subsequent access requests for criminal records as a condition of employment. As with the earlier legislation, data-users will require to give due consideration to the sort of information they retain. By including manual filing records in the legislation, there is the suggestion that this may herald the demise of such records and encourage everyone to computerise their record systems. The 1998 Act also includes a number of important exemptions for employers and educational establishments. There are also a number of exemptions in respect of law enforcement and security service.

Data protection principles

Part 1 of Schedule 1 to the 1998 Act contains the data protection principles. These are: **10.34**

1. Personal data shall be processed fairly and lawfully.

2. Personal data shall be obtained only for one or more specified and lawful purposes, and shall not be further processed in any manner incompatible with that purpose or those purposes.

3. Personal data shall be adequate, relevant and not excessive in relation to the purpose or purposes for which they are processed.

4. Personal data shall be accurate and, where necessary, kept up to date.

5. Personal data processed for any purpose or purposes shall not be kept for longer than is necessary for that purpose or purposes.

6. Personal data shall be processed in accordance with the rights of data subjects under the 1998 Act.

7. Appropriate technical and organisational measures shall be taken against unauthorised or unlawful processing of personal data and against accidental loss or destruction of, or damage to, personal data.

8. Personal data shall not be transferred to a country or territory outside the European Economic Area unless that country or territory ensures an adequate level of protection for the rights and freedoms of data subjects in relation to the processing of personal data.

Rights of data subjects and others

10.35   An individual is entitled

(a) to be given information by any data controller, where personal data, of which the individual is the data subject, is being processed by, or on behalf of, that data controller;

(b) if that is the case, to be given by the data controller a description of—

(i) the personal data of which that individual is the data subject,
(ii) the purposes for which they are being, or are to be, processed, and
(iii) the recipients or classes of recipients to whom they are, or may be, disclosed;

(c) to have communicated to him in an intelligible form—

(i) the information constituting any personal data of which that individual is the data subject, and
(ii) any information available to the data controller as to the source of that data; and

(d) where the processing by automatic means of personal data of which that individual is the data subject for the purpose of evaluating matters relating to him such as, for example, his performance at work, his creditworthiness, his reliability or his conduct, has constituted or is likely to constitute the sole basis for any decision significantly affecting him, to be informed by the data controller of the logic involved in that decision taking.[24]

Courts have the power to order data controllers to comply with a request from an individual.[25] The data controller is entitled to satisfy himself as to the identity of the person making the request and to charge a fee. The controller can refuse to comply with the request where information relating to another individual which can be identified from that information will be disclosed unless that other individual has consented to the disclosure, or it is reasonable in all the circumstances to comply with the request without the consent of that other individual. The obligation to supply data to the data subject requires the delivery of a copy in permanent form unless such copies are not possible, or will involve disproportionate effort, or the data subject agrees otherwise.[26] There is also an obligation on the data controller to provide unintelligible data with an accompanying explanation of terms.[27] The data controller is not required to supply or respond to repeated requests unless there is a reasonable interval between them.[28] Where the individual making the request for personal data is making a request to a data controller who is a credit reference agency, he may limit his request to personal data relevant to his financial standing, and shall be taken to have limited his request unless the request shows a contrary intention.[29]

Section 10 of the 1998 Act confers the right on the individual, at any time by notice in writing to a data controller, to require the data controller at the end of such period as is reasonable in the circumstances to cease, or not to begin, processing, or processing for a

---

[24]   Data Protection Act 1998 ("1998 Act"), s. 7(1).
[25]   *ibid.*, s. 7.
[26]   *ibid.*, s. 8(2).
[27]   *ibid.*, s. 8(2).
[28]   1998 Act, s. 8(3).
[29]   *ibid.*, s. 9(2).

specified purpose or in a specified manner, any personal data in respect of which he is the data subject, on the ground that, for specified reasons

(a) the processing of that data, or their processing for that purpose, or in that manner, is causing, or is likely to cause, substantial damage, or substantial distress to him or to another, and

(b) the damage or distress is, or would be, unwarranted. The data subject cannot object where he has already consented to the processing or where processing is necessary for contractual purposes. Moreover, objection cannot be made where the data controller is obliged to carry out the processing to meet a legal obligation or the processing is in the vital interests of the data subject.

An individual is entitled at any time, by notice in writing to any data controller, to require the data controller to ensure that no decision taken by, or on behalf of, the data controller which significantly affects that individual is based solely on the processing by automatic means of personal data in respect of which that individual is the data subject, for the purposes of evaluating matters relating to him such as, for example, his work performance, his creditworthiness, his reliability, or his conduct.[30]

In addition to the right to seek a court order compelling compliance, an individual who **10.36** suffers damage by reason of any contravention by a data controller of any of the requirements of the new legislation can seek compensation from the data controller for any damage occasioned.[31] It is also the right of a data subject to apply to the court seeking an order to rectify, block, erase or destroy that data and any other personal data in respect of which he is the data subject, which contains an expression of opinion which appears to the court to be based on inaccurate data.[32] The court may also order that the data controller notify third parties to whom the data has been disclosed of the rectification, blocking, erasure or destruction.[33] The court to which applicants will have to resort is the Court of Session or the sheriff court.[34] A child of sufficient age and maturity can exercise his rights under the Act. A child of 12 years of age and over is presumed to have sufficient understanding to exercise his rights.[35]

Section 17(1) of the 1998 Act provides that personal data must not be processed unless an entry in respect of the data controller is included in the register maintained by the Data Commissioner. Data controllers who wish to be included on the register must give notification to the Data Commissioner.[36] The notification will include registerable particulars and a general description of the measures to be taken for the purposes of complying with the seventh data protection principle. There is a duty on the data controller to keep their register entry up-to-date.[37] It is a criminal offence to process personal data without notification in the register entry. It is also an offence for a data controller not to keep his entry up-to-date. It is a defence to both of the foregoing offences that the data controller exercised all due diligence to comply with the duty.[38]

---

[30] 1998 Act, s. 12(1).
[31] *ibid.*, s. 13(1).
[32] *ibid.*, s. 14(1).
[33] *ibid.*, s. 14(3).
[34] *ibid.*, s. 15(1).
[35] *ibid.*, s. 66.
[36] *ibid.*, s. 18.
[37] *ibid.*, s. 20.
[38] See 1998 Act, s. 21.

The 1998 Act contains provisions under which the Secretary of State may empower data controllers to appoint independent data protection supervisors to oversee compliance with the Act.[39] It is not actually known how this will operate, but there is a clear implication that data controllers who appoint independent supervisors will be granted some exemption from the notification process.

10.37   Not surprisingly, considerable amounts of data are exempt from the provisions of the 1998 Act. Data required for the purpose of safeguarding national security is exempt.[40] Likewise data processed for:

(a) the prevention or detection of crime,

(b) the apprehension or prosecution of offenders, or

(c) the assessment or collection of any tax or duty or any imposition of a similar nature,

are exempt from the subject information provisions and non-disclosure provisions.[41]

The law also allows for limited disclosure of personal data to organisations with statutory functions so that they can process it free of subject information provisions. The exemption for these categories of data is not an exemption in the same way that national security exemption is. Nevertheless, it allows for considerable scope for public agencies to process data without persons knowing what data the authorities hold on them.

The Secretary of State may by order exempt from the subject information provisions, or modify those provisions in relation to personal data consisting of information as to the physical and mental health or condition of the data subject.[42] Similarly, the Secretary of State may by order exempt in relation to (a) personal data in respect of which the data controller is the proprietor of, or the teacher at, a school, and which consists of information relating to persons who are, or have been, pupils of the school, or (b) personal data in respect of which the data controller is an education authority in Scotland, and which consists of information relating to persons who are receiving, or have received, further education provided by the authority. It is further provided in section 30 that personal data being information (a) processed by government departments, local authorities or by voluntary organisations or other bodies designated by, or under, any order, and (b) appearing to the Secretary of State to be processed in the course of, or for the purposes of, carrying out social work in relation to the data subject or other individuals, may be exempted by the Secretary of State from the subject information provisions; or he may modify those provisions in respect of that data. In making this modification in respect of social work, the Act explicitly provides that the Secretary of State may do nothing which would be likely to prejudice the carrying out of social work.[43] One can readily imagine a number of situations where the data subject will be denied access to information held by social workers, and as such, one can anticipate these provisions being important in the work of social work departments. Currently there are regulations which control access to social work files which stipulate that access can be denied if it would identify a third party or if it would be detrimental to the physical or mental health of the client.[44]

[39]   *ibid.*, s. 23.
[40]   *ibid.*, s. 28.
[41]   1998 Act, s. 29.
[42]   *ibid.*, s. 30(1).
[43]   *ibid.*, s. 30(3).
[44]   Access to Personal Files (Social Work) (Scotland) Regulations 1989; Data Protection (Subject Access Modification) (Social Work) Order 1997.

Further exemptions for the processing of personal data exists in respect of professional, charitable, or health and safety-related regulatory activity.[45] The parliamentary ombudsman, the local ombudsman and other investigatory authorities are accordingly given some exemption so as not to prejudice the proper discharge of their functions.[46]

Access to Personal Files (Social Work) (Scotland) Regulations 1989

The Access to Personal Files (Social Work) (Scotland) Regulations 1989 are made under **10.38** section 3 of the Access to Personal Files Act 1987 ("1987 Act").[47] The 1987 Act applies to personal information contained in manual records maintained by a local authority for the purposes of its social work functions as defined in the Social Work (Scotland) Act 1968. Persons acting in an official capacity for a local authority have no right of access to personal information about themselves. Furthermore the 1987 Act does not apply to:

(a) automatically processed records as defined by the Data Protection Act 1984,

(b) the records of voluntary organisations or other bodies, even where they are directly involved with a local authority in the provision of a social work service,

(c) the records maintained by Reporters to Children's Panels, and

(d) the records of persons in prison or in a state hospital where local authorities act on behalf of the Secretary of State.

The term "manual records" means all records not automatically processed. They include files, reports, day books, card indexes, documents and all other written, typed or other manually maintained forms of record, containing all or part of the personal information relating to an individual held by the local authority, wherever the record is held. The definition of manual records also includes audio and visual recordings. Formal requests to a local authority for access must be made in writing. Regulation 2 entitles an individual who makes a request for access to personal information held by a local authority to be told by the local authority whether or not it holds any personal information relating to him and, if it does, to have access to any accessible personal information and be supplied, on request, with a copy of all or part of the record. If no personal information is held about the individual, or if all the personal information is restricted by one or more of the exemptions, it is sufficient to respond to the effect that the information held does not include personal information which the local authority is required to disclose. If any of the information recorded is not intelligible without explanation, the local authority is required under the regulations to give an explanation. Regulation 12 provides for an applicant dissatisfied with a local authority's decision, on his request for access or rectification or erasure of information, to make representations to a committee of the local authority. No special provision is made in the regulations about requests for access in respect of persons with mental disorders. Where a person considers all or part of the personal information disclosed to him is inaccurate, regulation 11 provides for application to be made to the local authority for the record to be corrected or erased. If the local authority agrees that all or part of the personal information

---

[45] 1998 Act, s. 31.

[46] See *Re Subpoena (Adoption Commissioner for Local Administration)* [1996] 2 F.L.R. 629.

[47] The Access to Personal Files Act 1987 is to be prospectively repealed by the Data Protection Act 1998 as that Act will cover manual files as well as computer generated ones. The 1989 Regulations remain in force for the time being and it seems likely will eventually be substituted by new regulations dealing with substantially the same issues.

is inaccurate, it must correct or erase such information. It is required to supply the individual, if requested, with a copy of the corrected information or the record from which it has been erased. Differences of view require to be noted on the record. Regulation 10(2) provides for access to personal information to be restricted where access to information by the subject is considered by the local authority to be likely to result in serious harm to his physical or mental health or emotional condition, or that of some other person. "Other person" may include staff of the authority. Withholding of information for this reason would be expected to be exceptional. Regulation 10(4) provides for personal information to be exempt from access if it is held for the purposes of the prevention or detection of crime or the apprehension or prosecution of offenders, and access to it would be likely to prejudice one of those purposes. Where an application is received from an individual for access to personal health information supplied by a health professional, the local authority is required under regulation 8 to consult the "appropriate health professional" on whether all or part of the information should be restricted.

Access to Medical Reports Act 1988 ("1988 Act")[48]

10.39   Individuals have the right to have access to any medical report relating to themselves which has been supplied by a medical practitioner for employment purposes or insurance purposes. Employers or insurers cannot make an application to a medical practitioner for a report relating to an individual unless they have notified the individual that they propose to make an application, and the individual has advised the applicant that he consents to the making of the application. Where the insurer or employer does notify the individual, they must also notify them of their right to withhold their consent, and also their right to access the report before or after it is supplied, and also their rights of amendment. Where the individual notifies the employer, or the insurer, that he wishes to have access to the medical report before it is supplied, the applicant must notify the medical practitioner of that fact at the time when the application is made, and also they must advise the individual of the making of their application for a report.

Where the medical practitioner has received notification that the applicant wishes to see the report, he must not supply the report unless he has given the individual access to it or a period of 21 days has elapsed without receiving any communication from the individual concerning arrangements for the individual to have access to the report. Even in circumstances where the applicant, employer, or insurer has not notified the medical practitioner but the individual themselves has contacted the medical practitioner and advises that he wishes sight of the report before it is forwarded, a medical practitioner must give the individual access to it, or at least wait 21 days to elapse from receiving notification from the individual. In providing access to the medical report, the medical practitioner may either make a copy of the report available to the individual for inspection, or supply him with a copy of it. Where an individual has been given access to the report, the report must not be supplied to the employer or insurer unless the individual has notified the medical practitioner that he consents to it being supplied. Before giving consent, an individual can request a medical practitioner to amend any part of the report which the individual considers to be incorrect or misleading. If the medical practitioner agrees with the individual's comments, he may proceed to amend the report accordingly. Alternatively, if he is not prepared to agree with the individual's comments, he must attach a statement of the individual's views in respect of any part of the report which he is declining to amend.

---

48   The following provisions can be found generally in ss. 1 and 3–8 of the Access to Medical Reports Act 1988.

Medical practitioners are required to keep copies of medical reports which they supply for employment and insurance purposes for a period of six months. Where the individual requests, a medical practitioner must give the individual access to any medical report relating to him which the practitioner supplied for employment and insurance purposes in the previous six months. Notwithstanding the right to access of medical records, section 7 of the 1988 Act states that a medical practitioner is not obliged to give an individual access to a medical report where in the opinion of the practitioner it is likely to cause serious harm to the physical or mental health of the individual or others, or would indicate the intentions of the practitioner in respect of the individual. Nor need a medical practitioner give an individual access to any part of a medical report where it is likely to reveal information about another person, or to reveal the identity of another person who has supplied information to the practitioner about the individual, unless (a) that person has consented, or (b) that person is a health professional who has been involved in the care of the individual and the information leads to or has been provided by the professional in that capacity. Where the medical practitioner intends to exercise his right of exemption, he must notify the individual of that fact. In circumstances where an individual considers that the requirements of the 1988 Act are not being complied with, they may make an application to the sheriff seeking an order compelling the person to comply with the requirement.

Access To Health Records Act 1990 ("1990 Act")[49]

The 1990 Act confers rights of access on patients to manually-held health records. The **10.40** legislation seeks to equalise the position in respect of the rights of access with information held on computer. The health record is defined in the Act as a record which

(a) consists of information relating to the physical or mental health of an individual who can be identified from that information, or from other information in the possession of the holder of the records; and

(b) has been made by, or on behalf of, a health professional in connection with the care of that individual.

As a broad definition "health professional" includes registered medical practitioners; registered dentists; registered opticians; registered pharmaceutical chemists; nurses, midwives or health visitors; osteopaths; chiropractors; clinical psychologists; child psychotherapists; speech therapists or music therapists employed by the health service; and scientists employed by the health service as a head of department.[50]

The holder of the record must give the applicant access to the record either by allowing them to inspect the record, or, in appropriate cases, an extract of the record. Alternatively, access may be occasioned by way of supplying a copy or an extract. It may also be the case that the record supplied was unintelligible without explanation and the legislation provides that where such circumstances arise, the holder of the record must supply an explanation of the terms contained in the extract.

An application can be made to access the health record of a deceased patient by the **10.41** patient's personal representative, or any person who may have a claim arising out of the patient's death. Access to the health record may be denied where the record includes a note

---

[49] The following provisions can be found generally in ss. 1, 3–6, 8 and 9 of the Access to Health Records Act 1990.

[50] Data Protection Act 1998, s. 69.

made at the patient's request that he did not wish access to be given. The record holder need not disclose any part of the record which in his opinion would disclose information which is not relevant to any claim which may arise out of the patient's death.

In all cases access may also be partially excluded where, in the opinion of the record holder, the information it would disclose is likely to cause serious harm to the physical and mental health of any individual, or that information relates to or is provided by an individual, other than the patient, or could be identified by that individual. Moreover, records made prior to the commencement of the 1990 Act may also be excluded from disclosure. It is not possible to exclude access to a record on the basis that it is likely to identify another individual where that individual has consented to the application, or where that individual is a health professional who has been involved in the health care of the patient. One cannot exclude information in the records dating back prior to the commencement of the Act where access is necessary in order to make intelligible any part of the record subsequent to that time. Section 5(3) of the 1990 Act states that access will not be given to any part of the record which in the opinion of the record holder would disclose (a) information provided by the patient in expectation it would not be disclosed to the applicant; or (b) information obtained as a result of any examination or investigation to which the patient consented in the expectation that the information would not be disclosed.

10.42 Where a person considers that the information contained in the health record to which he has been given access is inaccurate, he may apply to the holder of the record for a correction to be made. In turn, the record holder may be satisfied that the information is inaccurate and make the necessary correction, and if not satisfied, make in the part of the record in which the information is contained a note of the matter in respect of which the information is considered by the applicant to be inaccurate. In this context, inaccurate means incorrect, misleading or incomplete. Where an applicant is denied access to a health record, he may make an application to the sheriff court or the Court of Session seeking an order compelling the holder of the record to comply with their application. In order to determine whether to make such an order or not, the court itself has the power to inspect the record or part of it. On considering whether to grant an order or not, the court has the power to prevent disclosure of any record or part of it to the patient's representatives. Any contractual term which purports to require an individual to supply to another person a copy of a health record, or an extract from a health record to which he has been given access, is void.

INDEX